CW00405571

READING AS A PERCEPTUAL PROCESS

A historical perspective on "Reading as a perceptual process"

The figure on the cover of our book is intended to commemorate the Arabic scholar Ibn al-Haytham (Alhazen), who lived and worked in Iraq and Egypt around the turn of the first to the second Christian millennium (965–1040). He is considered the father of modern optics and was perhaps the first scientist to pursue an experimental approach to the study of visual perception on the basis of empirical anatomy and mathematical models.

The illustration is taken from a copy of Ibn al-Haytham's *Book of Optics* (Kitāb al Manāzir) now in the Süleymaniye Library Istanbul, (taken from Heller, 1988; see also Wade, 1998, p. 74). It demonstrates a detailed knowledge of the anatomy of the visual system including the visual pathways. This was the basis of Ibn al-Haytham's analyses of eye movement behaviour and, most important for the theme of this book, the role of perception in the understanding of written language.

Representative of his analyses of the reading process is the following quotation from the *Book of Optics*. To our knowledge, these remarkably prescient observations on the dual nature of word recognition represent the first published reference to issues that remain at the core of what is discussed in many contributions to the current volume.

> "For when a literate person glances at the form *abjad* written on a piece of paper, he will immediately perceive it to be *abjad* [a word denoting the Arabic alphabet] because of his recognition of the form. Thus from his perception that the '*a*' comes first and the '*d*' last, or from his perception of the configuration of the total form, he perceives that it is *abjad*. Similarly, when he sees the written name of Allāh, be He exalted, he perceives by recognition, at the moment of glancing at it, that it is Allāh's name. And it is so with all well-known written words which have appeared many times before the eye: a literate person immediately perceives what the word is by recognition, without the need to inspect the letters in it one by one. The case is different when a literate person notices a strange word which he has not come upon beforehand or the like of which he has not already read. For he will perceive such a word only after inspecting its letters one by one and discerning their meanings; then he will perceive the meaning of the word . . . "

Ibn al-Haytham, The Book of Optics, volume II, chapter 11, p. 129, ca. 1030, translated by A.J. Sabra, London, 1989.

References

Heller, D. (1988). On the history of eye movement recording. In: G. Lüer, U. Lass and J. Schallo-Hoffman (Eds.), Eye Movement Research. Physiological and Psychological Aspects. Toronto: Hogrefe.

Sabra, A.J. (1989). The Optics of Ibn al-Haytham. The Warburg Institute, University of London.

Wade, N. (1998). A Natural History of Vision. Cambridge, MA, MIT Press.

Reading as a Perceptual Process

Edited by

Alan Kennedy

Psychology Department
University of Dundee
Dundee DD1 4HN
Tayside, Scotland

Ralph Radach

Institute of Psychology
Technical University of Aachen
Jaegerstrasse 17
52064 Aachen
Germany

Dieter Heller

Institute of Psychology
Technical University of Aachen
Jaegerstrasse 17
52064 Aachen
Germany

Joël Pynte

CREPCO
Université de Provence
29 Av. Robert Schuman
13621 Aix-en-Provence
France

2000
ELSEVIER
Amsterdam — Lausanne — New York — Oxford — Shannon — Singapore — Tokyo

ELSEVIER SCIENCE Ltd
The Boulevard, Langford Lane
Kidlington, Oxford OX5 1GB, UK

© 2000 Elsevier Science Ltd. All rights reserved.

This dictionary is protected under copyright by Elsevier Science, and the following terms and conditions apply to its use:

Photocopying
Single photocopies may be made for personal use as allowed by national copyright laws. Permission of the Publisher and payment of a fee is required for all other photocopying, including multiple or systematic copying, copying for advertising or promotional purposes, resale, and all forms of document delivery. Special rates are available for educational institutions that wish to make photocopies for non-profit educational classroom use.

Permissions may be sought directly from Elsevier Science Global Rights Department, PO Box 800, Oxford OX5 1DX, UK; phone: (+44) 1865 843830, fax: (+44) 1865 853333, e-mail: permissions@elsevier.co.uk. You may also contact Global Rights directly through Elsevier=s home page (http://www.elsevier.nl), by selecting 'Obtaining Permissions'.

In the USA, users may clear permissions and make payments through the Copyright Clearance Center, Inc., 222 Rosewood Drive, Danvers, MA 01923, USA; phone: (978) 7508400, fax: (978) 7504744, and in the UK through the Copyright Licensing Agency Rapid Clearance Service (CLARCS), 90 Tottenham Court Road, London W1P 0LP, UK; phone: (+44) 171 631 5555; fax: (+44) 171 631 5500. Other countries may have a local reprographic rights agency for payments.

Derivative Works
Permission of the Publisher is required for all derivative works, including compilations and translations.

Electronic Storage or Usage
Permission of the Publisher is required to store or use electronically any material contained in this work.

Except as outlined above, no part of this work may be reproduced, stored in a retrieval system or transmitted in any form or by any means, electronic, mechanical, photocopying, recording or otherwise, without prior written permission of the Publisher.
Address permissions requests to: Elsevier Science Global Rights Department, at the mail, fax and e-mail addresses noted above.

Notice
No responsibility is assumed by the Publisher for any injury and/or damage to persons or property as a matter of products liability, negligence or otherwise, or from any use or operation of any methods, products, instructions or ideas contained in the material herein. Because of rapid advances in the medical sciences, in particular, independent verification of diagnoses and drug dosages should be made.

First edition 2000

Library of Congress Cataloging in Publication Data
A catalog record from the Library of Congress has been applied for.

British Library Cataloguing in Publication Data
A catalogue record from the British Library has been applied for.

ISBN: 0 08 043642 0

♾ The paper used in this publication meets the requirements of ANSI/NISO Z39.48-1992 (Permanence of Paper).
Printed in The Netherlands.

Reading as a Perceptual Process?

The title of this book may appear self-consciously provocative. Surely 'reading' is the name given to a set of essentially cognitive acts: lexical processing, the mapping between orthography and phonology, sentence parsing, conceptual integration, and so on? We know vastly more today about all of these than we did even ten years ago, but it remains questionable how, or even whether, they can be related to perceptual operations. This has little to do with the inadequacy of current experimental techniques, but is an epistemological question, stemming from the long tradition in psychology which usually views perceptual coding processes as autonomous from cognition. For many experimental psychologists, and perhaps the majority, a perceptual process is a mental operation without mentation: something fast, autonomous, data-driven and insulated from the vagaries of thought. From this perspective, even to talk of reading as a perceptual process may seem misguided. It is not our purpose here to lament this cultural divide. We simply note that its legacy is all too evident in many crucial aspects of reading research, such that work on the mechanisms underlying reading has become more than a little controversial. In particular, old experimental certainties are now under challenge and new quantitative theories clearly require a degree of explicit description not available to their more qualitative predecessors. The book charts some of these controversies and illustrates some initial tentative steps toward the integration of low-level 'perceptual' information into cognitive theories of reading. Naturally, in an edited volume, such a programme will find its expression more clearly in some contributions than in others, but all contributions summarise the state of the art in the relevant areas of experimental reading research.

The book is divided into five sections, dealing with various fundamental issues in current research: visual word processing; attention, information processing and eye movement control; the role of phonology in reading; syntax and discourse processing; and computational models and simulations.

Each section is accompanied by a commentary paper and we shall discuss both the choice of commentators and the nature of this process further below.

It will immediately be evident that the control and measurement of eye movements form a prominent theme. This is not, however, primarily a book about eye movements. It is simply that, in our opinion, a full understanding of the where and when of eye movement control is a prerequisite of any complete theory of reading, for it is precisely at this point that perceptual and cognitive processes interact. Unravelling the neural mechanisms controlling the movement of the eyes has been one of the great intellectual achievements of contemporary neurophysiology. In particular, models of this behaviour have strongly influenced psychologists interested in the deployment of attention across the visual field. Nonetheless, such models generally find no place for cognitive factors: " … those interested primarily in using eye movements to study reading seem to have little interest in the details of eye movements … whereas those interested in eye movements per se seem to be constantly worried that effects that those interested in language processing obtain are somehow artifacts associated with eye movements" [1]. Which raises the question of what status we attach to the tradition of research, from Javal and Huey, through Buswell and Tinker, to many (though not all) of the researchers represented in this book, pointing to an intimate link between cognitive operations on defined stimuli (typically letters or words) and the timing and location of eye fixations. To an astonishing degree, both properties appear to be under moment-to-moment cognitive control, exerted from lexical, syntactic, semantic and thematic levels. In different contexts, many of the chapters here demonstrate this fact and also, in different ways, address the question of how this might be reconciled with the notion of an autonomous oculomotor mechanism, driven by low-level properties of the visual field.

As part of the editorial process, we surveyed all contributors, asking what they considered to be fundamental developments and interesting recent findings in the field of experimental reading research and whether they could identify gaps in the field — possible topics for future research. We can hardly claim strict objectivity in this exercise (although few respondents simply cited their own work), but the results are interesting nonetheless. The 'hot topics' most commonly nominated feature to an encouraging degree in the present text: the relation between parafoveal and foveal visual processing of linguistic information; the role of phonology in fluent reading; and the emergence of statistical 'tuning' approaches to sentence parsing. Others, we capture rather more obliquely: for example the evolution of connectionist word processing.

Areas identified as relatively neglected were morphological processing (where there is general agreement that more research is needed), the time course and coordination of processing on different levels, and (perhaps inevitably) individual differences and varieties of reading. A second class of problems is related to methodology. There is agreement that the existence of a multiplicity of eye movement measures (and apparently equivalent measures defined in different ways) hampers the evaluation of empirical results. Finally, there is a class of problems relating to the need to integrate different viewpoints and research traditions, for example: work on naming often proceeds without reference to speech production; reading

---

1 Rayner, K. (1998). Eye movements and cognitive processes in reading, visual search, and scene perception. In: J.M. Findlay, R. Walker and R.W. Kentridge (Eds.), Eye Movement Research: Mechanisms, Processes and Applications. Oxford: Elsevier, pp. 2–22.

often occupies an area of the research landscape quite separate from that devoted to spelling; the relationship (if any) between data derived from word recognition paradigms and that derived from the study of eye movements in normal reading is still an unsettled issue. We have clearly reached a point where the separation of these lines of research is proving unhelpful. Of course, not all of these issues could be addressed, still less settled, in our book, but they are, at least, clearly spelled out in various chapters and in the commentaries. In this way we hope that the book not only samples the state of the art but also points to future directions for our field.

We do not propose summarising here the diverse specific issues raised in the book, but at least one point deserves special mention. This is the presentation of three attempts to develop quantitative models of reading. They are obviously far from perfect in simulating reading outside the laboratory context, but nonetheless they represent a significant departure in theory-building, something which would not have been possible ten years ago. We are closing in on models with a level of verifiability (and falsifiability) which will replace some of the heated debates of the past. We believe these models represent a quantum step in the maturation of reading research that is hardly being matched anywhere else in cognitive psychology.

Much of the work reported here was first presented at the 5th European Workshop on Language Comprehension organised in April 1998. The CNRS, the European Society for Cognitive Psychology and the Universities of Aix-en-Provence and Dundee generously supported the Workshop, which was held at the CNRS Luminy Campus near Marseilles. The first step towards publication of the book took the form of invitations to all the contributors to submit chapters.[2]

Each chapter was read and commented on by at least two other contributors (and in some cases, by outside referees). Revised versions comprising the five sections were then sent to a group of researchers the editors regarded as experts in their respective fields. The invitation to these commentators was to treat the chapters in a particular section as a launch pad for providing a review of the area from a broader perspective. A critical approach was encouraged, cushioned by the knowledge that chapter authors, having had their say, would have no further right to reply: their silence, therefore, reflects no more than the editors' wish to bring the book into print.

Alan Kennedy
Ralph Radach
Dieter Heller
Joël Pynte

---

2 Obviously, many chapters differ significantly from the original workshop contributions, following discussion and debate at the workshop itself and as a result of the later reviewing process.

Contents

Section 1. Visual Word Processing
    Section Editor: Dieter Heller

Section 2. Attention, Information Processing and Eye Movement Control
    Section Editor: Alan Kennedy

Section 3. Phonology in Reading
Section Editor: Ralph Radach

Section 4. Syntax and Discourse Processing
Section Editor: Joël Pynte

Section 5. Models and Simulations
Section Editor: Ralph Radach

Contributors

Cécile Beauvillain
Laboratoire de Psychologie Expérimentale, UMR 8581 CNRS, Université René Descartes, 28 rue Serpente, Paris 75006, France

Alice Binns
School of Psychology, University of Nottingham, Nottingham NG7 2RD, England

Jeannine Bock
Department of Psychology, University of Massachusetts, Amherst, MA 01003, USA

Marc Brysbaert
Department of Experimental Psychology, University of Ghent, Henri Dunantlaan 2, B-9000 Ghent, Belgium

Charles Clifton, Jr.
Department of Psychology, University of Massachusetts, Amherst, MA 01003, USA

Lucia Colombo
Dipartimento di Psicologia Generale, Via Venezia 8, 35139 Padova, Italy

Saveria Colonna
CREPCO, Université de Provence, 29 Av. Robert Schuman, 13621 Aix-en-Provence, France

Max Coltheart
Macquarie Centre for Cognitive Science, Macquarie University, Sydney NSW 2109, Australia

Meredyth Daneman
Department of Psychology, University of Toronto, Mississauga, Ontario, Canada, L5L 1C6

Heiner Deubel
Institute of Psychology, Ludwig-Maximilians-University Munich, Leopoldstrasse 13, D-80802 Munich, Germany

Tania Dukic
Arbetslivsinstitutet Väst, PO Box 8850, SE-402 72 Göteborg, Sweden

Brian P. Dyre
Department of Psychology, University of Idaho, Moscow, ID 83844-3043, USA

Martin H. Fischer
Psychology Department, University of Dundee, Dundee DD1 4HN, Tayside, Scotland

Jocelyn R. Folk
Department of Psychology, Kent State University, Kent, OH 44242, USA

Cheryl Frenck-Mestre
CREPCO, Université de Provence, 29 Av. Robert Schuman, 13621 Aix-en-Provence, France

Jonathan Grainger
Laboratoire de Psychologie Cognitive, Université de Provence, 29 Av. Robert Schuman, 13621 Aix-en-Provence, France

Seth Greenberg
Department of Psychology, Union College, Schenectady, NY 12308-3107, USA

Stefan Grondelaers
Laboratory of Experimental Psychology, Catholic University of Leuven, Tiensestraat 102, B-3000 Leuven, Belgium

Dieter Heller
Institute of Psychology, Technical University of Aachen, Jaegerstrasse 17, 52064 Aachen, Germany

Barbara Hemforth
Department of Computational Linguistics, University of the Saarland, Im Stadtwald, D-66041 Saarbrücken, Germany

Robin L. Hill
Department of Psychology, University of Dundee, Dundee, DD1 4HN, Tayside, Scotland

Jukka Hyönä
Department of Psychology, University of Turku, FIN-20014 Turku, Finland

Albrecht W. Inhoff
Department of Psychology, State University of New York, Binghamton, NY 13902-6000, USA

Arthur M. Jacobs
Insitute of Psychology, Catholic University Eichstaett, Ostenstr. 25, D-85071 Eichstaett, Germany

Alan Kennedy
Psychology Department, University of Dundee, Dundee DD1 4HN, Tayside, Scotland

Timothy S. Klitz
Department of Psychology, University of Minnesota, 75 East River Road, Minneapolis, MN 55455, USA

Lars Konieczny
Center for Cognitive Science, Institute of Computer Science and Social Research, Freiburg University, Friedrichstr 50, D-79098 Freiburg, Germany

Hye-Won Lee
Department of Psychology, University of Massachusetts, Tobin Hall, Amherst, MA 01003, USA

Gordon E. Legge
Department of Psychology, University of Minnesota, 75 East River Road, Minneapolis, MN 55455, USA

Stéphanie Mathey
Université Victor Segalen Bordeaux 2, UFR des Sciences de l'Homme, Laboratoire de Psychologie, 3 ter Place de la Victoire, 33076 Bordeaux, France

George W. McConkie
Beckman Institute, 405 North Mathews Avenue, University of Illinois at Urbana-Champaign, Urbana, IL 61801, USA

Don C. Mitchell
School of Psychology, University of Exeter, Washington Singer Laboratories, Perry Road, Exeter EX4 4QG, England

Robin K. Morris
Department of Psychology, University of South Carolina, Columbia, SC 29208, USA

Wayne S. Murray
Department of Psychology, University of Dundee, Dundee, DD1 4HN, Tayside, Scotland

Tatjana A. Nazir
Institute des Sciences Cognitives, 67, Bd Pinel, Lyon, France

J. Kevin O'Regan
Laboratoire de Psychologie Expérimentale, Institut de Psychologie, Centre Universitaire de Boulogne, 71 avenue Edouard Vaillant, 92774 Boulogne-Billancourt, Paris, France

Martin J. Pickering
Human Communication Research Centre, Department of Psychology, University of Glasgow, Glasgow G12 8QQ, Scotland

Alexander Pollatsek
Department of Psychology, University of Massachusetts, Tobin Hall, Amherst, MA 01003, USA

Joël Pynte
CREPCO, Université de Provence, 29 Av. Robert Schuman, 13621 Aix-en-Provence, France

Ralph Radach
Institute of Psychology, Technical University of Aachen, Jaegerstrasse 17, 52064 Aachen, Germany

Janina Radó
Graduiertenkolleg ILS, Universität Tübingen, Wilhelmstrasse 113, D-72074 Tübingen, Germany

Keith Rayner
Department of Psychology, University of Massachusetts, Tobin Hall, Amherst, MA 01003, USA

Erik D. Reichle
Department of Psychology, Carnegie Mellon University, Pittsburgh, PA 15213, USA

Eyal M. Reingold
Department of Psychology, University of Toronto, 100 St. George Street, Toronto, Ontario, Canada, M5S 3G3

Dave M. Stampe
Department of Psychology, University of Toronto, 100 St. George Street, Toronto, Ontario, Canada, M5S 3G3

Matt Starr
Department of Psychology, State University of New York, Binghamton, NY 13902-6000, USA

Piet Swanepoel
Universiteit van Suid-Afrika, Departement Afrikaans, PO Box 392, Pretoria 0001, South Africa

Bosco S. Tjan
NEC Research Institute, Princeton, NJ 08540, USA

Matthew J. Traxler

Department of Psychology, University of South Carolina, Columbia, SC 29208, USA

Geoffrey Underwood

School of Psychology, University of Nottingham, Nottingham, NG7 2RD, England

Roger van Gompel

Department of Psychology, University of Dundee, Dundee DD1 4HN, Tayside, Scotland

Hedderik van Rijn

Department of Psychology, University of Amsterdam, Roeterstraat 15, NL-1018 WB Amsterdam, The Netherlands

Dorine Vergilino

Groupe Exploration Oculaire et Perception Laboratoire de Pychologie Expérimentale UMR 8581 CNRS, Université René Descartes, 71 avenue Edouard Vaillant, 92774 Boulogne Billancourt, France

Françoise Vitu

Laboratoire de Psychologie Expérimentale, Institut de Psychologie, Centre Universitaire de Boulogne, 71 avenue Edouard Vaillant, 92774 Boulogne-Billancourt, France

Wietske Vonk

Max Planck Institute for Psycholingusitics, Nijmegen and Center of Language Studies, University of Nijmegen, P.O. Box 310, NL-6500 AH Nijmegen, The Netherlands

Stephanie Walker

Division of Psychology, Nottingham Trent University, Nottingham NG1 4BU, England

Daniel Zagar

Université de Bourgogne, Département de Psychologie, Laboratoire d'Etudes des Acquisitions et du Développement, CNRS ESA 5022, Faculté des Sciences, 6, Bd Gabriel, 21000 Dijon, France

Section 1

Visual Word Processing

Section Editor

Dieter Heller

CHAPTER 1

Traces of Print Along the Visual Pathway

Tatjana A. Nazir
ISC–CNRS, Lyon

Abstract

Skilled readers can recognize printed words during one single glance and they do so almost equally well for short as for long words. From a visual point of view the absence of a 'word length effect' is a rather surprising phenomenon. Given that every additional letter moves outer letters of a word farther into parafoveal vision, the probability that an entire word will be perceived during a fixation should decrease as words become longer. The word length effect which is expected but not observed with skilled readers is, however, noticed in beginning readers. Reading performance of first graders decreases linearly as words become longer and only after several years of reading experience word length ceases to influence performance. Curiously, a similar length effect can be observed after circumscribed lesions in temporo-occipital regions of the left hemisphere in premorbidly literate adults. What is acquired by skilled readers that made them recognize long words as easy as short words and that can be destroyed after localized brain lesions? With a series of examples that demonstrate strong correlations between eye movement pattern and reading performance I will try to argue that reading induces perceptual learning at early stages in the visual pathway. By this token perception of print becomes easy.

Reading as a Perceptual Process/A. Kennedy, R. Radach, D. Heller and J. Pynte (Editors)
© 2000 Elsevier Science Ltd. All rights reserved

The missing word length effect

When a skilled reader is asked to recognize a briefly presented 5-letter word displayed such that the eye is fixating either the first, the second, the third letter of the word and so forth, we observe a systematic variation of performance with the location of the eyes in the word: the word is recognized best when fixated slightly left of center and performance is better with the eyes fixating on the first compared to the last letter in the word (Fig. 1). Visual acuity and differences in the way letters are perceived in the two visual fields are major factors contributing to this variation in performance (Nazir, Jacobs and O'Regan, 1998).

When the reader is asked to recognize a 7- or a 9-letter word, a similar pattern of result emerges. Independent of word length performance varies with gaze location following an inverted u-shape function, although we notice that the 'viewing position effect' (VPE) becomes more pronounced as words become longer. The *height* of the VPE-curves, however, remains more or less the same. As will be outlined in the following, this latter point bears a theoretical problem.

Given the linear increase of the eye's minimum angle of resolution over the central 10° of the visual field (e.g., Olzak and Thomas, 1986), the probability of identifying single letters drops linearly as the distance from fixation increases. By multiplying these individual letter probabilities we can determine the theoretical probability that an entire letter string will be identified while the eye is fixating a certain location within the string. Table 1 illustrates the idea. In this example, the probability of identifying a directly fixated letter in a string of five letters is assumed

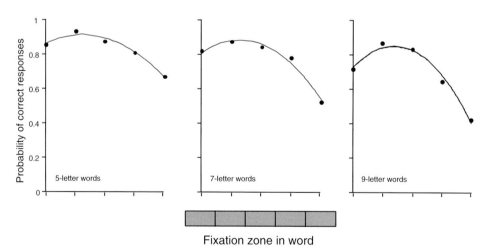

Fig. 1. Proportion of correct word recognition (in a task where participants were required to decide whether a briefly presented letter string was a word or not) as a function of the location of the eye in 5-, 7-, and 9-letters words. Replotted from Nazir (1993).

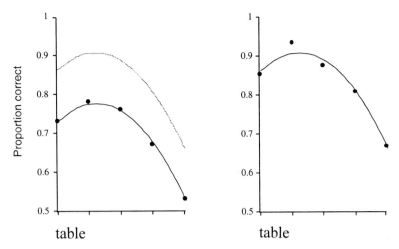

Fig. 2. Theoretical (left panel) and empirical word recognition data (right panel) as a function of fixation location in 5-letter words. Note that the shapes of the VPE-curves are almost identical. The difference in height of these curves comes from lexical factors. Words with different frequency of occurrence show a shift of the offset of the VPE-curve, with higher-frequency words being above those of lower frequency.

to be 1. Given the drop of acuity, the probability of identifying neighboring letters in the string will decrease by a constant value. In the present case this drop-off rate is arbitrarily set to 0.03 (the exact value depends on visual display conditions). Thus, the probability of recognizing the letter immediately to the right of the fixated letter is $(1 - 0.03) = 0.97$, for the following letters it is 0.94, 0.91, and so forth. For reasons that will be discussed later, this drop-off rate is stronger when letters are displayed in the left visual field by a ratio of $1:1.8$ (Nazir, O'Regan and Jacobs, 1991; see as well Bouma, 1973; Bouma and Legein, 1977; Hagenzieker, van der Heijden and Hagenaar, 1990; Nazir, Heller and Sussmann, 1992). Hence, when the probability to recognize a target letter drops from 1 at the center of gaze to $[1 - 0.03] = 0.97$ at a given eccentricity in the right visual field, it drops to $[1 - (0.03 \times 1.8)] = 0.946$ when the letter is presented at the same eccentricity in the left visual field. The theoretical probability of recognizing the entire letter string is given by multiplying these individual letter probabilities and is plotted in the last column of Table 1. Fig. 2 displays these data together with empirical data from Fig. 1, demonstrating strong agreements between prediction and observation (for an alternative model see Clark and O'Regan, 1999).

　　Fig. 3 displays theoretical VPE-curves for strings up to 9-letters length, calculated as in Table 1. Compatible with the empirical results (Fig. 1) the theoretical VPE becomes more pronounced as the length of the string increases. The *height* of

Table 1

Theoretical probability of recognizing a 5-letter string as a function of fixation location

Position of the fixated letter in the string	Recognition probabilities of individual letters, 5-letter string					Probability of recognizing the entire string
	1	2	3	4	5	
1	1	0.97	0.94	0.91	0.88	0.73
2	0.94	1	0.97	0.94	0.91	0.78
3	0.89	0.94	1	0.97	0.94	0.76
4	0.84	0.89	0.94	1	0.97	0.68
5	0.78	0.84	0.89	0.94	1	0.55

Note that the probability of recognizing the letter at fixation is set to 1. The drop-off rate is 0.03 going rightwards and (1.8×0.03) going leftwards. The probability of recognizing the entire letter string is calculated by multiplying individual letter recognition probabilities.

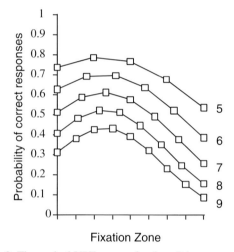

Fig. 3. Theoretical VPE-curves for 5- to 9-letters words.

these theoretical curves, however, drops systematically with every additional letter in the string. Thus, if word recognition were letter-based we should find signs of upgrading reading costs as words become longer [1]. It is worth noting that the ab-

1 Consistent word length effects in normal reading are observed when gaze duration is taken as dependent measures. However, this increase in the total time that the eyes spend in a word as words become longer is also observed in strings of z's (Rayner and Fischer, 1996). The length effect that appears when gaze duration is considered may therefore reflect oculomotor constraints rather than lexical processing.

sence of a word length effect in skilled reading is typically interpreted as indicating parallel letter processing during word recognition (LaBerge and Samuels, 1974; but for a different view see Just and Carpenter, 1987). Given the limits of acuity it is obvious, however, that performance should deteriorate with word length despite the fact that letters are processed in parallel. Hence, the missing word length effect in skilled reading is a puzzle that remains to be solved.

Conditions where word length does affect reading

Beginning readers and impaired readers

In contrast to skilled readers, systematic word length effects are noticed in beginning readers (Fig. 4). First graders recognize short words better than longer words independent of where in the word they are fixating. This length effect diminishes slowly as reading experience increases but disappears only after several years of reading experience (Aghababian and Nazir, in press). What takes place with experience is an adjustment of the height of the VPE-curves without apparent changes in their form. In other words, with increasing experience something about (long) words is learned that overcomes limits of acuity. Interestingly, children who do not develop normal reading skills (i.e., developmental dyslexia) persist in showing this length effect even after several years of instruction (Aghababian and Nazir, in prep.).

Word length effects can also be noticed after brain injuries in premorbidly literate adults. Relatively localized lesions in the temporo-occipital region of the left hemisphere produce a reading disorder called 'pure alexia'. This syndrome is characterized by slow reading in the absence of other marked neurobehavioral impairments (e.g., Behrman, Plaut and Nelson, 1998). The patients can pronounce words spelled to them, they can write to dictation but will have problems when asked to read what they wrote: reading latencies increase dramatically as the number of letters in words increases. According to some researchers pure alexia is caused by a general visuo-perceptual impairment that is not limited to the perception of print (Behrman and Shallice, 1995; Farah and Wallace, 1991; Sekuler and Behrman, 1996). According to the alternative view the deficit is the result of a dysfunction of mechanisms exclusively involved in reading (e.g., Patterson and Kay, 1982; Warrington and Shallice, 1980). The opposing character of these two theoretical positions seems to acknowledge that the nature of the impairment is not yet well understood.

Fig. 5 gives an example of the reading performance of such a patient as investigated by Montant, Nazir and Poncet (1998). The shape of the VPE-curves of this patient is not of the classic type because the patient was slightly impaired in perceiving stimuli displayed in his right visual field (for details see original

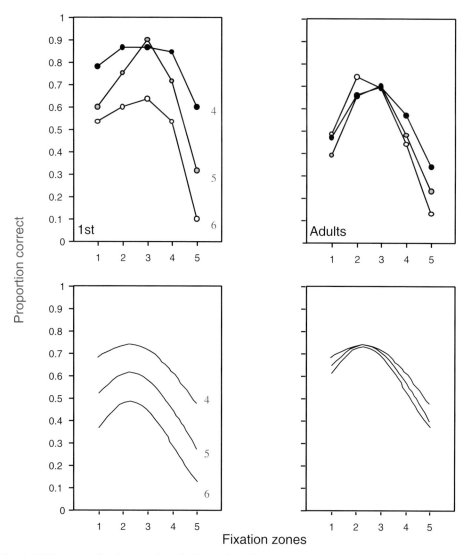

Fig. 4. VPE-curves for first graders (left panel) and adults (right panel) for words of different lengths. The top panel plots empirical data, the bottom panel theoretical data. While the data of first graders are coherent with the predictions, the results of adult readers are best described by an adjustment of the theoretical curves at their highest point. Replotted from Aghababian and Nazir (in press).

paper). Consequently, performance was best when words were fixated right of center, allowing most letters to fall into the intact left visual field. Within the present context the more interesting aspect of his performance, however, is the systematic drop of word identification scores as words become longer. Similar to

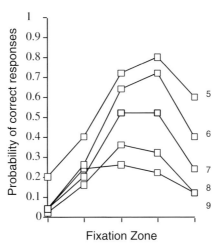

Fig. 5. VPE-curves for 5- to 9-letter words of a pure alexic patient (see text). Replotted from Montant et al., (1998).

first graders he recognized short words better than long words independent of where in the word he was fixating. On further examination this patient revealed a reduced capacity in using lexical knowledge to monitor incoming visual information from print. Thus, when required to choose — between two alternatives — the letter that was presented in a briefly displayed word, he would randomly choose the wrong alternative even though this alternative would not combine to give a word (i.e., choosing the letter 't' instead of the 'r' when displayed with the word <chair>). Based on the overall reading behavior of this patient it was concluded that the absence of length effects in skilled readers must result from a functional coupling between acquired (reading related) knowledge and visual input. The exact nature of this 'knowledge', however, was left unspecified.

Skilled readers

Under certain visual conditions word length effect also occurs in skilled reading. Letter and word recognition performance of skilled readers are generally better when the stimulus is displayed in the right as opposed to the left visual field. Interestingly, the inferiority of the left visual field increased as words become longer. That is, while words of different lengths are perceived almost equally well in the right visual field, in the left visual field performance drops as words become longer (e.g., Bouma, 1973; Bub and Lewine, 1988; Ellis, Young and Anderson, 1988; Faust, Kravetz and Babkoff, 1993; Malamed and Zaidel, 1993; Young and Ellis, 1985).

The difference in the way words are perceived in the two hemifields has repeatedly been attributed to cerebral hemispheric differences in processing written language (for a review see Bradshaw and Nettleton, 1983). As each hemifield projects entirely to the visual cortex of the contralateral hemisphere, word recognition is considered to be more efficient in the right visual field, because information is directed initially to the language-dominant hemisphere. A number of observations indicates, however, that the asymmetric functioning of the two hemispheres cannot entirely account for these results. The right visual field advantage in recognizing words develops during maturation of reading skill and is only fully present in pupils above grade seven (Forgays, 1953). Thus, although hemispheric specialization may play a role, reading experience clearly contributes to this asymmetry. Furthermore, while English words which are read from left to right are better perceived in the right visual field, reversed (or reduced) asymmetries are observed for words printed in Hebrew which is read from right to left (Mishkin and Forgays, 1952; Orbach, 1967). Reading habits seem therefore to constrain the way we perceive alphabetic materials in the two hemifields. Finally, a word length effect for Roman words can be reinstated in the right visual field when words are displayed in unusual visual formats (e.g., vertically), or when words are unfamiliar to the reader (i.e., pseudowords; Young and Ellis, 1985; see Fig. 6 below). Thus, reading competence in itself is not sufficient to account for the vanishing length effect in adult readers. Rather, familiarity with the visual configuration of the printed word seems to play a major role. Part of the 'knowledge' that is acquired with reading experience may therefore be of visual nature.

Early perceptual learning and reading

Perceptual learning is usually associated with the acquisition and storage of complex percepts, and is typically attributed to advanced stages of cortical processing.

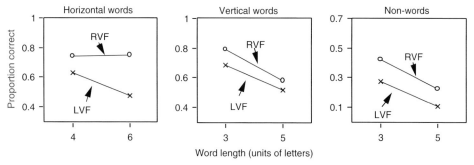

Fig. 6. Identification scores for words that were briefly displayed in the right or left visual field (RVF vs. LVF). Data are given as function of word length and plotted separately for three different display conditions. Left panel: horizontal words; middle panel: vertical words; right panel: non-words. Replotted from Young and Ellis (1985).

Results from psychophysical studies and from neuroscience suggest, however, that even at early stages of processing neuronal functional specificity is subject to experience (Gilbert, 1994). Practicing simple visual tasks, for instance, leads to improvements in performing them. This improvement, however, appears to depend on the precise configuration of the stimulus, including its orientation and location in the visual field. Thus, participants who learned to recognize an unfamiliar visual pattern displayed at one single location in the visual field may be significantly better at recognizing this pattern when displayed at the trained location than when displayed at other locations in the visual field (e.g., Ahissar and Hochstein, 1996). For this lack of generalization learning is thought to involve early stages of the visual pathway where receptive fields are small, relative to those seen at higher levels. However, the degree of specificity varies with the complexity of the training conditions, suggesting that learning can occur at various levels in the visual system (Ahissar and Hochstein, 1997): when training conditions are hard learning is specific to orientation and location, matching the fine spatial retinotopy exhibit by lower visual areas. For easy conditions by contrast, learning generalizes across orientation and retinal location, matching the spatial organization of higher areas. The time course over which learning takes place differs between studies. Some improvements develop over days, whereas other learning phenomena are observed over a few tens of trials within a single session (Gilbert, 1994). It is not entirely clear what distinguishes the long- and short-term learning effects. A necessary condition for learning to occur, however, is that the task is performed attentively (Ahissar and Hochstein, 1993). Although most 'perceptual learning' studies were conducted using simple tasks like vernier discrimination or texture segmentation (Fahle, Edelman and Poggio, 1995; Fiorentini and Berardi, 1981; Karni and Sagi, 1991), the same phenomenon is observed with more elaborate stimuli such as random checkerboards (Dill and Fahle, 1998; Nazir and O'Regan, 1990).

Granting that reading is a visual task, there is every reason to believe that perceptual learning also occurs during processing of print. Support for this assumption comes from the presence of remarkable correlations between eye movement patterns and word recognition performance. When the frequency of initially fixating different locations in a word during reading is compared to the probability that the word will be recognized while fixating these locations, a striking pattern emerges: word recognition performance is best from locations that are fixated most frequently during reading (Nazir et al., 1998). More precisely, statistics of where readers locate their initial fixations in words during natural reading show that eye movements are characterized by an asymmetric distribution of the landing site of the eye in words. Thus, independent of word length, there is a preference of the eye to land slightly before the center of a word (given the reading direction), and the probability of fixating the beginning of a word is higher than the probability of fixating the end (e.g., Rayner, 1979, for Roman script; Deutsch and Rayner, 1999, for Hebrew script). Although on-going linguistic processing modulates eye movement behavior during text reading (Rayner, Sereno and Raney, 1996), most authors agree that the location where the eye initially lands in words is mainly determined by low-level or visuo-motor factors (Vitu et al., 1995). That is, the apparent preference of the eye to land slightly before the center of words is essentially a consequence of rapidly moving the eye through a given visual stimulus configuration by using coarse visual information such as the spaces between words to guide the saccade (for more details see O'Regan, 1990; Rayner, 1998). Hence, it is not a strategy adopted by experienced readers for optimizing information extraction. Given that during natural reading the majority of words are fixated only once (Rayner and Pollatsek, 1989), these landing-site distributions provide a rough estimation of the frequency with which words are displayed at different locations in the visual field. When word recognition performance is considered, it turns out that performance varies with fixation location in the same way as the frequency of initial fixation. Performance is best when the word is fixated slightly before the center, and scores are higher for fixations at the beginning compared to the end of words (Fig. 7a). Thus, the frequency of having seen a word at certain locations in the visual field seems to modify the ease with which the word will be identified. It is interesting to note that this correlation even holds for 3-letter words for which the landing-site distribution has an atypical profile. In contrast to longer words the maximum of the landing-site distribution of short words is shifted beyond the word center towards the end of the words (Rayner, 1979, for Roman script; Deutsch and Rayner, submitted, for Hebrew script). As obvious from Fig. 7b the VPE-curve for 3-letter words follows this variation in the expected way.

A correlation between frequency of retinal exposure and performance is also evident in the results of the aforementioned laterality research. In fact, the reduced/absence of a word length effect in the right visual field and its presence in the left visual field could be predicted from the landing-site distribution. The left panel in Fig. 8 shows that the probability of landing at the beginning of a word varies only slightly between short and long words. However, the frequency of landing at the end of a word decreases significantly as words become longer. Note

---

Opposite page: Fig. 7. (a) Top panel. Distribution of landing positions in 5- and 9- letter Roman words, observed during reading (replotted from Vitu, O'Regan and Mittau, 1990). Bottom panel. Probability of correct responses for 5- to 9-letter words (in a task where participants were required to decide whether a briefly presented letter string was a word or not) as a function of the location of the eye on the word (replotted from Nazir, 1993). (b) Top panel. Distribution of landing positions in 3- and 5-letter Roman words, observed during reading (replotted from Rayner, 1979). Bottom panel. Probability of correct word identification for 3- to 5-letter words as a function of the location of the eye on the word (from Nazir, Nuerk and Jacobs, in prep.).

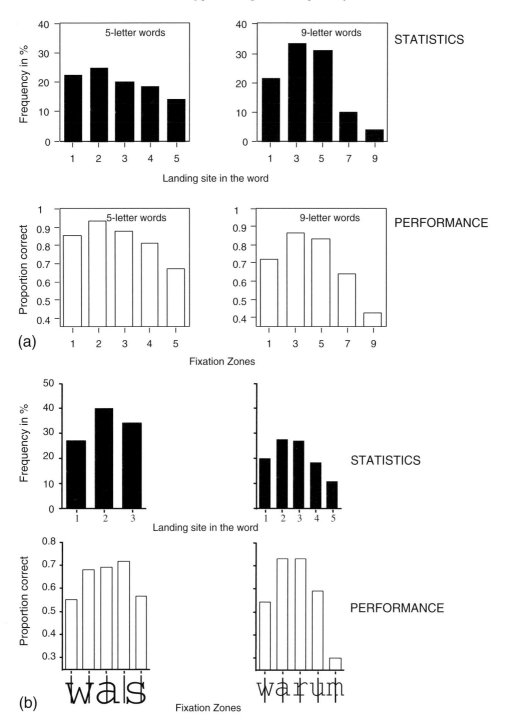

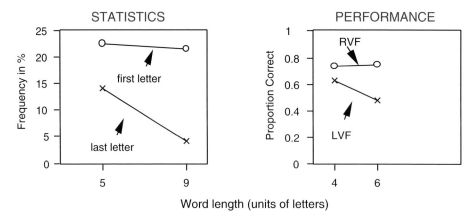

Fig. 8. Left panel gives the relative frequency to land on either the first or the last letter of 5- and 9-letter words during reading. Note, when fixating a word on the first letter, all but the first letter are presented in the RVF. When fixating on the last letter, all but the last letter are presented in the LVF (replotted from Vitu et al., 1990). Right panel gives probabilities of correct naming responses to briefly presented 4- and 6-letter words presented either in the RVF or the LVF. Replotted from Young and Ellis (1985, Experiment 5; low imageability words).

that when words are fixated at the beginning, all but the fixated letter falls into the right visual field. When words are fixated at the end, all but the last letter falls into the left visual field. Hence, the reduced/absence of a word length effect when words are presented in the right visual field and the presence of this effect in the left visual field (right panel of Fig. 8) does not necessarily indicate that written language is processed differently by the two hemispheres. Rather, length effects might depend on the frequency of having read printed words of various lengths displayed at different retinal locations. This claim finds support in the fact that at eccentricities beyond the perceptual span (e.g., further than 2–3° to the right of fixation; Rayner and Pollatsek, 1989), which corresponds to retinal locations at which words are usually not read, length effects are evident in the right visual field as well (Bouma, 1973; Fig. 9). Finally, the probability that the eyes land at regions around the center of a word varies only marginally between short and longer words (e.g., see statistics by McConkie et al., 1988; Rayner, 1979; Rayner and Fischer, 1996; Vitu et al., 1990). Hence, if the landing-site distribution is truly related to word recognition performance, word length effects should indeed level off as reading experience progresses.

The presence of strong correlations between eye movement patterns and word recognition performance, as outlined above, is suggestive of the idea that reading a word displayed at a given location in the visual field modifies the way the word is perceived when displayed anew at that location. Whether this correlation is also causal remains yet to be proven. However, given the emerging view that early

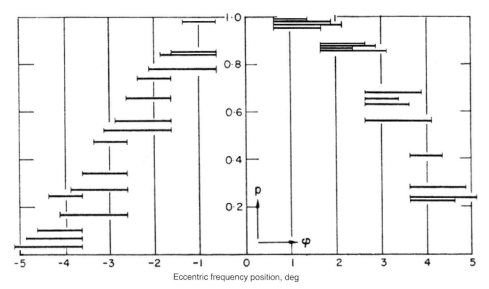

Fig. 9. Identification scores for words that were briefly displayed in the RVF or LVF. Data are displayed as a function of retinal eccentricity and plotted separately for words of different lengths (the length of the lines indicates word length). The left side gives scores in the LVF, the right side scores in the RVF. Replotted from Bouma (1973).

perceptual learning should occur for any visual feature that is processed attentively (Gilbert, 1994), let us suppose for a moment that the frequency of retinal exposure and visual word recognition performance were indeed causally related. What would this observation tell about reading?

A glance at the neural substrate of early perceptual learning

Most studies investigating the neural substrate of early perceptual learning have been conducted in sensory modalities other than the visual modality (Gilbert, 1994). Experiments in the somatosensory and auditory systems, for instance, have revealed that rehearsing a perceptual discrimination task gives rise to an expansion of the cortical territory that represents the stimulus (Recanzone, Merzenich, Jenkins, Grajski and Dinse, 1992; Recanzone, Schreiner and Merzenich, 1993; Wang, Merzenich, Sameshima and Jenkins, 1995; Weinberger, Ashe, Metherate, McKenna, Diamond and Bakin, 1990; cited in Gilbert, 1994). Thus, monkeys trained to detect differences in the frequency of tactile vibrations that were delivered to a constant skin site on a small part of one finger, improved their performance over several weeks of training. Concomitant to this behavioral progress the somatosensory cortex of these animals developed several changes, including an expansion of the cortical area that represented the restricted skin location trained in the behavioral task (Recanzone

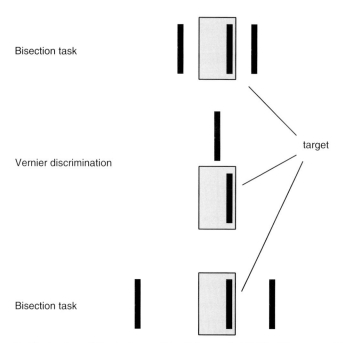

Fig. 10. Schematic illustration of the tasks used by Crist et al. (1997). The top and bottom panels show the bisection task, the central panel the vernier discrimination. The gray rectangle serves to indicate the trained retinal location. The black line within the rectangle is the target. Target location varied from trial to trial within the indicated retinal region. Training reduced the magnitude of target displacement that was necessary in order to indicate that the target was displaced towards the right or left reference line.

et al., 1992, cited in Gilbert, 1994). Comparable transformations were observed in the auditory system. In animals that were trained to discriminate small differences in the frequency of sequentially presented tones, behavioral changes were correlated to an increase of the cortical area that represented the trained frequency (Recanzone et al., 1993; Weinberger et al., 1990; cited in Gilbert, 1994). Cortical 'recruitment' alone, however, cannot account for the entire phenomenon. Perceptual learning is strongly modulated by the context within which the discrimination was performed and seems therefore to depend on feedback from higher-order cortical areas (Gilbert, 1998). Crist, Kapadia, Westheimer and Gilbert (1997), for instance, demonstrated that learning effects that were obtained in a bisection task (see top panel of Fig. 10) did not transfer to vernier discrimination (Fig. 10, central panel), although both tasks required judgments about the location of a target line within the same region in the visual field (see as well Fahle and Morgan, 1996). Learning generalized, however, to a similar bisection task in which the distance between the outer reference lines was doubled (bottom panel of Fig. 10).

If simple cortical recruitment were sufficient to explain improvements in performance, one would have expected that the effect of learning generalizes to all discrimination tasks involving a stimulus that activates cells in the critical cortical area (Crist et al., 1997). The specificity of learning effects to the trained retinal location on one side, but their dependency from the reference pattern with respect to which the judgment was made on the other side (i.e., two parallel lines placed laterally to the target vs. one parallel line fixed in position just above the target line), suggest that although part of the learning process takes place in early levels of visual processing, learning involves a complex network of cortical areas (Ahissar and Hochstein, 1997; Crist et al., 1997; Gilbert, 1998).

Following this view it can be presumed that if early perceptual learning takes place in reading, these learning effects may occur for some but not for all attributes of the visual word stimulus. In addition, even for those attributes that are subject to early perceptual learning, these learning effects should only be evident when the appropriate context conditions are met. As will be outlined in the following, by virtue of this context dependency, early perceptual learning could serve the analysis of the mechanisms that underlie the perception of complex patterns such as printed words.

In previous studies it has been demonstrated that the legibility of isolated Roman letters drops symmetrically to both sides of fixation as their distance from the center of gaze increases. Interestingly, this drop-off rate becomes asymmetric as the target letter is displayed embedded in a context of x's (e.g., xxxexx, where the letter 'e' represents the target; Bouma and Legein, 1977; Nazir et al., 1992). Like for entire words, the embedded individual target letter is better perceived when the string is displayed in the right rather than in the left visual field (LVF). Given the limited linguistic value that is represented by a string of x's, it seems unlikely that this visual field difference is triggered by the dominance of the left hemisphere for language. Rather, similar to the context dependency of the learning effects described for the line segment in Fig. 10, the left–right recognition difference that is induced by presenting the target letter within x's suggests that target perception is modulated by the configuration of the entire letter-string. This context dependency could be the imprint of processes that supports reading and, if well exploited, could therefore tell how orthographic strings are parsed in order to recognize *words*.

In a first attempt to investigate this possibility Nazir, Deutsch, Grainger and Frost (submitted) compared viewing dependent reading performance of Roman and Hebrew readers. Given the opposing reading directions (left to right in Roman scripts but right to left in Hebrew) the landing-site distributions of the eye during reading are mirror-reversed in these two scripts (Deutsch and Rayner, 1999). Learning effects that evolve with the frequency of retinal exposure should therefore come in reversed patterns and should be easily detectable. The native English and Hebrew readers were displayed with strings of identical letters of their respective alphabet. One character in the string was replaced by a target letter which had to be identified (e.g., xxxex in the Roman case). To manipulate the targets' context, strings were presented such that the observers fixated either the first or the last letter of a 5-letter string (i.e., x̱exxx or xxxex̱; the line indicates fixation location), or the center of a 9-letter string (i.e., xxxex̱xxxx). Thus, in both conditions targets appeared in the right as well as in the left visual field, and due to the selected string lengths (5- and 9-letters), target eccentricities were comparable in the two cases. The two display conditions allowed us to dissociate effects of absolute retinal location from effects that are related to the relative position of the target within the context of the string.

Similar to the results reported by Crist et al. (1997) for the bisection task, the results reported by Nazir et al. (submitted) demonstrated effects that were dependent on both the absolute retinal location of the target in the visual field and the relative position of the target within the string. In the 5-letter condition where letter strings were exposed in either the right or the left visual fields, readers of Roman scripts more accurately reported a Roman target letter when the string was displayed on the side in the direction of reading (i.e., in the right visual field). For readers of Hebrew (tested with Hebrew stimuli) this right visual field advantage disappeared, although it did not invert into a left visual field advantage. By contrast, when letter strings covered both visual fields simultaneously with fixation on the central letter (9-letter condition), the right visual field advantage for readers of Roman scripts reversed to favor the left visual field (see Heron, 1957, for similar results), while readers of Hebrew performed better when the target letter was presented in the right visual field; that is, performance was best for letter positions corresponding to the beginning of words in the respective script.

The variation of the left–right asymmetry between the two scripts suggests that letter legibility is affected by the frequency with which letters are read from a given location in the visual field (e.g., right or left of fixation). The inversion of this asymmetry within the same script suggests that on top of this frequency effect the legibility of individual letters is modulated by their relative spatial location within the string. These observations, though simple, seem to provide evidence that even at rather elementary stages of visual processing information extraction is already shaped to meet the demands of the system that enables word recognition.

Conclusion

From a simple visual point of view, reading, at least the way we do it, should not be possible. Limits of acuity combined with the rapidity with which skilled readers move their eyes through a text (4.8 words per second; Rayner and Pollatsek, 1989) should make it difficult to recognize words. Still, we read the way we read. The sample of data summarized in this chapter advances the hypothesis that word recognition is easy because of the involvement of pattern memory in reading. This notion is supported by the observation that certain skills, like the ability to recognize long words as easily as short words, can be neutralized by alterations of visual display conditions or by presenting words on retinal regions beyond the perceptual span of reading. The positive correlation between frequency of retinal exposure and word recognition performance, which is noticed throughout these examples, locates the sites of learning at fairly early stages of visual processing. The context-dependent variations of the legibility of individual letters within letter strings further suggest that higher-level constraints interact with the accumulating visual information at these early stages. If proven to be true, these learning effects would therefore indicate that reading modifies the functional organization of primary stages of sensory processing.

Final remarks

Only literates can come up with the correct pronunciation of a word that is orally spelled to them letter by letter. Yet, a literate person who decodes *print* in this letter by letter fashion will be termed dyslexic (cf., pure alexia). Between knowing how to decode printed graphemes and the ability to 'see words' lies a gap that has been neglected in current theories of visual word recognition. The indifference towards these visuo-perceptual aspects of reading stems in part from the view that early visual stages are common to the perception of all visual stimuli and are therefore not specific to reading. The present chapter proposes that this may not be true.

The significant role of visual processing stages in reading becomes evident when we consider what would be left of our reading skills if pattern memories that we acquire throughout our reading experience were erased and set to zero. To acquire some intuition about this, one needs to experience again what it is to learn a new script: transform your text from the Roman script into another alphabetic script (available on the computer) that is unfamiliar to you (e.g., [Cognitive psychology] could become [Χογνιτιωε πσψχηολογψ]). With a bit of effort it will take you a few hours until you can *easily* tell that [α] is [a], [β] is [b], etc. Note that neither the language nor the grapheme-to-phoneme conversion rules are affected by this manipulation. Once you are comfortable with the new alphabet, you can try to read whole words. In doing so, you will realize that despite your remaining knowledge of how to read, when deprived of the familiarity with the visual symbols you will find yourself elaborating letter–sound correspondences just like beginning readers do. An even more impressive experience comes with writing. Given that everything but the shape of the symbols remains equal in this experiment, once you have learned the new alphabet you will be able to write almost effortlessly. However, when you try to read the text that you wrote you will manifest symptoms of pure alexia: it will be hard to recognize the words that you just wrote. Obviously, nobody really doubts that pattern memories do matter to reading. The point advanced here is simply that these memories maybe found 'dispersed along the visual pathway', being less abstract than usually thought.

Acknowledgements

Preparation of this article was funded by a grant from the French–Israeli Association for Scientific Research and Technology (AFIRST) to the author. I would like to thank D. Heller, R. Frost, N. Kajii, K. O'Regan, R. Radach, E. Reingold, and S. Waxman for helpful comments during the preparation of this paper. Correspondence concerning this article should be addressed to Tatjana A. Nazir, Institut des Sciences Cognitives – CNRS, 67, Boulevard Pinel, 69675 Bron Cedex, France. Electronic mail may be sent to nazir@isc.cnrs.fr

References

Aghababian, V. and Nazir, T.A. (2000). Developing normal reading skills: aspects of visual processes underlying word recognition. Journal of Experimental Child Psychology (in press).

Aghababian, V. and Nazir, T.A. (in prep.). Identifying deviant reading behavior by looking at visual strategies.

Ahissar, M. and Hochstein, S. (1993). The role of attention in early perceptual learning. Proceedings of the National Academy of Science USA, 90, 5718–5722.

Ahissar, M. and Hochstein, S. (1996). Learning pop-out detection: specificities to stimulus characteristics. Vision Research, 36, 3487–3500.

Ahissar, M. and Hochstein, S. (1997). Task difficulty and the specificity of perceptual learning. Nature, 387, 401–406.

Behrman, M., Plaut, D.C. and Nelson, J. (1998). A literature review and new data supporting an interactive account of letter-by-letter reading. Cognitive Neuropsychology, 15 (1/2), 7–51.

Behrman, M. and Shallice, T. (1995). Pure alexia: a non spatial visual disorder affecting letter activation. Cognitive Neuropsychology, 12, 409–454.

Bouma, H. (1973). Visual interference in the parafoveal recognition of initial and final letters of words. Vision Research, 13, 767–782.

Bouma, H. and Legein, C.P. (1977). Foveal and parafoveal recognition of letters and words by dyslexics and by average readers. Neuropsychologia, 15, 69–80.

Bradshaw, J.L. and Nettleton, N.C. (1983). Human Cerebral Asymmetry. Englewood Cliffs, NJ: Prentice-Hall.

Bub, D. and Lewine, J. (1988). Different models of word recognition in the left and right visual fields. Brain and Language, 33, 161–188.

Clark, J.J. and O'Regan, J.K. (1999). Word ambiguity and the optimal viewing position in reading. Vision Research, 4, 843–857.

Crist, R.E., Kapadia, M.K., Westheimer, G. and Gilbert, C.D. (1997). Perceptual learning of spatial localization: specificity for orientation, position, and context. Journal of Neurophysiology, 78, 2889–2894.

Deutsch, A. and Rayner, K. (1999). Initial fixation position in Hebrew: influences of morphology and reading direction. Language and Cognitive Processes, 14, 393–421.

Dill, M. and Fahle, M. (1997). Limited translation invariance of human visual pattern recognition. Perception and Psychophysics, 60, 65–81.

Ellis, A.W., Young, A.W. and Anderson, C. (1988). Modes of word recognition in the left and right cerebral hemispheres. Brain and Language, 35, 254–273.

Fahle, M., Edelman, S. and Poggio, T. (1995). No transfer of perceptual learning between similar stimuli in the same retinal location. Vision Research, 35, 3003–3013.

Fahle, M. and Morgan, M. (1996). No transfer of perceptual learning between similar stimuli in the same retinal location. Current Biology, 6, 292–297.

Farah, M.J. and Wallace, M. (1991). Pure alexia as a visual impairment: a reconsideration. Cognitive Neuropsychology, 3, 149–177.

Faust, M., Kravetz, S. and Babkoff, H. (1993). Hemispheric specialization or reading habits: evidence from lexical decision research with Hebrew words and sentences. Brain and Language, 44, 254–263.

Fiorentini, A. and Berardi, N. (1981). Learning in grating waveform discrimination: specificity for orientation and spatial frequency. Vision Research, 21, 1149–1158.

Forgays, D.G. (1953). The development of differential word recognition. Journal of Experimental Psychology, 45, 165–168.

Gilbert, C.D. (1994). Early perceptual learning. Proceedings of the National Academy of Science USA, 91, 1195–1197.

Gilbert, C.D. (1998). Adult cortical dynamics. Physiological Review, 78, 467–485.

Hagenzieker, M.P., van der Heijden, A.H.C. and Hagenaar, R. (1990). The time courses in visual-information processing: some empirical evidence for inhibition. Psychological Research, 52, 13–21.

Heron, W. (1957). Perception as a function of retinal locus and attention. American Journal of Psychology, 70, 38–48.

Just, M.A. and Carpenter, P.A. (1987). The Psychology of Reading and Language Comprehension. Boston, MA: Allyn and Bacon.

Karni, A. and Sagi, D. (1991). Where practice makes perfect: evidence for primary visual cortex plasticity. Proceedings of the National Academy of Science USA, 88, 4966–4970.

LaBerge, D. and Samuels, S.J. (1974). Towards a theory of automatic information processing in reading. Cognitive Psychology, 6, 293–323.

Malamed, F. and Zaidel, E. (1993). Language and task effects on lateralized word recognition. Brain and Language, 45, 70–85.

McConkie, G.W., Kerr, P.W., Reddix, M.D. and Zola, D. (1988). Eye movement control during reading, I. The location of initial eye fixations in words. Vision Research, 28, 1107–1118.

Mishkin, M. and Forgays, G. (1952). Word recognition as a function of retinal locus. Journal of Experimental Psychology, 43, 43–48.

Montant, M., Nazir, T.A. and Poncet, M. (1998). Pure alexia and the viewing position effect in printed words. Cognitive Neuropsychology, 15 (1/2), 93–140.

Nazir, T.A. (1993). On the relation between the optimal and the preferred viewing position in words during reading. In: G. d'Ydewalle and J. van Rensbergen (Eds.), Perception and Cognition: Advances in Eye Movement Research. Amsterdam: North-Holland, pp. 349–361.

Nazir, T.A., Heller, D. and Sussmann, C. (1992). Letter visibility and word recognition: the optimal viewing position in printed words. Perception and Psychophysics, 52, 315–328.

Nazir, T.A., Jacobs, A.M. and O'Regan, J.K. (1998). Letter legibility and visual word recognition. Memory and Cognition, 26, 810–821.

Nazir, T.A., Nuerk, H.C. and Jacobs, A.M. (in prep.). Seeing three letter words.

Nazir, T.A. and O'Regan, K. (1990). Some results on translation invariance in the human visual system. Spatial Vision, 5, 81–100.

Nazir, T.A., O'Regan, J.K. and Jacobs, A.M. (1991). On words and their letters. Bulletin of the Psychonomic Society, 29, 171–174.

Nazir, T.A., Deutsch, A., Grainger, J. and Frost, R. Perceptual learning in reading: evidence from Roman and Hebrew readers. Perception and Psychophysics (submitted).

Olzak, L.A. and Thomas, J.P. (1986). Seeing spatial patterns. In: K.R. Boff, L. Kaufman and J.P. Thomas (Eds.), Handbook of Perception and Human Performance, Vol. II. New York: Wiley, pp. 7:1–7:56.

Orbach, J. (1967). Differential recognition of Hebrew and English words in right and left visual fields as a function of cerebral dominance and reading habits. Neuropsychologia, 5, 127–134.

O'Regan, J.K. (1990). Eye movements and reading. In: E. Kowler (Ed.), Eye Movements and their Role in Visual and Cognitive Processes. Amsterdam: Elsevier, pp. 395–453.

Patterson, K. and Kay, J. (1982). Letter-by-letter reading: psychological descriptions of a neurological syndrome. Quarterly Journal of Experimental Psychology, 34A, 411–441.

Rayner, K. (1979). Eye guidance in reading: fixation location within words. Perception, 8, 21–30.

Rayner, K. (1998). Eye movements in reading and information processing: 20 years of research. Psychological Bulletin, 3, 372–422.

Rayner, K. and Fischer, M. (1996). Mindless reading revisited: eye movements during reading and scanning are different. Perception and Psychophysics, 58, 734–747.

Rayner, K. and Pollatsek, A. (1989). The Psychology of Reading. Englewood Cliffs, NJ: Prentice-Hall.

Rayner, K., Sereno, S.C. and Raney, G.E. (1996). Eye movement control in reading: a comparison of two types of models. Journal of Experimental Psychology: Human Perception and Performance, 22, 1188–1200.

Recanzone, G.H., Schreiner, C.E. and Merzenich, M.M. (1993). Plasticity in the frequency representation of primary auditory cortex following discrimination training in adult monkeys. Journal of Neuroscience, 13, 87–103.

Recanzone, G.H., Merzenich, M.M., Jenkins, W.M., Grajski, K.A. and Dinse, H.R. (1992). Topographic reorganization of the hand representation in cortical area 3b of owl monkeys trained in a frequency discrimination task. Journal of Neurophysiology, 67, 1031–1056.

Sekuler, E.B. and Behrman, M. (1996). Perceptual cues in pure alexia. Cognitive Neuropsychology, 13, 941–974.

Vitu, F., O'Regan, J.K. and Mittau, M. (1990). Optimal landing position in reading isolated words and continuous texts. Perception and Psychophysics, 47, 583–600.

Vitu, F., O'Regan, J.K., Inhoff, A.W. and Topolski, R. (1995). Mindless reading: eye-movement characteristics are similar in scanning letter strings and reading texts. Perception and Psychophysics, 57, 352–364.

Wang, X., Merzenich, M.M., Sameshima, K. and Jenkins, W.J. (1995). Remodelling of hand representation in adult cortex determined by timing of tactile stimulation. Nature, 378, 71–75.

Warrington, E.K. and Shallice, T. (1980). Word-form dyslexia. Brain, 103, 99–112.

Weinberger, N.H., Ashe, J.H., Metherate, R., McKenna, T.M., Diamond, D.M. and Bakin, J. (1990). Retuning auditory cortex by learning: a preliminary model of receptive field plasticity. Concepts in Neuroscience, 1, 91–132.

Young, A.W. and Ellis, A.W. (1985). Different methods of lexical access for words presented in the left and right visual hemifields. Brain and Language, 24, 326–358.

CHAPTER 2

When WORDS with Higher-frequency Neighbours Become Words with No Higher-frequency Neighbour (Or How to Undress the Neighbourhood Frequency Effect)

Daniel Zagar
Université de Bourgogne and CNRS

and

Stéphanie Mathey
Université de Bordeaux 2

Abstract

"SATOR AREPO TENET OPERA ROTAS"
(The ploughman, with his plough, manages the work)

The influence of lexical similarity on word recognition has been discussed not only because of its theoretical impact but also because it is difficult to replicate. Among the multiplicity of the causes of this inconsistency one reason can be that *different* words were used in comparing words with higher-frequency neighbours (HFN) and words without HFN. In this experiment we chose French words for which the neighbourhood changes when they are written in UPPER case or in lower case. For example 'DEFI' has one HFN ('DEMI') but when it is displayed in lower case 'défi' has no HFN because 'demi' has no accent on the 'e'. Reaction times in a lexical decision task for these words were compared with a control condition in which there was no change in the neighbourhood when the word typography was changed ('NEON — néon'). The data showed a significant HFN effect: reaction times were longer on 'DEFI' than on 'défi' while no difference was observed between 'NEON' and 'néon'. Moreover the simulations ran with the IA model (McClelland and Rumelhart, 1981) showed the same pattern of results. These data confirm the reality of an inhibitory mechanism during visual word recognition.

Reading as a Perceptual Process/A. Kennedy, R. Radach, D. Heller and J. Pynte (Editors)
© 2000 Elsevier Science Ltd. All rights reserved

Introduction

Words from alphabetical languages are generated by the serial combination of a few letters (in French, there are about 60,000 words and 27 letters and 11 diacritic signs). However, because most of the letter combinations are not allowed, a large proportion of words have similar spelling. The word similarity was operationally defined by Coltheart, Davelaar, Jonasson and Besner (1977) as orthographic neighbourhood with *N* being "the number of different English words that can be produced by changing just one of the letters in the string to another letter, preserving letter positions" (p. 544). Statistics made on the TLF corpus (French lexical database; Imbs, 1971) show that 44.44% of the French three- to nine-letter words have at least one neighbour (see Table 1). This percentage dramatically increases for short words. Indeed, 96.25%, 88.81%, and 79.49% of three-, four- and five-letter words, respectively, have neighbours. Similar proportions can be found in English. Andrews (1997) reported statistical data computed from the Celex database and shows that 80.3 and 52% of four- and five-letter words have at least one higher-frequency neighbour.

In 1989, two papers reported an influence of orthographic neighbourhood on the word recognition process. First, Grainger, O'Regan, Jacobs and Segui (1989) reported that the presence of at least one neighbour of higher frequency than the stimulus word produced an interference in the word stimulus processing in both a lexical decision task and an eye movement study. Such a neighbourhood frequency effect (NFE) confirmed previous data obtained when measuring visual threshold duration (Havens and Foote, 1963; Newbigging, 1961). The data reported by Andrews (1989) were more surprising, because such results had never been reported before. She showed that a large *N* facilitated visual recognition of low-frequency words in both lexical decision and naming tasks. These two sets of results seemed to be contradictory because there is a strong probability for a low-frequency word with many neighbours to have at least one higher-frequency neighbour.

Since the publication of the papers of Andrews and Grainger et al. several attempts were made to resolve this apparent conflict (see for comprehensive reviews Andrews, 1997; Grainger and Jacobs, 1996; Mathey, submitted). The most extreme position was to deny the existence of the neighbourhood frequency effect. Sears, Hino and Lupker (1995) failed to replicate the experiment of Grainger et al. (1989). They found instead that higher-frequency neighbours facilitated the lexical decision responses to low-frequency words. They concluded that "these results would appear to call into question the existence of a true inhibitory effect of neighbourhood frequency" (p. 893).

A similar but milder argument was made by Andrews (1992). She noticed that the inhibitory NFE only occurred in lexical decision tasks, while the effect

Table 1

Neighbourhood size distribution according to N for three- to nine-letter words from the TLF database

N	Word length						
	3 (246) [a]	4 (1361)	5 (3154)	6 (5386)	7 (7411)	8 (8395)	9 (8371)
0	3.3	11.1	20.5	37.3	53.2	68.1	78.8
1	8.1	13.5	19	25.8	27.1	22.7	17.4
2	10.2	12.3	16.6	17.6	10.9	6.1	3.1
3	12.2	12	12.4	8.6	6	1.9	0.5
4	8.1	11.2	9.5	4.7	2	0.6	0.2
5	8.1	9.8	6.8	2.9	1.1	0.3	0.1
6	12.2	7.6	5.6	2.4	0.5	0.1	0
7	11	5.7	3.7	1.2	0.4	0.1	0
8	6.9	4.3	2.6	0.8	0.1	0.1	0
9	10.2	3.5	1.9	0.3	0.1	0.1	0
>9	9.8	6.5	0.9	0.4	0	0	0

[a] Value between brackets is number of words.

was facilitatory in word naming tasks. She suggested that "inhibitory effects of neighbourhood frequency may, therefore, arise in the decision stage of the lexical decision task rather than in lexical access" (p. 248). However, the same argument was used by Grainger (1992) in the opposite way. The facilitation effect observed in naming could be produced by a stage specific to creating phonological representation, and neighbours could facilitate performance when they are pronounced similarly to the stimulus word.

A third possible explanation is that facilitation and inhibition effects of neighbourhood are language-dependent (Andrews, 1997; Ziegler and Perry, 1998). In languages for which relationships between orthography and phonology are inconsistent, such as English, neighbours would facilitate word recognition. When languages are more regular, like French and Spanish, the competitive influence between neighbours may be more salient.

A fourth attempt to resolve the conflict was to assume that words were responded to on the basis of two different mechanisms: a pure lexical activation criterion and a global lexicon activation criterion (Grainger and Jacobs, 1996). According to the neighbourhood definition, large N words are similar to many more words in the lexicon than small N words. Consequently, they produce higher activity in the lexicon. When the words are responded to on the basis of the global lexicon activity (strategic criterion), large N words would produce shorter latencies than small N words because they look more 'familiar'. On the contrary, words with only one neighbour would not produce enough global lexical activity and then would be responded on a pure lexical activation criterion which is sensitive to neighbour higher-frequency inhibition.

A fifth possibility is that the influence of neighbourhood is complex when $N > 1$. The general idea is that when a word has more than one neighbour, the neighbours' influence on the word could be different from the simple addition of their inhibitory and/or facilitatory effects. The 'gang effect' described by McClelland and Rumelhart (1981) in the Interactive Activation (IA) model is a good example of such a complex interaction. They showed that a large set of ncighbours sharing the same three letters (called a gang) were more activated than another smaller one. The reason is that these words all work together to reinforce the common three-letter nodes and they thereby produce much stronger reinforcement for themselves. McClelland and Rumelhart illustrated this phenomenon by running the IA simulation with a non-word. Nonetheless, the rationale can be extended to words with more than one neighbour. Mathey and Zagar (2000) have run IA simulations, and demonstrated that when the neighbours belong to two different 'gangs', their inhibitory effect is less important than when they belong to the same gang. In addition, they reported empirical data that confirmed the IA model prediction. They compared lexical decision latencies for two different sets of two higher-frequency neighbour words. In the first set the word neighbours belonged to two different gangs (i.e. the French word *flanc* has two neighbours: *blanc* and *franc*). In the second one, both neighbours belonged to the same gang (i.e. *firme* and its neighbours *forme* and *ferme*). The data showed that participants responded faster to the former than to the later words, which suggested that when neighbours belong to different gangs they strongly competed each other, and their inhibitory influence on the stimulus word was weakened. In this article this effect was called the neighbourhood distribution effect (but see Johnson and Pugh, 1994 for different results). Generalising this effect, it could then be assumed that the competition effects between neighbours are larger when N is large than when it is small. Thus, large N words would be relatively less inhibited than small N words. Following this rationale, the N effect could be viewed (interpreted) as a diminution of an inhibitory effect rather than as a pure facilitatory one and the inhibitory neighbourhood frequency effect would be theoretically reconciled with the facilitatory N effect. This hypothesis will be examined in more detail in the next section.

An interesting feature of Mathey and Zagar's assumption is that the original IA model actually captures all the neighbourhood effects reported in the literature. The first part of this chapter will concentrate on a detailed examination of the IA model and of its mechanisms. The second part (Experiments 1 and 2) will provide some more evidence for the inhibitory mechanism of the IA model.

How the IA model of McClelland and Rumelhart (1981) accounts for neighbourhood effects

In the IA model, word-units are connected with all letters in each position of the word. A continuous flow of activation produces a progressive activation of all word-units that share letters with the stimulus (see Fig. 1). This architecture is a very simple analogy of how words are generated in alphabetical languages. The incoming information is distributed among all letters and activates word-units across a network of all possible connections between letter- and word-units.

The second mechanism is the intraword-unit inhibition: each word-unit sends inhibition to all other word-units. The functional property of this mechanism is to moderate the general activation produced by the continuous flow of entering activation from the stimulus towards all the lexicon. Indeed, the competition mechanism described by McClelland and Rumelhart guarantees that while a set of word detectors can be contacted by the input, only one of them will reach the recognition level.

The third mechanism is the word to letter activation (hereafter the reverberation mechanism): each activated word-unit sends feedback activation to letter-units that are compatible with its spelling. The functional property of this mechanism is to mimic an 'orthographic context'. With such a mechanism, the activation of a

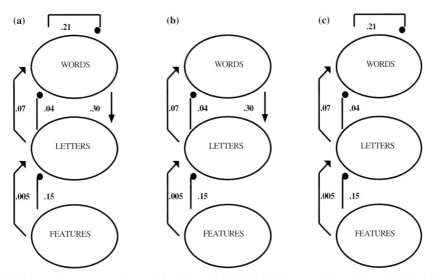

Fig. 1. Schematic representation of the IA model of McClelland and Rumelhart (1981): (a) IA model with default parameters; (b) 'pure' reverberation model; (c) 'pure' inhibition model. The arrows represent excitatory connections. The circular ends of connections represent inhibitory connections. The numbers represent the connection weights.

misperceived letter can be reinforced if it belongs to a word. For example the stimulus WOR? will activate the letters D and K, even if visual information about the last letter of the stimulus is not available.

While the IA model was originally designed to account for the word superiority effect (Reicher, 1969), it was subsequently used to simulate the inhibitory neighbourhood effect (Grainger and Jacobs, 1994, 1996; Jacobs and Grainger, 1992). However, it apparently failed to produce the N facilitation effect (Jacobs and Grainger, 1992), which was indeed very damaging for the model. The means used by Grainger and Jacobs (1996) to reconcile the IA model with the facilitatory N effect was to introduce a strategic component. In the multiple read-out model, words can be responded to with both the original word-unit activation criterion and with a 'global lexical activation criterion'. The global lexical activation is the sum of all word-unit activations produced by the stimulus. A word with a large neighbourhood will activate more word-units than a word with a small neighbourhood. When the words are responded to on the strategic criterion, large N words produce faster responses than small N words. The use of the strategic criterion in a lexical decision task also leads to the prediction that the N facilitation effect would be sensitive to the nonword aspect, and more precisely that it would be strengthened when the pseudowords are similar to the words (Jacobs and Grainger, 1994). However, this prediction was not confirmed (Mathey and Zagar, 2000).

On the other hand we have shown (Mathey and Zagar, 2000) that the IA model can capture the N facilitation effect. However, it is not straightforward to demonstrate this effect from simulations using natural (French or English) lexica. The reason is that it is difficult to disentangle the influence of various word variables. In the IA model, word activation is a function of at least three variables: word frequency (resting level of word-unit), N, and neighbourhood frequency. In order to study the effect of each of these variables on word-unit activation, the simplest way is to vary one of these variables while others are held constant. This led us to use the original IA model with artificial lexica as a heuristic tool.

Simulation with artificial lexica

Preliminary experiments (Mathey and Zagar, 2000; Zagar, 1995) indicated that word activation in the IA model is only sensitive to two factors: word resting level (which is a function of word frequency) and orthographic neighbourhood. Words differing from the stimulus by at least two letters have no influence at all on the activation course of the stimulus word. For example, a low-frequency French word (*loir*) was input into the simulation model in two different lexica in succession. Lexicon 1 was the natural French lexicon of four-letter words (977 words in all). Lexicon 2 was limited to the representations of the stimulus and its orthographic neighbours (*hoir, noir, voir, soir, loin*). The results of these simulations revealed that the stimulus activation levels were strictly identical for the two lexica (which was replicated for twenty other cases). Thus, contrary to PDP models (Feldman-Stewart and Mewhort, 1994), running IA simulations with small lexica produces exactly the same results as with a natural and large lexicon.

Neighbourhood frequency

Six artificial lexica of four-letter words were constructed in order to examine how the interactive activation model behaved with different neighbourhoods. Two frequency levels were tested (0.4 and 20 occurrences per million). In the 'no neighbour' condition the two lexica were reduced to the representation of one word (aaaa). In the 'neighbour' condition each lexicon was reduced to the representations of a word (aaaa) and of one neighbour (aaab). Two neighbour frequency levels were tested (73 and 3625 occurrences per million). Four lexica were constructed to represent the orthogonal combination of the two word frequencies and of the two neighbour frequencies. Simulations were run by inputting the artificial lexica into the interactive activation model with the default parameters (McClelland and Rumelhart, 1981).

Table 2 gives the results of the word stimulus simulations at cycle 17 (around the word identification). Comparing a hermit with a word with one neighbour showed that a neighbour always has an inhibitory effect, whatever its frequency (lower or

Table 2

Stimulus word activation at cycle 17 for a word simulated by the IA model when included in reduced artificial lexica, according to word stimulus resting level, neighbourhood size and neighbour resting level

	Stimulus word-unit resting level (aaaa)	
Resting level	−0.85	−0.45
No neighbour	0.67	0.68
1 neighbour (aaab) Neighbour frequency		
−0.55	0.63	0.65
−0.15	0.61	0.63

The correspondence between word frequency and resting level activation was given by the equation used by Jacobs and Grainger (1992) (resting level $= 0.177 \times \log_{10}(\text{freq } W) - 0.78$). Resting levels of −0.85, −0.45, −0.55 and −0.15 correspond respectively to the frequency values of 0.4, 73, 20 and 3625 occurrences per million.

higher than the target word). Moreover the inhibitory effect is proportional to the difference in frequency between the word and its neighbour.

Neighbourhood density

Another set of artificial lexica was constructed to describe the neighbourhood density effect. Three levels of N ($N = 4$, 8 and 12) and two neighbour frequencies (resting level $= -0.55$ and -0.15) were tested. These neighbourhood conditions were crossed with two word stimulus frequencies (resting level $= -0.85$ and -0.55). In addition, two neighbour distributions were used. In the 'one gang' condition (hereafter $G = 1$) each lexicon was made of the word stimulus and of N neighbours in the same letter position (for example when $N = 4$: *aaaa, aaab, aaac, aaad,* and *aaae*). In the opposite case, the neighbourhood of a four-letter word can be spread over the four letter positions, so $G = 4$ (for example when $N = 4$: *aaaa, baaa, acaa; aada,* and *aaae*). Lexica based on the same principles were built, with two or three neighbours at each letter position for respectively $N = 8$ and $N = 12$. Simulations were run with the IA model with the original default parameters.

When G was low ($G = 1$), the results (see Table 3) indicated that the stimulus word activation was inversely proportional to both neighbour frequency and N. In this case, the IA model did not provide any facilitation effect while N increased. Moreover, there is a neighbourhood frequency $\times$ N interaction. The effect of N

Table 3

Stimulus word activation at cycle 17 for a word simulated by the Interactive Activation Model, when included in reduced artificial lexica, according to word stimulus resting level, neighbour resting level, neighbourhood size (N) and number of gangs (G)

	Neighbourhood resting level					
	-0.55			-0.15		
N	4	8	12	4	8	12
$G = 1$						
Stimulus resting level						
-0.85	0.61	0.60	0.59	0.58	0.57	0.54
-0.45	0.63	0.64	0.63	0.61	0.60	0.59
$G = 4$						
Stimulus resting level						
-0.85	0.63	0.64	0.64	0.61	0.62	0.61
-0.45	0.65	0.66	0.66	0.64	0.64	0.64

was large when the difference in frequency between the word stimulus and its neighbours was great. In contrast, when the difference in frequency was small, increasing N from 4 to 12 did not produce any effect on word activation. The pattern of stimulus word activation was very different when G was high ($G = 4$). Increasing N from 4 to 12 did not inhibit word stimulus activation. On the contrary, a slight increase in activation was observed.

Finally there was a $G \times N$ interaction. More precisely, a word with a large N ($N = 12$) and a high G ($G = 4$) produced more activation (= 0.61) than a word with a small N ($N = 4$) and a low G ($G = 1$; activation = 0.58). This result confirms that the IA model with its default parameters can capture the N facilitation effect (Andrews, 1989, 1992). It also suggests that something interpreted as a 'facilitation effect' of N must be described within the IA framework as a relative lack of inhibition. Indeed a word with a large N is still inhibited when compared with a word of the same frequency and with no neighbour (activation = 0.67, see Table 2). However, the amount of inhibition is less significant (activation = 0.61 vs. 0.67) than for a word with few neighbours and a small G (activation = 0.58 vs. 0.67, see Tables 2 and 3). We will now examine which mechanisms are responsible for these effects.

Reverberation and competition within the IA model

In the IA framework, it is possible to disentangle the effects of reverberation and of inhibition by cutting off the appropriate connections. A 'pure' effect of reverberation is obtained when the word-to-word inhibition is eliminated (the initial parameter is set to zero, Fig. 1b). On the other hand, a 'pure' effect of inhibition is obtained when the parameter of the word-to-letter activation is set to zero (see Fig. 1c).

The same lexica as previously defined were used to run simulations with these two versions of the IA model. Activation of the stimulus words was taken at the 14th cycle because in the reverberation version of the model the words reached their asymptotic activation earlier. The effects of reverberation and of inhibition were obtained by comparing the stimulus word activation at cycle 14 with the activation of a word of the same resting level, but without any neighbour. In addition, we report the same measures with the original IA model. Table 4 gives the effects of reverberation, of inhibition and of combined reverberation and inhibition (IA model) for stimulus words of different neighbourhood.

The 'pure' reverberation model indicated that the reverberation mechanism always produced a facilitatory effect (between +0.03 and +0.16 depending on the characteristics of the neighbours, see Table 4). Increasing N accentuated this facilitation effect (the N effect was around +0.10). However, this augmentation reached its asymptote when $N = 8$. The neighbour frequency also increased the

Table 4

Neighbouring effect at cycle 14 for word simulated by a pure reverberation model, a pure inhibition model and the Interactive Activation model, when included in reduced artificial lexica, according to neighbour resting level, number of gangs (G) and neighbourhood size (N)

	Reverberation		Inhibition		IA model	
$G =$	1	4	1	4	1	4
Neighbour resting level $= -0.55$						
N						
1	+0.03	+0.03	−0.05	−0.05	−0.03	−0.03
4	+0.09	+0.10	−0.07	−0.07	−0.09	−0.07
8	+0.12	+0.14	−0.07	−0.07	−0.11	−0.07
12	+0.13	+0.15	−0.07	−0.07	−0.13	−0.08
N effect	+0.10	+0.12	−0.02	−0.02	−0.10	−0.05
Neighbour resting level $= -0.15$						
N						
1	+0.04	+0.04	−0.07	−0.07	−0.06	−0.06
4	+0.10	+0.11	−0.10	−0.10	−0.13	−0.09
8	+0.13	+0.15	−0.11	−0.11	−0.15	−0.09
12	+0.14	+0.16	−0.11	−0.11	−0.18	−0.10
N effect	+0.10	+0.12	−0.04	−0.04	−0.12	−0.04

The neighbouring effect at cycle 14 was calculated by removing the activation level of a word with no neighbour to the activation level of a same frequency word with neighbour(s). The N effect was calculated by removing (subtracting) the neighbouring effect of word with 1 neighbour to the neighbouring effect of word with 12 neighbours.

reverberation activation: the higher the frequency of a neighbour, the greater the reverberation. Neighbour frequency and N had additive effects on reverberation. Finally, it appeared that a high G accentuated the N effect on reverberation. The N effect was greater for a high than for a low G.

The 'pure' inhibition model showed that the neighbours produced inhibition whatever their number; moreover the inhibition effect grew with N (between −0.05 and −0.11 depending on the characteristics of the neighbours, see Table 4). However, it reached its asymptote earlier than the reverberation effect. Neighbour frequency had a strong influence on inhibition. In addition, the influence of neighbour frequency increased as N was higher. Finally G had no effect on the amount of inhibition.

The combined effect of reverberation and inhibition can be examined by comparing the results of the two previous models with the simulation results of the IA model. First, it can be observed that reverberation and inhibition effects were not additive. For instance, when $N = 1$ and $G = 1$ (see first line of Table 4) the neighbouring effect on word activation was +0.03 for the 'pure' reverberation model, -0.05 for the 'pure' inhibition model and -0.03 for the IA model. More-over, this interaction between the two mechanisms of reverberation and inhibition interacted with the G value. This three-way interaction can be seen in Table 4 when looking at the N effects. When $G = 1$ the N effects were respectively $+0.10$ and -0.02 for the 'pure' reverberation and inhibition models, while the combination of both mechanisms produced a -0.10 N effect in the IA model. It is as if the reverberation mechanism amplified the inhibition effect when G was low. In contrast, when $G = 4$, the N effects were respectively $+0.12$ and -0.02 for the 'pure' reverberation and inhibition models, while the combination of both mechanisms produced a -0.05 N effect in the IA model. The net result of reverberation and inhibition observed in the IA model was still inhibitory but slightly amplified by N. It is as if the amplification of the inhibition effect produced by the reverberation was less efficient when G was high than when it was low, in spite of the fact that the reverberation was higher in the high than in the low G condition.

Discussion

An important conclusion flowing from these results is that the IA model can theoretically capture the two main effects of neighbourhood. The presence of higher-frequency neighbours provoked an important drop of stimulus word acti-vation. The origin of this inhibition is clearly constituted by the word-to-word inhibition connections. Simulations with artificial lexica demonstrated that the amount of inhibition was proportional to the difference of frequency between the stimulus word and its neighbour.

The presence of several higher-frequency neighbours complicated the pattern of results because the reverberation mechanism produced a greater effect when G was high than when it was low. When G was low, the excitatory activation produced by the reverberation was not powerful enough to counterbalance the inhibitory effect. The net result was that increasing N continued to reduce the word stimulus activation. In contrast, when G was high there was no additional inhibitory effect. A word with a large N can be responded faster than a word with a small N, not because of the facilitatory effect of N, but because the neighbours of the large N are spread over several letter positions, while the neighbours of the small N word are concentrated on a single letter position.

Taken together, our simulation data were theoretically compatible with the neighbourhood effects reported in the literature for lexical decision tasks (LDTs): the IA model with its default parameters can capture not only the inhibitory NFE reported by Grainger and his colleagues (Grainger et al., 1989; Grainger, 1990), but also the facilitatory N effect (Andrews, 1989, 1992) and the facilitatory G effect (Mathey and Zagar, 2000).

However, the existence of the inhibitory mechanism remains questionable. Our simulations with the 'pure reverberation' model showed that both the *N* and *G* effects can be accounted for by the reverberation mechanism alone. The only experimental result that supports the hypothesis of an inhibitory mechanism is the NFE. The finding by Grainger et al. (1989) was important because it was a kind of psychological validation of this central mechanism of the IA model. Since Grainger et al.'s seminal work there have been several attempts to replicate the NFE in LDTs and unfortunately it does not appear very robust. We collected twelve papers examining the neighbourhood frequency effect with a LDT (see reviews by Andrews, 1997; Mathey, submitted). Seven of them reported an inhibitory effect in three languages: in French (Grainger et al., 1989; Grainger, 1990; Grainger, O'Regan, Jacobs and Segui, 1992; Grainger and Jacobs, 1996), in Spanish (Carreiras et al., 1997), and in English (Huntsman and Lima, 1996; Perea and Pollatsek, 1998). Four papers reported a null effect in French (Grainger and Jacobs, 1996; Mathey and Zagar, 2000), and in English (Forster and Shen, 1996; Sears et al., 1995). Finally, three papers reported a facilitation effect in French (Bozon and Carbonnel, 1996; Mathey and Zagar, 1996), and in English (Sears et al., 1995). As discussed by Forster and Shen (1996), one possible explanation of such an inconsistency can be that it is very difficult to match the experimental materials. Ideally, in order to obtain a pure NFE, words with and without higher-frequency neighbours should be matched according to several factors: word frequency, of course, but also word length, number of syllables, bigram frequency, and probably many other factors. This is of particular importance with the NFE because, contrary to the word frequency effect, the size of NFE is generally very small: between 20 and 40 ms. Thus, the ideal paradigm would be to use the same words in both conditions.

Experiment 1: the reality of the NFE

Such an ideal paradigm can be adopted in French, since it is possible to find words for which the neighbourhood changes as they are written in lower- or in upper-case letters. The reason is that French uses accents on some vowels (a, e, i, o, u) and that these accents are written in lower case, but not in upper case. For example, the French word *défi* has one HFN when it is written in upper case (*DEFI*): *DEMI*. But when it is written in lower case *demi* cannot be considered as a neighbour of *défi*, following the strict neighbourhood definition for the reason that there is no accent on *demi*. If *DEFI* takes longer to recognise than *défi* it is either because of the presence of a HFN or because of typography. This set of words was dubbed 'unstable condition'. In order to control for the influence of typography we selected words with an accent for which there is no neighbour either in lower case or in upper case ('stable condition', e.g. *néon*). The HFN effect was tested in both a LDT and a simulation study by the interaction between the two sets of words and typography.

Lexical decision task

Method

Participants
Ninety-eight undergraduate students from the University of Burgundy with normal or corrected-to-normal vision participated in this experiment for course credit. They all were native French speakers.

Stimuli and design
Thirty four- and five-letter words of low frequency were selected such that their orthographic neighbourhood was stable or unstable, according to the letter-case change. In the stable condition, the words had no neighbour, whatever the typography used. In the unstable neighbourhood condition, the words had no neighbour when presented in upper case, but had at least one higher-frequency neighbour when displayed in upper-case letters (see Table 5). Thirty pseudowords were constructed by changing one letter in a real French word. They all contained a letter with an accent. Two independent groups of participants were used. Each saw all the materials, either in upper case or in lower case.

Table 5

Statistical characteristics of Experiment 1 word materials

	Word condition			
	Stable		Unstable	
	Lower case	Upper case	Lower case	Upper case
Stimulus				
Example	néon	NEON	défi	DEFI
Log *F*	2.62	2.62	2.77	2.77
N	1.13	1.13	1.27	4.80
HFN	0	0	0	1.87
Higher-frequency neighbour	–	–	–	DEMI

Log F = mean word frequency per 100 million (in logarithms). N = number of neighbours. HFN = number of higher-frequency neighbours.

Procedure

Participants were tested with a standard lexical decision task. They were instructed to respond as quickly and accurately as possible. Twenty-eight practice trials were administered before receiving the experimental trials in different random orders. On each trial, a central fixation point was presented for 500 ms, followed by the stimulus. The stimulus remained on the screen until the participant responded by pressing one of two response keys ('Yes' or 'No'). 'Yes' responses (for words) were given with the dominant hand.

Results

Mean correct response latencies and error rates averaged over participants are presented in Table 6. Participant and item means were submitted to separate analyses of variance, reported as F_1 and F_2 after removing responses with latencies of greater than 1500 ms. Analysis of the word data revealed that responses to stable words were faster, $F_1(1, 96) = 54.57$, $p < 0.001$, $F_2(1, 28) = 5.25$, $p < 0.03$, than responses to unstable words. The main effect of typography was significant only in the item analysis, $F_1(1, 96) = 1.03$, $p > 0.10$, $F_2(1, 28) = 5.25$, $p < 0.03$. However, the interaction between typography and stability was significant in both the participant and item analyses, $F_1(1, 96) = 9.79$, $p < 0.01$, $F_2(1, 28) = 5.22$, $p < 0.04$. This interaction reflected the fact that responses to words in lower case were faster than responses to words in upper case in the unstable condition, that is when words in upper case had a higher-frequency neighbour. When words had no HFN, in either lower case or in upper case, there was no effect of typography.

Table 6

Mean lexical decision times (RTs) in ms, error rates (% E), and activation cycles for words in Experiment 1

| | Word condition | | | |
| | Stable | | Unstable | |
	Lower case	Upper case	Lower case	Upper case
LDT				
RTs	631	635	656	692
% E	4.94	4.87	8.87	9.67
IA simulation				
Activation cycle	17.07	17.13	17.40	18.73

Simulation study

Method

Stimuli
The same thirty words were run in two simulation studies. In the 'upper-case' simulation the lexicon was made up of all stimulus words, plus their neighbours. In the 'lower-case' simulation the neighbours of upper-case words were removed from the lexicon.

Procedure
Simulations were run with the IA model and its default parameters (McClelland and Rumelhart, 1981). The lexicon used by Jacobs and Grainger (1992) was slightly modified because the accents had to be taken into account as in the French lexical database (Imbs, 1971). The activation-based criterion (Jacobs and Grainger, 1992) was used to determine word identification cycle. This was set at 0.67, which represents 90% of the asymptotic activation values for words. The number of processing cycles to reach the threshold was used as the dependent variable.

Results

Mean word identification cycles are presented in Table 6. The word identification cycles for stable stimuli were identical for both 'upper-case' and 'lower-case' conditions (17.1 cycles). For unstable stimuli, words in 'upper case' took longer to reach the threshold (18.1 cycles) than the same words in 'lower case' (17.4 cycles). An analysis of variance with items as a random factor show a significant interaction between stability and 'typography', $F(1, 28) = 20.71$, $p < 0.0001$. Thus, the simulation data successfully captured the LDT experiment data.

Discussion

The LDT data replicated those of Grainger et al. (1989) and confirmed the psychological reality of the NFE: when words were written in upper case, that is in a typography for which they had a HFN, reaction times were 36 ms longer than for the same words written in lower case with the accent. The same comparison in the stable condition indicated that this difference was not a typography effect. When the typography was changed while the words still had no neighbour, reaction times were almost identical (+4 ms). The interaction between typography and stability confirmed that the presence of a HFN inhibited the visual word recognition process. Moreover, because the same words were used in both conditions, this inhibition cannot be attributed to factors such as the presence of a HFN. The simulation study produced a similar interaction. The number of cycles to reach the threshold was, of course, absolutely insensitive to the case change in the stable condition, whereas it was greater for 'upper-case' words in the unstable condition. These data provide strong support for the existence of an inhibitory mechanism.

Experiment 2: several HFNs

Simulation investigations with artificial lexica showed that the competition mechanism in the IA model still produced inhibition when N was increased from 1 to 4. The inhibition effect was also observed when N was increased from 4 to 12 for a large difference in frequency between the stimulus word and its neighbours. Such an inhibition should also be observed in LDT experiments when the number of HFNs is increased. However, this effect was never observed (Grainger et al., 1989). On the contrary, Grainger and colleagues reported facilitatory effects (Grainger and Jacobs, 1996). Nonetheless, it could be assumed that the inhibitory effect of large higher-frequency neighbourhood was masked by confounding variables as the NFE had been at times. Experiment 2 was designed to examine whether a large higher-frequency neighbourhood produces an inhibitory effect on LDT. The same lower–upper-case design as in Experiment 1 was used. In the experimental (unstable) condition the number of HFNs changed as the word was written in upper or in lower case, whereas in the stable condition the number of HFNs was constant in both cases. Two conditions of neighbourhood change were tested. In the first condition, the number of HFNs increased from, in average, 1.13 to 3.07. In the second condition the number of HFNs increased from 3.07 to 5.93.

Lexical decision task

Method

Participants
The same 98 undergraduate students from the University of Burgundy participated in this experiment.

Stimuli
Sixty four- and five-letter words with low frequency were selected so that their orthographic neighbourhood was stable versus unstable in upper and in lower case (Table 7). Fifteen of these words had one or two HFNs (mean HFN = 1.13) in

Table 7

Statistical characteristics of Experiment 2 word materials

	Word condition			
	Stable		Unstable	
	Lower case	Upper case	Lower case	Upper case
Stimulus with small N change				
Example	héron	HERON	môme	MOME
Log *F*	2.69	2.69	2.58	2.58
N	1.53	1.53	2.13	6
G	1.27	1.33	1.53	2.4
HFN	1	1	1.13	3.07
HFG	1	1	1	1.67
Higher-frequency neighbours	héros	HEROS	même	MEME
				MODE
Stimuli with large N change				
Example	débit	DEBIT	coût	COUT
Log *F*	2.63	2.63	2.49	2.49
N	3.13	4.33	4.13	9.2
G	1.87	2.07	2.4	3.13
HFN	2.4	2.53	3.07	5.93
HFG	1.73	1.73	2.07	2.73
Higher-frequency neighbours	débat	DEBAT	août	AOUT
	début	DEBUT	goût	BOUT
	dépit	DEPIT		COUP
				COUR
				GOUT
				TOUT

Log F = mean word frequency per 100 million (in logarithms). N = number of neighbours. G = number of gangs. HFN = number of higher-frequency neighbours. HFG = number of gangs with higher-frequency neighbours.

the lower-case condition and more than one in the upper-case condition (2 to 9; mean HFN = 3.07). In the corresponding stable condition, fifteen words were chosen for which the number of HFNs was 1, whatever the typography. Fifteen other words were selected for which the number of HFNs was more than 1 in the lower-case condition (2 to 6; mean HFN = 3.07) and the number of HFNs was higher in the upper-case condition (between 3 and 16; mean HFN = 5.93). The fifteen words of the corresponding stable condition were selected in order to match the number of HFNs with the unstable condition (between 2 and 4; mean HFN = 2.44).

Procedure and design
The procedure was the same as in Experiment 1. For half of the 98 participants, the words were presented in lower case and for the other half in upper case. All the participants responded to the four sets of words.

Results

Mean correct response latencies and error rates averaged over participants are presented in Table 8. Participant and item means were submitted to separate analyses of variance that were reported as F_1 and F_2 after removing responses with latencies greater than 1500 ms. None of the main effects was significant. The interaction between stability and typography was marginally significant when the number of HFNs changed from 1 to 2 and more, $F_1(1, 96) = 2.82$, $p < 0.10$, $F_2(1, 28) = 3.24$, $p < 0.10$, but not when the number of HFNs changed from 3 to 6.87.

Simulation study

Method

Stimuli
The same 60 words were ran in two simulation studies. In the 'upper-case' simulation, the lexicon was made of all stimulus words plus their HFNs. In the 'lower-case' simulation, the words that were neighbours of upper-case stimuli but not of lower-case stimuli were removed from the lexicon. The same procedure as in Experiment 1 was used.

Results

Mean word identification cycles are presented in Table 8. In the small change condition (mean HFNs = 1.13 to 3.07), the word identification cycles for stable stimuli were identical for both 'upper-case' and 'lower-case' conditions (17.67 cycles). For unstable stimuli, the identification cycle for words in 'upper case' took longer to reach threshold (18.86 cycles) than the same words in 'lower case' (18.33 cycles). Nonetheless, the interaction between stability and 'typography' failed to reach significance, $F(1, 28) = 3.80$, $p < 0.10$.

   In the large change condition (mean HFNs = 3.07 to 5.93), the word identification cycles for stable stimuli were slightly higher for the 'upper-case' compared with the 'lower-case' condition (18.53 cycles vs. 18.40 cycles). The same difference was observed for unstable stimuli (respectively 19.13 and 19 cycles for

Table 8

Mean lexical decision times (RTs) in ms, error rates (% E), and activation cycles for words in Experiment 2

	Word condition			
	Stable		Unstable	
	Lower case	Upper case	Lower case	Upper case
Small N change				
LDT				
RTs	654	669	641	674
% E	8.07	6.80	10.73	10.60
IA simulation				
Activation cycle	17.67	17.67	18.33	18.86
Large N change				
LDT				
RTs	631	643	641	671
% E	12.67	15.40	7.33	9.93
IA simulation				
Activation cycle	18.53	18.40	19.00	19.13

words in 'upper case' and in 'lower case'). The interaction between stability and 'typography' was not significant ($F(1, 28) = 1.26$, $p > 0.10$).

Discussion

One would expect that a change in the number of HFNs would produce either an inhibitory effect, following the IA predictions, or a facilitatory effect, following the experiment of Andrews (1989). However, no interaction at all between stability and typography was observed in our experiment. In addition, these results were confirmed in simulation studies. The IA simulations did not indicate either that words with about 1 HFN reached threshold significantly earlier than words with several HFNs, or that words with few HFNs were more activated than words with more HFNs. This lack of effect suggests that the materials were not perfectly designed.

One possible explanation is that the word typography manipulation modified not only the number of HFNs but also the number of gangs. We reanalysed the data by distinguishing three sets of words when both neighbourhood size and *G* were controlled (see Table 9). In the first set, the number of HFNs and HFG (higher-frequency gangs) were stable whatever the typography (control condition). In the second set, HFG was held constant and the number of HFNs varied from 2.46

Table 9

Statistical characteristics of the word materials, mean lexical decision times (RTs) in ms and activation cycles of the reanalysis of Experiment 2

	Word condition					
	HFN and HFG stable		HFN unstable, HFG stable		HFN and HFG unstable	
	Lower case	Upper case	Lower case	Upper case	Lower case	Upper case
No. of stimuli	28	28	13	13	19	19
Log F	2.64	2.64	1.40	1.40	1.68	1.68
N	2.18	2.61	3.54	7.23	3.00	7.84
G	1.54	1.68	2	2.31	1.95	3.00
HFN	1.68	1.68	2.46	4.23	1.74	4.53
HFG	1.36	1.36	1.69	1.69	1.37	2.47
LDT						
RTs	649	669	641	697	637	664
IA simulation						
Activation cycle	18.11	18.04	18.38	19.15	18.79	18.79

in lower case to 4.23 in upper case. Thus, the second set was a condition in which a 'pure' influence of the number of HFNs could be examined. Finally, in the third set the number of HFNs and HFG increased from lower-case to upper-case words.

The LDT data indicated that words in upper case were always responded to more slowly than words in lower case. However, the difference between latencies for upper and lower case was greater in the condition for which HFG was stable and the number of HFN increased (+56 ms) than for the control condition (+20 ms). A post-hoc analysis indicated a significant interaction between typography and these two sets of words, $F(1, 39) = 4.23$, $p < 0.05$. When the number of HFNs and HFGs increased with the typography change (third set of words), only a 26 ms difference was observed between words in upper and in lower case. This difference was very similar to the one observed in the control condition and no interaction was observed ($F < 1$).

Simulation data were analysed in the same way. The word identification cycles for the control stimuli were the same in both lower- and upper-case conditions (18.11 and 18.04 cycles), while for the condition in which the number of HFN increased while HFG was stable, they were lower in the upper than in the lower-case condition (18.38 and 19.15 cycles, respectively). A post-hoc analysis indicated a significant interaction between typography and HFN stability, $F(1, 39) = 24.07$; $p < 0.0001$. Such an interaction was not observed when the words of the third set were compared to those of the control condition ($F < 1$). Our experimental data were perfectly consistent with the simulation data and confirmed the inhibitory effect of a large higher-frequency neighbourhood. In addition, they showed that the word competition can be counterbalanced by the number of gangs. When HFG varied along with the number of HFNs no difference was observed between words in upper and lower case. It can plausibly be assumed that this effect was never previously observed because G and N are correlated.

General discussion

Our issue has been to focus on the two main mechanisms of the IA model (McClelland and Rumelhart, 1981): word-to-word inhibition and word-to-letter reverberation. The use of artificial lexica allows us to dismantle each of these mechanisms. First, the inhibitory mechanism is sensitive to N and neighbour frequency; both variables increase an inhibitory effect. Moreover, there is an interaction between these two variables. Second, the reverberation mechanism is sensitive to N, to neighbour frequency, and to G. All three variables increase the facilitation effect of reverberation. Third, the combined effect of reverberation and inhibition appears complex and suggests a $N \times G$ interactive influence. When there is only one gang, reverberation amplifies inhibition. When there are several gangs, the amplification effect of reverberation on inhibition is very weak. The consequence is that a word with several neighbours may be less inhibited when G is high than a word with few neighbours belonging to the same gang. This hypothesis receives some empirical support from Mathey and Zagar (2000) and could explain why high N words are responded to faster than low N words (Andrews, 1989, 1992).

Turning to the inhibition mechanism, the purpose of the present experiments was to explore the reality of the phenomenon in a LDT. Experiment 1 showed that WORDS (in upper case) with one HFN are responded to more slowly than the same words (in lower case) without a HFN. These data strongly support the existence of an inhibitory effect because in our experiment all confounded variables but typography were controlled. Whether other variables are able to mask the influence of competition when comparing two sets of different words in a lexical decision task remains an open issue (for example the number of phonographic neighbours, Peereman and Content, 1997).

Experiment 2 examined the influence of increasing the number of HFNs for which the IA model predicted an inhibitory effect. The results were in accordance with the IA prediction when the number of gangs was strictly controlled. This result provides surprising and new support in favour of the IA model. Indeed G was never controlled in previous experiments that examined the effect of increasing the number of HFNs (Grainger et al., 1989; Grainger and Jacobs, 1996).

Experiments 1 and 2 clearly establish the existence of an inhibition mechanism within the word recognition process. Whether inhibition can be an independent and localised process (as the word-to-word inhibition in the IA model) or an emergent property of a PDP model has to be examined. Up to now it is not clear how PDP models (Plaut, McClelland, Seidenberg and Patterson, 1996; Seidenberg and McClelland, 1989) can accommodate inhibition effects. For example, Grainger (1992) has suggested that the model of Seidenberg and McClelland (1989) seems unable to capture 'pure' inhibitory effects as produced by a higher-frequency neighbour (but see Andrews, 1997, p. 456, for an alternative hypothesis).

Experiment 2 confirmed the importance of a gang effect (see Mathey and Zagar, 2000). We assume that this effect is a manifestation of the reverberation mechanism into the IA framework. The gang effect (or N facilitation effect) rules out serial models of lexical access (Forster, 1976; Paap and Johansen, 1994; Paap, Newsome, McDonald and Schvaneveldt, 1982) because such models predict that a high N can only have an inhibitory effect on word recognition. In contrast, PDP models easily accommodate this effect. Seidenberg and McClelland (1989, p. 538) simulated a facilitatory effect of large N and also a $N \times$ frequency interaction.

We have shown how the IA model can account for what has been described in the literature as the 'neighbourhood conflict'. It remains for future research to explore in detail other features of this model.

S A T O R
A R E P O
T E N E T
O P E R A
R O T A S

(The ploughman, with his plough, manages the work)

Acknowledgements

We thank Ronald Peereman for fruitful discussions and Joël Pynte for his comments.

References

Andrews, S. (1989). Frequency and neighbourhood effects on lexical access: activation or search? Journal of Experimental Psychology: Learning, Memory, and Cognition, 15, 802–814.

Andrews, S. (1992). Frequency and neighbourhood effects on lexical access: lexical similarity or orthographic redundancy? Journal of Experimental Psychology: Learning, Memory, and Cognition, 18, 234–254.

Andrews, S. (1997). The effect of orthographic similarity on lexical retrieval: resolving neighbourhood conflicts. Psychonomic Bulletin and Review, 4, 439–461.

Bozon, F. and Carbonnel, S. (1996). Influence des voisins orthographiques sur l'identification de mots et de pseudomots. Revue de Neuropsychologie, 2, 219–237.

Carreiras, M., Perea, M. and Grainger, J. (1997). Effects of orthographic neighborhood in visual word recognition: cross-tasks comparisons. Journal of Experimental Psychology: Learning, Memory, and Cognition, 23, 857–871.

Coltheart, M., Davelaar, E., Jonasson, J.T. and Besner, D. (1977). Access to the Internal Lexicon. In: S. Dornic (Ed.), Attention and Performance VI. London: Academic Press.

Feldman-Stewart, D. and Mewhort, D.J.K. (1994). Learning in small connectionist networks does not generalize to large networks. Psychological Research, 56, 99–103.

Forster, K.I. (1976). Accessing the mental lexicon. In: R.J. Wales and E.W. Walker (Eds.), New Approaches to Language Mechanisms. Amsterdam: North-Holland, pp. 257–287.

Forster, K.I. and Shen, D. (1996). No enemies in the neighborhood: absence of inhibitory neighborhood effects in lexical decision and semantic categorization. Journal of Experimental Psychology: Learning, Memory, and Cognition, 22, 696–713.

Grainger, J. (1990). Word frequency and neighbourhood frequency effects in lexical decision and naming. Journal of Memory and Language, 29, 228–244.

Grainger, J. (1992). Orthographic neighborhoods and visual word recognition. In: R. Frost and L. Katz (Eds.), Orthography, Morphology, and Meaning. Amsterdam: Elsevier, pp. 131–146.

Grainger, J. and Jacobs, A.M. (1994). A dual read-out model of word context effects in letter perception: further investigations of the word superiority effect. Journal of Experimental Psychology: Human Perception and Performance, 20, 1158–1176.

Grainger, J. and Jacobs, A.M. (1996). Orthographic processing in visual word recognition: a multiple read-out model. Psychological Review, 103, 518–565.

Grainger, J., O'Regan, J.K., Jacobs, A.M. and Segui, J. (1989). On the role of competing word units in visual word recognition: the neighborhood frequency effect. Perception and Psychophysics, 45, 189–195.

Grainger, J., O'Regan, J.K., Jacobs, A.M. and Segui, J. (1992). Neighborhood frequency effects and letter visibility in visual word recognition. Perception and Psychophysics, 51, 49–56.

Havens, L.L. and Foote, W.E. (1963). The effect of competition on visual duration threshold and its independence of stimulus frequency. Journal of Experimental Psychology, 65, 6–11.

Huntsman, L.A. and Lima, S.D. (1996). Orthographic neighborhood structure and lexical access. Journal of Psycholinguistic Research, 25, 417–429.

Imbs, P. (1971). Etudes statistiques sur le vocabulaire français. Dictionnaire des fréquences. Vocabulaire littéraire des XIXe et XXe siècles. Centre de recherche pour un trésor de la langue française, CNRS, Nancy. Paris: Librairie Marcel Didier.

Jacobs, A.M. and Grainger, J. (1992). Testing a semistochastic variant of the interactive activation model in different word recognition experiments. Journal of Experimental Psychology: Human Perception and Performance, 18, 1174–1188.

Jacobs, A.M. and Grainger, J. (1994). Models of visual word recognition — sampling the state of the art. Journal of Experimental Psychology: Human Perception and Performance, 20, 1311–1334.

Johnson, N.F. and Pugh, K.R. (1994). A cohort model of visual word recognition. Cognitive Psychology, 26, 240–346.

Mathey, S. (submitted). Le rôle du voisinage orthographique lors de la reconnaissance des mots écrits. Revue Canadienne de Psychologie Expérimentale.

Mathey, S. and Zagar, D. (1996). Rôle du voisinage orthographique lors de la reconnaissance visuelle des mots de 4, 6 et 8 lettres. Revue de Neuropsychologie, 2, 205–217.

Mathey, S. and Zagar, D. (2000). The role of neighborhood distribution in visual word recognition: words with single and twin neighbors. Journal of Experimental Psychology: Human Perception and Performance, 26, 184–205.

McClelland, J.L. and Rumelhart, D.E. (1981). An interactive activation model of context effects in letter perception, Part 1. An account of basic findings. Psychological Review, 88, 375–407.

Newbigging, P.L. (1961). The perceptual redintegration of frequent and infrequent words. Canadian Journal of Psychology, 15, 123–131.

Paap, K.R. and Johansen, S. (1994). The case of the vanishing frequency effect: a retest of the verification model. Journal of Experimental Psychology: Human Perception and Performance, 20, 1129–1157.

Paap, K.R., Newsome, S.L., McDonald, J.E. and Schvaneveldt, R.W. (1982). An activation–verification model for letter and word recognition: the word-superiority effect. Psychological Review, 89, 573–594.

Peereman, R. and Content, A. (1997). Orthographic and phonological neighborhoods in naming: not all neighbors are equally influential in orthographic space. Journal of Memory and Language, 37, 382–410.

Perea, M. and Pollatsek, A. (1998). The effects of neighborhood frequency in reading and lexical decision. Journal of Experimental Psychology: Human Perception and Performance, 24 767–779.

Plaut, D.C., McClelland, J.L., Seidenberg, M.S. and Patterson, J.C. (1996). Understanding normal and impaired word reading: computational principles in quasi-regular domains. Psychological Review, 103, 56–115.

Reicher, G.M. (1969). Perceptual recognition as a function of meaningfulness of stimulus material. Journal of Experimental Psychology, 81, 274–280.

Sears, C.R., Hino, Y. and Lupker, J. (1995). Neighbourhood size and neighbourhood frequency effects in word recognition. Journal of Experimental Psychology: Human Perception and Performance, 21, 876–900.

Seidenberg, M.S. and McClelland, J.L. (1989). A distributed, developmental model of word recognition and naming. Psychological Review, 96, 523–568.

Zagar, D. (1995). La lecture: processus de base. Habilitation à diriger des recherches. Dijon: Université de Bourgogne.

Ziegler, J. and Perry, C. (1998). No more problems in Coltheart's neighborhood: resolving neighborhood conflicts in the lexical decision task. Cognition, 68, B53–B62.

CHAPTER 3

Words Likely to Activate Many Lexical Candidates Are Granted an Advantage: Evidence from Within-word Eye Movements

Joël Pynte
CNRS and University of Provence

Abstract

Eye movements were recorded during the reading of long words, which were presented in isolation at their optimal viewing position. Gaze durations were found to vary as a function of the number of lexical candidates consistent with the few letters located around the fixation point, with apparently shorter processing times for words likely to initially activate a large set of lexical candidates, as compared to few-candidate words. This facilitatory effect was interpreted as resulting from a word-to-letter activation feedback, in keeping with the proposals of Andrews (1989, 1992).

Reading as a Perceptual Process/A. Kennedy, R. Radach, D. Heller and J. Pynte (Editors)
© 2000 Elsevier Science Ltd. All rights reserved

Introduction

For the past ten years, the word recognition literature has been dominated by a debate as to whether the time necessary to identify a word depends on the sole intrinsic properties of that word (e.g. its orthographic regularity, its frequency of usage, etc.) or whether some other properties, linked to its orthographic 'neighbourhood' (i.e. the set of orthographically similar words likely to be confounded with the target word at an early stage of perceptual analysis) also play a role (for a comprehensive review see Andrews, 1997).

Most of the studies that have investigated this issue have adopted an orthographic similarity metric labelled N, which refers to the number of words that can be created by changing one letter of the target word (Landauer and Streeter, 1973; Coltheart et al., 1977; Chapter 2, this volume). For example, in a series of experiments that orthogonally manipulated N and word frequency, Andrews (1989, 1992) obtained a neighbourhood effect in both lexical decisions and naming tasks. More specifically, she found that lexical-decision and naming times for low-frequency words that had many neighbours were shorter than for low-frequency words with few neighbours. Simultaneously, Grainger, O'Regan, Jacobs and Segui (1989) demonstrated the importance of another neighbourhood metric, namely the frequency of neighbours, relative to the frequency of the target word. They reported that the presence of a single high-frequency word in the lexical neighbourhood of the stimulus word is sufficient for lengthening lexical decision latencies. These results clearly conflict with those of Andrews. Although the metrics used to assess neighbourhood influences are clearly different in each series of experiments, they are certainly not independent. If a low-frequency word has many neighbours (the situation studied by Andrews), it is likely that one of them will be frequent, and this puts us in the situation used by Grainger et al. (1989) that is, a low-frequency word with a more frequent neighbour. Yet, opposite findings have been reported, with a facilitatory effect of neighbourhood size in Andrews' case, and an inhibitory effect of neighbourhood frequency in Grainger et al.'s case. In spite of this discrepancy, both findings can apparently be accommodated in the framework of the interactive activation model of lexical access of McClelland and Rumelhart (1981). For example, the results of Grainger et al. (1989) are consistent with the notion, embodied in the interactive activation model, that identification involves competition between activated word neighbours in order to select the lexical representation that is the best match with the input stimulus. As for Andrews' results, they can be interpreted as deriving from top-down feedback from the word level to the letter level, an hypothesis which seems to imply the existence of both bottom-up and top-down activation links between letter positions and lexical representations.

The discrepancy between the findings of Andrews and those of Grainger et al. has led some authors to look for alternative explanations, however. For example, the argument has been made that facilitatory and inhibitory effects might reflect different subprocesses, or 'stages' of lexical access, with one or the other being privileged as a function of experimental conditions. For example, in the activation–verification model of Paap, Newsome, McDonald and Schvaneveldt (1982), candidate activation and target selection are assumed to operate at two distinct processing steps. It could be argued, in this framework, that in Andrews's experiments, a response occurred before identification had been fully completed, and that performance in this case mainly reflected the activation stage of lexical access. This suggestion is consistent with the high error rate found in these studies. By contrast, in Grainger et al.'s experiments, participants may have been led to adopt a more cautious behaviour, thus emphasising the verification stage.

Such a view is clearly at odds with the philosophy behind the interactive activation model that basically sees word recognition as a unitary process, with all letters being apprehended in parallel, and both feed-back activation and lateral inhibition occurring simultaneously. One can doubt whether either of these assumptions are justified, however. As noted by Andrews (1997) in many studies conducted in the framework of the interactive activation model it is not always clear whether the conclusions that have been drawn actually derived from empirical evidence, or whether they were merely taken for granted, as a consequence of the metric used for assessing orthographic similarities. Andrews (1997) mentions, for example, the assumption that words are coded in terms of position-specific letter representations, which is central to the interactive activation model, and seems to be implicit in the very notion of orthographic neighbourhood.

In fact, there are good reasons to think that all letter positions do not contribute in the same way to lexical access, and that the position of the critical letters (i.e., the letters whose replacement produces neighbours) might, in fact, be important. It is a well known fact that visual acuity rapidly decreases as soon as one moves away from the centre of the fovea, which means that the few letters located around the fixation point are less likely to be misidentified (and thus less likely to activate neighbours) than letters located outside the area around the fixation point. Letters further away from the fixation point are probably more likely to be misidentified and thus more likely to permit the activation of neighbours. In an experiment that systematically varied the position of the fixation point, Grainger, O'Regan, Jacobs and Segui (1992) found virtually no neighbourhood effect when the word was presented in such a way that the critical letter (i.e. the letter likely to generate a higher-frequency neighbour) coincided with the fixation point. This result can easily be interpreted if one admits that the fixated position is the one where the probability of correctly identifying the critical letter is the highest, and thus the probability that a lexical competitor will be activated the lowest. Part of the neighbourhood effects reported in the literature could possibly be reinterpreted in terms of such perceptual constraints. For example, the finding that several candidates are apparently activated before a stimulus word is eventually identified is entirely consistent with the notion that perceptual analysis is initially restricted to a few central letters. Similarly, selection of a single lexical representation could, in part, derive from purely bottom-up processes, as more perceptual information becomes available from more and more remote positions.

Additional evidence in favour of a multi-stage view of lexical access can be found in the pattern of eye movements as words are inspected. Long words in particular often receive more than one fixation, and one can wonder how recognition might proceed under such circumstances. The role of within-word eye movements in lexical access was examined by Pynte (1996) in a situation where participants were forced to fixate the 'optimal viewing position' (O'Regan, Lévy-Schoen, Pynte and Brugallière, 1984) of long words sharing all but a few letters with a higher-frequency potential competitor (e.g., the low-frequency French word 'imbriquer' shares all but its two beginning letters with the high-frequency word 'fabriquer', whereas 'recouvrer' shares all but its two end letters with the high-frequency 'recouvrir'). The results indicated that refixations were mainly directed towards the critical part of the stimulus (e.g. more left refixations in the case of 'imbriquer', and more right refixations in the case of 'recouvrer').

Words' neighbours also exert an influence in continuous reading. In an experiment recently published by Perea and Pollatsek (1998), participants had their eye movements recorded while they were reading continuous text. Target words with either no higher-frequency neighbours or at least one higher-frequency neighbour were embedded in a sentential context. The inhibitory effect of Grainger et al. (1992) was replicated in this situation. The reading data, furthermore, indicate that this inhibitory effect tended to occur quite late in lexical processing, with longer fixations recorded on the text immediately following the words with higher frequency neighbours (as well as more regressions back to these words). Perea and Pollatsek (1998) interpret these effects as being lexical in nature, and most probably linked to the selection stage of lexical access.

As far as the activation stage of lexical access is concerned, potential neighbourhood effects are to be expected on early measures of visual inspection, such as first fixation, or gaze durations. In a new series of eye-tracking experiments, Pollatsek, Perea and Binder (1999) failed to find any such early facilitatory effect, however. On the contrary, they reported that neighbourhood size had a late inhibitory effect on the duration of the fixations recorded on the following word. However, since the same words gave rise to the classical facilitatory effect in another experiment using the lexical decision task, there is a possibility that the inhibitory effect found in the reading experiment occurred as lexical processing was interfacing with higher-order processing (e.g. integration of the word meaning in the sentential context). Let us assume that sentential integration starts before the selection of a single lexical entry has been completed. The integration process can be assumed to be more complex for high-*N* words (that is when many candidates can be assumed to be still active) than for low-*N* words (for which the number of activated candidates is presumably low). It is possible that the facilitatory effect of having a large neighbourhood, found in the lexical decision task, was masked by such integration processes in the reading experiment.

A more general source of difficulty, which might have prevented any clear facilitatory effect from showing up in the experiment of Pollatsek et al., relates to the fact that orthographic neighbours can be responsible for both facilitatory and inhibitory effects. This difficulty can theoretically be bypassed in the framework of a multi-stage approach of lexical access, since, in this framework, the set of candidates initially activated during the first fixation made on the stimulus word is not necessarily identical to the set of close neighbours that will eventually compete for recognition. Such a distinction is very difficult to make in practice, however, at least as far as 4- or 5-letter words are concerned (the size used by Pollatsek et al.). Things are probably different for long words, provided it is assumed (1) that an initial set of candidates is activated on the sole basis of the few letters around the fixation point, and (2) that only close competitors are likely to exert inhibition. The expression 'close competitor' could be defined, for example, as referring to words sharing almost all their letters with the stimulus word and, in any case, more letters than the few initially identified ones.

The interest in using long words is illustrated in Table 1, which indicates the average number of words consistent with a given cluster of letter (in rows: 2 to 9 letters located around the fixation point) as a function of word length (in columns: 4- to 11-letter words). The fixation point is assumed to be located on the letter

Table 1

Average number of activated candidates for 4- to 10-character words, assuming that only a few central letters (number varying from 2 to 9 characters) initially contibute to lexical access

Central cluster	Word length						
	4-char	5-char	6-char	7-char	8-char	9-char	10-char
2 char	8.81	18.70	19.73	25.42	35.53	33.84	29.79
3 char	0.64	1.83	4.11	5.33	4.66	4.56	5.07
4 char	0	0.21	0.86	1.15	1.27	1.23	2.09
5 char		0	0.09	0.33	0.43	0.51	0.57
6 char			0	0.06	0.14	0.23	0.33
7 char				0	0.03	0.16	0.18
8 char					0	0.02	0.03
9 char						0	0.01
N	896	2120	3487	4555	4994	4681	3854

immediately left of the centre (exhaustive counting from the BRULEX data-base, Content and Radeau, 1988). For example, for 9-letter words (6th column), there are 4.56 words of that length on average (excluding the target word itself) that contain the same trigram in positions 3, 4, and 5. In contrast, the number of 4-letter words containing the same three 'middle' letters is 0.64 on average (excluding the target word itself). These values illustrate the notion that long words are more likely to produce early facilitatory effects than short ones, if one assumes that the amount of facilitation elicited during the early stages of the recognition process depends on the number of lexical candidates activated by the few letters located around the fixation point.

The aim of the experiment reported in this chapter was to revisit the question raised by Pollatsek et al. (1999) and more precisely to examine whether the number of candidates likely to be activated during the first fixation made on a long word can influence the total time spent on the word. In order to avoid any interference from sentential integration processes (see above), isolated word presentation was used.

Method

Participants

Thirty-two psychology students at the University of Provence, Aix-en-Provence, volunteered for participating in the experiment. All were native speakers of French with normal vision.

Task and apparatus

Participants were asked to read series of three words (plus an additional probe word) presented successively at the centre of the display monitor of a PC computer. They controlled stimulus presentation with a button connected to the computer. Words were displayed in lower case, except for the probe, which was in upper case. Participants had to decide whether the probe had been presented in the previous series of three words. The word of interest here was the second one (the target). It was presented in such a way that its fourth letter coincided with the location previously occupied by the fixation point. The first and third words were always relatively short (three or four letters long) and were aimed at keeping the eye in the middle of the screen where the target was to be presented. Eye movements were monitored by using a standard spectacle-mounted infrared limbus tracking device. Output from the horizontal detectors from the right eye was sampled every 5 ms. During the experiment, the participant's head was restrained with a dental-composition bite bar and adjustable head- and chin-rest. Prior to each block of four trials, participants completed a calibration procedure. They were asked to look one at a time at five points located in a line in the area to be occupied by the stimulus material. The system was accurate to approximately ±0.5 characters.

Linguistic materials

The description of the linguistic materials only concerns target words (the second word in each series). All target words were nine letters long and were presented so that the initial fixation was located on the fourth letter. Sixty target words were presented, among which twenty were high-frequency words (mean: 229 per million), twenty were medium-frequency words (mean: 12 per million), and twenty were low-frequency words (mean: 2 per million). Moreover, the orthographic familiarity of the trigrams located at positions 345 and 456 was varied. For half the words, these trigrams were familiar (mean probability of occurrence: 0.0018, see Content and Radeau, 1988), whereas for the other half, they were unfamiliar (mean probability of occurrence: 0.00018). The target words also differed from the point of view of the number of candidates likely to be activated from the four letters located at positions 3, 4, 5, and 6. A candidate was defined here as any 9-letter word containing these four letters at these positions. Half the target words had no such candidates (few-candidate condition), whereas for the other half there was at least one (mean: 1.40, many-candidate condition). Since it can be suspected that the visual system might be somewhat inaccurate at determining word lengths, a new metric was defined by including the number of 8- and 10-letter candidates (i.e. a candidate is now defined as any 8-, 9-, or 10-letter word containing the same letters as the stimulus word at positions 3, 4, 5 and 6). The obtained mean values were 4.83 and 0.33 for the many- and few-candidate conditions, respectively. One can also suspect the visual system to be inaccurate at determining letter positions. A third metric was thus used, namely the number of 9-letter words containing the same four letters at any location, except for the first and the last ones. According to this new definition, the set of candidates associated with the word 'veritable' includes all those 9-letter words containing the sequence 'rita' at positions 2345, 3456, 4567, or 5678 (-rita----, --rita---, ---rita--, ----rita-). The obtained values were 4.10 and 0.13 for the many- and few-candidate conditions, respectively (13.07 and 0.60, respectively, if both length and positions are assumed to be inaccurate).

Procedure and design

A trial began with a fixation point made of two dots. The participant's initial button pressing replaced it with the first word. Subsequent button presses displayed successive words in the series, until the fourth press, where an upper-case probe word appeared. The participant responded to this word (was it in the previous series of three?) by pressing one of two buttons located under his/her left and right hands (see Pynte, 1996 for a more detailed description of this procedure). A practice session of twelve trials was given, followed by 60 experimental trials. For half of the trials, the probe word was one of the three previous ones (either the first, the second, or the third) and called for a 'yes' answer. For the other half, it was a completely new, 3-, 4-, or 9-character word (sometimes orthographically or semantically related to one of the previous three words), and called for a 'no' answer. Only the visual inspection of the second word in each experimental series was analysed. This was done according to a 2 (many vs. few candidates) × 2 (familiar vs. unfamiliar trigrams) × 3 (high-, medium- or low-frequency words) design. All three factors were within-participant/between-item factors.

Results

On average, 2.19 saccades per trial were recorded, with a majority of first saccades being directed towards the target word's beginning (see Fig. 1). Moreover, the direction of the first saccade was influenced by the factors manipulated in the experiment in a rather complex way (see the percentage of left-going first saccades for each condition of the experiment in the first column of Table 2; $F_1(2, 62) = 17.09$, $p < 0.05$, $F_2(2, 48) = 9.00$, $p < 0.05$, for the interaction between word frequency and trigram familiarity; $F_1(1, 31) = 20.96$, $p < 0.05$, $F_2(1, 48) = 10.23$, $p < 0.05$, for the interaction between trigram familiarity and number of candidates). A possible account for these effects will be considered in the Discussion section. For the time being, it must be noted that specific inspection strategies are likely to influence first fixation durations. As indicated in Fig. 2, when the first saccade was directed towards the right end of the word, its latency

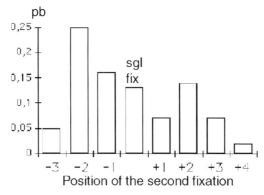

Fig. 1. Distribution of first saccades as a function of direction and size.

Table 2

Mean percentages of left-going first saccades (% lft), first fixation durations (fix1) and gaze durations (ms) as a function of word frequency, trigram familiarity and number of candidates

Trigrams:	Many candidates						Few candidates					
	familiar			unfamil.			familiar			unfamil.		
	% lft	fix1	gaze	% lft	fix1	gaze	% lft	fix1	gaze	% lft	fix1	gaze
Word freq.												
High	81	384	924	56	421	930	63	387	954	59	389	1017
Medium	61	403	944	61	406	961	63	439	968	74	377	992
Low	60	427	925	60	396	971	56	421	980	78	382	996

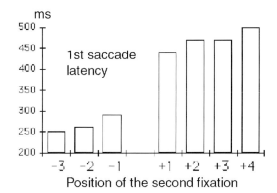

Fig. 2. First saccade latencies as a function of location and size.

was much higher (469 ms for right-going saccades vs. 271 ms for left-going ones; $F_1(1, 31) = 1558.30$, $F_2(1, 48) = 4489.42$). Clearly, such huge asymmetries cannot be ignored if one wishes to avoid possible artefacts when examining the locus of a particular effect during visual inspection.

Table 2 also indicates the mean first fixation and gaze durations (sum of all the fixations recorded while the target word was displayed on the screen) for each condition of the experiment. Six percent of the trials ended up in an incorrect answer to the probe and were excluded from the analysis. First fixation durations did not seem to be clearly affected by any of the three factors manipulated in the experiment, except for a marginally significant effect of trigram familiarity (410 ms vs. 390 ms for familiar and unfamiliar trigrams, respectively; $F_1(1, 31) = 3.06$, $F_2(1, 48) = 3.33$), and a series of complex interactions mimicking those revealed in the direction-of-first-fixation analysis. By contrast, the analysis of gaze durations revealed a significant main effect of Number of candidates and Trigram familiarity, with shorter gazes for the many-candidate condition than for the few-candidate condition (943 vs. 984 ms, $F_1(1, 31) = 16.61$, $p = 0.05$, $F_2(1, 48) = 14.96$, $p < 0.05$), and for familiar trigrams than for unfamiliar trigrams (949 vs. 978 ms, $F_1(1, 31) = 6.90$, $p < 0.05$, $F_2(1, 48) = 6.41$, $p < 0.05$). No effect of word frequency (Fs < 1), and no interaction between any of the factors (all Fs < 1.4) were found for this measure.

The lack of any clear effect in the first fixation analysis probably derives from the fact that this measure mixed two quite different types of first fixations. For those trials where a single fixation was recorded, first fixation durations corresponded to the total time spent on the stimulus word. By contrast, in the case of a multi-fixation strategy, the first fixation corresponds to only part of the time spent on the word. Since saccade latencies are likely to vary as a function of the direction the saccade to be launched (see Fig. 2), the consequence is that first fixation durations possibly reflect specific inspection strategies that may have been adopted in a given condition. In order to avoid this difficulty, it seems necessary, in the case of a multi-fixation trial, to sum up all the fixations recorded for this trial, which corresponds to the definition of gaze duration. However, given the task that was used in the present experiment, which did not put any time pressure upon participants, and the large number of fixations that were recorded for each trial, including some fixations located outside the stimulus word, it seems unreasonable to assume that the gaze durations given in Table 2 correctly reflect identification times and, as a consequence, to draw any conclusion concerning the effects showing up on this measure.

What is needed here is a method for excluding any 'irrelevant' fixations, without introducing any bias linked to specific inspection strategies. Since it was difficult to decide which fixations had to be excluded, it was decided to carry out a series of analyses, progressively restricting the area of inspection from nine characters (full word) to only one (single fixation case). For example, the 4-character analysis excluded all trials involving a fixation located outside a cluster of four characters around the fixation point (positions - -3456- - -). The proportion of trials meeting the criterion for each analysis is plotted in Fig. 3. For example, 90% of the trials were included for the 9-character analysis (which means that 10% of the trials involved at least one fixation located outside the target word).

Interestingly, the proportion of trials that was taken into account in the 3-, 2-, and 1-letter analyses was greater for the many-candidate condition than for the few-candidate condition ($F_1(1, 31) = 5.54$, 8.72, 11.23, $p < 0.05$; $F_2(1, 48) = 5.10$, 10.01, 8.26, $p < 0.05$, respectively), suggesting that fewer letters were inspected, on average, in the many-candidate condition. No other main effect approached significance (Fs < 1).

In Figs. 4–6, the corresponding mean gaze durations are plotted as a function of word frequency, trigram familiarity, and number of candidates, respectively. Not surprisingly, gaze durations get shorter as the recording zone becomes narrower,

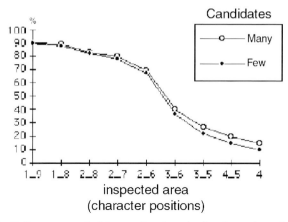

Fig. 3. Percentage of trials meeting the criterion for each analysis.

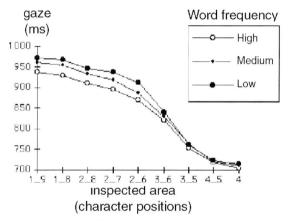

Fig. 4. Mean gaze durations as a function of word frequency, for inspection areas ranging from nine to one characters.

with a relatively sharp drop as soon as the inspected area reaches a critical size which seems to correspond to 5 or 4 characters. Similarly, the factors manipulated in the experiment seem to exert their influence mainly for those trials involving at least one fixation outside a cluster of 4 characters around the fixation point. For example, a clear frequency effect was found in the 6- and 5-character analyses ($F_1(2, 62) = 4.48$ and 4.63, $p < 0.05$; $F_2(2, 48) = 5.33$ and 5.47, $p < 0.05$, respectively), but not in the 4-, 3-, 2- and 1-character analyses ($F_1(2, 62) = 1.63$, $1,67$, < 1, and 3.01; $F_2(2, 48) = 2.15$, 1.74, < 1, and 2.85, respectively). Note that extending the zone of inspection above 6 characters did not help much ($F_1(2, 62) = 2.56$, 3.09, 2.98, and $F_2(2, 48) = 2.15$, 3.12, 3.33, for the 9-, 8-, and 7-character analyses, respectively).

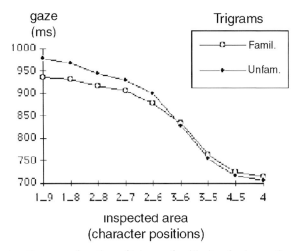

Fig. 5. Mean gaze durations as a function of trigram familiarity, for inspection areas ranging from nine to one characters.

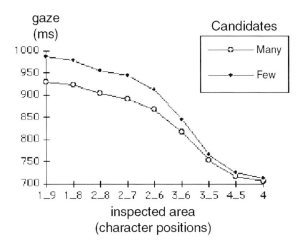

Fig. 6. Mean gaze durations as a function of number of candidates, for inspection areas ranging from nine to one characters.

As far as orthographic familiarity is concerned, opposite effects were observed above and below this 5-character size limit, with an advantage (shorter gaze durations) to familiar trigrams for inspection areas ranging from 9 to 6 characters ($F_1(1, 31) = 8.66, 7.14, 6.19, 4.50, p < 0.05$, and $F_2(1, 48) = 8.69, 7.88, 5.00, 4.41, p < 0.05$, respectively), a lack of difference for inspection areas ranging from 5 to 3 characters, and an advantage to unfamiliar trigrams for the 2-character and single-fixation analyses ($F_1(1, 31) = 4.22, 7.14, p < 0.05$, and $F_2(1, 48) = 4.92$,

10.44, $p < 0.05$, respectively). Whatever the reason for such a cross-over, it seems reasonable to admit that gazes restricted to two characters do not provide a good estimation of the time necessary to identify the stimulus word as a whole.

In contrast to the above observations, it is interesting to note that the main factor of interest in this experiment, namely number of candidates, exerted its influence all over the range of inspection areas, including when the zone of inspection taken into account was as narrow as three characters ($F_1(1, 31) = 23.99, 24.51, 19.52, 17.92, 17.65, 10.14, 5.22, p < 0.05$, and $F_2(1, 48) = 17.13, 18.49, 19.18, 24.09, 17.69, 10.68, 5.64, p < 0.05$, for inspection areas ranging from 9 to 3 characters, respectively). The effect was only marginally significant for the 2-character and single-fixation analyses however ($F_1(1, 31) = 3.81, 3.60$, and $F_2(1, 48) = 4.09, 3.94$, respectively). This pattern of results suggests that the gaze durations recorded in the present experiment correctly indexed word recognition processes, at least as far as the effect of the number of candidates is concerned. Interestingly, this factor did not interact with word frequency in any of the analyses (all Fs < 1.5), except for a hint of an interaction in the 9-letter subject analysis ($F_1(2, 62) = 3.28$, $F_2(2, 48) = 1.56$). Neither the interaction of number of candidates and trigram familiarity, nor the three-way interaction were significant (all Fs < 1.9).

Discussion

The main outcome of the experiment reported in this chapter was the finding that words likely to activate a large set of candidates were more rapidly identified than words that did not. Importantly, this result was obtained in French, suggesting that facilitatory effects of neighbourhood size might not be restricted to English, as it has sometimes been argued (see Andrews, 1997, for a discussion). Moreover, the present facilitatory effect was found for low-frequency words as well as for medium- or high-frequency ones. Since it may be assumed that the set of candidates comprised some high-frequency words for all three types of words, one has to admit that some higher-frequency competitors were activated in the case of low-frequency stimulus words. Still, this apparently did not prevent a facilitatory effect from showing up. A possible account for the results of the present experiment is the suggestion of Andrews (1989, 1992) that activated candidates might send back top-down activation, thus facilitating letter identification. However, before speculating about how this could translate in terms of visual inspection, it may be wise to wonder whether alternative interpretations can be formulated.

Facilitatory effects of neighbourhood size have sometimes been ascribed to processes other than identification of the printed word. For example, Andrews (1997) noted that a disproportionate number of 4- and 5-letter words' neighbours are created by changes at the first position, which means that most of the high-*N* stimulus words that have been used in experiments probably had a familiar ending. This leaves open the possibility that neighbourhood effects are really due to phonological rather than orthographic structure. As shown by Treiman et al. (1995), familiar word endings (corresponding to rime units) provide systematic cues to inconsistent pronunciations in English, and might, in fact, reflect the interface between orthography and phonology in this language. Clearly such criticisms cannot apply to the present experiment, which was conducted in French (rimes are thought to play a much weaker role in French, see Andrews, 1997). Moreover, it should be noted that the degree of orthographic familiarity of the stimulus words was controlled in the present experiment, at least as far as the four letters located around the fixation point were concerned. Importantly, the manipulation of the number of candidates led to systematic gaze differences, irrespective of trigram familiarity. This suggests that the facilitatory effect that was found is probably lexical in nature, and cannot be interpreted in mere terms of sub-lexical orthographic and/or phonological coding.

Another criticism that has often been presented relates to the fact that the recorded performance, in terms of processing time, does not necessarily reflect the time necessary to identify the target word. For example, it has been argued that the lexical decision task, which has been used extensively in the area of neighbourhood effects, might reflect strategic decision-related processes rather than lexical retrieval (Balota and Chumbley, 1984; Gordon, 1983). It should be noted, from this point of view, that the task used in the present experiment did not involve any decision on the target word itself, since the participant's response was delayed until the probe word was presented.

It has also been suggested that, under some circumstances, lexical decisions might be based on information about activation levels in the lexical network as a whole. By globally monitoring the overall level of lexical activation, an assessment of the probability that a match will be achieved can be made, and hence it is possible that a correct lexical decision could be made long before the final activation pattern is reached (Coltheart, Davelaar, Jonasson and Besner, 1977; Grainger and Jacobs, 1996; Monsell, Doyle and Haggard, 1989; Paap and Johansen, 1994). This criticism also applies to eye movement measures. For example, Pollatsek and Rayner (1989) argued that the decision to move the eye towards the next word in continuous reading might be triggered by the level of global lexical activation reaching some threshold (see also Chapter 27, this volume). It is possible that some of the within-word eye movements that were recorded in the present experiment were actually due to such a mechanism. However, it should be remembered that, in the present experiment, the manipulation of the lexical activation level (i.e. number of candidates) produced an effect whatever the gaze measure that was used (from single fixations to total gazes), and it is likely that at least one of the measures of gaze that have been analysed would correspond to full identification time.

Assuming that this is indeed the case, it remains to be explained why such an effect showed up in the present experiment, whereas Pollatsek et al. (1999) failed to find any clear facilitatory effect of neighbourhood size on gaze durations. As suggested in the introduction of this chapter, the answer must probably be looked for in the length of the words that were used in each study (four or five letters in Pollatsek et al.'s, as opposed to nine in the present experiment). In the case of long words, it was argued, only a few central letters are initially clearly identified, and the set of candidates initially activated can be assumed to comprise all the words sharing these few central letters and having a similar length. Moreover, the correlate of this assumption is that there are some other letters (e.g. those located too far away relative to the fixation point) that are not immediately identified, and can consequently benefit from the word-to-letter feedback hypothesised by Andrews (1989, 1992). It is interesting to note, from this point of view, that eccentric letter positions were apparently granted an advantage (e.g. received less fixations) in the many-candidate condition, as compared to the few-candidate condition (since many-candidate words elicited more single fixations or gazes restricted to two or three letters).

This interpretation may seem contradictory with the notion, defended in a previous paper (Pynte, 1996) that refixations might be aimed at distinguishing the target word from higher-frequency competitors (in a series of four experiments, refixations were found to be mainly directed towards those letters that were critical from this point of view). However, it should be noted that the number of candidates was maintained approximately constant in these experiments (only the position of critical letters was varied). Moreover, no effect was found on gaze durations (only the direction of saccades differed across conditions). The result of the present experiment suggests that lexical candidates might actually exert their influence on visual inspection in two ways. On the one hand, refixations might be less necessary for many-candidate words than for few-candidate words (because of word-to-letter feedback activation). On the other hand, refixations, if any, would be preferentially directed towards the end of the word where lexical information is.

A post hoc analysis was conducted in order to determine whether a similar tendency could be found in the present data. Each stimulus word was first ascribed a value indexing the relative 'informativeness' of its left vs. right edge. More precisely, this value corresponded to the difference between the number of candidates that could be eliminated by inspecting the word's beginning (first letter) and the number of candidates that could be eliminated by inspecting the word's end (last letter). This value was then compared to the proportion of leftward relative to rightward first saccades for each word. The correlation happened to be significant ($r = 0.41$, $p < 0.05$), with more left-going first saccades for information-at-beginning words, and more right-going ones for information-at-end words. This correlation can account for the complex pattern of interactions mentioned at the beginning of the Result section.

Another aspect of the results that remains to be explained is the general tendency, illustrated in Figs. 1 and 2, to preferentially inspect the target word from left to right (higher probability and shorter latencies for left- than for right-going first saccades). Since lexical information is generally located at words' beginnings, an interpretation in terms of lexical processing seems possible here too. In order to illustrate this point, the mean number of neighbours (Coltheart et al.'s definition) likely to be generated by each letter position for 8-, 9- and 10-letter words was calculated.

As can be seen in Fig. 7, clear differences do exist. The number of neighbours likely to be generated by positions 3, 4, or 5 is quite large, on average. However, since these positions are close to the preferred landing position, it is unlikely that the corresponding letters would be misperceived in normal reading. This leaves us with position 1 on the one hand, and positions 8 and 9 on the other hand, as the main sources of potential ambiguity. Although the distribution for 9-letter words does not provide any cues for explaining the mainly left-to-right inspection strategy that seems to have been adopted in the present experiment (there seems to be as much ambiguity at a 9-letter word's beginning and end), a clear difference does show up for the 8- and 10-letter distributions. This may be enough to justify a general strategy that may be adopted for all long words, whatever their precise length. It is conceivable that expert readers have adapted their inspection strategies to the statistical properties of their language, so that, on average, refixations will be more frequently located on those letter positions that are more frequently ambiguous, in the language as a whole. In this framework, the longer latencies obtained for rightward first saccades, as compared to leftward ones, suggest that rightward first saccades may result from a modification of this strategy (for example by inhibiting the initially left-going first saccade).

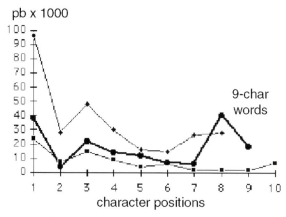

Fig. 7. Probability that a neighbour will be generated for each letter position, for 8-, 9- and 10-character words.

References

Andrews, S. (1989). Frequency and neighborhood effects on lexical access: activation or search? Journal of Experimental Psychology: Learning, Memory and Cognition, 15, 802–814.

Andrews, S. (1992). Frequency and neighborhood effects on lexical access: lexical similarity or orthographic redundancy? Journal of Experimental Psychology: Learning, Memory and Cognition, 18, 234–254.

Andrews, S. (1997). The effect of orthographic similarity on lexical retrieval: resolving neighborhood conflicts. Psychonomic Bulletin and Review, 4, 439–461.

Balota, D.A. and Chumbley, J.I. (1984). Are lexical decisions a good measure of lexical access? The role of word frequency in the neglected decision stage. Journal of Experimental Psychology: Human Perception and Performance, 10, 340–357.

Coltheart, M., Davelaar, E., Jonasson, J.T. and Besner, D. (1977). Access to the internal lexicon. In: S. Dornic (Ed.), Attention and Performance VI. Hillsdale, NJ: Erlbaum, pp. 535–555.

Content, A. and Radeau, M. (1988). Données statistiques sur la structure orthographique du français. Cahiers de Psychologie Cognitive, special issue, pp. 1–87.

Gordon, B. (1983). Lexical access and lexical decision: mechanisms of frequency sensitivity. Journal of Verbal Learning and Verbal Behavior, 22, 24–44.

Grainger, J. and Jacobs, A. (1996). Orthographic processing in visual word recognition: a multiple read-out model. Psychological Review, 103, 518–565.

Grainger, J., O'Regan, K., Jacobs, A. and Segui, J. (1989). On the role of competing word units in visual recognition: the neighborhood frequency effect. Perception and Psychophysics, 45, 189–195.

Grainger, J., O'Regan, K., Jacobs, A. and Segui, J. (1992). Neighborhood frequency effects and letter visibility in visual word recognition. Perception and Psychophysics, 51, 49–56.

Landauer, T.K. and Streeter, L.A. (1973). Structural differences between common and rare words: failure or equivalence assumptions for theories of word recognition. Journal of Verbal Learning and Verbal Behavior, 12, 119–131.

McClelland, J.L. and Rumelhart, D.E. (1981). An interactive activation model of context effects in letter perception, Part 1. An account of basic findings. Psychological Review, 88, 375–407.

Monsell, S., Doyle, M. and Haggard, P. (1989). Effects of frequency on visual word recognition tasks. Where are they? Journal of Experimental Psychology: General, 118, 43–71.

O'Regan, K., Lévy-Schoen, A., Pynte, J. and Brugallière, B. (1984). Convenient fixation location within isolated words of different length and structure. Journal of Experimental Psychology: Human Perception and Performance, 10, 250–257.

Paap, K. and Johansen, S. (1994). The case of the vanishing frequency effect: a retest of the verification model. Journal of Experimental Psychology: Human Perception and Performance, 26, 1129–1157.

Paap, K., Newsome, S.L., McDonald, J.E. and Schvaneveldt, R.W. (1982). An activation–verification model for letter and word recognition: the word superiority effect. Psychological Review, 89, 573–594.

Perea, M. and Pollatsek, A. (1998). The effects of neighborhood frequency in reading and lexical decision. Journal of Experimental Psychology: Human Perception and Performance, 24, 767–779.

Pollatsek, A., Perea, M. and Binder, K. (1999). The effects of neighborhood size in reading and lexical decision. Journal of Experimental Psychology: Human Perception and Performance, 25, 1142–1158.

Pollatsek, A. and Rayner, K. (1989). Eye movement and lexical access in reading. In: D.A. Balota,

G.B. Flores d'Arcais and K. Rayner (Eds.), Comprehension Processes in Reading. Hillsdale, NJ: Erlbaum, pp. 143–163.

Pynte, J. (1996). Lexical control of within-word eye movements. Journal of Experimental Psychology: Human Perception and Performance, 22 (4), 958–969.

Treiman, R., Mullenix, J., Bijeljac-Babic, R. and Richmond-Welty, E.D. (1995). The special role of rimes in description, use, and acquisition of English orthography. Journal of Experimental Psychology: General, 124, 107–136.

CHAPTER 4

Processing of Finnish Compound Words in Reading

Jukka Hyönä
University of Turku

and

Alexander Pollatsek
University of Massachusetts

Abstract

In this chapter, we report data from four experiments on the identification of Finnish two-noun compound words during reading. In the experiments, we independently varied the frequency of the first and second compound word constituents and the frequency of the whole word; we also varied the constituent lengths while holding the length of the word and the frequencies constant. The primary processing measures were the durations and locations of eye fixations landing on the compound word. The data showed (a) that the frequency of the initial constituent influenced the duration of first fixation on the target word as well as later processing, (b) effects of second constituent frequency did not show up until the second fixation, whereas (c) the effects of word frequency emerged as early as the second constituent effect and perhaps even earlier. This pattern of data is consistent with a parallel dual-route model that assumes that the identification of compound words occurs via a direct look-up route and a decomposition route operating in parallel. The locations of fixations were affected both by the constituent length and constituent frequency. A refixation landed further into the word (a) the longer the initial constituent, and (b) the higher the frequency of either the first or second constituent. The frequency of the first constituent also produced a small but reliable effect on the incoming saccade. These frequency effects are largely consistent with a processing difficulty hypothesis, which posits a mechanism that is capable of fine-tuning the saccade length as a function of moment-to-moment fluctuations in the difficulty of carrying out lexical access. Finally, we also report data on the pupil size, which indicate

Reading as a Perceptual Process/A. Kennedy, R. Radach, D. Heller and J. Pynte (Editors)
© 2000 Elsevier Science Ltd. All rights reserved

that the pupil size on the first fixation on the target word is larger than on the second fixation, possibly indicating that the identification process of long words requires more effort during the initial than later stages.

Introduction

In this chapter, we report and summarize data bearing on the question of how compound words are identified in reading, as revealed by readers' eye fixation patterns. In cognitive psychology, a wealth of studies have been conducted to study the process of identifying printed words, but the majority of them has suffered from two shortcomings: the studies have focused on (a) the identification of short words and (b) words presented in isolation. Surprisingly little is known of how longer words, such as compounds, are processed during normal, continuous reading.

The registration of readers' eye movements has proved to be a very fruitful way to study word identification during reading. Readers' eye behavior consists of two components, fixations and saccades, that are assumed to be governed by relatively independent mental mechanisms (Rayner and McConkie, 1976; Rayner and Pollatsek, 1981). The visual intake of information takes place during eye fixations, and saccades bring new information to the foveal vision for scrutiny. The *when* mechanism that governs the duration of fixations decides when to terminate a fixation to move on in text, while the *where* mechanism that controls for the saccadic amplitude guides the eye to a specific location in text.

According to a widely held view (see e.g., Pollatsek and Rayner, 1990), the duration of fixations in reading is under the control of cognitive factors. It has been demonstrated that the fixation duration on a word reflects the speed with which the fixated word is accessed in the mental lexicon. [1] Moreover, higher-order comprehension processes are capable of influencing the duration of individual fixations (see Rayner, 1998; Rayner and Sereno, 1994, for a review). In contrast, there are models that assign only a minor role to cognitive factors in controlling fixation durations. For example, in the strategy-tactics model proposed by O'Regan (1992), fixation durations are largely controlled by the location of a fixation on a word. That is, it is assumed that if a fixation is positioned non-optimally for word identification (e.g., in the beginning of the word), a short fixation will ensue that is not influenced by cognitive processing. On the other hand, it is conceded that a fixation located optimally near the center of the word will be longer and may be

---

1 However, according to a recent computational model of readers' eye behavior (Reichle, Pollatsek, Fisher and Rayner, 1998; see also Chapter 27), this may not be due to completion of lexical access, but instead to a 'familiarity check' of the word that is also influenced by lexical variables such as word frequency.

affected by cognitive factors. (However, see O'Regan, Vitu, Radach and Kerr, 1994, for a less extreme position.)

The computation of where a saccade should be targeted is generally assumed to be carried out primarily under the guidance of low-level visual features of the text. Specifically, the *where* decisions in reading are believed to be made on the basis of word length and spacing information so that saccades are targeted to the center of the word to yield an optimal perception of the word. It has been shown that the eyes typically fixate somewhat to the left of the center of a word (the so-called *preferred landing position*). To achieve this, a saccade to a long word will be longer than to a short word, and a saccade leaving a long word will be longer than from a short word. However, there is some evidence, although disputed, that other, more linguistic, features of a word may be capable of influencing where the eyes fixate it. Hyönä, Niemi and Underwood (1989) showed that the incoming saccade lands further into the word for words in which the crucial information for identification is at the end. The generality of the finding was challenged by Rayner and Morris (1992), who could not replicate it using stimuli adopted from Underwood, Clews and Everatt (1990). There is also evidence, still undisputed, that orthographic regularity has a potential to influence the saccade trajectory. Hyönä (1995) and Beauvillain, Doré and Baudouin (1996) showed that a fixation lands closer to the word beginning when the word has an irregular letter cluster in the beginning (see also Chapter 11).

We think that this *when–where* distinction needs to be refined to be word-based (McConkie and Zola, 1984), or possibly constituent-based (see below). That is, there are abundant data that cognitive variables such as the word's frequency and its predictability from prior context influence both (a) the probability of fixating a word and (b) the number of fixations it receives given that it is fixated (see Rayner and Pollatsek, 1989, for a review). Hence, we think it is more appropriate to make the distinction between the decision of which word (or other meaningful unit) to fixate and *where* on the word to fixate (see also Radach and McConkie, 1998). The former can be viewed as similar to a *when* decision as it is a decision of whether it is time to move on to a subsequent word and is heavily affected by cognitive variables, and the latter is a decision about *where* to land on a word, and seems largely uninfluenced by cognitive factors. Of course, a key question of interest with compound words is whether aspects of the constituents (such as their frequencies) have an influence on where readers fixate within a word.

In the following, we report data on the processing of long compound words as reflected in factors that affect the *when* decision (i.e., is it time to move on to the next word or constituent?) and factors that affect the *where* decision (i.e., where to target a saccade within a word or constituent). To date, very little is known about how long compound words are identified during reading. We started out with a working hypothesis that the identification of long compounds occurs in three sequential stages: (1) the initial constituent is identified, (2) the second constituent is identified, and (3) the constituents are 'glued' together to form a meaning for the whole word. We suspected that this simple model of ours would not provide the ultimate description of the identification process, but we wanted to see how far we can get with such a straightforward stage model.

The experiments

In the experiments, we employed long (12–14 characters) two-noun compound words that typically receive more than one fixation. The compound words were embedded in single sentences, and readers were instructed to read the sentences for comprehension. There were 24 or 25 participants in each experiment. In all experiments, there were two compound word conditions and the number of words per condition varied between 20 and 51. Two target words, one from each compound word type, were paired, and the sentence frames for each word pair were identical up through the word following the target word.[2] A typical sentence pair (taken from Experiment 2) is as follows, with the target word in italics. The target words appeared near the beginning of sentences, but never as either the first word of the sentence nor in the initial or final position of a line. Eye movements were recorded using the EYELINK system (SR Research Ltd.).

Low-frequency second constituent condition

"Tukholmassa *pommihysteria* onnistui valtaamaan tavallisten ihmisten mielet." (In Stockholm the bomb hysteria managed to overwhelm the minds of ordinary people.)

High-frequency second constituent condition

"Tukholmassa *kuorokonsertti* onnistui kohtuullisesti, vaikka pitkä konserttikiertue oli uuvuttanut kuorolaisia." (In Stockholm the choral concert succeeded moderately well, although the long concert tour had tired the singers.)

Our three-stage model assumes that properties of the initial constituent (e.g., constituent frequency and constituent length) affect an early processing stage, properties of the second constituent affect a relatively later processing stage, and properties of the whole word (while constituent properties are matched) affect a still later processing stage. Although there is no one-to-one correspondence between different processing stages and eye fixation measures, a processing sequence can be discerned from readers' eye movement protocols: the initial fixation on the compound word reflecting the initial processing stages, the second fixation reflecting later processing stages as well, and a possible third fixation reflecting

---

2 In Experiment 2, only the length of the next word was equated.

still later stages. Thus, to the extent our model is correct, the properties of the initial constituent should have an effect on the duration and/or location of the initial fixation made on the compound word, although they may also have an effect on the duration and/or location of subsequent fixations as well. But what is crucial for our model, the effect of the initial constituent should begin to be seen at the earliest possible point, whereas the properties of the second constituent are not likely to influence the initial fixation. Instead, the second constituent properties would probably affect the location and/or duration of the second fixation made on the word. Finally, the properties of the whole word should not affect the eye movement record until the properties of the second constituent do.

In the following, we summarize the results of four experiments, in which different compound word features were manipulated (for a more detailed report of the experiments, see Hyönä and Pollatsek, 1998, for Experiments 1 and 4; and Pollatsek, Hyönä and Bertram, 2000, for Experiments 2 and 3).[3] We also report some new results from follow-up analyses conducted on a subset of the complete data set. For the new analyses, detailed statistics will be reported (for the other results, the reader is asked to consult Hyönä and Pollatsek and Pollatsek et al., for more detail).

In Experiment 1, the frequency of the first constituent was manipulated while controlling for the familiarity of the whole word,[4] the frequency of the second constituent and the length of both constituents. In Experiment 2, the frequency of the second constituent was varied while controlling for the frequencies of the first constituent, and the whole word and the lengths of both constituents. Finally, in Experiment 3, the frequency of the whole word was manipulated while matching the frequency and length of both constituents. In Experiment 3, also a set of frequency-matched and length- matched high and low frequency monomorphemic words were included against which the frequency effects for compound words could be compared. We present the data separately for the duration of fixations (i.e., the *when* decisions) and for the location of fixations (i.e., the *where* decisions). In Experiment 4, the length of the two constituents was varied (but the length of the whole word and the frequencies of the constituents and the whole word were

---

3 The experiment numbering we have adopted here is for ease of exposition and is not the chronological ordering of the experiments. What we are referring to Experiment 1 here is Experiment 2 of Hyönä and Pollatsek (1998) and what we are referring to as Experiment 4 here is Experiment 1 of Hyönä and Pollatsek. What we are referring to as Experiments 2 and 3 here are Experiments 1 and 2, respectively, of Pollatsek et al. (2000).

4 At the time of study, we did not have a representative word corpus available so that the words were matched using a familiarity rating instead of frequency counts. However, we subsequently did get the frequencies; follow-up analyses indicated that the small whole-word frequency difference apparent for the two types of compound words did not modulate the pattern of results.

controlled for): in one condition, the initial constituent was short (3–5 characters) and the second long (8–11 characters), and in the other condition, the initial constituent was long (8–11 characters) and the second short (3–5 characters).

In the final section, we report analyses in which pupil size was employed as a putative measure of cognitive effort (see Kahneman, 1973) during word identification. There is evidence reported in the literature suggesting that fluctuations in the processing load during language comprehension and production tasks are reflected in the pupil size (see Beatty, 1982, for a review of the earlier studies). That is, the pupil has shown to dilate with increasing task difficulty. For example, Hyönä, Tommola and Alaja (1995) showed that the relative difficulty of repeating back and translating auditorily presented English and Finnish words was reliably reflected in pupil size, and Just and Carpenter (1993) demonstrated that complexity of syntactic processing during reading is reflected in pupil size. However, to our knowledge no previous study has tried to employ pupillometry to study lexical access during reading.

When decisions

In this section, we begin by summarizing data on durations of individual fixations. The central issue here is to examine the validity of our three-stage model outlined above, which assumes that the frequency of first and second constituents as well as the whole-word frequency all affect the identification process, but at different points in time.

In Experiment 1, the first fixation duration on the compound words was significantly longer when the initial constituent was low-frequency than when it was high-frequency. This early effect of initial constituent frequency is consistent with the model's prediction and indicates that morphemic components of words are playing an active role early in processing. The effect of first constituent frequency also spilled over to the second and third fixations, the second fixations being significantly longer and the probability of making a third fixation significantly greater for low-frequency initial constituents. But what is crucial for the model, the effect emerged early (i.e., during the first fixation). Also consistent with the model, the frequency of the second constituent influenced processing in Experiment 2, but later in the time-course than the effects of the first constituent. Although the effect showed up in the duration of the second fixation, the duration of the initial fixation remained unaffected. The strongest effect of second constituent frequency, however, was on the probability of making a third fixation on the word, which was clearly greater for compounds with a low-frequency second constituent.

On the other hand, the pattern of results of Experiment 3, where the whole-word frequency was manipulated, was not completely in line with the simple three-stage model. The model predicts that whole word frequency effects should appear later than those of the second constituent frequency. However, in the data, word frequency effects emerged no later, and possibly earlier, than the second constituent frequency effect. The whole-word frequency affected the second fixation duration and the probability of making a third fixation on the word at least as strongly as the second constituent frequency. There was even an indication that it affected the first fixation duration: there was a 6-ms difference that proved significant in the subject analysis (but it was non-significant in the item analysis). These data are thus problematic for the three-stage model, which predicts a later effect of whole-word frequency than for second constituent frequency (see below for further discussion).

The results from Experiments 1 and 2 suggest that the frequencies of the constituents of compound words affect the identification process pretty much the same way they would if they were separate words. The first fixation (which typically landed on the initial constituent) was influenced by the frequency of the initial constituent, while the second fixation (which typically landed on the second constituent) was influenced by the frequency of the second constituent (see Hyönä and Pollatsek, 1998; Pollatsek et al., 2000). To examine further whether this is the case, we conducted a follow-up analysis of the data of Experiments 1 and 2. In these analyses, constituents were treated as if they were separate words, and fixation durations were analyzed accordingly. We employed four eye fixation measures: (a) the duration of the first fixation on a constituent; (b) the gaze duration on a constituent (i.e., the sum of fixations before exiting a constituent); (c) the probability of fixating a constituent during the 'first-pass reading' (if the initial fixation on the word landed on the second constituent, the first constituent was considered to be skipped or if the second constituent was not fixated, it was considered to be skipped); and (d) the probability of fixating a constituent during the second-pass reading. (To initiate a second pass, the reader needed to regress back from the second to the first constituent; all fixations that followed such a regression were considered second-pass fixations).

As indicated above, in Experiment 1, the frequency of the initial constituent was manipulated.[5] Perhaps not surprisingly, the *when* fixation measures on the first constituent were similar to what they would have been if it was a separate word (see Table 1). That is, when the initial constituent was low-frequency, the duration of the first fixation on it was 14 ms longer ($F_1(1, 23) = 14.83$, $p = 0.001$, $F_2(1, 27) = 29.68$, $p < 0.001$), the 'gaze duration' on it was 86 ms longer ($F_1(1, 23) = 37.36$, $p < 0.001$, $F_2(1, 27) = 88.65$, $p < 0.001$), and it was skipped during first-pass reading 19% less often ($F_1(1, 23) = 105.29$, $p < 0.001$,

---

5 The average length of the initial constituent was 6.0 characters for the frequent constituent and 7.6 characters for the infrequent constituent. In Experiment 2, the average length of the frequent second constituent was 7.4 and that of the infrequent second constituent 6.6. It is highly unlikely that these minor differences in constituent lengths could account for the observed effects.

Table 1

First fixation duration (in ms), gaze duration (in ms), and probability of fixation (first-pass and second-pass reading) for compound words with a frequent and an infrequent first morpheme, separately for the first and second constituent (Experiment 1)

	Fixation measures on 1st constituent		Fixation measures on 2nd constituent	
	Frequent 1st constituent	Infrequent 1st constituent	Frequent 1st constituent	Infrequent 1st constituent
First fixation duration	183	197	198	193
Gaze duration	229	315	274	208
Probability of fixation				
First pass	0.78	0.97	0.82	0.66
Second pass	0.06	0.17	0.02	0.06

$F_2(1, 27) = 15.80$, $p < 0.001$). The probability of coming back to it after having fixated the second constituent (i.e., what we are calling 'second-pass reading') was also greater when the initial constituent was low-frequency ($F_1(1, 23) = 51.52$, $p < 0.001$, $F_2(1, 27) = 10.23$, $p < 0.01$).

There were also some significant effects of the first constituent frequency on fixation times on the second constituent; however, some were quite different from 'spillover' effects commonly seen when reading separate words. Most notably, when the initial constituent was low-frequency, the gaze duration on the second constituent was actually 66 ms *shorter* ($F_1(1, 23) = 30.49$, $p < 0.001$, $F_2(1, 27) = 22.54$, $p < 0.001$). (The initial fixation on the second constituent was also 5 ms shorter, but p-values were >0.20.) In addition, the probability of skipping the second constituent during the first-pass reading was actually greater when the initial constituent was low-frequency ($F_1(1, 23) = 46.83$, $p < 0.001$, $F_2(1, 27) = 22.89$, $p < 0.001$). However, the probability of fixating the second constituent during the second-pass reading was more 'normal': it was greater when the initial constituent was low-frequency ($F_1(1, 23) = 15.83$, $p = 0.001$, $F_2(1, 27) = 4.02$, $p = 0.055$).

The latter result, together with an increased number of second-pass fixations on the first constituent, indicate that compounds with a low-frequency first constituent were generally refixated more often. However, the other fixation time results on the second constituent are quite counterintuitive if one views fixation times on a constituent as a simple reflection of processing that constituent or simple spillover effects from processing the prior constituent. One possible explanation for those apparently counterintuitive results is that the mean frequencies of the second constituents were not perfectly equated between the two conditions: the high-frequency first constituents had on average somewhat lower-frequency second

Table 2

First fixation duration (in ms), gaze duration (in ms), and probability of fixation (first-pass and second-pass reading) for compound words with a frequent and an infrequent second morpheme, separately for the first and second constituent (Experiment 2)

	Fixation measures on 1st constituent		Fixation measures on 2nd constituent	
	Frequent 2nd constituent	Infrequent 2nd constituent	Frequent 2nd constituent	Infrequent 2nd constituent
First fixation duration	214	214	197	217
Gaze duration	354	311	216	262
Probability of fixation				
First pass	0.96	0.94	0.62	0.80
Second pass	0.14	0.26	0.05	0.14

constituents (188 vs. 288 per million). However, this relatively small frequency difference is not particularly likely to produce the fairly large differences in gaze duration or skipping. Instead, we suspect that processing of the two constituents did not neatly relate to where people were fixating. First, note that the probability of initially skipping the first constituent was quite different between the low- and high-frequency first constituents. Thus, one possible reason for the increased gaze duration on the second constituent for high-frequency first constituents is that the constituent, though skipped, was not fully processed, necessitating 'catch up' processing when the second constituent was processed. In addition, some of the increased gaze duration on the first constituent in the infrequent first constituent condition could have reflected increased processing on the second constituent.

In sum, the data of Table 1 suggest that though the constituents may be acting somewhat like separate words, there are ways in which the processing of them is more interrelated than for separate words. This could be true either for linguistic reasons (e.g., that even transparent compounds are not linguistically like separate words) or because the lack of a space between them alters where the eye lands. We will return to this issue in the next section.

In Experiment 2, the frequency of the initial constituent was matched, but the frequency of the second constituent differed considerably between the two compound word types. As expected, when the second constituent was low-frequency, the duration of first fixation on it was 20 ms longer ($F_1(1, 23) = 22.75$, $p < 0.001$, $F_2(1, 31) = 5.63$, $p = 0.02$), and the gaze duration on it was 46 ms longer ($F_1(1, 23) = 37.19$, $p < 0.001$, $F_2(1, 31) = 25.20$, $p < 0.001$). Moreover the second constituent was skipped 18% less often when it was low-frequency ($F_1(1, 23) = 69.43$, $p < 0.001$, $F_2(1, 31) = 32.77$, $p < 0.001$; see Table 2). In addition, there was one reliable 'first-pass' effect on the first constituent: the gaze duration on the initial constituent was 43 ms *less* when the second constituent was low-frequency ($F_1(1, 23) = 27.02$, $p < 0.001$, $F_2(1, 31) = 7.51$, $p = 0.01$). Note, however, that there was no effect of second constituent frequency on the first fixation duration of the first constituent, nor much of an effect on the probability of skipping the first constituent ($F_1(1, 23) = 4.00$, $p = 0.06$, $F_2(1, 31) = 2.00$, $p > 0.1$). Hence, the evidence for the effects of processing the second constituent during the first pass on the first constituent was fairly modest.

Interestingly, the probability of making a second-pass fixation on both the first and second constituents was significantly greater for low-frequency second constituents ($F_1(1, 23) = 36.21$, $p < 0.001$, $F_2(1, 31) = 15.80$, $p < 0.001$, and $F_1(1, 23) = 24.74$, $p < 0.001$, $F_2(1, 31) = 16.32$, $p < 0.001$, respectively). This suggests that difficulty in processing the second constituent led to reprocessing of the entire word.

To sum up the follow-up analyses of Experiment 2, most of the results are reasonably consistent with the two constituents being processed sequentially. Almost all the measures indicated that the second constituent frequency affected only first-pass measures on the second constituent. However, the finding that gaze duration on the first constituent was longer with a high-frequency second constituent calls for an explanation. As the probability of fixation data indicate, high-frequency second constituents were skipped more frequently than low-frequency constituents. What this probably indicates is that there are occasions when the last fixation on the initial constituent (either the first or second fixation) is near enough to the boundary between the two constituents to allow processing of the second constituent, and that, on some occasions, this fixation is lengthened because the second constituent is processed and then skipped. This would be analogous to the finding that fixation duration on word n is lengthened when word $n + 1$ is skipped (Hogaboam, 1983; Pollatsek, Rayner and Balota, 1986).

More generally, however, the patterns of data from Experiments 1 and 2 suggest that even transparent compound words are not processed the way they would be if they were two separate words. Although we indicated above that some part of the difference may be linguistic, there is recent evidence from German (Inhoff, Radach and Heller, in press) that at least part of the difference is due to the lack of spaces between the constituents. Most notably, German readers were actually faster to process German compounds when spaces were inserted between the constituents even though the resulting separated compound words were both unfamiliar and grammatically illegal.

Above we have presented evidence showing that the frequency of compound word constituents influences fixation durations pretty much the same way that word frequency does. This evidence is consistent with our working hypothesis, which assumes that compound words are identified via their constituents. However, the finding from Experiment 3 that the effect of whole-word frequency shows up relatively early during the encoding process suggests that a completely serial model is not viable. Thus, the complete pattern of results suggests that there may be two identification mechanisms operating in parallel: (a) a mechanism that decomposes the compound word into its constituents and tries to identify the word via its constituents (the *decomposition route*), and (b) another mechanism that tries to access the mental lexicon by using the word's full form as an entry (the *full-form route*). If one assumes that the two mechanisms operate in parallel, one can explain both the observation that whole-word frequency exerts a relatively early effect and the findings that constituent frequencies influence compound word processing when word frequency is controlled for. (Search models like the one by Taft and Forster, 1976, cannot account for our results; see Hyönä and Pollatsek, 1998; Pollatsek et al., 2000.)

Before closing this section, we would like to discuss the model of O'Regan (1992), which posits that fixation location is the primary determinant of fixation durations in words and that fixation durations are influenced by cognitive factors only under special circumstances (i.e., when a fixation is optimally positioned around the word's center). We conducted analyses of the frequency effects observed in Experiments 1–3 as a function of initial landing position (we compared fixations landing on character positions 0–4 to those landing on character positions 5–9). In Experiment 1, the frequency of initial constituent affected the duration of the first fixation when it was positioned around the word's center, but did not do so for fixations landing in the word's beginning (i.e., positions 0–4). A similar trend was observable in Experiment 2 (in which the frequency of the second constituent was varied), but the effects did not prove statistically significant. In Experiment 3 (in which whole-word frequency was varied), there was not even a hint that the frequency effect was modulated by the initial fixation location. In all, there is some support (but not consistent) for O'Regan's hypothesis that the location of the initial fixation crucially determines whether frequency affects the duration of individual fixations (see also Rayner, Sereno and Raney, 1996; for effects of fixation position on fixation duration, see also Chapter 7). In contrast, there is ample evidence for the view that cognitive factors related to word identification determine fixation durations in words. Moreover, the follow-up analyses of Experiments 1 and 2 that we presented above indicate that fixation durations are modulated by the frequency of the constituent of a compound word that is being fixated.

Where decisions

In this section, we summarize data on individual fixation locations and saccade lengths. The issue here is to what extent constituent properties of compound words have the potential to influence where fixations in a word land. In Experiment 4, the length of the compound word constituents was manipulated, and in Experiments 1–3, the frequency of the constituents or the whole word was varied.

The effect of constituent length

With respect to the effect of constituent length, we reasoned that if constituents are treated similarly to separate words (note that the constituents were not separated by a space or hyphen), the incoming saccade into the compound word and the first forward saccade in the word should go farther into the word when the initial constituent is longer. The prediction concerning the incoming saccade is based on an assumption that the compound word is decomposed parafoveally into its constituents while still fixating on the previous word, and this information is then utilized in saccadic programming. (Most probably, the target would be the middle of the first constituent.) The prediction about the location of the second fixation merely assumes that the decomposition into constituents is accomplished some time during the first fixation. If it is, then fixations targeted either to the center of the first constituent or to the center of the second constituent should be further to the right when the first constituent is long. (Because there is no previous evidence for morphological decomposition of words before they are fixated — see Inhoff, 1989, Lima and Inhoff, 1985 — the former prediction seemed less likely to be true.)

As it turned out, the location of initial fixation did not differ between the long and short initial constituents. However, reliable effects of constituent length were observed for the first within-word saccade. First, when the first constituent was long, the first forward within-word saccade was launched further toward the end of the word (i.e., closer to the center of the second constituent) than when the first constituent was short. This is analogous to the finding that an exit saccade from a long word is longer than from a short word. Second, the probability of making a regression back to the beginning of the word was significantly greater for compounds with a short initial constituent. This makes sense as the mean location of initial fixation on the word was on the 5th letter, which is a less optimal landing site for identifying a short (3–5 characters) initial constituent. In other words, when the initial constituent was skipped over (the saccade presumably being guided by the length of the entire word), a regressive saccade was often launched toward the beginning of the word.

The finding that the length of the initial constituent affected the saccadic trajectory of the forward refixations suggests that saccadic programming is affected by compound word constituents in a manner similar to that when two words are separated by a space. However, there was evidence indicating that saccadic programming in the absence or presence of spaces between morphemes is not identical. First, as indicated above, the initial fixation was on the 5th letter of the compound word, which means that the first constituent, when short, was typically skipped over resulting in an increased tendency to program a regressive saccade toward the word beginning. Second, the first forward refixation did not land optimally (i.e., near the center of the second constituent), but was further into the word than would be expected for the short initial constituent and not as far into the word as would be expected for the words with long initial constituents. Thus, fixation locations in long compound words appear to be a compromise between a pure morphological guidance mechanism and a pure visual (i.e., space-guided) mechanism. In morphemic guidance, the reader needs to recognize the boundary between the constituents and use that information in targeting the subsequent refixation. However, Hyönä and Pollatsek (1998) showed that the frequency of the morpheme-spanning bigram was not responsible for the morphemic effects. Thus it appears that morphological structure of compound words did affect fixation locations, and that the effect was not due to a low bigram frequency at the constituent boundary popping out as a visually salient feature. (Other potential low-level artifacts were also ruled out by Hyönä and Pollatsek, 1998.)

The effect of constituent frequency

The predictions concerning fixation locations in Experiments 1–3, where constituent frequency or whole-word frequency was manipulated, were derived from the *processing difficulty hypothesis* of saccadic computation proposed by Hyönä (1995; see also Henderson and Ferreira, 1990). According to the hypothesis, the perceptual span around the fixation from which useful information is picked up is narrowed down with increasing difficulty in parafoveal and foveal processing. Thus, when a word in foveal or parafoveal vision is low-frequency, less parafoveal processing will be done, which should then lead to a shorter forward saccade.

There is some previous evidence in support of the processing difficulty hypothesis. Beauvillain et al. (1996) and Hyönä (1995) observed that the initial fixation tends to land closer to the beginning of a word having an irregular letter cluster in the beginning part of the word. By assuming that an irregular letter cluster in the word's beginning is more difficult to process parafoveally, these findings can be interpreted as being consistent with the processing difficulty hypothesis. Second, Kennison and Clifton (1995) manipulated foveal and parafoveal load by varying the frequency of two adjacent words. When both words $N - 1$ and N were of low frequency (i.e., when both foveal and parafoveal load was high when fixating on $N - 1$), the probability of skipping over the word N was decreased for good readers (i.e. readers with a high working memory span). For readers with a low working memory span, on the other hand, the skipping rate was highest when the foveal and parafoveal load was low (i.e., when both words were high-frequency). Thus, the Kennison and Clifton study suggests that foveal and parafoveal processing difficulty can affect saccadic trajectory during reading, at least in the sense of programming saccades to skip over entire words.

In Experiments 1–3, we tested the validity of the processing difficulty hypothesis by examining the effects of constituent frequency on saccadic programming. In Experiment 1, where the frequency of the initial constituent was varied, we observed that the incoming saccade into the compound word landed somewhat closer to the word beginning [6] and the second fixation (preceded by a forward saccade) clearly landed closer to the word beginning when the initial constituent was of low frequency. These findings are consistent with the processing difficulty hypothesis, as they suggest that both the difficulty in parafoveal preprocessing (as indexed by the effect in the incoming saccade) and in foveal processing (as indexed by the effect in the within-word saccade) [7] are capable of influencing the saccade trajectory during reading.

The processing difficulty hypothesis was further tested against the data of Experiments 2 and 3. The hypothesis predicts that in Experiment 2, where the frequency of the second constituent was varied, the location of the second fixation in the word will be closer to the word beginning for compounds with a low-frequency than a high-frequency second constituent. This is because during the initial fixation on the compound word parafoveal processing of the second constituent is more difficult when it is of lower frequency. On the other hand, the landing site of the incoming saccade into the word is not predicted to differ between the two conditions, because the frequency of the initial constituent was equated and it would be highly unlikely that properties of the second constituent would influence saccadic programming from a long distance.

The data were consistent with the above predictions. The landing site of the initial fixation was very similar for the two word types, and the location of the second fixation was closer to the word beginning with a low-frequency second constituent (although the effect was reliable only in the subject analysis). The third prediction concerning the data of Experiment 2 is that the saccade leaving the word would be shorter when the second constituent is low in frequency, because increased difficulty in processing the second constituent would hamper with the parafoveal processing of the subsequent word thus leading to a shorter exit saccade.

———————————

6 Subsequent regression analyses indicated that the frequency effect on the initial landing position could not be accounted for by differences in the initial trigram frequency.

7 The effect cannot be explained by the predictability of the second constituent based on the first constituent (i.e., a longer saccade associated with an easily predictable second constituent). The predictability of the second constituent was actually much higher for low-frequency first constituents, as there were only one or two compound words in the dictionary starting with a particular low-frequency constituent (for high-frequency first constituents, there was a minimum of 45 compounds starting with a particular first constituent).

We conducted an analysis of the length of the exit saccade separately for the trials when there were exactly one or two fixations on the compound word. For the one-fixation trials, the length of the exit saccade was in the predicted direction (the means in character spaces were 11.51 and 11.87, for the low- and high-frequency second constituents, respectively), but the effect was far from significant ($F_1 < 1$; it should be noted that there were a lot of missing data for the one-fixation trials). There was also no effect on saccade length in the analysis of two-fixations trials ($F_1(1, 23) = 2.85$, $p > 0.1$, $F_2 < 1$). If anything, the trend is in the opposite direction to what was predicted (the means were 12.47 and 12.23, for the low- and high-frequency second constituents, respectively).

With regard to the low- and high-frequency compound words employed in Experiment 3, the processing difficulty hypothesis does not predict any difference for the length of the incoming saccade, because the frequency of the initial constituent was carefully matched between low- and high-frequency compounds. On the other hand, the predictions concerning the first within-word saccade and the exit saccade (i.e., the saccade leaving the word) depend on when the effect of compound word frequency is assumed to 'kick in'. If the frequency effect shows up relatively early in processing, the first within-word saccade should be affected, but if it appears only very late, as predicted by our three-stage model, only the saccade leaving the word would be influenced by the compound word frequency.

The data did not reveal any effects of word frequency on landing positions; the locations of the initial and second fixations on the compound words were not affected by word frequency. Moreover, the length of the exit saccade remained unaffected by word frequency. The length of the exit saccade was analyzed separately for trials with a single fixation (the data for 6 subjects had to be discarded due to missing data points) or with two fixations on the target word. For compound words, word frequency did not exert any significant effects on exit saccade either for single fixation trials ($t_1(17) = 1.85$, $p = 0.08$, $t_2 < 1$), or for two fixation trials ($t_1(23) < 1$, $t_2 < 1$). If anything, the trend was in the opposite direction to that predicted. That is, there was a longer exit saccade for low-frequency compounds: for the single fixation trials, the means were 9.74 vs. 10.85 character spaces, and for the two fixation trials, 9.62 vs. 9.25 character spaces, for low- and high-frequency compounds, respectively. For the monomorphemic words, the effect of word frequency was also non-significant, both for the single fixation trials ($t_1(21) < 1$, $t_2 < 1$) and for the two fixation trials ($t_1(23) < 1$, $t_2 < 1$).

In sum, the following effects were predicted by the processing difficulty hypothesis and observed in the data: (a) the frequency of the initial constituent influenced the location of both first and second fixations on the word; (b) the frequency of the second constituent influenced the location of the second fixation on the word. On the other hand, the processing difficulty hypothesis predicted two effects that did not occur: (1) an effect of second constituent frequency on the length of the exit saccade; and (2) an effect of whole-word frequency on the location of second fixation and on the length of the exit saccade.

One way of reconciling the pattern of results is to suggest that intra-word saccades are affected by processing difficulty, while inter-word saccades are not. However, the finding that the incoming saccade was affected by the frequency of the initial constituent, poses a problem for this interpretation (as the effect is small in size, it should probably be replicated before basing any really strong conclusions on it, however). We offer another view which is based on the notion that frequency effects associated with the fixated word would not spill over to the parafoveal processing of the next word, at least in so far as saccadic programming is concerned. In other words, a compound word is identified to a sufficient degree during its fixation before attention is shifted and a saccade is programmed to a succeeding word. This notion would explain why the frequency effect does not carry over to the exit saccade. On the other hand, intra-word saccades are affected as they are intimately linked with the ongoing identification of the currently fixated word. Finally, entry saccades are influenced, because attention shifts to the to-be-fixated word prior to executing a saccade to it, and consequently the frequency of initial constituent is capable of affecting the saccadic trajectory.

Pupil size

As noted above, pupil size has been shown to reflect differences in the attentional effort needed to carry out various information processing tasks (see Beatty, 1982; Kahneman, 1973). However, we do not know of any study where cognitive effort associated with lexical access during reading has been examined using the pupillometric method. The EYELINK tracker used in collecting the data also measured the size of the pupil, so we were in a position to employ this measure to determine whether pupil diameter would reflect differences in the relative ease in identifying long compound words (i.e., larger pupil size reflecting more effort). In the following, we report a detailed analysis of the pupil size for the data of Experiment 2 accompanied with an additional analysis of the data from Experiment 3. We employed pupil diameter as the measure to comply with the tradition in the field (the other available option would have been pupil area). [8]

Because of the relatively small number of observations on the third fixation, we concentrated our analysis of the mean pupil size on the first two fixations

---

8 The pupil diameter was recorded in pixels, but in the absence of any baseline measure we were
   unable to convert the pixels into any absolute measure, such as millimeters. Thus, we measured
   only relative changes in pupil diameter.

Table 3

Pupil diameter (in pixels) as a function of second constituent frequency and whether the initial fixation landed on letters 0–4 or letters 5–8 of the target word in Experiment 2

	Region 1: Fix1 on 0–4		Region 2: Fix1 on 5–8		Mean
	Frequent 2nd constituent	Infrequent 2nd constituent	Frequent 2nd constituent	Infrequent 2nd constituent	
First fixation	53.9	53.0	52.1	52.8	53.0
Second fixation	52.3	51.5	51.1	51.7	51.7

made on the target words in Experiment 2 (the one in which the frequency of the second constituent was varied). As seen in Table 3, there was a tendency for the pupil size to be larger in the frequent constituent condition (apparently contrary to the effort hypothesis), but the frequency effect was not significant, even averaged over the two fixations: $F_1(1, 23) = 2.22$, $p > 0.1$, $F_2(1, 31) = 2.31$, $p > 0.1$. However, the difference in pupil size between the two fixations was highly reliable: $F_1(1, 23) = 61.0$, $p < 0.001$, $F_2(1, 31) = 21.9$, $p < 0.001$. This effect is potentially interesting as it suggests that encoding a word takes more effort in its initial stages and less effort as the candidates are narrowed down. Obviously, there are many potential stimulus artifacts that might also explain the effect. One is that the fixation locations are different on the two fixations and thus there could be differential luminance levels. However, because the first fixation is nearer the space between the words (which is a source of increased luminance when the background is light), one might expect the opposite effect to the one we observed (i.e., smaller pupil size near the beginning of the word).

One way to assess potential artifacts is to analyze pupil *size* conditional on the initial landing position. There does appear to be a location effect of initial fixation location, as pupil size on the first fixation was larger when the initial fixation location was closer to the beginning of the word ($F_1(1, 23) = 7.96$, $p = 0.01$, $F_2(1, 31) = 5.51$, $p = 0.025$; see Table 3). The decrease in pupil size from first to second fixation, however, can not be completely due to the fixation location. In the above analysis, the mean pupil size was still significantly smaller on the second fixation than on the first, even when the initial fixation location was around the word center (i.e., on characters 5–9; $F_1(1, 21) = 40.7$, $p < 0.001$, $F_2(1, 30) = 60.8$, $p < 0.001$). Unfortunately, this comparison is not perfect as the mean first fixation location in these cases was 6.07, as contrasted with 8.05 for the mean second fixation location. As a result, we did a second analysis in which we tried to equate fixation locations even more closely. In this analysis, we only examined trials on which the first fixation was to the left of the 6th letter of the word. This restriction led to the

Table 4

Pupil diameter (in pixels) as a function of word frequency and word type (compound vs. monomorphemic words) in Experiment 3

	Compound words		Monomorphemic words		Mean
	Low frequency	High frequency	Low frequency	High frequency	
First fixation	57.0	57.0	56.5	56.3	56.7
Second fixation	55.0	55.5	54.5	54.6	54.9

mean first fixation location actually being slightly further into the word than the mean second fixation location (7.9 vs. 7.5). Unfortunately, this restriction led to a smaller set of data, but there was still a pupil size difference between first and second fixation (53.5 vs. 53.0), which was significant ($F_1(1, 13) = 7.41, p < 0.017$). (Because pupil size differed widely between participants, item analyses based on widely differing numbers of data points from different participants seemed pointless.)

Another possible artifact that could have produced the pupil size difference between the first and second fixation is the differing size of the saccade preceding the fixation (although we have not found any reports of such an artifact). That is, saccades from word to word are longer than intraword saccades. To try to control for this, we conducted an analysis in which only trials were examined in which the fixation prior to landing on the target word was within four characters of the space preceding the target word and the first fixation on the target word was within the first four characters of the target word. In addition, all trials on which there were regressive saccades were eliminated. This did not exactly equate for mean saccade length, as the mean saccade length prior to the first fixation was 5.7 characters and the mean saccade length prior to the second fixation was 4.8 characters. Again, these restrictions led to elimination of a lot of data; however, the difference in pupil diameter between the first and second fixations (51.3 vs. 50.2 pixels) was still significant, $F_1(1, 13) = 77.1$ with $p < 0.001$, and because the size of the effect was just about the same size as in the main analysis (where there was a large difference in mean saccade size), we doubt whether the small remaining difference in saccade size could be the cause of the difference in pupil size.

A highly reliable fixation order effect was also found in the pupil size data of Experiment 3, where high- and low-frequency compounds and length-matched and frequency-matched monomorphemic words were employed as stimuli ($F_1(1, 18) = 203.6, p < 0.001$; see Table 4). Here we wanted to examine a possible artifact that was not considered in the previous analysis: that the duration of the first fixation tends to be longer than that of the second fixation. Thus, we did a regression analysis by items, in which the pupil diameter was predicted from both the fixation duration and the fixation number (either first or second). If the fixation order effect in pupil size is merely an artifact of fixation duration, fixation duration should predict pupil size and fixation number should exert no effect. However, the regression analysis showed that fixation duration had virtually no predictive power and fixation order essentially predicted the entire effect.

In Experiment 3, word frequency did not exert an effect on pupil size, $F_1 < 1$, but there was a marginally significant effect of word type, $F_1(1, 18) = 3.79$, $p = 0.067$, suggesting that the average pupil size for compound words was slightly larger than for monomorphemic words. Although the finding is only suggestive, it is consistent with the view that compound words would be more effortful to identify than monomorphemic words. The gaze duration data are in line with this view by showing a 60-ms decrement for the monomorphemic words over the compound words.

Across the two experiments, the data on pupil size strongly suggest that encoding a long word takes more effort in its initial stages and less effort as the potential lexical candidates are narrowed down. Thus, it may be worthwhile in future eye movement research on word identification to include the pupil size as an additional measure to assess relative processing effort.

One may argue against our interpretation that the fixation order effect is due to mental effort by pointing out that the pupil is known to dilate fairly slowly in response to a triggering event. The peak amplitude is typically observed only approximately 1000 ms after the beginning of an experimental trial (Beatty, 1982), and the dilation is shown to begin with a delay of about 300 ms (Hoeks and Levelt, 1993). As a typical fixation during reading lasts about 200–250 ms, a skeptic would claim that the duration of initial fixation does not last long enough to reflect changes in the relative mental effort related to the identification of the fixated word. We do not think this is a valid argument, because it is now well established that the processing of a given word is already initiated while fixating on the previous word. Because of this parafoveal preprocessing, the triggering event for the pupil dilation may appear well before making the first fixation on the target word, and thus it is not at all implausible that an effect can be detected during the initial fixation. Perhaps a part of the effect could be explained as a reaction to the length of the word (long words being more effortful to identify). However, assuming that the difference between the monomorphemic and compound words is real, word length cannot be the only explanation for the pupil dilation effect.

Summary

The above data indicate that Finnish compound words are decomposed into their primary constituents on-line (at least some of the time), and that this decomposition influences both *when* and *where* decisions. Most importantly, the frequencies of the first and second constituents each affect both how long the constituent is fixated and how long the whole compound is fixated. In addition, the time course of processing is consistent with a serial processing model, in which the first constituent is processed prior to the second. However, a pure decomposition model is not tenable, as the frequency of the whole word has an effect which surfaces in the eye movement record at least as early as the effects of the frequency of the second constituent.

The pattern of fixation duration data are compatible with a parallel dual-route model (see also Pollatsek et al., 2000), which assumes that two processes go on in parallel when accessing morphologically complex words — one that tries the access by looking up an entry in the mental lexicon that directly corresponds to the processed word as a whole, and another that decomposes the word into its morphological constituents and accesses the word meaning via the constituents. The finding that constituent frequencies reliably influence individual fixation durations is evidence supporting the existence of a decomposition route, and the finding that the whole-word frequency exerts an early effect in processing is evidence for a direct look-up route. Moreover, by assuming that these two processes occur in parallel, we are in the position to explain both that the access of the initial constituent would generally start to occur at least as rapidly as access of the whole word (i.e., that initial constituent effects occur before whole-word effects) and that second constituent effects would not necessarily have to occur after whole-word effects but that the two could overlap in time.

Our analyses of the constituents as if they were separate words also indicated that significant processing of the second constituent occurred when the first constituent was fixated, resulting in the frequency of the first constituent having significant effects on the probability that the second constituent was fixated, and the gaze duration on the second constituent. In contrast, there was little effect of the frequency of the second constituent on initial processing of the first constituent. The only effect was on the gaze duration on the first constituent, and this effect could have been due to refixations on the first constituent that were intended as initial fixations on the second constituent.

These data suggest that although compound word constituents to some extent may behave like separate words, there is considerably more overlap in their processing than is the case with separate words. First, the effect of word frequency does not typically spill over to the processing of next word, a finding that is at odds with our observation that the processing of first constituent continues when fixating the second constituent. Second, with words it is typically not the case that the frequency of the parafoveal word to the right of the fixated word exerts an effect prior to its fixation (but see Kennedy, 1998; Chapter 8), again a finding we observed for compound word constituents. Thus, compound word identification does not reduce to the identification of the constituents as if they were separate words.

Properties of the constituents also affected where on the word a saccade landed. Most notably, the length of the initial morpheme affected where the refixations on the compound word were directed, even when word length and various frequency measures were controlled. This indicated that the size of constituents can guide saccadic targeting decisions even in the absence of spaces between them (and in the absence of other lower-level cues such as low bigram frequencies at constituent boundaries). The frequency of the constituents also influenced where a word is fixated (both the initial fixation and refixations). The latter effects are most parsimoniously explained by a processing difficulty hypothesis, which assumes that saccadic amplitude can be affected by foveal and parafoveal processing difficulty. Note that the constituent length effect can not be plausibly explained in this way, as fixations go further into a word when the first constituent is long (and hence, all other things being equal, would be harder to process).

The processing difficulty hypothesis can take two forms. According to one version, processing difficulty influences the probability of fixating or skipping a word (or a compound word constituent) and the probability of making a refixation on a word (or constituent). According to a stronger version, saccade length can also be affected by processing difficulty in a graded fashion (see Radach and McConkie, 1998, for a similar distinction). The former version translates to a *when* decision in the sense that the decision of where to saccade next is governed by how hard a foveal or parafoveal word or constituent is to process. In other words, it assumes that processing difficulty only influences which word or constituent is selected as the target for a saccade. The latter version of the hypothesis adds a mechanism which is capable of fine-tuning the exact saccadic amplitude as a function of foveal or parafoveal processing difficulty. In other words, a mechanism is postulated that directly modulates the saccade amplitude computation. It is this latter version that has created some controversy (Radach and McConkie, 1998; see also Chapter 7).

The weaker version of the processing difficulty hypothesis that is generally accepted by the eye movement community was supported by the finding that high-frequency constituents were selected as the saccadic targets less often than low-frequency constituents. On the other hand, we also found evidence for the more controversial version of the hypothesis: fine-tuning of the saccadic amplitude was carried out by the readers on the basis of the frequency of compound word constituents. This leads us to conclude that processing difficulty influences both the target selection as well as the amplitude of saccades in reading.

Finally, we observed some evidence suggesting that the size of the pupil may reflect the difficulty of accessing long words in reading with the pupil being larger during the initial processing stages and relatively smaller during the later stages. As this is apparently the first time a relationship is observed between pupil size and lexical access during reading, it awaits confirmation by corroborative evidence from future studies.

References

Beatty, J. (1982). Task-evoked pupillary responses, processing load, and the structure of processing resources. Psychological Bulletin, 91, 276–292.

Beauvillain, C., Doré, K. and Baudouin, V. (1996). The 'center of gravity' of words: evidence for an effect of the word-initial letters. Vision Research, 36, 589–604.

Henderson, J.M. and Ferreira, F. (1990). Effects of foveal processing difficulty on the perceptual span in reading: implications for attention and eye movement control. Journal of Experimental Psychology: Learning, Memory, and Cognition, 16, 417–429.

Hoeks, B. and Levelt, W.J.M. (1993). Pupillary dilation as a measure of attention: a quantitative system analysis. Behavior Research Methods, Instruments, and Computers, 25, 16–26.

Hogaboam, T.W. (1983). Reading patterns in eye movement data. In: K. Rayner (Ed.), Eye Movements in Reading: Perceptual and Language Processes. New York: Academic Press, pp. 309–332.

Hyönä, J. (1995). Do irregular letter combinations attract readers' attention? Evidence from fixation locations in words. Journal of Experimental Psychology: Human Perception and Performance, 21, 68–81.

Hyönä, J., Niemi, P. and Underwood, G. (1989). Reading long words embedded in sentences: informativeness of word halves affects eye movements. Journal of Experimental Psychology: Human Perception and Performance, 15, 142–152.

Hyönä, J. and Pollatsek, A. (1998). Reading Finnish compound words: eye fixations are affected by component morphemes. Journal of Experimental Psychology: Human Perception and Performance, 24, 1612–1627.

Hyönä, J., Tommola, J. and Alaja, A.M. (1995). Pupil dilation as a measure of processing load in simultaneous interpretation and other language tasks. Quarterly Journal of Experimental Psychology, 48A, 598–612.

Inhoff, A.W. (1989). Lexical access during eye fixations in reading: are word access codes used to integrate lexical information across interword fixations. Journal of Memory and Language, 28, 444–461.

Inhoff, A.W., Radach, R. and Heller, D. (in press). Complex compounds in German: Interword spaces facilitate segmentation but hinder assignment of meaning. Journal of Memory and Language.

Just, M.A. and Carpenter, P.A. (1993). The intensity dimension of thought: pupillometric indices of sentence processing. Canadian Journal of Experimental Psychology, 47, 310–339.

Kahneman, D. (1973). Attention and Effort. Englewood Cliffs, NJ: Prentice-Hall.

Kennedy, A. (1998). The influence of parafoveal words on foveal inspection time: evidence for a processing trade-off. In: G. Underwood (Ed.), Eye Guidance in Reading and Scene Perception. Oxford: Elsevier, pp. 149–179.

Kennison, S.M. and Clifton, C. (1995). Determinants of parafoveal preview benefit in high and low working memory capacity readers: implications for eye movement control. Journal of Experimental Psychology: Learning, Memory, and Cognition, 21, 68–81.

Lima, S.D. and Inhoff, A.W. (1985). Lexical access during eye fixations in reading: effects of word-initial letter sequence. Journal of Experimental Psychology: Human Perception and Performance, 11, 272–285.

McConkie, G.W. and Zola, D. (1984). Eye movement control during reading: the effects of word units. In: W. Prinz and A.T. Sanders (Eds.), Cognition and Motor Processes. Berlin: Springer, pp. 63–74.

O'Regan, J.K. (1992). Optimal viewing position in words and the strategy-tactics theory of eye movements in reading. In: K. Rayner (Ed.), Eye Movements and Visual Cognition: Scene Perception and Reading. New York: Springer, pp. 334–354.

O'Regan, J.K., Vitu, F., Radach, R. and Kerr, P.W. (1994). Effects of local processing and oculomotor factors in eye movement guidance in reading. In: J. Ygge and G. Lennerstrand (Eds.), Eye Movements in Reading. Oxford: Pergamon, pp. 329–348.

Pollatsek, A., Hyönä, J. and Bertram, R. (2000). The role of morphological constituents in reading Finnish compound words. In press.

Pollatsek, A. and Rayner, K. (1990). Eye movements and lexical access in reading. In: D.A. Balota, G.B. Flores d'Arcais and K. Rayner (Eds.), Comprehension Processes in Reading. Hillsdale, NJ: Erlbaum, pp. 143–163.

Pollatsek, A., Rayner, K. and Balota, D.A. (1986). Inferences about eye movement control from the perceptual span in reading. Perception and Psychophysics, 40, 123–130.

Radach, R. and McConkie, G.W. (1998). Determinants of fixation positions in words during reading. In: G. Underwood (Ed.), Eye Guidance in Reading and Scene Perception. Oxford: Elsevier.

Rayner, K. (1998). Eye movements in reading and information processing: 20 years of research. Psychological Bulletin, 124, 372–422.

Rayner, K. and McConkie, G.W. (1976). What guides a reader's eye movements. Vision Research, 16, 829–837.

Rayner, K. and Morris, R.K. (1992). Eye movement control in reading: evidence against semantic preprocessing. Journal of Experimental Psychology: Human Perception and Performance, 18, 163–172.

Rayner, K. and Pollatsek, A. (1981). Eye movement control during reading: evidence for direct control. Quarterly Journal of Experimental Psychology, 33A, 351–373.

Rayner, K. and Pollatsek, A. (1989). The Psychology of Reading. Englewood Cliffs, NJ: Prentice Hall.

Rayner, K. and Sereno, S.C. (1994). Eye movements in reading: psycholinguistic studies. In: M.A. Gernsbacher (Ed.), Handbook of Psycholinguistics. San Diego, CA: Academic Press, pp. 57–81.

Rayner, K., Sereno, S.C. and Raney, G.E. (1996). Eye movement control in reading: a comparison of two types of models. Journal of Experimental Psychology: Human Perception and Performance, 22, 1188–1200.

Reichle, E.D., Pollatsek, A., Fisher, D.L. and Rayner, K. (1998). Towards a model of eye movement control in reading. Psychological Review, 105, 125–157.

Taft, M. and Forster, K.I. (1976). Lexical storage and retrieval of polymorphemic and polysyllabic words. Journal of Verbal Learning and Verbal Behavior, 15, 607–620.

Underwood, G., Clews, S. and Everatt, J. (1990). How do readers know where to look next? Local information distributions influence eye fixations. Quarterly Journal of Experimental Psychology, 42A, 39–65.

CHAPTER 5

Perceiving Spatial Attributes of Print

Martin H. Fischer
University of Dundee

Abstract

Reading is a spatial activity, with the eyes moving from one fixation location to the next to pick up spatially distributed information. Despite this fact, our current understanding and modeling of reading tends to ignore the relevance of spatial cognition in reading. Several findings suggest that spatial attributes of a text can affect its reading. Evidence from sentence and paragraph processing is reviewed, and new results on word and letter processing are described. It is proposed that readers maintain a page-based spatial representation of the text, and that normal reading involves the activation of biased cognitive representations of word length, possibly due to attentional scaling within an orthographic processing module. Finally, current models of reading and of visuo-spatial cognition are briefly considered as possible frameworks for further investigations of the role of spatial cognition in reading.

Reading as a Perceptual Process/A. Kennedy, R. Radach, D. Heller and J. Pynte (Editors)
ⓒ 2000 Elsevier Science Ltd. All rights reserved

Perceiving spatial attributes of print

Reading research has generated cognitive models that account for much of a skilled reader's behavior, such as fixation times on certain regions of text. Yet, reading is also a spatial activity, with the eyes moving from one fixation location to the next to pick up spatially distributed information. Despite this fact, our understanding and modeling of reading tends to ignore the relevance of spatial cognition in reading: current models of reading are predominantly based on temporal measures of performance (word naming and lexical decision latencies, reading speed, eye fixation times), and relatively few investigators have looked at the role of spatial variables in reading (see below). No doubt, the time-based approach to reading has been and continues to be successful. However, in the present chapter, the focus is on spatial cognition in reading, a perspective that can contribute to our better understanding of reading.

Technology has modified how we read. Today, many of us read more from computer screens than from paper. Consider the example of internet browsing. The visual layout of a given text depends on the size of the display window of the internet browser, and the order in which we encounter propositions depends on whether and how we select keywords embedded in the currently displayed document. Normally, localizing such keywords is supported by highlighting (color, underlining, blinking), but it remains to be investigated whether and how keyword selection also depends on the reader's memory for the spatial layout of the text. Clearly, the change from linear to nonlinear reading strategies will affect (and interact with) our cognitive representation of the text. For example, the unfamiliar non-linearity of hypertext documents makes it easy to loose track of one's position in the text. We might experience this problem even when using our word processor. An analog to this phenomenon of "being lost in hyperspace" (Dillon, McKnight and Richardson, 1990) has never been reported to occur during the reading of hardcopies, even though in both cases we only see a segment of the text at a time. Current theorizing cannot account for this observation, due to the absence of a comprehensive theory of spatial cognition in reading. The spatial coding hypothesis (Kennedy, 1992) is an exception to this general state of affairs. It considers a text like any other visual object: although subsequent information processing will yield phonological, syntactic, and semantic representations of the text, according to the spatial coding hypothesis the initially apprehended information about the spatial attributes of the text remains available in working memory, including its layout and the location of propositions within the text. Kennedy (1992) reviewed further evidence in support of spatial coding, but left open the question of how such spatial codes are generated, maintained, and subsequently retrieved. Today the available evidence on spatial cognition during reading remains scattered.

To provide a structure for the reader, this chapter is organized hierarchically. After reviewing spatial coding at the more global levels of sentences, paragraphs and texts, I will turn to the spatial coding of words before addressing finally the perception of spatial extent of single letters. The last section of this chapter briefly sketches two theoretical frameworks within which spatial cognition in reading might be investigated further.

Spatial coding of text

How accurately can we determine the location of a text segment from which we previously extracted semantic information? To address this question, Christie and Just (1976) had subjects read a passage that then remained visible on a computer screen. Eye movements were monitored during subsequent questioning about the content of each sentence. Subjects fixated a start location below the passage before they were asked each question, and their subsequent first fixation in the passage could be used to assess sentence location memory. Subjects spontaneously fixated on the probed sentence in 31% of the trials, indicating a good ability to remember sentence locations within a paragraph.

Eye movement behavior during normal reading provides further clues to the spatial representation of texts. Readers tend to initiate regressive eye movements from an ambiguous region (a word or phrase) toward a previously inspected text segment for disambiguation or to locate the referent of an anaphor (e.g., Frazier and Rayner, 1982; Kennedy and Murray, 1987). Given the limit of the perceptual span in reading (see Rayner and Pollatsek, 1989, Chapter 4), large and purposeful regressions cannot be based on immediate visual input. Their occurrence implies that readers either directly remember the locations of words, or else can quickly reconstruct their location (see also Radach and McConkie, 1998). Return sweeps are a special case of long-range regressions where a reader directs the eyes to the beginning of a new line of text after fixating near the end of the current line. The return sweep has a typical behavioral signature: a shorter than average fixation is followed by the regressive sweep of less than unity gain into the new line's beginning, followed by either a longer than average fixation or a correction for undershooting. Leisman (1978) assumed that the return sweep is guided by a stored representation of text coordinates, but Hofmeister, Heller and Radach (1997) found no effects of different text layout manipulations on the return sweep signature, casting doubt on Leisman's proposal.

There is behavioral evidence of spatial representations of text, in addition to eye movement studies, to which we now turn. Rothkopf (1971) was probably the first to investigate memory for spatial locations in reading systematically. His subjects read 12 pages of a novel (roughly 250 words per page) and then tried to answer 32 questions about its contents. Each answer was followed by an attempt to localize the relevant item first within one quarter of the entire text and then within one eighth (effectively analyzed as one fourth) of a page. A test for uniformity of the distribution of localization judgments showed that the within-page localization of items was most frequently made toward the region in which the item had actually appeared. A similar trend in this direction was present in the more global, text-based judgments. Rothkopf also reported individual differences such that readers who answered the content questions more accurately also had a better localization score (correlation of $r = 0.66$). Finally, this study provided a first indication that the spatial memory for texts may be page-based: subjects did better when asked to locate an item in one of four regions of a page than in one of four regions of the entire text.

In a similar study (Zechmeister et al., 1975), text passages of six pages were presented to the readers, either with or without prior instruction about the role of spatial location in a subsequent memory test. After reading the passage, subjects answered, for each of 16 items, first a fill-in question and then localized the filled-in item; the results were quite interesting. Reading times were not reliably slower for the group of readers who knew that they would be tested about spatial knowledge than for the uninformed group (16.1 vs. 15.9 min). One possible interpretation of this result is that it was not necessary for readers to modify their reading strategy to accommodate a spatial coding requirement because it is part of normal reading. However, the informed group also did not perform better on the localization test than the uninformed group. Item and location memory were both above chance and were positively correlated, such that there was a higher probability of localizing an item when it was remembered correctly than when it was not remembered in the fill-in test ($p = 0.58$ vs. 0.34). This result could argue for an overall benefit from selective attention to both item and location information during reading. However, it is equally possible that the available (item or location) information may have acted as a retrieval cue for the other part of this information. This latter interpretation was, however, ruled out by a second study where localization performance did not improve when subjects received the correct item information prior to their localization attempt. Finally, there was consistently poorer localization performance for items in the lower right quadrant of a page. Given the densely printed information (roughly 600 words per page), this suggests a gradual loading of a hypothetical location tagging mechanism during reading but no spill-over of this load from one page to the next. Both this absence of spill-over and the superior page-based localization in Rothkopf's (1971) study suggest that the physical page might provide an allocentric reference frame for spatial representations of texts. Such an account implies a hierarchical cognitive representation of the text in a form that matches the physically available pages.

Two recent studies looked at the accuracy with which readers remember the location of information after processing either an entire paragraph or a single sentence. Baccino and Pynte (1998, Experiment 3) assessed localization accuracy for target words at the paragraph level, using a probe localization task. Their subjects first read passages of around 80 words that either included or did not include a perspective shift (from third to first person). After the text was masked, a single probe word appeared below the passage and subjects had to move the mouse cursor to this word's location or the location of its synonym in the text body. The authors reasoned that the perspective shift provided an incentive to store the location of its occurrence for future reinspection. In agreement with this notion, target localization was faster and less variable after a perspective shift. The surface form of the target (synonym vs. identical to the probe) did, however, not affect localization accuracy. Using a similar approach, Fischer (1999) presented single sentences on a computer screen and, upon termination of the sentence display, asked readers to indicate with a mouse cursor the position that had been occupied by one probe word from each sentence. Localization scores showed primacy and recency effects. Localization times and errors suggested that memory for word locations was limited to the last one or two words of a sentence and that the remaining word positions were reconstructed through sequential retrieval of the sentence's surface structure. This was true for complete as well as for incomplete sentences, although one would expect an additional incentive to retain location information from sentences that had not yet been comprehended (e.g., to control regressive eye movements). These findings imply a relatively shallow span for word location memory that can be augmented through item information.

Finally, some more indirect evidence of spatial cognition during reading is available. For example, sentences that contain imaginable statements take longer to read and verify than sentences with abstract content (Eddy and Glass, 1981; see also Brooks, 1967; and the section below entitled 'Theories for spatial cognition in reading'). The fact that this processing difficulty does not occur when sentences are given auditorily suggests that the visual processing of text during reading engages cognitive resources that are also used for the generation of visuo-spatial images during comprehension. To be sure, reading is possible without spatializing the text: text elements can be presented one after the other at the same place around a reader's fixation (the so-called rapid serial visual presentation or RSVP technique; e.g., Juola, 1988), leading to reading rates many times those of normal reading. Text can also be scrolled along underneath the reader's fixation point (the billboard technique) without loss of comprehension. But clear support for an advantage of spatialized over non-spatialized reading comes from a study by Kennedy and Murray (1984): reading spatially distributed text leads to higher syntactic sensitivity compared to reading text that is presented sequentially at a single location even though in both conditions the reader may only see one word at a time. Spatialized text is also easier to comprehend than RSVP text (e.g., Masson, 1983; Potter,

Kroll and Harris, 1980). These findings indicate that the spatial distribution of text supports some of the cognitive activities normally involved in reading.

In summary, the data on spatial cognition at more global levels of reading suggest that skilled readers establish a spatial representation of the text. Functional aspects of this representation, such as its mechanism of generation, capacity, and accessibility are currently not well understood. It is also unclear whether such a representation might be generated automatically (Hasher and Zacks, 1979; Logan, 1998) or through controlled processing (e.g., Fischer, 1999; Naveh-Benjamin, 1987, 1988). Further research should address the possible interactions between spatial and phonological working memory in reading, and the hypothesis that spatial representations of text might be page-based and are thus tightly linked to the hardcopy formats familiar from reading acquisition. Such research might be informed by observations regarding the spatial coding of subunits of a text, such as words and their letters. We turn to these latter issues next.

Spatial coding of words

Given the central status of the word concept for our understanding of the cognitive operations involved in reading, the processing of spatial information from words deserves special attention. Two recent studies provide indirect support for the spatial coding of words, both making use of well-known aspects of human performance. The first study utilized a spatial compatibility phenomenon to demonstrate the spatial coding of words. Spatial compatibility refers to the fact that a spatial stimulus attribute is spontaneously linked up with a spatial response dimension, such that responding with the left hand is faster and more accurate when the relevant stimulus is also located on the left side and vice versa. This holds even when location is a task-irrelevant stimulus attribute. When asked to indicate the presence of a target letter in a word by pressing a button, subjects do so faster with their left hand for targets in the beginning of the word, and faster with their right hand for targets in the end of the word (Mapelli, Umilta, Nicoletti, Fanini and Capezzani, 1996). This result suggests that visual word perception normally involves the processing of a left–right dimension, an idea running against the widespread assumption of parallel coding of letters (see also Kwantes and Mewhort, 1999).

A second study utilized a perceptual grouping phenomenon to demonstrate spatial coding of words. Neurologically healthy adults bisected horizontal lines with long- and short-word flankers, using a pencil. Bisection is a standard method to infer the representation of spatial extent of the bisected stimulus: errors into one direction indicate that this part of the stimulus appears subjectively larger than the other side (see Heilman, Watson and Valenstein, 1985). Flankers can cue attention to either side of a line, but Fischer (1994) showed that perceptual grouping of the cue with the line might be an alternative cause for modified bisection performance. In the presently relevant experiment (Fischer, 1996, Experiment 1), the flankers were pairs of 3- and 6-character monosyllabic words with controlled frequency that had to be named before bisecting each line. Line bisection was overall quite accurate, but showed a systematic bias toward the longer of the two flanker words, indicating that differences in word length of only 3 characters (about 1° of visual angle) are cognitively represented and can reliably influence spatial behavior.

Reading and spelling errors in dyslexic readers and in patients with brain lesions provide further evidence in support of spatial coding of words in hierarchically organized maps, such as a feature map, a letter shape map, and a graphemic buffer (e.g., Caramazza and Miceli, 1989; for review see Riddoch and Humphreys, 1993). These studies rely on the fact that parietal lobe injuries often lead to a contralateral representational deficit called 'hemispatial neglect' (e.g., Heilman et al., 1985). For example, Caramazza and Hillis (1990) reported that a 77-year-old left-handed woman with a left parietal stroke made reading and spelling errors only in the right halves of words, regardless of word length or topographic arrangement (horizontal, vertical, mirror-reversed). Based on the performance of this stroke patient the authors concluded " ... that order information in orthographic representations is coded spatially in a word-centered coordinate system; that is, in a spatially defined coordinate frame whose center corresponds to the midpoint of a canonical, orientation-invariant representation of the word and not the midpoint of the word stimulus" (p. 267). It may, however, seem premature to infer general properties of lexical representations from the examination of only a single person who is, in addition, left-handed with left-sided brain damage. The left hemisphere is normally dedicated to language processing, and left-handedness may or may not alter this specialization. Two lines of evidence indicate that caution is indeed warranted, as they show (a) that spatial attributes of words have a special representational status and (b) that word orientation does affect spatial performance.

Consider first the special status of word length coding. Sieroff, Pollatsek and Posner (1988) found that both left- and right-parietal stroke patients identified many letters of tachistoscopically presented words correctly, while they showed contralateral extinction of letters in non-words. Thus, there was no lateralized spatial performance deficit associated with words despite the parietal lesion. A line bisection experiment by Brunn and Farah (1991, Experiment 2) also argues for a special status of word length information in some neglect patients. Prior to each bisection attempt, their parietal patients reported words, pseudowords, or non-words that were presented horizontally above horizontal lines. The patients' line bisection bias improved most when lines were combined with words, suggesting that words somehow counteracted the hemispatial neglect associated with the perception of lines.

Consider now the role of word orientation. Nichelli, Venneri, Pentore and Cubelli (1993) reported a patient who made errors on the final letters of words printed in a top-down direction but on the initial letters of words printed in a bottom-up direction. The spatial compatibility effect for target letter detection (Mapelli et al., 1996; see above) also depended on the congruency of stimulus orientation with response orientation and did not obtain with vertically presented stimuli. Finally, Fischer (1996) asked healthy subjects to bisect English words and non-words directly after reading them aloud. This method is thought to provide most direct evidence on how the spatial extent of words is perceived and provided two interesting findings. First, words tended to be bisected toward their beginning, despite their continuous visual presence. And second, this was true only for horizontally printed words and not for vertical words or horizontal non-words. These observations suggest that the spatial representation of words is non-veridical and orientation-dependent.

Let us now take a closer look at the systematic bias in word bisection. This observation may have important implications. Current theories of eye movement control in reading all share the implicit assumption that the location of word centers is perceived correctly. Given this assumption, it is surprising to find that, in normal reading, there is a pervasive tendency to first fixate to the left of the true word center. This preference for the left side of newly encountered words has been termed the preferred viewing position effect (henceforth: PVP effect) and has sparked considerable interest because one would expect skilled behavior such as reading to be optimized. From a perceptual point of view it would indeed be optimal to fixate the center of new words to project the maximum number of letters onto high-acuity areas of the retina. To account for the apparently suboptimal PVP effect, a number of hypotheses have been put forth. These assume, for example, an oculomotor origin of the bias (Coeffe and O'Regan, 1987; McConkie et al., 1988) or a role of information distribution in words (Clark and O'Regan, 1999; Underwood, Bloomfield and Clews, 1988; Underwood, Clews and Everatt, 1990; but see Hyönä, 1995; Radach and Kempe, 1993; Rayner and Morris, 1992). It is currently not clear which combination of factors can account for this pervasive fixation preference to the left of a word's center in reading (for a recent review see Radach and McConkie, 1998). The important point is that all current accounts of the PVP effect assume veridical word length coding. Fischer's (1996) observation of a word bisection bias with unlimited viewing time does, however, suggest that this assumption might be unwarranted. Therefore, it was important to replicate and extend this finding that was originally obtained with English nouns. Two new experiments are now described, showing that the word bisection bias also holds in a different language and extends to other word classes. Line bisection as a control condition excludes purely visual or motor accounts of this result. The word bisection bias increases with word length, just as the PVP effect does.

Word bisection experiments

In the first experiment, 4 men and 12 women between 18 and 36 years participated after giving their informed consent. All subjects were right-handed with normal or corrected vision. Subjects reported to be neurologically healthy and were naive with respect to the hypotheses of the study. Subjects were run individually in a quiet laboratory room with a dim background light. They were seated on a height-adjustable office chair in front of a Philips 4 CM 2299 Autoscan Professional Color monitor with 20 inch diagonal screen size. Stimuli were presented in black on a white background, and no head restraint was used. An Apple 4400/200 Power-Mac controlled stimulus presentation and response collection. Horizontal and vertical screen resolution were 1024 and 768 pixel, respectively. Responses were with the right hand on a one-button Apple Desktop Bus Mouse II.

Ten adjectives and 10 verbs, all with a length of 16 characters (char) and printed frequency of less than 6/6 million, were selected from a computerized database of German language (Celex, 1995). Length and frequency were controlled to minimize variability of judgments in the present study (see Experiment 2 for different lengths and frequencies). Letters were presented in nonproportional Monaco font and in uppercase to prevent effects of ascenders or descenders on perceived word center. Using large 45-point type, letter size was 34 by 26 pixel or 13×10 mm, yielding about $1.3°$/char at a viewing distance of about 50 cm. Twenty line stimuli were generated on-line from the word stimuli by first plotting the corresponding word in white color (which is not visible on white background) at its pre-assigned coordinates. Connecting then the first and last pixel of this invisible word with a black line of 1 pixel width (plus adjustments for the differential use of the pixel matrix for different initial and final characters) insured that lines had the same length and spatial position on the screen as the corresponding words. Average line length was 416 pixel or 160 mm.

The line and word bisection tasks were blocked and presented in a counter-balanced order across subjects to control unspecific learning effects. Words were shown in a random sequence, one at a time, at randomly chosen locations on the screen. When the subject pressed the mouse button, a word appeared horizontally on the screen, together with a 1 mm narrow and 9 mm long vertical pointer. Subjects named each word aloud before indicating its perceived midpoint by moving the pointer, or said 'line' before each line bisection attempt to equate overall task demands. The pointer responded only to horizontal displacements of the mouse, and it did so only after 600 ms of stimulus exposure. This emphasized priority of the naming task and avoided attention capture from the moving pointer. The pointer always appeared at the screen center so that it had to be moved to the left and to the right side about equally often. Pressing the mouse button terminated the stimulus display and yielded a measure of bisection accuracy, where negative values indicated a shorter distance from the pointer to the stimulus begin than to its end. Pilot testing had shown that observers can localize the beginning and ending of words within ± 2 pixel with this method, and that the effect of particular start or end letters in the stimuli is negligible.

Bisection performance was calculated by subtracting the distance between pointer position and the first pixel of the word from the distance between pointer position and the last pixel of the word. Thus, a negative score indicates an error toward the left, i.e., toward the word beginning. Average bisection performance was determined for each subject, and two-tailed t-tests were performed on all group means.

Average word bisection bias across both word classes was -10.2 pixel or -0.39 char (SD 9 pixel). This value differed reliably from accurate bisection performance, $t(15) = -5.57$, $p = 0.0001$. Average verb bisection bias was -10.7 pixel or -0.41 char (SD 13 pixel), also differing reliably from accurate performance, $t(15) = -3.37$, $p = 0.005$. Finally, average adjective bisection bias was -9.5 pixel or -0.37 char (SD 11 pixel), $t(15) = -3.48$, $p = 0.003$. Thus, both word classes had a similar left bias, as indicated by the absence of significant difference between them, $p > 0.7$. Average bisection performance for horizontal lines was -4.2 pixel (SD 13 pixel). This result did not differ reliably from accurate bisection, $t(15) = -1.31$, $p = 0.21$. It does, however, differ significantly from the average word bisection bias of the same subjects, $t(15) = 2.49$, $p = 0.0249$. This finding insures that the perceptual bias in word bisection is related to the lexical nature of the stimulus material and rules out a purely motor account of word bisection bias.

The first experiment showed that there is a robust and general left-bias specific to the perceived middle of words. A second experiment assessed visual and lexical contributions to this word bisection bias. Visual factors were investigated by manipulating the length of the words. Lexical factors were investigated by comparing bisection accuracy for lines and words. A total of 38 German nouns were selected according to length and frequency (Celex, 1995). They were all of high frequency (mean: 120/6 million, range 51 to 471) but differed systematically in length and number of syllables. Specifically, there were ten monosyllabic 5-char words. Further, there were ten 13-char words, five having 3 syllables and five with 6 syllables. Thus, the effect of number of syllables on word bisection performance could be assessed independently from the number of characters. Finally, ten 9-char words consisted of 4 syllables. They could be contrasted against eight 17-char words with 4 syllables to assess the effect of number of characters on word bisection performance independently from the number of syllables. Line stimuli were generated on-line as before. Average line length was 107 mm (range: 50 to 170 mm).

The 16 subjects from Experiment 1 also participated in this study. The same apparatus and procedure were used. Subjects bisected either 38 horizontal lines or 38 horizontal words in two counterbalanced blocks, naming each word or saying

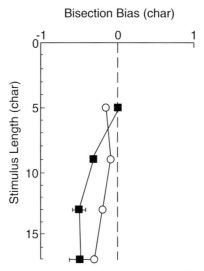

Fig. 1. Bisection bias (in characters) for words (squares) and for lines (circles) of equal length.

'line' prior to bisection. Each line appeared at the same random location on the screen as the corresponding word with the same horizontal extent. Data were analyzed as before.

The results are shown in Figs. 1 and 2. Consider first word bisection performance as a function of word length. The average bisection score for 5-char words was +0.6 pixel (SD 3.4 pixel), which corresponds to +0.02 char and does not differ from accurate bisection, $t(15) = 0.1$, $p = 0.94$. As word length increased to 9 char, a reliable bisection bias of −8.0 pixel or −0.31 char (SD 5.8 pixel) emerged, $t(15) = -5.57$, $p = 0.0001$. The bias increased further to −12.5 pixel or −0.48 char (SD 9.1 pixel) with 13-char words, $t(15) = 5.47$, $p = 0.0001$. The difference between the 9- and 13-char conditions was reliable, $t(15) = 2.87$, $p = 0.0116$. Finally, the average bisection score for 17-char words was −11.7 pixel or −0.45 char (SD 14 pixel), $t(15) = -3.22$, $p = 0.0058$. Thus, there was no further change in word bisection performance with further increase of word length, $t(15) = 0.38$, $p = 0.712$.

To check whether the number of syllables had an impact on word bisection performance, separate bisection scores were determined for the 13-char words made of 3 or 6 syllables. Average bisection with 3- and 6-syllable words was −15.82 pixel (SD 10.8 pixel) and −9.11 pixel (SD 10.5 pixel), respectively. This corresponds to −0.61 char and −0.35 char, respectively. Both scores differed reliably from zero, with $t(15) = -5.87$, $p = 0.0001$ and $t(15) = -3.47$, $p = 0.0034$, respectively. There was a reliable decrease of the bias with increasing number of syllables, $t(15) = 2.73$, $p = 0.0156$, possibly due to the syllable border near word center. Finally, the distribution of bisection judgments across word lengths is depicted in Fig. 2.

M.H. Fischer

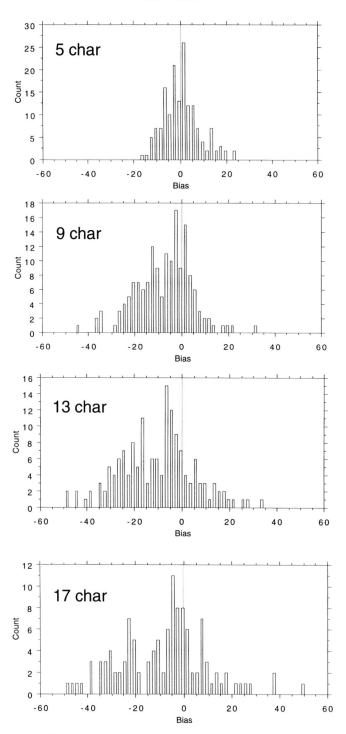

Fig. 2. Distribution of bisection bias (in pixels) for words, separately for the four word lengths investigated. Each character of a word was 26 pixels wide.

With line bisection, a different picture emerged (see Fig. 1). Subjects bisected short lines with an average bias of −4.3 pixel or 11.2 mm (SD 3.6 pixel), which was different from accurate bisection performance, $t(15) = -4.8$, $p = 0.0002$. The average bias was somewhat reduced for lines with an intermediate length corresponding to 9 char. The score of −2.5 pixel or 6.5 mm (SD 7.3 pixel) was not reliably different from accurate performance, $t(15) = -1.18$, $p = 0.2559$. Longer lines, corresponding to the 13- and 17-char words, were bisected with left biases of −4.6 pixel or 12 mm (SD 7.9 pixel) and −7.1 pixel or 18.5 mm (SD 14.4 pixel), respectively. These biases were both marginally reliable, $t(15) = -2.34$, $p = 0.0332$ and $t(15) = -1.97$, $p = 0.0675$, respectively. Finally, average bisection bias was again stronger with words than with lines of equal length, $t(15) = 2.23$, $p = 0.0416$.

These findings replicate and extend the observations on the cognitive representation of word length reported in Fischer (1996). In that study, American students bisected English nouns with a pencil and exhibited a similar left bias. Also, their bisection bias extended to pronounceable pseudowords but not to letter strings without consonants. And finally, the word bisection bias for English words was reliably stronger in bilingual Hebrew–English subjects compared to native English readers bisecting the same words (see also Fischer, 2000).

Fischer (1996, 2000) proposed that the bias in perceived word length may be related to the cognitive process of lexical access. Lexical access has often been conceived as inherently directional, starting at the beginning of a word and progressing to its end (for reviews see Marslen-Wilson, 1989). Specifically, the beginning of a word or a morpheme is used to generate a set of candidate interpretations of the stimulus (a 'cohort'), among which subsequently processed information can then efficiently select the correct interpretation. This directional and sequential lexical access strategy makes it important to represent word beginnings as saliently as possible to avoid erroneous cohort recruitment and subsequent delays or identification errors. To optimize candidate selection for the lexical interpretation of orthographic stimuli, the cognitive system might thus specifically attend to the word's beginning, which leads to an over-representation of the initial part of the word relative to its actual physical extent. According to the *attentional scaling hypothesis*, attending distorts the cognitive representation of spatial stimulus extent (for similar evidence see Prinzmetal and Wilson, 1997 and Robertson and Kim, 1999). Pseudowords and words from an unfamiliar language (or orthography) might demand repeated attempts at lexical access (see also Price, Wise and Frackowiak, 1996). The subsequent spatial bias would then reflect the increased saliency of this stimulus segment after prolonged selective attending.

Although the cohort model of lexical access was originally developed for speech perception, recent results by Kwantes and Mewhort (1999) suggest that its basic mechanism might also apply to visual word recognition, contrary to the widely held belief of parallel letter processing in visual word recognition. These authors showed that the position of the uniqueness point in a word does affect naming latency, contrary to prior reports. The word bisection bias and the PVP effect in reading might then both be a consequence of attention allocation during lexical processing: readers bisect the *perceived* word length, and they direct their eyes to the *perceived* word center during reading. Although the effect size of the word bisection bias is smaller than the PVP effect, note that the bisection error exhibits a similar increase with word length (Radach and McConkie, 1998; Rayner, 1979). The attentional scaling hypothesis thus provides an alternative to previous accounts of the PVP effect discussed above: it assumes that a functionally scaled cognitive representation and not a veridical image of the visual stimulus is processed toward lexical access. A direct test of the attentional scaling hypothesis would be to compare the PVP effect and the size of the word bisection bias within the same subjects and for the same stimulus materials: the hypothesis predicts a positive correlation between these two spatial measures of reading performance.

Spatial coding of letters

The comparison of bisection performance for lines and words suggests that spatial attributes of orthographic information are processed somehow differently by the visual system of skilled readers. Studies in which subjects evaluated spatial aspects of single letters provide additional evidence that there is indeed a systematic bias associated with their perception: we tend to misperceive even the most basic aspects of the spatial layout of orthographic information. Consider first a study by Carrasco and Sekuler (1993), who presented so-called Navon stimuli to their subjects. Small letters were arranged to form a large letter, and the sizes of all small letters were varied. Subjects rated whether the letters in the horizontal component of the global stimulus were larger, smaller, or equal to the letters that made up its vertical component. The authors found that viewers overestimated the horizontal extent of the local letter components, and that this illusion was not affected by an instruction to either focus on the height or the width dimension. Note that this result is contrary to what one might expect from the well-known horizontal–vertical illusion, supporting the idea of distorted spatial perception of orthographic information in the brain.

Investigating the spatial perception of regular letters, Skottun and Freeman (1983) reported that the height of letters is overestimated by a constant proportion of about 20% once the spacing between letters is larger than a critical value of about 3 min of arc. This result was obtained with a variety of psychophysical procedures. It agrees with the notion of an over-representation of the spatial extent of attended orthographic stimuli, which could also lead to the word bisection bias. Before we accept a role of this effect in word perception and reading, however, some open questions need to be addressed. Importantly, Skottun and Freeman (1983) only used letter heights below 6 min of arc, whereas letter sizes typically encountered in reading are well above 12 min (e.g., McCormick and Sanders, 1982). This raises the question whether the overestimation was truly dependent on orthographic information processing: did the subjects identify the letters they assessed? Because they might have been told that they were shown letters, a conceptual contribution to the reported effect cannot be ruled out (Appelman and Mayzner, 1981; Frith, 1984). Another concern is with the direction of causality in the relation between perceived spacing and perceived height. The data only indicated that smaller physical inter-letter spacing went with smaller estimates of letter height. Inter-letter spacing might, however, also be subject to perceptual biases as a function of letter height. Specifically, due to lateral masking the spacing could appear smaller with larger flanking stimuli. If perceived spacing is also affected by stimulus height, then either bias can be mapped as a joint function of the values on both the relevant and the irrelevant dimension, and the psychophysical function of the underlying mechanism can be estimated. Two new experiments were conducted to address these issues.

Experiments on letter perception

Six naive students with normal or corrected to normal vision participated without payment. Subjects were seated in front of a monochrome monitor (Atari sm 124, 21×13 cm display area, 640×400 pixels resolution). The black stimuli had a luminance of 6 cd/m^2, and the white background had a luminance of 120 cd/m^2. For each trial, the subject saw two letters in the center of the screen, drawn without serifs to enable accurate assessment of height and spacing. Both height and spacing of the letters varied independently and were either 6 or 21 pixels (equivalent to 2 or 7 mm, respectively). To preserve letter quality, the large stimuli had 5 pixels stroke width and the small stimuli had 2 pixels stroke width. Below the letter pair, and within two degrees of visual angle, a reference bar with the same stroke width as the letter was displayed with an offset from the relevant stimulus dimension. The reference bar had either a short or a long initial extension (1 or 40 pixels) to obtain judgments from both ascending and descending psychophysical procedures for each condition, which were subsequently averaged. The length of the reference bar had to be manipulated by means of two mouse buttons in steps of 1 pixel until it subjectively matched the dimension of relevance. If the subject matched the inter-letter spacing, the length of the reference bar varied horizontally. For height judgments the bar's length changed vertically. The dimension of relevance was also spelled out at the bottom of the screen to minimize confusion with respect to the change of instructions between trials.

Table 1

Stimulus dimensions for Experiments 1 and 2 [a]

Stimulus size	Viewing distance in Experiment 1			Viewing distance in Experiment 2		
	60 cm	120 cm	180 cm	150 cm	250 cm	350 cm
Small: 2 mm, 6 pixel	11.5	5.7	3.8	4.6	2.8	2.0
Large: 7 mm, 21 pixel	40.1	20.1	13.4	16.0	9.6	6.9

[a] The tabulated values are visual angles in minutes of arc.

The two dimensions of the stimulus were varied between 3.8 and 40.1 min of arc by changing the viewing distance. Keeping the physical stimulus constant makes the interpretation of judgments more straightforward. Due to this method each judgment was made under two different values of the respective context dimension. For example, the letter of 3.8 min height was matched in the context of either 3.8 or 13.4 min letter spacing (see Table 1). Such covariation of letter size and letter spacing is typical for regular text and allowed to efficiently assess the perceptual bias on both dimensions. Each subject was tested at viewing distances of 60, 120, and 180 cm, measured from display surface to cornea. Order of conditions was counterbalanced across subjects. Two letter heights, two letter separations, and two relevant dimension tasks yielded eight experimental conditions per viewing distance. These were given in random order at each viewing distance. The display was available for inspection until the subject was satisfied with his/her reproduction.

The average bias in perception of height was 4.4 min, and the average bias in perception of spacing was 3.7 min, $t(71) = 0.36$, $p > 0.7$. The absence of a main effect for Dimension of Judgment, $F(1, 5) = 0.73$, $p > 0.4$, $MS_e = 22.23$, confirmed that the differences between height and spacing judgments were not reliable. A significant main effect of True Stimulus Size, $F(5, 25) = 27.82$, $p < 0.001$, $MS_e = 8.23$, indicated that the larger stimulus size yielded larger reproduction errors. A main effect of Size of Context, $F(1, 5) = 187.44$, $p < 0.001$, $MS_e = 0.55$, indicated that a large context increased the perceptual bias. An interaction of Dimension of Judgment and Size of Context, $F(1, 5) = 68.18$, $p < 0.001$, $MS_e = 1.53$, indicated that context size mainly affected the perception of spacing.

Fig. 3 shows how the physical letters (open triangles) were misperceived in both height (horizontal displacement) and spacing (vertical displacement of circle). Letters with equal height and spacing (corresponding to the six triangles on a hypothetical diagonal with a slope of 1 in Fig. 3) were overestimated by approximately the same amount in height as in spacing. This is indicated by the

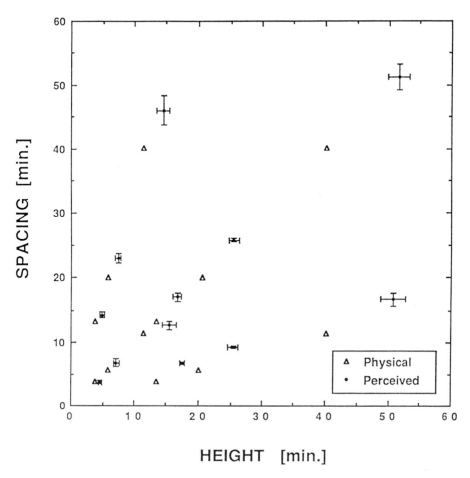

Fig. 3. True and perceived letter height and spacing. Physical stimuli are depicted as triangles, average judgments across subjects are depicted as circles (with 1 Standard Error of the Mean).

fact that the corresponding perceived stimuli (black dots) roughly map on the same hypothetical diagonal. At the same time there was overestimation of spacing for all asymmetric letter configurations.

The linear regression equation

$$\text{Perceived Letter Height} = 1.28 \times \text{True Letter Height} + 0.04$$

predicted 98% of the variability in height judgments. Letter height was always overestimated, as indicated by rightward displacement of the black dots (perceived) from the corresponding triangles (physical stimuli) in Fig. 3. This finding shows that the perceptual illusion first reported by Skottun and Freeman (1983) holds for letter

Table 2

Regression weights for the context factor in Experiment 1 [a]

Dimension of judgment	Overall context weight ($n = 72$)		Average context weight ($n = 6$)	
	True	Perceived	True	Perceived
Height	0.01 (n.s.)	0.01 (n.s.)	0.01 (n.s.)	0.01 (n.s.)
Spacing	0.15 (**)	0.11 (**)	0.14 (**)	0.12 (**)

[a] The tabulated values are nonstandardized beta weights as derived from regression analyses in which the true value of either dimension of judgment was included as first predictor of that judgment.
n.s. = nonsignificant contribution; ** = significant at the 0.01 level.

sizes in the range of normal text. Overestimation of letter heights was not affected by letter spacing. The average overestimation was 27.3% (standard deviation 4.7) with small spacings and 27.7% (standard deviation 1.7) with large spacings, $t(5) = 0.18$, $p > 0.8$. These values correspond to the estimate of 20% provided by Skottun and Freeman and confirm that overestimation of letter height is independent of letter spacing. This is further substantiated by the fact that a (nonstandardized) regression weight of 0.01 for True Letter Spacing as an additional predictor of Perceived Letter Height was not reliable in a multiple regression analysis, $t(69) = 0.34$, $p > 0.7$. A t-test on regression weights from individual subjects, $t(5) = 0.79$, $p > 0.2$, yielded the same average context weight and confirmed that True Letter Spacing did not contribute to height perception. Similar results were obtained for Perceived Letter Spacing as an additional predictor, $t(69) = 0.42$, $p > 0.6$, and $t(5) = 1.29$, $p > 0.2$, respectively. The results of both analyses are summarized in Table 2.

Spacing was also overestimated, as indicated by upward displacement of the black dots (perceived) from the corresponding triangles (physical stimuli) in Fig. 3. The linear regression equation

$$\text{Perceived Letter Spacing} = 1.19 \times \text{True Letter Spacing} + 0.72$$

predicted 96% of the variability in all spacing judgments. Thus, the 'perceived spacing illusion' is as strong as the height illusion. For spacing judgments in the context of large letters, the amount of overestimation ranged from 77.8 to 27.8% for spacings from 3.8 to 40.1 min, respectively; for the small-letter context the bias of spacing judgments was smaller throughout (average 10.5%, standard deviation 7.7), $t(5) = 3.3$, $p < 0.05$. This finding suggests an influence of letter height on perceived spacing. In a multiple regression analysis the beta weight of 0.15 for True Letter Height as an additional predictor of Perceived Letter Spacing was reliable, $t(69) = 5.64$, $p < 0.001$. A t-test on beta weights from individual subjects, $t(5) = 5.53$, $p < 0.01$, confirmed that the coefficient for True Letter Height as context variable was reliably different from zero. Similar results obtained for Perceived Letter Height as an additional predictor of Perceived Letter Spacing, $t(69) = 5.64$, $p < 0.001$, with the coefficient being 0.11 in an overall multiple regression, and $t(5) = 8.03$, $p < 0.01$, and a coefficient of 0.12 in a t-test on beta weights from individual subjects. The results of both analyses are also summarized in Table 2. Hence, letter height contributes significantly to perceived inter-letter spacing.

The first experiment found systematic overestimation of both letter height and letter spacing and thus replicated and extended a finding of Skottun and Freeman (1983). There were, however, some problems with an interpretation in terms of dedicated orthographic processing in the brain: the height bias could be unrelated to the letter quality of the stimuli, and the spacing bias could be due to phosphor irradiation (from the white spacing onto the black letters). A second experiment with rectangle stimuli displayed in positive or negative display polarity clarified these issues. The same apparatus and method as in Experiment 1 were used and the range of viewing distances was extended to investigate the perception of height and spacing of non-letter stimuli with a visual angle between 2 and 16 min of arc. The predictions for spacing judgments are straightforward. Consider the negative polarity display: the spacing between rectangles is black, and the reference bar is white. If irradiation has an effect, then the perceived spacing will be reduced by irradiation from the white flankers; the white reference bar will at the same time be overestimated in its extension. Both effects will work together and yield smaller spacing judgments with negative displays than with positive displays. With respect to height judgments, this experiment is exploratory. Finding no reliable overestimation of rectangle height would support the notion of a processing advantage specific to letters, presumably due to the activation of internal representations. If, on the other hand, height judgments exhibit the same overestimation bias as letters, then this effect indicates a perceptual or response bias.

Six new naive students with normal or corrected to normal vision participated without payment. Pairs of rectangles of 6 pixels width and 6 or 21 pixels height were presented with 6 or 21 pixels spacing, as measured from adjacent inner sides. The width of both rectangles and of the reference bar were constant throughout the experiment. Method of stimulus presentation and data collection were the same as in Experiment 1. Displays were driven with 120 and 6 cd/m^2. The rectangles were white in the negative display mode and black in the positive display mode. The polarity reversal simply changed all white areas of the screen into black and vice versa.

Two rectangle heights, two separations, and two relevant dimension instructions (matching the height or the separation) were completely crossed and assessed in random order at each of three viewing distances (150, 250, and 350 cm, see Table 1). The sequence of polarity levels and viewing distances was counterbalanced across subjects. The data were analyzed as for Experiment 1, with Display Polarity as an additional factor.

The average bias in perception of height was 1.12 min with positive displays and 1.16 min with negative displays, $t(71) = 0.95$, $p > 0.3$. The average bias in perception of spacing was 1.75 min with positive displays and 1.37 min with negative displays, $t(71) = 3.57$, $p < 0.001$. Hence, spacing judgments were smaller with negative than with positive displays, while height judgments were not affected by display polarity. The main effect of Display Polarity was only marginally significant, $F(1, 5) = 4.69$, $p < 0.1$, $MS_e = 0.44$. The interaction of Display Polarity with Dimension of Judgment was marginal, $F(1, 5) = 5.99$, $p < 0.06$, $MS_e = 0.53$, supporting the notion that only spacing judgments tended to be affected by the polarity manipulation. The judgments on rectangles were equally accurate across levels of stimulus size, as indicated by the absence of a main effect of Stimulus Size, $F(1, 5) = 1.05$, $p > 0.4$, $MS_e = 0.12$. Judgments were not equally accurate for the two dimensions, as indicated by a main effect of Dimension of Judgment, $F(1, 5) = 15.08$, $p < 0.05$, $MS_e = 0.85$. The average bias in perception of spacing was 1.56 min, whereas the average bias in height perception was only 1.14 min. A main effect of Size of Context, $F(1, 5) = 62.96$, $p < 0.001$, $MS_e = 0.1.06$, showed that larger context increased the size of the bias. An interaction between Size of Context and Dimension of Judgment, $F(1, 5) = 36.55$, $p < 0.002$, $MS_e = 0.57$, showed that context affected perception of spacing more than perception of height, replicating the finding of Experiment 1.

Fig. 4 shows how the rectangles (depicted as triangles) were misperceived in both height (horizontal displacement) and spacing (vertical displacement of circles). Rectangles with equal height and spacing (corresponding to the six triangles on a hypothetical diagonal with a slope of 1 in Fig. 4) were almost accurately estimated in height but considerably underestimated in spacing. This is indicated by the fact that the corresponding perceived stimuli (black dots) roughly map on a hypothetical diagonal with a slope < 1. At the same time there was overestimation of spacing for all asymmetric rectangle configurations.

Height judgments were more accurate with rectangles than with letters (cf. Figs. 1 and 2, note different scaling). The linear regression equation

$$\text{Perceived Rectangle Height} = 1.41 \times \text{True Rectangle Height} - 1.33$$

predicted 85% of the variability in all height judgments. There was no evidence for underestimation of rectangle height below 3 min of spacing. This finding suggests that the height illusion, as first reported by Skottun and Freeman (1983) and replicated in the first experiment of the present study, does depend on the stimuli being letters and does not generalize to non-letter stimuli.

Multiple regression analyses showed that rectangle spacing affected perceived rectangle height. True Rectangle Spacing as an additional predictor of Perceived

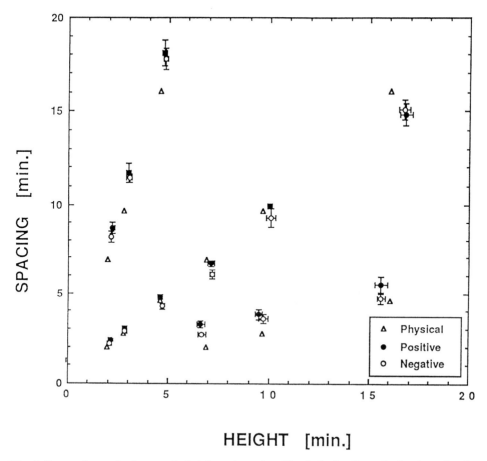

Fig. 4. True and perceived rectangle height and spacing. Physical stimuli are depicted as triangles, average judgments across subjects are depicted as circles (with 1 Standard Error of the Mean). Dots represent positive display (black rectangles on white background); circles represent negative display (white rectangles on black background).

Rectangle Height was reliable in a multiple regression analysis of height judgments with positive displays, $t(69) = 2.06$, $p < 0.05$, but only marginally reliable with negative displays, $t(69) = 1.98$, $p < 0.06$. Average regression weights were reliable in t-tests based on the subject's individual beta coefficients obtained from judgments on positive displays, $t(5) = 13.39$, $p < 0.01$, and negative displays, $t(5) = 5.10$, $p < 0.01$. The respective regression weights and statistics are summarized in Table 3.

Perceived Rectangle Spacing was a reliable additional predictor of height judgments with positive displays, $t(69) = 3.21$, $p < 0.01$, and with negative displays, $t(69) = 2.91$, $p < 0.01$. Average regression weights were also reliable with

Table 3

Regression weights for the context factor in Experiment2 [a]

Dimension of judgment	Overall context weight ($n = 72$)		Average context weight ($n = 6$)	
	True	Perceived	True	Perceived
Positive display				
Height	0.15 (*)	0.15 (**)	0.15 (**)	0.16 (**)
Spacing	0.29 (**)	0.23 (**)	0.29 (**)	0.24 (**)
Negative display				
Height	0.14 (n.s.)	0.13 (**)	0.12 (**)	0.13 (**)
Spacing	0.28 (**)	0.22 (**)	0.28 (**)	0.22 (**)

[a] The tabulated values are nonstandardized beta weights as derived from regression analyses in which the true value of either dimension of judgment was included as first predictor of the judgment.
n.s. = nonsignificant contribution; * = significant at the 0.05 level; ** = significant at the 0.01 level.

positive displays, $t(5) = 15.13$, $p < 0.01$, and negative displays, $t(5) = 6.98$, $p < 0.01$. Regression weights and statistics are summarized in Table 3. Hence, the perception of rectangle height is predicted more accurately when perceived rather than true stimulus context is considered.

The vertical displacements of average judgments away from the triangles indicate misperception of spacing (see Fig. 4). The linear regression equation

$$\text{Perceived Rectangle Spacing} = 1.43 \times \text{True Rectangle Spacing} - 0.98$$

predicted 82% of the variability in all spacing judgments. Multiple regression analyses showed a strong contribution of stimulus context to the spacing bias. True Rectangle Height as an additional predictor of Perceived Rectangle Height was reliable in a multiple regression analysis of height judgments with positive displays, $t(69) = 4.11$, $p < 0.01$, and with negative displays, $t(69) = 3.78$, $p < 0.01$. Average regression weights were equally reliable in t-tests based on the subject's individual beta coefficients obtained from judgments on positive displays, $t(5) = 11.56$, $p < 0.01$, and negative displays, $t(5) = 6.40$, $p < 0.01$.

Perceived Rectangle Height was reliable as an additional predictor of spacing judgments with positive displays, $t(69) = 5.30$, $p < 0.01$, and with negative displays, $t(69) = 4.64$, $p < 0.01$. Average regression weights were also reliable with positive displays, $t(5) = 12.08$, $p < 0.01$, and negative displays, $t(5) = 6.54$, $p < 0.01$. All regression weights and statistics are summarized in Table 3.

The marginally significant effect of display polarity can be observed in Fig. 4. Circles (reflecting judgments on negative displays) are mostly below the dots and are also closer to the triangles than the dots. The significantly smaller judgments of black as opposed to white spaces (see above) supports an explanation of spacing bias in terms of phosphor irradiation. Because height judgments were largely unaffected by display polarity, they are probably influenced by a different process.

Due to the larger viewing distances the stimuli in Experiment 2 were smaller on average (5.97 min) than the stimuli in Experiment 1 (15.76 min). To compare letter perception with rectangle perception, perceived stimulus height was divided by true stimulus height for all judgments made in Experiments 1 and 2 with positive displays; the analogous transformation was performed on the spacing judgments. The transformed data from both experiments were then compared with a *t*-test across all judgments and with a *t*-test based on mean relative judgments from the six subjects in each experiment.

The average relative judgment on heights in Experiment 1 was 1.28 (range 1 to 1.75), and the average relative judgment on spacings was also 1.28 (range 0.67 to 1.92). For positive displays in Experiment 2 the average relative judgment on heights was 1.13 (range 0.83 to 1.79), and the average relative judgment on spacings was 1.28 (range 0.92 to 2.07). *t*-Tests comparing all judgments on letters against all judgments on rectangles yielded a significant difference for height judgments, $t(71) = 4.43$, $p < 0.01$, but no difference for spacing judgments, $t(71) = 0.07$, $p > 0.9$. Similar findings obtained from one-tailed *t*-tests on mean relative judgments of the subjects, showing a significant difference between letters and rectangles for height judgments, $t(5) = 2.21$, $p < 0.05$, but no difference for spacing judgments, $t(5) = 0.03$, $p > 0.4$. These comparisons support the claim that there is larger overestimation of height for letter stimuli as compared to rectangle stimuli. They further show that the spacing judgments were not affected by the nature of the flankers.

In summary, both the height and spacing of letters were overestimated. The effect extended beyond the range of letter sizes investigated by Skottun and Freeman (1983) and might thus generalize to the perception of text during reading. Overestimation of letter height was approximately constant and did not depend on letter spacing. The absence of a similar height bias for rectangles suggests an underlying conceptual cause of this illusion. This notion is further supported by the absence of an effect of display polarity on height judgments. Spacing judgments were significantly larger with positive than with negative displays, and they were not affected by the nature of the flankers, suggesting that the underlying cause of these biases is probably perceptual. The overestimation of letter heights remained approximately constant over a wide range of letter separations. Because increased letter spacing reduces lateral masking (Bouma, 1970), this result casts doubt on the proposal that the mechanism responsible for the height illusion is related to lateral masking, as was proposed by Skottun and Freeman (1983). A study by Loomis (1978) also argues against this proposal. He found that letters cause slightly stronger lateral masking than rectangles (his Experiment 2), also demonstrating that letters have different processing qualities compared to shapes. These results on letter perception fit nicely with the previously discussed results on biased perception of word length; together, these observations suggest that orthographic stimuli receive special processing that enhances their spatial attributes. Future studies should include assessments of perceived letter width to further clarify the cognitive representation of spatial attributes of print for reading.

Theories for spatial cognition in reading

As the previous sections illustrated, investigations of the perception and representation of spatial attributes of print can reveal surprising biases that may well contribute to eye movement control and reading. It is thus important to know if and how domain-specific models of human performance can provide frameworks for *both* spatial cognition and reading. To address this question, one exemplary model from the domain of reading and one from the domain of spatial working memory will be described. Of course, other models are available and may be equally promising.

Consider first a computational model of reading. Legge, Klitz and Tjan (1997; see also this volume) recently proposed a computational model of reading that is capable of simulating some of the spatial behavior of normal- as well as low-vision readers. In this model, new fixation positions are selected to minimize the overall number of saccades, based on visual, lexical, and oculomotor considerations. The specific computational constraints are: (1) the information from the visual span with a given span size and possible retinal damage; (2) the number of alternative words in the lexicon that match the currently known information about the next to-be-identified word; and (3) saccadic accuracy in the light of oculomotor noise, as modeled with a Gaussian distribution of error.

As an example of the model's workings, consider a situation where a reader without retinal damage has identified the letters 'wou' as the rightmost letters in her visual span. Based on a search of her lexicon, she might then be able to predict that this word must be either 'would' or 'wound' (no context is available). To decide between these two alternatives, she should then select the new fixation site to align the first new letter with the left boundary of her visual span. The actual new landing site might, however, be affected by random saccadic error. On average, the strategy of left-justification of each new word on the high-resolution area of foveal vision yields a preferred viewing position effect as an emergent phenomenon.

This model seems to have important limitations with respect to the temporal domain of eye movement behavior, which shall not be discussed here. With respect to spatial behavior the model appears only moderately convincing. The basic assumption that each new saccade moves the eye to the first character beyond the visual span of the current fixation yields unrealistic saccade length distributions. They depend on span size and saccadic noise, but typically underestimate the amount of regressions, as regressions in normal reading are solely due to oculomotor noise. Furthermore, word skipping, which occurs when a forthcoming word is highly predictable from previous context and from parafoveal cues, is limited in the model to short words that fit into the visual span. More important, the model does not address the fixation linking problem, i.e., it is not clear how the reader actually knows where each new fixation is located, given that each saccade contains an unknown error component. Nevertheless, Legge's model is a first step toward theorizing about spatial cognition in reading. To be fair, we have only reviewed its performance with respect to normal reading, whereas the authors stress the model's applicability to eye behavior of patients with scotomas and retinal diseases. It seems that the model can easily be extended to incorporate spatial representations. An example would be a parameter representing perceived word length (independently assessed with the word bisection technique, see above), which could be included into saccade length computation to yield more realistic landing distributions.

A prominent model of working memory has been developed by Baddeley (1986, 1990, 1998). He suggested a functional subdivision of working memory into a central executive and two slave systems, the visuo-spatial sketchpad (VSSP) and the phonological loop. The phonological loop holds and manipulates speech-based information, whereas the VSSP does the same for visual and spatial information. The importance of the phonological loop for fluent reading has been well documented (e.g., articulatory suppression; for review see Baddeley, 1986), but to address the present issue of spatial cognition in reading we will focus on the VSSP. Attributes of the VSSP have been investigated mostly in dual-task experiments, assuming that two tasks can be performed simultaneously only to the degree that they do not tax the same processing resources or structures. For example, subjects generated from a verbal description a mental image of how several numbers were located in a 4×4 array (the Brooks task). Imagery performance was tested during two versions of a disruption task: one group tried to simultaneously trace a pendulum with a light beam while being blindfolded (a spatial nonvisual task with acoustic feedback). Another group tried to simultaneously make brightness judgments (a visual non-spatial task). The stronger imagery decrement (relative to a single-task condition) when the Brooks task was paired with the pendulum task has been taken to identify the visuo-spatial sketchpad as a spatial, nonvisual memory (Baddeley and Lieberman, 1980). Interestingly, Brooks himself (Brooks, 1968) reported that his task can be performed better with auditorily presented material than with printed instructions. This finding supports the notion that reading involves a spatial memory component.

These initial experiments on the nature of the VSSP have since been followed up by other researchers and with different paradigms (see e.g., Baddeley and Hitch,

1994). This work shows that this theoretical framework for working memory is also well-suited for an assessment of spatial cognition in reading, a task that involves visual–spatial as well as phonological representations. Such tests could combine various spatial tasks with reading and obtain measures of reading performance. An important issue should be the interaction of the subcomponents of working memory.

Conclusion

Current theorizing focuses on temporal aspects of eye movement control and tends to ignore the impact of spatial representations on reading behavior. Consequently, there is currently only scattered empirical evidence available to clarify the cognitive operations involved in spatial cognition during reading. Some of this evidence and theorizing has been brought together in this chapter, addressing spatial coding at the global levels of text, paragraph, and sentence processing before reporting systematic biases of spatial cognition at the levels of word and letter processing. It was hypothesized that the spatial representation of a text is page-based, and that the cognitive representation of word length is biased. This bias might reflect an attentional strategy for lexical access, and might be based on activation of dedicated orthographic processing modules in the brain. Understanding the spatial coding of text might lead to more comprehensive theories of reading.

Acknowledgements

I thank Arthur Jacobs and two anonymous reviewers for their help with a previous version of this paper.

References

Appelman, I.B. and Mayzner, M.S. (1981). The letter-frequency effect and the generality of familiarity effects on perception. Perception and Psychophysics, 30, 436–446.

Baccino, T. and Pynte, J. (1998). Spatial encoding and referential processing during reading. European Psychologist, 3 (1), 51–61.

Baddeley, A.D. (1986). Working Memory. Oxford: Oxford University Press.

Baddeley, A.D. (1990). Human Memory: Theory and Practice. Boston, MA: Allyn and Bacon.

Baddeley, A.D. (1998). Recent developments in working memory. Current Opinion in Neurobiology, 8, 234–238.

Baddeley, A.D. and Hitch, G.H. (1994). Developments in the concept of working memory. Neuropsychology, 8, 485–493.

Baddeley, A.D. and Lieberman, K. (1980). Spatial working memory. In: R.S. Nickerson (Ed.), Attention and Performance VIII. Hillsdale, N.J.: Erlbaum, pp. 521–539.

Bouma, H. (1970). Interaction effects in parafoveal letter recognition. Nature, 226, 177–178.

Brooks, L.R. (1967). The suppression of visualization by reading. Quarterly Journal of Experimental Psychology, 19, 289–299.

Brooks, R.L. (1968). Spatial and verbal components in the act of recall. Canadian Journal of Psychology, 22, 349–368.

Brunn, J.L. and Farah, M.J. (1991). The relation between spatial attention and reading: evidence from the neglect syndrome. Cognitive Neuropsychology, 8, 59–75.

Caramazza, A. and Hillis, A.E. (1990). Spatial representation of words in the brain implied by studies of a unilateral neglect patient. Nature, 346, 267–269.

Caramazza, A. and Miceli, G. (1989). Orthographic structure, the graphemic buffer and the spelling process. In: C. von Euler, I. Lundberg and G. Lennerstrand (Eds.), Brain and Reading. London: Macmillan, pp. 257–268.

Carrasco, M. and Sekuler, E.B. (1993). An unreported size illusion. Perception, 22, 313–322.

Celex (1995). The CELEX lexical database (Vol. Release 2). Nijmegen: Centre for lexical information. Max-Planck Institute for Psycholinguistics.

Christie, J.M. and Just, M.A. (1976). Remembering the location and content of sentences in a prose passage. Journal of Educational Psychology, 68, 702–710.

Clark, J.J. and O'Regan, J.K. (1999). Word ambiguity and the optimal viewing position in reading. Vision Research, 39, 843–857.

Coeffe, C. and O'Regan, J.K. (1987). Reducing the influence of non-target stimuli on saccade accuracy: predictability and latency effects. Vision Research, 27, 227–240.

Dillon, A., McKnight, C. and Richardson, J. (1990). Navigation in hypertext: a critical review of the concept. In: D. Diaper et al. (Eds.), Interact '90. Amsterdam: Elsevier/North-Holland, pp. 587–592.

Eddy, J.K. and Glass, A.L. (1981). Reading and listening to high and low imagery sentences. Journal of Verbal Learning and Verbal Behavior, 20, 333–345.

Fischer, M.H. (1994). Less attention and more perception in cued line bisection. Brain and Cognition, 25, 24–33.

Fischer, M.H. (1996). Bisection performance indicates spatial word representation. Cognitive Brain Research, 4, 163–170.

Fischer, M.H. (1999). Memory for word locations in reading. Memory, 7, 79–116.

Fischer, M.H. (2000). Word center is misperceived. Perception (in press).

Frazier, L. and Rayner, K. (1982). Making and correcting errors during sentence comprehension: eye movements in the analysis of structurally ambiguous sentences. Cognitive Psychology, 14, 178–210.

Frith, U. (1984). A curious effect with reversed letters explained by a theory of schema. Perception and Psychophysics, 16, 113–116.

Hasher, L. and Zacks, R.T. (1979). Automatic and effortful processes in memory. Journal of Experimental Psychology: General, 3, 356–388.

Heilman, K.M., Watson, R.T. and Valenstein, E. (1985). Neglect and related disorders. In: K.M. Heilman and E. Valenstein (Eds.), Clinical Neuropsychology, Oxford: Oxford University Press, pp. 243–293.

Hofmeister, J., Heller, D. and Radach, R. (1997). The return sweep in reading. Paper at the 9th European Conference on Eye Movements, Ulm, Sept. 23–26.

Hyönä, J. (1995). Do irregular letter combinations attract readers' attention? Evidence from fixation locations in words. Journal of Experimental Psychology: Human Perception and Performance, 21, 68–81.

Juola, J.F. (1988). The use of computer displays to improve reading comprehension. Applied Cognitive Psychology, 2, 87–95.

Kennedy, A. (1992). The spatial coding hypothesis. In: K. Rayner (Ed.), Eye Movements and Visual Cognition: Scene Perception and Reading. New York: Springer, pp. 379–396.

Kennedy, A. and Murray, W.S. (1984). Inspection times for words in syntactically ambiguous sentences under three presentation conditions. Journal of Experimental Psychology: Human Perception and Performance, 10, 833–849.

Kennedy, A. and Murray, W.S. (1987). Spatial coordinates in reading: comments on Monk (1985). Quarterly Journal of Experimental Psychology, 39A, 649–656.

Kwantes, P.J. and Mewhort, D.J.K. (1999). Evidence for sequential processing in visual word recognition. Journal of Experimental Psychology: Human Perception and Performance, 25, 376–381.

Legge, G.E., Klitz, T.S. and Tjan, B.S. (1997). Mr. Chips: an ideal-observer model of reading. Psychological Review, 104, 524–553.

Leisman, G. (1978). Ocular-motor system control of position anticipation and expectancy. In: J.W. Senders, D.F. Fisher and R.A. Monty (Eds.), Eye Movements and Higher Psychological Functions. Hillsdale, N.J.: Erlbaum, pp. 195–207.

Logan, G.D. (1998). What is learned during automatization? II Obligatory encoding of spatial location. Journal of Experimental Psychology: Human Perception and Performance, 24, 1720–1736.

Loomis, J.M. (1978). Lateral masking in foveal and eccentric vision. Vision Research, 18, 335–338.

Mapelli, D., Umilta, C., Nicoletti, R., Fanini, A. and Capezzani, L. (1996). Prelexical spatial representations. Cognitive Neuropsychology, 13, 229–255.

Marslen-Wilson, W. (1989). Lexical Representation and Process. Cambridge, MA: MIT Press.

Masson, M.E.J. (1983). Conceptual processing of text during skimming and rapid sequential reading. Memory and Cognition, 11, 262–274.

McConkie, G.W., Kerr, P.W., Reddix, M.D. and Zola, D. (1988). Eye movement control during reading, I. The location of initial fixations on words. Vision Research, 28, 1107–1118.

McCormick, E.J. and Sanders, M.S. (1982). Human Factors in Engineering and Design (5th ed.). New York: McGraw-Hill.

Naveh-Benjamin, M. (1987). Coding of spatial location information: an automatic process? . Journal of Experimental Psychology: Learning, Memory and Cognition, 13, 595–605.

Naveh-Benjamin, M. (1988). Recognition memory of spatial location information: another failure to support automaticity. Memory and Cognition, 16, 437–445.

Nichelli, P., Venneri, A., Pentore, R. and Cubelli, R. (1993). Horizontal and vertical neglect dyslexia. Brain and Language, 44, 264–283.

Potter, M.C., Kroll, J.F. and Harris, C. (1980). Comprehension and memory in rapid sequential reading. In: R. Nickerson (Ed.), Attention and Performance VIII. Hillsdale, N.J.: Erlbaum, pp. 98–118.

Price, C.J., Wise, R.J.S. and Frackowiak, R.S.J. (1996). Demonstrating the implicit processing of visually presented words and pseudowords. Cerebral Cortex, 6, 62–70.

Prinzmetal, W. and Wilson, A. (1997). The effect of attention on phenomenal length. Perception, 26, 193–205.

Radach, R. and Kempe, V. (1993). An individual analysis of initial fixation positions in reading. In: G. D'Ydewalle and J. v. Rensbergen (Eds.), Perception and Cognition. Amsterdam: Elsevier/North-Holland, pp. 213–225.

Radach, R. and McConkie, G. (1998). Determinants of fixation positions in words during reading.

In: G. Underwood (Ed.), Eye Guidance in Reading and Scene Perception. Amsterdam: Elsevier/North-Holland, pp. 77–100.

Rayner, K. (1979). Eye guidance in reading: fixation locations in words. Perception, 8, 21–30.

Rayner, K. and Morris, R.K. (1992). Eye movement control in reading: evidence against semantic preprocessing. Journal of Experimental Psychology: Human Perception and Performance, 18, 163–172.

Rayner, K. and Pollatsek, A. (1989). The Psychology of Reading. Englewood Cliffs, N.J.: Prentice Hall.

Riddoch, M.J. and Humphreys, G.W. (1993). Visual aspects of neglect dyslexia. In: D.M. Willows, R.S. Kruk and E. Corcos (Eds.), Visual Processes in Reading and Reading Disabilities. Hillsdale, N.J.: Erlbaum, pp. 111–136.

Robertson, L.C. and Kim, M.-S. (1999). Effects of perceived space on spatial attention. Psychological Science, 10, 76–79.

Rothkopf, E.Z. (1971). Incidental memory for location of information in text. Journal of Verbal Learning and Verbal Behavior, 10, 608–613.

Sieroff, E., Pollatsek, A. and Posner, M.I. (1988). Recognition of visual letter strings following injury to the posterior visual spatial attention system. Cognitive Neuropsychology, 5, 427–449.

Skottun, B.C. and Freeman, R.D. (1983). Perceived size of letters depends on inter-letter spacing: a new visual illusion. Perception and Psychophysics, 23, 111–112.

Underwood, G., Bloomfield, R. and Clews, S. (1988). Information influences the pattern of eye fixations during sentence comprehension. Perception, 17, 267–278.

Underwood, G., Clews, S. and Everatt, J. (1990). How do readers know where to look next? Local information distributions influence eye fixations. Quarterly Journal of Experimental Psychology, 42A, 39–65.

Zechmeister, E.B., McKillip, J., Pasko, S. and Bespalec, D. (1975). Visual memory for place on the page. Journal of General Psychology, 92, 43–52.

CHAPTER 6

Saccadic Inhibition and Gaze Contingent Research Paradigms

Eyal M. Reingold and Dave M. Stampe
University of Toronto

Abstract

In several gaze contingent reading studies (e.g., Blanchard, McConkie, Zola and Wolverton, 1984; McConkie, Underwood, Zola and Wolverton, 1985) the text was masked at a fixed delay from the beginning of fixation, and the fixation duration distributions exhibited dips. McConkie, Reddix and Zola (1992) interpreted these dips as reflecting a disruption to automatic, parallel encoding or registration processes that are time locked to the onset of the visual pattern on the retina. Processing disruption causes an eye movement disruption after a constant transmission delay in the neural system. We propose an alternative explanation to the processing disruption hypothesis which suggests that the display change produced saccadic inhibition with maximum inhibition occurring at a constant latency following the onset of the display change. The purpose of the research reported in this chapter was to disentangle these two alternative explanations.

In the reported experiment we recorded eye movements from subjects performing a reading comprehension task or a visual search task. In each of these tasks we employed two paradigms. In the first paradigm, the display change occurred at a fixed delay following the end of a saccade (beginning of fixation). We will refer to this as the fixed delay paradigm (henceforth FDP). The FDP is in essence a gaze contingent paradigm. Two fixed delays of 110 ms and 158 ms were used. In addition, we developed another paradigm which will be referred to as the random delay paradigm (henceforth RDP) in which the display change could occur at any point in time, thus at a random delay from the end of a saccade (beginning of fixation). The saccadic inhibition hypothesis predicts an identical inhibition profile across the three experimental conditions (FDP 110 ms, FDP 158 ms and RDP) in each

Reading as a Perceptual Process/A. Kennedy, R. Radach, D. Heller and J. Pynte (Editors)
© 2000 Elsevier Science Ltd. All rights reserved

task whereas the processing disruption hypothesis predicts differences across conditions. The results of the present experiment are consistent with the saccadic inhibition hypothesis and are difficult to reconcile with the processing disruption hypothesis. We discuss implications for reading research and examine the plausibility that the superior colliculus is the neurophysiological locus of saccadic inhibition.

Introduction

The use of eye movement measures as dependent variables in the study of complex visual tasks such as reading, visual search and scene perception, has provided important evidence for the understanding of the processes underlying performance in these tasks (see Rayner, 1998, for a recent review). Nowhere is this more true than in the context of reading research. In the past 25 years an impressive body of knowledge emerged as a result of studies employing eye movement measurement to study reading. One of the most important advantages of eye movement techniques over other research paradigms is that the unobtrusive nature of the measurement procedure allows for preserving the ecological validity of reading complex sentences or passages without requiring the use of secondary tasks and responses unrelated to reading. In addition to providing important data which can be analyzed off-line, real time monitoring of gaze position permits the introduction of display changes that are contingent on the spatial or temporal characteristics of eye movements. Such methodology is referred to as a *gaze contingent display paradigm*, and combines the ecological validity of naturalistic reading with a degree of experimental control comparable to tachistoscopic presentation. For example, McConkie and Rayner (1975) introduced the *moving window technique* in which illegible or mutilated text was presented outside the boundaries of a region of intact text centred on the point of gaze (i.e., the window). As gaze position changed so did the location of the window. By manipulating the size of the window it was possible to estimate the useful field of view or perceptual span in reading. In another gaze contingent paradigm referred to as the *invisible boundary technique* (Rayner, 1975) a single display change is introduced once the eye crosses an invisible location in the text. This paradigm was used to study what kind of information is extracted from words subsequent to the fixated word (i.e., parafoveal processing). A thorough review of gaze contingent methodology and related findings is beyond the scope of the present chapter (see Rayner, 1998).

The starting point for the present investigation was research by McConkie and his colleagues (e.g., Blanchard et al., 1984; McConkie et al., 1985, 1992) which employed a gaze contingent masking paradigm. In this paradigm a region of the text was masked at one or more delays after the start of fixation. For example

Blanchard et al. (1984) briefly masked the text at delays of 50 ms, 80 ms, or 120 ms after the fixation began. The mask was presented for 30 ms followed by the reappearance of the text. Although not reported in the original paper, McConkie et al. (1992) reported that in this study the stimulus change produced a large dip in the frequency distribution of fixations beginning about 80 to 90 ms following the visual change. This effect was attributed to a disruption of massively parallel, automatic registration or encoding processes which operate to provide utilization processes with the information required for reading comprehension (henceforth the processing disruption hypothesis). This model assumed that following the onset of fixation a time locked fixed sequence of registration processes extract visual information from the text. At the termination of this sequence visual information becomes available for use by higher level processes, but the time at which this information is actually used is variable (i.e., registration but not utilization processes are time locked to the beginning of fixation). A mask appearing during the period in the fixation when registration processes are active will result in a constant delay of the next saccade rendering a certain range of fixation durations less probable and resulting in the dip in the fixation distribution. The constant delay is a function of the fact that the mask disrupts the same point in the time locked processing sequence, and after the neural delay required to transmit the disruption through the saccadic control and generation structures, the eye movements are affected.

However, it is possible that the dips observed in the fixation distributions may result from a reflexive, low level saccadic inhibition effect which is time locked to the flicker associated with the presentation of the mask (henceforth the saccadic inhibition hypothesis). A crucial prediction of the processing disruption hypothesis is that the disruption caused by the mask should vary as a function of fixation onset to mask delay. This is the case because the mask may or may not affect registration processes depending upon the length of the delay. If the mask appears once registration processes are complete, fixation durations may still be impacted because of disruption to utilization processes. However, this disruption should not result in distribution dips because utilization processes are not time locked and consequently the nature and the magnitude of the disruption should vary across fixations. To test this it is possible to use several masking delays. If all masking delays produce fixation dips and if these dips occur at the same latency across masking delays (i.e., dip latency corresponds to mask delay plus a constant reflecting neural transmission times) then the saccadic inhibition hypothesis is confirmed. If, however, the timing or existence of dips varies across mask delays then the processing disruption hypothesis is validated.

Although, as mentioned earlier, Blanchard et al. (1984) included multiple mask delays, McConkie et al. (1992) did not report the timing of the dips in the different delay conditions. However, a careful examination of a different study by McConkie et al. (1985) provides tentative support for the saccadic inhibition interpretation. In one condition a region of the text to the left or right of fixation was replaced by a letter mask during the saccade preceding the fixation followed by the reappearance of text at a delay of 100 ms from fixation onset (immediate condition). In another condition the text was replaced with a letter mask following the first 100 ms of the fixation (delayed condition). Note that the saccadic inhibition hypothesis would predict no difference in the timing of dips across conditions because the text to mask, or mask to text flicker always occurs at 100 ms into the fixation. In contrast, the processing disruption hypothesis predicts very different results across conditions because registration processes are less likely to be impacted in the delayed condition relative to the immediate condition. Standard fixation distributions were shown just for the immediate condition and the dips appear to have identical timing in these distributions (McConkie et al., 1985, Fig. 3). In addition, McConkie et al. (1985) did provide cumulative fixation distribution curves (McConkie et al., 1985, Fig. 4). In such curves a dip would be reflected by a deceleration in the slope followed by an acceleration in the slope. The point of minimum slope within this region represents the centre of the dip in a fixation duration distribution. An examination of the cumulative curves indicates that this point occurs with the same timing across all conditions (at fixation duration of about 240 ms). Thus, the results from this study support the conclusion that following the flicker (the change between mask to text or vice versa) saccadic inhibition was produced and that the latency to maximum inhibition was constant across conditions.

The strategy of employing multiple mask delays to disentangle the saccadic inhibition hypothesis versus the processing disruption hypothesis can be taken to its logical extreme by abandoning the gaze contingent procedure altogether, and presenting a display change randomly without considering the point in the fixation at which such a change occurs (i.e., the RDP procedure). Such a procedure would produce a continuum of fixation onset to display change delays. If the fixation distribution dips observed by McConkie et al. (1992) reflect an effect which is time locked to the display change associated with the mask, then the results from the RDP should demonstrate a dip in the frequency of saccades at a certain temporal range following the display change. In other words, if the reduction in saccadic probability is time locked to the flicker rather than to fixation onset it should be evident in the RDP condition even though fixation onset to display change delays are allowed to vary. If, however, as predicted by the processing disruption hypothesis, display changes occurring at different points in the fixation affect different processes, no such dips time locked to the display change should be observed.

An empirical comparison of the FDP versus RDP

The goal of the present experiment was to compare the effects on eye movements of a variety of display changes across the RDP and FDP conditions. If the effects demonstrated by McConkie and his colleagues represent a low level saccadic inhibition effect, then such effects should be evident regardless of the saccade producing task. In fact, Van Diepen, De Graef and d'Ydewalle (1995) in a study that employed a gaze contingent masking paradigm in a visual search task demonstrated effects similar to the ones reported by McConkie and his colleagues. The subjects in this study searched line drawings of everyday scenes for non-objects. The appearance of the mask was delayed relative to the end of a saccade (beginning of fixation) by 17, 46, 76 or 121 ms. All fixation duration distributions in the masking conditions exhibited a dip with longer masking delays resulting in the dip occurring at longer fixation durations. In contrast, a no-mask condition did not produce a dip. These results are consistent with the saccadic inhibition hypothesis, and consequently, we included a visual search task in addition to a reading comprehension task.

   Fig. 1 illustrates the display changes that were employed in both the reading (panels A and B) and visual search (panels C and D) tasks. In reading the text was either replaced for 33 ms with a black screen or displaced by 0.6 degrees vertically for the same duration resulting in the subjective experience of a flicker or a jitter respectively. In the visual search task subjects scanned for checkerboard targets embedded in scenes of residential interiors. In this task the normal image was replaced for 33 ms by either a luminance matched blank image or by a 1.0 cy/° Gaussian blurred version of the image.

   In the FDP conditions in both tasks two fixed delays (110 ms and 158 ms) between the beginning of fixation and the display change were used. In the RDP conditions in both tasks the display change could occur at any point in time during the fixation, thus at a random delay from the end of a saccade (beginning of fixation). As explained earlier the saccadic inhibition hypothesis predicts an identical inhibition profile across the three experimental conditions (FDP 110 ms, FDP 158 ms and RDP) in each task whereas the processing disruption hypothesis predicts differences across conditions.

Method

Subjects

Two groups of ten subjects were tested. One group performed the visual search task and the other group performed the reading comprehension task. All subjects had normal or corrected to normal vision, and were paid $10.00 for a single one hour session.

Apparatus and display generation

The eye tracker employed in this research was the SR Research Ltd. Eyelink system. This system has high spatial resolution (0.005°), and a sampling rate of 250 Hz (4 ms temporal resolution). The Eyelink headband has three cameras, allowing simultaneous tracking of both eyes and of head position for head-motion compensation. By default, only the subject's dominant eye was tracked in our studies. The Eyelink system uses an Ethernet link between the eye tracker and display computers for real-time saccade and gaze position data transfer. The system also performs saccade and blink detection on-line for the FDP paradigm. In the present study the configurable acceleration and velocity thresholds were set to detect saccades of 0.5° or greater.

Displays were generated using an S3 VGA card and a 17-inch ViewSonic 17PS

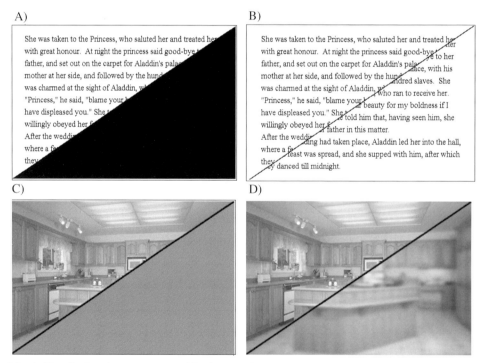

Fig. 1. The display change types used in the experiment. Reading: black (A) versus displaced (B); visual search: blanked (C) versus blurred (D). The normal image is shown above the diagonal and the transient image below. The duration of all display changes was 33 ms.

monitor. The display had a resolution of 360 by 240 pixels, with a frame rate of 120 Hz. At the 60 cm viewing distance the display subtended a visual angle of 30° horizontally and 22.5° vertically.

A 9-point calibration was performed at the start of each block of trials, followed by 9-point calibration accuracy test. Calibration was repeated if any point was in error by more than 1°, or if the average error for all points was greater than 0.5°. Before each trial, a black fixation target was displayed at the centre of the display. The subject fixated this target and the reported gaze position was used to correct any post-calibration drift errors. The background of the target display had the same luminance as the image to be displayed during the trial, to minimize pupil size changes.

Display changes were generated by displaying a transient image beginning at a vertical retrace, and restoring the normal display 4 retraces (33 ms) later. The transient images for the visual search task were a grey field matched in luminance (blanked condition) or a 1.0 cy/° Gaussian blurred version of the image presented during the trial (blurred condition). In the reading experiment the transient images were a black screen (black condition) or a 0.6° vertically displaced version of the text (displaced condition).

In the FDP condition, a display change was generated at a fixed delay of either 110 or 158 ms after the end of each saccade made by the subject. These delays were verified using an artificial eye and an optical sensor. In the RDP condition the interval between consecutive display changes varied randomly between 250 and 350 ms in the visual search task and between 300 and 400 ms in the reading task. Subjectively it was very difficult to distinguish between the three experimental conditions.

The reading comprehension task

Subjects read a short story for comprehension and enjoyment. The text was presented in black (brightness = 4 cd/m^2) on a white background (brightness = 68 cd/m^2). Proportional spaced font was used with an average of 2.2 characters per degree of visual angle and an average of 10 lines per screen. For each of the two display change types 12, 12 and 24 screens were read in the FDP 110 ms, FDP 158 ms, and RDP conditions, respectively. The pairing of screens to conditions was determined randomly for every subject. Screens were pages of text in the story, and were presented in the same order to all subjects. Subjects were told that they would be asked questions about the content of the story when they finished reading. They answered over 93% of these questions accurately indicating that they complied with the instructions, and were not simply scanning the text. When subjects finished reading a screen they pressed a button to proceed to the next screen.

The visual search task

In this task subjects searched for four targets embedded in greyscale images of residential interiors. Average brightness across images was 27 cd/m^2. Targets were 0.5° by 0.5° checkerboard patterns with 35% contrast, and were locally matched in luminance to the picture background in order to make search difficult and generate numerous saccades per trial. Subjects were allowed up to 30 s for each trial. Subjects were asked to press a button as they fixated each of the targets. If subjects located all the targets before the deadline they terminated the trial by pressing another button. Overall, across subjects the accuracy of target detection was over 89%. For each of the two display change types totals of 64, 64 and 128 trials were used in the FDP 110 ms, FDP 158 ms, and RDP conditions, respectively. Trial order and the pairing of stimuli to conditions were randomly determined for every subject.

Results

Histograms of fixation duration distributions collapsed across all subjects in a given condition are plotted in Fig. 2. An inspection of this figure indicates that the FDP conditions in both the visual search task (panel C) and reading comprehension task (panel A) replicated the results obtained in previous gaze contingent studies. In particular, the fixation duration distributions for the FDP conditions exhibited a dip. In both tasks the location of the dip across the two delay conditions (i.e., 110 vs. 158 ms) was displaced by approximately the difference between the delays (48 ms). In contrast, no dip was seen in the histograms of fixation duration distributions for the RDP condition in either task (panels B and D).

Whereas the fixation duration distributions for the RDP versus the FDP conditions appear on the surface to be very different, a re-plotting of the results from the RDP condition reveals a striking similarity. This is shown in Fig. 3 which plots the proportion of saccades by latency after the display change, using saccades and display change data from the eye movement file and collapsing across all subjects in a given RDP condition. It is important to understand why the dips in the fixation duration distributions were present in the FDP conditions and absent in the RDP conditions. In the FDP conditions the display change is time locked to the beginning of fixation. Given that saccadic inhibition is time locked to the display change it is in effect also time locked to the beginning of fixation in this paradigm. As a result only a narrow band of fixation durations is affected, resulting in the dips in the distribution of fixation durations. The RDP pattern reflects a condition in which the display change delay varies continuously (i.e., not time locked to the beginning of fixation). As the value of the display change delay increases, the range

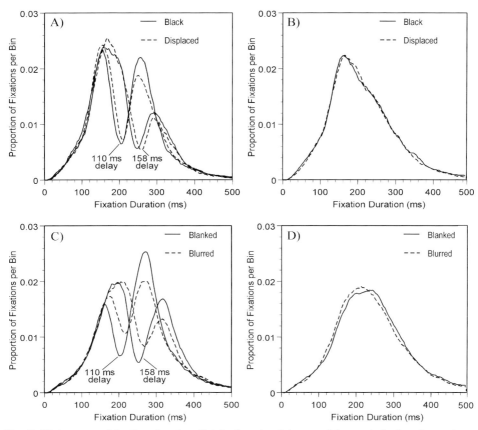

Fig. 2. Histograms of fixation duration distributions by delay condition and display change type. (A) Reading: FDP 110 and FDP 158. (B) Reading: RDP. (C) Visual search: FDP 110 and FDP 158. (D) Visual search: RDP. (Bin size = 4 ms.)

of affected fixations corresponds to longer fixation durations. Once the data are summed across all display change delays the dip is no longer apparent because it occurs at different points for different delays. In other words, in the FDP condition only a narrow range of fixation durations is affected, hence the dip; whereas in the RDP condition a wide range of fixation durations is affected, hence the absence of the dip. In order to reveal the inhibition in the RDP condition the data have to be plotted with reference to the latency from display change (Fig. 3) rather than latency from the beginning of fixation (i.e., fixation duration distribution, Fig. 2).

In order to be able to compare the findings across the FDP and RDP conditions, histograms of saccadic frequency by latency from display change were produced for each subject and each RDP condition (such as the one shown in Fig. 3). As

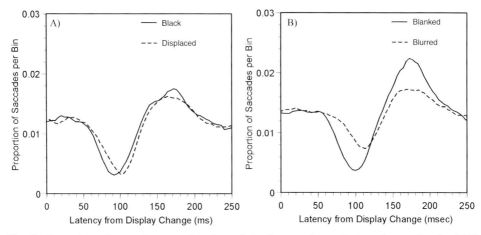

Fig. 3. Proportion of saccades as a function of the latency from display change for the RDP conditions. (A) Reading: black versus displaced. (B) Visual search: blanked versus blurred. (Bin size = 4 ms.)

Table 1

Mean latency to maximum inhibition by task and display change type (standard errors are shown in parentheses)

Task	Display change type	Latency to maximum inhibition (ms)		
		110 ms delay	158 ms delay	random delay
Reading	Black	95.6 (1.4)	93.2 (1.3)	91.2 (1.8)
	Displaced	101.2 (1.3)	100.0 (1.2)	101.2 (1.3)
Visual search	Blanked	96.4 (1.6)	97.2 (1.6)	99.8 (1.5)
	Blurred	107.6 (2.2)	112.4 (2.1)	110.4 (1.4)

well, fixation duration histograms were produced for each subject and each FDP condition (such as the one shown in Fig. 2). For RDP histograms the latency to maximum inhibition for each subject and condition was computed as the latency to the centre of the dip. For FDP histograms the latency to maximum inhibition was computed as the fixation duration corresponding to the centre of the dip minus the fixed delay in that condition (i.e., 110 ms or 158 ms). This delay is subtracted because the inhibition is time locked to the onset of the display change rather than the beginning of fixation. For each task and display change type average latency to maximum inhibition by condition is shown in Table 1.

For each task a repeated measures ANOVA was performed which crossed display change type (for reading: black versus displaced; for visual search: blanked versus blurred) with delay condition (FDP 110 ms, FDP 158 ms, RDP). The only significant effect in both ANOVAs was the main effect of display change type (both F-values > 84.3, both p-values < 0.001). For the reading task this main effect demonstrates that latency to maximum inhibition is shorter for the black versus the displaced display change type in all delay conditions. For the visual search task this main effect indicates that latency to maximum inhibition is shorter in the blanked versus the blurred display change type in all delay conditions. These consistent effects of display change type likely reflect differences in the neural delays associated with visual processing of the display changes employed. More importantly for the present purpose, the main effect of delay condition was not significant for either the reading or the visual search task (both F-values < 2.85, both p-values > 0.08). As shown by an inspection of Table 1 within each display change type latencies to maximum inhibition across the RDP and FDP conditions are very similar. To further highlight the similarity of the saccadic inhibition profiles across the RDP and FDP delay conditions, Fig. 4 plots the proportion of saccades by latency from display change for all three delay conditions in each of the four tasks by display change type conditions (panels A, B, C, and D). For the two FDP conditions this is equivalent to aligning the fixation duration distributions by subtracting the value of the delay from each fixation duration and plotting values greater than zero. As can be seen in Fig. 4, the dip is present and appears to be similar in shape and latency for all of the FDP and RDP conditions in all four panels.

Although the dip is quite similar across all three delay conditions, the pattern before and after the dip differs. This occurs because the two FDP conditions depend on the underlying shape of the fixation duration distribution. That is, a fixed delay causes the dip to occur at a particular point along the continuum of fixation durations. In contrast, the RDP pattern reflects a condition in which the display change is not time locked to the beginning of fixation and therefore the inhibition profile does not preserve the fixation duration distribution. Accordingly, only the RDP condition reveals the true nature of the saccadic interference effect. An inspection of these conditions in Fig. 4 indicates that for the first 50 ms following the display change the proportion of saccades remains flat. In all likelihood these saccades are unaffected by the display change and therefore may serve as a baseline. At a later point the proportion of saccades decreases below baseline constituting the dip and then increases above baseline constituting the peak, which likely reflects the recovery from inhibition. Finally, following the peak the proportion of saccades returns to baseline levels.

In addition to computing latency to maximum inhibition it is important to estimate the latency to the onset of inhibition. This is only possible for the RDP condition because it is the only condition which provides a baseline for saccadic frequency. However, latency to inhibition onset in the current experiment could

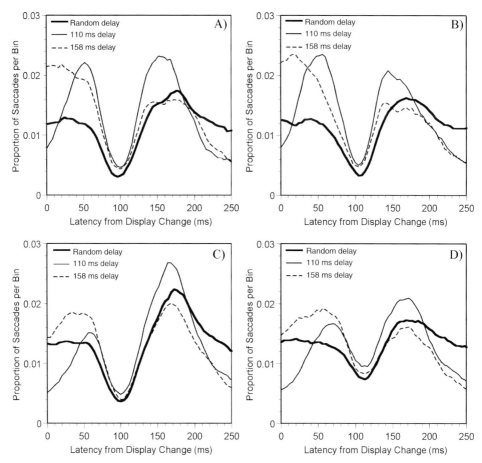

Fig. 4. Proportion of saccades as a function of the latency from display change for the FDP and RDP conditions for each display change type. (A) Reading black. (B) Reading displaced. (C) Visual search blanked. (D) Visual search blurred. (Bin size = 4 ms.) FDP histograms are aligned by subtracting the value of the delay from each fixation duration and plotting values greater than zero.

only be estimated across all ten subjects in a given RDP condition. This is the case because individual histograms were too noisy. To achieve this for each condition the average proportion of saccades and the standard deviation for the first twelve bins (equivalent to the first 48 ms following display change) in the aggregate histogram (i.e., Fig. 3) were computed. The point at which the proportion of saccades decreased to 3 standard deviations below this average was determined as the onset of inhibition in each condition. The latencies to inhibition onset as well as the number of saccades in the aggregate histogram are shown for each RDP condition in Table 2. Inspection of this table reveals that saccadic inhibition can

Table 2

Latency to inhibition onset and number of saccades in the aggregate RDP histograms (shown in Fig. 3) by task and display change type

Task	Display change type	Onset (ms)	Saccades (count)
Reading	Black	62.9	19982
	Displaced	69.4	20239
Visual search	Blanked	67.8	34206
	Blurred	70.6	33523

start as early as 60 to 70 ms following the onset of the display change. These short latencies as well as the strong similarity in the inhibition profile across RDP and FDP conditions provide strong support for the hypothesis that the documented dips in fixation duration distributions in gaze contingent masking paradigms reflect a low level, reflexive oculomotor effect (i.e., saccadic inhibition) rather than a higher level disruption to encoding processes.

Discussion

A crucial prediction of the processing disruption hypothesis is that the nature of the disruption should vary across different display change delays. In contrast, the saccadic inhibition hypothesis postulates that, regardless of the point in the fixation at which the display change occurs, a time locked stereotyped inhibition pattern follows. Our results are consistent with the latter but not with the former prediction. In addition, the short onset latencies in the RDP conditions clearly support a reflexive, low level oculomotor effect.

If saccadic inhibition is a low level reflexive oculomotor response, then is this phenomenon relevant to reading research? There are at least two potential ways in which saccadic inhibition may be relevant to reading research. First, as should be clear from our discussion of the research by McConkie and his colleagues, saccadic inhibition is important to consider when interpreting the results obtained using any gaze contingent masking paradigm, as well as any other gaze contingent reading paradigm which involves a display change during fixation (e.g., the fast priming paradigm; Sereno and Rayner, 1992; see also Fischer, 1999, and Morrison, 1984, for additional examples of such paradigms). Of course, this consideration is generally relevant for gaze contingent techniques, rather than specific to reading research. However, given the pivotal role that gaze contingent paradigms had, and continue to have, in the development of the understanding of reading processes (see Rayner, 1992, 1998), such a methodological consideration may be of some importance to this field. A similar concern regarding the potential influence of visible flicker in gaze contingent paradigms was advanced by O'Regan (1990). However, this researcher was particularly concerned about display changes which were supposed to occur during the saccade preceding the critical fixation, but due to implementation difficulties, were actually visible during the first few milliseconds of the fixation. Recently, Inhoff, Starr, Liu and Wang (1998) demonstrated that such briefly visible flickers at fixation onset do not constitute an important factor in the interpretation of results from gaze contingent paradigms. In contrast, the results of the present study clearly demonstrate the importance of saccadic inhibition induced by a flicker occurring later during the fixation for the interpretation of data from gaze contingent studies.

Second, if it can be shown that any component of the latency or strength of saccadic inhibition is sensitive to higher level attentional or cognitive influences, then it may be possible to use this effect to study processes which underlie task performance, and which may be specific to reading. This is not unlike the use of physiological measures such as event related potentials (ERPs) to study performance in complex cognitive tasks including reading. Research in progress in our lab indicates that higher level processes may modulate the strength of the saccadic inhibition effect, and consequently, the patterns of saccadic inhibition may be used to study these processes.

The RDP methodology introduced here has several advantages over traditional gaze contingent paradigms (i.e., FDP) for studying the saccadic inhibition phenomena. First, the technical implementation of gaze contingent methodology is challenging and expensive in terms of both software and hardware, and consequently may not be widely available to researchers. Second, the RDP reflects a continuous rather than a discrete manipulation of saccade to display change delay. Consequently the RDP reveals the pattern of saccadic inhibition independent of the shape of the fixation duration distribution. Finally, the RDP allows estimation of the baseline saccadic frequency, which enables the computation of additional measures such as the magnitude and duration of the dip and the peak. We are currently evaluating a variety of dip and peak measures. In addition, research employing the RDP is being conducted in our lab to assess the influence of stimulus factors (i.e., the nature of displays and transient images) as well as observer factors (e.g., attentional and strategic factors) on the pattern of saccadic inhibition.

The current findings of saccadic inhibition in complex visual tasks must be compared with findings from previous psychophysical and neurophysiological studies. Several psychophysical studies reported inhibition or slowing of saccades following the presentation of a visual event which was displayed at the same time or after the presentation of the saccadic target (e.g., Ross and Ross, 1980, 1981; Walker, Deubel, Schneider and Findlay, 1997). Walker et al. (1997) suggested that the neurophysiological locus of the saccadic inhibition they observed may be related to inhibitory processes in the superior colliculus. In the next section we will consider the plausibility of this collicular hypothesis of saccadic inhibition in light of the present findings and the available knowledge concerning the neurophysiology of the saccadic system.

Saccadic inhibition and the neurophysiology of the saccadic system

A network of cortical areas and subcortical structures acts to control saccades and visual attention. A simplified depiction of selected neural structures and their interconnections is shown in Fig. 5 (for more detailed reviews see Moschovakis, Scudder and Highstein, 1996; Schall, Morel, King and Bullier, 1995; Wurtz and Goldberg, 1989). In the cerebral cortex, the frontal eye fields (FEF) and the supplementary eye fields (SEF) act to generate voluntary saccades. In parietal cortex, the lateral intraparietal area (LIP) can generate saccades as well. All these cortical regions are connected by direct projections, and indirectly via the pulvinar

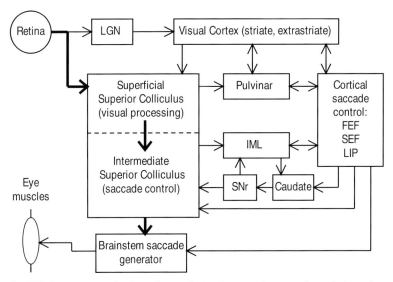

Fig. 5. A simplified summary of selected neural structures and connections that are known to be involved in saccade production and visual attention. Data flow in saccade generation proceeds clockwise from the retina to the eye muscles, through structures involved in visual input, saccade control, and the saccade generator. Arrows depict monosynaptic or polysynaptic neural connections which are either excitatory and/or inhibitory. Thick arrows represent the fastest pathway for saccadic inhibition (see Table 4). FEF = frontal eye fields; IML = internal medullary lamina of the thalamus; LGN = lateral geniculate nucleus; LIP = lateral intraparietal area; SEF = supplementary eye fields; SNr = substantia nigra pars reticulata.

Table 3

Summary of visual latencies in selected saccadic control structures [a]

Area	Cell type	Visual latency (ms)	Reference
Superior colliculus	Pandirectional	40–50 (small spot)	Goldberg and Wurtz (1972)
		35–47 (bright flash)	Rizzolatti et al. (1980)
	Buildup	~70 (very dim LED)	Dorris et al. (1997)
Frontal eye fields	Visuomovement	67	Schall (1991)
Supplementary eye fields	Visuomovement	92	Schall (1991)
Lateral intraparietal	Visuomovement	60–140	Yin and Mountcastle (1977)

[a] Latencies are means (single numbers) or ranges as reported by the authors.

nucleus and internal medullary lamina of the thalamus, in a network that may coordinate visual attention as well as saccades. The FEF and SEF have direct projections to the saccade generator in the brainstem. Each of the cortical areas also has a direct projection to the superior colliculus, and an indirect projection through the basal ganglia (caudate nucleus and substantia nigra). The superior colliculus is the central element in subcortical saccade production. It receives projections from most other saccade-producing areas, has fast visual input, and its neurological mechanisms are beginning to be understood in detail.

The time course of events in the visual system, such as the transduction of light into neural signals and the transmission and processing of these signals, determines the latency of neural events in the superior colliculus and other saccadic control neural structures. Thus, delays of visual input determine in part the latencies of saccades and of saccadic inhibition. The latencies of neural activity following visual input for each of several saccadic control structures are summarized in Table 3. Caution must be used when comparing values of visual latencies across studies in Table 3, as these are known to decrease as the size and contrast of stimuli are increased. The display changes employed in the present experiment far exceed the size of the stimuli used in the studies summarized in Table 3, and consequently, would be expected to produce faster latencies. This may be offset at least in part by the fact that when experimental conditions are equated, latencies obtained with human subjects are known to be longer than latencies obtained with monkeys, such as the ones summarized in Table 3. Nevertheless, an inspection of the latencies in Table 3 clearly reveals that only the superior colliculus, which receives visual input in as little as 35 ms, is a candidate for mediating the fast inhibition onset latencies we obtained (60 to 70 ms). Although the visual input latencies to cortical saccadic control structures are too slow to produce the early part of the saccadic inhibition pattern we observed, these structures may contribute to the latter part of the inhibition pattern, thus extending its duration. Fig. 5 illustrates the direct

Table 4

Time course of saccadic inhibition for the direct collicular pathway (shown in Fig. 5)

Area	Visual input latency	Internal delay	Effects of electrical stimulation	Estimated inhibition latency [a]
Superior colliculus	35–70 (see Table 3)	5–10 ms (Lee et al., 1997)	~20 ms to delay saccade (Munoz et al., 1996)	60–100 ms

[a] Inhibition latency is estimated as the sum of the superior colliculus input latency, internal delay and output latency.

collicular pathway to saccadic inhibition and Table 4 summarizes evidence which indicates that this pathway is capable of producing inhibition onset values as short as 60 ms, which is consistent with our findings. Accordingly, in the remainder of this section we will review in some detail the available neurophysiological evidence regarding the role of the superior colliculus in saccadic production and its potential relevance to the interpretation of the saccadic inhibition phenomena.

The superior colliculus: structure, connectivity, and function

The superior colliculus (SC) is uniquely situated to provide fast oculomotor responses to visual inputs. The SC receives direct retinal input, and collicular output directly activates the saccade generator in the brainstem. Lesions of the superior colliculus abolish the fast ('express') saccades in monkeys (Schiller, Sandell and Maunsell, 1987), the latency of which is thought to approach the limits imposed by delays in the visual and saccadic system (Fischer and Weber, 1993; Pare and Munoz, 1996). The SC is a central structure in the saccade control network, receiving converging projections from many cortical areas involved with visual attention and saccades. Collicular output is sent to the cortex through the pulvinar nucleus and the internal medullary lamina of the thalamus (IML), which may serve to coordinate visual attention as well as saccades. In addition, the SC has connections with many of the subcortical structures involved with saccades and pursuit, including the substantia nigra and cerebellum.

The superior colliculus is divided on its midline into left and right colliculi, each of which receives visual input from and commands saccades to the contralateral (opposite) visual hemifield. Each SC consists of several alternating layers of grey and white tissue, which have been grouped by function into the superficial, intermediate, and deep layers. The superficial SC contains largely visually responsive cells. The intermediate SC contains buildup and burst neurons (Munoz and Wurtz, 1995a), which fire in advance of and during saccades and project to the saccade generator in the brainstem. The deep SC may be involved in multimodal orienting behaviours and in combined eye–head gaze shifts (for a review, see Sparks and Hartwich-Young, 1989).

Both the visual inputs to the superficial SC and the motor responses of the intermediate SC are organized in a retinotopic map (Robinson, 1972). The foveal area of the visual field is represented at the rostrolateral pole of the SC, and stimulation of the intermediate layer of the SC in this area evokes small saccades (Robinson, 1972) or prevents the production of saccades (Munoz and Wurtz, 1993a,b). The peripheral visual field is represented in the caudal SC, and larger saccades are evoked by stimulation of this region.

The motor map in intermediate SC and the visual map in superficial SC appear to be aligned. It has been found (e.g., Goldberg and Wurtz, 1972; Kadonya, Wolin and Massopust, 1971) that cells in the superficial SC respond to locations in the visual field that are close to those that the cells immediately below them in the intermediate layer command saccades to. Excitatory synaptic connections have been demonstrated between the superficial and intermediate layers of the SC (Lee, Helms, Augustine and Hall, 1997; Mooney et al., 1988; Moschovakis, Karabelas and Highstein, 1988), suggesting the vertical columnar organization of the SC.

The intermediate layer of the superior colliculus is the most important for the present context. This layer of the SC contains several types of premotor cells, which fire before and during saccades. These cells have been classified according to their pattern of activity, and by their position and depth in the intermediate layer (Munoz and Wurtz, 1995a,b). The upper part of the intermediate SC contains burst neurons (BNs), which fire strongly before and during saccades but are otherwise inactive. The deep part of the intermediate SC contains buildup neurons (BUNs), which show increasing activity before saccades and may also fire strongly during saccades. The most rostral part of the deep layer of the intermediate SC contains fixation neurons (FNs) (Munoz and Wurtz, 1993a,b) which are active during fixations and pursuit but pause just before and during saccades. These cells are limited to the fixation zone, which has been estimated to cover the rostral 0.72 mm of the SC (Munoz and Wurtz, 1995b).

All classes of cells in the intermediate SC may show transient bursts of activity in response to visual events. This neuronal activity may be generated by the visual cells in the superficial SC, and carried through vertical connections to the intermediate SC. Neurons in the intermediate SC can have both a visual receptive field and a movement field. The movement field is the set of saccade directions and amplitudes that a neuron fires to command, which typically move the eye to a small region of the visual field. The visual receptive field and movement field typically overlap, and the combination of these has been called the neuron's response field (Dorris, Pare and Munoz, 1997). Visual activity in both the superficial and intermediate SC may be modulated by descending projections from striate and extrastriate cortex (Lee et al., 1997; Wurtz and Mohler, 1976). The intermediate SC also receives projections from several cortical regions which are involved in saccade planning and visual attention: the frontal eye fields (Segraves and Goldberg, 1987), supplementary eye fields (Shook, Schlag-Rey and Schlag, 1990), and lateral intraparietal area (Lynch, Graybiel and Lobeck, 1985). These projections may serve to suppress unwanted saccades and to command saccades by imposing the desired pattern of activation onto the intermediate layers of the SC. The frontal eye field connections are known to achieve this by a pattern of inhibition and excitation of the intermediate SC (Schlag-Rey, Schlag and Dassonville, 1992). Movement neurons in the frontal eye fields have excitatory connections to neurons in the intermediate SC that produce saccades similar in amplitude and direction to those produced by the FEF neurons that project to them. Other SC neurons that produce saccades incongruent to those induced by the FEF neurons will be inhibited (Schlag-Rey et al., 1992).

Another control pathway to the SC is via the basal ganglia. Both the FEF and SEF project to the caudate nucleus (CN), which sends inhibitory projections to the substantia nigra pars reticulata (SNr) which in turn sends inhibitory projections to the intermediate SC. Cells in the SNr appear to change activity in a sequential fashion as required to carry out saccadic tasks, firing tonically and pausing to allow SC activity and saccades. The caudate nucleus appears to be active only during performance of well-learned tasks such as reading, with neurons firing to inhibit the SNr and disinhibit the SC (for a review, see Hikosaka and Wurtz, 1989).

The intermediate SC commands saccades through its connections to the brainstem saccade generator. A network of excitatory and inhibitory interneurons within the superior colliculus shapes neural activity before and during saccades. The current understanding of the collicular circuitry is shown in Fig. 6, which is derived from Munoz and Istvan (1998). These authors found that electrical stimulation of FNs in the fixation zone at the rostral pole of the SC strongly inhibited BNs and also inhibited BUNs to a lesser degree. In turn, stimulation of both BNs and BUNs inhibited the FNs. This suggests a pattern of mutual inhibitory connections which may prevent the FNs and BNs from being active at the same time, thus forcing the SC to switch quickly between saccade (BNs active) and fixation (FNs active) states. FNs in the left and right colliculi are connected by strong excitatory connections, ensuring that both colliculi are in the same state. The lesser inhibition of BUNs by FNs allows moderate preparatory activity in these neurons before saccades (Munoz and Istvan, 1998).

Inhibition also occurs between BNs and BUNs in different regions of the SC, as shown in Fig. 6. The majority of neurons inhibit each other, and inhibitory connections are also present between neurons in the left and right colliculi. However, there is strong evidence that each neuron also excites nearby neurons within 1 to 2 mm (McIlwain, 1982; Meredith and Ramoa, 1998; Munoz and Istvan, 1998).

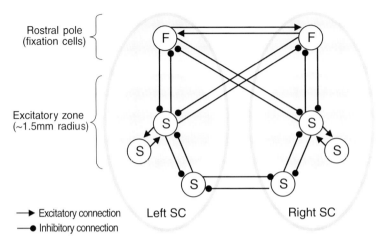

Fig. 6. Summary of excitatory and inhibitory interactions in the superior colliculus. Fixation zones of the left and right colliculi excite each other to act as a unit, while inhibition between and within caudal areas of the colliculi acts as a winner-take-all competition network to select a saccade target. Local excitatory zones act to produce active regions to encode saccades. Connections in the figure after Munoz and Istvan, 1998. F = fixation neurons; S = saccade neurons (BN or BUN).

Models using this pattern of excitation of nearby neurons and inhibition of distant neurons produced winner-take-all competition to select between distant saccade targets, while shaping the local region of neural activity seen during saccadic bursts (Van Opstal and Van Gisbergen, 1989a,b). This connectivity also contributes to the merging of activity that leads to the global effect, in which saccades to two closely spaced visual targets tend to land midway between the targets (Edelman and Keller, 1998; Findlay, 1982; Ottes, Van Gisbergen and Eggermont, 1984).

The activities of fixation, buildup, and burst cells before and during saccades to visual targets has been studied in detail (Anderson, Keller, Gandhi and Das, 1998; Dorris and Munoz, 1998; Dorris et al., 1997; Munoz and Wurtz, 1993a, 1995a,b). The pattern of activity during saccades and fixations is illustrated in Fig. 7. During a fixation, FNs are active and BNs are silent. In preparation for a saccade, activity of BUNs in the area of the colliculus corresponding to the saccadic target increases and may be accompanied by a decrease in FN activity. About 20 ms prior to the saccade, BUNs and BNs both burst to command the saccade and activity of FNs is almost completely suppressed.

Throughout the course of the saccade, the BN activity remains limited to an area of the SC about 1.4 mm in diameter, the location of which encodes the saccade amplitude and direction (Munoz and Wurtz, 1995b). BUNs also burst in this area during the saccade, and lower levels of BUN activity spread rostrally towards the fixation zone as the saccade progresses (Munoz and Wurtz, 1995b; but see Anderson et al., 1998). Shortly before the end of the saccade, the fixation zone is

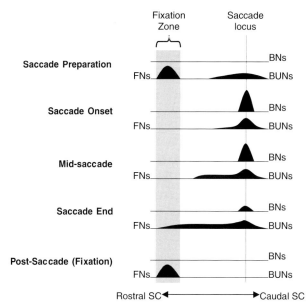

Fig. 7. Behaviour of intermediate superior colliculus neurons before, during, and after saccade. Height of curves shows activity levels of neurons at various positions in the SC. Burst neurons (BNs) are active during the saccade. Buildup neurons (BUNs) are active before the saccade to compute the goal. During the saccade (BUNs) show spreading activity that reaches the fixation zone at the end of the saccade. Fixation neurons (FNs) are active between saccades, but pause during the saccade to let BNs fire. (After Munoz and Wurtz, 1995b.)

reactivated and the BNs and BUNs stop firing. One possible role for the spread of BUN activity during the saccade is as a neural integrator of the saccade pulse (Optican, 1995). According to this model, when BUN activity reaches the fixation zone, the FNs are reactivated and shut off the brainstem saccade generator (Munoz and Wurtz, 1995b; but see Aizawa and Wurtz, 1998).

Activity of BUNs before a saccade has been shown to be correlated with motor preparation, which can be manipulated by changing the predictability of the location of the saccade target (Dorris and Munoz, 1998) or by changing the number of potential targets (Basso and Wurtz, 1997). Presaccadic activity in monitored BUNs was highest when the location of the saccade target was predictable and was within the response field of the neuron. Conversely, presaccadic activity was lowest when the target location was uncertain or was unlikely to be in the response field of the neuron. The presaccadic BUN activity was also highly correlated with the saccadic reaction time on a trial-by-trial basis, with high activity preceding the shortest reaction times (Dorris and Munoz, 1998).

The probability of very low latency (express) saccades also increases when BUN activity is high (Dorris et al., 1997). These saccades are thought to be triggered directly by visual input to the BUNs caused by the onset of the saccade target. When presaccadic activity in the BUNs is high enough, this additional visual input may cause the total BUN activity to reach the threshold required to produce a saccade immediately (Dorris et al., 1997; Edelman and Keller, 1996).

Visually evoked saccadic inhibition may also be a result of activity in the intermediate superior colliculus caused by changes in visual input (i.e., the display change). Visually evoked activity in BUNs associated with the irrelevant transient image may act through inhibitory connections within the intermediate SC to reduce presaccadic activity in other BUNs (Munoz and Istvan, 1998). Such lateral inhibition of BUNs corresponding to the saccadic target may delay the onset of saccades (Dorris and Munoz, 1998). Alternatively, the visual activity associated with the transient visual event might stimulate FNs, which would also inhibit presaccadic activity in BUNs throughout the SC. The small size of the classical fixation zone (Munoz and Wurtz, 1993a,b) would limit the source of this inhibition to visual changes near the fovea, although it has been proposed that FNs may be present in an extended fixation zone as far as 10° from the fovea (Findlay and Walker, 1999; Gandhi and Keller, 1995, 1997). This extended fixation zone is based on the interruption of saccades by electrical stimulation of the SC outside the area of the classical fixation zone (Gandhi and Keller, 1995).

The latency of saccadic inhibition caused by either BUN or FN excitation may be estimated from the latencies of visual activity in the intermediate SC, and the interval required for a reduction of presaccadic activity to delay the saccade (see Fig. 5 and Table 4). Visual latencies in the superficial SC are as low as 35 ms for strong stimuli and the delay in transmission between the superficial and intermediate SC is probably about 5 to 10 ms (Lee et al., 1997) for a predicted minimum latency of 40 ms in the intermediate SC. Visual latencies of 60–70 ms were reported for BUNs by Munoz and Wurtz (1995a), but these longer latencies may be due to the very dim LEDs used as stimuli in their study. The latency at which FN activity can act to delay saccades can be estimated from a study by Munoz and Wurtz (1993b), in which electrical stimulation of FNs could delay saccades when delivered as little as 20 ms before the saccade onset. The estimated minimum latency of saccadic inhibition is then equivalent to the visual latency in the intermediate SC (40 ms) plus the latency at which such activity can delay saccades (20 ms), for an estimated latency of 60 ms. This is in good agreement with the 60–70 ms latency of the onset of the saccadic inhibition demonstrated in the present experiment. The above timing example used findings of FN stimulation, but the latency of inhibition of BUNs within the SC is similar when either FNs (1.8 ms in ipsilateral SC, 3.6 ms in contralateral SC) or BUNs (1.3 ms for ipsilateral SC, 3.0 ms in contralateral SC) are stimulated (Munoz and Istvan, 1998). This suggests that saccadic inhibition produced by either of the two mechanisms would result in similar latencies.

In conclusion, the evidence reviewed here, as well as the present findings, may help to elucidate the nature and characteristics of visually evoked saccadic inhibition. This phenomenon appears to be a fast reflex of the oculomotor system, which acts in response to changes in visual input to suppress the production of saccades. The visual changes do not need to be relevant to the task being performed in order to evoke saccadic inhibition. The exact characteristics of the visual change may influence the timing and pattern of saccadic inhibition. These effects are likely due to differences in visual input latencies for different display changes. The fast onset of saccadic inhibition suggests that its likely locus is the superior colliculus. However, cortical control structures may produce saccadic inhibition with longer latencies extending the total duration of inhibition. Finally, what role could visually evoked saccadic inhibition play in everyday visual perception and oculomotor behaviour? The visual system is unable to process new input during saccades resulting in a momentary disruption. Saccadic inhibition may serve to give the brain time to process the arrival of changes in visual input by delaying the execution of saccades. These saccades may be rescheduled or cancelled depending upon the relevance of the visual event.

Acknowledgements

Preparation of this paper was supported by a grant to Eyal Reingold from the Natural Science and Engineering Research Council of Canada. We wish to thank Elizabeth Bosman, Doug Munoz, Tatjana Nazir, Ralph Radach and an anonymous reviewer for their helpful comments on an earlier version of this paper. Part of the data reported in this chapter was presented at the ninth European Eye Movement Conference (Reingold and Stampe, 1997; Stampe and Reingold, 1997).

References

Aizawa, H. and Wurtz, R.H. (1998). Reversible inactivation of monkey superior colliculus, I. Curvature of saccadic trajectory. Journal of Neurophysiology, 79 (4), 2082–2096.

Anderson, R.W., Keller, E.L., Gandhi, N.J. and Das, S. (1998). Two-dimensional saccade-related population activity in superior colliculus in monkey. Journal of Neurophysiology, 80 (2), 798–817.

Basso, M.A. and Wurtz, R.H. (1997). Modulation of neuronal activity by target uncertainty. Nature, 389 (6646), 66–69.

Blanchard, H.E., McConkie, G.W., Zola, D. and Wolverton, G.S. (1984). Time course of visual information utilization during fixations in reading. Journal of Experimental Psychology: Human Perception and Performance, 10, 75–89.

Dorris, M.C. and Munoz, D.P. (1998). Saccadic probability influences motor preparation signals and time to saccadic initiation. Journal of Neuroscience, 18 (17), 7015–7026.

Dorris, M.C., Pare, M. and Munoz, D.P. (1997). Neuronal activity in monkey superior colliculus related to the initiation of saccadic eye movements. Journal of Neuroscience, 17 (21), 8566–8579.

Edelman, J.A. and Keller, E.L. (1996). Activity of visuomotor burst neurons in the superior colliculus accompanying express saccades. Journal of Neurophysiology, 76 (2), 908–926.

Edelman, J.A. and Keller, E.L. (1998). Dependence on target configuration of express saccade-related activity in the primate superior colliculus. Journal of Neurophysiology, 80 (3), 1407–1426.

Findlay, J.M. (1982). Global visual processing for saccadic eye movements. Vision Research, 22 (8), 1033–1045.

Findlay, J.M. and Walker, R. (1999). A model of saccade generation based on parallel processing and competitive inhibition. Behavioral and Brain Sciences, 22 (4), 661–674.

Fischer, M.H. (1999). An investigation of attention allocation during sequential eye movement tasks. Quarterly Journal of Experimental Psychology, 52 (3), 649–647.

Fischer, B. and Weber, H. (1993). Express saccades and visual attention. Behavioral and Brain Sciences, 16, 553–610.

Gandhi, N.J. and Keller, E.L. (1995). Interrupting saccades by electrical stimulation of the superior colliculus determines an extended fixation zone. Society for Neuroscience Abstracts, 21, 468.2.

Gandhi, N.J. and Keller, E.L. (1997). Spatial distribution and discharge characteristics of superior colliculus neurons antidromically activated from the omnipause region in monkey. Journal of Neurophysiology, 78 (4), 2221–2225.

Goldberg, M.E. and Wurtz, R.H. (1972). Activity of superior colliculus in behaving monkey, I. Visual receptive fields of single neurons. Journal of Neurophysiology, 35 (4), 542–559.

Hikosaka, O. and Wurtz, R.H. (1989). The basal ganglia. In: R.H. Wurtz and M.E. Goldberg (Eds.), The Neurobiology of Saccadic Eye Movements. Amsterdam: Elsevier, pp. 257–282.

Inhoff, A.W., Starr, M., Liu, W. and Wang, J. (1998). Eye-movement-contingent display changes are not compromised by flicker and phosphor persistence. Psychonomic Bulletin and Review, 5 (1), 101–106.

Kadonya, S., Wolin, L.R. and Massopust, L.C., Jr. (1971). Photically evoked unit activity in the tectum opticum of the squirrel monkey. Journal of Comparative Neurology, 142, 495–508.

Lee, P.H., Helms, M.C., Augustine, G.J. and Hall, W.C. (1997). Role of intrinsic synaptic circuitry in collicular sensorimotor integration. Proceedings of the National Academy of Science, USA, 94 (24), 13299–13304.

Lynch, J.C., Graybiel, A.M. and Lobeck, L.J. (1985). The differential projection of two cytoarchitectonic subregions of the inferior parietal lobule of macaque upon the deep layers of the superior colliculus. Journal of Comparative Neurology, 235 (2), 241–254.

McConkie, G.W. and Rayner, K. (1975). The span of the effective stimulus during a fixation in reading. Perception and Psychophysics, 17, 578–586.

McConkie, G.W., Reddix, M.D. and Zola, D. (1992). Perception and cognition in reading: where is the meeting point? In: K. Rayner (Ed.), Eye Movements and Visual Cognition: Scene Perception and Reading. New York, NY: Springer-Verlag, pp. 293–303.

McConkie, G.W., Underwood, N.R., Zola, D. and Wolverton, G.S. (1985). Some temporal characteristics of processing during reading. Journal of Experimental Psychology: Human Perception and Performance, 11, 168–186.

McIlwain, J.T. (1982). Lateral spread of neural excitation during microstimulation in the intermediate gray layer of cat's superior colliculus. Journal of Neurophysiology, 47 (2), 167–178.

Meredith, M.A. and Ramoa, A.S. (1998). Intrinsic circuitry of the superior colliculus: pharmacophysiological identification of horizontally oriented inhibitory interneurons. Journal of Neurophysiology, 79 (3), 1597–1602.

Mooney, R.D., Nikoletseas, M.M., Hess, P.R., Allen, Z., Lewin, A.C. and Rhoades, R.W. (1988). The projection from the superficial to the deep layers of the superior colliculus: an intracellular horseradish peroxidase injection study in the hamster. Journal of Neuroscience, 8 (4), 1384–1399.

Morrison, R.E. (1984). Manipulation of stimulus onset delay in reading: Evidence for parallel programming of saccades. Journal of Experimental Psychology: Human Perception and Performance, 10, 667–682.

Moschovakis, A.K., Karabelas, A.B. and Highstein, S.M. (1988). Structure–function relationships in the primate superior colliculus, II. Morphological identity of presaccadic neurons. Journal of Neurophysiology, 60 (1), 263–302.

Moschovakis, A.K., Scudder, C.A. and Highstein, S.M. (1996). The microscopic anatomy and physiology of the mammalian saccadic system. Progress in Neurobiology, 50 (23), 133–254.

Munoz, D.P. and Istvan, P.J. (1998). Lateral inhibitory interactions in the intermediate layers of the monkey superior colliculus. Journal of Neurophysiology, 79 (3), 1193–1209.

Munoz, D.P., Waitzman, D.M. and Wurtz, R.H. (1996). Activity of neurons in monkey superior colliculus during interrupted saccades. Journal of Neurophysiology, 75 (6), 2562–2580.

Munoz, D.P. and Wurtz, R.H. (1993a). Fixation cells in monkey superior colliculus, I. Characteristics of cell discharge. Journal of Neurophysiology, 70 (2), 559–575.

Munoz, D.P. and Wurtz, R.H. (1993b). Fixation cells in monkey superior colliculus, II. Reversible activation and deactivation. Journal of Neurophysiology, 70 (2), 576–589.

Munoz, D.P. and Wurtz, R.H. (1995a). Saccade-related activity in monkey superior colliculus, I. Characteristics of burst and buildup cells. Journal of Neurophysiology, 73 (6), 2313–2333.

Munoz, D.P. and Wurtz, R.H. (1995b). Saccade-related activity in monkey superior colliculus, II. Spread of activity during saccades. Journal of Neurophysiology, 73 (6), 2334–2348.

Optican, L.M. (1995). A field theory of saccade generation: temporal-to-spatial transform in the superior colliculus. Vision Research, 35 (2324), 3313–3320.

O'Regan, J.K. (1990). Eye movements in reading. In: E. Kowler (Ed.), Eye Movements and their Role in Visual and Cognitive Processes: Reviews of Oculomotor Research. Amsterdam: Elsevier, pp. 395–454.

Ottes, F.P., Van Gisbergen, J.A. and Eggermont, J.J. (1984). Metrics of saccade responses to visual double stimuli: two different modes. Vision Research, 24 (10), 1169–1179.

Pare, M. and Munoz, D.P. (1996). Saccadic reaction time in the monkey: advanced preparation of oculomotor programs is primarily responsible for express saccade occurrence. Journal of Neurophysiology, 76 (6), 3666–3681.

Rayner, K. (1975). The perceptual span and peripheral cues in reading. Cognitive Psychology, 7, 65–81.

Rayner, K. (1992). Eye movements and visual cognition: introduction. In: K. Rayner (Ed.), Eye Movements and Visual Cognition: Scene Perception and Reading. New York, NY: Springer-Verlag, pp. 1–7.

Rayner, K. (1998). Eye movements in reading and information processing: twenty years of research. Psychological Bulletin, 124, 372–422.

Reingold, E.M. and Stampe, D.M. (1997). Transient saccadic inhibition in reading. Paper presented at the 9th European Conference on Eye Movements, Ulm.

Rizzolatti, G., Buchtel, H.A., Camarda, R. and Scandolara, C. (1980). Neurons with complex visual properties in the superior colliculus of the macaque monkey. Experimental Brain Research, 38 (1), 37–42.

Robinson, D.A. (1972). Eye movements evoked by collicular stimulation in the alert monkey. Vision Research, 12 (11), 1795–1808.

Ross, L.E. and Ross, S.M. (1980). Saccade latency and warning signals: stimulus onset, offset, and change as warning events. Perception and Psychophysics, 27 (3), 251–257.

Ross, S.M. and Ross, L.E. (1981). Saccade latency and warning signals: effects of auditory and visual stimulus onset and offset. Perception and Psychophysics, 29 (5), 429–437.

Schall, J.D. (1991). Neuronal activity related to visually guided saccadic eye movements in the supplementary motor area of rhesus monkeys. Journal of Neurophysiology, 66 (2), 530–558.

Schall, J.D., Morel, A., King, D.J. and Bullier, J. (1995). Topography of visual cortex connections with frontal eye field in the macaque: convergence and segregation of processing streams. Journal of Neuroscience, 15 (6), 4464–4487.

Schiller, P.H., Sandell, J.H. and Maunsell, J.H. (1987). The effect of frontal eye field and superior colliculus lesions on saccadic latencies in the rhesus monkey. Journal of Neurophysiology, 57 (4), 1033–1049.

Schlag-Rey, M., Schlag, J. and Dassonville, P. (1992). How the frontal eye field can impose a saccade goal on superior colliculus neurons. Journal of Neurophysiology, 67 (4), 1003–1005.

Segraves, M.A. and Goldberg, M.E. (1987). Functional properties of corticotectal neurons in the monkey's frontal eye field. Journal of Neurophysiology, 58 (6), 1387–1419.

Sereno, S.C. and Rayner, K. (1992). Fast priming during eye fixations in reading. Journal of Experimental Psychology: Human Perception and Performance, 18, 173–184.

Shook, B.L., Schlag-Rey, M. and Schlag, J. (1990). Primate supplementary eye field, I. Comparative aspects of mesencephalic and pontine connections. Journal of Comparative Neurology, 301 (4), 618–642.

Sparks, D.L. and Hartwich-Young, R. (1989). The deep layers of the superior colliculus. In: R.H. Wurtz and M.E. Goldberg (Eds.), The Neurobiology of Saccadic Eye Movements. Amsterdam: Elsevier, pp. 213–256.

Stampe, D.M. and Reingold, E.M. (1997). Transient saccadic inhibition in gaze contingent viewing. Paper presented at the 9th European Conference on Eye Movements, Ulm.

Van Diepen, P.M.J., De Graef, P. and d'Ydewalle, G. (1995). Chronometry of foveal information extraction during scene perception. In: J.M. Findlay, R. Walker and R.W. Kentridge (Eds.), Eye Movement Research: Mechanisms, Processes, and Applications. Amsterdam: Elsevier, pp. 349–362.

Van Opstal, A.J. and Van Gisbergen, J.A. (1989a). A nonlinear model for collicular spatial interactions underlying the metrical properties of electrically elicited saccades. Biological Cybernetics, 60 (3), 171–183.

Van Opstal, A.J. and Van Gisbergen, J.A. (1989b). A model for collicular efferent mechanisms underlying the generation of saccades. Brain Behavior and Evolution, 33 (2-3), 90–104.

Walker, R., Deubel, H., Schneider, W.X. and Findlay, J.M. (1997). Effect of remote distractors on saccade programming: Evidence for an extended fixation zone. Journal of Neurophysiology, 78, 1108–1119.

Wurtz, R.H. and Goldberg, M.E. (Eds.) (1989). The Neurobiology of Saccadic Eye Movements. Amsterdam: Elsevier.

Wurtz, R.H. and Mohler, C.W. (1976). Organization of the monkey superior colliculus: enhanced visual response of superficial layer cells. Journal of Neurophysiology, 39 (4), 745–765.

Yin, T.C. and Mountcastle, V.B. (1977). Visual input to the visuomotor mechanisms of the monkey's parietal lobe. Science, 197 (4311), 1381–1383.

COMMENTARY ON SECTION 1

From Print to Meaning via Words?

Jonathan Grainger
CNRS and Université de Provence

Reading researchers generally ascribe a privileged status to the individual word as a fundamental building block in the process of deriving meaning from text, and the various contributions to the section on visual word processing in the present volume are no exception. This is likely due to the fact that, unlike speech, print provides reliable cues to word boundaries. It is implicitly assumed that the human brain will capitalize on this critical information and hence develop a whole-word based system for reading comprehension (at least in non-agglutinative languages such as English and French with relatively limited word length). Moreover, as noted by Reichle, Pollatsek, Fisher and Rayner (1998), most words in a given text are indeed fixated during reading. Thus, the great majority of members of the subgroup of the reading research community that specifically investigate printed word perception believe (a) that they are studying one fundamental representational unit of the reading process, and (b) that the standard word recognition paradigms (e.g., lexical decision, naming, perceptual identification, semantic categorization) using isolated word stimuli offer an appropriate method of study.

However, the special role assigned to individual words, and the paradigms typically used to investigate visual word recognition, have not gone unchallenged. One of the motivations behind these challenges was the observed divergences in effects of variables measured using more 'naturalistic' techniques (i.e., eye-movement measures on words embedded in sentence contexts) compared to effects obtained with the standard word recognition paradigms, as well as divergences among these paradigms themselves. Some good examples are provided in the section on visual word processing of the present volume. In my commentary on this section I will briefly analyze the various theoretical and methodological attacks on the above mentioned assumptions, and I will conclude with some suggestions for how to reconcile the apparently opposing viewpoints. The criticisms can be divided into two main categories, theoretical and methodological, to be dealt with in turn.

Reading as a Perceptual Process/A. Kennedy, R. Radach, D. Heller and J. Pynte (Editors)
© 2000 Elsevier Science Ltd. All rights reserved

Theoretical attacks on the classic notion of lexical representation

At a theoretical level, the privileged position of individual words as theoretically relevant units of analysis in the study of reading has been criticized from essentially two camps: (i) those who question the utility of the classic notion of lexical representation; and (ii) those who claim that the morpheme, rather than the whole word, is the more appropriate basic unit for the translation of perceptual codes into meaning. These two lines of criticism are not mutually exclusive, but will be analyzed separately in what follows.

Critique I: There is no mental lexicon

Before the arrival of PDPism in the nineteen eighties, the basic idea of a mental lexicon had gone largely uncriticized ever since its introduction over twenty years before, and the formalization of the notion in models such as Forster's (1976) and Morton's (1969). Knowledge about words was thought to be stored in the form of word-sized representations grouped together in a single general lexicon, or across several more specialized lexica. Perhaps the earliest theoretical attack on this widely adopted position was launched by those who were convinced that applying the backpropagation learning algorithm (Rumelhart, Hinton and Williams, 1986) to three-layered networks (i.e., with a layer of hidden units intervening between input and output units) provided the answer to all that we ever wanted to know about word recognition (Plaut, McClelland, Seidenberg and Patterson, 1996; Seidenberg and McClelland, 1989). Mark Seidenberg has probably been the most fervent preacher of the anti-lexicon view and his position has been clearly stated in several papers (e.g., Seidenberg, 1990, 1995).

The essential claim is that the use of distributed representations[1] to code the learned associations between input and output patterns in word processing stands in contradiction to the classic notions of lexical representation and lexical access, in that there is no longer one specific unit that serves only to represent one specific word. Seidenberg (1990) suggested that the 'error' made by the classic word recognition researcher arises from applying a perceptual–representational isomorphism: the units of representation in the mind are thought to correspond to the basic perceptual units in speech and reading. However, Besner, Twilley, McCann and Seergobin (1990), among others, have already pointed out that the use of distributed representations does not necessarily do away with the notion of a mental lexicon, and that adopting a connectionist perspective (involving the concept

---

1 According to Van Gelder (1992), a representation is genuinely distributed if, roughly speaking, " ... it is representing many items using exactly the same resources (p. 176)."

of activation rather than access, for example) is in no way incompatible with the classic notion of lexical representation (e.g., McClelland and Rumelhart, 1981). It suffices to examine the larger framework of the Seidenberg and McClelland (1989) model to realize that the layer of hidden units that would be used to map orthography onto meaning, for example, may well turn out to resemble the orthographic input lexicon of several classic models (see Page, 2000, for an examination of this possibility).

The debate, therefore, should not focus on the question of whether or not there is something like a mental lexicon in our heads, but whether or not the backpropagation algorithm applied to three-layered networks with hidden units provides a better means of understanding the main phenomena that have been observed in the field, compared to alternative connectionist or non-connectionist accounts. On this point, it has been argued in several recent papers (e.g., Grainger and Jacobs, 1998; Page, 2000) that there are some good reasons for preferring a localist[2] as opposed to a distributed connectionist approach to cognitive modeling (in general, and not just for visual word recognition). Without going into any detail here, it is worth mentioning two of the advantages discussed by Grainger and Jacobs (1998) under the headings of *continuity* and *transparency*.

The advantage of continuity is illustrated in two main ways. Firstly in terms of the link with pre-existing models, typically expressed in a verbal and/or boxological format (see Jacobs, this volume), that have already stood the test of extensive empirical research. Page and Norris (1998) speak of a "symbiosis between verbal theorizing and quantitative modeling". The other aspect of continuity is reflected in the principle of nested modeling. Adopting this approach facilitates the process of model-to-model comparison. Models differing by a single feature (e.g., interactivity, Jacobs and Grainger, 1992), can be compared, and different variants of the model can compete in strong inference (see Chapter 2). Localist connectionist models offer greater transparency in the mapping between model structure and model behavior. Although the identifiability of complex algorithmic models is a non-trivial problem, the use of localist as opposed to distributed representations appears to provide a clear advantage here. Algorithmic models of the localist connectionist variety may offer the best trade-off between clarity/transparency and formality/precision (Jacobs, Rey, Ziegler and Grainger, 1998). Greater transparency leads to improved interpretability and therefore to clearer empirical predictions, thus fulfilling Popper's criterion of falsifiability. The chapter by Zagar and Mathey in the present

---

2 According to Grainger and Jacobs (1998) "localist representations are simple processing units (as used by all connectionist models) that can be usefully interpreted as standing for a single meaningful entity in the target world (p. 1)."

volume provides a good example of how the transparency of localist connectionist models can help isolate the specific mechanisms that determine the model's ability to simulate observed data patterns.

Independently of this general and important question of cognitive modeling, the solution, I believe, to such conflicts in the field of visual word recognition, is to do away with the notion of a unitary lexical representation to be replaced by the notion of orthographic, phonologic, and semantic representations, that must at some level correspond to whole words. Thus the criticisms of Seidenberg and others are justified when launched against the notion of a unitary lexical representation that perhaps only a minority of researchers would defend today. Abandoning a unitary lexical representation does not, however, eliminate the need for whole-word representations of orthographic and phonological information. Applications of the backpropagation algorithm have provided some very interesting insights into how such orthographic and phonological codes might be learned through experience. However, the time is ripe to explore alternative learning algorithms and to confront the predictions generated by specific algorithms with data obtained from children learning to read. Such learning algorithms should, for example, explain how the limits of visual acuity are progressively counteracted via experience with printed language, such that long words become as easy to recognize as short words in a single glance (see Chapter 1).

Critique II: Morphemes not words

Another line of attack has, more naturally, been launched by specialists of spoken language comprehension (Marslen-Wilson, Zhou and Ford, 1996). The fact that there is often no clear indication of word boundaries in the speech signal raises the possibility that listeners have learned to access meaning from sound via units smaller than the whole word (in this respect, printed language provides the simplest definition of what a whole word is: any meaningful string of letters bounded by spaces). However, linguists define the morpheme as the smallest unit that is directly associated with meaning. Morphologically complex words contain a stem and at least one affix (prefix or suffix) such that the whole-word form can be broken down into several morphemic units. Based on the linguistic definition of the morpheme as the smallest meaning-bearing unit of speech, Marslen-Wilson et al. (1996) proposed that the core representation of lexical information is morphologically based around abstract representations of stems [3].

---

3 D. Heller pointed out that there is evidence from analyses of pause durations in continuous speech indicating that intervals between successive words are reliably longer than the intervals between morphemes (Vollrath, 1994; Krueger and Vollrath, 1996). This would work in favor of a whole-word based segmentation process for speech.

Marslen-Wilson et al.'s proposal is best analyzed within the more general debate in the morphology literature concerning the role of an obligatory morphological decomposition during language comprehension. One can summarize the two extreme positions in this debate in terms of where morphological codes are hypothesized to be located in the processing hierarchy from perceptual codes to meaning. I will call these two opposing positions the *sublexical* hypothesis and the *supralexical*[4] hypothesis of morphological representation. According to the sublexical hypothesis, morphological representations are contacted before whole-word representations in the process of language comprehension. In this view, a given word stimulus is first parsed into its morphological components before the word can be recognized as a whole (Taft, 1994; Taft and Forster, 1975). According to the supralexical hypothesis, morphological representations are contacted after whole-word representations. On presentation of a morphologically complex word such as *remake*, units corresponding to the root *make* and the affix *re* will receive activation from the whole-word representation, and send back activation to all whole-word representations that are compatible with the root or the affix. In this way, root representations impose an organization on the lower-level form representations in terms of so-called morphological families.

The evidence in favor of some form of explicit representation of morphology is now impressive, be it from research on spoken or printed word perception. However, what is critical with respect to the attack on a word-based account of extracting meaning from perceptual codes, is that there is also plenty of evidence for the involvement of whole-word codes in the processing of morphologically complex words. For example, the results presented by Hyönä and Pollatsek (Chapter 4) show that even in a morphologically rich language like Finnish where a morphological parsing principle is optimized, whole-word characteristics continue to influence eye-movement patterns. Thus, the current evidence suggests that both whole-word and morpheme-based analyses can proceed simultaneously. The critical question is therefore not whether one can do away with whole-word representations, but how word-sized codes and morphemic codes interact in language comprehension. In our quest to understand the reading process, we need to know whether morphemic representations can be derived independently of the whole word (i.e., a parsing system that searches for known morphemes within the letter string, as in the sublexical hypothesis described above), or whether morphemes are derived from whole-word representations and then used to guide eye movements for more fine-grained analysis (the supralexical hypothesis of morphological representation).

---

4 In the words sublexical and supralexical, "lexical" refers to the representation of whole-word orthographic and phonological forms.

One thing seems clear at least, that inspection strategies for long complex words as revealed by eye-movement studies, will continue to provide extremely valuable information on these critical issues (see, e.g., Inhoff, Radach and Heller, 2000). It is in this particular area of research that the combined use of eye-movement techniques and the standard word recognition paradigms, including priming methodology, has already shown the utility of a multi-task approach to be discussed in more detail below.

Validity of the standard paradigms

At a methodological level, it is the ecological validity of standard word recognition paradigms that has often been called into question. Many researchers who preferentially use eye-movement measures to study the reading process have questioned the relevance of paradigms such as the lexical decision task for understanding fluent reading for meaning. This line of criticism can be split into two components: one concerns the belief that eye-movement measures provide a more direct reflection of the 'normal' reading process, and the other concerns the validity of studying words presented in isolation as opposed to words embedded in normal sentence contexts. Standard word recognition paradigms (lexical decision, perceptual identification, naming, semantic categorization) are guilty on both fronts.

These criticisms, however, are only justified to the extent that one assumes that experimental techniques such as word naming and lexical decision can be used to tap into what Balota (1990) referred to as the 'magic moment' in word recognition. This is defined as "the point in time where the subject has recognized the word but has yet to access meaning" (Balota, 1990, p. 9). Balota went on to examine the major paradigms used to study visual word recognition in order to evaluate the extent to which they might provide a window to this hypothetical magic moment. All of the standard paradigms, including eye-movement measures, failed this test. Response measures in each paradigm were shown to be sensitive to factors over and above those that are involved recognizing a word form. There are at least two possible consequences of this failure: either one abandons using these paradigms, or one seeks a more appropriate means of relating what is observed with these techniques to the models and theories that we wish to test. Following the second option leads to the development of the notion of *functional overlap* combined with the adoption of a multi-task approach, to be explained in what follows.

However, first let us note that few word recognition researchers today would argue in favor of this discrete stage version of the magic moment hypothesis, and even fewer would argue that any one paradigm would provide a precise means of measuring this, if it did exist[5]. As stated by Seidenberg and McClelland (1989), " ... there is no lexical access stage common to all word recognition tasks; there are simply orthographic, phonological, and semantic computations. Within this framework, the primary question concerns how the readers' knowledge of the correlations among these codes is represented, how they are computed, and how the computed codes are used in performing different tasks (p. 560)." What all our on-line behavioral paradigms allow us to measure is a decision time[6], a moment in time at which some mechanism decides that a behavioral response can be made (in the form of a button press, an articulation, or an eye movement). The trick then is to be able to relate the decision time to basic processes in reading by specifying exactly how the decision is made (on the basis of what information, and how that information is translated into a response). Luckily, this is exactly what many researchers are now doing with paradigms such as lexical decision (e.g., Grainger and Jacobs, 1996), word naming (e.g., Kawamoto, Kello, Jones and Bame, 1998), as well as with eye-movement paradigms (e.g., Rayner, 1998; Reichle et al., 1998).

In what follows I will discuss one specific research strategy aimed at bringing together data obtained from paradigms with or without eye-movement measures. Finally, I will analyze some examples of divergences and convergences in the empirical data that are highlighted in the chapters of Section 1 of the present volume.

Functional overlap and a multi-task approach

One solution for the harmonious integration of reading research and visual word recognition research is the systematic application of a multi-task approach where eye-movement measures are not considered as the panacea to the ills of word nerds[7] but simply as another performance measure that has its own intrinsic methodological strengths and weaknesses (see Inhoff and Radach, 1998). Advocat-

---

5 A concrete example of an application of the magic-moment assumption (at least in a weaker, non-discrete, version) is provided by Grainger and Jacobs (1996). Within the framework of their multiple read-out model (MROM), these authors proposed a response-generation mechanism based on unit activity in whole-word representations, called the M criterion. This criterion was considered special in that tasks that were assumed to uniquely involve this criterion were considered to index "normal word recognition". However, the special status of the M criterion has since been called into question by Perea, Carreiras and Grainger (1999).

6 Eye-movement paradigms also allow fixation position to be examined.

7 Colloquial American English referring to any person who takes the study of isolated printed word perception seriously.

ing a multi-task approach is not new. This has been standard practice in the field of visual word recognition for over a decade now, even to the point that publication of data was only accepted when the same pattern was obtained in at least two different paradigms (typically lexical decision and naming). The basic logic was that if the same effects are obtained in two different paradigms then they must reflect basic processes in word recognition. However, this purely empirical (theoretically blind) multi-task approach is insufficient, and can even lead to the wrong conclusions when in fact different mechanisms are at the basis of the same effects observed in different tasks (see, for example, Hudson and Bergman's, 1985, discussion relative to effects of word length in lexical decision and naming).

A multi-task approach must be supplemented with a clear theoretical analysis of the mechanisms that determine performance in a given task, how these mechanisms relate to those hypothesized to be operational in normal reading outside of the laboratory, and how they relate to the mechanisms hypothesized to be operational in other tasks used to study word recognition and reading. This is the basis of the strategy for modeling functional overlap (Jacobs and Grainger, 1994). This concept relates the ideas that (i) there is a reasonable overlap between the functional mental structures and processes involved in generating responses in laboratory tasks, and those involved in mapping print-to-meaning during normal reading, and (ii) there is no model-free way of determining this functional overlap.

Assuming that the orthographic, phonological, morphological, and semantic codes that underlie normal reading comprehension are automatically activated on presentation of a printed word, independently of the paradigm being used, then applying the notion of functional overlap requires defining how these different codes are used to generate a given response in a given paradigm. Within an activation framework, the simplest means of describing speeded response generation is in terms of response criteria set on dimensions of activity, such that when a given activation level is attained, a response is generated. According to the multiple read-out approach (Grainger and Jacobs, 1996), several response criteria can be used simultaneously in any given task. In speeded RT paradigms, it is the first response criterion to be reached that determines performance on a given trial, but different criteria can be the source of response generation across different trials. Initial modeling efforts should therefore provide a minimal specification of (i) how code formation develops over time on presentation of a printed word (in terms of activation of code-specific representations, for example), and (ii) what codes are necessary and/or sufficient to perform a given task.

Finally, more fine-grained analyses of specific paradigms should provide the basis for a complete understanding of task-specific and task-independent mechanisms in reading. The chapter by Reingold and Stampe in the present volume is an excellent example of such fine-grained analysis of gaze-contingent research paradigms. These authors demonstrate how changes in the visual display result in saccadic inhibition, hypothesized to provide the brain with more time to process the new information made available by the display change.

Converging–diverging data from eye-movement measures and other paradigms

Some of the chapters in the section of visual word processing provide key examples of the type of divergences in effects of a given variable across different paradigms that can, and must be integrated within a common theoretical framework by applying the above mentioned strategy of modeling functional overlap. The case of two critical variables will be examined here: word length and orthographic neighborhood.

The chapter by Tatjana Nazir provides an account, in terms of perceptual learning, for why increasing word length does not give rise to poorer performance in word identification tasks with skilled adult readers. Although the 'missing word length effect' observed in the perceptual identification task is indeed an intriguing finding, a complicated pattern of word length effects appears when one examines results obtained with other paradigms. Nazir (foot)notes, for example, that effects of word length are observed in gaze duration measures, but suggests that since similar effects are also obtained with z-strings, this is likely to reflect oculomotor constraints rather than lexical processing. There is, however, some evidence that lexical decision and word naming latencies are also adversely affected by increasing word length (e.g., Hudson and Bergman, 1985; O'Regan and Jacobs, 1992), although it remains to be clarified whether these effects are actually due to confounded variables (e.g., Weekes, 1997). Since Hudson and Bergman (1985) demonstrated that the magnitude of length effects in naming and lexical decision is affected by list-context (presence of non-words intermixed with words in the naming task, type of non-word in the lexical decision task), word length would appear to be affecting highly task-specific processes in each of these paradigms. Future theoretical work must specify the length-sensitive processes that can influence performance in these tasks, to be tested by further manipulations of word length, task, and list-context.

The chapter by Martin Fischer examines how word length information might be coded during reading. On the basis of word bisection experiments, Fischer concludes that normal reading involves the activation of orthographic representations with biased spatial extent; that is with exaggerated word beginnings. This biased cognitive representation would explain the word beginning asymmetry observed in initial saccade landing site distributions (see, e.g., Chapter 11), since a strategy to fixate the word's beginning would in fact lead the eyes to the perceived (biased) center of the word. Of course, one could turn this explanation on its head and hypothesize that the observed bias in word bisection is due to the specific characteristics of the landing distribution function (this being due to purely oculomotor constraints). The critical question is therefore what information do participants use in order to bisect a word? Is it indeed some form of biased orthographic representation that is being bisected, or is the brain using on-line eye-fixation information to infer the location of the word's center?

The chapters by Nazir and Fischer serve to remind us that some of the most elementary questions concerning printed word perception remain unanswered. For progress to be made in this field, we need to know more about the most basic aspects of orthographic processing: How the individual letters of a word, with such large variations in visibility, are coded for their identity and their position (thus involving length information) to form the orthographic code that enables further phonological, morphological, and semantic processing. Improving our knowledge in this area will surely help resolve some of the (apparent) conflicts that appear with the manipulation of more complex variables such as orthographic neighborhood, phonology, and morphology.

Closer to my own research interests lie the conflicting effects of orthographic neighborhoods. The chapter by Daniel Zagar and Stéphanie Mathey, and the chapter by Joel Pynte introduce the critical issues that are at stake here, while illustrating the fundamental problem of diverging effects across paradigms. Some of the divergences may be due to uncontrolled variables, such as the variable referred to as G (number of Gangs) by Zagar and Mathey (see also the work on neighborhood spread by Johnson and Pugh, 1994), or phonologically defined neighborhoods (Andrews, 1997; Ziegler and Perry, 1998). Some may be due to cross-linguistic differences (Andrews, 1997; Van Heuven, Dijkstra and Grainger, 1998). Some of these divergences, however, may be expected on the basis of the particular paradigm being used.

Zagar and Mathey's chapter provides a particularly interesting manipulation that allows the authors to have a within-item manipulation of orthographic neighborhood (presence or absence of higher frequency orthographic neighbors using the definition of an orthographic neighbor given by Coltheart, Davelaar, Jonasson and Besner, 1977), thus getting rid of the problem of confounding variables. The results show inhibition from the presence of higher frequency neighbors, a result simulated by the Interactive Activation model (McClelland and Rumelhart, 1981), and in line with prior work using between-item manipulations of the same variable in French (e.g., Grainger, O'Regan, Jacobs and Segui, 1989, 1992). These inhibitory effects of neighborhood frequency have been observed in several different paradigms including those using eye-movement measures (Grainger et al., 1989; Perea and Pollatsek, 1998), and across different languages (Dutch, English, French, Spanish). The results of Perea and Pollatsek (1998) suggest that these effects arise late in processing, as the reading system settles on a unique representation of the target word. As further noted by these authors, this may explain why certain studies have failed to observe any inhibitory effect of neighborhood frequency in the lexical decision task. In these particular studies (Forster and Shen, 1996; Sears, Hino and

Lupker, 1995) participants showed faster RTs and higher error rates, and might therefore have been making a lexical decision response before complete target identification. The multiple read-out model of Grainger and Jacobs (1996) predicts exactly this pattern of results. Slow and accurate responding in lexical decision reflects unique word identification subject to within-level inhibition from other activated word units as in the Interactive Activation model (McClelland and Rumelhart, 1981). Faster and more error-prone performance reflects responding on the basis of global lexical activation, thus removing the competitive influence of high frequency neighbors.

However, research investigating the effects of number of orthographic neighbors or neighborhood density has somewhat complicated the picture. Increasing the number of orthographic neighbors generally facilitates responding in lexical decision and naming (e.g., Andrews, 1989, 1992; Sears et al., 1995) while inhibitory effects are generally observed in tasks requiring unique word identification (e.g., Carreiras, Perea and Grainger, 1997; Van Heuven et al., 1998; Ziegler, Rey and Jacobs, 1998). This task-dependent pattern has been accounted for within the framework of the multiple read-out model. Increasing neighborhood density increases the number of words that are significantly activated by the target, therefore increasing the amount of global lexical activation. Increasing the number of words that compete for identification slows processing in tasks that require unique identification, but can facilitate performance in word naming where these competing words all contribute toward activation in articulatory units (to the extent that the orthographic neighbors are also phonological neighbors, Peereman and Content, 1997). Finally, as argued by Grainger and Jacobs (1996), positive lexical decision responses can be accurately generated (depending on the non-word characteristics) on the basis of global lexical activation, hence the facilitatory effects of neighborhood density observed in this task. So what about eye-movement measures?

The chapter by Joël Pynte in the present volume provides an initial response to this question. The results of this study show that increasing the number of words that share the four central letters of a 9-letter target word, causes a decrease in gaze duration on the target. If one accepts that this modified definition of orthograhic neighborhood will provide a reasonable reflection of the number of words that are partially activated by the stimulus (although one may wonder why the external letters were not included in this measure), then this study actually confirms the predictions of Reichle et al. (1998). In the Reichle et al. model (see Chapter 27), gaze duration is determined by a familiarity measure of the fixated word (where familiarity could be operationalized as global lexical activation). The familiarity measure is used to signal that identification of the word currently processed is almost complete and that an eye movement out of that word should therefore be programmed. Thus Reichle et al. were led to predict facilitatory effects of neighborhood density in gaze duration measures, the pattern observed by Pynte [8].

Unfortunately, Pollatsek, Perea and Binder (1999) have failed to observe a facilitatory effect using the classic (i.e., Coltheart et al., 1977) measure of orthographic neighborhood with 4- and 5-letter words (see also Grainger et al., 1989). As suggested by Pynte, this divergence may be due to the fact that Pollatsek et al.'s stimuli were embedded in sentence contexts and may therefore have been influenced by meaning integration processes (the same is true for the paradigm used by Grainger et al.). The multiple meanings generated by words with many neighbors may indeed hinder this process. This is clearly a critical question for future research, where eye movement measures should be compared in words presented in normal sentences (where reading comprehension is required) with words presented in nonsense, but otherwise comparable sequences of words.

Finally, it is clear that the definition of similarity neighborhoods is another critical point for future investigation. Such developments must be made on the basis of improved knowledge concerning the type of information about letter identity and letter position that is made available upon a single fixation. The present discussion has focused on the role of individual words in the mapping of print to meaning. However, in alphabetic languages such as English and French, the starting point for this process is the individual letter. Improving our knowledge of the most fundamental processes in printed word perception will allow us to develop more accurate accounts of the macroscopic phenomena we observe with our standard paradigms, with or without eye movements.

Conclusions

In this commentary on the section on visual word processing I have examined the status of whole-word representations as basic units in the process of mapping print to meaning. Some theoretical attacks on the fundamental role played by whole-word representations were presented, followed by a discussion of some standard criticisms of the classic word recognition paradigms. It is concluded that a multi-task approach combined with the theoretical notion of functional overlap provides the means by which reading research using eye movement measures, and research on visual word recognition using the classic paradigms in this field, can be integrated within a single theoretical and methodological framework.

---

8 Work showing inhibitory influences of orthographic neighborhood in eye movement measures can also be interpreted within the framework of the Reichle et al. model. In this model the final resolution of word n will influence processing on word $n + 1$, since this determines the moment at which covert attention is directed to the following word, thus determining the moment at which (full) processing is initiated on this word.

Acknowledgements

I would like to thank Ralph Radach who provided excellent detailed comments on an earlier version of this work.

References

Andrews, S. (1989). Frequency and neighborhood size effects on lexical access: Activation or search? Journal of Experimental Psychology: Learning, Memory, and Cognition, 15, 802–814.

Andrews, S. (1992). Frequency and neighborhood effects on lexical access: Lexical similarity or orthographic redundancy? Journal of Experimental Psychology: Learning, Memory, and Cognition, 18, 234–254.

Andrews, S. (1997). The effects of orthographic similarity on lexical retrieval: Resolving neighborhood conflicts. Psychological Bulletin and Review, 4, 439–461.

Balota, D.A. (1990). The role of meaning in word recognition. In: D.A. Balota, G.B. Flores D'Arcais and K. Rayner (Eds.), Comprehension Processes in Reading. Hillsdale, NJ: Erlbaum, pp. 9–32.

Besner, D., Twilley, L., McCann, R. and Seergobin, K. (1990). On the connection between connectionism and data: Are a few words necessary? Psychological Review, 97, 432–446.

Carreiras, M., Perea, M. and Grainger, J. (1997). Effects of orthographic neighborhood in visual word recognition: Cross-task comparisons. Journal of Experimental Psychology: Learning, Memory, and Cognition, 23, 857–871.

Coltheart, M., Davelaar, E., Jonasson, J.T. and Besner, D. (1977). Access to the internal lexicon. In: S. Dornic (Ed.), Attention and Performance VI. London: Academic Press, pp. 535–555.

Forster, K.I. (1976). Accessing the mental lexicon. In: R.J. Wales and E.W. Walker (Eds.), New Approaches to Language Mechanisms. Amsterdam: North-Holland, pp. 257–287.

Forster, K.I. and Shen, D. (1996). No enemies in the neighborhood: Absence of inhibitory neighborhood effects in lexical decision and semantic categorization. Journal of Experimental Psychology: Learning, Memory and Cognition, 22, 696–713.

Grainger, J. and Jacobs, A.M. (1996). Orthographic processing in visual word recognition: A multiple read-out model. Psychological Review, 103, 518–565.

Grainger, J. and Jacobs, A.M. (1998). On localist connectionism and psychological science. In: J. Grainger and A.M. Jacobs (Eds.), Localist Connectionist Approaches to Human Cognition. Mahwah, NJ: Erlbaum, pp. 1–38.

Grainger, J., O'Regan, J.K., Jacobs, A.M. and Segui, J. (1989). On the role of competing word units in visual word recognition: The neighborhood frequency effect. Perception and Psychophysics, 45, 189–195.

Grainger, J., O'Regan, J.K., Jacobs, A.M. and Segui, J. (1992). Neighborhood frequency effects and letter visibility in visual word recognition. Perception and Psychophysics, 51, 49–56.

Hudson, P.T.W. and Bergman, M.W. (1985). Lexical knowledge in word recognition: Word length and word frequency in naming and lexical decision tasks. Journal of Memory and Language, 24, 46–58.

Inhoff, A.W. and Radach, R. (1998). Definition and computation of oculomotor measures in the study of cognitive processes. In: G. Underwood (Ed.), Eye Guidance in Reading and Scene Perception. Oxford: Elsevier, pp. 29–53.

Inhoff, A.W., Radach, R. and Heller, D. (2000). Complex compounds in German: Interword spaces facilitate segmentation but hinder assignment of meaning. Journal of Memory and Language, 42, 23–50.

Jacobs, A.M. and Grainger, J. (1992). Testing a semistochastic variant of the interactive activation model in different word recognition experiments. Journal of Experimental Psychology: Human Perception and Performance, 18, 1174–1188.

Jacobs, A.M. and Grainger, J. (1994). Models of visual word recognition — Sampling the state of the art. Journal of Experimental Psychology: Human Perception and Performance, 20, 1311–1334.

Jacobs, A.M., Rey, A., Ziegler, J.C. and Grainger, J. (1998). MROM-p: An interactive activation, multiple read-out model of orthographic and phonological processes in visual word recognition. In: J. Grainger and A.M. Jacobs (Eds.), Localist Connectionist Approaches to Human Cognition. Mahwah, NJ: Erlbaum, pp. 147–188.

Johnson, N.F. and Pugh, K.R. (1994). A cohort model of visual word recognition. Cognitive Psychology, 26, 240–346.

Kawamoto, A.H., Kello, C.T., Jones, R. and Bame, K. (1998). Initial phoneme versus whole-word criterion to initiate pronunciation: Evidence based on response latency and initial phoneme duration. Journal of Experimental Psychology: Learning, Memory, and Cognition, 24, 862–885.

Krueger, H.P. and Vollrath, M. (1996). Temporal analysis of speech patterns in the real world using the LOGOPORT. In: J. Fahrenberg and Myrtek (Eds.), Ambulatory Assessment. Computer-Assisted Psychological and Psychophysiological Methods in Monitoring and Field Studies. Seattle: Hogrefe and Huber, pp. 103–113.

Marslen-Wilson, W.D., Zhou, X. and Ford, M. (1996). Morphology, modality, and lexical architecture. In: G. Booij and J. van Marle (Eds.), Yearbook of Morphology 1996. Amsterdam: Kluwer.

McClelland, J.L. and Rumelhart, D.E. (1981). An interactive activation model of context effects in letter perception: Part I. An account of basic findings. Psychological Review, 88, 375–407.

Morton, J. (1969). Interaction of information in word recognition. Psychological Review, 76, 165–178.

O'Regan, J.K. and Jacobs, A.M. (1992). Optimal viewing position effect in word recognition: A challenge to current theory. Journal of Experimental Psychology: Human Perception and Performance, 18, 185–197.

Page, M. (2000). Connectionist modelling in psychology: A localist manifesto. Behavioral and Brain Sciences, in press.

Page, M. and Norris, D. (1998). Modelling immediate serial recall with a localist implementation of the primacy model. In: J. Grainger and A.M. Jacobs (Eds.), Localist Connectionist Approaches to Human Cognition. Mahwah, NJ: Erlbaum, pp. 227–256.

Peereman, R. and Content, A. (1997). Orthographic and phonological neighborhoods in naming: Not all neighbors are equally influential in orthographic space. Journal of Memory and Language, 37, 382–410.

Perea, M., Carreiras, M. and Grainger, J. (1999). Blocking by word frequency and neighborhood density. Manuscript submitted for publication.

Perea, M. and Pollatsek, A. (1998). The effects of neighborhood frequency in reading and lexical decision. Journal of Experimental Psychology: Human Perception and Performance, 24, 767–779.

Plaut, D.C., McClelland, J.L., Seidenberg, M.S. and Patterson, K.E. (1996). Understanding normal and impaired word reading: Computational principles in quasi-regular domains. Psychological Review, 103, 56–115.

Pollatsek, A., Perea, M. and Binder, K. (1999). The effects of neighborhood size in reading and lexical decision. Manuscript submitted for publication.

Rayner, K. (1998). Eye movements in reading and information processing: 20 years of research. Psychological Bulletin, 124, 372–422.

Reichle, E.D., Pollatsek, A., Fisher, D.L. and Rayner, K. (1998). Toward a model of eye movement control in reading. Psychological Review, 105, 125–157.

Rumelhart, D.E., Hinton, G.E. and Williams, R.J. (1986). Learning internal representations by error propagation. In: D.E. Rumelhart, J.L. McClelland and the PDP research group (Eds.), Parallel Distributed Processing: Explorations in the Microstructure of Cognition (Vol. 1). Cambridge, MA: Bradford Books.

Sears, C.R., Hino, Y. and Lupker, S. (1995). Neighborhood size and neighbor frequency effects in word recognition. Journal of Experimental Psychology: Human Perception and Performance, 21, 876–900.

Seidenberg, M.S. (1990). Lexical access: Another theoretical soupstone? In: D.A. Balota, G.B. Flores D'Arcais and K. Rayner (Eds.), Comprehension Processes in Reading. Hillsdale, NJ: Erlbaum, pp. 33–71.

Seidenberg, M.S. (1995). Visual word recognition: An overview. In: P. Eimas and J.L. Miller (Eds.), Handbook of Perception and Cognition: Language. New York: Academic Press.

Seidenberg, M.S. and McClelland, J.L. (1989). A distributed, developmental model of word recognition and naming. Psychological Review, 96, 523–568.

Taft, M. (1994). Interactive-activation as a framework for understanding morphological processing. Language and Cognitive Processes, 9, 271–294.

Taft, M. and Forster, K.I. (1975). Lexical storage and retrieval of prefixed words. Journal of Verbal Learning and Verbal Behavior, 14, 638–647.

Van Gelder, T. (1992). Defining distributed representation. Connection Science, 4, 175–192.

Van Heuven, W.J.B., Dijkstra, A. and Grainger, J. (1998). Orthographic neighborhood effects in bilingual word recognition. Journal of Memory and Language, 39, 458–483.

Vollrath, M. (1994). Automatic measurement of aspects of speech reflecting motor coordination. Behavior Research Methods, Instruments, and Computers, 26, 35–40.

Weekes, B.S. (1997). Differential effects of number of letters on word and nonword naming latency. Quarterly Journal of Experimental Psychology, 50A, 439–456.

Ziegler, J.C. and Perry, C. (1998). No more problems in Coltheart's neighborhood: Resolving neighborhood conflicts in the lexical decision task. Cognition, 68 (2), 53–62.

Ziegler, J.C., Rey, A. and Jacobs, A.M. (1998). Simulating individual word identification thresholds and errors in the fragmentation task. Memory and Cognition, 26, 490–501.

Attention, Information Processing and Eye Movement Control

Section Editor

Alan Kennedy

CHAPTER 7

Relations Between Spatial and Temporal Aspects of Eye Movement Control

Ralph Radach and Dieter Heller
Technical University of Aachen

Abstract

Models of eye movement control in reading and other complex cognitive tasks need to specify the oculomotor, perceptual and cognitive variables that determine *when* an eye movement is initiated and *where* it is intended to land. In recent years a large amount of data has accumulated on both aspects of eye guidance, but far less attention has been paid to their interrelations. The dominant view in the literature is that spatial and temporal aspects of eye movement control are independent and need to be accounted for separately. This is in contrast to evidence suggesting that influences of fixations on subsequent saccades and vice versa exist as part of local fixation patterns.

In this chapter a number of specific hypotheses are developed and examined on the basis of a very large corpus of reading data and crucial aspects tested using data from two recent reading experiments. Our results indicate that there are significant influences of where-parameters on when-decisions: processing time savings on the current fixation appear to be a function of the distance to the preceding fixation location. On the other hand there is only very limited evidence for influences of when-decisions on subsequent where-computations: fixation durations do generally not predict fixation positions on the next word. The proposition that fixation durations are inflated before word-skipping does not find empirical support in our data.

Reading as a Perceptual Process/A. Kennedy, R. Radach, D. Heller and J. Pynte (Editors)
© 2000 Elsevier Science Ltd. All rights reserved

Introduction

Over the last two decades research on eye movement control in reading has accumulated an immense body of scientific evidence (Rayner, 1978, 1998). This research has focussed on both spatial and temporal aspects of eye guidance. At the very beginning of modern computer-based eye movement research, more then 20 years ago, there was also considerable interest in their interrelations. For example, in their now classic paper, Rayner and McConkie (1976) examined eye movement data from six subjects reading passages of prose. Discussing several alternative candidate models of eye movement control, they examined the possibility of correlations between fixation durations and the amplitude of the saccades prior to or following fixations. They assumed that, if such a correlation were to be found, this could be taken as evidence that temporal and spatial aspects of eye movement control are governed by a single mechanism such as a gain control or memory buffer mechanism. However, since the correlations in their data set ranged only from −0.08 to 0.13, they dismissed this idea in favor of models that include two separate control mechanisms. Similar results were obtained by Andriessen and de Voogd (1973) and by Kliegl, Olson and Davidson (1983). In addition, the finding of differential consequences of eye movement contingent display changes on saccade amplitudes vs. fixation durations (Rayner and Pollatsek, 1981) has also contributed to the widespread view that spatial and temporal aspects of eye guidance are basically independent and need to be accounted for separately (e.g. McConkie, 1983; Rayner, 1998; Rayner and Pollatsek, 1989). [1]

The early correlation studies were conducted with the intention of finding *global* interrelations without considering the possibility that on a more *local* level dependencies may exist that are washed out when computing a general correlation. Two possible mechanisms are of particular interest. First, it may be that the fixation duration within a word varies as a function of the distance from which the incoming saccade was launched. A large number of studies used the moving window technique of eye movement contingent display changes to show that the region of effective vision for the extraction of letter information spans from the beginning of the current word to about 8 to 9 letters to the right of the fixation position (e.g. Pollatsek, Rayner and Balota, 1986; Rayner, Well and Pollatsek, 1980; Rayner, Well, Pollatsek and Bertera, 1982; Underwood and McConkie, 1985). In a related line of research, the boundary technique of display changes was used to show that there is a substantial increase in fixation duration on a target word when

---

[1] An important exclusion is the 'strategy and tactics' theory of O'Regan (1990), which asserts that a spatial parameter, the fixation position within a word, partially determines a temporal parameter, the fixation duration. O'Regan also explicitly suggests that fixation duration mediates the landing position of the subsequent saccade.

parafoveal preview of the word is denied on the prior fixation (for a review see Rayner and Pollatsek, 1989). McConkie and Zola (1987) demonstrated that within the effective span of letter identification there is a sharp decline in performance with increasing eccentricity of the critical letters relative to the current fixation. The spatial distribution of letter identification performance in a given perceptual span is both a function of perceptual and attentional factors (see also the discussion by O'Regan (1990) on differences between visual and perceptual span).

The evidence on the letter identification span suggests that there should be a systematic relation between saccade launch distance and subsequent fixation duration. When a fixation is located relatively close to the next target word, effective parafoveal preprocessing is more likely, and hence the fixation on the target word can be shorter. Although this hypothesis seems straightforward, there have been so far only two studies that have contributed evidence to test it empirically in a normal reading situation. Pollatsek et al. (1986) partitioned the data set of a sentence-reading experiment (see also Balota, Pollatsek and Rayner, 1985) according to the distance of the prior fixation from 4–8-letter target words into near (3–5 characters), middle (6–8) and far (>8 characters) distance cases. Although they did not find an effect of distance on the first fixation on the target word, there was a significant decrease in gaze duration from 289 ms for the far condition to 258 ms for the near condition. Heller and Müller (1983) introduced empty spaces within lines of print to vary the distance between a pre-target word and a subsequent target word. This manipulation resulted in an increased amplitude of the saccade to the target word and an associated significant increase in fixation duration on the target. In the current chapter we will take these findings as a starting point and examine the relation between saccade launch distance and fixation duration in greater detail on the basis of a large corpus of reading data.

A second class of potential relations between spatial and temporal aspects of eye movement control concerns the influence of fixation duration on the extent of subsequent saccades. This problem has two aspects. If a word has been selected as a saccade target, it is possible to ask how the current fixation duration (the 'latency' of the saccade) influences the resulting fixation position within the target word. A second question is whether the current fixation duration is related to the decision to fixate or skip a subsequent word. There is an accumulating body of evidence in both basic oculomotor research (for a recent review see Findlay and Walker, 1999) and reading research (e.g. Radach and McConkie, 1998; Rayner, Sereno and Raney, 1996) suggesting that saccade target selection and amplitude programming are based on different mechanisms or modules of the eye movement control system (see also Chapter 4). We will therefore deal with both aspects separately.

With respect to the first problem, the relation between 'latency' and subsequent fixation position, a number of different hypotheses seem plausible. In the study already mentioned, Pollatsek et al. (1986) examined the duration of the prior fixation as a function of its distance from the target word. They found that there was a tendency for fixation to be longer when readers fixated farther away from a target word and that gaze duration on the preceding word was significantly increased for longer distances. Pollatsek, Rayner and Balota saw their results as suggesting that "there are places in text where more complete processing of the material fixated (and that just to the right of fixation) takes more time but then leads to longer saccades." (p. 127). This idea can be generalized to the proposition that longer fixation durations should allow for more processing of letters to the right of the current fixation location which, in turn, may lead to a larger subsequent saccade. Thus initial fixation positions within words may be shifted to the right for longer preceding fixations. We will refer to this idea as the *preprocessing hypothesis*. The preprocessing hypothesis is more or less in the spirit of what has been called the 'perceptual span control hypothesis' of eye movement control (O'Regan, 1990; O'Regan, Vitu, Radach and Kerr, 1994). Although it may appear very plausible, it does not seem to be in harmony with more recent views on the relation between visual attention, linguistic processing and saccade generation.

For example, Henderson and Ferreira (1990, 1993) found that the difficulty of a fixated word is negatively related to the efficiency of parafoveal preprocessing of the next word. This has contributed to the recent development of an eye movement control model in which the programming of a saccade to the next word is time-locked to an initial stage of lexical processing (a familiarity check) and the (re-)allocation of attention to the word is time-locked to the completion of lexical access on the current word (Reichle, Pollatsek, Fisher and Rayner, 1998; see also Chapter 27). The processing time for lexical access is assumed to be a constant multiple of the time required for the familiarity check, leading to an increasing disparity between the two time components as word frequency decreases. Consequently, when fixation duration on a word increases as a function of processing difficulty, this will result in less parafoveal processing and, given that preprocessing and saccade amplitude are related at all (for a discussion see Inhoff, 1989), may lead to a shorter saccade to the parafoveal word. The idea that initial fixation positions within words may be shifted to the left for longer preceding fixations will be referred to as the *negative preprocessing hypothesis*.[2]

A very different perspective derives from a more low-level view of eye movement control. In his 'strategy and tactics' theory of eye movement control, O'Regan (1990, 1992) sees target specification for a saccade as a process of spatial filtering,

---

2 We do not wish to imply that the negative preprocessing hypothesis follows necessarily from a sequential attention shift model of eye movement control. However, given the proposition by Rayner et al. (1996, p. 1189) that " ... readers often move their eyes to a position in a following word at or beyond the margin from which information was obtained parafoveally in the previous fixation", the hypothesis seems well within the more general scope of 'local processing models'.

passing from lower to higher spatial frequencies as latency increases (see also Deubel, Wolf and Hauske, 1984). In these terms, the later an eye movement is triggered, the more accurate will be the specification of its target position. An important empirical basis for this idea is found in an experiment by Coëffe and O'Regan (1987) who instructed subjects to make a saccade to a visually marked target letter within a parafoveally presented string. They found that delaying saccade onset (by asking subjects to remain fixated at the center of the display until a fixation marker was switched off) resulted in an increase in the spatial precision of the primary saccade toward the target letter. In their paradigm, saccades tended to overshoot near targets and to undershoot far targets. Both of these tendencies were markedly reduced for longer latencies, leading to a convergence in saccade landing positions toward the target. Assuming these results may be generalized to a normal reading situation, it would follow that saccades following longer fixations should land closer to the 'optimal viewing position', at or near the word center (O'Regan, 1990). Support for this *convergence hypothesis* has been provided by McConkie, Kerr, Reddix and Zola (1988) who reported evidence suggesting that for longer preceding fixations there are fewer overshoots for saccades coming from near launch sites, and fewer undershoots for saccades coming from remote launch sites.

A final hypothesis may be derived from the fact that most of the visual information necessary to program the next saccade is acquired very early during the current fixation (Pollatsek and Rayner, 1982). Hence, the total duration of this fixation may be irrelevant to the amplitude of this saccade. This *no relation hypothesis* seems particularly plausible when reading is seen as a visual 'dual task' with text processing as the primary component and saccade programming playing only a secondary role. The processing of low-level visual information used for saccade preparation may be quite distinct from the visual processing of finer detail used for letter and word identification. There is a strong and systematic oculomotor error tendency in the landing positions for progressive saccades that appears to be part and parcel of low-level saccade generation routines. Radach and McConkie (1998) described this in terms of a linear 'landing position function' relating launch site and mean landing position. They have also demonstrated that this distance effect almost disappears (i.e. landing positions cluster at the target word center) when the routine pattern is interrupted and interword regressions are programmed and executed. The basis of this striking difference may be that more visual processing resources can be invested in programming a single regression (similar to Coëffe and O'Regan's 1987 experiment), whereas the normal progressive saccade routine has to operate on the basis of minimal low-level cues and does therefore not profit from a longer latency during the prior fixation.

After discussing a number of general hypotheses on the relation between fixation duration and subsequent saccade extent, we will now consider a special case that has received extensive attention in the literature, the non-fixating or 'skipping' of words during reading. There has been a controversial debate on whether word-skipping is based primarily on low-level factors like spatial distance and word length or whether it is a result of linguistic processing (see e.g. McConkie, Kerr and Dyre, 1994; O'Regan et al., 1994; Rayner et al., 1996). Perhaps the final word in this dispute has come from a recent meta-analysis by Brysbaert and Vitu (1998) who showed that although most of the variance in the available data on word-skipping can be accounted for by low-level variables, there is, nonetheless, a significant influence of cognitive factors like word frequency and contextual constraint.

The question that will be raised in this chapter is whether there is a systematic increase in fixation duration before a word is skipped. This problem is of considerable theoretical importance. Rayner and Pollatsek (1987) initially claimed that fixation durations before word-skipping are inflated to allow for the completion of lexical processing of the to-be-skipped word. O'Regan (1990) accounted for the same finding in a diametrically opposite way, asserting that prolonged fixations are not a *consequence* but a *precondition* of word-skipping which is possible if and because fixations happen to be long.

Within the context of sequential attention shift theories of eye movement control, an increased fixation duration before skipping is taken to indicate that, due to success in lexical processing on the next (parafoveal) word, a saccade toward this word is cancelled. Consequently, the word can be skipped. For example, Rayner and Pollatsek (1989, p. 169) illustrate this idea with a chart on the time course of processing events during fixations, where a 50 ms interval is assigned to saccade cancellation in the case of skipping the next word. Two studies are often cited as evidence that such an effect exists. One is the sentence-reading experiment by Pollatsek et al. (1986) who reported for the 5% target word-skipping cases in their study an increase in prior fixation duration of 21 ms relative to non-skipping cases. The second is a study by Hogaboam (1983) examining fixation durations in passage reading as a function of different patterns of fixation, as defined by combinations of incoming and outgoing progressive and regressive saccades. However, in his comparison of cases where a subsequent word is fixated vs. skipped there was only a 4 ms increase in fixation duration before skipping (table 18.3, p. 317). The fixation pattern analyses presented by Hogaboam are very interesting, but, as he did not control for word length and fixation position, they may be vulnerable to several sources if confounding (see below). There is also no indication as to whether the small difference of 4 ms was significant.

More recently, Reichle, Pollatsek, Fisher and Rayner (1998) reported that across their corpus of sentence reading data the fixation duration cost of skipping the next word was 38 ms. Their EasyReader model (see also Chapter 17) predicted much higher costs, progressing from 100 ms in a more basic version to 173 ms in the most complex final version. This difference is interesting and underscores the importance of the effect for implementing sequential attention shift models of eye movement control that rely on saccade cancellation and reprogramming.

The claim that fixation durations before skipping are inflated has recently been questioned by McConkie et al. (1994) who, on the basis of a large corpus of reading data, plotted virtually identical fixation duration distributions for skipping and non-skipping cases. In an attempt to find more evidence on the problem, we looked at a total of 22 publications dealing with word-skipping (including all studies referred to in Brysbeart and Vitu's meta-analysis) with the surprising result that in none of these studies was the fixation duration before skipping reported. To broaden the empirical base for the discussion we will analyze fixations before skipping versus not skipping the next word, taking into account the fixation position within the origin word. We will also examine data from recent sentence-reading experiments (see Chapter 11) that appear adequate to test the *prolongation hypothesis*.

General methodology

Most of the results reported in this chapter are based on analyses of a large corpus of reading data collected from four participants as they read a German translation of the first two parts of the novel Gulliver's Travels (about 160 book pages).[3] The text was presented on a 15-inch VGA in pages of 5 to 7 double-spaced lines of up to 72 ASCII characters. Each letter corresponded to approximately 0.25° of visual angle at a viewing distance of 80 cm. Participants were instructed to read the text at their normal pace in order to comprehend the main ideas and to be prepared to answer questions at the end of each of 32 text segments. Eye movements were recorded using a generation 5 Dual-Purkinje eye tracker sampling at a rate of 1000 Hz. The calibration routine used is described in McConkie (1983) and algorithms used for saccade identification can be found in McConkie, Wolverton and Zola (1984).

After excluding blinks, cases of track loss and fixations outside the page, matrices of 47989, 47826, 59857 and 64226 valid saccade–fixations pairs were available for the four participants, respectively. In all analyses regarding the relation between a fixation on a target word and parameters of the preceding saccade or fixation, cases with punctuation on the target word or on the preceding word were excluded.

---

3 The data used in this study were collected by the first author while at the University of Illinois in Champaign/Urbana. We are indebted to George McConkie, Gary Wolverton, Paul Kerr and John Grimes.

Similarly, in all analyses regarding the relation between a fixation on a target word and parameters of the following saccade, cases with punctuation on the target word and the following word were eliminated. To avoid interference with specific fixation patterns at the beginning or end of the line (Heller, 1982) we considered only target words that were more then two words away from the line margins.

The quasi-experimental approach employed to analyze the corpus data is different from the typical design of a reading experiment, where specific text material can be constructed in a way that allows the outcome to support or contradict a certain hypothesis. The key technique used here is the method of orthogonal sampling (Kliegl et al., 1983) where, in a given subset of data, a number of variables is controlled (held constant) while a target variable is examined by comparing cases with different values of that variable. This methodology is particularly useful when aspects of oculomotor behavior cannot be experimentally manipulated. For example, it is not possible to control where the eyes go during free viewing, but given a large enough number of observations, orthogonal sampling makes it possible to separate out very fine grain effects of saccade launch sites and landing positions on linguistic processing and eye guidance (Radach, 1996; Radach and McConkie, 1998).

A major confounding factor that needs to be controlled in our analyses is the influence of the fixation position within the critical word on the duration of the fixation. As O'Regan et al. (1994) and Vitu and O'Regan (1995) have demonstrated, there is an inverted u-shaped relation between initial fixation position and fixation duration for both one-fixation and two-fixation cases (see below, Fig. 2, right panel and Fig. 7). Within his strategy and tactics theory O'Regan (1990, 1992) suggested that when the eyes land at a non-optimal location at the word beginning or ending, a refixation is quickly executed that brings the eyes to the opposite end of the word. While O'Regan sees these refixations as the result of a specific 'within-word tactic', we believe on the basis of both evidence on landing positions (Radach and McConkie, 1998) and fixation duration distributions (Radach, Heller and Inhoff, 1999), that it is more adequate to interpret them as corrective movements directed toward the word center (see also Jacobs, 1987). Despite these minor differences, it is quite clear that the proportion of refixations is exceedingly high at word beginnings and endings and, most importantly, that fixations before refixations tend to be relatively short (e.g. Kliegl et al., 1983; O'Regan et al., 1994; Rayner et al., 1996). Taking these two tendencies together, it follows that fixation positions within critical words need to be considered as a potential source of variance in fixation duration. [4]

---

4 As Rayner et al. (1996) have noted, the position effect on fixation duration is greatly attenuated for single fixation cases. However, in the current context there is no reason to distinguish between initial fixations on the critical word that are or are not followed by a refixation when examining the influence of saccade launch distance on fixation duration.

On a more general level, the relation between corpus studies and controlled experimentation, as we see it, is twofold: on the one hand, effects that are found in controlled experiments should be capable of validation in normal reading to show that they can be generalized to a more ecologically valid reading situation. If an effect needs very specific materials with extreme variations of experimental variables to manifest itself, it may be of limited explanatory significance for normal reading. On the other hand, corpus analyses may be particularly vulnerable to certain methodological problems (for example, the influence of variables not considered in the sampling scheme, or hidden interactions creating phantom results). For this reason, it is prudent, whenever possible, to confirm findings of corpus analyses in controlled experiments. Following this idea, some critical aspects of our results will be re-examined in two experiments in the second part of the chapter.

Relations between saccade launch distance and subsequent fixation duration

To test the hypothesis that the eccentricity of a target word is related to the duration of the first fixation on the target, mean fixation durations on 5- to 8-letter words were computed as a function of saccade launch distance. The results are shown as individual plots in the left panel of Fig. 1. For each participant

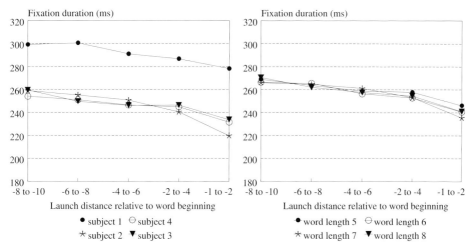

Fig. 1. Initial fixation durations on 5- to 8-letter words as a function of the distance between saccade launch position and word beginning ($n = 17\,464$). The empty space before the target word is coded as the leftmost landing position. Left panel: individual data for 4 subjects. Each graph represents between 1505 and 6248 observations. Right panel: averaged data for word length of 5 to 8 letters. Each graph represents between 2544 and 5824 observations.

there is a marked increase in fixation duration with increasing launch distance. The mean differences between the farthest vs. nearest launch sites considered are 21 ms, 40 ms, 26 ms and 22 ms for our four subjects. As indicated by Kruskal–Wallis tests, this effect is highly significant for each subject ($\chi^2(4) = 49.47$, $\chi^2(4) = 214.42$, $\chi^2(4) = 63.78$ and $\chi^2(4) = 13.74$ for subject 1 to 4, respectively, all $p < 0.01$). The right panel of Fig. 1 indicates that the relation between saccade launch distance and initial fixation duration is only marginally influenced by the length of the target word within the 5- to 8-letter word length range considered. This justifies collapsing data across word length in further analyses.[5]

A possible objection to these results could be that they are compromised by influences of the landing position within the target word. To deal with this problem, two points need to be considered. First, as discussed in the general methodology section, the distribution of mean fixation durations as a function of initial landing position takes the form of an inverted 'u' with a maximum at, or slightly left of, the word center. Second, it is well known that launch distance and landing position within the target word are linearly related, such that for every 1-letter decrement in launch distance the subsequent landing position moves about half a letter further into the word (McConkie et al., 1988; Radach and McConkie, 1998; Chapter 11). For far launch distances there will be a substantial undershoot of the word center whereas for near launch sites the mean landing position will be near or even slightly to the right of the word center (Radach and Kempe, 1993). Taking these two tendencies together, it follows that the effect of launch distance on fixation duration goes *against* the influence of the within-word distribution of fixation duration. That is, if the landing position does have an effect on fixation duration, it will be to attenuate the launch distance effect. To examine the role of within-word fixation location, mean fixation duration on different fixation positions within target words were plotted as a function of saccade launch distance in Fig. 2.

The left panel of Fig. 2 shows the data with launch distance on the abscissa. Both factors, fixation position and launch distance, appear to contribute independently to the variability of fixation durations. For each letter position within the target word, the effect of launch distance is significant ($\chi^2(4) = 86.43$, $\chi^2(4) = 74.46$, $\chi^2(4) = 72.40$, $\chi^2(4) = 114.11$, $\chi^2(4) = 59.42$, for letter positions 0 to 5; all $p < 0.01$ and $\chi^2(4) = 11.60$; $p < 0.05$ for letter position 6). As shown in the right panel of Fig. 2, the inverted 'u' function of fixation duration within words is present for all launch distances, although somewhat attenuated for very near

---

5 Individual Kruskal–Wallis tests for all launch distances indicate that in 19 of the 20 conditions the effect of word length is negligible. The only exclusion is a 12 ms difference between word length 5 and 7 at launch distance 1/2 in subject 3 ($\chi^2(3) = 9.72$; $p < 0.05$).

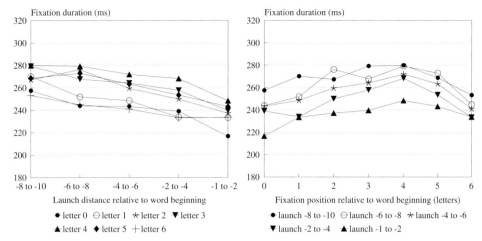

Fig. 2. Initial fixation duration as a function of saccade launch distance for fixation positions within 5- to 8-letter target words ($n = 17\,464$). The empty space before the target word is coded as landing position 0. Data are averaged such that each subject and word length is given equal weight. Left panel: data plotted with launch distance on the abscissa. Right panel: data plotted with fixation position on the abscissa. Graphs represent between 1037 and 3235 observations.

launches. The effect of launch site mainly consists in a vertical displacement of this function.

Relations between fixation duration and subsequent saccade landing position

The second class of relations to be considered concerns the influence of the prior fixation duration, the 'latency' of the incoming saccade, on the initial fixation position. There are two major methodological problems with such an analysis. First, a fixed range of fixation durations (as used e.g. by McConkie et al., 1988) creates the possibility that subjects with relatively low or high mean fixation durations are misrepresented, in the sense that a given fixation duration value may be close to the average in one subject but constitute an exceptionally long fixation for another subject. As shown in Fig. 1, one of our readers differs markedly from the others in making substantially longer fixations. It would therefore be inappropriate to set general margins for short vs. long fixation. Second, a related, more technical, problem is that when data from several subjects are taken together, it may be that unequal numbers of cases contribute to cells. An observed effect could be mediated, or even created, by this kind of sampling asymmetry.

To avoid these problems, for our four readers the individual distributions of prior fixation durations were partitioned for two word-length ranges (5- to 6- and 7- to

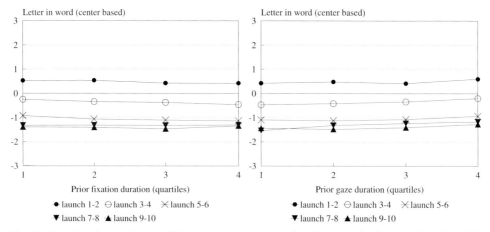

Fig. 3. Mean landing position within the target word as a function of prior fixation duration. Left panel: landing position as function of prior fixation duration. Right panel: landing position as a function of prior gaze duration. Pooled data for 4 subjects. Graphs represent between 2288 and 4631 observations.

8-letter words) and five launch distance ranges (-1 to -10 in 2-letter steps). For each of the 40 cells of this sampling scheme, quartiles of the fixation duration distributions were computed, leading to a total of 160 subsets of 'very short', 'short', 'long' and 'very long' prior fixation durations. These subsets provide the independent variables for analyses of mean initial saccade landing positions as illustrated in Fig. 3. In the figure, mean landing position is shown as a function of launch distance for 5- to 8-letter words.

As it is apparent from the figure, there are only small effects of prior fixation duration on saccade landing positions. In nonparametric Kruskal–Wallis analyses, carried out separately for the 40 cells of the sampling scheme, effects are significant in 12 cases. In 11 of these cells mean landing positions shift to the left for increased fixation duration. This is the case for 5 conditions in subject 2 and for 5 conditions in subject 3. This argues strongly against the preprocessing hypothesis, but there is also no clear support for the convergence hypothesis, as the predicted rightward shift for farther launch distances appears only as a weak nonsignificant trend in some conditions. As the right panel of Fig. 3 indicates, in contrast to the data for fixation duration, there is a suggestion that longer gaze durations are associated with more rightward landing positions within the target word. In fact, in 15 of the 40 cells landing positions are significantly shifted to the right following longer gaze durations. A plausible explanation for this pattern of results can be derived from Radach and Kempe's (1993) finding that landing site distributions are considerably shifted to the right when the prior fixation was a refixation on the preceding word. Since longer gaze durations are mainly due

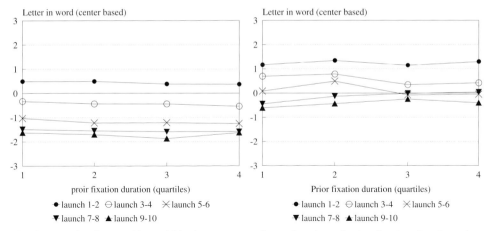

Fig. 4. Mean landing position within the target word as a function of prior fixation duration when exactly one fixation was made on the previous word. Left panel: pooled data for subjects 1 to 3 (10 381 observations). Right panel: data for subject 4 (1116 observations).

to increases in the number of refixations (e.g. Blanchard, 1985; for a discussion see Inhoff and Radach, 1998) and refixations are generally of shorter duration than single fixations (e.g. Kliegl et al., 1983; O'Regan et al., 1994; Rayner et al., 1996) it follows that a shorter preceding (re-)fixation is equivalent to a longer preceding gaze duration. These considerations point to the possibility that it is not the prior fixation or gaze duration per se but the fixation pattern (single vs. refixation) on the previously fixated word that mediates the subsequent fixation position.

To examine this account and to dissociate the effect of the prior fixation pattern from a possible residual effect of preceding fixation duration on landing position, we recomputed the data shown in Fig. 3 (left panel) including only cases where the previous word had received a single fixation. For three of our four readers, this resulted in a weakening of the tendency for landing positions to be shifted to the left after longer fixations, to an extent that prevented it from being significant in any of the conditions (see Fig. 4, left panel). However, in subject 4 a qualitatively different pattern of results emerged. As shown in the right panel of Fig. 4, landing positions clearly converge toward the word center. When counting only launches from −3 to −10,[6] the difference between landing positions resulting from far vs. near launches is reduced almost by half when comparing the highest to the lowest quartile of prior fixation duration.

---

6 The data for positions -1 and -2 immediate left of the word beginning (13.6%) are likely to include many saccades that were aimed at this word but missed it due to oculomotor undershoot, resulting in a 'landing position' rather then a true 'launch site'.

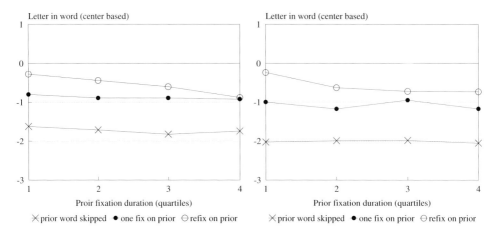

Fig. 5. Saccade landing position as a function of prior fixation duration for cases where the previous word was skipped, received one fixation, or was refixated. Left panel: pooled data from subjects 1 to 3 for launch distance −5 to −6 relative to the word beginning (3017 observations). Right panel: pooled data from subjects 1 to 3 for launch distance −7 to −8 relative to the word beginning (4171 observations).

For subjects 1 to 3 we attempted to further investigate the relation between the previous fixation pattern, prior fixation duration and landing position. For launch distances 5 to 6 and 7 to 8, where a sufficient number of observations was available, the respective (subject × word length) cells were again split as a result of whether the preceding fixation was a single fixation, a refixation or had skipped a short word. For these pattern-specific cells, prior fixation duration was again partitioned into quartiles. The resulting pattern of results is depicted inFig. 5. As expected, there is a large vertical displacement of the mean landing position curve as a function of fixation pattern. For skipping and single fixation cases there is no significant influence of prior fixation duration on saccade landing position. However, for refixation cases there is an additional effect of the prior fixation duration itself: the shorter this duration, the farther to the right the following landing position ($\chi^2(3) = 10.96$, $p < 0.05$ for launch distance 4 to 5, and $\chi^2(3) = 15.50$, $p < 0.01$ for launch distance 6 to 7).

Are fixation durations prolonged before word-skipping?

A first step to examine this question was to take the observations presented in Fig. 3 and plot prior fixation duration in relation to launch distance separately for single fixation, skipping, and refixation cases. As Fig. 6 shows, this analysis again replicates the finding that refixations are considerably shorter than single fixations.

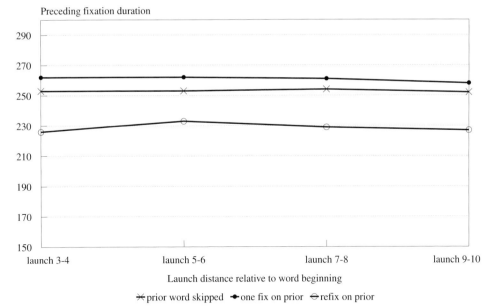

Fig. 6. Mean fixation duration as a function of launch distance for cases where the prior word was not fixated (skipped), received one fixation, or was refixated. Data are replotted from Fig. 3.

More importantly, it is clear that when plotted as a function of launch distance, fixation durations before skipping the previous word are slightly *shorter* in comparison to single fixation cases. Following the line of discussion introduced when considering the relation between launch distance and subsequent fixation duration, it can be assumed that this difference is due to a confound with within-word fixation position. When a short word to the left of the target is skipped, the fixation before skipping will often be on the rightmost letters of the word fixated. Hence, when compared to single fixation cases from the same launch distance, the respective fixations will be of shorter duration.

To avoid this confound, it is necessary to take into account the position-dependent variation of fixation durations within the word from which a critical saccade was launched. As in Fig. 2 (right panel) we started from a plot of mean fixation duration as a function of fixation position. A possible further confound with within-word fixation pattern (refixations) on the current word was prevented by using only observations where the critical word received one fixation. These data were partitioned as a function of whether a progressive saccade departing from the current word (word N) landed on the next $(N + 1)$ or second next word $(N + 2)$ to the right. In Fig. 7, results are presented for saccades starting from words of length 5 and 8, indicating that now there is virtually no relation between fixation duration and subsequent fixation probability. Statistical analyses of these

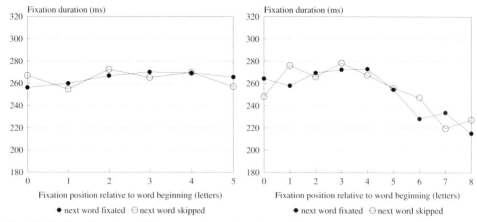

Fig. 7. Fixation duration within a word as a function of fixation position for cases where the subsequent word is fixated vs. skipped. Left panel: pooled data of subjects 1 to 4 data for word length 5 (3709 observations with next word fixated vs. 1857 observations with next word skipped.). Right panel: pooled data of subjects 1 to 4 data for word length 8. (1419 observations with next word fixated vs. 679 observations with next word skipped.)

data, again using nonparametric Kruskal–Wallis tests, did not yield any significant results.

Experimental investigations of selected hypotheses

In this section we will test some of the hypotheses developed during the first part of the chapter using data from two recent sentence reading experiments. [7]

Experiment 1: relation between launch distance and subsequent fixation duration

The data for experiment 1 were taken from a study on the processing of very long German words during reading (Inhoff, Radach and Heller, 2000). Complex compound nouns consisting of 3 noun constituents as in 'Datenschutzexperte' (dataprotectionexpert) served as stimuli. These target words contained between 15 and 25 characters, with the mean length amounting to 18 characters. All targets were regular German words, rated 'meaningful' and relatively 'familiar' in an independent survey.

---

7 The two experiments were carried out in collaboration with Albrecht Inhoff, SUNY Binghamton (Inhoff et al., 2000) and Wietske Vonk and Hedderik Van Reijn, Max-Planck-Institute of Psycholinguistics and KMU, Nijmegen (see Chapter 11).

Two factors were varied. One factor was the potential diagnostic value of the bigram separating the second and third constituent as a cue to identify the constituent boundary, determined by statistical bigram frequency measures. The second factor was whether the compound word was written in the standard form (Datenschutzexperte), with the constituent initial letters in upper case (DatenSchutzExperte), or with constituents separated by blank spaces, providing a distinct visuo-spatial marking (Daten schutz experte). While the first factor, bigram diagnosticity, turned out not to be significant, the second factor influenced viewing duration measures. Although the spaced condition constituted an orthographically illegal and unfamiliar format, it led to substantial savings in reading time. For the analyses to be reported here, we selected only stimuli from the unspaced conditions. [8]

Target words were embedded in declarative sentences where they occupied neither sentence beginning nor sentence final positions. All target nouns were preceded by an adjective with a length of at least five letters, to increase the probability of a pre-target-to-target fixation sequence. Eye movements were recorded using an AMTech 4 infrared pupil reflection eye tracker running at 500 Hz. A more detailed description of stimuli, apparatus and design can be found in Inhoff et al. (2000).

Each of the 24 participants read 80 target words in the critical conditions. These data were used to test the hypothesis that there is a systematic relation between the position from which a saccade is launched and the duration of the subsequent saccade. From our analyses of the corpus data reported earlier we could expect that the duration of the initial fixation within a word is affected by fixation position relative to the word boundaries. Looking at the experimental data, there is a marked increase of mean fixation duration from 185 ms for fixations on the first letter to 279 ms for fixations on letter seven. This difference is, of course, highly significant as indicated by a Kruskal–Wallis test on the pooled data set ($\chi^2(6) = 200.47$, $p < 0.001$). It is evident that this constitutes a major confound with potential effects of launch distance. A similar confound could be expected when fixation positions approach the end of the word. The mean letter position for the third fixation within our target words following a progressive saccade is 13.8 ($SD = 3.63$). There is indeed a tendency for fixation durations to become somewhat shorter when this fixation lies closer to the right word boundary. For example, the mean fixation duration at letter position 13 is 251 ms as compared to 233 ms at letter 16. Although this difference is smaller compared to the figures for the first fixation, the effect is significant on the 5% level ($\chi^2(6) = 13.04$, $p = 0.04$) as indicated by

---

8 Following Pollatsek et al. (1986), we believe that averaging over these data is reasonable, as the design was completely factorial so that possible influences of the experimental variables are counterbalanced on all presented analyses.

Table 1

Mean fixation duration as a function of saccade launch distance [a]

	Launch distance		
	Far	Medium	Near
First fixation	237 (73)	245 (70)	261 (71)
Second fixation	263 (66)	248 (64)	233 (71)
Third fixation	244 (70)	227 (63)	213 (68)

[a] For first fixation, launch distance is determined relative to the word beginning, for the second and third fixation it is the distance to the previous fixation within the same target word. Means of individual SD's are shown in parentheses.

a Kruskal–Wallis test, including the seven most frequent landing positions (10 to 16). Although we will report results for the third fixation cases, these data must be treated with some caution.

The mean landing position for the second fixation within target words following a progressive saccade is 10.4 (SD = 3.1). As indicated by a Kruskal–Wallis test on the pooled data for the seven most frequent landing positions (6 to 12) there is no significant effect of landing position on the duration of these fixations ($\chi^2(6) = 9.31$, $p > 0.05$). This indicates that the duration of the second fixation within very long target words is independent of fixation position and can therefore be used to test our hypothesis. For this within-word analysis, the launch distance variable simply takes the form of the distance in letter positions to the previous fixation. For each subject, individual ranges of far, medium and near launches were determined such that the available observations were partitioned into subsets of about equal size. Typical subset boundaries used were -2 to -4 for near launches, -4 to -6 for medium and -7 to -10 for far launches. The actual mean launch distances amounted to -4.02, -5.77 and -7.74 for the second fixation and -3.74, -5.70 and -7.91 for the third fixation.

Table 1 shows the effect of launch distance on the fixation duration. For the first fixation there is a nonsignificant increase of duration for *near* launches relative to the word beginning, which can be attributed to the fact that the respective saccades land further into the word ($F(1, 23) = 3.10$, $p > 0.05$). The respective mean landing positions for the first fixation are 3.17 for near launches, 4.49 for medium and for 5.91 for far launches, corresponding to mean launch distances of 3.18, 5.70 and 8.24. For both second and third fixations, however, there is a significant increase of fixation duration when the incoming saccade is launched from a *more distant* location within the very long target word [$F(1, 23) = 6.90$, $p < 0.01$ for the second fixation and $F(1, 23) = 4.06$, $p < 0.05$ for the third fixation].

Table 2

Fixation duration before leaving an 8- to 10-letter noun as a function of whether a subsequent word is fixated vs. skipped [a]

Word length	Proportion of words skipped	Prior fixation duration	
		Skipping cases	Non-skipping cases
3	13.4	220 (66)	236 (62)
4	21.1	211 (61)	209 (52)
5 and more	65.9	210 (61)	236 (78)

[a] Means of individual SD's are shown in parentheses. The methodology of the experiment is described in more detail in Chapter 11.

These findings are in line with our hypothesis and confirm the results of the corpus analyses. In general, the results also show that the examination of launch distance effects is difficult due to the potential confounding with landing position effects. This problem will be present in every study where data cannot be partitioned by landing position for each participant. In the experiment presented here, the use of extremely long target words allows for the study of the relation between saccade launch distance and the duration of the subsequent fixation without interference from nearby word boundaries.

Experiment 2: fixation durations before word-skipping

Experiment 2 is a sentence-reading experiment where 8–10-letter target words were embedded in story frames that formed either a neutral or moderately positive context. The critical experimental variation concerned the orthographic saliency of the word beginning, defined in terms of the token frequency of the initial trigram. The methodology of the experiment is reported in more detail in Chapter 11. The design has some similarities with the experiment reported by Pollatsek et al. (1986) who also used stimuli from a sentence-reading experiment including a variation of sentential context (see also Balota et al., 1985).

We took the stimulus words of the Vonk et al. experiments as a starting point and examined the fixation duration for cases where the subsequent post-target word was either fixated or skipped. This approach has two advantages. First, characteristics of the word on which the critical fixation takes place, such as word length and word frequency and morphemic structure as well as the length and frequency of the preceding word, are well controlled. Second, due to the variation of word length within the post-target words, cases can be studied where a relatively large number of words are skipped. Table 2 shows the fixation duration before leaving the target word for cases where a 3-letter, 4-letter or a longer word followed. As can be expected, there is a strong effect of word length on the skipping rate for the subsequent word. It is also clear from the table that, for this data set, fixation durations before word-skips are not prolonged.

General discussion

The analyses of the corpus data showed that in accordance with our hypothesis there is a systematic relation between saccade launch distance and subsequent fixation duration. This basic result is consistent with similar findings by Heller and Müller (1983) and Pollatsek et al. (1986). The effect is evident for all within-word fixation positions, but, as might be expected, appears slightly more pronounced for fixations on the first letters of the target word. Its size is in the order of what has been reported as 'preview benefits' when conditions with and without parafoveal preview are compared (for a recent review see Rayner, 1998). The general conclusion that can be drawn is that the effectiveness of parafoveal preprocessing during reading is directly related to the eccentricity of the target word. It is particularly interesting that this relation between launch distance and subsequent fixation duration also holds when the eyes land at the rightmost letter positions within the target word. As Inhoff (1989) proposed, one consequence of parafoveal letter processing may be to raise the activation level of lexical entries that are compatible with the initial letters of the target. In this case, it should be an effective contribution to word recognition to supplement such preliminary evidence with information on the identity of letters that received less processing during the prior fixation.

With respect to relations between prior fixation duration and saccade landing position, there was no evidence in favor of a *preprocessing hypothesis* suggesting that landing positions are shifted to the right following longer fixations. A second hypothesis, suggesting that landing positions should *converge* toward the word center (the optimal viewing position) after longer fixations, also finds no support in the data of three readers. This points to the possibility that two plausible interpretations of variation in fixation durations during reading do not have a firm empirical base. First, it appears that a prolonged fixation does not necessarily coincide with more effective parafoveal preprocessing. Second, it may not be adequate to interpret fixation durations generally in terms of latencies for subsequent saccades, with longer latencies resulting in more precision (a reduced deviation of landing sites from the word center) in the positioning of the eyes.

Concerning the two remaining hypotheses, the situation is more complex. Our finding of a tendency for longer fixation durations and shorter gaze durations to lead to a leftward shift can be explained in part by a decomposition of prior fixation patterns occurring before the saccade into the critical word is executed. When the data are partitioned according to whether there was no fixation, a single fixation, or two fixations on the prior word it becomes clear that these conditions lead to a substantial shifting of mean landing positions on the target word (Radach and Kempe, 1993). For skipping and single fixation cases there is almost no residual effect of prior fixation duration, whereas in the case of a prior refixation there is a small but significant leftward shift with increasing fixation duration. This leads to an interesting differential interpretation: when the preceding fixation was on the second last word or was a single fixation on the last word, processing resources might have been extensively occupied with processing the fixated and/or the to-be-skipped word. In this case, results of parafoveal preprocessing may often become available too late to influence saccade generation. [9]

Only when the preceding fixation was a refixation on the last word does there appear to be a relation between its duration and the following landing position, with shorter fixations (indicating less processing on the prior word) associated with saccades that bring the eyes further into the next word. Assuming that refixations are triggered at a point during the initial fixation, when only preliminary results of lexical processing are available (O'Regan, 1992; Reichle et al., 1998), it is likely that a certain proportion of these refixations may turn out to be unnecessary for the completion of word processing. If this is the case, resources will become available to process the critical target word, be it in terms of a moving processing spotlight (Chapter 27) or a gradient shift (Chapter 9). Hence, more complete processing will indeed lead to a larger saccade into the next word as originally proposed by Pollatsek et al. (1986). The respective refixations will, of course, be of relatively short duration, producing the observed effect.

Contrary to the results discussed above, subject 4 showed a marked convergence of saccade landing positions towards the word center. In general, eye movement patterns in this reader are somewhat irregular (Radach, 1996). He executed an exceptionally large proportion of regressions and needed considerably more saccades and fixations to achieve an appropriate level of text comprehension. As discussed by Radach and Kempe (1993), the usual dissociation between 'preferred' and 'optimal' viewing position, related to the occurrence of a saccadic launch distance error (McConkie et al., 1988), is absent in this subject. Instead, the landing positions of his progressive interword saccades tend to cluster near the word center, just as recently shown to be the case for regressions in all 4 subjects (Radach and McConkie, 1998). Interestingly, the deviation of subject 4 is restricted to saccade targeting and/or programming, as he shows identical patterns of results in all other analyses reported in this chapter. He appears to lack the ability to leave the process of saccade programming to low-level routines and may instead be forced to program progressive

---

9 An alternative, rather implausible interpretation could be that preprocessing and negative preprocessing cases cancel each other out exactly, such that a null result is produced.

interword saccades in a more deliberate way. This suggests that it is indeed possible to generate saccades in reading in a way similar to single goal-directed saccades (for an experimental demonstration see Coëffe and O'Regan, 1987) but that this mode of control is not the default for normal reading.

With respect to the question of whether fixation durations are longer before word-skipping we found no evidence for such an effect in either the corpus analysis or the sentence-reading experiment by Vonk et al. (Chapter 11). If the prolongation hypothesis continues to find no empirical support in further studies, what would be the theoretical consequences? It may appear as if this would be particularly damaging to sequential attention shift models of eye movement control in reading, as these models explain word-skipping in terms of the cancellation of a saccade to word $N + 1$, and its replacement with a saccade to word $N + 2$. This is assumed to require additional time, hence fixation durations before skipping should be inflated.

Such a mechanism was first proposed by Morrison (1984) who was influenced by the work of Becker and Jürgens (1979) on saccades to double-step targets. We have recently carried out a double-step experiment using step eccentricities of two degrees that are relatively close to the amplitude of reading saccades (Radach and Heller, 1998; for a similar approach see Findlay and Harris, 1984). Our results closely replicate those of other double-step studies in finding the typical amplitude transition function for uncrossed steps (e.g. Deubel et al., 1984). We also found an increased latency for 'skip-over' responses, but this latency is not a function of the time interval between the two steps. Under the assumptions that (1) the programming of two saccades can occur partially in parallel, but (2) saccade cancellation and reprogramming is still a time-consuming process, costs should be relatively small when this process starts very early (e.g. after 50 ms) and much larger when it starts late (e.g. after 125 ms), at a time when the initially planned saccade is close to being fully specified and almost committed to action. However, contrary to this prediction, it turned out that the latency of skip-over saccades was not increased when the critical target step occurred later. It appears that saccade reprogramming takes place when enough time is available during the latency period, no matter what the total latency is (for a discussion of the theoretical background see Becker, 1989).

If replacing one saccadic goal by another in a double-step paradigm does not per se lead to longer latencies, there is no reason to assume that word-skipping in reading should be related to longer preceding fixation durations. Seen from this perspective, the double-step results indicate that finding no inflation of fixation duration before word-skipping cannot be taken as evidence against sequential attention models, as finding the opposite could not be taken as evidence in favor of these models. [10]

---

10 We are in sympathy with the idea that saccades are sometimes cancelled and reprogrammed during reading, as this is the most parsimonious way to explain the occurrence of very

In summary, our results confirm and extend findings by Heller and Müller (1983) and by Pollatsek et al. (1986) in showing that there is a systematic relationship between the launch position of a saccade and the duration of a subsequent fixation. Hence, there appears to be a significant influence of where-parameters on when-decisions: processing time savings on the current fixation are a function of the distance to the preceding fixation location. On the other hand there is only very limited evidence for influences of when-decisions on subsequent where-computations: fixation durations generally do not predict fixation positions on the next word. A tendency for shorter fixations to be followed by saccades that land further into the target word can be explained to a large extent by a difference in landing positions after refixations. When landing positions of saccades coming from refixations are considered, there appears to be a small negative preprocessing effect: longer fixations associated with a slight leftward shift in landing position. It is interesting to note that this finding conforms to the *processing difficulty hypothesis*, proposed by Hyönä and Pollatsek (Chapter 4), to account for landing site effects of orthographic regularity.

The pattern of results reported is not restricted to the task of reading. Nattkemper and Prinz (1987) reported experiments using a continuous search task (Neisser, 1963), where letters are arranged in lines similar to text and participants instructed to search for defined target letters. As noted here, there was a strong positive relation between saccade amplitude and subsequent fixation duration and also no indication of any effect of fixation duration on the amplitude of the following saccade. The same pattern of results has recently emerged in an applied study on visual inspection in an industrial setting (Nies, Heller, Radach and Bedenk, 1998). Subjects were instructed to search for very small targets on the surface of glass tubes for TV monitors. Again, longer saccades were followed by shorter fixations, although there was no relation between fixation duration and subsequent saccade amplitude. Given this convergence of findings from different domains, we may conclude that the interrelations between spatial and temporal aspects of eye movement control in reading described in this chapter represent one special case of more fundamental regularities of visual information processing and saccade generation.

Returning to the classic question raised by Rayner and McConkie (1976): what are the implications of our results for models of eye movement control in reading? The principal division between a spatial and a temporal processing stream has become one of the core elements of basic saccade generation models

---

short duration fixations (Radach et al., 1999). However, since the frequency of these 'fast fixations' shows large individual variation, we tend to believe that saccade re-programming varies accordingly, giving rise to doubts that this process is a default mechanism responsible for every case of word-skipping.

both on the neurobiological and functional level (e.g. Findlay and Walker, 1999; Van Gisbergen and Van Opstal, 1989). Therefore, finding that saccade launch distance and subsequent fixation durations are systematically related can hardly be taken to indicate that spatial and temporal decisions are governed by a unified control process. However, the empirical evidence presented in this chapter does indicate that *results* of spatial decisions can have immediate consequences for local processing and hence co-determine temporal aspects of eye movement control in reading.

References

Andriessen, J.J. and de Voogd, A.H. (1973). Analysis of eye movement patterns in silent reading. IPO Annual Progress Report, 8, 30–35.

Balota, D.A., Pollatsek, A. and Rayner, K. (1985). The interaction of contextual constraints and parafoveal visual information in reading. Cognitive Psychology, 17, 364–390.

Becker, W. (1989). Metrics. In: R.H. Wurtz and M.E. Goldberg (Eds.), The Neurobiology of Saccadic Eye Movements. Amsterdam: Elsevier, pp. 13–61.

Becker, W. and Jürgens, R. (1979). An analysis of the saccadic system by means of double step stimuli. Vision Research, 19, 967–984.

Blanchard, H.E. (1985). A comparison of some processing measures based on eye movements. Acta Psychologica, 58, 1–15.

Brysbaert, M. and Vitu, F. (1998). Word skipping: implications for theories of eye movement control in reading. In: G. Underwood (Ed.), Eye Guidance in Reading and Scene Perception. Oxford: Elsevier, pp. 125–147.

Coëffe, C. and O'Regan, J.K. (1987). Reducing the influence of non-target stimuli on saccade accuracy: predictability and latency effects. Vision Research, 27, 227–240.

Deubel, H., Wolf, W. and Hauske, G. (1984). The evaluation of the oculomotor error signal. In: A.G. Gale and F. Johnson (Eds.), Theoretical and Applied Aspects of Eye Movement Research. Amsterdam: Elsevier, pp. 55–62.

Findlay, J.M. and Harris, L.R. (1984). Small saccades to double-stepped targets moving in two dimensions. In: A.G. Gale and F. Johnson (Eds.), Theoretical and Applied Aspects of Eye Movement Research. Amsterdam: Elsevier, pp. 71–78.

Findlay, J.M. and Walker, R. (1999). A model of saccade generation based on parallel processing and competitive inhibition. Behavioral Brain Sciences, 12, 697–698.

Heller, D. (1982). Eye movements in reading. In: R. Groner and P. Fraisse (Eds.), Cognition and Eye Movements. Berlin: Deutscher Verlag der Wissenschaften, pp. 139–154.

Heller, D. and Müller, H. (1983). On the relationship between saccade size and fixation duration in reading. In: R. Groner, C. Menz, D.F. Fisher and R.A. Monty (Eds.), Eye Movements and Psychological Functions: International Views. Hillsdale, NJ: Erlbaum, pp. 287–302.

Henderson, J.M. and Ferreira, F. (1990). Effects of foveal processing difficulty on the perceptual span in reading: implications for attention and eye movement control. Journal of Experimental Psychology: Learning, Memory, and Cognition, 16 (3), 417–429.

Henderson, J.M. and Ferreira, F. (1993). Eye movement control during reading: fixation measures foveal but not parafoveal processing difficulty. Canadian Journal of Experimental Psychology, 47, 201–221.

Hogaboam, T.W. (1983). Reading patterns in eye movement data. In: K. Rayner (Ed.), Eye Movements in Reading. New York: Academic Press, pp. 309–332.

Inhoff, A.W. (1989). Parafoveal processing of words and saccade computation during eye fixations in reading. Journal of Experimental Psychology: Human Perception and Performance, 15, 544–555.

Inhoff, A.W. and Radach, R. (1998). Definition and computation of oculomotor measures in the study of cognitive processes. In: G. Underwood (Ed.), Eye Guidance in Reading and Scene Perception. Oxford: Elsevier, pp. 29–54.

Inhoff, A.W., Radach, R. and Heller, D. (2000). Complex compounds in German: Interword spaces facilitate segmentation but hinder assignment of meaning. Journal of Memory and Language, 42, 23–50.

Jacobs, A.M. (1987). On the role of blank spaces for eye-movement control in visual search. Perception and Psychophysics, 41, 473–479.

Kliegl, R., Olson, R.K. and Davidson, B.J. (1983). On problems of unconfounding perceptual and language processes. In: K. Rayner (Ed.), Eye Movements in Reading and Perceptual and Language Processes. New York: Academic Press, pp. 333–343.

McConkie, G.W. (1983). Eye movements and perception during reading. In: K. Rayner (Ed.), Eye Movements in Reading. Perceptual and Language Processes. New York: Academic Press, pp. 65–96.

McConkie, G.W., Kerr, P.W. and Dyre, B.P. (1994). What are 'normal' eye movements during reading: toward a mathematical description. In: J. Ygge and G. Lennerstrand (Eds.), Eye Movements in Reading. Oxford: Elsevier, pp. 315–327.

McConkie, G.W., Kerr, P.W., Reddix, M.D. and Zola, D. (1988). Eye movement control during reading, I. The location of initial eye fixation on words. Vision Research, 28, 1107–1118.

McConkie, G.W., Wolverton, G.S. and Zola, D. (1984). Instrumentation considerations in research involving eye movement contingent stimulus control. In: A.G. Gale and F. Johnson (Eds.), Theoretical and Applied Aspects of Eye Movement Research. Amsterdam: Elsevier, pp. 39–47.

McConkie, G.W. and Zola, D. (1987). Visual attention during eye fixations while reading. In: M. Coltheart (Ed.), Attention and Performance XII: The Psychology of Reading. London: Erlbaum, pp. 385–401.

Morrison, R.E. (1984). Manipulation of stimulus onset delay in reading: evidence for parallel programming of saccades. Journal of Experimental Psychology: Human Perception and Performance, 10, 667–682.

Nattkemper, D. and Prinz, W. (1987). Saccade amplitude determines fixation duration: evidence from continuous search. In: J.K. O'Regan and A. Lévy-Schoen (Eds.), Eye Movements: From Physiology to Cognition. Amsterdam: Elsevier, pp. 269–277.

Neisser, U. (1963). Decision-time without reaction-time: experiments in visual scanning. American Journal of Psychology, 76, 376–385.

Nies, U., Heller, D., Radach, R. and Bedenk, B. (1998). Eye movements during free search on a homogenous background. In: W. Becker, H. Deubel and T. Mergner (Eds.), Current Oculomotor Research: Physiological and Psychological Aspects. New York: Plenum, pp. 269–277.

O'Regan, J.K. (1990). Eye movements and reading. In: E. Kowler (Ed.), Reviews of Oculomotor Research: Vol. 4. Eye Movements and Their Role in Visual and Cognitive Processes. Amsterdam: Elsevier, pp. 395–453.

O'Regan, J.K. (1992). Optimal viewing positions in words and the strategy-tactics theory of eye movements in reading. In: K. Rayner (Ed.), Eye Movements and Visual Cognition: Scene Perception and Reading. New York: Springer, pp. 333–354.

O'Regan, J.K., Vitu, F., Radach, R. and Kerr, P. (1994). Effects of local processing and oculomotor factors in eye movement guidance in reading. In: J. Ygge and G. Lennerstrand (Eds.), Eye Movements in Reading. New York: Pergamon Press, pp. 329–348.

Pollatsek, A. and Rayner, K. (1982). Eye movement control in reading: the role of word boundaries. Journal of Experimental Psychology: Human Perception and Performance, 8, 817–833.

Pollatsek, A., Rayner, K. and Balota, D.A. (1986). Inferences about eye movement control from the perceptual span in reading. Perception and Psychophysics, 40, 123–130.

Radach, R. (1996). Blickbewegungen beim Lesen. Psychologische Aspekte der Determination von Fixationspositionen (Eye movements in reading. Psychological aspects of fixation position control). Münster/New York: Waxmann.

Radach, R. and Heller, D. (1998). Spatial and temporal aspects of eye movement control. Fifth European Workshop on Language Comprehension, Luminy, April 2nd–April 4th.

Radach, R., Heller, D. and Inhoff, A.W. (1999). Occurrence and function of very short fixation durations in reading. In: W. Becker, H. Deubel and T. Mergner (Eds.), Current Oculomotor Research: Physiological and Psychological Aspects. New York: Plenum, pp. 321–331.

Radach, R. and Kempe, V. (1993). An individual analysis of fixation positions in reading. In: G. d'Ydevalle and J. Van Rensbergen (Eds.), Perception and Cognition. Advances in Eye Movement Research. Amsterdam: Elsevier, pp. 213–225.

Radach, R. and McConkie, G.W. (1998). Determinants of fixation positions in words during reading. In: G. Underwood (Ed.), Eye Guidance in Reading and Scene Perception. Oxford: Elsevier, pp. 77–100.

Rayner, K. (1978). Eye movements in reading and information processing. Psychological Bulletin, 85, 618–660.

Rayner, K. (1998). Eye movements in reading and information processing: 20 years of research. Psychological Bulletin, 124, 372–422.

Rayner, K. and McConkie, G.W. (1976). What guides a reader's eye movements? Vision Research, 16, 829–837.

Rayner, K. and Pollatsek, A. (1981). Eye movement control during reading: evidence for direct control. Quarterly Journal of Experimental Psychology, 33A, 351–373.

Rayner, K. and Pollatsek, A. (1987). Eye movements in reading: a tutorial review. In: M. Coltheart (Ed.), Attention and Performance XII: The Psychology of Reading. London: Erlbaum, pp. 327–362.

Rayner, K. and Pollatsek, A. (1989). The Psychology of Reading. Boston, MA: Prentice-Hall.

Rayner, K., Sereno, S.C. and Raney, G.E. (1996). Eye movement control in reading: a comparison of two types of models. Journal of Experimental Psychology: Human Perception and Performance, 22, 1188–1200.

Rayner, K., Well, A.D. and Pollatsek, A. (1980). Asymmetry of the effective visual field in reading. Perception and Psychophysics, 27, 537–544.

Rayner, K., Well, A.D., Pollatsek, A. and Bertera, J.H. (1982). The availability of useful information to the right of fixation in reading. Perception and Psychophysics, 31, 537–550.

Reichle, E.D., Pollatsek, A., Fisher, D.L. and Rayner, K. (1998). Towards a model of eye movement control in reading. Psychological Review, 105, 125–157.

Underwood, N.R. and McConkie, G.W. (1985). Perceptual span for letter distinctions during reading. Reading Research Quarterly, 20, 153–162.

Van Gisbergen, J.A.M. and Van Opstal, A.J. (1989). Models. In: R.H. Wurtz and M.E. Goldberg (Eds.), The Neurobiology of Saccadic Eye Movements. Amsterdam: Elsevier, pp. 69–101.

Vitu, F. and O'Regan, J.K. (1995). A challenge to current theories of eye movements in reading. In: J. Findlay, R.W. Kentridge and R. Walker (Eds.), Eye Movement Research: Mechanisms, Processes and Applications. Amsterdam: Elsevier, pp. 381–392.

CHAPTER 8

Attention Allocation in Reading: Sequential or Parallel?

Alan Kennedy
University of Dundee

Abstract

In this chapter I consider some of the consequences of adopting the assumption that reading is a form of surrogate listening, and that readers typically process text sequentially, each word in turn. Most current models of eye movement control assign a significant role to the idea that attention is allocated in a serial-sequential fashion to successive words, but there are significant signs of strain in this position. First, reinspections, word-skipping, preview and spill-over effects cannot easily be accommodated in a model where visual attention is allocated on a strictly serial basis; second, there is evidence from a number of sources suggesting a degree of mutual interaction (or cross-talk) in the processing of successive words in text. Such data pose a serious challenge to sequential attention-allocation models.

Reading as a Perceptual Process/A. Kennedy, R. Radach, D. Heller and J. Pynte (Editors)
© 2000 Elsevier Science Ltd. All rights reserved

Reading versus listening

When processing spoken sentences, there is very little the listener can do to simplify the task. Successive words arrive at a rate determined by the speaker and must be dealt with more or less immediately. There is the possibility of retaining information in short-term memory, but this is of limited capacity. It follows that some complexities which are acceptable in the written form become inconsiderate, or incomprehensible, when spoken. Even such a simple stylistic variation as the passive is relatively unusual in speech (Goldman-Eisler, 1968) and structural ambiguities such as reduced complements, reduced relatives, multiply-embedded structures and other tools of the psycholinguist's trade are rare in speech and, if used at all, must be flagged with elaborate markers of intonation, stress and pausing. These radical differences in the nature of the stimulus, comparing speech and writing, may have powerful consequences for processing. Thus, although 'later' properties of the signal can influence 'earlier' processing decisions (for example, changing segmentation) this does not arise from violations in the temporal sequence of the relevant properties, but from operations over the integrated signal. The auditory stimulus is simply not under the hearer's control. In contrast, the temporal order in which written words are examined is determined by the reader's scanning strategies, which will almost certainly involve both within- and between-word reinspections and word-skips. The argument I want to develop is that this contrast in the demands of speech and writing has largely been ignored in psycholinguistic theory [1].

This chapter will deal first with the assumption that reading is a form of sur-rogate listening. This has had a profound effect on the development of theories of reading and, in particular, underlies the proposition that the reader processes text sequentially, each word in turn (Just and Carpenter, 1980; Morrison, 1984; Reichle, Pollatsek, Fisher and Rayner, 1998). I will then briefly discuss models of eye movement control which assign a significant role to the notion of se-quential allocation of attention and consider two significant sources of strain in this 'canonical' position: (1) the fact that reinspections, word-skipping, preview and spill-over effects cannot easily be accommodated in a model where visual attention is allocated on a strictly serial basis; (2) evidence suggesting a signifi-cant degree of mutual interaction (or cross-talk) in the processing of successive words.

---

1 See, for example, the claim by Ferreira and Clifton (1986) that " ... there is no reason to doubt that the syntactic processing strategies used by listeners and readers would be the same."

Parsing and the spatial code

Written text is normally available as a spatially extended object on a printed page or screen and can be inspected at will (Christie and Just, 1975; Kennedy, 1983, 1986, 1992). This bestows a unique advantage on the reader, as distinct from the listener, because reinspection can be deployed as a reprocessing option. One consequence of this is that the cost of incorrect initial structural analysis is higher when processing speech, where reinspection is obviously not possible (Murray, Watt and Kennedy, in prep.). To illustrate this point, I will consider first the role played by spatial coding in the parsing of one class of structurally ambiguous sentence when visually presented and then examine in the next section how the same materials are parsed in the auditory modality.

(1) The teacher noticed one girl from her class in school activities.
(2) The teacher noticed that one girl from her class had school uniform.
(3) The teacher noticed one girl from her class had school uniform.
(4) The teacher noticed one girl from her class in school activities had arrived late.

The temporary structural ambiguity in sentences like (3), induced by the omission of the overt complementiser 'that', has been extensively studied (Frazier and Rayner, 1982; Holmes, Kennedy and Murray, 1987; Rayner and Frazier, 1987). The balance of evidence supports an early suggestion of Frazier and Rayner that subjects parse such sentences initially (i.e. up to the point where the local ambiguity is resolved) by adopting as a preferred analysis the default 'direct-object' form, as in (1). That is, the words 'one girl' are attached as the object of the verb 'noticed'. In the case of sentence (3), the reader becomes aware of a garden-path when the word 'had' is encountered and the incorrect parsing decision must then be revised. There is considerable controversy over factors which determine the initial preferred analysis (Kennedy, Murray, Jennings and Reid, 1989; Mitchell, 1994), but this is unimportant in the present context. The critical point is that when an initial analysis turns out to be wrong, the sentence can be reanalysed relatively easily through a process of reinspection. Frazier and Rayner consider three possible reinspection strategies: (a) backing up through the text, looking at each word in turn in reverse order; (b) making a saccade back to the beginning of the sentence (or line) and re-reading ab initio; (c) re-reading selectively by making a saccade to the point where the faulty parsing attachment was made. The data generally support (c): subjects make a saccade to the region 'noticed one', presumably in an attempt to un-do the mistaken parsing decision. Note, however, that this is only possible because the sentence remains available for reinspection and enough spatial information is retained to allow the reader to make saccades to specific locations. This second point needs to be stressed, because saccades made in the service of reanalysis can be quite large: acuity falls off very rapidly from the central fixation point, and it is doubtful if such saccades could be controlled accurately by physical identification of their landing site.

Auditory parsing

It is instructive to compare performance on the identical structures presented as speech. Murray et al. (in prep.) did this using a mispronunciation detection task [2] to provide the critical performance measures. The pattern of results is strikingly different from that obtained with visual presentation. In the auditory mode, there is no difference in performance between the reduced and full complement structures (2) and (3), whereas the apparently simpler 'direct-object' structure (1) is invariably more difficult to process. Why should the structure easiest to process when written be hardest to process when listened to? The answer must surely lie in the fact that a single preferred structural analysis represents a relatively low-risk strategy for the reader, but a high-risk strategy for the listener. This is not to deny that ambiguity imposes a real-time penalty for the reader: there is ample evidence that this is the case. But if an initial parse turns to be out incorrect a repair process is readily available, under-pinned by spatially coded information. This is in stark contrast to the situation facing the hearer, where the ephemeral nature of the signal being processed means that the risk of an early commitment to any particular structure is great. The only safe alternative is to undertake a degree of parallel processing of structure [3]. The paradoxical difficulty of sentences like (1) now becomes more explicable, because the hearer cannot know whether such a sentence is to be parsed as a 'direct-object' construction, or whether it represents the initial part of a more complex reduced complement such as (4).

Single-location reading: an auditory analogue

If these apparent differences between speech and writing are fundamental, it should be possible to demonstrate a processing penalty if we remove from the words of text the crucial aspect of 'spatial adjacency'. This can easily be achieved by presenting individual words at a fixed spatial location, as a kind of 'surrogate speech' in which reanalysis can no longer be defined in terms of reinspection. The question is, does

---

2 The necessary control for possible cues to structure from intonation and stress was achieved using cross-splicing.

3 There are a number of possible parallel structural analyses, but this theoretical question is not relevant to the visual–auditory comparison.

this incur a processing deficit? At first sight, the evidence on the question appears clearly negative. Reading is not only possible under 'single-location' presentation conditions (Bouma and de Voogd, 1974; Juola, Ward and McNamara, 1982; Monk, 1985), some researchers have even suggested that it is *better* (Cocklin, Ward, Chen and Juola, 1984). However, before accepting the rather unpalatable conclusion that eye movements might hinder reading (Rubin and Turano, 1992, 1994) it should be noted that single-location presentation actually solves one processing problem for the reader. Although it is assumed that words in normal text are looked at in their correct order, this 'order', at least for the beginning reader, is actually defined by the underlying speech-code being represented, rather than by the sequence of fixations over a particular spatial array. Indeed, a crucial part of what is acquired in the skill of reading involves recovering a temporal sequence from a given spatial array (Murray and Kennedy, 1988). Only for the fluent reader can words be seen as 'objects' to be looked at in a number of possible sequences (McConkie and Zola, 1987), with both word-skipping and reinspection conceived of as events taking place over a stable spatial array. It is the solution of this spatio-temporal mapping problem which ensures that the sequence of fixations indicated at (5) does *not* lead to the mental representation 'The wise man rarely visited the temple in old hidden forest'. That is, the representation arising from the temporal sequence of fixations 7, 8, 9, 10 and 11 can be overridden by the property of spatial adjacency. Thus, the demonstration that reading is *possible* under single-word presentation conditions does not, of itself, adequately dispose of the notion that useful information is provided by physical adjacency.

        1   2   3   4   5   6 9   7   10   8   11
(5) The wise man rarely visited the old Temple hidden in the forest

Kennedy and Murray (1984) set out to examine this by comparing the effects of 'spatialised' and 'non-spatialised' modes of display on the analysis of temporary syntactic ambiguity. We looked at the closure ambiguity illustrated in the comparison between (6) and (7). As in the analysis of reduced complements, adopting the sequence 'the huge old book' as the 'direct object' of the verb in (7) leads to a parsing failure when the word 'fell' is encountered. Subjects read the sentences by pressing a button to reveal one word at a time in either a 'cumulative' display mode, in which words built up across the screen until the whole sentence was visible, or in a 'central' mode, in which words appeared successively at the same location in the middle of a screen. Mean inter-response times were computed in the zones indicated.

(6) While the teacher was reading | the huge old book | it fell off the | table.
(7) While the teacher was reading | the huge old book | fell off the | table.

Average inter-response times in the second zone ('the huge old book') can serve as a baseline. This was 300 ms in the central presentation mode and 330 ms in

```
┌──────────────────────────────────────────────────────────────────────┐
│         Spatialised                          Non-Spatialised           │
│   t1: The                                         The                  │
│   t2:     old                                     old                  │
│   t3:        man                                  man                  │
│   t4:           walked                            walked               │
│   t5: The old man walked home.        The old man walked home.         │
└──────────────────────────────────────────────────────────────────────┘
```

Fig. 1. Spatialised and non-spatialised presentation modes used by Pynte, Kennedy, Murray and Courrieu (1988).

the cumulative mode and, as expected, these times did not differ between the two sentence types. Relative to sentences like (6), we would expect times in the third zone in (7) to reflect the closure ambiguity (with a clause boundary after the word 'reading'). This was clearly so, *but only in the cumulative presentation mode*, where the average time of 470 ms in (7) was significantly slower than the 370 ms found in (6). In the central presentation mode, in contrast, there was absolutely no difference between the two sentence types, with mean times about the same as in zone 2. Subjects appear not to notice the structural ambiguity when denied the opportunity to see words in different spatial locations.

Pynte, Kennedy, Murray and Courrieu (1988) examined whether this 'on-line' effect could also be demonstrated in later processing. They used the two presentation modes illustrated in Fig. 1. The experimental sentences, up to the penultimate word, were presented either with each word in the same location (non-spatialised) or occupying different spatial locations (spatialised). In both cases, the final word was presented along with the rest of the sentence. Eye movements over this full sentence display were then analysed for evidence of differential effects induced by the two presentation modes.

The materials consisted of sentences like (8) and (9) containing a pronoun ('it' in the example given [4]), the correct referent of which was only evident when the final segment was read.

(8) The clause surprised the crowd because it was ... imposed without debate.
(9) The clause surprised the crowd because it was ... used to receiving notice.

The two presentation modes induced very different patterns of reinspection, related to the degree to which subjects were able to deploy pragmatic rules to decide which of the two interpretations was correct. In particular, systematic reinspection of the first noun and the verb *only* occurred following spatialised presentation. We argue from this that denying subjects information in the form of spatial adjacency does not simply produce a global penalty at input, it triggers specific

---

4 The experiment was run in French, which is better adapted to capture this particular ambiguity, since there is no equivalent of the English gender-neutral pronoun 'it' in French.

problems with pronominal anaphoric reference. Interestingly, such relationships are essentially coded in terms of relative position and, in fact, frequently lead to selective reinspection (Kennedy, 1978).

The control of reinspections

The evidence reviewed so far provides prima facie grounds for disputing the proposition that reading is some kind of 'visual listening'. First, whether or not the processor has continuing access to material after initial analysis influences parsing strategies in the two modalities: for the reader, the initial inspection of a word secures not only its identity (i.e. *what* it is), but also *where* it lies, and this latter spatially coded information permits selective reinspection, a mode of reanalysis unavailable to the listener. Second, although more controversial, spatial adjacency itself appears to provide a processing advantage at input (see also Baccino and Pynte, 1994). This latter issue is taken up in the next section.

Further evidence on the first of these two propositions has recently been provided by an ingenious analysis of progressive and regressive saccades in normal reading (Radach and McConkie, 1998). It is generally accepted that the balance of evidence points to predominantly low-level control over the location of initial progressive saccades in text (McConkie, Kerr, Reddix and Zola, 1988; O'Regan, 1990). Targeting is on the basis of information about the length of the next word to be fixated. Thus, for readers of English a simple algorithm such as 'aim for the centre of one of the blobs lying to the right of the current fixation' accounts for virtually all the variance in forward eye movement control. Claims that lexical or sub-lexical properties of upcoming words influence where they are initially fixated (Inhoff, Briihl and Schwartz, 1996; Underwood, Clews and Everatt, 1990) have proved difficult to replicate (Radach and Kempe, 1993; Rayner and Morris, 1992). It is possible that very irregular-looking adjacent words may influence initial fixation position (Hyönä, 1995; Hyönä and Pollatsek, in press), but any effect obtained is small (see also Brysbaert and Vitu, 1998).

Radach and McConkie illustrated the operation of this 'dumb' control mechanism by demonstrating that the relationship between initial landing position and launch site for forward saccades in normal reading is close to linear. Relevant data from a large corpus of eye movements, derived from four subjects each reading half of the novel *Gulliver's Travels*, are shown in Fig. 2, upper panel. For each shift of one character in launch position there is a corresponding shift of about one third to one half of a character in landing position. This function obtains over the whole range of launch positions likely to be found in normal reading. Furthermore, both within- and between-word forward saccades show the same relationship, with no difference apparent between saccades programmed within a currently fixated word

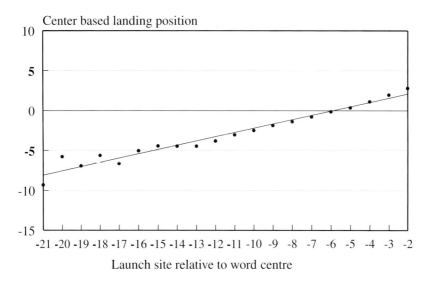

Launch site relative to word centre

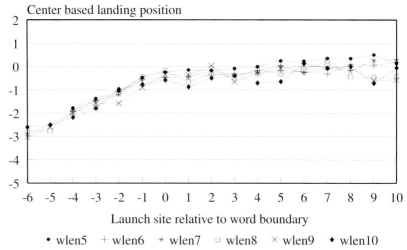

Launch site relative to word boundary

• wlen5   + wlen6   ⋆ wlen7   □ wlen8   × wlen9   ◆ wlen10

Fig. 2. The upper panel shows estimated mean landing position on words (9–11 characters in length) as a function of the launch site of progressive saccades, relative to the word centre. The slope of the linear regression function is 0.53 ($r^2 = 0.96$). Launch distances of 5 or less include cases where the progressive saccade was launched from within the word. The lower panel shows mean landing positions (averaged over words 5–10 characters in length) of regressive fixations as a function of launch site. The x axis is numbered relative to the space following the target word. Negative launch sites indicate saccades from within a word. The data are derived from pooled data from four subjects. (Figure re-drawn from Radach and McConkie, 1998.)

and those to an adjacent word to the right. We may conclude that what determines where the eyes land is primarily where they are launched from (see Chapter 11 for a detailed discussion). There are relatively small effects of word length and local fixation patterns, but very little evidence of cognitive control. In marked contrast, an equivalent analysis of inter-word eye movements launched to sites already inspected shows a virtually flat relationship between extent and accuracy (see Fig. 2, lower panel). In this case, landing position is close to the target word's centre, regardless of launch position (see also Vitu, McConkie and Zola, 1998). The outcome strongly suggests a degree of spatial control over saccades to 'already-inspected' sites. To put it simply, subjects appear to know *where* previously inspected words lie (for a discussion of the co-ordinate system used to code this information, see: Baccino and Pynte, 1994; Kennedy, 1983, 1986; Kennedy and Baccino, 1995).

(10) The novels in the library has started to go mouldy with the damp.   novels
(11) The workmen were leaning on their spades by the side of the road.   shovels

Kennedy and Murray (1987) provided an experimental demonstration of a closely related point. Subjects read sentences like (10) and (11). After reading the final word, a target appeared which was either a word from the sentence or a close synonym of a word. Subjects were instructed to press a button if the target was present in the displayed sentence. Although not demanded by the task, large regressive eye movements were often made from the target towards the equivalent word in the sentence. The materials were constructed so that this distance varied from a few characters to over 70 characters. However, the accuracy of regressive saccades was remarkably high, whatever their extent, with an average absolute error of about 2.6 characters, relative to the centre of the target word, for close targets and 2.8 characters for remote targets. That is, consistent with the findings of Radach and McConkie, saccades almost invariably landed on their target, however remote the launch site. The absence of a relationship between saccade size and accuracy was further confirmed by an analysis of the correlation between these measures in the full data set, which was effectively zero, with $r = 0.09$.

Eye movement control: processing 'word objects'

I want now to turn to the second, and more controversial, of the two propositions noted in the previous section. In what way might spatial adjacency provide a processing advantage at input? As we have seen, early attempts to account for the control of saccades in reading (e.g. Bouma and de Voogd, 1974) considered that words in text were processed in a manner roughly analogous to words in speech.

Each was looked at in turn, mimicking the temporal sequence which would obtain if it had been heard rather than seen. The concept of the 'word object' thus found a place in the literature (McConkie and Zola, 1984), capturing simultaneously the idea of low-level physical control over saccades and the processing of each word as a cognitive event bounded by the time spent inspecting it. The proposal that processing begins when the eyes first fall on a word and ends with the launch of the saccade to the next word (Carpenter and Just, 1983) was further buttressed by an appeal to the concept of *visual attention*. Reading as a form of surrogate listening seems entirely plausible if we envisage attention as a serial-sequential mechanism, of limited capacity, deployed over the printed page like a spotlight switched to each word in turn. Of course, to the extent that this metaphor itself rests on the notion of 'word objects' it is somewhat circular. It has, nonetheless, underpinned models of eye movement control in reading over the past twenty years.

Serial-sequential attention allocation

The most clearly articulated statement of this class of theory is the Morrison (1984) serial model of eye movement control in reading [5]. This proposes that visual inspection and visual attention can be decoupled (McConkie, 1979; Posner, 1980; Posner and Cohen, 1984). Assume that the eyes are initially fixating a given word n, which is thus undergoing foveal processing. Some time later, when a criterion level of processing (for example, lexical access) has been reached, attention shifts discretely to the next word, $n + 1$. At the same time, the reader programs an inter-word saccade. Thus, for a period of time, the eyes remain fixating word n while word $n + 1$ is processed in the parafovea. This prior processing is cashed in when the parafoveal target is eventually inspected directly, in the form of a *preview advantage*: words which have previously been located in parafoveal vision are more rapidly identified when eventually fixated (for a discussion see Rayner and Pollatsek, 1989). It follows from this description that Morrison saw the size of any preview advantage as related to the time to program a saccade, and thus approximately constant. The reference to parallel programming in the model (see footnote 5) points to the possibility that further saccades (to words $n + 2$ or even $n + 3$) may be programmed if the criterion level of processing is reached for whatever parafoveal target is currently attended to. Obviously, if two attentional shifts actually occur, words will be skipped.

---

5 I will adopt this terminology rather than the more common 'parallel-programming model' because the parallel component in Morrison's model is strictly restricted to the programming of overlapping saccades.

This model is limited in several respects. First, it makes no predictions about *where* saccades are directed. Second, it does not deal with the effects of syntax or any other higher-level properties of text, such as anaphor resolution. Finally, as we shall see, it attaches a rather peculiar status to reinspections. Morrison's model has, nonetheless, been enormously influential as defining what the bones of a theory of eye movement control in reading might look like, notwithstanding the fact that certain aspects of the model could not be verified. The most significant problem relates to the prediction, noted above, that the parafoveal preview effect should be roughly constant. Information collected from a word in the parafovea should not vary as a function of foveal processing load for the simple reason that an attentional shift only occurs when the foveal criterion has been exceeded. Henderson and Ferreira (1990) showed that this is not the case: preview advantage is plainly modulated by foveal difficulty. In different experiments, they changed word frequency or local syntactic load (adding or removing a complementiser in a garden-path sentence) and measured consequential changes in preview advantage. Both manipulations produced similar results: the time taken to process a previewed word varies as a function of foveal load. For example, in one experiment a 13 ms preview advantage following an easy, high-frequency, foveal item was reduced to 3 ms in the case of a hard, low-frequency, word. In effect, if word n is particularly difficult, no preview advantage is found. Foveal-on-parafoveal interactions can be interpreted quite naturally in terms of a modulation of the perceptual span by current processing load (Rayner and Pollatsek, 1989), but such an interpretation cannot be derived from Morrison's model, as originally conceived, because processing interactions of this kind are incompatible with the operation of a sequential, time-locked, attentional mechanism.

Revisions to the Morrison model

After considering several alternatives, the solution proposed by Henderson and Ferreira was to add a saccadic deadline to the Morrison model. They suggested that a point is reached during foveal inspection when a saccade becomes inevitable, regardless of whether the 'criterial level' of foveal processing has been reached. When this deadline expires, a saccade will be prepared, but with a target location within the current word, since that is where attention remains directed. On some occasions (perhaps the majority) processing of the foveal word will be completed before this intra-word saccade is actually executed, in which case attention will switch to word $n + 1$ and a second saccade will be programmed. The deadline assumption predicts a foveal-on-parafoveal interaction because any time spent shifting attention *within* the foveal word cannot, by definition, also be committed to the parafoveal processing of word $n + 1$. Unfortunately, there is not much empirical evidence that the operation of a saccade programming deadline of this kind is responsible for the obtained foveal-on-parafoveal interaction. For example, the revised model predicts that if the foveal word is actually refixated, the preview advantage should return to a value equivalent to the time to program a saccade. It is relatively straightforward to measure whether a reduction in preview benefit is restricted to cases where the foveal word received only a single fixation, but attempts to show this have proved negative (Schroyens, Vitu, Brysbaert and d'Ydewalle, 1999). Much the same conclusion can be derived from studies by Kennison and Clifton (1995) and Vitu and O'Regan (1995), both of which fail to show any hint of bimodality in distributions of single-fixation durations on words, such as would be found if a deadline were operating. In any case, the observation that when two fixations are made on a word, the first is usually shorter (Kliegl, Olson and Davidson, 1982)[6] is fatal for the notion of a processing deadline.

Reichle et al. (1998) have recently offered a more convincing revision of the Morrison model. They propose that the trigger for an attentional shift and for an inter-word saccade cannot be the *same* cognitive event, namely completion of processing on the currently fixated word. Not only foveal-on-parafoveal modulation of the preview effect, but also reports of 'spill-over' effects (Rayner and Duffy, 1986) strongly suggest that processing difficulty on one word can modulate the processing load on subsequent words. If, as the Morrison model demands, a primary inter-word saccade is only programmed when the criterial level of processing on the current foveal word has been exceeded, such 'inherited' processing difficulties should not occur. Reichle et al. make the suggestion that an eye movement and an attentional shift are triggered by different cognitive events. An eye movement is programmed as soon as a preliminary (i.e. pre-lexical) familiarity check on the fixated word is completed, whereas the crucial attentional shift takes place only when lexical access is achieved. Fig. 3 illustrates how, by decoupling attention and eye movement programming in this way, the model can predict foveal-on-parafoveal effects. Furthermore, it predicts the occurrence of both word-skipping and short-duration fixations and produces a good quantitative fit to observations of fixation duration and refixation rate as a function of word frequency. It should be noted, however, that the notion of sequential attention allocation remains central to the model, which is strictly serial. That is, the difficulty of a foveal stimulus may influence the amount of useful information available from a parafoveal target, but effects in the opposite direction are not predicted. Properties of a word in the parafovea cannot influence current foveal processing for the simple reason

---

6 I am grateful to Ralph Radach for pointing out that Henderson and Ferreira appear to have overlooked this reference.

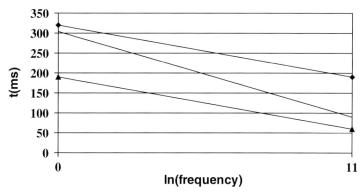

Fig. 3. How foveal frequency modulates preview benefit in the model of Reichle et al. (1998). The bottom line represents the time to complete the familiarity check (i.e. trigger an eye movement) as a function of log word *n* frequency. The top line indicates when the eye movement is executed, a fixed time after completion of the familiarity check. The middle line shows when lexical access is completed (i.e. an attentional switch to word *n* + 1 occurs), as a function of log word *n* frequency. The vertical distance between the upper two lines represents the time between completing lexical access of word *n* and making a saccade to word *n* + 1. The lower the word frequency, the smaller this time interval. (Figure re-drawn from Reichle et al., 1998.)

that such information is not available until the crucial attentional switch has taken place.

Processing from multiple sites

There is a paradox in the Morrison model and its various revisions, including sophisticated versions such as that of Reichle et al. It stems, I believe, from the parallel between listening and reading implicit in the notion of sequential attention allocation, a parallel which has become firmly embedded in the canonical view of eye movement control, notwithstanding the fact that the serial-sequential nature of speech is precisely the property which a writing system can avoid. The question is, do any significant conclusions flow from this? As a first step towards an answer it is worthwhile asking whether the terms 'fovea' and 'parafovea' actually support the processing distinction asked of them in models involving sequential attention allocation. Do they have unique roles in reading, or should we treat the point of fixation as an "arbitrary spatial reference without special processing qualities" (Legge, Klitz and Tjan, 1997)? Although acuity varies continuously across the visual field (Bouma, 1973; O'Regan, 1989), visual processing is, nonetheless, essentially parallel, and the influence of this fact on processing efficiency is not trivial. Information from across the visual field as a whole is capable of influencing processing from any given point of inspection (Schiepers, 1980). Indeed, it might be more defensible to characterise the deployment of visual attention as a 'zoom' rather than a 'switch' (Eriksen and St. James, 1986), with each fixation defined, not so much as a clearly demarcated 'event', but as a train of events in which stimulus information of increasing specificity becomes available over time. Perhaps it is time to question the fundamental assumption of the attention-switching model: do 'word objects' really constitute the primary visual stimulus in reading and, if so, are they *necessarily* processed sequentially?

An alternative view is that attention is distributed across the visual field in parallel (Hoffman, 1998; McClelland and Mozcr, 1986). This is not to deny the privileged status of the fovea, since it is over this region that high-quality feature information becomes rapidly available. But, from a parallel-processing point of view, information from other regions of the visual field will also influence processing throughout each fixation. For example, in a study of normal reading, Blanchard, McConkie, Zola and Wolverton (1984) briefly masked a fixated word after a carefully controlled interval and replaced it with another word, differing by just one letter. If we assume that this (nonvisible) change occurred after attention had shifted to an adjoining word, it should not have been detectable and only the first word should have been reported. In the experiment of Blanchard et al. this was often the case, but subjects sometimes also reported seeing both words and sometimes they saw only the second, even when the change took place as late as 120 ms after initial fixation on the first word. This experiment is difficult to interpret, but offers a challenge to the idea of attention-switching because it suggests that information in the fovea and parafovea may be processed throughout a fixation. That is, beyond the point in time where parafoveal influences are known to occur.

The notion that attention might be shared between locations appears to conflict with neurophysiological evidence implicating attention in the *selection* of saccade targets (Klein, 1980; Wurtz, Goldberg and Robinson, 1980) and with the associated, and widely accepted, view of attention as a metaphorical 'spotlight'. But alternative neurophysiological models interpret the available behavioural evidence in terms of competitive interactions between simultaneous, spatially separated, stimuli (e.g. Desimone, 1998). For example, Hoffman (1998) has recently suggested that atten-tion can be allocated to more than one *discrete* location simultaneously. In any case, it is an objection which cannot be pressed too far by proponents of the sequential attention-allocation position since, even in its most recent version (Reichle et al., 1998), the claim is made that foveal processing continues up to the point of lexical access, while, at the same time, a parafoveal target is selected and a saccade towards it prepared. Henderson (1992), in a careful review, sees it as essentially an empirical question: foveal-on-parafoveal interactions, spill-over effects and the preview effect *can* be interpreted in terms of parallel allocation of attention, but, for Henderson, the evidence does not point that way. In the next section I want to reconsider just how convincing that evidence is.

Parafoveal-on-foveal effects

As noted, modulation of the preview effect by foveal load is compatible with a degree of parallel processing. It could, for example, be interpreted in terms of the expansion or contraction of the perceptual span (Henderson and Ferreira, 1993). But it may equally well be interpreted in terms of competition for attentional resources, as a delay in switching attention, or as a change in the relative timing of a pre-lexical familiarity check (the interpretation favoured by Reichle et al., 1998). On the other hand, the interpretation of any obtained modulation in the reverse direction (i.e. 'parafoveal-on-foveal' effects) would be much less ambiguous (see also Chapters 9 and 10). If the difficulty of an as-yet-unfixated word influences processing efficiency on a currently fixated word, such an outcome is plainly incompatible with the sequential allocation of attention, although it would not, of course, be incompatible with a parallel-processing account.

Until recently, the evidence for parafoveal-on-foveal cross-talk was generally negative. Two studies are commonly cited. First, Carpenter and Just (1983) used linear regression techniques to partition variance in gaze duration in normal reading between a number of measures, including length and word frequency. Features of word $n + 1$ had negligible effects on fixation times on word n. The problem with this conclusion, however, is that Carpenter and Just found no apparent modulation of preview advantage, in the form of an n on $n - 1$ interaction. It seems possible that the regression technique was simply too insensitive to deal with the issue. Second, Henderson and Ferreira (1993) manipulated the frequency of successive words embedded in short sentences. This study showed a clear preview effect, but processing time on word n was not influenced by the frequency of word $n + 1$. Indeed, foveal inspection time was slightly *shorter* when the word lying in the parafovea was of low rather than high frequency. It appeared that, as predicted by the serial-sequential attention-allocation model, parafoveal information only became available *after* a foveal word had been processed. Unfortunately, there are also some unsatisfactory aspects to this study. In particular, refixation rate on the foveal word was very low, suggesting that the stimulus items defined as 'difficult' were relatively easy to process. Furthermore, the manipulation of word frequency was itself problematic. For the chosen manipulation of difficulty to be effective, it would have been necessary for words to be completely identified in the parafovea and little is known about the circumstances under which this occurs (Rayner and Sereno, 1994). It may have been more sensible to manipulate sub-lexical properties of the parafoveal target, such as initial letter frequency (Lima and Inhoff, 1985; Pynte, Kennedy and Murray, 1991; Rayner, 1978; Rayner, McConkie and Zola, 1980). Thus, although the outcome provides no support at all for operation of parafoveal-on-foveal cross-talk, there is a real possibility that the chosen parafoveal manipulation was ineffective. It may be premature, on the basis of this null effect, to conclude that parafoveal-on-foveal effects do not occur.

Kennedy (1995, 1998) reexamined the question using the 'looks–means' decision task described by Kennedy and Murray (1996). Participants viewed a fixation marker, which was then replaced by the simultaneous display of a string of three words. The marker ensured tight control over fixation position on the third letter of the initial 'prompt', which was invariably either the word 'looks' or the word 'means'. Depending on which of these was presented, participants judged whether the two adjacent words had the same spelling or the same meaning. All the experimental materials were allocated to the 'looks' condition and measures were made *on the prompt word* as a function of the properties of the parafoveal target (in particular, its length, word frequency, and the type and token frequency of its initial three letters). Surprisingly, given the apparent simplicity of the task, the prompt word was refixated about 15% of the time. Furthermore, refixation probability was systematically influenced by both the length and frequency of the target: with significantly *more* refixations on the prompt when the parafoveal target word was short or of high frequency. Restricting the analysis to cases where the prompt was not refixated, there was an effect of the length of the target on fixation duration, but no effect of target word frequency. That is, the obtained frequency effect was restricted to a measure of gaze and primarily driven by changes in refixation rate. However, it was not the case that properties of the target failed altogether to influence behaviour on the prompt. Rather, there was a strong effect of the type frequency of the target's initial letters on prompt fixation duration. Parafoveal targets sharing initial letters with many other words were associated with shorter fixation duration on the (foveal) prompt word.

There was a near-significant tendency for first fixation duration on the target itself to be longer on low-frequency words and a highly significant effect of frequency, in the same direction, for the measure of target gaze duration. The importance of these observations lies in their direction, which take the form of orthodox frequency effects. This argues against the proposition that there may have been something peculiar about the experimental materials which gave rise to the effects of the target's properties on prompt refixation rate. Analysis of the rate of within-word refixation on the target was used to answer the question as to whether gaze differences stemmed from more fixations or longer fixations, or both. The data showed that variation in gaze durations as a function of the manipulated properties of target words did not arise from more fixations alone. Rather, there was a higher incidence of right-going refixations when the initially fixated region of the target was uninformative, suggesting a form of spatial control, with a higher probability of the eyes shifting towards the other, possibly more informative, end of the word. The best explanation of this pattern of data as a whole is in terms of distributed processing, with extended times inspecting the prompt traded off in shorter times on the foveal target, and vice versa. The correlation between time spent on the prompt and on the target was highly significant, and negative. Hill and Murray (Chapter 22) arrive at a similar conclusion regarding processing trade-offs between fixations on two adjacent words.

These data show very clear parafoveal-on-foveal interactions and a tempting conclusion is that parafoveal difficulty acts to modulate foveal processing time (i.e. both refixation rate and fixation duration), with 'difficulty' defined in terms of physical visibility, word frequency, or the constraint provided by a target word's initial letters. Since, for different reasons, long words or low-frequency words are difficult to identify, an early inter-word saccade may be launched towards parafoveal targets with such properties. The effect of the type frequency of the target's initial trigram is less easy to account for in these terms, because the outcome points to an early inter-word saccade associated with cases where many, rather than few, other words shared the target's initial letters. This is discussed further in the next section.

Parafoveal cross-talk revisited

The data described in the preceding section comment on two important theoretical issues. First, foveal processing appears to be modulated by parafoveal difficulty, possibly in the direction of shorter times for more difficult (unfixated) targets. With regard to length and frequency, the obtained effects certainly appear inverted, with shorter inspection times associated with more difficult parafoveal targets. It is hard to escape an interpretation of such a pattern of results in terms of process monitoring, with the mechanism guiding the eyes sensitive to moment-to-moment processing success. When parafoveal information is difficult to acquire, foveal processing, on the average, is terminated earlier. Obviously, any interpretation in these terms runs counter to the strictly 'dumb' control mechanism implicit in many current models of eye movement control (O'Regan, Vitu, Radach and Kerr, 1994; Rayner and Morris, 1992; Reichle et al., 1998). More importantly, parafoveal cross-talk of this kind represents a serious challenge to the principle of serial-sequential attention allocation. Regardless of whether an inter-word saccade is triggered by word identification or by the completion of a preliminary familiarity check, once attention is switched from word n to $n + 1$, it is not possible for properties of $n + 1$ to influence behaviour on n. However, since the theoretical cost of challenging this outcome is relatively high, it is worth considering some possible objections.

The most obvious problem relates to the task. The looks–means task is obviously a weak analogue of normal reading and could well have induced task-specific strategies. For example, since the prompt was invariably either the word 'looks' or 'means', and was seen up to two hundred times in a session, it is plausible that deep processing (of either prompt or target) would be discouraged. Possibly both words came to be treated as a single entity, processed from an 'extremely sub-optimal' viewing position [7]. Certainly, the prompt word itself imposed a very low foveal load. A more general objection can be raised with respect to any laboratory task. Many eye movement effects found in laboratory studies of words viewed in isolation (e.g. the effects of word frequency on fixation duration, or the effect of initial landing position on gaze or refixation rate) become much less reliable when examined in the context of normal reading (Rayner, 1995; but see also Vitu, O'Regan and Mittau, 1990). Claims regarding eye movement control in reading which rest on the use of simplified laboratory tasks are bound to be viewed with some suspicion.

The clothing-search task

I have recently completed out some further experimental work (Kennedy, in press) attempting to address the methodological objections raised in the previous section while, at the same time, obtaining data on parafoveal-on-foveal effects using a wider range of materials and a less restricted experimental procedure. A variant of the 'clothing-search' task was used (Schroyens et al., 1999). Subjects were still asked to read a sequence of three words, but a different set of unrelated words occurred on each trial. In particular, the crucial initial word (the equivalent of the prompt in the looks–means task) varied from trial to trial. The task was to spot rare occurrences of an article of clothing (which were always allocated to filler items). Foveal load on each trial was at a level characteristic of normal reading. The task has reasonable face validity because each word must be processed for meaning and there is no way the decision can be made on the basis of minimal physical features, such as the occurrence of a single letter.

   Two experimental manipulations were employed. In the first, as in the looks–means task, the display was arranged so that the initial fixation invariably fell at the third letter of word 1. In the second, an attempt was made to reduce the effect of the rather artificial predetermined initial fixation point. One way achieving this would have been to embed the experimental materials into sentences (the route followed by Henderson and Ferreira, 1993, and Kennison and Clifton, 1995), but this brings its own problems. As Kennison and Clifton point out, launch position on the first word in normal reading is necessarily uncontrolled and refixations inevitably result in a rather subtle confounding between the frequency of the first

---

7 This account is ruled out if a privileged status is accorded to the space between consecutive words, but it is compatible with the 'word-group' hypothesis suggested by Radach (1996).

word and the visibility of the second. This confounding is systematic and gives rise to a paradoxical outcome: since refixations are less probable on high-frequency words, the word following a high-frequency word in normal reading may be harder than normal to process. Thus, to draw completely unambiguous conclusions about parafoveal processing a given target word must be in the parafovea at the same eccentricity across the manipulated conditions, something which is effectively impossible to achieve using a completely unconstrained task. The alternative is to introduce more normal reading dynamics directly into the task, while maintaining control over both the experimental materials and physical aspects of the display. This was the solution adopted in the second manipulation.

A variant of a procedure first employed by Vitu (1991) was used. Following a fixation mark, participants were confronted with a sequence like:

zzzzz zzzzzz zzzzz abbey enemy

with initial fixation on the third letter of the first z-string and instructed to examine each string in turn. Once a saccade passed an invisible boundary, defined as the final letter of the second z-string, the third z-string was replaced by the word 1 for that trial, producing, for example, the display:

zzzzz zzzzzz trade abbey enemy

As before, the fixation mark ensured a stable initial fixation point, but thereafter a sequence of saccades was executed towards the three experimental items.

The materials for the experiment comprised the sets of 96 five-letter and 96 nine-letter words described in Kennedy (1998). For each word length, there were eight sets of twelve target words, selected to meet a criterion (Kuçera and Francis, 1967) defining: (1) high and low values of word frequency (244 vs. 8 per million); (2) high and low values of the number of words in the norms having the same initial letters (148 vs. 12); and (3) high and low values of the token frequency of their initial three letters (2925 vs. 175). There were also 192 five-letter words, all with a frequency greater than 90 per million, allocated as an initial word (i.e. the equivalent of the 'prompt' in the looks–means task). Each subject received a different random allocation of these initial words to targets. Finally, stimulus word triples were constructed by the addition of a third word, 4–8 letters in length, selected at random from 192 words with a frequency between 70 and 90 per million. Sets of word triples thus comprised word 1 ('trade' in the example above), the target word ('abbey'), and a final control word ('enemy'). There were also 40 sets of word triples employed as fillers, constructed from words of varying frequency, 4–8 letters in length. Twenty words denoting items of clothing were randomly allocated to one of the three possible positions in half the fillers.

Consider first the case where the experimental procedure determined an initial

Table 1

Data derived from the task involving initial fixation

	Five-letter target		Nine-letter target	
	High WF	Low WF	High WF	Low WF
(A) Fixed initial fixation:				
Word 1 fixation duration				
High type frequency	291	288	288	288
Low type frequency	296	278	289	285
Target fixation duration				
High type frequency	264	259	241	246
Low type frequency	246	269	243	253
(B) Initial z-strings:				
Word 1 gaze duration				
High type frequency	284	282	261	260
Low type frequency	272	268	265	267
Target gaze duration				
High type frequency	328	330	373	389
Low type frequency	320	356	361	407

(A) Initial fixation on character position 3 on word 1: 'single-case' fixation duration (ms) on word 1 as a function of (1) length, (2) word frequency and (3) type frequency of the initial trigram of a parafoveal target lying one character to the right of word 1. The table also shows first fixation duration on the target as a function of the same properties. (B) Initial fixation on a sequence of z-strings, followed by a sequence of saccades towards word 1: gaze duration (ms) on word 1 and on the target as a function of the same variables shown in (A).

fixation point on character 3 of word 1 [8]. As in the looks–means task, there was a significant tendency to refixate this word as a function of the length of the parafoveal target word. The pattern of these refixations took the same form, with an increased tendency to shift the eyes within the current stimulus if the 'down-stream' target word was short rather than long. Refixation probability was 0.12 when the target was short and 0.09 when it was long. Virtually all refixations were right-going, serving to bring the target word closer to the fixation point. Thus, to arrive at an estimate of parafoveal cross-talk from a fixed foveal location, uncontaminated by systematic changes in prompt refixation rate, a separate analysis was carried out on those cases (i.e. about 90% of the data) where the prompt was fixated once. These data are shown in the first two rows of Table 1. Since there were no effects of the token frequency of the target's initial letters, the data are shown collapsed over

8 These data are discussed in more detail in Kennedy (in press).

this variable. There was a significant effect of target word frequency, with fixation duration significantly *longer* when the target word was a high-frequency word (high = 291 ms, low = 285 ms). For this task, and perhaps particularly when the target word is short, lexical properties of an unfixated parafoveal target clearly act to modulate foveal inspection time. The outcome is consistent with the results of the looks–means task, suggesting that parafoveal processing difficulty acts to trigger an early inter-word saccade. Table 1 also shows quite strikingly how processing on word 1 is traded off when the target is eventually inspected directly. An analysis of total processing time (word 1 gaze plus target first fixation duration) showed no effect of any of the manipulated variables. Parafoveal-on-foveal cross-talk is obviously not restricted to the conditions of low foveal load characteristic of the looks–means task: indeed, it appears to be relatively ubiquitous. However, it remains the case that the experimental procedure employed was unlike normal reading. In particular, it is worrying, given the extreme simplicity of the task, that the absolute level of inspection time on word 1, which was 40–50 ms longer than might obtain in normal reading. The second, z-string, manipulation addressed this issue by providing a better approximation to normal reading dynamics with a sequence of saccades prior to the initial fixation on the experimental items.

The relevant data are shown in section (B) of Table 1, again collapsed over the variable of target token frequency. Measured gaze duration (270 ms) was, in fact, reliably shorter than in the task involving initial fixation on word 1 (295 ms). In this respect, average gaze duration in the z-string task represents a reasonable approximation to values found in normal reading (e.g. Kennedy, 1998; Rayner, 1995, table 2). The average refixation rate on word 1 was 0.10, but since it did not vary systematically with any of the manipulated variables, separate treatment of 'single-fixation' cases was not called for. As is evident in Table 1, by far the largest effect exerted on word 1 gaze derived from the length and the initial trigram frequency of the parafoveal target word. Gaze on word 1 was reliably longer for short targets (short = 276 ms, long = 263 ms), the direction of this effect confirming previous observations that foveal gaze is reduced in the presence of long parafoveal targets. There was also a significant interaction between target length and the type frequency, or constraint, of the target's initial trigram. For short parafoveal targets, gaze on word 1 was significantly shorter when target shared its initial letters with few other words (high frequency = 283 ms; low frequency = 270 ms). The small difference in the opposite direction for long targets did not approach significance.

In contrast to the manipulation where subjects began each trial with a steady fixation on word 1, there were no effects of target word frequency. The pattern of results found for the looks–means task hints at a possible explanation, since for that task the effects of word frequency were only evident when there was opportunity for relatively long inspection time on the prompt. The determining factor appears to be the effective availability of parafoveal information, with effects of parafoveal word frequency on foveal inspection time either when the eyes are very close to the target for part of the time (particularly when the target is short) or when relatively extended parafoveal inspection occurs. Inspection time overall was shorter in the z-string task and it appears plausible that this restricted parafoveal lexical processing, while allowing strong sub-lexical effects (e.g. initial letter constraint). Fortunately, this speculation can be tested directly by means of a post-hoc analysis of word 1 gaze, restricted to relatively long individual fixation durations, where an effect of target word frequency would be predicted. This analysis was carried out on the z-string data set, treating all individual prompt fixations < 200 ms as missing cases. As predicted, a reliable frequency effect was obtained, taking the same 'inverted' form (high frequency = 287 ms, low frequency = 277 ms). This outcome supports the idea that parafoveal lexical processing is associated with extended foveal inspection. There was also clear evidence of a processing trade-off in this task, with analyses on the combined word 1 and target gaze showing no reliable effects of any of the manipulated variables. Finally, as Table 1 shows (at least for short targets), time on word 1 was shorter when the target word was highly constrained. This conflicts with the robust effect of type frequency found in the looks–means task. Further work will be needed to resolve this discrepancy, but the most likely account is in terms of mutual interactions between properties of foveal and parafoveal items (Kennedy, Pynte and Ducrot, in prep.).

The data from the z-string experiment serve to dispel reservations regarding the low ecological validity of the looks–means task. The principal risk of any laboratory task is that subjects may develop specific strategies which do not demand lexical processing and the experiment may end up delivering data of little relevance to normal reading. The z-string experiment escapes this criticism: lexical processing was not only possible, it was essential to effective performance on the task and, as Table 1 illustrates, both the size and direction of the word frequency effect on the target word, when it was eventually inspected, were in the expected direction. Furthermore, apart from the gaze duration on the very first z-string (which, at 288 ms, was rather long) all other parameters of eye movement behaviour fell easily within the normal range, with values of gaze duration on both word 1 and the target very similar to those found in studies of text and sentence processing. Similarly, average saccade extent approaching word 1 (6.4 characters) and approaching the target (6.2 characters) were within the normal range.

The question raised was whether parafoveal-on-foveal cross-talk can be demonstrated under conditions involving a genuine foveal load and involving a more naturalistic task. The answer is clearly positive. Regarding the effect of target length, inspection of a foveal stimulus is generally shorter, and refixation rate lower, when the next word is long (nine letters) rather than short (five letters). The most parsimonious account of this outcome (which is also consistent with the results as a whole) is that less parafoveal processing is possible when the target is long, and a primary inter-word saccade is launched earlier when processing is restricted by low visibility of a target. Such a claim is, of course, controversial to the extent that it implies a degree of process monitoring and suggests that parafoveal processing may have immediate rather than delayed effects on the processes of eye movement control. But parafoveal cross-talk was not restricted to the effects of length. Although the token familiarity of the target word's initial letters had little effect on prompt processing time, both the word frequency of a target word and the ability of its initial letters to constrain its identification had powerful effects. Contrary to the conclusions of Henderson and Ferreira (1993)[9], a parafoveal processing burden has clear effects on concurrent foveal processing.

Conclusion

These data, together with other data presented in this section of the present volume, represent a serious challenge to models of eye movement control in reading based on the sequential allocation of attention. I have suggested that such models initially appealed to the concept of sequential attention allocation because reading was seen as a kind of surrogate listening. Inter-word spaces thus came to play a crucial role as cues to segmentation: determining where successive saccades are launched as words are processed 'in order'. In this context it is clear why suggestions that 'unspaced text' (i.e. without any inter-word spaces) can be read quite well (Epelboim, Booth and Steinman, 1993) should be seen as peculiarly subversive and rejected with vigour (Rayner and Pollatsek, 1996; see also Epelboim, Booth and Steinman, 1996). Partly this is because inter-word spaces effectively underpin the notion that the 'primitive object level' in reading is the word. But, more importantly, they define the boundary of attention. Thus, while it has long been accepted that parallel processing of letters takes place *within* the word (Slowiaczek and Rayner, 1987), processing *between* words has been seen as necessarily sequential. The historical antecedents of this view can be found in the seductive, but fallacious, belief that the processing demands of listening and reading are effectively identical. But this is to ignore the fact that text is a spatially extended array allowing for substantial processing interactions between words in parallel. It will, of course, be argued that abandoning the sequential assumption removes much of the explanatory power and elegance of the attention-switching approach. In the original Morrison

---

9 In fact, as noted in the Introduction, Henderson and Ferreira (1993) also found that the time spent inspecting a foveal target was *shorter* when the word in the parafovea was difficult. Although nonsignificant, the obtained difference (high frequency = 252 ms, low frequency = 244) was of about the same magnitude as that found in the experiments reported here.

model, a simple monitoring of 'foveal processing success' was enough to determine the timing of the primary inter-word saccade. Notwithstanding the fact that the most recent attention-switching model (Reichle et al., 1998) permits saccade preparation in the absence of an attentional shift, if processing over more than one location must be taken into account, the nature of the control structure becomes undeniably more complicated. But the serial-sequential attention-allocation hypothesis cannot easily survive a demonstration that properties of words in the parafovea (physical, sub-lexical and lexical) influence current foveal processing and future models of the reader's eye movements will need to acknowledge this fact.

Acknowledgements

I am deeply indebted to Albrecht Inhoff, Wayne Murray, Joël Pynte, Ralph Radach and Françoise Vitu for many helpful comments on earlier versions of this chapter. The experimental work described was supported in part by a grant from the European Union under the BIOMED Programme (Grant No BMHI-CT94-1441).

References

Baccino, T. and Pynte, J. (1994). Spatial coding and discourse models during text reading. Language and Cognitive Processes, 9, 143–155.

Blanchard, H.E., McConkie, G.W., Zola, D. and Wolverton, G.S. (1984). Time course of visual information utilization during fixations in reading. Journal of Experimental Psychology: Human Perception and Performance, 10, 75–89.

Bouma, H. (1973). Visual interference in the parafoveal recognition of initial and final letters of words. Vision Research, 13, 767–782.

Bouma, H. and de Voogd, A.H. (1974). On the control of eye saccades in reading. Vision Research, 14, 273–284.

Brysbaert, M. and Vitu, F. (1998). Word-skipping: implications for theories of eye movement control in reading. In: G. Underwood (Ed.), Eye Guidance in Reading and Scene Perception. Oxford: Elsevier, pp. 135–147.

Carpenter, P.A. and Just, M.A. (1983). What your eyes do while your mind is reading. In: K. Rayner (Ed.), Eye Movements in Reading: Perceptual and Language Processes. New York: Academic Press, pp. 275–305.

Christie, J. and Just, M.A. (1975). Remembering the location and content of sentences in a prose passage. Journal of Educational Psychology, 68, 702–710.

Cocklin, T.G., Ward, N.J., Chen, H.C. and Juola, J.F. (1984). Factors influencing readability of rapidly presented text segments. Memory and Cognition, 12, 431–442.

Desimone, R. (1998). Visual attention mediated by biased competition in extrastriate visual cortex. Philosophical Transactions of the Royal Society (Biological Sciences), 353, 1245–1256.

Epelboim, J., Booth, J.R. and Steinman, R.M. (1993). Reading unspaced text: implications for theories of eye movements. Vision Research, 34, 1735–1766.

Epelboim, J., Booth, J.R. and Steinman, R.M. (1996). Much ado about nothing: the place of space in text. Vision Research, 36, 465–470.

Eriksen, C.W. and St. James, J.D. (1986). Visual attention within and around the field of focal attention: a zoom lens model. Perception and Psychophysics, 56, 277–287.

Ferreira, F. and Clifton, C., Jr. (1986). The independence of syntactic processing. Journal of Memory and Language, 25, 348–368.

Frazier, L. and Rayner, K. (1982). Making and correcting errors during sentence comprehension: eye movements in the analysis of structurally ambiguous sentences. Cognitive Psychology, 14, 178–210.

Goldman-Eisler, F. (1968). Psycholinguistics: Experiments in Spontaneous Speech. London: Academic Press.

Henderson, J.M. (1992). Visual attention and eye movement control during reading and picture viewing. In: K. Rayner (Ed.), Eye Movements and Visual Cognition. New York: Springer, pp. 260–283.

Henderson, J.M. and Ferreira, F. (1990). Effects of foveal processing difficulty on the perceptual span in reading: implications for attention and eye movement control. Journal of Experimental Psychology: Learning, Memory and Cognition, 16, 417–429.

Henderson, J.M. and Ferreira, F. (1993). Eye movement control during reading: fixation measures foveal but not parafoveal processing difficulty. Canadian Journal of Experimental Psychology, 47, 201–221.

Hoffman, J.E. (1998). Visual attention and eye movements. In: H. Pashler (Ed.), Attention. Hove: Psychology Press, pp. 119–150.

Holmes, V.M., Kennedy, A. and Murray, W.S. (1987). Syntactic ambiguity and the garden path. Quarterly Journal of Experimental Psychology, 39A, 277–294.

Hyönä, J. (1995). Do irregular letter combinations attract readers' attention? Evidence from fixation locations in words. Journal of Experimental Psychology: Human Perception and Performance, 21, 68–81.

Hyönä, J. and Pollatsek, A. (1998). Reading Finnish compound words: eye fixations are affected by component morphemes. Journal of Experimental Psychology: Human Perception and Performance, 24, 1612–1627.

Inhoff, A.W., Briihl, D. and Schwartz, J. (1996). Compound effects differ in reading, on-line naming, and delayed naming tasks. Memory and Cognition, 24, 466–476.

Juola, J.F., Ward, N.J. and McNamara, T. (1982). Visual search and reading of rapid serial presentations of letter strings, words and texts. Journal of Experimental Psychology: General, 111, 208–227.

Just, M.A. and Carpenter, P.A. (1980). A theory of reading: from eye fixations to comprehension. Psychological Review, 87, 329–354.

Kennedy, A. (1978). Eye movements and the integration of semantic information during reading. In: M.M. Gruneberg, R.N. Sykes and P.E. Morris (Eds.), Practical Aspects of Memory. London: Academic Press, pp. 484–490.

Kennedy, A. (1983). On looking into space. In: K. Rayner (Ed.), Eye Movements in Reading: Perceptual and Language Processes. New York: Academic Press, pp. 237–250.

Kennedy, A. (1986). The case for place: text arrangement and reading skill — Invited Tutorial Review. Current Psychological Research and Reviews, 5, 94–104.

Kennedy, A. (1992). The spatial coding hypothesis. In: K. Rayner (Ed.), Eye Movements and Visual Cognition. New York: Springer, pp. 379–397.

Kennedy, A. (1995). The influence of parafoveal words on foveal inspection time. AMLaP-95 Conference, Edinburgh.

Kennedy, A. (1998). The influence of parafoveal words on foveal inspection time: evidence for a processing trade-off. In: G. Underwood (Ed.), Eye Guidance in Reading and Scene Perception. Oxford: Elsevier, pp. 149–223.

Kennedy, A. (in press). Parafoveal processing in word recognition. Quarterly Journal of Experimental Psychology.

Kennedy, A. and Baccino, T. (1995). The effects of screen refresh rate on editing operations using a computer mouse pointing device. Quarterly Journal of Experimental Psychology, 48A, 55–71.

Kennedy, A. and Murray, W.S. (1984). Inspection-times for words in syntactically ambiguous sentences under three presentation conditions. Journal of Experimental Psychology: Human Perception and Performance, 10, 833–849.

Kennedy, A. and Murray, W.S. (1987). Spatial coding and reading: some comments on Monk (1985). Quarterly Journal of Experimental Psychology, 39A, 649–718.

Kennedy, A. and Murray, W.S. (1996). Eye movement control during the inspection of words under conditions of pulsating illumination. European Journal of Cognitive Psychology, 8, 381–403.

Kennedy, A., Murray, W.S., Jennings, F. and Reid, C. (1989). Parsing complements: comments on the generality of the principle of minimal attachment. Language and Cognitive Processes, 4, 51–76.

Kennedy, A., Pynte, J. and Ducrot, S. (in prep.). Mutual interactions of foveal and parafoveal properties of words in continuous reading.

Kennison, S.M. and Clifton, C. (1995). Determinants of parafoveal preview benefit in high and low working memory capacity readers: implications for eye movement control. Journal of Experimental Psychology: Learning, Memory and Cognition, 21, 68–81.

Klein, R. (1980). Does oculomotor readiness mediate control of visual attention? In: R.S. Nickerson (Ed.), Attention and Performance VIII. Hillsdale, NJ: Erlbaum, pp. 259–276.

Kliegl, R., Olson, R.K. and Davidson, B.J. (1982). Regression analyses as a tool for studying reading processes: comments on Just and Carpenter's eye fixation theory. Memory and Cognition, 10, 287–296.

Kuçera, H. and Francis, W.N. (1967). Computational Analysis of Present-Day American English. Providence, RI: Brown University Press.

Legge, G.E., Klitz, T.S. and Tjan, B.S. (1997). Mr. Chips: an ideal-observer model of reading. Psychological Review, 104, 524–553.

Lima, S.D. and Inhoff, A.W. (1985). Lexical access during eye fixations in reading: effects of word–initial letter sequence. Journal of Experimental Psychology: Human Perception and Performance, 11, 272–285.

McClelland, J.L. and Mozer, M.C. (1986). Perceptual interactions in two-word displays: familiarity and similarity effects. Journal of Experimental Psychology: Human Perception and Performance, 12, 18–35.

McConkie, G.W. (1979). On the role and control of eye movements in reading. In: P.A. Kolers, M.E. Wrolstad and H. Bouma (Eds.), Processing of Visible Language: Vol. I. New York: Plenum Press, pp. 37–48.

McConkie, G.W., Kerr, P.W., Reddix, M.D. and Zola, D. (1988). Eye movement control during reading: I. The location of initial eye fixations on words. Vision Research, 29, 1107–1118.

McConkie, G.W. and Zola, D. (1984). Eye movement control during reading: the effects of word units. In: W. Prinz and A.T. Sanders (Eds.), Cognition and Motor Processes. Berlin: Springer, pp. 63–74.

McConkie, G.W. and Zola, D. (1987). Visual attention during eye fixations while reading. In: M. Coltheart (Ed.), Attention and Performance XII: The Psychology of Reading. Hillsdale, NJ: Erlbaum, pp. 385–401.

Mitchell, D.C. (1994). Sentence parsing. In: M.A. Gernsbacher (Ed.), Handbook of Psycholinguistics. New York: Academic Press, pp. 375–409.

Monk, A.F. (1985). Theoretical note: co-ordinate systems in visual word recognition. Quarterly Journal of Experimental Psychology, 37A, 613–626.

Morrison, R.E. (1984). Manipulation of stimulus onset delay in reading: evidence for parallel programming of saccades. Journal of Experimental Psychology: Human Perception and Performance, 10, 667–682.

Murray, W.S. and Kennedy, A. (1988). Spatial coding and the processing of anaphor by good and poor readers: evidence from eye movement analyses. Quarterly Journal of Experimental Psychology, 40A, 693–718.

Murray, W.S., Watt, S.M. and Kennedy, A. (in prep.). Modality, processing options and the Garden Path. Memory and Language (submitted).

O'Regan, J.K. (1989). Visual acuity, lexical structure and eye movements in word recognition. In: B. Elsendoorn and H. Bouma (Eds.), Working Models of Human Perception. London: Academic Press, pp. 261–292.

O'Regan, J.K. (1990). Eye movements and reading. In: E. Kowler (Ed.), Eye Movements and Their Role in Visual and Cognitive Processes. Amsterdam: Elsevier, pp. 395–453.

O'Regan, J.K., Vitu, F., Radach, R. and Kerr, P. (1994). Effects of local processing and oculomotor factors in eye movement guidance in reading. In: J. Ygge and G. Lennerstrand (Eds.), Eye Movements in Reading. New York: Pergamon Press, pp. 329–348.

Posner, M.I. (1980). Orienting of attention. Quarterly Journal of Experimental Psychology, 32, 3–25.

Posner, M.I. and Cohen, Y. (1984). Components of visual orienting. In: H. Bouma and D. Bouwhuis (Eds.), Attention and Performance X. Hove: Erlbaum, pp. 531–556.

Pynte, J., Kennedy, A. and Murray, W.S. (1991). Within-word inspection strategies in continuous reading: time course of perceptual, lexical and contextual processes. Journal of Experimental Psychology: Human Perception and Performance, 17, 458–470.

Pynte, J., Kennedy, A., Murray, W.S. and Courrieu, P. (1988). The effects of spatialisation on the processing of ambiguous pronominal reference. In: G. Luer, U. Lass and J. Shallo-Hoffman (Eds.), Eye Movement Research: Physiological and Psychological Aspects. Göttingen: Hogrefe.

Radach, R. (1996). Blickbewegungen beim Lesen: Psychologische Aspekte der Determination von Fixationspositionen (Eye Movements in Reading). Münster: Waxmann.

Radach, R. and Kempe, V. (1993). An individual analysis of initial fixation positions in reading. In: G. d'Ydewalle and J. Van Rensbergen (Eds.), Perception and Cognition: Advances in Eye Movement Research. Amsterdam: Elsevier, pp. 213–225.

Radach, R. and McConkie, G.W. (1998). Determinants of fixation positions in words during reading. In: G. Underwood (Ed.), Eye Guidance in Reading and Scene Perception. Oxford: Elsevier, pp. 77–100.

Rayner, K. (1978). Eye movements in reading and information processing. Psychological Bulletin, 85, 618–660.

Rayner, K. (1995). Eye movements and cognitive processes in reading, visual search, and scene perception. In: J.M. Findlay, R. Walker and R.W. Kentridge (Eds.), Eye Movement Research: Mechanisms, Processes and Applications. Amsterdam: North-Holland, pp. 3–21.

Rayner, K. and Duffy, S.A. (1986). Lexical complexity and fixation times in reading: effects of word frequency, verb complexity, and lexical ambiguity. Memory and Cognition, 14, 191–201.

Rayner, K. and Frazier, L. (1987). Parsing temporarily ambiguous complements. Quarterly Journal of Experimental Psychology, 39A, 657–673.

Rayner, K., McConkie, G.W. and Zola, D. (1980). Integrating information across eye movements. Cognitive Psychology, 12, 206–226.

Rayner, K. and Morris, R. (1992). Eye movement control in reading: evidence against semantic pre-processing. Journal of Experimental Psychology: Human Perception and Performance, 18, 163–172.

Rayner, K. and Pollatsek, A. (1989). The Psychology of Reading. Englewood Cliffs, NJ: Prentice-Hall.

Rayner, K. and Pollatsek, A. (1996). Reading unspaced text is not easy: comments on the implications of Epelboim et al.'s (1994) study for models of eye movement control in reading. Vision Research, 36, 461–465.

Rayner, K. and Sereno, S. (1994). Regressive eye movements and sentence parsing: on the use of regression-contingent analysis. Memory and Cognition, 22, 281–285.

Reichle, E.D., Pollatsek, A., Fisher, D.L. and Rayner, K. (1998). Towards a model of eye movement control in reading. Psychological Review, 105, 125–157.

Rubin, G.S. and Turano, K. (1992). Reading without saccadic eye movements. Vision Research, 32, 895–902.

Rubin, G.S. and Turano, K. (1994). Low vision reading with sequential word presentation. Vision Research, 34, 1723–1733.

Schiepers, C. (1980). Response latency and accuracy in visual word recognition. Perception and Psychophysics, 27, 71–81.

Schroyens, W., Vitu, F., Brysbaert, M. and d'Ydewalle, G. (1999). Visual attention and eye-movement control during reading: the case of parafoveal processing. Quarterly Journal of Experimental Psychology, 52A, 1021–1046.

Slowiaczek, M.L. and Rayner, K. (1987). Sequential masking during eye fixations in reading. Bulletin of the Psychonomic Society, 25, 175–178.

Underwood, G., Clews, S. and Everatt, J. (1990). How do readers know where to look next? Local information distributions influence eye fixations. Quarterly Journal of Experimental Psychology, 42A, 39–65.

Vitu, F. (1991). The influence of parafoveal pre-processing and linguistic context on the optimal landing position effect. Perception and Psychophysics, 50, 58–75.

Vitu, F., McConkie, G.W. and Zola, D. (1998). In: G. Underwood (Ed.), Eye Guidance in Reading and Scene Perception. Oxford: Elsevier, pp. 101–124.

Vitu, F. and O'Regan, J.K. (1995). A challenge to current theories of eye movements in reading. In: J.M. Findlay, R. Walker and R.W. Kentridge (Eds.), Eye Movement Research: Mechanisms, Processes and Applications. Amsterdam: North-Holland, pp. 381–392.

Vitu, F., O'Regan, J.K. and Mittau, M. (1990). Optimal landing position in reading isolated words and continuous text. Perception and Psychophysics, 47, 583–600.

Wurtz, R.H., Goldberg, M.E. and Robinson, D.L. (1980). Behavioural modulation of visual responses in the monkey: stimulus selection for attention and movement. Progress in Psychobiology and Physiological Psychology, 9, 43–83.

CHAPTER 9

Allocation of Visuo-Spatial Attention and Saccade Programming During Reading

Albrecht W. Inhoff
State University of New York at Binghamtom

Ralph Radach
Technical University of Aachen

Matt Starr
State University of New York at Binghamtom

and

Seth Greenberg
Union College

Abstract

Current conceptions of visuo-spatial and lexical processing during reading (e.g., Reichle, Pollatsek, Fisher and Rayner, 1998) assume that attention confines recognition processes to a single word at a time and that interword saccades are triggered by the completion of an initial stage of lexical processing while attention is exclusively allocated to the fixated word. Three experiments examined these assumptions by determining whether readers obtained useful lexical information to the right and left of fixation prior to the initiation of interword saccades. The results of Experiment 1 reveal that lexical information from a parafoveal word to the right of fixation can be obtained before a saccade to this word is committed to action. The results of Experiments 2 and 3 show that readers obtain useful lexical information from a target word to the left of fixation, irrespective of whether the target is subsequently reread. These findings indicate that more than one word is attended at a time during a fixation, that successive areas of attention overlap, and that programming of a saccade to a parafoveally visible word is not completed before attention is allocated to it.

Reading as a Perceptual Process/A. Kennedy, R. Radach, D. Heller and J. Pynte (Editors)
© 2000 Elsevier Science Ltd. All rights reserved

Introduction

The written language signal differs fundamentally from the spoken language signal. In contrast to auditory speech, where the signal is dynamic and sequential, written language is static and a multitude of spatially ordered symbols can be available at each point in time. Speech and script also differ in that the listener receives an ordered set of speech symbols, whereas it is up to the reader to adhere to and follow the spatial ordering of visible language symbols.

Moreover, reading differs from listening in that the encoding of a sequence of linguistic symbols requires overt action and decision making (see also Chapter 8). This is because high-acuity visual processing, necessary for the identification of visual symbols, is confined to a relatively small part of the retina, the fovea (corresponding to the 'line of sight') and adjacent parafovea (e.g., Riggs, 1965; for an excellent review see O'Regan, 1990). Irrespective of the potential number of concurrently available visual language symbols, only a limited set of symbols can thus be identified at a time. To overcome these limitations readers move the eyes along lines of print, deciding when and where to move the eyes, so that different segments of text are brought into high-acuity vision. Knowledge of word order is used in the decision making so that saccades can be directed toward successive units of text (though readers occasionally move to prior text for rereading). But to be effective, saccadic decision making must also be coordinated with the success of linguistic analyses, as the eyes must be at or near successive words of text from which linguistic information is sought. The effective coordination of saccade programming and linguistic computations thus constitutes a unique and pivotal element of skilled reading.

Readers acquire useful linguistic information when the eyes are relatively stationary (fixated) in between saccades. Experiments manipulating the visibility of text during individual fixations showed that more information is obtained to the right of fixation than to the left in left-to-right reading (see Rayner and Pollatsek, 1989; Rayner, 1998, for reviews on alphabetic text; and Inhoff and Liu, 1998, for Chinese text). Other experiments showed that the asymmetric shape of effective vision (the perceptual span) is reversed, extending farther to the left when right-to-left ordered Hebrew text is read (Pollatsek, Bolozky, Well and Rayner, 1981) and when reverse-ordered (right-to-left) English text is read (Inhoff, Pollatsek, Posner and Rayner, 1989). The asymmetric horizontal extension of effective vision contrasts with its vertical focusing, as readers usually do not obtain any information from words below a fixated line (Inhoff and Briihl, 1991; Inhoff and Topolski, 1992; Pollatsek, Raney, LaGasse and Rayner, 1993). Spatial asymmetries in the horizontal and the vertical focusing of the perceptual span indicate that readers actively select the spatial area of to-be-analyzed text during a fixation so that they obtain pertinent information from a directly fixated word and the next word(s) within the current line of text.

Spatial selectivity during a fixation is generally assumed to be related to the allocation of visual attention. The current chapter examines readers' allocation of visual attention to text for the purpose of word identification and text comprehension rather than the allocation of visual attention for the purpose of saccade generation. [1]

There is broad agreement in the research community that words constitute functional units for the programming of saccades and for lexical analyses. According to sequential attention-shift models, processing selectivity during reading is accomplished by allocating attention to each individual word in the text until it is recognized. Once recognized, attention is shifted to the next word, yielding a strictly serial, speech-like ordering of recognized words (Henderson and Ferreira, 1990; Inhoff, Pollatsek, Posner and Rayner, 1989; Morrison, 1984; Pollatsek and Rayner, 1990; Rayner and Pollatsek, 1989; Reichle, Pollatsek, Fisher and Rayner, 1998). In the original attention-shift model (Morrison, 1984), completion of lexical access of a fixated word was assumed to lead to a shift of attention to the next word, which, in turn, triggered an eye movement to this word. While this model could explain several features of eye behavior during reading, such as parafoveal preview benefit and word skipping, it also has limitations. For example, it does not include mechanisms to deal with refixations on the current word and regressions back to previously read text. Furthermore, this model could not account for the influence of foveal processing difficulty on the preview benefit from a parafoveal word (for a more detailed discussion see Chapter 27).

To overcome these limitations, a new feature was introduced in the latest version of sequential attention models: a relative decoupling of attention shift and saccade programming [2] allowing for some flexibility in the temporal ordering of attention shift and saccade execution. (Rayner, Reichle and Pollatsek, 1998; Reichle et al., 1998). Word recognition is assumed to involve an initial stage, during which global familiarity is established and lexical access is imminent, and a subsequent stage

---

1 Although almost never considered, the distinction of two different visual selection mechanisms is critical to any attention-based theory of eye movement control. One reason for this is that a single mechanism drawing from a unified resource pool would require that attention is allocated to two places at the same time (Hoffman, 1998). As shown, e.g., by Morris, Rayner and Pollatsek (1990), the target for the next interword saccade is specified very early during a fixation, while 'attention' is assumed to be still focused on the currently fixated word (see below).

2 We will use the term 'saccade programming' when referring to the parameterization of saccades in general. By 'saccade initiation' or 'commitment to action' we will refer to a stage where an imminent saccade has passed a point of no return and can no longer be delayed by linguistic information (McConkie, 1983). This is not necessarily identical to the transition point between Reichle et al.'s (1998) labile and nonlabile saccade programming stages as they refer to the modifiability of spatial saccade parameters.

during which a specific lexical form is accessed so that meaning can be retrieved. Completion of a fixated word's familiarity assessment initiates programming of an interword saccade to the next word in the text and successful access of lexical word form and word meaning initiates a corresponding shift of attention. The programming of an interword saccade thus precedes a corresponding shift of attention; however, since programming of the saccade consumes time, the actual execution of the saccade can lag behind the shifting of attention, which accounts for parafoveal preview benefits. The processing times required to complete both word processing stages are a function of lexical properties of the word such as word frequency, recency of usage, number of lexical neighbors, etc. Their relation, as implemented in the model simulation, is such that the time necessary to complete lexical access is a constant multiple of the time required for the familiarity check. This relation leads to an increasing disparity between both time components as word frequency decreases, which can account for the reduced parafoveal preview benefit when a more difficult word is processed foveally (see below). Similar to previous versions of sequential attention-shift models, interword saccades are triggered by the completion of a certain amount of lexical processing (familiarity check) and usually arrive at the target word only *after* a shift of attention to this word has taken place (see Reichle et al., 1998, fig. 6). On some occasions, when the completion of lexical access takes more time than expected on the basis of the familiarity check, the eyes may be sent to the next word some time *before* a shift of attention can take place. In this case, the saccade is directed back at fixated text, as readers are assumed to be unable to obtain information from a fixated but unattended word. According to Reichle et al. (1998), this mechanism accounts for regressive saccades during reading (for a detailed discussion of regressions see Chapter 12). In sum, the new model (see also Chapter 27) adds flexibility to saccade programming but it does not abandon central claims of prior attention-shift models: the programming of an interword saccade is started as the result of completing an initial stage of lexical processing while attention is exclusively allocated on the fixated word. We will refer to this central claim as the 'sequential attention assumption'.

A formalized version of Reichle et al.'s (1998) model yielded simulated results that were remarkably similar to empirical findings. The empirical support for core assumptions of the model has remained equivocal, however. In particular, there is conflicting evidence as to whether readers can obtain useful linguistic information from the next (parafoveal) word at a time when an interword saccade is not yet committed to action and, according to the sequential attention-shift assumption, no such information should be available. Consistent with sequential attention-shift models, Henderson and Ferreira (1993) showed that the viewing duration on a target word (*N*) was unaffected by the processing difficulty of the next word in the text. In their study, participants read sentences in which a target (*N*) word was followed either by a short or long word that had either a high- or low-frequency of occurrence. Virtually all targets received at least a single fixation, the duration of which was independent of the length and word frequency of the following word. According to sequential attention models, this occurred because the saccade to the parafoveal ($N + 1$) word was committed to action before this word was attended, i.e., before any useful linguistic information could be obtained from it.

Using a word classification task, in which readers were asked to determine whether a pair of two successively fixated words were visually or semantically similar, Kennedy (1998) showed, however, that sublexical properties of the second member of the pair influenced the gaze duration (the cumulated value of all fixations on a word until the eyes move to the right or left of it) of the first member of the pair (see also Kennedy, in press, and Chapter 8). In a recent sentence reading experiment, Inhoff, Starr and Schindler (in press) obtained effects of a parafoveally visible preview on the viewing duration of a fixated word. In our study, participants read declarative sentences that contained a critical two-word sequence consisting of the target and post-target word. For instance, in the sentence "They had to wait for the traffic light to turn green", *traffic* constituted the target word and *light* constituted the post-target word. Four parafoveal post-target viewing conditions were created. One in which the contextually appropriate post-target was visible during all fixations (baseline condition), one in which the post-target word was shown in upper-case (*LIGHT*), one in which the post-target word was replaced with a sequence of dissimilar and orthographically illegal lower-case characters (*govpq*), and one in which it was replaced with a contextually inconsistent lower-case word (*smoke*). Eye-movement-contingent display changes were used to display the post-target base word in lower case (*light*) in all conditions when the eyes moved to the right of the target word. Under these conditions, target gazes were substantially shorter in the baseline condition than in the upper-case and random-letter post-target preview conditions, indicating that readers responded to the visual distinctiveness (upper case) and the orthographic familiarity (randomness of the letter sequence) of the post-target preview. However, not all preview manipulations increased target gazes. Notably, the contextual consistency of the post-target preview word had no overall effect on target gazes.

To accommodate these findings, sequential attention-shift models could be modified. Access to word meaning could be confined by visuo-spatial attention to one word at a time, whereas extraction of visual and orthographic information could encompass all words within the range of effective vision, including a parafoveally visible post-target preview. Hence, readers obtained visual and orthographic information from the parafoveal preview, but no semantic information, prior to the programming of a saccade to it. Though this modification has the advantage of accommodating the current results, it also has major disadvantages. In particular, it implies that there can be temporal gaps in the word recognition process and that the word recognition process can be put on hold at various stages. If, for instance, readers obtained useful orthographic information from the parafoveal word before the fixated word was recognized, then further processing, including the accessing of the parafoveal word's meaning would have to enter a wait state until attention arrived. This wait state would have to be entered, irrespective of the success with which parafoveal word recognition progressed prior to the arrival of attention.

Recent results by Murray (1998) raise the possibility that readers can complete the recognition of a parafoveally visible word while a saccade out of the foveal word is not yet initiated, and hence, according to the sequential attention assumption, attention is still focused on the fixated word. Using a sentence comparison task, in which readers decided whether two successively read sentences were identical, Murray (1998) showed that the last fixation on the initial noun phrase of a sentence (the target expression) was shorter when the subsequently fixated verb (post-target expression) was a plausible continuation (e.g., *the hunters [target] stacked [post-target]* ...) than when it was an implausible continuation (e.g., *the bishops stacked* ...). Readers thus obtained semantic information from the post-target expression before it was fixated.

Allocation of attention may differ in sentence comparison and sentence reading tasks, however, as sentence comparison and sentence reading could impose functionally distinct demands. Readers rarely encounter a succession of two identical or nearly identical sentences, and they rarely face the instruction to compare the contents of successively read sentences. Effects of task demands were evident in a comparison of reading and search tasks, with effects of word frequency being prominent in reading but not in search (Rayner and Raney, 1996). Experiment 1 was thus conducted to determine whether recognition of a post-target word could affect the programming of a saccade toward it when the experimental task comprises normal sentence reading.

Experiment 1

We constructed sentences in which a target word was followed by a post-target word that was either a semantically associated word or an unassociated word. In contrast to Murray (1998), we manipulated the context-independent semantic relatedness of target and post-target words, rather than context-dependent plausibility, as effects of context-independent semantic relatedness accrue relatively fast (e.g., Neely, 1977). The experiment also included a repetition condition in which target and post-target words were nearly identical, the assumption being that readers should be particularly likely to obtain useful orthographic information and lexical information from the post-target word when target and post-target words are nearly identical. The main prediction was straightforward: if readers obtained useful lexical information from the post-target word prior to the programming of a saccade to it, then target viewing durations should be a function of the relatedness of target and post-target words.

Method

Participants
Forty-two State University of New York undergraduate students participated for pay or experimental course credit in the experiment. All participants had normal vision, classified themselves as good readers, and were naive with respect to the purpose of the experiment.

Materials
Twenty-four sentence targets sentences were constructed each containing a target word. None of the targets occupied the two sentence-initial or sentence-final word locations. Each target could be followed by one of three different post-target words. In one post-target condition, referred to as *target repetition* condition, target and post-target words were nearly identical. In another post-target condition, target and post-target words were strongly *associated* according to the norms of Postman and Keppel (1970). In a final condition, target and post-target words were *unassociated*. All post-target words were nouns. The three post-target words that could follow a particular target word were matched for word length, concreteness, and syllabic structure. An attempt was also made to match the three pairs for word frequency. In the repetition condition, the word frequency of post-target words ranged from 3 to 2455 per million, with a mean of 271. The ranges in the associated and unassociated post-target words were 1 to 5145 and 1 to 878, respectively, with corresponding means of 327 and 183. An ANOVA, that compared word frequencies in the three conditions (repetition, associated, unassociated), indicated that the differences between means were not statistically reliable, $F < 1$. All sentences formed syntactically correct and meaningful expressions. A sample sentence with a target and its three different post-target words is shown in Table 1. Three lists were created each of which contained a target paired with a different post-target word. To avoid the detection of target–post-target relationships, each of the three lists also contained 50 filler sentences, none of which contained a word repetition or a highly associated word pair.

Apparatus
Participants were tested in a sound-insulated, dimly illuminated room. A 60-Hz noninterlaced VGA monitor was used to display text (640 × 480 pixels) that was shown in light green on a black background. The distance between readers' eyes

Table 1

A sample sentence, with the target *mother's*, and the three types of post-target words

---

Repetition condition
Did you see the picture of her mother's mother at the meeting?
                                    *   *

Associated condition
Did you see the picture of her mother's father at the meeting?
                                    *   *

Unassociated condition
Did you see the picture of her mother's garden at the meeting?
                                    *   *

The asterisk indicates a hypothetical target to post-target word fixation sequence.

and the monitor was set at 70 cm; at this viewing distance, each letter of text subtended approximately 0.33° of visual angle.

Eye movements were recorded via a fifth-generation dual-Purkinje SRI eye-tracking system. Viewing was binocular but eye movements were recorded from the right eye only. The system has a relative spatial resolution of <10 min of arc and its output was linear over the vertical and horizontal range of the visual display. Analog input from the eye tracker was digitized via a Data Translation 2801-A A-to-D converter housed in a personal computer. The computer controlled the visual display and stored horizontal and vertical fixation coordinates every 2 ms.

Procedure
Participants were tested individually. When a participant arrived in the laboratory, a bite bar was prepared that served to reduce head movements during the experiment. A two-dimensional calibration of the eye-tracking system began the experiment. During calibration, the participant was requested to fixate four monitor positions (left top, right top, left bottom, right bottom) as they sequentially appeared on the screen and to manually depress a mouse button when the indicated location was accurately fixated. Button pressing resulted in the sampling of horizontal and vertical fixation location values for 150 ms. The X/Y A-to-D converter values were then mapped onto the corresponding CRT locations. After calibration was completed, eight character-size squares were illuminated, forming an octagon and the participant's fixation location was indicated on the screen via a green $1/3$ character-size cursor grid. The participant was asked to fixate each of the illuminated locations. During this calibration check phase, the participant's eye position was examined. The participant was reminded that the task was not to move

the cursor into the illuminated square but to merely look at the center of each square. The calibration was considered successful when the computer generated eye position (the green cursor) deviated by no more than one character space from the center of each of the eight squares.

After successful calibration, the participant was asked to fixate a one-character size marker at the left side of the screen and to depress a button to display a passage of text. Button pressing initiated the recording of eye movements and replaced the fixation marker with a sentence, so that the first character of the initial word of the sentence overlay the fixation marker. After sentence reading was completed, participants were asked to manually press another button, which replaced the sentence with the fixation marker and terminated the recording of eye movements for the trial. Reading for sentence meaning was encouraged and participants were occasionally asked to repeat or paraphrase the most recently read sentence. After this, the accuracy of the calibration was checked and, if inaccuracies were detected, a new calibration was initiated. Subsequently, the participant was asked to look at the fixation marker and to initiate the presentation of the next sentence.

Design

Three lists were used and each participant read one list. All lists contained the identical targets, but each target was paired with a different post-target word in each of the lists. List assignment was counterbalanced across three successive participants.

Data analyses

The continuous record of fixation locations was used to determine target and post-target fixation durations. A target word was considered fixated when the point of fixation fell on one of its constituent letters or the blank space preceding it. Similar to Kennedy (1998) and Murray (1998) we measured the first-fixation duration on the target words and cumulated target viewing durations (gaze durations) that included the time spent re-fixating the target before the post-target word was fixated. First fixations and gazes were also used as primary measures in a large number of other psycholinguistic investigations (for methodological background see Inhoff, 1984; Inhoff and Radach, 1998; for a recent review of psycholinguistic research see Rayner and Sereno, 1994).

Instances in which the first recorded fixation of a sentence was on the target word and instances in which the first target fixation followed a regression back to the target were excluded from analysis. Approximately 5% of the data were lost due to hardware failures. All other data were analyzed using a within-subjects analysis of variance (ANOVA) with the factor target–post-target relationship (repetition, associated, unassociated).

Table 2

First-fixation durations, gaze durations (in ms), and interword saccade size as a function of the target–post-target word pair type

Target word	Target–post-target word pair		
	Repetition	Associated	Unassociated
First-fixation durations	216 (36)	216 (38)	226 (39)
'Potential error' fixations	215 (43)	216 (37)	227 (42)
'Nonerror' fixations	219 (52)	219 (50)	226 (58)
Gaze durations	262 (52)	268 (50)	288 (56)
'Potential error' fixations	265 (71)	272 (66)	297 (71)
'Nonerror' fixations	263 (93)	253 (70)	274 (80)

Standard deviations are shown in parentheses.

Results

First-fixation durations and *gaze durations* on target words, as a function of the target–post-target relatedness, are shown in Table 2.

Effects of relatedness were evident in the first-fixation durations, $F(2, 82) = 3.20$, $p < 0.05$ and gaze durations, $F(2, 92) = 5.55$, $p < 0.01$. Paired comparisons revealed significantly shorter target first-fixation durations and target gazes when target and post-target words were identical (repetition condition) than when they were unassociated, $t(41) = 2.45$, $p < 0.025$ and $t(41) = 2.95$, $p < 0.01$, respectively. Furthermore, first-fixation durations and gaze durations on targets were shorter in the associated than the unassociated condition, $t(41) = 1.95$, $p < 0.059$, and $t(41) = 3.02$, $p < 0.01$, respectively. First-fixation durations in the repetition and associated conditions were nearly identical, with the difference amounting to 0 ms and 6 ms, respectively.

Effect sizes, notably in the first-fixation duration durations, were relatively small, raising the possibility that they could have resulted from oculomotor variation. Specifically, an effect of the relatedness of the post-target word on target viewing could have occurred because on some occasions an eye movement intended for the post-target word could have positioned the eyes at the ending letters of the target word. If this was the case, then some target fixations could have reflected the demands of post-target processing rather than the demands of target processing, effectively confounding target and post-target analyses.[3]

---

3 The Gaussian distribution of landing positions of progressive interword saccades aimed at the next word peaks about halfway between word beginning and word center (e.g., Reichle et al., 1998, and Chapter 11). Due to systematic oculomotor variation, the distribution is truncated at

Table 3

Post-target processing in Experiment 1 consisting of skipping rates, interword saccades to subsequently fixated post-target words, first fixations, and post-target gazes

| | Target–post-target word pair | | |
	Repetition	Associated	Unassociated
Skipping rates (%)	12.6 (1.6)	12.5 (1.2)	9.5 (1)
Interword saccade size (character)	7.1 (1.3)	7.1 (1.1)	7.1 (1)
First fixation durations (ms)	239 (50)	229 (44)	232 (49)
Gaze durations (ms)	292 (63)	276 (60)	276 (60)

Standard deviations are shown in parentheses.

To examine this possibility, target first-fixation durations and gaze durations were partitioned into two approximately equal-size sets. One set of 'potential error' fixations comprised the four ending character spaces of the target. The second set of likely 'nonerror' fixations comprised all other target fixations. If effects of the post-target word on target viewing durations were due to incorrectly specified saccades, then they should be evident in 'potential error' fixations but not in 'nonerror' fixations. Supplementary analyses with the factor target-fixation location (potential error vs. nonerror), also shown in Table 2, argue against this possibility, as they revealed no significant contribution of intra-target fixation location. Statistically, this was expressed in a negligible interaction of fixation location and parafoveal word type for first-fixation durations and gaze durations, both $F < 1$.

Table 3 shows the skipping rate for the post-target word, size of the interword saccade to the post-target word, and the viewing duration of the post-target word when it was fixated. Skipping was a function of post-target type, $F(2, 82) = 3.43$, $p < 0.05$, being more common in the repetition condition than the unassociated condition, $t(41) = 2.89$, $p < 0.01$, and also being slightly more common in the associated condition than the unassociated condition, though this difference did not approach statistical significance, $t(41) = 1.18$, $p > 0.24$. However, neither interword saccade size nor post-target viewing were a function of the type of post-target word, both $F < 1$.

Discussion

The relatedness of a fixated target and parafoveally visible post-target word determined target viewing durations. First-fixation duration and gaze duration on the

---

the word beginning, indicating that a considerable number of these saccades actually land at the ending letters of the current word (for a detailed discussion see Radach and McConkie, 1998).

target decreased when target and post-target words contained the same letter sequence and when they were associated. These results extend the findings of Murray
(1998) by showing that semantic properties of parafoveally visible words affect target viewing duration even when the task requires typical sentence reading. Hence,
access to the meaning of a parafoveally visible word can precede the initiation of an
interword saccade into this word. This finding clearly contravenes the sequential attention assumption, according to which programming of interword saccades occurs
when attention is focused on the fixated word, i.e., before any useful linguistic can
be obtained from the next word in the text.

The more effective processing of the parafoveally visible post-target word in the
associated condition than in the unassociated condition was not reflected, however,
in shorter viewing durations when the post-target word was subsequently fixated.
Presumably, this occurred because our highly associated word sequences, such
as *mother's father*, are less common in written language than our unassociated
word sequences, such as *mother's garden*. Larger parafoveal preview benefits
in the associated condition thus could have been offset by increased sentence
comprehension difficulties.

Experiment 2

Sequential attention-shift models of oculomotor control maintain that allocation of
attention progresses unidirectionally from the fixated word to the next. According
to this view, allocation of attention to a word must prevent the acquisition of useful
lexical information to its left (in left-to-right ordered text). In a recent study, Binder,
Pollatsek and Rayner (in press) showed, however, that readers do obtain semantic
information to the left of a *fixated* word. In the study, Binder et al. (in press) changed
the identity of a target word when it was visible to the left of fixation (during the
saccade that moved the eyes to the right of the target area) by replacing it either
with a contextually related word or with an unrelated word. The target replacement
was implemented only during the first post-target fixation, and no display change
occurred in a control condition. The results showed that the left-of-fixation display
change had no effect on the duration of the post-target fixation that followed the
display change. The word change to the left of fixation increased, however, the
time spent *rereading* the target, with less time spent rereading the target when its
replacement was consistent than when it was context-inconsistent.

Reichle et al.'s (1998) attention-shift mechanism can accommodate this finding
by assuming that readers obtain effective lexical information to the left of fixation
when the saccade moved the eyes to the next word in the text before a corresponding
shift of attention took place. On occasion, the change in word identity to the left
of fixation thus occurred at an attended, though nonfixated, location. The finding

that effects of the left-of-fixation word change were confined to target rereadings corroborates this view.

Binder et al.'s (in press) results do indicate that readers obtained lexical information from a word to the left of fixation when it was subsequently reread. Their results do *not* imply, however, that no useful semantic information was obtained to the left of fixation in the absence of rereading. The idea that left-of-fixation information acquisition is a deviation from normal reading that must manifest itself in the eye movement record (e.g., in terms of rereading or at least an inflated viewing duration for the fixated word) is valid only under the precondition that the sequential attention assumption is true. We decided to use a performance parameter whose interpretation does not depend on the validity of a particular eye movement control theory. Specifically, a forced-choice task was used to determine whether a word shown to the left of fixation was perceived during sentence reading.

Similar to Binder et al., target sentences were used in which a target word, that was visible to the right of fixation and during fixation, was replaced with a different word as soon as the eyes moved to its right. Readers viewed, for instance, one target, *sack*, before and during its fixation and another target, *rack*, after the eyes moved to the right of the target's location. Oculomotor responses to the left-of-fixation word change were not of primary interest. Instead, each sentence reading was followed by a forced-choice task and performance in this task was evaluated. Three forced-choice words were shown, one consisting of the left-of-fixation word, one consisting of the right-of-fixation (and fixated) target, and one consisting of a new word that was not shown during prior sentence reading. To reduce effects of guessing, the right- and left-of-fixation words were equally compatible with sentence context. Acquisition of useful lexical information to the left of fixation was expected to yield a higher selection rate for the word to the left of fixation than for the new word. Moreover, if acquisition of useful lexical information to the left of fixation was an anomaly, occurring only when a saccade off the target was executed before a corresponding shift of attention took place, then the word change to the left of fixation should have no effect when only those instances are considered in which no target rereading occurred. Experimentally, this should be expressed in a substantially higher forced-choice selection rate for the left-of-fixation word when instances of target rereading are included than when they are excluded.

Method

Subjects

Thirty undergraduate students who were enrolled in an introductory psychology course at the State University of New York at Binghamton participated in the eye-tracking study for course credit. All students had normal vision and none of them was familiar with the purpose of the experiment.

Materials

Thirty-six word pairs were selected. The two members of each pair shared all characters, except the beginning character. The two members were matched on word length, word frequency, word type, and concreteness. Word length ranged from 3 to 5 characters. Half of the target pairs were high-frequency word pairs, with a mean word frequency of 234 per million (Kuçera and Francis, 1967), the remaining word pairs were low-frequency words, with a mean word frequency of nine per million. A target sentence was written for each pair, with the constraint that both members would occupy the same sentence location and would yield meaningful and syntactically correct expressions. None of the targets occupied either the two sentence-initial or the two sentence-final locations. An attempt was made to match the contextual consistency of the two members of each target pair. A rating task was devised in which each sentence target was shown with both members of the target pair. For instance, the targets containing the high-frequency target pair *wall/ball* and the low-frequency pair *rack/sack* were presented as "The neighbor hit the wall/ball with a bar", and "I bought a new laundry sack/rack to have more space in my room".

The line below each sentence was blank except for dotted word-size underlinings beneath the two members of the target pair. Twenty subjects, none of whom participated in the reading experiment, were asked to judge the contextual appropriateness of each member of the target pair, and to note their judgement on the underlined space below each judged word. A scale from 1 to 10 was used with 1 indicating a poor contextual fit and 10 indicating a perfect contextual fit. The results showed that targets were considered context-appropriate, with a mean appropriateness rating of 6.5. The two members of a pair were considered matched when their mean appropriateness rating differed by no more than two units. Initially, four target sentences did not meet this criterium; they were rewritten and presented to four new raters who considered the revised targets matched.

Each sentence was accompanied by three forced-choice alternatives. Two of these alternatives consisted of the two members of the target pair; a third choice, the new word, was either similar to the two members of the target pair, e.g., *hall* constituting the new target for the target pair *wall/ball* target pair, or dissimilar, e.g., *rope* constituting the new target for the *rack/sack* target pair. The position of the three choice alternatives was randomly assigned.

Apparatus

The hardware setup of Experiments 1 and 2 were virtually identical, except that all text was shown within a 111 (vertical) by 480 (horizontal) window of the CRT. The vertical CRT display area was reduced to achieve a 200 Hz vertical refresh rate (for details see Inhoff and Liu, 1998). All text was shown in standard ASCII format.

Procedure

The procedures of Experiments 1 and 2 were similar, with participants reading meaningful sentences, while their eye movements were monitored. There were, however, two major changes and one minor change. Major changes included the implementation of eye-movement-contingent display changes to the left of a fixated target and the addition of a forced-choice task. The minor change involved the alignment of the fixation marker with sentence onset. In contrast to Experiment 1, where the fixation marker coincided with the first character of the sentence, the left side fixation marker was placed four character spaces to the left of the first character of the sentence, so that sentence reading was initiated with a progressive saccade.

To implement eye-movement-contingent display changes, a visuo-spatial boundary was defined that consisted of the first pixel to the right of the target word. When the eyes crossed this boundary, the previously visible target word was replaced by the alternate member of the target pair, e.g., *ball* was replaced with *wall*, or vice versa. This replacement was shown as long as the eyes remained to the right of the target, i.e., until sentence reading was completed. The replacement was reversed when the eyes regressed to the left of the target location. During each sentence reading, both members of the target pair were thus displayed, one member being visible when the target location was to the right of fixation and when the target location was fixated and the other member being visible when the target location was to the left of fixation. The high display refresh rate was used to implement display changes within approximately 5 ms of traversing the critical boundary (for technical details see Inhoff and Liu, 1998).

After the sentence was read and erased from the screen, clicking of the mouse did not result in the presentation of another sentence. Instead, it displayed a sequence of three choice alternatives that were ordered from left to right. Each choice was preceded by a number, e.g., (1) wall, (2) hall, (3) ball, or (1) rope, (2) sack, (3) rack, and the readers were instructed to choose the target that was shown during the prior sentence reading by pressing the corresponding number on the numerical pad of the keyboard. The visibility of text during a typical trial is illustrated in Table 4. Readers were not informed that more than one target could have been shown during sentence reading. When in doubt, readers were instructed to choose the target that was most visible during sentence reading. The identity of the choice was recorded by the computer. The to-be-read materials also contained 40 filler sentences whose reading was not followed by a forced-choice task.

Design and data analyses

Two lists were constructed, each containing the same set of 36 sentence foils. The two lists differed in the visibility of the word pair member that was presented to the right vs. left of fixation, so that a target that was visible to the right of fixation and during its fixation on one list was visible to the left of fixation on the other list,

Table 4

A sample sentence with a sequence of three fixations indicated by an asterisk below the line of text

---

Sample sentence:
I bought a new laundry rack/sack to save space in my dorm room.

Visible text:
I bought a new laundry rack to save space in my dorm room.
                          *

I bought a new laundry rack save space in my dorm room.
                             *

I bought a new laundry sack to save space in my dorm room.
                                *

One fixation occupies pre-target text, one is positioned on the target, and one occupies post-target text. Available forced-choice alternatives: (1) rope, (2) sack, (3) rack.

and vice versa. List assignment was counterbalanced over two consecutive subjects. Performance on the forced-choice task was of primary interest. Target selection was analyzed using an analysis of variance (ANOVA) with the factors word frequency of the target word (high vs. low) and location of the target word during sentence reading (left of fixation, right of fixation and at fixation, new word). The data of one reader were excluded because the forced-choice responses were not mapped onto proper keyboard entries.

Results

Forced-choice performance, as a function of target word frequency (high and low) and the location of the target during sentence reading (left vs. right of fixation), is shown in Table 5. As expected, the location of the target during sentence reading had a profound effect on target selection, readers generally choosing the member of the target pair that was visible to the right of fixation and at fixation (72%), rather than the member of the pair that was visible to the left of fixation (24%). In addition, choices were considerably higher for the left-of-fixation target than for the new word that was never shown during sentence reading (3%). The main effect of target location was robust, $F(2, 56) = 250.0$, $p < 0.01$, as were the supplementary contrasts of the right (fixation) target vs. left target, $F(1, 28) = 124.27$, $p < 0.01$, and of the left target vs. new word, $F(1, 28) = 76.98$, $p < 0.01$. Readers were also somewhat more likely to choose the right side (or fixated) target when a high-frequency target pair was used than when a low-frequency pair was used, $F(2, 56) = 3.18$, $p < 0.05$.

As noted before, acquisition of useful information to the left of fixation can

Table 5

Selection rates as a function of the target–target correspondence (target type) in Experiment 2

Target location	Target word type		
	HF	LF	
Right of fixation	37.1 (1.5)	35 (1.2)	72.1
Left of fixation	11 (1.4)	13 (1.1)	24
New	1.7 (0.5)	1.7 (0.5)	3.4
With rereadings removed:			
Right of fixation	35 (2)	36 (1.3)	71
Left of fixation	10.3 (1.5)	14 (1.3)	24.3
New	2.3 (0.5)	1.4 (0.5)	3.7

Standard errors of the mean are shown in parentheses.

be consistent with Reichle et al.'s (1998) sequential attention-shift model, when assuming that readers acquired lexical information to the left of fixation only when attention had been retained at that location after the eyes were moved to the right. To test this account, all trials were removed in which target rereading occurred. This resulted in the exclusion of 14% of the forced-choice trials (most rereadings were performed by 3 of the 29 readers). The results showed that removal of rereading trials had virtually no effect on decision making (see Table 5). Again, there was a robust effect of target location, $F(2, 56) = 217.2$, $p < 0.01$, with the right-of-fixation (fixated) target being chosen on 71% of the trials, the left-of-fixation target being chosen on 24% of the trials and the new word being chosen on 4% of the trials. Paired comparisons revealed, again, a higher selection rate for the right-of-fixation (fixated) target than the left-of-fixation target, $F(1, 28) = 108.2$, $p < 0.01$, and a higher selection rate for the left-of-fixation target than the new word, $F(1, 28) = 60.02$, $p < 0.01$.

A sequential attention-shift model must predict that instances in which readers obtained useful information to the left of a fixated word should coincide with instances in which no useful information was obtained to the right of a fixated word, as attention cannot be allocated to right and left of a fixated word during a fixation. Readers should therefore have obtained little or no information from the word to the right of the target when the left of fixation target was selected in the corresponding forced-choice task. Experimentally, this should be expressed in longer post-target fixation durations for left target choices than for right (fixated) target choices. In contrast to this prediction, the duration of the first post-target fixation was slightly shorter (259 ms) when the left-of-fixation target was chosen than when the right-of-fixation (and fixated) target was chosen (267 ms), though this difference did not approach significance, $t < 1$.

Additional examinations of oculomotor activity during sentence reading revealed several expected findings. Target skipping occurred on approximately 31% of the trials, which is similar to previously reported skipping rates for 3- to 5-character words (Vitu, O'Regan, Inhoff and Topolski, 1995), and readers spend less time viewing high-frequency targets than low-frequency targets. [4] The corresponding frequency effect was marginally significant in the first-fixation durations (263 ms and 272 ms for high- and low-frequency targets, respectively, $t[28] = 1.76$, $p < 0.09$) and significant in the gaze durations (272 ms and 294 ms for high- and low-frequency words, respectively, $t[28] = 2.34$, $p < 0.05$).

Discussion

The main results of Experiment 2 were straightforward. Readers obtained useful lexical information from a target word to the left of fixation, irrespective of whether this was accompanied by target rereading. Rather than being an anomaly, i.e., occurring only in instances in which the eyes moved off the target before it was recognized, acquisition of effective lexical information to the left of fixation thus appears to be an element of the normal reading process. Moreover, acquisition of useful lexical information to the left of fixation did not appear to hamper the acquisition of useful information to the right of a fixated word, as the duration of the post-target fixation was not increased when the left-of-fixation target was selected.

It is unlikely that acquisition of useful information to the left of fixation was due to the display change manipulation that could have attracted attention to the left of fixation. Several considerations argue against this possibility. Readers rarely, if ever, noticed the left-of-fixation display change. Furthermore, the rate with which the left-of-fixation target was chosen was independent of saccade direction. If choice of the left-of-fixation target was due to an artifactual pull of attention to the left, then left-of-fixation rates should have been higher when target viewing (or skipping) was followed by regressive saccade, which was not the case. We (Inhoff, Starr, Liu and Wang, 1998) also showed that minor delays (of a few ms) in the implementation of eye-movement-contingent display changes do not have a discernible effect on readers' use of parafoveally visible information.

Our current results thus confirm one aspect of Binder et al. (in press), that readers can obtain useful lexical information to the left of a fixated word. They demand, however, a different theoretical account. In fact, close examination of Binder et al.'s findings also reveals several findings that are difficult to reconcile with Reichle et al.'s (1998) attention-shift model. First, readers in Binder et al. (in

---

4 When the target word was skipped, participants selected the right-of-fixation target on 76% of the trials, the left target on 23%, and the new word on 5%.

press) did not notice the left-of-fixation display change, even though the identity of all characters of the left-of-fixation word was changed. If this visually distinct word display change had occurred at an attended location, as must be claimed by a sequential attention-shift model, then some awareness of a major display change should have been exhibited. Second, a sequential attention-shift model must predict that readers are more likely to retain attention to the left of fixation when the attended word is unpredictable than when it is predictable. Unpredictable words are more difficult to recognize than predictable words, making it more likely that a saccade to subsequent text is programmed and executed before these words are recognized. This should have been expressed in a larger left-of-fixation replacement effect when the originally shown target word was unpredictable. In contrast to this, replacement of the target to the left of fixation yielded a numerically smaller (20 ms) effect when the originally viewed word was unpredictable. Third, readers seemed to obtain useful information to the left of a fixated word only when the left-of-fixation change occurred no more than four characters to the left of the fixated word. For sequential attention-shift models, this finding poses a paradox: on the one hand, readers are assumed to program interword saccades *prior* to the identification of the fixated word; on the other hand, the saccade programming mechanisms must have had knowledge about the success of the target word's identification. That is, the system must have known that the fixated word would *not* be recognized prior to the launching of the saccade, so that the executed saccade could keep the eyes near the attended word.

Experiment 3

Relatively high selection rates for left-of-fixation targets, irrespective of whether the target was reread, argue against sequential attention-shift models only if selection of a word target was based on the acquisition of useful lexical information during sentence reading. The validity of this assumption can be challenged, however, as selection of the left-of-fixation target could have occurred when readers no longer had any useful target information when the forced-choice task was performed. The meaning of both members of the target pair was compatible with the previously read sentence content; the meaning of new targets, by contrast, was generally unrelated to prior sentence content. When readers did not retain useful target information, they could have guessed that the appropriate choice consisted of either the right- or left-of-fixation target, yielding a relatively high selection rate for the left-of-fixation target, especially when the left-of-fixation target had a higher frequency of occurrence than the right-of-fixation target.

Experiment 3 examined whether selection of the left-of-fixation target in Experiment 2 was based on context-constrained guessing. The experiment was identical to Experiment 2, except that there was no change in the identity of the right-of-fixation target word; that is, the same target was visible to the right of fixation, during fixation, and to the left of fixation. If the choice of the left-of-fixation target in Experiment 2 was based on guessing, then forced-choice selection of this target word in Experiment 3 should be identical to the forced-choice selection of this target in Experiment 2.

Method

Subjects
Eighteen undergraduate students participated for course credit. All had normal vision. None of the students had participated in any aspect of Experiment 2.

Materials
The same target word pairs, target-containing sentences, and forced-choice alternatives were used as in Experiment 2.

Apparatus
The identical hardware setup was used as in Experiment 2.

Procedure and design
The procedures of Experiments 2 and 3 were identical with one exception: there was no display change during sentence reading. Readers viewed only one member of the target word pair during sentence reading, which was visible when it was to the right of fixation, when it was directly fixated, and when the eyes had moved to the right of it. Again, two lists were constructed, one list containing one member of the target pair and the other list containing the alternate member.

Results and discussion

The results of Experiment 3 revealed negligible effects of context-constrained guessing. On almost all trials, readers selected the previously read target in the forced-choice task, with target selection rate amounting to 94%. The context-consistent second member of the target word pair, that was never shown during sentence reading, and the context-inconsistent new word, that was also never shown during sentence reading, were rarely chosen, their selection rates amounting to 5% and 1%, respectively. Readers thus appeared to be quite successful at identifying the right-of-fixation and fixated target word during sentence reading, ruling out the possibility that choice of the left-of-fixation target in Experiment 2 was based on guessing.

Statistical comparisons of the forced-choice performance in Experiments 3 and 2 corroborate this view. Selection of the right-of-fixation target occurred significantly more often in Experiment 3 than in Experiment 2, $F(1, 44) = 49.49$, $p < 0.01$. Presumably this occurred because the same word was present to the right of fixation and later to the left of fixation in Experiment 3 but not in Experiment 2. Furthermore, the context-consistent forced-choice alternative was selected more often when it was shown to the left of fixation, as occurred in Experiment 2, than when it was not shown during sentence reading, as occurred in Experiment 3, $F(1, 44) = 40.41$, $p < 0.01$, again indicating that readers obtained useful information from the word that was visible to the left of fixation. The new word was also selected more often in Experiment 2 than in Experiment 3, $F(1, 44) = 6.97$, $p < 0.01$.

General discussion

Effective reading requires that the eyes are either at or near to-be-recognized words of text. According to sequential attention-shift models, coordination is accomplished by linking the saccade programming mechanism to lexical processing and covert shifts of attention. Covert attention is assumed to confine linguistic analyses to one word at a time, and shifts of attention are assumed to move the attentional spotlight unidirectionally to successive words of text after they have been recognized. Programming of an interword saccade to new text requires that a fixated word is attended, so that a first stage of lexical processing, comprising the specification of its familiarity, can be performed. The start of saccade programming to the next word is followed by a shift of attention after the current word is fully recognized. The timing constraints laid out by Reichle et al. (1998) suggest that the executed saccade will in most cases land at the target word shortly after the attentional beam has arrived; hence, the eyes are usually at or near the location of text from which useful linguistic information is obtained.

Experiment 1 examined one claim of sequential attention-shift models, that the programming of an interword saccade toward a parafoveally visible new word is triggered when a certain stage of lexical processing on the currently fixated word is completed and attention is still focused on this word. Experiment 2 examined whether acquisition of useful lexical information to the left of a fixated word is an anomaly, occurring only when an interword saccade to new text was executed before the attended (and previously fixated) word was recognized. The results of both experiments are in empirical disagreement with these contentions. In contrast to the predictions of Reichle et al.'s (1998) attention-shift model, readers obtained useful lexical information to the right of the fixated word in Experiment 1 before a saccade to the next parafoveal word was committed to action. Furthermore, acquisition of useful lexical information from a target word to the left-of-fixation word was not an anomaly; instead, it appeared to be part and parcel of normal reading, occurring irrespective of whether the target was reread.

There are two different lines of reasoning along which our results can be interpreted. First, we could maintain the idea that attention is confined to one single word at a time but postulate that different words can be attended to and processed at different times during a fixation. This view is consistent with results reported by Blanchard, McConkie, Zola and Wolverton (1984) who briefly masked words some time after fixation onset and replaced these words with different alternatives. In a forced-choice task similar to our task in Experiments 2 and 3, participants often reported a word that was present during the second halve of the critical fixation. This occurred when, according to the sequential attention hypothesis, attention should have been centered already on the next or even second next word. Such a finding can be taken to indicate that although attention is confined to one word at a time, the temporal coordination between effective lexical processing and eye movement control is much more flexible than predicted by sequential attention models. However, to accommodate our finding of lexical processing of words to the left of fixation, something like an 'attentional regression' has to be postulated (for a discussion of 'mental regressions' see Duffy, 1992). This should lead to a disruption or a delay in the processing of the fixated word. As discussed earlier, there is no evidence for such a pattern in our data.

These considerations led us to favor a second line of interpretation. Rather than assuming that attention confines word recognition to individual words during reading, we propose that all words within the range of effective vision are attended and subjected to lexical analyses, i.e., more than one word may be processed concurrently during a fixation (for similar views see also Inhoff et al., in press, and Schroyens, Vitu, Brysbaert and d'Ydewalle, 1999). Within this multi-unit range of visuo-spatial attention, resources may be unevenly allocated; but even if more attention was allocated to one unit (word) within the range of effective vision than to its spatially adjacent neighbors, it would not need to exclude the linguistic analysis of the target's neighbors, as they would be the recipients of some attentional resources. LaBerge and Brown (1989) and LaBerge, Brown, Carter and Bash (1991) suggested that viewers estimate the importance of different segments of a visual array to focus attention. Specifically, a gradient value is determined that controls the allocation of attention to different segments of the spatially contiguous array, with the highest value being assigned to the most important segment and progressively lower values being assigned to spatially adjacent neighbors. [5]

---

5 Our results are also in harmony with a more principled departure from attention-shift models. Findlay and Walker (in press) have presented a general theory of saccade generation based on parallel processing and competitive inhibition within a saliency map. Potential targets are

During reading, the specification of the gradient could be a function of fixation location and of the success of linguistic analyses. The fixated word offers the highest visual resolution, and a higher gradient value could be assigned to it than to its spatially adjacent neighbors. Furthermore, a higher gradient value could be assigned to words that are difficult to recognize than to words that are easy to recognize. Successful recognition of a word (or a sub-word unit or a sequence of words) could lead to a gradient adjustment, increasing the allocation of attention to nonrecognized neighboring units and decreasing the allocation of attention to the identified unit. Such dynamic adjustments to the center of attention could lead to the programming of corresponding saccades, which now would be directed toward, rather than away from, the locus of attention.

According to this view, acquisition of useful linguistic information from fixated and parafoveally visible words is concurrent (though more effective for the fixated word). Hence, properties of a parafoveally visible word and with it the relationship between fixated and parafoveally visible words can affect the programming of interword saccades. As successively attended areas of text generally overlap, so that a word that is at the focus of attention during one fixation may still be attended, though to a lesser degree, during the fixation of the next word in the text, acquisition of linguistic information to the left of fixation becomes part of normal reading.

The attention gradient conception also accounts for dynamic changes in the acquisition of useful information from parafoveal words prior to the programming of an interword saccade. Specifically, less information will be obtained from parafoveal neighbors prior to the programming of an interword saccade when a fixated word is difficult to recognize than when it is easy to recognize, as less attention can be allocated to the parafovea when the fixated word demands more resources (e.g., Henderson and Ferreira, 1990; Kennison and Clifton, 1995). Orthogonal to this, more information will be obtained from parafoveal words prior to the programming of an interword saccade when parafoveal words are easy to recognize than when they are difficult to recognize, as fewer resources need to be allocated to obtain useful information from 'easy' words (Inhoff and Rayner, 1986; Kennison and Clifton, 1995).

Rather than being a qualitatively different type of model, the gradient-shift model can be considered a generalized version of attention-shift models, generalization being accomplished by relaxing assumptions concerning the allocation of attention. The gradient can become functionally equivalent to a sequential attention-shift

---

represented on a spatial map with the order of preference specified by saliency values that vary as a function of both low level and cognitive input. This theory can be applied to reading (Radach, submitted) and may provide a useful framework for an alternative model in which both linguistic processing and oculomotor factors contribute to eye movement control and the concept of attention shifts is not required to explain saccade generation.

mechanism under some conditions, e.g., when words, or other of to-be-identified or to-be-deciphered expressions, are exceedingly difficult to process. In this case, all resources could be allocated solely to a fixated unit until it was recognized (or deciphered), and successively attended areas of text would be nonoverlapping.

References

Binder, K.S., Pollatsek, A. and Rayner, K. (in press). Extraction of a fixated word to the left of a fixation in reading. Journal of Experimental Psychology: Human Perception and Performance.

Blanchard, H.E., McConkie, W., Zola, D. and Wolverton, G.S. (1984). Time course of visual information utilization during fixations in reading. Journal of Experimental Psychology: Human Perception and Performance, 10, 75–89.

Duffy, S.A. (1992). Eye movements and complex comprehension processes. In: K. Rayner (Ed.), Eye Movements and Visual Cognition: Scene Perception and Reading. New York: Springer, pp. 333–354.

Findlay, J.M. and Walker, R. (1999). A model of saccade generation based on parallel processing and competitive inhibition. Behavioral and Brain Sciences, 22, 1031–1050.

Henderson, J.M. and Ferreira, F. (1990). Effects of foveal processing difficulty on the perceptual span in reading: Implications for attention and eye movement control. Journal of Experimental Psychology: Learning, Memory, and Cognition, 16, 417–429.

Henderson, J.M. and Ferreira, F. (1993). Eye movement control during reading: fixation measures foveal but not parafoveal processing difficulty. Canadian Journal of Experimental Psychology, 47, 201–221.

Hoffman, J.E. (1998). Visual attention and eye movements. In: H. Pashler (Ed.), Attention. Hove: Psychology Press, pp. 119–153.

Inhoff, A.W. (1984). Two stages of word processing during eye fixations in the reading of prose. Journal of Verbal Learning and Verbal Behavior, 23, 612–624.

Inhoff, A.W. and Briihl, D. (1991). Semantic processing of unattended text during selective reading: how the eyes see it. Perception and Psychophysics, 49, 289–294.

Inhoff, A.W. and Liu, W. (1998). The perceptual span and oculomotor activity during the reading of Chinese sentences. Journal of Experimental Psychology: Human Perception and Performance, 24, 20–34.

Inhoff, A.W., Pollatsek, A., Posner, M. and Rayner, K. (1989). Covert attention and eye movements during reading. Quarterly Journal of Experimental Psychology, 41a, 63–89.

Inhoff, A.W. and Radach, R. (1998). Definition and computation of oculomotor measures in the study of cognitive processes. In: G. Underwood (Ed.), Eye Guidance in Reading and Scene Perception. Oxford: Elsevier, pp. 29–53.

Inhoff, A.W. and Rayner, K. (1986). Parafoveal word processing during eye fixations in reading: effects of word frequency. Perception and Psychophysics, 40, 431–439.

Inhoff, A.W., Starr, M., Liu, W. and Wang, J. (1998). Eye-movement-contingent display changes are not compromised by flicker and phosphor persistence. Psychonomic Bulletin and Review, 5, 101–106.

Inhoff, A.W., Starr, M. and Schindler (in press). Is the processing of words during a fixation of text strictly serial? Perception and Psychophysics.

Inhoff, A.W. and Topolski, R. (1992). Lack of semantic activation from unattended text during passage reading. Bulletin of the Psychonomic Society, 30, 365–366.

Kennedy, A. (1998). The influence of parafoveal words on foveal inspection time: evidence for a processing trade-off. In: G. Underwood (Ed.), Eye Guidance in Reading and Scene Perception. Oxford: Elsevier, pp. 149–179.

Kennedy, A. (in press). Parafoveal processing in word recognition. Quarterly Journal of Experimental Psychology.

Kennison, S.M. and Clifton, C. (1995). Determinants of parafoveal preview benefit in high and low working memory capacity readers: implications for eye movement control. Journal of Experimental Psychology: Learning, Memory, and Cognition, 21, 68–81.

Kuçera, H. and Francis, W.N. (1967). Computational Analysis of Present-Day American English. Providence, RI: Brown University Press.

LaBerge, D. and Brown, V. (1989). Theory of attentional operations in shape identification. Psychological Review, 96, 101–124.

LaBerge, D., Brown, V., Carter, M. and Bash, D. (1991). Reducing the effects of adjacent distractors by narrowing attention. Journal of Experimental Psychology: Human Perception and Performance, 17, 65–76.

McConkie, G.W. (1983). Eye movements and perception during reading. In: K. Rayner (Ed.), Eye Movements in Reading. Perceptual and Language Processes. New York: Academic Press, pp. 65–96.

Morris, R.K., Rayner, K. and Pollatsek, A. (1990). Eye movement guidance in reading: the role of parafoveal letter and space information. Journal of Experimental Psychology: Human Perception and Performance, 10, 268–281.

Morrison, R.E. (1984). Manipulation of stimulus onset delay in reading: evidence for parallel programming of saccades. Journal of Experimental Psychology: Human Perception and Performance, 10, 667–682.

Murray, W.S. (1998). Parafoveal pragmatics. In: G. Underwood (Ed.), Eye Guidance in Reading and Scene Perception. Amsterdam: North-Holland, pp. 181–200.

Neely, (1977). Semantic priming and retrieval from semantic memory: role of inhibitionless spreading activation and limited capacity attention. Journal of Experimental Psychology: General, 106, 226–254.

O'Regan, J.K. (1990). Eye movements and reading. In: E. Kowler (Ed.), Reviews of Oculomotor Research, Vol. 4. Eye Movements and Their Role in Visual and Cognitive Processes. Amsterdam: Elsevier, pp. 395–453.

Pollatsek, A., Bolozky, S., Well, A.D. and Rayner, K. (1981). Asymmetries in the perceptual span for Israeli readers. Brain and Language, 14, 174–180.

Pollatsek, A., Raney, G.E., LaGasse, L. and Rayner, K. (1993). The use of information below fixation in reading and visual search. Canadian Journal of Experimental Psychology, 47, 179–200.

Pollatsek, A. and Rayner, K. (1990). Eye movements and lexical access in reading. In: D.A. Balota, G.B. Flores d'Arcais and K. Rayner (Eds.), Comprehension Processes in Reading. Hillsdale, NJ: Erlbaum, pp. 143–164.

Postman, L. and Keppel, G. (1970). Norms of Word Association. New York: Academic Press.

Radach, R. (1999). Top down influences on saccade generation in cognitive tasks (commentary). Behavioral and Brain Sciences, 22, 1055.

Radach, R. and McConkie, G.W. (1998). Determinants of fixation positions in words during reading. In: G. Underwood (Ed.), Eye Guidance in Reading and Scene Perception. Oxford: Elsevier, pp. 77–100.

Rayner, K. (1998). Eye movements in reading and information processing: 20 years of research. Psychological Bulletin, 124, 372–422.

Rayner, K. and Pollatsek, A. (1989). The Psychology of Reading. Englewood Cliffs, NJ: Prentice Hall.

Rayner, K. and Raney, G. (1996). Eye movement control in reading and visual search: effects of word frequency. Psychonomic Bulletin and Review, 3, 238–244.

Rayner, K., Reichle, E.D. and Pollatsek, R. (1998). Eye movement control in reading: an overview and model. In: G. Underwood (Ed.), Eye Guidance in Reading and Scene Perception. Oxford: Elsevier, pp. 243–268.

Rayner, K. and Sereno, S. (1994). Regressive eye movements and sentence parsing: on the use of regression-contingent analysis. Memory and Cognition, 22, 281–285.

Reichle, E.D., Pollatsek, A., Fisher, D.L. and Rayner, K. (1998). Towards a model of eye movement control in reading. Psychological Review, 105, 125–157.

Riggs, L.A. (1965). Visual acuity. In: C.H. Graham (Ed.), Vision and Visual Perception. New York: Wiley.

Schroyens, W., Vitu, F., Brysbaert, M. and d'Ydewalle, G. (1999). Eye movement control during reading: foveal load and parafoveal processing. Quarterly Journal of Experimental Psychology, 52A, 1021–1046.

Vitu, F., O'Regan, K., Inhoff, A.W. and Topolski, R. (1995). Mindless reading: eye movement characteristics are similar in scanning strings and reading text. Perception and Psychophysics, 57, 352–364.

CHAPTER 10

Attentional Demands on the Processing of Neighbouring Words

Geoffrey Underwood
University of Nottingham

Alice Binns
University of Nottingham

and

Stephanie Walker
Nottingham Trent University

Abstract

In this chapter we describe two eye-tracking experiments that were conducted to investigate how foveal and parafoveal information is used in eye movement control. Characteristics of neighbouring words were manipulated and interference effects resulting from increases in processing difficulty were observed. Findings from these experiments suggest that neighbouring interference effects are bi-directional, with increases in processing difficulty leading to a disruption of both the currently fixated and the next-to-be fixated word. These findings are discussed with reference to current attention-based models of eye movement control and it is suggested that our data offer support to parallel attention-based but not to sequential attention-based models of eye guidance.

Reading as a Perceptual Process/A. Kennedy, R. Radach, D. Heller and J. Pynte (Editors)
© 2000 Elsevier Science Ltd. All rights reserved

Introduction

In the two experiments reported in this chapter we investigate how foveal and parafoveal information is used to guide eye movements in reading. Much of the current thinking in eye movement control has been influenced by the notion of the *perceptual span* (i.e. that region from which effective information is acquired during a fixation). Previous research has shown that the perceptual span is asymmetric (Pollatsek, Bolozky, Well and Rayner, 1981), with its extent ranging from 3 to 4 letters to the left of fixation (Underwood and McConkie, 1985), to a maximum of approximately 15 letters to the right (McConkie and Rayner, 1975). To account for this perceptual span asymmetry, researchers have considered how visuo-spatial attention may be allocated to words during reading, and over recent years there has been considerable interest in attention-based theories of eye movement control (e.g. Henderson and Ferreira, 1990; Morrison, 1984; Rayner, Reichle and Pollatsek, 1998).

Researchers who have posited these current attention-based models of eye guidance all claim, to a larger or smaller extent, that attention moves *sequentially*, from word to word and from left to right, within the perceptual span. For example, in Morrison's model of eye movement control (Morrison, 1984), attention is sequentially allocated, first to the foveal word (n), and then to the parafoveal word ($n + 1$). According to Morrison, eye location and visual attention are, in the first instance, directed at the foveal word. After the processing of this word has reached some criterion level, for example, when word n has been identified, attention is redirected towards the next, $n + 1$, word, and processing of this word begins. The redirection of attention towards the parafoveal word also serves as a signal for the programming of the next saccade to begin. Since saccade programming takes up a fixed amount of time, it is possible that processing of the parafoveal word is completed (i.e. the parafoveal word is identified) before programming for the next saccade is completed. Under these circumstances attention is redirected from word $n + 1$ to the following word ($n + 2$), the saccade to word $n + 1$ is cancelled (i.e. fixation of $n + 1$ is skipped), and the programming of a saccade to word $n + 2$ is initiated.

Under this account of sequential attention allocation, time taken for saccade programming, and hence time spent on parafoveal word processing, remains constant irrespective of foveal word processing difficulty. Thus one prediction of Morrison's model is that foveal processing load should not influence parafoveal processing. However, recent findings do not altogether support this kind of processing framework. For example, Henderson and Ferreira (1990), using eye contingent displays, showed how foveal processing load influenced parafoveal processing; as the difficulty of the foveal word increased, the amount of information acquired from the parafoveal word decreased. As a result of their findings Henderson and Ferreira

(1990) suggested the inclusion of a maximum fixation duration (i.e. a fixation 'deadline') within Morrison's original model. Under this more recent version of Morrison's sequential attention-based model of eye guidance, once the fixation deadline has been reached the next saccade is instigated irrespective of the current state of processing. By introducing a fixation cut-off and programming deadline into Morrison's original model, Henderson and Ferreira were able to account for their effect of foveal processing load on parafoveal processing. Under their amended sequential attention-based account of eye guidance, when a foveal word is easy to process, the criterion level of processing required to shift attention is reached before the programming deadline, and under these circumstances the eye guidance system will work exactly as Morrison predicted, with the parafoveal word being processed in the time it takes to program and execute a saccade. However, when the foveal word is difficult to process, the attentional shift criterion may not be achieved before the programming deadline is reached, and when this occurs saccade programming will begin before attention has moved to the parafoveal word. If the processing criterion is reached soon after the programming deadline, then attention will move to the parafoveal word. However, attention will be focused on the parafoveal word for less time than it takes to program a saccade, and therefore the neighbouring word will receive less parafoveal processing than Morrison predicted. Thus, when the foveal word is difficult to process, the reader will engage in less parafoveal processing.

Although the inclusion of a deadline within Morrison's model was used to explain Henderson and Ferreira's (1990) findings, more recent evidence reported by Kennison and Clifton (1995) suggests that this cannot be the case. Kennison and Clifton examined the fixation duration distributions for high and low frequency words and found no evidence to support the claim that a fixation cut-off was operating during the processing of low frequency words, and therefore, their data are inconsistent with the notion of a fixation deadline within a sequentially allocated attentional-based account of eye movement control.

Reichle, Pollatsek, Fisher and Rayner (1998, see also Rayner et al., 1998) have recently reported a quantitative model of eye movement control. Their E-Z Reader model is, essentially, a computer simulation program that largely implements, but also modifies, Morrison's model of eye movement control (Morrison, 1984). Reichle et al. (1998) suggest that to account for the reported findings of a foveal load influence on parafoveal processing (e.g. Henderson and Ferreira, 1990; Kennison and Clifton, 1995), shifts in covert attention must be decoupled from eye movement programming. Therefore one important difference between E-Z Reader and Morrison's model (Morrison, 1984) is that within E-Z Reader the signal to shift attention is decoupled from the signal that initiates programming of a saccade. Rayner et al. (1998) suggest that this somewhat controversial change to the original model is justified since the majority of previous studies that have posited a tight coupling between the two signals tend to rely on paradigms in which 'exogenous' signals drive eye movements. Rayner and colleagues also cite a study conducted by Stelmach, Campsall and Herdman (1997) in which attentional shifts were found to be independent of saccades (see Rayner et al., 1998, p. 255). Within E-Z Reader, to facilitate the decoupling between the shift of attention and the saccadic programming signal, lexical processing is divided into two stages: a familiarity check and complete lexical access. The first stage, the familiarity check, involves as assessment of overall similarity of the processed word to the entire contents of the lexicon, and if some criterion level of similarity is determined, eye movement programming begins. However, attention does not shift to the next word until lexical access has been completed (i.e. at the second stage of lexical processing). Reichle et al. argue that when the foveal word is difficult to process the time between completion of the familiarity check and lexical access will be longer than when the foveal word is easy to process. Therefore, when the foveal word is difficult to process, the next (parafoveal) word will be processed for less time before the saccade is executed. Thus, the model of Reichle et al. (1998) is able to account for the influence of foveal load on parafoveal processing.

Although E-Z Reader provides us with a useful quantitative framework for future research, it nevertheless relies to an extent on the notion of *sequential* allocation of attentional resources to the words being processed. However, some of the findings from experiments that have investigated readers' perceptual spans have proved difficult to explain within a sequential attention-based model of eye guidance. For example, Rayner (1986) found that the perceptual spans of beginning readers were smaller than those of skilled readers. Rayner also reported that the span of skilled readers reduced in size when they were reading difficult text. Rayner explained his results in terms of competition for attentional resources between the fixated (foveal) and parafoveal words, with beginning readers being required to allocate a greater proportion of their attentional resources to the fixated word. Once again, these data and Rayner's explanation of them are difficult to account for within a sequential attention allocation model.

The notion of differential and competitive attentional resource allocation between foveal and parafoveal words (cf. Rayner, 1986) is an interesting one since it suggests the possibility that rather than attention being allocated in a sequential fashion, first to foveal and then to parafoveal words, it is instead shared between neighbouring foveal and parafoveal words. This would then constitute a *parallel* rather than a *sequential* model of attention allocation for eye guidance. Although the possibility of a parallel attention-based model of eye movement control has been considered by researchers in the area, until recently it has largely been dismissed (e.g. Henderson, 1992; Henderson and Ferreira, 1993). Within a parallel attention allocation model, when attentional demands of the fixated word increase, there would be less resources available for parafoveal processing, and this would be evidenced by a decrease in any parafoveal preview benefit. Conversely, when attentional demands of the as-yet unfixated parafoveal word are high, we would expect less resources to be available for foveal word processing. Hence two predictions for a parallel attention allocation model in eye guidance would be that (1) foveal load influences parafoveal processing, and (2) parafoveal load influences foveal processing.

As we saw earlier, there has been some reported evidence that supports the first of these predictions: an effect of foveal processing load on parafoveal processing. Henderson and Ferreira (1990) reported findings suggesting that when foveal processing load was high the preview benefit gained from a parafoveal word was reduced, compared to when foveal processing load was low. In that experiment 'high' and 'low' foveal processing loads were measured in terms of their word frequencies, with low frequency words corresponding to a high foveal processing load, and with high frequency words representing a low foveal processing load. However, one problem with this study, and also with the study reported by Kennison and Clifton (1995), was that measures were taken using an eye contingent 'boundary' technique, in which the words in the display changed in some way as readers' eyes moved over them. Whilst eye contingent displays are a useful tool in reading research, they do not approximate well to normal reading tasks, and as such, their use may be limited when drawing conclusions about eye movement control.

As far as the second of our two predictions is concerned, that there should be an influence of parafoveal load on foveal processing, the reported evidence is somewhat contradictory. Henderson and Ferreira (1993) reported data from an experiment in which they failed to find an influence of parafoveal load on foveal word processing. In their experiment, Henderson and Ferreira (1993) varied the frequency, syntactic class and length of the parafoveal word and measured foveal word processing. Findings from their study suggested that manipulations of these characteristics of the parafoveal word had no influence on processing of the fixated word, and thus, according to these researchers, their data could not be explained in terms of a parallel attention allocation model. Instead, these researchers suggested that their data could be explained by a sequential attention model of eye guidance (Henderson and Ferreira, 1990, Henderson and Ferreira, 1993). In some ways, this is a similar model to the one proposed by Reichle et al. (1998, see also Rayner et al., 1998), with proponents of both models arguing that a parafoveal word is not processed until the foveal word has been accessed in the lexicon.

However, there is some evidence that supports the notion of a parafoveal-to-foveal processing influence. For example, Rayner (1978) reported evidence to show that fixation durations were influenced by the position of a word in a line of text. Whereas the first fixation on a line tended to be long, the last fixation was comparatively shorter. Rayner used this evidence to argue that the last fixation on a line is shorter because less parafoveal information is available to the right of the fixation point. More recently, Brysbaert and Vitu (1998), in their discussion of previously reported data on word skipping, suggested that current sequential attention-based theories of eye movement control are probably incorrect. They propose a new model to account for word skipping in which parafoveal and foveal words are processed in parallel, but with a delay between the two. In support of their claim that processing of foveal and parafoveal information takes place in parallel, they cite some empirical evidence reported by Schroyens, Vitu, Brysbaert and d'Ydewalle (in press). Finally, Kennedy (1998) reported an experiment in which the findings suggested that gaze duration on a foveal word was shorter when a parafoveal target word was long (nine vs. five letters) and of low frequency, once again indicating an influence of parafoveal load on foveal word processing.

One issue needing to be addressed, therefore, is that of why there are these seemingly contradictory findings for effects of parafoveal-to-foveal processing. Perhaps one explanation for the failure of Henderson and Ferreira (1993) to find an influence of parafoveal load on foveal word processing lies with the nature of the parafoveal word manipulations used in that particular experiment. Manipulations involving word frequency, syntactic class and word length are typically used to investigate foveal word processing, but evidence from previous studies has suggested that it is the initial letters of a parafoveal word that play an important role in parafoveal processing difficulty (e.g. Briihl and Inhoff, 1995). Therefore, it is possible that any influence of parafoveal load on foveal processing may have been missed by Henderson and Ferreira (1993). On the other hand, although Kennedy (1998) did find an influence of both parafoveal word length and word frequency on foveal processing, he utilised a two-word comparison task rather than a natural reading task. Thus there is the possibility with Kennedy's experiment that the findings may not generalise to normal reading. One indication of this is that Kennedy (1998) also reports some analyses from a corpus of eye movement recordings taken from four native German speakers during a natural reading task. Findings from these analyses suggest that foveal word fixations were longer when parafoveal words were of low frequency, thus supporting the notion of a parafoveal-to-foveal word influence.

In view of the limitations of some of the previous research that has addressed the issue of foveal load influence on parafoveal processing (e.g. Henderson and Ferreira, 1990), and of the contradictory findings from previous empirical studies that have investigated the influence of parafoveal load on foveal word processing (e.g. Henderson and Ferreira, 1993, vs. Kennedy, 1998), the two experiments reported here were conducted to investigate the influence of foveal load on parafoveal processing (Experiment 1), and the influence of parafoveal load on foveal processing (Experiment 2). In these two experiments a more natural reading task was utilised, and manipulation of foveal and parafoveal load was undertaken using word characteristics that were suitable for the particular items of interest.

Experiment 1: the influence of foveal load on parafoveal processing

In this first experiment we investigated whether or not the difficulty of processing a foveal target word (n) had an influence on the processing of the next word ($n + 1$). Processing difficulty of the foveal word was manipulated by varying length and frequency of a target word (n) which was embedded in a sentence. Parafoveal processing of the following word (i.e. word $n + 1$) was measured by investigating pre-fixation (i.e. preview) processing benefit.

Method

Participants
Twenty students from the University of Nottingham participated in this experiment. All were native English speakers, had normal, uncorrected vision and were paid £5.

Materials
Three hundred target words (word n), were selected from Kuçera and Francis (1967), on the basis of their length and frequency. Twenty words each of high frequency (greater than 150 per million; mean frequency = 583), medium frequency (between 30 and 70 per million, mean frequency = 47), and low frequency (less than 10 per million, mean frequency = 5) were selected for each of five word lengths between 3 and 7 letters. A further 300 words were selected to be $n + 1$ words (i.e. the words that followed the target words). These words were all 6 letters in length and were of medium frequency (between 10 and 30 per million, mean frequency = 18).

Each target word n was paired with a word $n + 1$ and these 300 word pairs were included in sentences of no longer than 50 characters in length, including spaces. Two n, $n + 1$ word pairs appeared in each sentence, giving a total of 150 sentences, each of which could be displayed on a single line of the viewing screen. Target words never appeared as the first, penultimate, or final word in a sentence. An example of a test sentence is given below, with the target (n) words italicised and the $n + 1$ words underlined:

"At the *huge* mosque a *war* victim begged for money"

Sentences were organised into groups of either seven or eight to form short 'stories', which were presented to participants in random order. Four practice sentences, constructed in a similar fashion to the test sentences, preceded presentation of the 150 test sentences.

A short comprehension test was constructed to ensure that participants had read and understood the sentences. A criterion of 80% correct performance on this test was set, and only data from participants meeting this criterion were included in the analyses.

Apparatus

An SRI Dual Purkinje Generation 5.5 eyetracker (Fourward Technologies) was used to monitor participants' eye movements. Their gaze location was monitored by the eyetracker every millisecond, and information concerning their sequence of eye fixations and start and end times was obtained from the sampled output. Sentences were presented on a VDU at a viewing distance of 70 cm, with four characters being displayed per degree of visual angle. Although participants used both eyes during the reading task, only the right eye was monitored by the tracker.

Procedure

During the experiment participants' head movements were minimised by use of a bite bar and head restraint. For each participant, the eye-tracking system was calibrated at the beginning of the experiment and recalibration was undertaken at the end of each group of seven or eight test sentences (i.e. at the end of each 'story'). Each participant was presented with four practice sentences followed by the 150 test sentences. The participant pressed a key to indicate they had finished reading a sentence, and the next sentence was then displayed. Throughout the course of the experiment participants were given four short breaks, during which times short comprehension tests were administered to assess knowledge of the preceding test sentences.

Results

All participants reached the criterion of 80% correct performance on the reading comprehension test, and therefore no participant's data were excluded from the following analyses on the basis of poor comprehension. All fixations <80 ms and within one character of the previous or subsequent fixation were merged, and any fixation of <40 ms which fell more than three characters away from the previous or subsequent fixation was excluded. Data from seven percent of test sentences were excluded due to tracker loss, with these being distributed evenly across conditions.

Measures taken included the total reading times for the target word (n) during the first pass (i.e. excluding regressive fixations), the 'prior fixation' location of word $n + 1$, and the duration and number of fixations of word $n + 1$ on the first pass, and these were subjected to further analyses. Prior fixation locations were classed as being either 'near', in which the fixation immediately before fixation of word $n + 1$ was within four characters of the first letter of word $n + 1$, or 'far', in which the fixation immediately before fixation of word $n + 1$ was further than four characters from the first character of word $n + 1$. Analyses were conducted on target word (n) data and on parafoveal word ($n + 1$) data, and these are reported below.

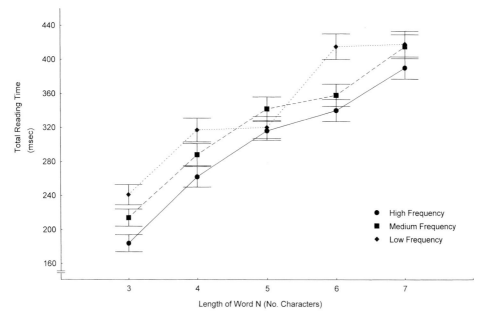

Fig. 1. Effects of length and frequency on word *N* reading time.

Target word (n) reading times: effects of length and frequency

The mean total reading time for the target word (*n*) as a function of its length and frequency is shown in Fig. 1.

A 3 (low, medium, or high word frequency) × 5 (word length of 3, 4, 5, 6, or 7 letters) ANOVA was conducted on these data, across both subjects (F_1) and items (F_2). A significant main effect of word length of word *n* on its total reading time was observed ($F_{1(4,76)} = 73.66$, $p < 0.001$, $MS_e = 341425$; $F_{2(4,5546)} = 102.42$, $p < 0.001$, $MS_e = 6358912$). All pairwise comparisons between means of the five different word lengths showed significant differences; total reading time was affected by each increase in word length between 3 and 7 letters (all *t*-values >2.77, all *p*-values <0.01). There was also a significant main effect of word frequency of word *n* on its total reading time ($F_{1(2,38)} = 25.23$, $p < 0.001$. $MS_e = 49144$; $F_{2(2,5546)} = 14.89$, $p < 0.001$, $MS_e = 924514$). Comparisons between means of target word frequencies revealed that readers spent longer reading low frequency words compared to either medium ($t_1 = 3.35$, $p < 0.01$, $t_2 = 2.3$, $p < 0.05$) or high ($t_1 = 7.1$, $p < 0.001$, $t_2 = 5.33$, $p < 0.001$) frequency target words. Participants also took longer to read medium than high frequency target words ($t_1 = 3.75$, $p < 0.001$, $t_2 = 3.04$, $p < 0.01$). There was no interaction between target word length and target word frequency ($F_{1(8,152)} = 2.05$, $p > 0.05$. $MS_e = 5542$; $F_{2(8,5546)} = 1.67$, $p > 0.05$, $MS_e = 103478$).

It appears, therefore, that when either target words were longer, or they were of lower frequency, readers required longer reading times. Implications of these findings, in terms of attentional demands of the target word, are that (1) long words are more attentionally demanding than short words, and (2) low frequency words are more attentionally demanding than high frequency words. Either one of these two manipulations (long vs. short words *or* low vs. high frequency words) could thus be considered a suitable method of influencing the processing difficulty of a target word. Since word length and word frequency did not interact in the total reading time analyses, subsequent analyses of word frequency effects were collapsed over all five word lengths.

Word $n + 1$ processing effects
Processing of word $n + 1$ was measured in terms of its pre-fixation (preview) processing benefit. Reading time indices used as measures of pre-fixation processing benefit were first fixation duration of word $n + 1$ and the total number of fixations on word $n + 1$. Prior fixation locations of word $n + 1$ were classed as either *near* fixations (i.e. within four characters of the first letter of word $n + 1$) or *far* fixations (i.e. further than four characters away from the first letter of word $n + 1$).

Duration of first fixation on word $n + 1$
The mean duration of the first fixation on word $n + 1$ as a function of the location of the prior fixation (near or far) and word n word frequency are shown in Fig. 2.

A 3 (low, medium or high target word frequency) $\times$ 2 (near or far prior location fixation) ANOVA was conducted on these data. There was a main effect of prior location fixation, which was significant by items (F_2) and approached significance by subjects (F_1), $F_{1(1,19)} = 4.31$, $p < 0.06$, $MS_e = 3480$; $F_{2(1,292)} = 8.24$, $p < 0.01$, $MS_e = 17369$): first fixations on word $n + 1$ were shorter when the prior fixation was located within four characters of the first character of this word. The main effect of target (n) word frequency was also significant, $F_{1(2,38)} = 8.0$, $p < 0.01$, $MS_e = 2282$; $F_{2(2,294)} = 4.43$, $p < 0.05$, $MS_e = 14257$). A comparison between means showed that first fixations on $n + 1$ were longer when target words were of low frequency than when they were of high frequency ($t_1 = 4.0$, $p < 0.01$, $t_2 = 2.98$, $p < 0.01$). There was no interaction between target word frequency and prior fixation location ($F_{1(2,38)} < 1$; $F_{2(2,294)} < 1$).

Total number of fixations on word $n + 1$
The means of the total number of fixations on word $n+1$ as a function of the location of the prior fixation (near or far) and word n word frequency are shown in Fig. 3.

A 3 (word frequency) $\times$ 2 (prior fixation location) ANOVA was conducted on these data. There was a main effect of prior fixation location, $F_{1(1,19)} = 72.74$, $p < 0.001$, $MS_e = 2.21$; $F_{2(1,294)} = 152.35$, $p < 0.001$, $MS_e = 14.1$). The total

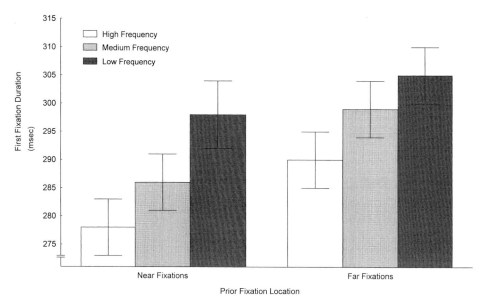

Fig. 2. Effect of frequency on word N upon first fixation duration of word $N + 1$.

number of fixations on word $n + 1$ were fewer when the prior fixation location was 'near' (i.e. within four characters of the first character of this word). There was also a main effect of target (n) word frequency, $F_{1(4,76)} = 5.34$, $p < 0.01$. $MS_e = 0.05$; $F_{2(2,294)} = 3.73$, $p < 0.05$, $MS_e = 0.39$). Comparison between these means showed that participants made more fixations on word $n + 1$ when target words were of low frequency than when they were of high frequency ($t_1 = 3.19$, $p < 0.01$, $t_2 = 2.71$, $p < 0.01$). The interaction between target word frequency and prior fixation location approached significance by subjects, but was not significant by items ($F_{1(2,38)} = 3.12$, $p < 0.06$, $MS_e = 0.04$; $F_{2(2,294)} < 1$). Comparison of means showed that readers gained a significant pre-fixation processing benefit (i.e. near vs. far prior fixation location) at all three levels of target word frequency (all t-values > 6.53, all p-values < 0.01). However, the pre-fixation benefit associated with high frequency target words was numerically larger than the benefit associated with either low frequency (0.34 vs. 0.25) or medium frequency (0.34 vs. 0.23) target words (see Fig. 3).

These findings suggest that the target word frequency did affect the pre-fixation processing benefit derived from word $n + 1$. Findings from both the first fixation duration and the total number of fixations suggest that readers spent more time fixating and made more fixations on word $n + 1$ when the prior fixation location was 'far' (i.e. further than four characters away from the first letter of word $n + 1$) than when it was 'near', and when target words were of low frequency compared to when they were of high frequency.

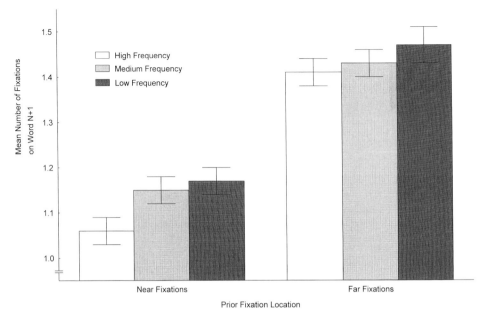

Fig. 3. Effect of frequency on word N upon number of fixations on word $N + 1$.

Discussion

Taken overall, the findings from Experiment 1 suggest that readers engaged in more parafoveal processing (i.e. they made more 'near prior fixation location' fixations) when the target word (n) frequency was high than when it was low, and these data therefore support the findings reported by Henderson and Ferreira (1990) that there is an influence of foveal word load on parafoveal processing.

Although so far we have accounted for our findings in terms of parafoveal benefit, an alternative explanation for these data is that of *spill-over effects* (e.g. Ehrlich and Rayner, 1983; Henderson and Ferreira, 1990). According to Ehrlich and Rayner, the processing of one particular word may affect reading times of words that follow it, and thus *spill-over effects* are those effects that although expected on word n, also appear on word $n + 1$. Henderson and Ferreira (1990) suggested that although some of the reading time differences they observed on neighbouring word pairs n, $n + 1$ could be attributed to differences in the amount of parafoveal processing taking place, some of the observed differences could well have been due to spill-over effects. As far as the data reported from Experiment 1 are concerned, if low frequency words are, as our data suggest, more attentionally demanding than high frequency words, then any increase in difficulty that they cause may well spill-over into the processing of the neighbouring ($n + 1$) word. Thus, it is possible that our observed differences in reading times, rather than being due to differences in parafoveal processing per se, are instead due to continued processing of word *n* when word *n* + 1 was being fixated.

The data from this current experiment, in keeping with those of Henderson and Ferreira (1990), are problematic for Morrison's sequential attention-based model of eye guidance (Morrison, 1984). However, the findings reported here are nevertheless in keeping with the sequential attention-based eye guidance models proposed by Henderson and Ferreira (1990, Henderson and Ferreira, 1993) and also by Reichle et al. (1998; see also Rayner et al., 1998), since both of these models are able to account for an influence of foveal load on parafoveal processing.

Under a parallel attention-based account of eye guidance, in which attention is seen as a limited resource that is shared between foveal and parafoveal stimuli, we would expect that increasing the parafoveal load would cause foveal processing to be disrupted. Also, since a parallel attention-based model of eye guidance would predict that foveal and parafoveal words are processed in parallel from the beginning of a fixation, we would predict that any influence of parafoveal processing difficulty would disappear when foveal processing was made easier. These predictions are tested in Experiment 2.

Experiment 2: the influence of parafoveal load on foveal processing

Experiment 2 was conducted to investigate the influence of parafoveal load on foveal processing. In this experiment parafoveal processing difficulty was varied by manipulating the informativeness of the initial letter sequence of word *n* + 1 (Underwood, Clews and Everatt, 1990). Foveal processing in this experiment was manipulated by use of different anaphoric reference relationships (e.g. Garrod, O'Brien, Morris and Rayner, 1990).

Method

Participants
Thirty-six native English speakers took part in this experiment. All had normal or corrected-to-normal vision, and those with corrected-to-normal vision wore soft contact lenses. Participants were paid £3 each.

Materials
Initially, 47 test passages were constructed, following the same restraints as in the study reported by Garrod et al. (1990). Each passage contained four sentences. The second sentence in each passage contained an antecedent which implicitly refer-enced a particular category member, and the context surrounding the antecedent strongly suggested the referenced category member. The final sentence of each

passage contained either an anaphoric (e.g. the rake) or a non-anaphoric (e.g. a rake) noun phrase. An example of a test passage is as follows.

> "Autumn was almost over and the leaves were piling up. Peter told his son to go to the shed and get the tool with the long handle and metal prongs. The boy soon returned and Peter began the job. He found the rake compact and easy to handle."

These 47 test passages were pre-screened to ensure that only one category member was implied by the context, and as a result of this procedure, seven items were removed, leaving a total of 40 sentences for use in the experiment.

The anaphoric/non-anaphoric target noun phrase (n) in sentence four of each passage was followed, in every instance, by a 7-letter word (word $n + 1$) with a frequency of less than 18 per million (mean frequency = 6; Kuçera and Francis, 1967). The initial trigrams of these words were either informative or redundant. Informativeness was defined according to three criteria: initial trigram frequency (total trigram frequency $\leq$ 9 per 20,000; Mayzner and Tresselt, 1965), initial bigram frequency (bigram frequency $\leq$ 9 per 20,000; Mayzner and Tresselt, 1965), and the number of same-length words sharing the same initial trigram (informative beginning words shared initial trigrams with <6 other 7-letter words). Redundant word beginnings had initial trigram frequency >20 per 20,000 (Mayzner and Tresselt, 1965), initial bigram frequencies >20 per 20,000 (Mayzner and Tresselt, 1965), and shared their initial trigrams with >30 other 7-letter English words. A one-way between groups ANOVA conducted on the frequencies of these words revealed no significant differences in frequencies between informative and redundant beginning words ($F_{1(1,78)} < 1$).

Four versions of each passage were constructed, such that (1) the noun phrase (NP) in the final sentence was either anaphoric or non-anaphoric, and (2) word $n + 1$ had either an informative or a redundant beginning. The four possible versions of the final sentence for the example test passage presented earlier, this time with the 7-letter $n + 1$ words italicised, are presented below.

He found the rake *compact* and easy to handle	Redundant beginning/Anaphoric NP
He found the rake *awkward* and cumbersome to handle	Informative beginning/Anaphoric NP
He found a rake *compact* and easy to handle	Redundant beginning/Non-anaphoric NP
He found a rake *awkward* and cumbersome to handle	Informative beginning/Non-anaphoric NP

Four sets of materials were compiled, with each set containing ten test passages in each of these four different conditions. Across the four sets each passage appeared once in each condition. Four additional passages were similarly constructed and were presented to subjects prior to presentation of the test passages. A comprehension test was also constructed, and this was administered to participants during the course of the experiment.

Apparatus and procedure
The apparatus and procedure were the same as described for Experiment 1.

Results

Target noun phrases were classed as having been fixated when a reader's fixation point fell on either one of its component letters or on one of the blank spaces that preceded or followed it. Word $n + 1$ was considered to have been fixated when one of its component letters was fixated. As in the previous experiment, all fixations <80 ms and within one character of the previous or subsequent fixation were merged, and any fixation of <40 ms which fell more than three characters away from the previous or subsequent fixation was excluded. A small amount of data (1.7%) was also excluded from further analyses due to tracker loss.

Analyses were conducted on measures of target noun phrase processing, and on word $n + 1$ processing, and these are reported below.

Target noun phrase processing
Reading time indices used in the analyses of the target noun phrase included first fixation durations and first pass reading times. Due to the nature of the experimental manipulation, the length of the target noun phrases varied across conditions, and therefore first pass reading times were calculated by dividing the raw reading times by the number of characters in the region of interest. This procedure resulted in a *millisecond per character* measure. Although it is indisputable that words have psychological reality, we can see in Experiment 1 that word length can have strong and systematic effects on reading times. For this reason we are including the measure here in addition to reading time per word measures.

The total mean durations of the first fixation on the target noun phrase (n) as a function of noun phrase type (anaphoric vs. non-anaphoric) and informativeness of the initial trigram of word $n + 1$ are shown in Fig. 4.

A 2 (anaphoric vs. non-anaphoric noun phrase type) $\times$ 2 (informative vs. redundant initial trigram) ANOVA was conducted on these data. There were main effects of both noun phrase type ($F_{1(1,35)} = 6.28$, $p < 0.05$, $MS_e = 5339$, $F_{2(1,39)} = 6.01$, $p < 0.05$, $MS_e = 6856$) and informativeness ($F_{1(1,35)} = 4.23$, $p < 0.05$, $MS_e = 4087$, $F_{2(1,39)} = 4.8$, $p < 0.05$, $MS_e = 4392$). Participants' first fixation duration was shorter when either the target noun phrase (n) type was anaphoric, or when word $n + 1$ had a redundant initial trigram. There was no interaction between noun phrase type and informativeness (all F-values <1).

The total mean first pass reading times (ms/char.) for the target noun phrase (n) as a function of noun phrase type (anaphoric vs. non-anaphoric) and informativeness of the initial trigram of word $n + 1$ are shown in Fig. 5.

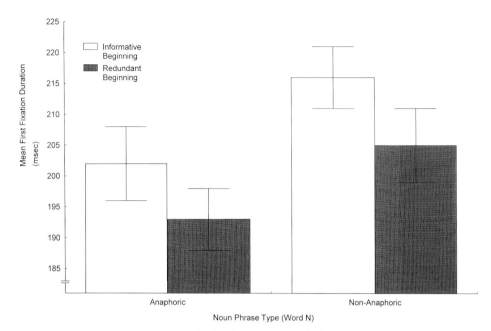

Fig. 4. First fixation on word N.

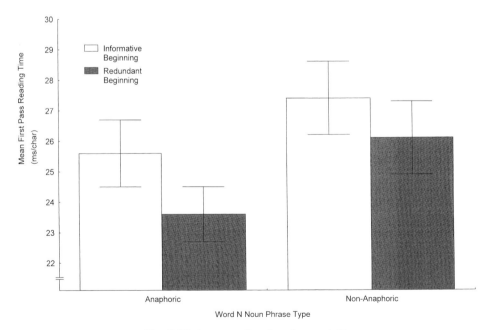

Fig. 5. First pass reading time for word N.

A 2 (noun phrase type) $\times$ 2 (informativeness) ANOVA was conducted on these data. Once again there were main effects of both noun phrase type ($F_{1(1,35)} = 7.72$, $p < 0.01$, $MS_e = 160$, $F_{2(1,39)} = 5.1$, $p < 0.05$, $MS_e = 181$) and informativeness ($F_{1(1,35)} = 11.79$, $p < 0.01$, $MS_e = 236$, $F_{2(1,39)} = 5.59$, $p < 0.05$, $MS_e = 114$). In keeping with the analysis of first fixation duration, participants' first fixation duration was found to be significantly shorter when either the target noun phrase (n) type was anaphoric, or when word $n + 1$ had a redundant initial trigram. There was no interaction between noun phrase type and informativeness (all F-values <1).

Thus it appears from our data that reading times for the target noun phrase, as measured by first fixation duration and first pass reading times, are sensitive to the informativeness of the initial trigram of the neighbouring word.

Parafoveal word ($n + 1$) processing
As in Experiment 1, parafoveal processing was measured in terms of pre-fixation processing benefit. Reading time indices used included first fixation durations of word $n + 1$ and first pass reading time for word $n + 1$. In this experiment, however, these measures were taken as functions of target noun phrase type (anaphoric vs. non-anaphoric), informativeness of the initial trigram of word $n + 1$ (informative vs. redundant word beginning, and prior fixation location ('near' vs. 'far'). As before, prior location fixations for word $n + 1$ were considered to be either *near* fixations (i.e. within four characters of the first letter of word $n + 1$) or *far* fixations (i.e. further than four characters away from the first letter of word $n + 1$).

The mean first fixation durations for word $n + 1$ as a function of target noun phrase type, informativeness of initial trigram, and prior fixation location are shown in Fig. 6.

A 2 (anaphoric vs. non-anaphoric target NP) $\times$ 2 (informative vs. redundant initial trigram) $\times$ 2 (near vs. far prior fixation location) ANOVA was conducted on these data. There was a main effect of prior fixation location ($F_{1(1,35)} = 57.06$, $p < 0.001$, $MS_e = 205570$, $F_{2(1,39)} = 23.2$, $p < 0.001$, $MS_e = 137597$): first fixation durations were significantly shorter when the prior fixation location was near (i.e. within four characters of word $n + 1$). There was a main effect of informativeness, which was significant by items and approached significance by subjects ($F_{1(1,35)} = 3.48$, $p < 0.08$, $MS_e = 15177$, $F_{2(1,39)} = 4.52$, $p < 0.05$, $MS_e = 20137$): first fixations were shorter when the parafoveal word ($n + 1$) had a redundant beginning. There was also a main effect of target noun phrase type, but this was significant by subjects only ($F_{1(1,35)} = 4.21$, $p < 0.05$, $MS_e = 14718$, $F_{2(1,39)} < 1$): readers made shorter first fixations on word $n + 1$ when the preceding noun phrase was anaphoric. The interaction between target noun phrase type, informativeness, and prior fixation location was significant by subjects but not by items ($F_{1(1,35)} = 4.87$, $p < 0.05$, $MS_e = 17891$, $F_{2(1,39)} < 1$). No other effects approached significance.

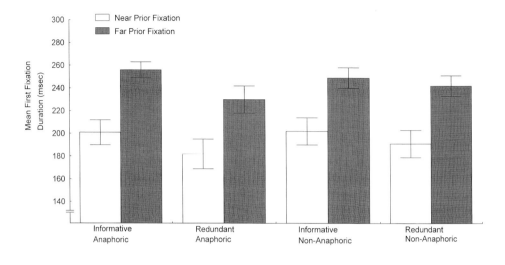

Noun Phrase Type of Word N and
Initial Trigram Informativeness of Word N+1

Fig. 6. First fixation duration for word $N + 1$.

The first pass reading times (ms) for word $n + 1$ as a function of target noun phrase type, informativeness of initial trigram, and prior fixation location are shown in Fig. 7.

A 2 (anaphoric vs. non-anaphoric target NP) $\times 2$ (informative vs. redundant initial trigram) $\times 2$ (near vs. far prior fixation location) ANOVA was conducted on these data. There was a main effect of prior location fixation ($F_{1(1,35)} = 36.01$, $p < 0.001, MS_e = 212748, F_{2(1,39)} = 39.6, p < 0.001, MS_e = 268426$): first pass reading times for word $n + 1$ were shorter when the prior fixation location was near (i.e. within four characters of word $n + 1$). There was also a significant main effect of informativeness ($F_{1(1,35)} = 6.91, p < 0.05, MS_e = 38782, F_{2(1,39)} = 6.99$, $p < 0.05, MS_e = 49572$): first pass reading times were shorter when word $n + 1$ had a redundant beginning. No other effects approached significance.

Discussion

The purpose of Experiment 2 was to test the predictions made by sequential attention- and parallel attention-based models of eye guidance, with regard to the effects of parafoveal processing load on foveal processing. To investigate this issue, we examined whether or not increased parafoveal processing load caused foveal processing to be disrupted (i.e. by manipulating the informativeness of the parafoveal word beginning), and we also investigated whether the influence

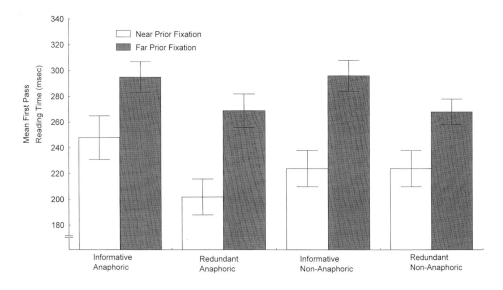

Fig. 7. First pass reading time for word $N + 1$.

of parafoveal load difficulty disappeared when foveal load was manipulated to make it easier (i.e. when an anaphoric phrase was used instead of a non-anaphoric phrase). Analyses of data from both first fixation durations and first pass reading times in Experiment 2 showed that when the parafoveal word had an informative initial trigram the foveal word was fixated for longer than when it had a redundant initial trigram, irrespective of foveal processing difficulty. It appears from the data reported here that informative word beginnings induced longer fixations on the previous word, suggesting that parafoveal load did have an influence foveal word processing. Our findings also replicate those of Garrod et al. (1990), in that participants in this study took longer to read non-anaphoric noun phrases than they did anaphoric noun phrases.

If, under a parallel attention-based account of eye guidance, attention is seen as a limited capacity resource shared between foveal and parafoveal stimuli, then we would expect that when the parafoveal word is attentionally demanding, less resources would be available for foveal processing. Under such an account, when the foveal word is easy to process, the demands of the parafoveal word would not influence foveal processing, but when both foveal and parafoveal words are difficult to process, the demands of the two words may exceed the available attentional resources, and this would lead to disruption of foveal word processing. Thus we would have expected an interaction between foveal and parafoveal processing load, and this was not apparent in our data. Our data do, however, support our original predictions to some extent in that we did find an influence of parafoveal load on foveal processing, and therefore we have some support for a parallel attention-based account of eye movements. One explanation for a failure to find an interaction between foveal and parafoveal processing difficulty may have been that our anaphoric noun phrases (i.e. the 'easy' foveal stimuli) were sufficiently attentionally demanding to produce a conflict of resources even when the parafoveal word was difficult to process.

Findings from Experiment 2 are not entirely consistent with the predictions made by a sequential attention-based model of eye guidance. However, the data are consistent with a parallel attention-based account, such as the one discussed, but subsequently dismissed, by Henderson and Ferreira (1993). Data reported by Kennison and Clifton (1995) are also consistent with a parallel attention-based account, and those researchers suggested on the basis of their findings that a feasible alternative to a sequential allocation of attention in eye guidance would be a model where attention is viewed as "a gradient . . . focused around the centre of vision and extending out in the direction of the ensuing saccade" (Kennison and Clifton, 1995, pp. 78–79). This description sounds remarkably similar to the parallel allocation model described but dismissed by Henderson and Ferreira (1993).

Conclusions

The purpose of these two experiments was to investigate how foveal and parafoveal information is used to guide eye movements in reading. In Experiment 1, we investigated whether or not foveal load influences parafoveal processing, and in Experiment 2 we investigated the influence of parafoveal load on foveal processing.

Findings from Experiment 1 revealed that when foveal load was high (i.e. foveal words were of low frequency) readers engaged in less parafoveal word processing than when foveal load was low, and this supports previously reported findings suggesting that there is an influence of foveal word load on parafoveal processing. These findings, in keeping with those of Henderson and Ferreira (1990), are problematic for Morrison's sequential attention-based model of eye guidance (Morrison, 1984), since Morrison's model predicts that foveal processing load would have no influence on parafoveal influence. However, the data from this first experiment could be accounted for by the sequential attention-based models proposed by Henderson and Ferreira (1990, 1993) and by Reichle et al. (1998).

Findings from Experiment 2 revealed that when parafoveal words had informative initial trigrams, readers' fixation times on the previous word were longer than when the parafoveal words had redundant initial trigrams. These data show

how features of the parafoveal word are able to influence reading time measures for the foveal word. Overall, our findings, that parafoveal load influences foveal processing, are inconsistent with sequential attention-based models of eye guidance (e.g. Henderson and Ferreira, 1990, 1993; Reichle et al., 1998), and instead lend support to a parallel allocation of attention model of eye movement.

Taken together, the findings from these two experiments show how certain characteristics of neighbouring words (e.g. word frequencies, informativeness of initial letters of a word) serve to disrupt processing in a bi-directional fashion, with increased processing demands resulting in disruption of both the currently fixated word and the next-to-be fixated word.

In summary, the findings of our two experiments do not support current sequential attention-based models of eye guidance (e.g. Morrison, 1984; Henderson and Ferreira, 1990; Reichle et al., 1998), since these would predict that there would be no influence of either foveal-to-parafoveal or parafoveal-to-foveal word processing. Instead our findings are much more in keeping with a parallel attention-based model of eye movement control, in which there is shared allocation of attention to neighbouring foveal and parafoveal words.

Acknowledgements

We are grateful to Alan Kennedy, Albrecht Inhoff and Cécile Beauvillain for their comments on an earlier draft of this chapter. Simon Liversedge helped with the analysis and interpretation of Experiment 2.

References

Briihl, D. and Inhoff, A.W. (1995). Integrating information across fixations during reading: the use of orthographic bodies and of exterior letters. Journal of Experimental Psychology: Learning, Memory, and Cognition, 21, 55–67.

Brysbaert, M. and Vitu, F. (1998). Word skipping: Implications for theories of eye movement control in reading. In: G. Underwood (Ed.), Eye Guidance in Reading and Scene Perception. Oxford: Elsevier, pp. 125–147.

Ehrlich, K. and Rayner, K. (1983). Pronoun assignment and semantic integration during reading: eye movements and immediacy of processing. Journal of Verbal Learning and Verbal Behavior, 22, 75–87.

Garrod, S., O'Brien, E.J., Morris, R.K. and Rayner, K. (1990). Elaborative inferencing as an active or passive process. Journal of Experimental Psychology: Learning, Memory, and Cognition, 16, 250–257.

Henderson, J.M. (1992). Visual attention and eye movement control during reading and picture viewing. In: K. Rayner (Ed.), Eye Movements and Visual Cognition. New York: Springer-Verlag, pp. 260–283.

Henderson, J.M. and Ferreira, F. (1990). Effects of foveal processing difficulty on the perceptual span in reading: implications for attention and eye movement control. Journal of Experimental Psychology: Learning, Memory, and Cognition, 16, 417–429.

Henderson, J.M. and Ferreira, F. (1993). Eye movement control during reading: fixation measures reflect foveal but not parafoveal processing difficulty. Canadian Journal of Experimental Psychology, 47, 201–221.

Kennedy, A. (1998). The influence of parafoveal words on foveal inspection time: evidence for a processing trade-off. In: G. Underwood (Ed.), Eye Guidance in Reading and Scene Perception, Oxford: Elsevier, pp. 149–179.

Kennison, S.M. and Clifton, C. (1995). Determinants of parafoveal preview benefit in high and low working memory capacity readers: implications for eye movement control. Journal of Experimental Psychology: Learning, Memory, and Cognition, 21, 68–81.

Kučera, H. and Francis, W.N. (1967). Computational Analysis of Present-Day American English. Providence, RI: Brown University Press.

Mayzner, M.S. and Tresselt, M.E. (1965). Tables of single letter and bigram frequency counts for various word length and letter position combinations. Psychonomic Monograph Supplement, 1 (2), 13–32.

McConkie, G.W. and Rayner, K. (1975). The span of the effective stimulus during a fixation in reading. Perception and Psychophysics, 17, 578–586.

Morrison, R.E. (1984). Manipulation of stimulus onset delay in reading: evidence for parallel programming of saccades. Journal of Experimental Psychology: Human Perception and Performance, 10, 667–682.

Pollatsek, A., Bolozky, S., Well, A.D. and Rayner, K. (1981). Asymmetries in the perceptual span for Israeli readers. Brain and Language, 14, 174–180.

Rayner, K. (1978). Eye movement latencies for parafoveally presented words. Bulletin of the Psychonomic Society, 11 (1), 13–16.

Rayner, K. (1986). Eye movements and the perceptual span in beginning and skilled readers. Journal of Experimental Child Psychology, 41, 211–236.

Rayner, K., Reichle, E.D. and Pollatsek, A. (1998). Eye movement control in reading: an overview and model. In: G. Underwood (Ed.), Eye Guidance in Reading and Scene Perception. Oxford: Elsevier, pp. 243–268.

Reichle, E.D., Pollatsek, A., Fisher, D.L. and Rayner, K. (1998). Towards a model of eye movement control in reading. Psychological Review, 105 (1), 125–157.

Schroyens, W., Vitu, F., Brysbaert, M. and d'Ydewalle, G. (1999). Eye movement control during reading: Foveal load and parafoveal processing. Quarterly Journal of Experimental Psychology, 52A, 1021–1046.

Stelmach, L.B., Campsall, J.M. and Herdman, C.M. (1997). Attention and ocular movements. Journal of Experimental Psychology: Human Perception and Performance, 23, 823–844.

Underwood, G., Clews, S. and Everatt, J. (1990). How do readers know where to look next? Local information distributions influence eye fixations. Quarterly Journal of Experimental Psychology, 42A, 39–65.

Underwood, N.R. and McConkie, G.W. (1985). Perceptual span for letter distinctions during reading. Reading Research Quarterly, 20 (2), 153–162.

CHAPTER 11

Eye Guidance and the Saliency of Word Beginnings in Reading Text

Wietske Vonk
Max Planck Institute for Psycholingusitics and University of Nijmegen

Ralph Radach
Technical University of Aachen

and
Hedderik van Rijn
University of Nijmegen

Abstract

It is generally agreed that the spatial distribution of landing positions of initial progressive saccades into words is primarily determined by low-level factors such as launch distance and target word length. At the same time there is a lively and highly controversial discussion on whether higher-level cognitive processing can modulate the extent of these saccades. In this chapter we investigate whether the orthographic saliency of a word beginning affects the initial saccade landing position. Dutch 10–12-letter NN-compounds with either high or low frequency of the initial trigram served as targets. They were embedded into declarative sentences that provided story frames creating a moderately positive vs. neutral context. Results indicate that there is indeed a small but reliable effect of initial trigram frequency on landing position over a large range of saccade launch positions. There was no influence of sentence context on the landing position in the word, although context did prove to be effective on first-fixation duration, number of fixations and gaze duration. It is concluded that the landing position of saccades within words is modulated by higher-order information, probably of an orthographic nature.

Reading as a Perceptual Process/A. Kennedy, R. Radach, D. Heller and J. Pynte (Editors)
© 2000 Elsevier Science Ltd. All rights reserved

Introduction

Background: parafoveal processing and eye movement control

The importance of parafoveal processing for information acquisition and eye movement control has been one of the most important subjects of experimental reading research during the last 25 years. It has been shown in numerous studies that readers, while fixating a word, often preprocess the beginning letters (and sometimes all letters) of the next parafoveally available word. The effective region of letter identification is generally assumed to span from the beginning of the current word to about 8 or 9 letters to the right of the fixation position. [1] The most obvious consequence of this parafoveal processing is a reduction of word viewing time when the adjacent word is eventually fixated (for reviews see Rayner, 1998; Rayner and Pollatsek, 1989). Measures of reading time sensitive to parafoveal preview effects include mean fixation duration, the duration of the first of several fixations and a variety of gaze duration (word reading time) measures (for a recent overview and discussion see Inhoff and Radach, 1998). Interestingly, there appears to be no contribution of semantic or morphological information to parafoveal preprocessing (e.g., Inhoff, 1989; Lima and Inhoff, 1985; Rayner, Balota and Pollatsek, 1986; but see below our discussion of possible compound morpheme effects). Instead, what is integrated from one fixation to another appears to be an abstract letter code, as changing case in a mIxEd CaSe font between preview and target word fixation does not diminish preview benefits (McConkie and Zola, 1979; Rayner, McConkie and Zola, 1980). As might be expected, the efficiency of parafoveal processing is a function of the distance between target and pre-target fixation (see, e.g., Chapter 7 for a detailed discussion).

With respect to spatial eye movement parameters, extrafoveal information processing plays an important role in two respects: during every fixation a target word for the ensuing saccade needs to be selected and an intended fixation location within this target word has to be determined. This is usually seen as two relatively independent spatial decisions. While the target selection decision appears to be co-determined by low-level visuomotor and cognitive factors (see below), the landing site specification is usually assumed to be based solely on low-level information such as word length and distance to the target word (e.g., Radach and McConkie, 1998; Rayner, Sereno and Raney, 1996). The present chapter will deal with data that appear to cast doubt on the pure low-level nature of landing site determination and present a new experiment aimed at testing the controversial hypothesis that linguistic features of a word can influence the saccade landing position when the word is initially fixated.

---

1 There is now evidence indicating that some parafoveal processing of information to the left of the currently fixated word is possible (Binder, Pollatsek and Rayner, 1999; see also Chapter 9).

The role of low-level and cognitive factors for spatial aspects of eye movement control

The decision about which word to select next for fixation has been the subject of intensive discussion during the last decade, with one position claiming that 'word skipping' is due to low-level factors (O'Regan, 1990) and one position asserting that it is the result of parafoveal lexical processing (e.g., Rayner and Pollatsek, 1989). The latter position has been particularly influential, as it provides a basis for an important class of eye movement control models, the sequential attention models. The basic idea is that eye movements are always preceded by movements of attention, conceptualised as a lexical processing spotlight. If a parafoveal word is easy to process, it may be recognised during the current fixation, which will cause a further movement of attention to the following word. This, in turn, will lead to the cancellation of an initially planned saccade to the next parafoveal word and, hence, the skipping of that word. The latest version of this idea is presented in Chapter 27 by Rayner, Reichle and Pollatsek. Problems related to sequential attention models of eye movement control are discussed in detail in Chapter 9 by Inhoff, Radach, Starr and Greenberg.

The low-level factors involved in word skipping were first quantified by Kerr (1992) (see also McConkie, Kerr and Dyre, 1994) in his analyses of a large corpus of English reading data. He showed that the probability of fixation can be predicted reasonably well using a simple model including just two variables: word length and target word eccentricity. However, this does not necessarily mean that word skipping is determined entirely by low-level processes, as larger and more distant words are also more difficult to process and therefore less likely to be parafoveally identified. The controversy around the role of high-level (lexical and contextual) factors in word skipping has recently been resolved in an excellent review by Brysbaert and Vitu (1998). They presented a meta-analysis of several sentence reading experiments, including seven studies manipulating the easiness of parafoveal words and eight studies manipulating contextual constraints. When assessing the relative contribution of word difficulty and context against word length, however, they found that only a modest portion of the variance (4% for difficulty and 11% for context) can be explained by cognitive factors.[2] While this account emphasises the predominance of low-level factors, it also establishes a significant influence of linguistic processing on fixation probability. As we will see below, there is much less consensus about the determinants of fixation positions within words.

---

2 When interpreting these results, it should be kept in mind that parameters that represent cognitive influences (e.g., ratings of contextual constraint) are perhaps not as reliable as plain measures of low-level factors like saccade launch distance. Also, word length may also be seen as a 'lexical' parameter as it is likely to be used as a source of information in lexical processing.

When a word has been selected to be the target of a saccade, the intended landing position within this word needs to be specified. The specified target co-ordinates are then used to compute and execute a saccade that attempts to bring the eyes to the desired target. The actual landing positions of the saccades that go into the target word form a Gaussian distribution with a peak about halfway between word beginning and word centre. The peak of the landing site distribution has been named the 'preferred' viewing position (Rayner, 1979) as opposed to the 'optimal' viewing position, indicating a fixation location near the word centre at which information acquisition is most effective (e.g., O'Regan, 1990). McConkie, Kerr, Reddix and Zola (1988) have shown that the preferred viewing position distribution is mainly the result of two underlying low-level factors: launch distance and word length. These analyses have subsequently been replicated and extended by McConkie, Kerr and Dyre (1994), Radach and Kempe (1993) and Radach and McConkie (1998), adding the location on the line of text and the prior fixation pattern as additional factors of influence. There is also some influence of prior fixation and gaze durations on initial landing positions, which is discussed in Chapter 7 of the current volume by Radach and Heller.

The starting point of the account proposed by McConkie and his co-workers of the preferred landing position is the assumption that the word centre serves as the default saccade goal. Empirical support for this idea comes both from tachistoscopic word recognition studies (Brysbaert, Vitu and Schroyens, 1996; Nazir, Heller and Sussmann, 1992; O'Regan and Jacobs, 1992) as well as from reading data showing that the minimal probability of refixating the same word occurs when fixating locations near the word centre (e.g., McConkie, Kerr, Reddix, Zola and Jacobs, 1989; Radach and Kempe, 1993; Rayner, Sereno and Raney, 1996; Vitu, O'Regan and Mittau, 1990). Most recently, Radach and McConkie (1998) added a further argument showing that regressive inter-word saccades that bring the eyes back to previously read words tend to land at the word centre over a large range of word lengths and launch distances.

If the word centre indeed is the intended target, why does the preferred viewing position distribution peak considerably left of this location and why do many saccades undershoot the intended word (as indicated by the truncation of the distribution at the word beginning)? McConkie et al. (1988) and Radach and McConkie (1998) explain this as a result of a saccadic distance effect: when the saccade is launched near to the target word, it follows a tendency to overshoot the word centre, when the saccade is launched far from the target, the result is a tendency to undershoot. Interestingly, saccades tend to go to the word centre when the launch distance is close to the average individual saccade amplitude. The relation between launch position and landing site can be expressed quantitatively in a simple linear *landing position*: for every 1-letter increment in launch distance relative to the word centre, there is an increase in estimated mean landing position in the order of 0.4 to 0.5 letters. An increase in word length does not change the slope of this function but leads to a change in its intercept. As Radach and McConkie (1998) show, the landing position continues to be linear for launch sites of up to −21 characters relative to the word centre and thus spans over the entire range of saccade amplitudes found in reading.[3] This indicates that the phenomenon must be visuomotor rather than perceptual in nature (Poulton, 1981). It is incompatible with other previously proposed accounts of the preferred viewing position based on the notions of 'centre of gravity' (O'Regan, 1990; Vitu, 1991) and parafoveal letter processing (Rayner, Sereno and Raney, 1996).

Are there linguistic influences on initial fixation positions in reading?

If the distribution of inter-word saccade landing position is primarily determined by low-level factors, as suggested in the last section, is there still room for initial landing positions to be mediated by linguistic variables? Following Underwood and Radach (1998), we will refer to such higher-level influences as 'cognitive landing site effects'. As will be shown below, the literature on this subject is extremely controversial with results ranging from demonstrating significant influences of cognition on inter-word saccade landing positions to results that appear to speak strictly against such effects. Our discussion will be centred around two questions: under what circumstances do cognitive landing site effects occur and what characteristics of parafoveal words can be made responsible for their occurrence?[4]

Evidence in favour of cognitive landing site effects

The discussion about cognitive landing site effects started with a series of experiments reported by Everatt and Underwood (1992), Hyönä, Niemi and Underwood (1989), Underwood, Clews and Everatt (1990) and by Underwood, Hyönä and Niemi (1987). They obtained stimuli with 'uneven distributions of information' in pilot studies where subjects were asked to guess words on the basis of their first 5

---

3 When saccades depart from very far launch sites, many will fall short of the target word. Here, as in all other cases, the landing position function is determined by using the available observations for a given launch distance and target word length to compute *estimated* means of a Gaussian landing position distribution.

4 We will refer to potentially influential linguistic characteristics of word beginnings in two different respects: *orthographic saliency*, as defined by *token* letter cluster frequency, is based on the frequency of a word beginning in a particular language. In contrast, word beginning *informativeness* can be statistically defined by *type* letter cluster frequency, that is the number of words in a language that share the same beginning. In some studies informativeness has been determined as the frequency of correctly guessing the word on the basis of just the beginning and/or by counting the words in a dictionary that share the same beginning.

or 6 vs. last 5 or 6 letters. The selected words were presented within short sentences that subjects were asked to read. The general result from these studies was that the eyes tended to land further into words when the informative part was at the end as compared to cases where it was at the beginning. This landing position effect was initially interpreted on lexical–semantical grounds, arguing that fixations are attracted further into words that have an informative ending.

As Hyönä (1993) points out, this argument is far from decisive, as the words with informative beginnings vs. endings differed in several respects. For example, in the study by Hyönä, Niemi and Underwood (1989) most words with informative beginnings had a productive derivational ending, whereas all words with informative endings were NN-compounds. At the same time, orthographic redundancy, as indicated by positional bigram frequencies, was markedly different for the two groups of stimuli. The idea that during reading lexical–semantic information can be picked up from the second half of a parafoveal word and subsequently used for eye guidance is in conflict with a large body of data on parafoveal preprocessing in both word recognition and reading (Balota and Rayner, 1991; Inhoff, 1982; Rayner, Balota and Pollatsek, 1986) and has provoked severe criticism (Rayner and Morris, 1992).

In recent years, Underwood and his co-workers have adopted a more cautious viewpoint in the controversy around possible lexical–semantic preprocessing effects. Everatt, Bradshaw and Hibbard (1998) discuss two experiments in which the sentence context prior to the critical word was manipulated. In one study, the general context either primed the critical words that contained an informative beginning or ending or was neutral. In another study, the critical words were preceded by a word with which they were either semantically related or semantically unrelated. In both experiments there was a reliable effect of informativeness on landing position, but neither type of contextual constraint was found to mediate this effect. As the authors point out, this can be seen as evidence against the idea that cognitive landing position effects are produced by semantic preprocessing.

In his review of cognitive landing site effects, Hyönä (1993) emphasises 'orthographic saliency', denoting the relative orthographic regularity of the word beginning, as the best candidate for a factor that could 'pull' or 'attract' the eyes towards a particular region within a word. A direct test of this hypothesis was presented by Hyönä (1995). He compared three types of stimuli: words with a derivational ending, compound words containing an identical first half but an orthographically less frequent ending and words with an orthographically infrequent beginning. The most important result with regard to the current discussion was that while there was no difference between the first two word types, saccades into words with less regular beginnings landed about 1/3 character closer to the word beginning. Interestingly, the bulk of the effect was due to additional fixations made on the space before the critical word in the case of infrequent-beginning words. Similar results were reported by Beauvillain, Doré and Baudouin (1996), in an orthographic decision task involving the recognition of single words displayed to the right of a central fixation mark. They found that saccade landing positions in this task are shifted to the left for target words with orthographically irregular beginning letters.

Another class of cognitive landing site effects appears to have been demonstrated by Inhoff, Briihl and Schwartz (1996). In a study designed to investigate effects of word morphology in reading and naming tasks, they compared eye movements into three types of 9-letter target words: monomorphemic words (e.g., arthritis, cathedral), suffixed words (e.g., heartless, sainthood) and compound words with 3- to 5-letter first constituents (e.g., gunpowder, timetable). As an unexpected result, they found that initial saccades went significantly further into compound words (mean landing position 4.4) as compared to suffixed (mean landing position 3.9) and monomorphemic words (mean landing position 3.7). [5]

Hyönä and Pollatsek (1998, experiment 2) recently reported an experiment in which they varied the lexical frequency of the initial 5- to 6-letter constituent morphemes of Finnish NN-compounds. When the initial constituents were of low frequency, the initial saccade into the 12–14-letter target words landed slightly closer to the word beginning. The interpretation suggested for this result is based on a processing difficulty hypothesis originally proposed by Hyönä (1995). According to this hypothesis, a parafoveal low-frequency word will narrow down the span of effective preprocessing which in turn will lead to a shorter forward saccade (see Chapter 4). Although this account appears straightforward and plausible, it leaves open the crucial question *which* type of information (orthographic, morphological or lexical) is parafoveally processed and *how* results of this processing could affect saccade generation.

Evidence against cognitive landing site effects
From the beginning of the research on the subject, cognitive landing site effects have turned out to be fragile and difficult to replicate. For example, in a study similar to the initial experiment (Hyönä, Niemi and Underwood, 1989), Underwood, Bloomfield and Clews (1989) did not find a difference in landing position between words with differing word-internal information structure. Rayner and Morris (1992), amongst other points, argued that in some of the experiments by Underwood et al. the sentence context preceding the target word was not controlled. They took the stimuli of one experiment where this condition was met (Underwood, Clews and Everatt, 1990, experiment 2), reduced the set of items by some that were not

---

5 Using the published target words of Inhoff, Briihl and Schwarz (1996), we have computed their initial trigram and first two bigram frequencies with the result that the observed results cannot be attributed to differences in orthographic saliency.

applicable in American English and repeated the experiment. However, unlike the authors of the original experiment, they did not find a difference in initial saccade landing positions between words with informative beginning vs. ending.

In a recent study, Liversedge and Underwood (1998) attempted to test the hypothesis that a cognitive landing site effect may be strengthened when processing load on the foveal word is low and more resources can be allocated to parafoveal processing. In a first experiment, foveal processing load was manipulated by inserting a category word before the target word referring to an antecedent noun phrase which was either a typical or atypical instance of the category. In a second experiment, the target word was preceded by a possessive pronoun referring to an antecedent noun phrase with a stereotypical gender which was either congruous or incongruous with the gender of the pronoun. Contrary to the author's expectation, in both experiments there was no main effect of word beginning saliency (initial trigram frequency) on the landing position of the first saccade into target words. Only in a subsequent analysis of the second experiment, including items with the shortest vs. longest gaze durations in the pre-target region, saccades tended to land somewhat further into words containing frequent beginnings.

An experiment that appears to be particularly damaging to the cognitive landing site idea was carried out by Kerr (1992). He asked subjects to read a classic novel for comprehension while their eye movements were recorded. At certain places in the text, target words were (among other conditions) replaced with either strings of XXXX or letter strings that were created by scrambling the original words to make them maximally dissimilar to regular English orthography. When the eyes made a saccade into the target string, was the original word was restored. The result from this study that is most relevant for our discussion is that Kerr did not find any difference in landing position between the two types of manipulated strings and carefully matched cases with normal word previews. This is strong evidence against a default role of parafoveal letter processing in the determination of initial saccades into words.

Kerr's result is in harmony with other failures to find effects of word beginning frequency and redundancy in corpus reading studies. Radach (1996) looked for cognitive landing site effects by analysing a total of 40 conditions (5 launch distance ranges × 2 word length ranges × 4 participants) within his 49,000 word corpus of German reading data. For each condition he compared mean landing position as a function of the quartiles of initial trigram informativeness (i.e. the number of word forms that share the same initial trigram). Among the 40 conditions there were only 4 significant differences and only 2 of these were in the direction predicted by the 'informativeness hypothesis' as put forward by Underwood and colleagues. Two similar analyses were carried out with token trigram frequency and word frequency as the dependent variables, again with negative results. On the basis of the same corpus of reading data, Radach and Kempe (1993) compared initial landing positions for nouns beginning with the trigram Sch ... , by far the most common and redundant word beginning in German, with control words beginning with S ... that were matched for word length and word frequency. Although both classes of words differ almost by a factor of 10 in initial trigram frequency, there was no landing site difference. A similar corpus analysis was reported by Rayner, Sereno and Raney (1996), who on the basis of accumulated data from several reading experiments found no differences in landing position distributions for low- vs. high-frequency words.

Interim summary and rationale of our experiment

From our discussion of results in favour vs. against cognitive landing site effects, a number of conclusions can be drawn.

(1) Cognitive landing site effects have so far been found only in experiments in which participants read single sentences, but not in situations where subjects were asked to read substantial amounts of text. This points to the possibility that such effects are to some extent due to reading strategies used in particular experimental situations. A very 'careful' strategy with a maximum of mobilised processing resources may be adopted when reading one sentence at a time to follow a specific instruction (e.g., to memorise the surface structure of the sentence, or verify the occurrence of a target word). In contrast, reading an entire book chapter during a session may lead to a more relaxed strategy with much less emphasis on a detailed analysis of every available piece of visual and linguistic information (for a discussion of 'careful' vs. 'risky' reading strategies see O'Regan, 1992).[6]

(2) Cognitive landing site effects appear to require quite severe manipulations of target word variables. In most successful experiments, the target words either had a very high guessing probability (e.g., greater than 89% in the initial Underwood et al. studies) or very salient beginning letter clusters. A good example is the study by Hyönä (1995), who used Finnish loan words with second and third bigram frequencies that were virtually zero, certainly the most extreme variation of word beginning saliency in any specific language. This casts doubt on whether the demonstrated effects can be generalised to default behaviour in normal reading.

(3) The reviewed literature leads to the conclusion that cognitive landing site effects, when they occur, are due to variations in the orthographic regularity of word beginnings. There appears to be a tendency to find no differences between medium saliency and low-saliency conditions and to find differences between low- or

---

6 Careful sentence-by-sentence reading and colloquial book reading are both frequent variations of normal reading behaviour. We do not intend to suggest that one is more typical, diagnostic or ecologically valid than the other. Some aspects of information processing and eye movement control will be identical in both situations while others may differ.

medium- vs. high-saliency conditions. Thus, as Hyönä (1995) suggested, irregular letter clusters appear to 'pop out', causing atypical saccades into target words.

(4) The studies by Hyönä and Pollatsek (1998) and by Inhoff, Briihl and Schwartz (1996) suggest that there may be a second type of landing site effect: some very familiar first constituents of compound words might be recognised parafoveally and subsequently 'skipped', leading to a shift in the spatial distribution of initial landing sites. Such an effect has been considered as a possibility by Rayner and Morris (1992). Its verification or rejection will require new experiments including variations of orthographic vs. lexical (compound) word beginning frequency measures.

The present study has two purposes. First, we intend to test whether an orthographic effect on initial landing position can be obtained using a less extreme variation of word beginning saliency than the studies by Beauvillain et al. (1996) and Hyönä (1995). By 'less extreme' we mean the selection of target words that produces a large contrast but is still representative of the language as a whole. A selection that is adequate for this purpose can be obtained by drawing target words from the upper and lower end of a distribution of orthographic saliency in a given language. A demonstration of a landing site effect using such a representative sample is of theoretical importance because it would indicate that a modulation of saccade amplitudes by sublexical parafoveal processing is not just an atypical response to nearly irregular letter clusters with frequencies of occurrence near zero, but instead is part of regular reading behaviour. With respect to the problem of designing a situation that leads to careful reading but is sufficiently ecological, we decided to embed target words in story frames including several lines of text, thus avoiding the extremes of single-sentence vs. passage reading.

Second, we investigate the question of whether an orthographic landing site effect can be mediated by contextual constraint. Contextual effects on temporal eye movement parameters and/or word skipping have been demonstrated in several studies (e.g., Ehrlich and Rayner, 1981; Rayner and Well, 1996; Schustack, Ehrlich and Rayner, 1987; Zola, 1984). Of particular importance is the study by Balota, Pollatsek and Rayner (1985) on the role of context in parafoveal processing. They combined high vs. low contextual constraint with either identical, visually similar or visually dissimilar target word previews in an eye-movement-contingent display study. The main result was that context increased the preprocessing benefit for identical and visually similar previews in terms of fixation duration on the target word and also increased the number of cases in which the target word was skipped. The authors conclude that when words are predictable, readers use more detailed parafoveal visual information, which, in turn, is used to activate lexical representations of target words.

So far, there has been no attempt to combine a manipulation of contextual constraint with a variation of orthographic word beginning saliency. The two context experiments by Everatt, Bradshaw and Hibbard (1998), that we have already discussed above, used the 'informativeness' measure of the word beginning rather than its orthographic saliency. Our rationale in using a context manipulation in the current study is that context, if effective in increasing the efficiency of parafoveal information acquisition, may also interact with the visual information used to produce cognitive landing site effects.

Method

General design and materials

The present study used a two-level variation of orthographic trigram saliency (high and low token trigram frequency) and contextual constraint (positive and neutral context). Dutch compounds, consisting of two nouns with, in some cases, one or two linking graphemes, served as the stimuli. The length of the first stem was 4 or 5 characters, and the entire compound had a length of 8 to 10 characters. This range of word length was chosen to minimise the likelihood of target words being skipped during reading. The use of the noun–noun compounds allowed us to strictly control the morphemic structure of the critical words. [7]

Orthographic saliency was determined by using the token initial trigram frequency based on all nouns of word length 4 to 20 in the Dutch CELEX corpus [8] (Baayen, Piepenbrock and van Rijn, 1993). Nouns with nonalphabetic characters, such as - and ', and nouns starting with a capital were not included. In this subset of nouns 115,000 word forms remained. To derive the high and low levels of this factor, first the initial token trigram frequency distribution was tabulated from the tokens of these word forms. Then the word forms were added for each trigram. Finally, the lowest and highest two deciles of word forms were determined. This procedure yielded a trigram frequency for the boundary of the lower two deciles of 20 per million words and a trigram frequency for the boundary of the higher two deciles of 381 per million words. From the word forms in these lower deciles and higher deciles the target words were chosen. Only words that, according to four native speakers of Dutch, belong to standard familiar Dutch, served as the target words. This resulted in target words with mean initial trigram frequencies of 8 per million words (SD = 5.7) for low-saliency

---

7 For reasons not related to the purpose of the current chapter, there were also sentences with shorter targets consisting of the first constituent of our compounds. Results with respect to this variation will be reported elsewhere.

8 The Dutch CELEX corpus is based on approximately 42.3 million words.

target words and of 903 per million words (SD = 558) for high-saliency target words.

The target words were embedded in declarative sentences. Since our study is concerned with eye movements in 'normal reading', we considered it desirable that the target words were embedded in a text of at least two lines and appeared never earlier than on the second line. These story frames were also used to build up context in a way similar to Balota et al. (1985). However, rather than using word repetition (Ehrlich and Rayner, 1981) or a strong association between an adjective and a subsequent noun (Zola, 1984) or between a noun and a subsequent noun (Balota et al., 1985), which often will constitute a compound in Dutch, a sentence-contextual constraint was used to create a positive and a neutral context. Table 1 presents an example of the materials.

To allow for comparisons between conditions, great care was taken during item construction to meet the following conditions.

(1) The word preceding the target compound was an adjective of 5 to 8 letters, the word preceding this adjective was an article. The word length range for the adjectives was chosen on the basis of analysing a corpus of reading data to maximise the proportion of cases with one fixation on the word before the target. This is an important constraint, as it has been shown that the number of fixations on the preceding word has a large effect on initial landing position, even when the saccade launch distance is identical (Radach and Kempe, 1993).

(2) The two words prior to the target word had to be identical for the positive and neutral context conditions.

(3) To ensure that sentence or clause wrap up effects did not mediate eye movement parameters within the target area, the actual sentence had to continue after the target for at least three words on the same line. Also, after the target the critical sentence never continued with a relative clause or a co-ordinate or sub-ordinate clause that needed a comma after the target word.

(4) The target had to be at least the fifth word of a sentence.

(5) To exclude interference with return sweep effects within the critical region (Hofmeister, Heller and Radach, 1999) targets had to be preceded by at least four words on the current line of text.

The contextual constraint was operationalised as a word's predictability in a given context as established in a sentence completion task. The aim was to have in the positive context the target word moderately predictable, and in the neutral context plausible but not predictable. Initially, about 60 items were constructed for the low-saliency condition and the same number for the high-saliency condition. Sixteen participants were presented with fragments of these items, that is, the items up to and including the adjective prior to the target word. They were asked to complete the fragment into an acceptable full sentence. A positive context was defined as being a context that invited 40% or more of the participants to continue

Table 1

Example materials with English glosses and translations

(1) High-saliency trigram, positive context.
Bart ging van huis en stak de sleutel bij zich. Toen hij de sleutel langs zijn been omlaag voelde glijden, werd hij eraan herinnerd dat hij **een kapotte broekzak** had die nodig gerepareerd moest worden.

*Bart left home and took the key with him. When he the key along his leg down felt sliding, was he reminded that he **a torn trouser pocket** had that urgently mending needed.*
(Bart left home and took the key with him. When he felt the key sliding down his leg, he was reminded that he had a torn trouser pocket that urgently needed mending.)

(2) High-saliency trigram, neutral context.
Bart kwam hollend naar de badkamer om een pleister uit het medicijnkastje te halen. Hij had zich bij het maken van **een kapotte broekzak** met een naald lelijk in zijn vinger geprikt.

*Bart came running to the bathroom in order a band-aid from the medicine cupboard to get. He had himself in the mending of **a torn trouser pocket** with a needle badly in his finger pricked.*
(Bart came running to the bathroom to get a band-aid from the medicine cupboard. He had pricked himself badly in his finger with a needle when he was mending a torn trouser pocket.)

(3) Low-saliency trigram, positive context.
In Westerns werden Indianen bijna altijd beschouwd als de slechteriken met primitieve gewoontes. Er werd vaak verteld dat zij gevangen tegenstanders midden in het dorp vastbonden aan **de heilige totempaal** om hen dan te offeren aan hun goden.

*In westerns were Indians almost always considered as the bad guys with primitive practices. It was frequently related that they captured enemies in the centre of the village tied to **the holy totem pole** in order them then to sacrifice to their gods.*
(In westerns, Indians were almost always considered as the bad guys with primitive practices. It was frequently related that they tied captured enemies to the holy totem pole in the centre of the village to sacrifice them then to their gods.)

(4) Low-saliency trigram, neutral context.
Afgelopen weekend waren meneer en mevrouw De Winter naar het Volkenkundig Museum in Leiden geweest. Zij hadden daar vooral **de heilige totempaal** van een Noord-Amerikaanse indianenstam bewonderd.

*Last weekend had Mr. and Mrs. de Winter to the Ethnological Museum in Leiden been. They had there particularly **the holy totem pole** of a Northern American Indian tribe admired.*
(Last weekend, Mr. and Mrs. de Winter had been to the Ethnological Museum in Leiden. There they had particularly admired the holy totem pole of a Northern American Indian tribe.)

with the target word or with a word that started with the target trigram and had a close semantic match with the target word, and that, in addition, led participants to produce less than 20% identical other words. In this way, the positive context is biasing moderately positively towards the target word, and is not biasing towards an alternative word. A neutral context was defined as a context that induced not more than 12.5% target words and less than 20% identical other words. In this way, the neutral context is not biasing negatively. Only those items that satisfied the criteria were used in the experiment.

There were 48 items in each of the trigram saliency groups. In addition to the experimental items, 12 practice items and 4 starter items were constructed which preceded each of the two experimental blocks. They were similar in all relevant aspects to the experimental items. The total number of items presented to a participant was 116. To provide participants with a meaningful task, verification statements were constructed for about 25% of the items. Counterbalanced sets of materials were constructed. Each of the four versions of an experimental item was assigned to a different set and each set contained the same number of items in each condition. One pseudo-random order for the texts was constructed, under the constraint that the same condition never occurred twice in succession.

Subjects, equipment and procedure

Twenty-eight native Dutch speakers, students from the University of Nijmegen, were paid to participate in the eye-tracking experiment. All of them had normal, uncorrected vision. They were naive with respect to the aim of the experiment.

An AMTECH ET3 infrared pupil-reflection eye tracker was used to collect the eye movement data (for a description of the apparatus see Katz, Mueller and Helmle, 1987). The system has a relative spatial resolution in the order of a few minutes of arc and, depending on the calibration, an absolute accuracy of about 0.25°. The data were recorded with a sampling rate of 200 Hz. Only the movements of the right eye were recorded, although vision was binocular. Head movements were restricted by the use of a chin rest, a forehead rest, and a bite-bar. Saccades were identified using a simple velocity threshold algorithm. The velocity threshold for including a data point into a saccade was set to 0.30°/s, and the minimum saccade amplitude was 0.20°.

The stimuli were displayed on a 17-inch monitor in 800×600 pixel mode. The texts were presented in a standard Courier font face and a line spacing of 1.5 as dark text on a light grey background. A character subtended 9 pixels. One degree of visual angle was equivalent to 3.6 character positions.

During the preparation of the bite-bar, the experiment and the procedures of calibration and recalibration were explained. Each block of texts was preceded by and concluded with a calibration. A text trial started with a so-called recalibration, by means of which the data can be corrected for possible head movements. The recalibration display was followed by an asterisk indicating the location of the beginning of the text. Participants were asked not to blink when reading the texts, but only at the start of a recalibration. However, they had to look properly at the asterisk again before pressing the button in the arm-rest that started the presentation of the text. The participants were instructed to read the texts carefully, at their normal pace. After 25% of the texts a verification statement was presented. The participants had to indicate whether the statement was true or false according to the content of the text by pressing either the button in the left-hand arm-rest or the button in the right-hand arm-rest. The experiment lasted 40 to 50 min.

Results and discussion

Landing positions, fixation durations and gaze durations on the target word in first pass reading were analysed. The space before the target word was included in the critical word region and was defined as position 0. The characters were numbered according to their serial position counting from left to right. The landing positions in this chapter are reported in characters. However, the statistical analyses were based upon pixels, and not rounded off before the analyses. The gaze duration on the target word was defined as the time between the beginning of the first fixation and the end of the last fixation on the target word, so that the gaze duration includes saccade time.

Not all landing position observations were included in the analysis set. The data did not include observations from skimming, defined in number of fixations on the critical line left of the target word and in terms of launch distance. Furthermore, observations after regressions, observations from a return sweep, very short saccades and drift, and blinks were excluded from analysis. This resulted in the following criteria for inclusion in the analysis set. The number of non-regressive fixations on the line before the target word was two or more, the launch distance was less than or equal to fifteen characters, the saccade size was one character or more, the net drift during the relevant fixation was less than 0.5 character, and there was no blink in two fixations prior to the first fixation on the target word and no blink on the target word itself. Furthermore, observations of individual fixations with a duration less than 50 ms and more than 600 ms were excluded. Finally, one half percent of the data were lost due to track loss or calibration problems. As a result of these exclusions, 13% of the potential first-fixation data points were eliminated.

An overview of the proportion of first fixations landing to the right of the left boundary of the target word, i.e. fixations on the target word, and also fixations to the right of the target word if it was skipped, is presented as a function of launch site and landing position in Table 2. In addition, Table 2 contains partitions of the proportions for the number of fixations on the target word (one, two and more than two fixations) and for the number of fixations on the preceding adjective if the fixation was launched from this adjective (single fixation vs. one and more than one fixation). The table shows that 10% of the target words were skipped. Furthermore, it shows that almost two thirds of the data were single fixations on the target word,

Table 2

Proportion of first fixations on the target word and to the right of the target word if skipped as a function of launch site and landing position, together with partitions (in italic) for number of fixations on the target word and number of fixations on the preceding adjective

Landing position	Launch site				Total
	Prior to determiner	Determiner	Adjective No. of fixations in adjective		
			≥ 1	$= 1$	
In target word	0.08	0.15	0.68		0.90
No. of fixations:					
One	*0.05*	*0.09*	*0.49*	*0.45*	*0.64*
Two	*0.02*	*0.04*	*0.14*	*0.13*	*0.20*
More than two	*0.01*	*0.01*	*0.04*	*0.03*	*0.06*
Over target word	0.00	0.01	0.09		0.10

and that most of the landings on the target were launched from the adjective prior to the target word, almost all of those being fixated once.

Landing positions

In Fig. 1 the distribution of the initial landing positions on the target word (90% of the data) is plotted, separately for high trigram-saliency words and for low trigram-saliency words. The curves peak at the 4th character, replicating, as has been done many times, the preferred viewing location phenomenon. More importantly, the initial fixations on the high trigram-saliency words seem more to the right in the word than the initial fixation on the low trigram-saliency words. These data were analysed with a repeated measurement ANOVA with the binary factors trigram saliency and contextual constraint as within-subject variables. [9] The mean landing positions over subjects as a function of these factors are presented in Table 3. The overall mean was 4.43 characters, that is almost half way into the fourth character. There was a small, but significant effect of trigram saliency ($F(1, 27) = 6.45$, $MS_e = 37.06$, $p < 0.05$), no effect of contextual constraint ($F < 1$), and no significant interaction between trigram saliency and contextual constraint ($F(1, 27) = 1.92$, $MS_e = 47.26$, $p = 0.18$).

---

9 No $F2$ statistics are reported in this chapter, because, as can be seen shortly, we decided to analyse the data with a repeated measurement regression analysis, and to interpret the results based on the latter analyses only.

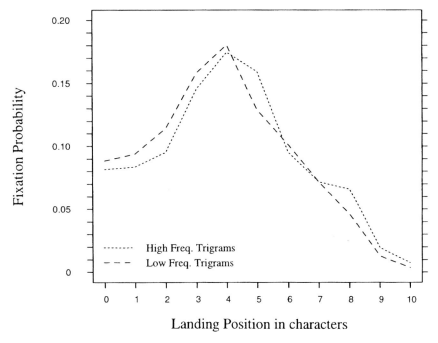

Fig. 1. Landing position distribution for all initial fixations on the target word, separately for words beginning with high-saliency trigrams and words beginning with low-saliency trigrams.

Table 3

Mean landing position (in number of characters) on the target word as a function of trigram saliency and contextual constraint

Context	Trigram saliency	
	Low	High
Neutral	4.39	4.51
Positive	4.17	4.64

The effect of trigram saliency, although significant by the ANOVA test, is small: the difference between the means of subjects' means, 4.28 and 4.58, is 0.3 characters (see Table 3), the difference between the 'raw' means, i.e. the means of the individual data points (4.24 and 4.49), is 0.25 characters.

When investigating landing positions in normal reading of text, one has no control over how frequently readers fixate or skip the target word nor over from what sites readers launch their saccades. It is well known that an important predictor for landing positions is the launch distance of the saccades leading to the landing positions. Because we had no control over the launch positions in the experiment, it is quite possible that the actual launch positions are not orthogonal to the factors of interest, trigram saliency and contextual constraint. A possible influence of launch position on the obtained trigram saliency effect should be eliminated in the analysis. In addition, we wanted to exclude the possibility that the obtained effect can be attributed to the frequency of the target word, or the length of the word following the target word (as its length may also influence the fixation pattern on the target, Vitu, 1991). Finally, we wanted to exclude any influence of the length of the target word. Although length was controlled between conditions, overall length effects might arise because of missing data. Therefore, the data were analysed with the repeated measurement regression analysis described by Lorch and Myers (1990) (method 3, multiple predictor model). Dummy coded subject variables and dummy coded item version variables were entered in the analysis (cf. Pedhazur, 1982). The confounding variables launch position, log frequency of the target word, length of the target word and length of the word following the target word were entered as the main predictors. Tested were trigram saliency and the contextual constraint. This analysis replicated the results of the previous analysis. The effect of initial trigram saliency on the landing position on the target word was again significant ($F(1, 24) = 20.68$, $MS_e = 190.84$, $p < 0.001$), and the effect of contextual constraint again was not ($F < 1$). [10]

To obtain a more detailed view of the relation between launch site and landing position, the landing positions were plotted against launch positions (Fig. 2). Launch positions coming from farther away than 10 characters were not plotted, because there were very few observations in that class. [11] To avoid biases caused by the choice of bin width, a scatterplot smoother, *lowess*, was used in plotting the lines (Venables and Ripley, 1998, p. 326).

The figure shows an effect of trigram saliency on the landing position on the target, and there is no indication that the effect is less pronounced for near than for far launch sites. The trigram saliency effect on the landing position appears to exist even for relatively far launch sites.

The slope of the landing position is 0.5, indicating that for every increment in launch distance the landing position within the target word is shifted by about half a character.

----

10 When the log frequency of the preceding adjective was added to the predictor variables, the results were the same.

11 When saccades launched from left of the determiner are discarded (8% of the data), the same repeated measurement regression analysis produced for trigram saliency $F(1, 24) = 38.37$, $MS_e = 124.22$, $p < 0.001$ and for contextual constraint $F < 1$.

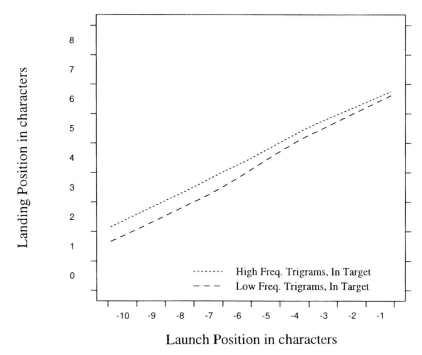

Launch Position in characters

Fig. 2. Landing position distributions for initial fixations on the target as a function of launch site, separately for target words beginning with high-saliency trigrams and target words beginning with low-saliency trigrams.

Context effect

None of the analyses revealed any effect of contextual constraint on landing position. To address the question of whether the context manipulation was effective at all, the fixation duration of the initial fixation and the gaze duration on the target word were analysed. First, the data were analysed using a repeated measurement ANOVA with the factors contextual constraint and trigram saliency as within-subject variables. The mean fixation duration and mean gaze duration over subjects as a function of these factors are presented in Table 4 and Table 5, respectively.

There was an effect of contextual constraint ($F(1, 27) = 13.05$, $MS_e = 527.77$, $p < 0.001$), an effect of trigram saliency ($F(1, 27) = 9.97$, $MS_e = 320.91$, $p < 0.01$), and no interaction between trigram saliency and contextual constraint ($F < 1$) on the initial fixation duration. For the gaze duration, there was a main effect of contextual constraint ($F(1, 27) = 8.23$, $MS_e = 1100.09$, $p < 0.01$), a main effect of trigram saliency ($F(1, 27) = 8.57$, $MS_e = 1405.90$, $p < 0.01$), and an interaction between contextual constraint and trigram saliency ($F(1, 27) = 3.83$,

Table 4

Mean fixation durations (in ms) of initial fixations on the target word as a function of trigram saliency and contextual constraint

	Trigram saliency	
Context	Low	High
Neutral	248	237
Positive	232	222

Table 5

Mean gaze durations (in ms) on the target word as a function of trigram saliency and contextual constraint

	Trigram saliency	
Context	Low	High
Neutral	282	275
Positive	273	243

$MS_e = 979.71$, $p = 0.06$). In the positive context the difference between the saliency conditions was more pronounced.

In the analysis with the same repeated measurement regression technique as described above, the log frequency of the target word was entered as the main predictor. The contextual constraint and trigram saliency factors were tested. Again, for the initial fixations, the effect of contextual constraint was significant ($F(1, 24) = 15.13$, $MS_e = 3977.15$, $p < 0.001$), as was the effect of trigram saliency ($F(1, 24) = 5.26$, $MS_e = 3045.71$, $p < 0.05$). The same applies to the gaze duration: a significant effect for contextual constraint ($F(1, 24) = 7.73$, $MS_e = 15504.14$, $p = 0.01$), and a significant effect of trigram saliency ($F(1, 24) = 8.97$, $MS_e = 7438.80$, $p < 0.01$).

Clearly, the context manipulation was effective. This makes the fact that no effect of contextual constraint on landing position was obtained very interesting. Although context influences the duration of first fixation and gaze on a word, it does not affect the landing position on that word.

Supplementary analyses

Number of fixations on target word
It is well known that spatial and temporal eye movement parameters differ for cases in which the target word receives exactly one vs. more fixations. For ex-

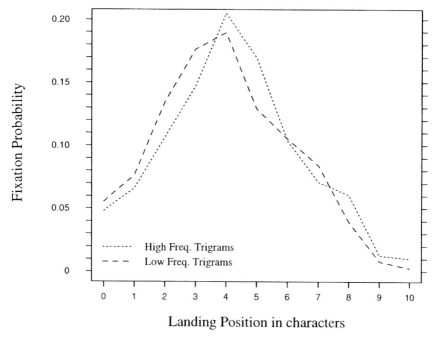

Fig. 3. Landing position distributions for single fixations on the target word, separately for words beginning with high-saliency trigrams and words beginning with low-saliency trigrams.

ample, landing positions are farther into the word and fixation durations are longer for single fixations as compared to the first of two fixations (Kliegl, Olson and Davidson, 1983; O'Regan, 1990; O'Regan, Vitu, Radach and Kerr, 1994; Rayner, Sereno and Raney, 1996). In their study on cognitive landing site effects, Underwood, Clews and Everatt (1990) took this difference into account and distinguished between single and refixation cases. Following this approach, we present landing position distributions based exclusively on single fixation observations in Fig. 3.

As in the previously mentioned studies, the proportion of fixations on the beginning of the target word is clearly less for single fixations (Fig. 3) than for the complete set of initial fixations on a word (Fig. 1). More importantly, the fixations on the high-saliency trigram words seem in Fig. 3 (as in Fig. 1) more to the right in the word than the fixations on the low-saliency trigram words. The same repeated measurement regression technique as described above, with launch position, log frequency of the target word, length of the target word, and length of the word following the target word entered as the predictor variables, was performed for single-fixation cases. The results were as before, i.e. the effect of initial trigram saliency on the landing position on the target word was significant ($F(1, 24) = 8.80, MS_e = 254.56, p < 0.01$), and the effect of contextual constraint was not ($F < 1$).

Fixation pattern on preceding word

As indicated above, Radach and Kempe (1993) found that the fixation pattern on the preceding word affected the landing position on the target word. We have already taken the log frequency of the preceding adjective into account by treating it as a predictor in one of the analyses: excluding the possible influence of the frequency of the adjective did not change the overall effect of trigram saliency on landing position. We now address the question of whether the number of fixations on the word preceding the target word affects the obtained saliency effect.

In two analyses with the same repeated measurement regression technique as described above, launch position, log frequency of the target word, length of the target word and length of the word following the target word were again entered as the predictor variables. In the first analysis, trigram saliency and contextual constraint were tested for the subset of fixations on the target word that were launched from the preceding adjective (75% of the observations on the target word). Again, the effect of initial trigram saliency on the landing position on the target word was significant ($F(1, 24) = 23.42, MS_e = 134.56, p < 0.001$), and the effect of contextual constraint was not ($F < 1$). The second analysis, testing trigram saliency and contextual constraint for the subset of fixations launched from the adjective when it was fixated only once (68% of the observations on the target word), provides similar results: the effect of trigram saliency was significant ($F(1, 24) = 24.77, MS_e = 148.56, p = 0.0001$), and the effect of contextual constraint was not ($F < 1$).

For the last set of data, i.e. the subset of first fixations in the target word launched from the adjective when it was fixated once, landing positions were plotted against launch positions (Fig. 4). The figure shows clearly the effect of trigram saliency, and no interaction between trigram saliency and launch site.

Frequency of the first stem of the target compound

As described above, Inhoff, Briihl and Schwartz (1996) found that the landing position was slightly closer to the target centre when compound words were fixated than when suffixed and monomorphemic targets were fixated. We addressed the question of whether the frequency of the first stem could have affected the obtained result. In a repeated measurement regression analysis with the same predictors as before, which also included the trigram frequency of the target word as a predictor, the frequency of the first stem of the target was tested. There was no effect on landing position: $F < 1$. When the effect of first stem frequency was tested without

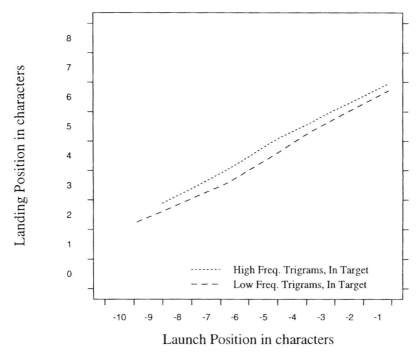

Fig. 4. Landing position distributions for initial fixations on the target word launched from the singly fixated adjective as a function of launch site, separately for target words beginning with high-saliency trigrams and target words beginning with low-saliency trigrams.

entering the trigram frequency as a predictor, the outcome was the same: $F < 1$. This result cannot simply be taken as evidence that stem frequency cannot affect landing position, because stem frequency was not included as an experimental variable in the experiment. However, we can rule the possibility out that first-stem frequency was a confounding factor in the experiment: in an analysis using the same predictors as before, but adding the frequency of the first stem as a predictor, the effect of trigram saliency remained highly significant ($F(1, 24) = 21.02$, $MS_e = 187.37$, $p = 0.001$).

Summary and conclusion

The results of our experiment are straightforward. We obtained a relatively small, but reliable effect of the orthographic saliency of word-initial letters on the positioning of the initial fixation within 8–10-letter target words. A variation of initial trigram frequency in the order of about 8 vs. 900 per million leads to a 0.3-letter shift in the mean landing position of the initial saccade. In a number of additional analyses it was shown that this result cannot be attributed to the number of fixations on the target word, the fixation pattern on the preceding word or the frequency of the initial constituent of the compound target word. A manipulation of contextual constraint, involving a moderately positive vs. neutral context, did not alter saccade landing positions, although context was effective in determining fixation durations on the target. Our results closely replicate the linear relation between saccade launch distance and landing position described by McConkie et al. (1988). To our knowledge, this is the first demonstration of this *landing position* in a controlled sentence reading experiment. The slope of the landing position function is 0.5, indicating that for every increment in launch distance the mean landing position within the target word is shifted to the left by about half a character.

There are, in principle, two different ways in which the saccade generation system may have produced the observed effect of initial trigram saliency. As discussed by Radach and McConkie (1998), such a difference can indicate that a large portion of the critical saccades are changed in a *graded* fashion by less than 1 character. On the other hand, it can also mean that in about 5% of the observations a *discrete* decision is made to skip the entire target word or its first stem, leading to an increase of the respective saccade amplitudes in the order of 6 characters. This kind of discrete influence can be observed in terms of more than one peak or a large plateau in saccade landing position distributions in situations when alternative decisions have to be made, such as refixating a low-frequency word vs. executing a saccade to the next parafoveal word.

There is evidence that can be taken to indicate that at least some discrete influence was present in previous studies that have found cognitive influences on saccade landing positions. One example is the experiment by Hyönä (1995), where much of the effect was due to atypical saccades landing on the space before target words with irregular beginnings. Another interesting example is the study by Underwood, Clews and Everatt (1990), who noted that their landing position effect was not caused by a change in saccade amplitude. This points to the possibility that orthographic features of a parafoveal word can cause extra refixations on the preceding word, a phenomenon that has also been described as 'refixations on the prompt' in the word comparison paradigm of Kennedy (1998).

In our data, none of these irregularities are present. The shape of the landing site distributions for high- and low-saliency targets are very similar and the slopes of the respective landing position functions are virtually identical. Although not impossible, it is quite unlikely that this pattern is produced by a discrete mechanism.

An interpretation in terms of a graded influence does also find support from a more theoretical point of view. Looking at the chronometry of processing and eye movement control decisions during a fixation, it is clear that there is a point in time where a saccade is committed to action and the movement becomes irrevocable

(McConkie, 1983; Rayner and Pollatsek, 1989). It may appear plausible to assume that the specification of the saccade amplitude lasts only until the decision to move is made. However, evidence from basic oculomotor research indicates that this is indeed not the case. Amplitude computation and movement decision can be seen as based on independent processing streams operating in parallel. The latest point in time at which the triggering of the saccade can be influenced is considerably earlier in comparison to the minimal modification time for a saccade amplitude. This indicates that the decision to move the eyes is taken *before* saccade amplitude computation is finished (for a detailed discussion see Deubel, 1994). Particularly convincing arguments for this view come from results of double-step experiments by Becker and Jürgens (1979) and Hou and Fender (1979). Discussing these studies, Becker (1989) suggests that new information calling for a change of saccade direction may arrive too late to block the decision for the previously required direction but may still be able to modify the amplitude of the impending saccade. By analogy, in our experiment, results of parafoveal letter processing may become available too late to initiate cancellation and reprogramming of a saccade to the target word, but may still be able to modify its amplitude.

This line of discussion is also relevant to our finding that context does not influence the positioning of the initial fixation within target words. This result is in line with a failure to find context effects by Everatt and Underwood (1992), although the two studies cannot be directly compared, as they used words with high vs. low informative beginnings. A possible objection to our context manipulation could be that the high-context condition included only cases where 40% or more subjects responded with the intended target word in a cloze task. This is certainly a moderate rather than 'strong' context. However, it was our intention to use a type of context that is relevant to a normal reading situation, including story frames that a reader is likely to encounter in natural text outside the laboratory. [12] As mentioned above, our context manipulation was quite effective in producing a significant difference in the fixation duration on the target. A similar effect of low vs. medium contextual constraint on first-fixation duration (10 ms) has been reported by Rayner and Well (1996). However, in their study this contrast did not lead to a difference in the probability of fixating their 4–10-letter target words. When comparing high to medium context, fixation probability was 10% lower in the high-context condition while there was no difference in fixation duration.

Why did the context manipulation not lead to an effect on saccade landing position? It may seem contradictory that there is no such effect, given that we just

---

12 In this context, 40% and more is a rather high figure, e.g., in comparison to Kerr (1992), who had difficulties finding places in a classic novel where more than 20% of his participants gave the desired answer in a cloze task.

proposed that amplitude adjustments can be made after the decision to move has been taken. There are in fact several demonstrations that context can influence the movement decision as indicated by word skipping rates (for a review see Brysbaert and Vitu, 1998). The time window for an effect of parafoveal orthography on saccade amplitude is certainly of longer duration than the time window for an effect of parafoveal lexical processing on the movement decision. Orthographic information is available earlier and, as we have proposed above, the processing window closes later for amplitude specification. However, the important difference may be that contextual constraint is a top-down influence that presumably has its effects primarily on the *lexical* rather than on the *visual–orthographic* level of word processing (see Commentary on Section 1, for a discussion of 'lexical' processing). When parafoveal visual processing specifies candidates for the lexical identity of the next parafoveal word (Inhoff, 1989), context information will contribute to the lexical activation of contextually compatible candidates relative to those that are less compatible, and thus effectively speed up lexical access. However, this context information, although effective, may not (or not early enough) be fed down to the level of visual letter processing in a way that can be used by the saccade generation system to remodulate the impending saccade.

Hyönä (1995) accounts for his finding of a cognitive landing site effect in terms of a general *processing difficulty hypothesis* stating that when a foveal or parafoveal word is difficult, the 'perceptual span' for letter processing narrows down, leading to a shorter inter-word saccade (see also Chapter 4). Converging evidence comes from a corpus analysis by Radach and Heller (Chapter 7), who found a tendency for longer fixations to be followed by saccades that land closer to the word beginning. If a long fixation duration is taken as evidence for difficult word processing, the *negative preprocessing hypothesis* proposed by Radach and Heller becomes very similar to Hyönä and Pollatsek's processing difficulty hypothesis.

It is interesting to note that landing position effects of the kind found in our experiment and in the studies by Hyönä (1995) and Hyönä and Pollatsek (1998) are incompatible with current sequential attention shift models of eye movement control in reading (Reichle, Pollatsek, Fisher and Rayner, 1998; see also Chapter 27). These models claim that attention is focused on a particular word until lexical access on this word is achieved. Saccade programming is initiated when a preliminary stage of lexical processing (labelled familiarity check) is completed. Neither the time of triggering for this saccade nor its amplitude is assumed to be influenced by parafoveal preprocessing. This is clearly not in harmony with any orthographic landing site effect. To accommodate such an effect within the framework of sequential attention models, parafoveal processing must be allowed to modify the parametrisation of saccades *prior to* and/or *after* the decision to move has been made. It may seem that one of the scenarios described by Morrison (1984) could accommodate saccade amplitude adjustments. Specifically, he proposed that there are cases when successful parafoveal processing of a subsequent word ($N+1$) occurs relatively fast, but too late to cancel the default saccade to this word. Temporal overlap between the programming of saccades to $N+1$ and $N+2$ may then result in a saccade amplitude that brings the eyes to a location somewhere between the two intended target positions. This is similar to an amplitude transition function as described in double-step experiments (for a review see Becker, 1989). Looking at the results of our experiment, this account may explain a rightward shift of landing positions for words with more salient beginnings (when the first constituent of our compounds is seen as a 'word'). However, since the reason for the amplitude shift lies in the fact that the fixation on '$N+1$' is no longer necessary, its duration should be reduced to an oculomotor minimum latency (see Morrison, 1984, who explicitly proposed this scenario to account for very short fixations). This is clearly not the case in our data.

A less constrained version of attention-based models that is principally compatible with cognitive landing site effects is the attentional gradient model (see Chapter 9). The basic idea is that fine adjustments in the spatial distribution of visual processing resources may provide a base for a graded refinement of saccade amplitude. It may be that the peak of the attentional gradient is shifted toward letter clusters that are difficult to process or, alternatively, that the peak is directed beyond very familiar letter combinations that have already received sufficient processing. Although these alternatives may sound straightforward, they are still based on speculation rather than on empirical data. The idea that feedback from parafoveal letter processing is able to modify saccade amplitudes should thus be seen with some caution until verified in more specific experiments.

A similar theoretical perspective can be derived from the recent general model of saccade generation by Findlay and Walker (1999). They postulate that the selection of saccade targets is based on parallel processing and competitive inhibition within a two-dimensional spatial saliency map. Potential saccade targets are represented as competing saliency peaks and a saccade is elicited when a single peak has emerged as a winner. Among the factors made responsible for saccade target specification is *intrinsic saliency*, seen primarily as a property of visual contours and high-contrast areas. It is suggested that long- and medium-term learning and adaptive processes modify the intrinsic saliency of visual information, explicitly including unusual orthographic patterns. However, determining the 'intrinsic' saliency of a word beginning will require a minimum of parafoveal orthographic processing rather than simple pattern recognition, as readers will perhaps not keep in memory representations of letter clusters that are *unlikely* to form word beginnings. There are two interesting differences between the saliency map model and the attentional gradient account discussed above. First, Findlay and Walker do not believe that the concept of 'attention' is necessary to explain the process of saccade generation at all. Second, the existence of more than one peak of saliency opens the possibility that a saccade amplitude shift could be the result of spatial integration between two competing saccade targets without a need for saccade cancellation and reprogramming.

In sum, the present study adds a further piece to a growing body of evidence suggesting that small adjustments in saccade amplitude in response to orthographic features of parafoveal words are possible. This modulation is not restricted to irregular or unfamiliar letter combinations, but appears to be part and parcel of normal reading behaviour. As the above discussion may have shown, it is not easy to integrate this *cognitive landing site* effect into current theoretical thinking on visual processing and saccade control. Although it is clear that the greater part of the variance in saccade amplitude specification is explained by low-level variables like saccade launch distance and target word length, the orthographic saliency effect will also have to be part of future theories and models of eye movement control in reading.

References

Baayen, R.H., Piepenbrock, R. and van Rijn, H. (1993). The Celex Lexical database. (CD-ROM). Linguistic Data Consortium. Philadelphia, PA: University of Pennsylvania.

Balota, D.A., Pollatsek, A. and Rayner, K. (1985). The interaction of contextual constraints and parafoveal visual information in reading. Cognitive Psychology, 17, 364–390.

Balota, D.A. and Rayner, K. (1991). Word recognition processes in foveal and parafoveal vision: the range of influence of lexical variables. In: D. Besner and G.W. Humphreys (Eds.), Basic Processes in Reading: Visual Word Recognition. Hillsdale, NJ: Erlbaum, pp. 198–232.

Beauvillain, C., Doré, K. and Baudouin, V. (1996). The 'center of gravity' of words: evidence for an effect of the word-initial letters. Vision Research, 36, 589–604.

Becker, W. (1989). Metrics. In: R.H. Wurtz and M.E. Goldberg (Eds.), The Neurobiology of Saccadic Eye Movements. Amsterdam: Elsevier, pp. 13–61.

Becker, W. and Jürgens, R. (1979). An analysis of the saccadic system by means of double step stimuli. Vision Research, 19, 967–983.

Binder, K.S., Pollatsek, A. and Rayner, K. (1999). Extraction of information to the left of the fixated word in reading. Journal of Experimental Psychology: Human Perception and Performance, 25, 1162–1172.

Brysbaert, M. and Vitu, F. (1998). Word skipping: implications for theories of eye movement control in reading. In: G. Underwood (Ed.), Eye Guidance in Reading and Scene Perception. Oxford: Elsevier, pp. 125–147.

Brysbaert, M., Vitu, F. and Schroyens, W. (1996). The right visual field advantage and the optimal viewing position effect: on the relation between foveal and parafoveal word recognition. Neuropsychology, 10, 385–395.

Deubel, H. (1994). The Anatomy of a Single Refixation. Unpublished Habilitation Thesis. University of Munich.

Ehrlich, S.F. and Rayner, K. (1981). Contextual effects on word perception and eye movements during reading. Journal of Verbal Learning and Verbal Behaviour, 20, 641–655.

Everatt, J., Bradshaw, M.F. and Hibbard, P.B. (1998). Individual differences in reading and eye movement control. In: G. Underwood (Ed.), Eye Guidance in Reading and Scene Perception. Oxford: Elsevier, pp. 223–242.

Everatt, J. and Underwood, G. (1992). Parafoveal guidance and priming effects during reading: a special case of the mind being ahead of the eyes. Consciousness and Cognition, 1, 186–197.

Findlay, J.M. and Walker, R. (1999). A model of saccade generation based on parallel processing and competitive inhibition. Behavioral and Brain Sciences, 22, 661–721.

Hofmeister, J., Heller, D. and Radach, R. (1999). The return sweep in reading. In: W. Becker, H. Deubel and T. Mergner (Eds.), Current Oculomotor Research: Physiological and Psychological Aspects. New York: Plenum, pp. 349–358.

Hou, R.L. and Fender, D.H. (1979). Processing of direction and magnitude information by the saccadic system. Vision Research, 19, 1421–1426.

Hyönä, J. (1993). Eye Movements during Reading and Discourse Processing. Psychological Research Reports. University of Turku.

Hyönä, J. (1995). Do irregular letter combinations attract readers' attention? Evidence from fixation locations in words. Journal of Experimental Psychology: Human Perception and Performance, 21, 68–81.

Hyönä, J., Niemi, P. and Underwood, G. (1989). Reading long words embedded in sentences: informativeness of word parts affects eye movements. Journal of Experimental Psychology: Human Perception and Performance, 15, 142–152.

Hyönä, J. and Pollatsek, A. (1998). Reading Finnish compound words: eye fixations are affected by component morphemes. Journal of Experimental Psychology: Human Perception and Performance, 24, 1612–1627.

Inhoff, A.W. (1982). Parafoveal word perception: a further case against semantic preprocessing. Journal of Experimental Psychology: Human Perception and Performance, 8, 137–145.

Inhoff, A.W. (1989). Parafoveal processing of words and saccade computation during eye fixations in reading. Journal of Experimental Psychology: Human Perception and Performance, 15, 544–555.

Inhoff, A.W., Briihl, D. and Schwartz, J. (1996). Compound word naming in reading, on-line naming and delayed naming tasks. Memory and Cognition, 24, 466–476.

Inhoff, A.W. and Radach, R. (1998). Definition and computation of oculomotor measures in the study of cognitive processes. In: G. Underwood (Ed.), Eye Guidance in Reading and Scene Perception. Oxford: Elsevier, pp. 77–100.

Katz, B., Mueller, K. and Helmle, H. (1987). Binocular eye movements recording with ccd arrays. Neuro-Ophthalmology, 7, 81–91.

Kennedy, A. (1998). The influence of parafoveal words on foveal inspection time: evidence for a processing tradeoff. In: G. Underwood (Ed.), Eye Guidance in Reading and Scene Perception. Oxford: Elsevier, pp. 149–180.

Kerr, P.W. (1992). Eye Movement Control during Reading: The Selection of Where to Send the Eyes. Unpublished Doctoral Dissertation. University of Illinois at Urbana-Champaign.

Kliegl, R., Olson, R.K. and Davidson, B.J. (1983). On problems of unconfounding perceptual and language processes. In: K. Rayner (Ed.), Eye Movements in Reading: Perceptual and Language Processes. New York: Academic Press, pp. 333–343.

Lima, S.D. and Inhoff, A.W. (1985). Lexical access during eye fixations in reading: effects of word initial letter sequence. Journal of Experimental Psychology: Human Perception and Performance, 13, 272–285.

Liversedge, S.P. and Underwood, G. (1998). Foveal processing load and landing position effects in reading. In: G. Underwood (Ed.), Eye Guidance in Reading and Scene Perception. Oxford: Elsevier, pp. 201–221.

Lorch, R.F. and Myers, J.L. (1990). Regression analyses of repeated measures data in cognitive research. Journal of Experimental Psychology: Learning, Memory, and Cognition, 16, 149–157.

McConkie, G.W. (1983). Eye movements and perception during reading. In: K. Rayner (Ed.), Eye Movements in Reading: Perceptual and Language Processes. New York: Academic Press, pp. 65–96.

McConkie, G.W., Kerr, P.W. and Dyre, B.P. (1994). What are 'normal' eye movements during reading: toward a mathematical description. In: J. Ygge and G. Lennerstrand (Eds.), Eye Movements in Reading. Oxford: Elsevier, pp. 315–327.

McConkie, G.W., Kerr, P.W., Reddix, M.D. and Zola, D. (1988). Eye movement control during reading, I. The location of initial eye fixation on words. Vision Research, 28, 1107–1118.

McConkie, G.W., Kerr, P.W., Reddix, M.D., Zola, D. and Jacobs, A.M. (1989). Eye movement control during reading, II. Frequency of refixating a word. Perception and Psychophysics, 46, 245–253.

McConkie, G.W. and Zola, D. (1979). Is visual information integrated across successive fixations in reading?. Perception and Psychophysics, 25, 221–224.

Morrison, R.E. (1984). Manipulation of stimulus onset delay in reading: evidence for parallel programming of saccades. Journal of Experimental Psychology: Human Perception and Performance, 10, 667–682.

Nazir, T.A., Heller, D. and Sussmann, C. (1992). Letter visibility and word recognition: the optimal viewing position in printed words. Perception and Psychophysics, 52, 315–328.

O'Regan, J.K. (1990). Eye movements and reading. In: E. Kowler (Ed.), Reviews of Oculomotor Research, Vol. 4: Eye Movements and their Role in Visual and Cognitive Processes. Amsterdam: Elsevier, pp. 395–453.

O'Regan, J.K. (1992). Optimal viewing position in words and the strategy-tactics theory of eye movements in reading. In: K. Rayner (Ed.), Eye Movements and Visual Cognition: Scene Perception and Reading. New York: Springer, pp. 333–354.

O'Regan, J.K. and Jacobs, A.M. (1992). Optimal viewing position effects in word recognition: a challenge to current theory. Journal of Experimental Psychology: Human Perception and Performance, 18, 185–197.

O'Regan, J.K., Vitu, F., Radach, R. and Kerr, P. (1994). Effects of local processing and oculomotor factors in eye movement guidance in reading. In: J. Ygge and G. Lennerstrand (Eds.), Eye Movements in Reading. New York: Pergamon, pp. 329–348.

Pedhazur, E.J. (1982). Multiple Regression in Behavioral Research: Explanation and Prediction (2nd ed.). New York: Holt, Rinehart and Winston.

Poulton, E.C. (1981). Human manual control. In: V.B. Brooks (Ed.), Handbook of Physiology, Sect. 1, Vol. II, Part 2. Bethesda: American Physiology Society, pp. 1337–1389.

Radach, R. (1996). Blickbewegungen beim Lesen. Psychologische Aspekte der Determination von Fixationspositionen. (Eye Movements in Reading. Psychological Aspects of Fixation Position Control.) Münster: Waxmann.

Radach, R. and Kempe, B. (1993). An individual analysis of initial fixation positions in reading. In: G. d'Ydewalle and J. van Rensbergen (Eds.), Perception and Cognition. Advances in Eye Movement Research. Amsterdam: North-Holland, pp. 213–225.

Radach, R. and McConkie, G. (1998). Determinants of fixation positions in reading. In: G. Underwood (Ed.), Eye Guidance in Reading and Scene Perception. Oxford: Elsevier, pp. 77–100.

Rayner, K. (1979). Eye guidance in reading: fixation locations within words. Perception, 8, 21–30.

Rayner, K. (1998). Eye movements in reading and information processing: 20 years of research. Psychological Bulletin, 124, 372–422.

Rayner, K., Balota, D.A. and Pollatsek, A. (1986). Against parafoveal semantic preprocessing during eye fixations in reading. Canadian Journal of Psychology, 40, 473–483.

Rayner, K., McConkie, G.W. and Zola, D. (1980). Integrating information across eye movements. Cognitive Psychology, 12, 206–226.

Rayner, K. and Morris, R.K. (1992). Eye movement control in reading: evidence against semantic preprocessing. Journal of Experimental Psychology: Human Perception and Performance, 18, 163–172.

Rayner, K. and Pollatsek, A. (1989). The Psychology of Reading. Englewood Cliffs, NJ: Prentice Hall.

Rayner, K., Sereno, S.C. and Raney, G.E. (1996). Eye movement control in reading: a comparison of two types of models. Journal of Experimental Psychology: Human Perception and Performance, 22, 1188–1200.

Rayner, K. and Well, A.D. (1996). Effects of contextual constraint on eye movements in reading: a further examination. Psychonomic Bulletin and Review, 3, 504–509.

Reichle, E.D., Pollatsek, A., Fisher, D.L. and Rayner, K. (1998). Toward a model of eye movement control in reading. Psychological Review, 105, 125–157.

Schustack, M.W., Ehrlich, S.F. and Rayner, K. (1987). Local and global sources of contextual facilitation in reading. Journal of Memory and Language, 26, 322–340.

Underwood, G., Bloomfield, R. and Clews, S. (1989). Information influences the pattern of eye fixations during sentence comprehension. Perception, 17, 267–278.

Underwood, G., Clews, S. and Everatt, J. (1990). How do readers know where to look next? Local information distributions influence eye fixations. Quarterly Journal of Experimental Psychology, 42A, 39–65.

Underwood, G., Hyönä, J. and Niemi, P. (1987). Scanning patterns on individual words during the comprehension of sentences. In: J.K. O'Regan and A. Levy-Schoen (Eds.), Eye Movements: From Physiology to Cognition. Amsterdam: North-Holland, pp. 467–477.

Underwood, G. and Radach, R. (1998). Eye guidance and visual information processing: reading, visual search, picture perception and driving. In: G. Underwood (Ed.), Eye Guidance in Reading and Scene Perception. Oxford: Elsevier, pp. 1–27.

Venables, W.N. and Ripley, B.D. (1998). Modern Applied Statistics with S-PLUS (2nd ed.). New York: Springer.

Vitu, F. (1991). The existence of a center of gravity effect during reading. Vision Research, 31, 1289–1313.

Vitu, F., O'Regan, J.K. and Mittau, M. (1990). Optimal landing position in reading isolated words and continuous texts. Perception and Psychophysics, 47, 583–600.

Zola, D. (1984). Redundancy and word perception during reading. Perception and Psychophysics, 36, 277–284.

CHAPTER 12

Regressive Saccades and Word Perception in Adult Reading

Françoise Vitu
CNRS–Université René Descartes

and

George W. McConkie
Beckman Institute–University of Illinois at Urbana-Champaign

Abstract

Three explanations for the occurrence of regressive eye movements during reading are described. Predictions are derived from one of these, the word identification explanation. These predictions are tested by analyzing a large corpus of eye movement data from 4 adult readers. The likelihood of regressing is directly related to the length of the prior saccade and to the probability the saccade skipped a word. The likelihood of regressing to a skipped word is influenced by variables that affect the perceptibility of that word. The likelihood of making inter- and intra-word regressions are often affected differently by the variables studied, indicating the importance of maintaining this distinction. The results are generally compatible with a word identification explanation of regressions during reading, though this is probably not the only basis on which regressive saccades occur.

Reading as a Perceptual Process/A. Kennedy, R. Radach, D. Heller and J. Pynte (Editors)
© 2000 Elsevier Science Ltd. All rights reserved

Regressive saccades and word perception in adult reading

People read by making a series of saccadic eye movements along the line of text, separated by pauses (eye fixations) during which the text can be perceived. Most of these saccades are progressive (forward), but occasionally regressive (backward) saccades occur. Most of the research on eye movement control during reading has focused on understanding the distance and timing of progressive saccades; less is known about the occurrence and control of regressive eye movements (see for reviews, Brysbaert and Vitu, 1998; O'Regan, 1990; Rayner, 1998). The purpose of the study described below was to examine the effects of some local text conditions on the likelihood of making regressions, and on where the regressions take the eyes when they occur, in eye movement data from skilled, adult readers.

Three primary types of explanation have been given to account for regressive saccades during reading. The first is that regressions are initiated in response to oculomotor aiming errors on the prior saccade and thus serve as corrective saccades (Taylor, 1971; see also, Shebilske, 1975). The clearest example of this is the corrective saccades that often occur following return sweeps that attempt to take the eyes to the beginning of the next line of text. The eyes often appear to fall short of the beginning of the line, leading to the initiation of a regressive movement following an unusually short eye fixation and having a length determined by the distance of the eyes from the left edge of the text on that line (Andriessen and DeVoogd, 1973; Shebilske and Fisher, 1983). The fact that regressions are more likely to occur following eye fixations that lie toward the ends of words, thus bringing the eyes back to an earlier part of the word, might also represent corrective saccades, though this has not been established (see O'Regan and Lévy-Schoen, 1987).

A second explanation is that regressive saccades are the result of difficulties or failures in word identification (Bouma, 1978; Bouma and DeVoogd, 1974; Pollatsek and Rayner, 1990; Shebilske, 1975). For example, if the eyes leave a word before its identification is complete, it may be necessary to bring them back to it in order to complete the identification process. Alternatively, if the eyes land too far to the right of the center of a word or on the following word, there may be inadequate visual information from the beginning of the attended word to distinguish it from its orthographic neighbors. Thus, a regression to an earlier part of the word may be required in order for identification to occur. Finally, if the system is having difficulty identifying a word, the eyes may be kept on it for an additional eye fixation in order to provide more processing time, which may involve the making of a regression.

A third explanation, proposed by a number of authors, is that regressive saccades occur in response to comprehension failures associated with high-level syntactic and semantic processes in understanding the text (Bouma and DeVoogd, 1974; Buswell, 1920; Hochberg, 1976; Just and Carpenter, 1980; Shebilske, 1975; Shebilske and Fisher, 1983). The most compelling evidence for this hypothesis comes from sentence processing studies which show that regressive saccades are more likely to occur in semantically or syntactically ambiguous sentences: when the eyes reach the disambiguating region of such a sentence, a regressive saccade is frequently initiated that brings the eyes back to the ambiguous portion of the sentence or to the beginning of it (see Rayner and Pollatsek, 1989, for a review).

Of course, these explanations are not necessarily exclusive. Different regressive movements may be made on different bases, and it is even possible that a given regression may be multiply determined.

In a recent study involving an a-posteriori analysis of 5th grade children's eye movements in normal reading, Vitu, McConkie and Zola (1998) present some findings that are compatible with the second, word identification explanation of regressive eye movements. First, regressions are more likely following the execution of longer progressive saccades (see also, Andriessen and DeVoogd, 1973; Lesèvre, 1964), and when the prior progressive saccade skips over one or more words. Second, when the eyes skip over a word, the regression likelihood depends on visual and lexical characteristics of that word, as well as on the prior saccade's launch site and landing position relative to the word's beginning (or how far from the word the eyes were located preceding and following skipping). The regression likelihood is higher for long and low-frequency skipped words, which are less likely to have been identified in parafoveal vision (Brysbaert, Vitu and Schroyens, 1996; Inhoff and Rayner, 1986). Regression likelihood is also higher for cases with more distant launch sites, and landing positions, thus providing less complete visual information from it due to reduced visual acuity in peripheral vision (Brysbaert et al., 1996). On the other hand, for cases in which no word was skipped, the regression likelihood shows no regular pattern with factors that reduce the perceptibility of the previously fixated word, a fact that suggests that the word-identification explanation might only account for regressive saccades initiated following word skipping.

A limitation of the Vitu et al. (1998) study is that no distinction was made between inter- and intra-word regressions, that is, between regressions that return the eyes to a prior word and regressions that occur within the destination word (where the prior saccade ended). In contrast, it is clear from recent research that the control of regressive saccades is word-based, each saccade being intended for a particular word (Radach and McConkie, 1998; Vitu et al., 1998). Thus, a word identification explanation must be tested by examining regressions taking the eyes to specific words. For example, it seems likely that inter-word regressions will be initiated more frequently when the immediately preceding word presents processing difficulties. Such difficulties might result when that word is longer and therefore less perceptible, or is of lower frequency, particularly when it has been skipped during the previous saccade. However, the frequency of intra-word regressions, those within the destination word, may not vary with these characteristics of the prior word. An exception to this could occur if the same factors that affect the perceptibility of the skipped word change the eyes' initial landing position in the destination word since landing position is known to influence the likelihood of making an intra-word regression (O'Regan and Lévy-Schoen, 1987; Radach and McConkie, 1998).

The present chapter continues the investigation of the relationship between regressive saccades and word identification processes during reading by presenting results from the analysis of a very large corpus of eye movement data from 4 adults reading a book presented one line at a time on a computer screen (Kerr, 1992). Inter- and intra-word saccades were considered separately. The data were partitioned in ways that made it possible to examine the effects of several word characteristics that influence the perceptibility of words: (1) the length of the prior progressive saccade which is related to the retinal eccentricity of the word to which the eyes are sent; (2) the type of event that characterized the prior saccade (whether or not a word was skipped); (3) the length of the critical word (the skipped word in word-skip cases, and the origin word in non-word skip cases); (4) the launch site of the saccade in word skip or the position in the origin word of the initial fixation for non-skip cases; and (5) the frequency of occurrence in the language of the skipped or the origin word. A series of predictions was developed from the word identification explanation and the data were examined to determine whether they are consistent with these predictions.

Data selection and analysis

The present corpus of eye movement data collected on 4 adults reading a classical novel originally consisted of a set of 369,186 fixations (see Kerr, 1992). All fixations and saccades that were made on a line of text were considered for analysis, except those containing a blink, as well as initial and final fixations on a line of text, or fixations followed by a premature return sweep. This resulted in a total of 189,848 fixations. From this set, quintuples were identified, each consisting of three successive fixations together with the two intervening saccades. The word toward which the eyes were directed during the first fixation in each quintuple will be referred to as the 'origin word'. The word fixated following the first saccade (hence, during the second fixation) is referred to as the 'destination word'. Thus, origin and destination are relative to the first saccade in the quintuple. One or more words lying between the origin and destination word, will be referred to as 'skipped words'. Saccade lengths were measured in letter position units. The only quintuples used in the following analyses were those in which (1) the first saccade was progressive, (2) the destination word had not been previously fixated, (3) the destination word was not the first or last word on the line, (4) the destination word was not preceded or followed by punctuation, (5) no skipped word had been previously fixated, and (6) if there was no skipped word, the origin word had not been previously fixated. After selection, the total number of quintuples available for analysis was 101,083, with a total of 55,742 cases in which a word was skipped (16161, 16955, 10313, 4497, 1323, respectively for 2- to 6-letter skipped words), and 30,720 cases in which the saccade took the eyes to the immediately following word (2195, 4809, 5134, 5095, 3571, 3591, respectively for 2- to 7-letter origin words in non-skip cases).

The analyses examined the likelihood that the second saccade in the quintuple was regressive, and, if so, also examined the location of the third (following) fixation (that is, the likelihood of going to the skipped or origin word vs. remaining on the destination word), under a variety of conditions. Three dependent variables were used, corresponding respectively to the overall regression likelihood, and the likelihood of inter- and intra-word regressions. Proportions were calculated for each subject, and these were then averaged across subjects. In this way, the weight of individual subjects' contributions to the final values was not influenced by the number of fixations that qualified for a particular condition. Analyses of variance were run on proportions obtained from the different individual subjects. This method of selecting and partitioning the data sometimes left few data points in a particular condition for individual subjects; when this occurred, the results for those conditions were not included in the presentations and analyses of variance described below. Thus, the data presented are for conditions in which each of the subjects had adequate data: more than 18 data points per subject in each condition. There were four exceptions to this in which a subject had 5, 5, 9 or 15 cases in a condition.

Results

The data are presented in three parts: (1) the overall frequency of regression and the effects of two variables on this frequency: length of the prior saccade and whether or not that saccade skipped a word; (2) the influence of the characteristics of the skipped word on regressions; and (3) the influence of characteristics of the origin word on regressions when no word was skipped. In each case we consider whether the results are compatible with a word identification explanation of regressive saccades.

Overall frequency of regressions

General characteristics

For the subjects tested, 15.3% of all within-line saccades were regressive. The average size of within-line regressive saccades was −5.4 letters, the average size of within-line progressive saccades was 9.5 letters, and the average fixation duration was 219 ms. Of the progressive saccades, 62% skipped at least one word (with 43% skipping only one word), and among the fixated words, 7.2% received at least two consecutive fixations during their first encounter (first pass).

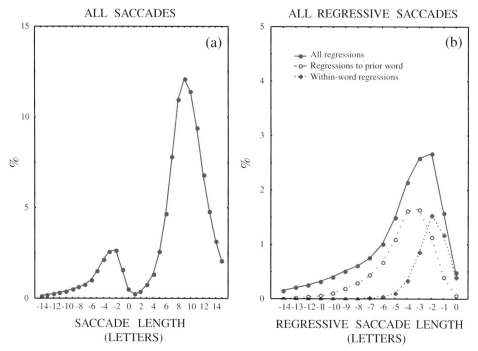

Fig. 1. (a) Frequency distribution of saccade lengths measured in letter-position units, for the combined data from 4 adult readers. (b) Frequency distribution of the lengths of all regressive saccades together with its two main component distributions, that for regressions to the prior word, and that for within-word regressions.

Fig. 1 presents the frequency distribution of all saccade lengths and the two composite frequency distributions that form the regressive saccade part of the distribution (including regressions within the destination word, and regressions to the prior word(s)). This figure shows that most regressive saccades are comparatively short. Component regressive saccade length distributions show that within-word regressions and regressions to the immediately preceding word constitute most of the regressions (77%) during reading. The within-word regressive saccades are necessarily much shorter than regressions to the prior word. This result is compatible with the hypothesis proposed by Radach and McConkie (1998; see also, Vitu et al., 1998) that the control of regressive saccades is word-based, and confirms the necessity of considering both types of saccades separately when analyzing the regression likelihood.

Of regressive saccades, 79% were preceded by a progressive eye movement. In those instances, 62% regressions occurred after one or several words were skipped (with 37% after a single word skip), 28% after the previous word was fixated, and 10% after a refixation of the same word occurred.

Prior saccade length

In a prior study, we have shown that the regression likelihood for 5th grade children is a function of prior saccade length: the longer the prior saccade, the higher the regression likelihood (Vitu et al., 1998; see also, Andriessen and De-Voogd, 1973). The present data indicate that adults show this same phenomenon for saccades longer than 6 characters, as seen in Fig. 2a. For prior saccades longer than 6 characters, the regression likelihood increases significantly with prior saccade length ($F(5, 15) = 8.01$, $p < 0.001$). For shorter saccades, regression likelihood decreases with prior saccade length, although the effect was not significant in this range ($F(3, 9) = 1.57$). The global effect of prior saccade length was non-significant ($F(8, 24) = 0.94$). A quadratic analysis of variance also reveals no significant trend when all saccade lengths are considered ($F(1, 3) = 5.19$).

Word-skip vs. non-word skip cases

A first prediction from the word identification explanation is that regressions occur more frequently when a word has been skipped than when no word is skipped.

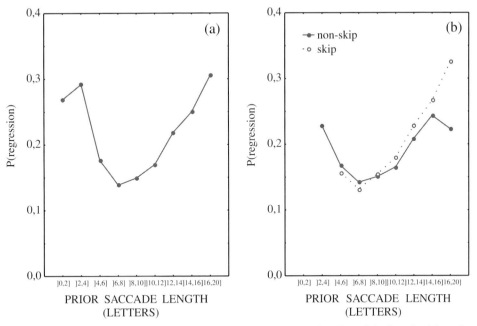

Fig. 2. The overall likelihood of making a regressive saccade as a function of the length of the prior progressive saccade, presented in two-letter intervals with a larger final interval: (a) presenting all data, and (b) presenting data separately for cases in which the prior saccade skipped one or several words (skip-cases), and cases in which the prior saccade did not skip a word ('non-skip' cases).

This is because skipped words are retinally more eccentric than fixated words, and hence, on average provide less visual information. In addition, since a word is more likely to be skipped with longer saccades, word-skip cases might be responsible for the effect reported above of prior saccade length on regression likelihood. Fig. 2b presents the frequency of regressing as a function of prior saccade length, plotted separately for skip and non-skip cases. While there do appear to be more regressions in the skip condition at least for saccades longer than 8 letters, the global effect of prior saccade event (tested on prior saccade length intervals going from 4 to 20 letters) was not statistically significant ($F(1, 3) = 5.28$). It is only for prior saccade length intervals going from 10 to 20 letters, that the difference between skip and non-skip cases is significant ($F(1, 3) = 11.48$, $p < 0.05$). Thus, the prediction is upheld, but only partially. On the other hand, the effect of prior saccade length is still present ($F(6, 18) = 2.63$, $p < 0.05$; for saccade length intervals going from 4 to 20 letters), being as great when words are not skipped as when they are (the interaction between prior saccade length and prior saccade event was not significant: $F(6, 18) = 1.56$).

A limitation of the above analysis is that it failed to distinguish between intra- and inter-word regressions. It may be that only inter-word regressions, and specifically those taking the eyes back to the skipped word, are stimulated by the failure to identify a skipped word; intra-word regressions may be produced by similar identification difficulty, but with respect to the destination word rather than the skipped word. Fig. 3 presents the frequency of inter- and intra-word regressions as a function of prior saccade length, and for skip and non-skip cases (here, inter-word regressions include only those taking the eyes to the prior skipped or origin word, respectively). Fig. 3a indicates that for saccades longer than 6 letters, increasing the saccade length increases inter-word regressions ($F(6, 18) = 4.94$, $p < 0.005$), but only when a word has been skipped ($F(6, 18) = 7.40$, $p < 0.0005$); when no word is skipped there is a slight, non-significant tendency for regressions to drop in frequency as saccade length increases ($F(6, 18) = 1.41$). As a result, more inter-word regressions occur in skip cases than in non-skip cases for saccades longer than 6 letters. The difference between skip and non-skip cases was not significant ($F(1, 3) \leq 3.20$), but the interaction between prior saccade length and prior saccade event was significant ($F(6, 18) = 6.67$, $p < 0.001$). This pattern of data is compatible with the word identification explanation for inter-word regressions.

In contrast, Fig. 3b indicates that intra-word regressions increase with saccade length ($F(6, 18) = 3.68$, $p < 0.05$) for both skip and non-skip cases ($F(6, 18) = 4.19$, $p < 0.01$, and $F(6, 18) = 3.43$, $p < 0.05$, respectively), though this increase is greater in the latter. The interaction between prior saccade length and prior saccade event was significant ($F(6, 18) = 2.85$, $p < 0.05$). Thus, intra- and inter-word regressions respond differently to differences in the prior saccade event.

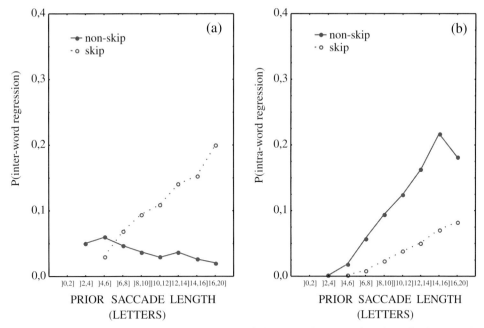

Fig. 3. Likelihood of inter-word (a) and intra-word (b) regressions as a function of prior saccade length for word-skip and non-skip cases. Inter-word regressions took the eyes to the prior skipped or origin word (in skip and non-skip cases, respectively), and intra-word regressions remained on the destination word.

Summary

Two types of within-line regressive saccades have been identified here: (1) inter-word regressions, most of which return the eyes to the immediately preceding word; and (2) intra-word regressions that necessarily bring the eyes closer to the beginning of the destination word than the initial location of the eye fixation on it. Inter- and intra-word regressions respond differently to the prior saccade event. Inter-word regressions are more likely following a progressive saccade that skips a word, and following longer progressive saccades. In contrast, intra-word regressions are most likely following longer progressive saccades that do not skip a word.

Influence of skipped word characteristics

Skipped word length

Previous study has shown that longer words presented briefly in parafovea are less likely to be identified than are shorter words (Brysbaert et al., 1996). The word identification explanation thus predicts that longer skipped words should cause more inter-word regressions taking the eyes to the skipped word than do shorter skipped words. Fig. 4a indicates that there are more regressions overall when a longer word is skipped rather than a shorter word, with all skipped word lengths showing a strong saccade length effect. Fig. 4b shows that when only inter-word regressions (those taking the eyes back to the skipped word) are considered, the effect of word length is even greater. Analyses of variance run on 2- to 5-letter words indeed reveal a significant effect of both skipped word length and prior saccade length on overall regression likelihood ($F(3, 9) = 6.81$, $p < 0.05$, $F(5, 15) = 9.05$, $p < 0.01$, respectively), and inter-word regression likelihood ($F(3, 9) = 6.48$, $p < 0.05$, $F(5, 15) = 8.47$, $p < 0.001$, respectively). These results are compatible with the word identification explanation of regressions, though there is an alternative possible explanation for this pattern that is discussed below. Fig. 4c indicates that, for intra-word regressions, word length has the opposite effect, with longer skipped words leading to fewer regressions, though this difference is not statistically significant ($F(3, 9) = 2.32$).

Launch site relative to skipped word
The retinal eccentricity of a word affects its perceptibility, with words lying further into the visual periphery being more difficult to identify (Bouma, 1978; Brysbaert et al., 1996). Thus, the word identification explanation of regressions predicts that the location of the fixation prior to the saccade that skips a word will affect the likelihood of regressing, and particularly of regressing to the skipped word. These regressions should be more frequent when the location of the prior fixation, or launch site for the saccade, is further from the skipped word. Fig. 5a, 5c and 5e are consistent with this prediction, showing that as the launch site moves further from the skipped word (indicated by increasing launch site values, which measure the distance of the eyes from the space in front of the word) the inter-word regression likelihood increases; this occurs consistently for 3-, 4- and 5- to 6-letter words. Analyses of variance actually show that the effect of launch site on inter-word regression likelihood was non-significant for all prior saccade length intervals (which were tested separately), except for intervals going from 10 to 12 characters, and 14 to 16 characters, where the effect was only marginally significant: $F(3, 9) = 2.88$, $p < 0.10$, and $F(3, 9) = 6.90$, $p < 0.10$, respectively. Intra-word regressions, presented for skipped words of different lengths in Fig. 5b, 5d and 5f, show the opposite pattern: at any given saccade length, greater launch distances produce reduced regression frequencies. However, the effect of launch site was non-significant for all saccade length intervals.

An analysis of all regressions, ignoring the distinction between inter- and intra-word regressions, shows no significant effect of launch site on regression frequency. This might be attributed to the opposite effects launch site has on inter- and intra-word regression likelihood.

The retinal eccentricity of a skipped word during the fixation after it was skipped

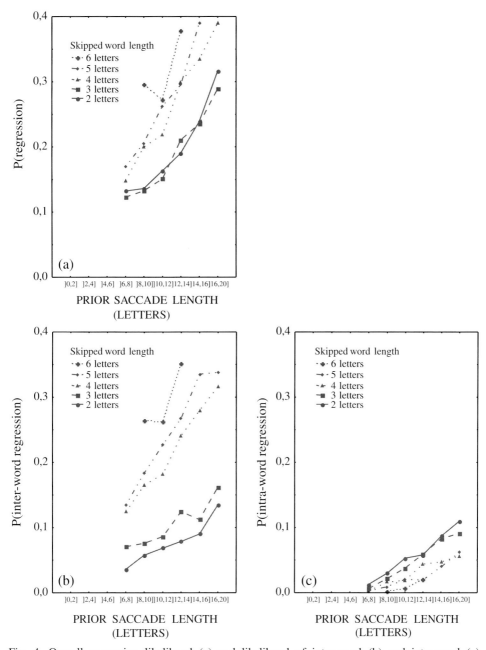

Fig. 4. Overall regression likelihood (a) and likelihood of inter-word (b) and intra-word (c) regressions as a function of prior saccade length for cases in which a word was skipped, and plotted separately for skipped words of different lengths. Since short words are more likely to be skipped, the present analyses are restricted to skipped word lengths of 2 to 6 letters. For 2- to 5-letter skipped words, data are presented for prior saccade lengths ranging between 6 and 20 letters; for 6-letter skipped words, data are presented for prior saccade lengths between 8 and 14 letters.

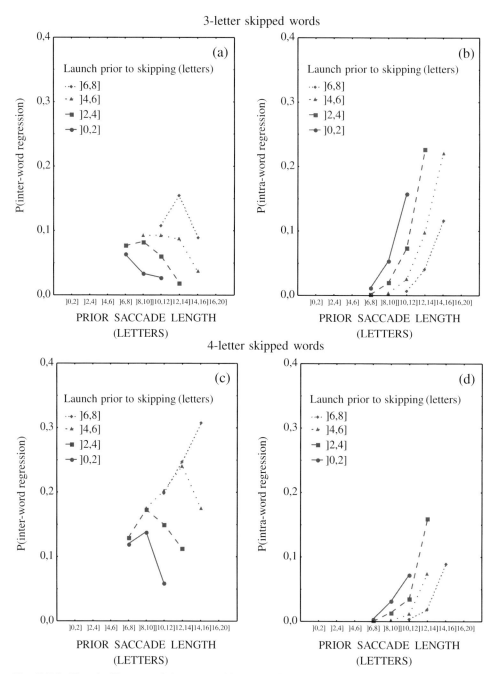

Fig. 5. Likelihood of inter-word (a, c, e) and intra-word (b, d, f) regressions as a function of prior saccade length, for cases in which a word was skipped, and plotted separately for cases in which that saccade was launched from different distances (launch sites) to the left of the space before a skipped word. Launch sites are presented in two-letter intervals. (a, b) Data for 3-letter skipped words. (c, d) Data for 4-letter skipped words. (e, f) Data for 5-letter skipped words.

5- & 6-letter skipped words

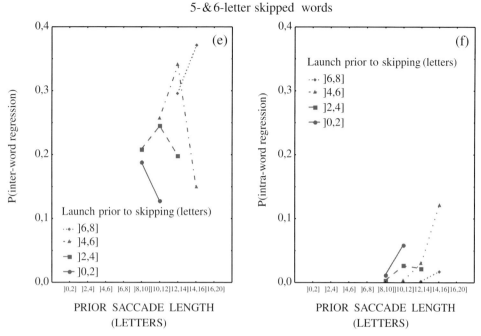

Fig. 5 (continued).

does not appear to affect the likelihood of regressing to it in quite the way predicted by the word identification explanation. When saccade length and launch site are held constant, then increasing the word length actually brings the end of the skipped word closer to the current fixation location. As Fig. 5a, 5c and 5e indicate, inter-word regressions are still more likely following the skipping of longer words, even though the distance from eye to word is reduced. Furthermore, when skipped word length and launch site are held constant, then increasing the saccade length causes the eyes to land farther from the word. Fig. 5a, 5c and 5e indicate that under these conditions increasing the saccade length produces no significant effect on inter-word regression frequency, even though the distance from eyes to word is increasing. Thus, it appears that retinal eccentricity of the skipped word, and the degree of visibility permitted by it, is having little influence on the inter-word regression likelihood.

In contrast, there is still a clear effect of prior saccade length on intra-word regression likelihood, with longer saccades leading to more regressions. This pattern of results might be accounted for by the fact that longer prior saccades bring the eyes further from the beginning of the destination word, which increases the area occupied by the word that lies to the left of the fixation point, and, hence, increases the possibility of making a regressive saccade within the word (see O'Regan and

F. Vitu & G.W. McConkie

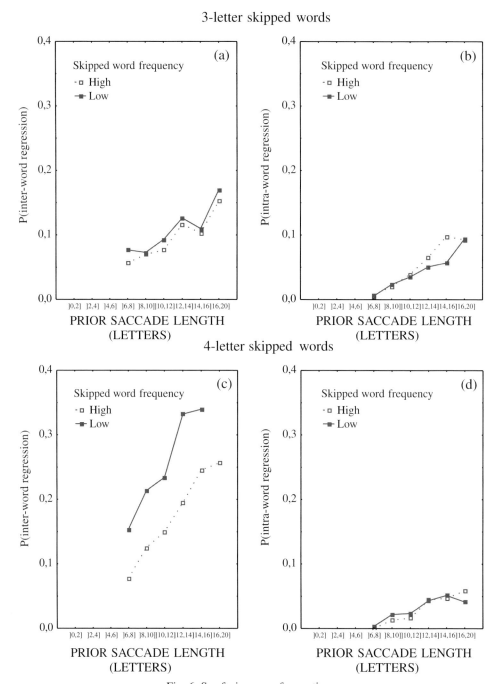

Fig. 6. See facing page for caption.

5-&6-letter skipped words

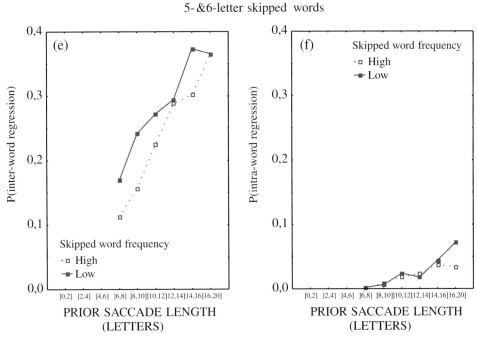

Fig. 6. Likelihood of inter-word (a, c, e) and intra-word (b, d, f) regressions as a function of the length of the prior saccade, for cases in which a word was skipped, and plotted separately for high- vs. low-frequency skipped words: (a, b) presenting data for 3-letter skipped words, (c, d) for 4-letter words, and (e, f) for 5- and 6-letter skipped words combined. The high- and low-frequency sets were defined using the frequency counts given by the Brown corpus (Kuçera and Francis, 1970), such that approximately the same number of cases was available in each set of words of a given length, and with words of moderate frequency excluded. Since longer words tend to have lower frequencies, the criteria used to define high- and low-frequency sets differed for words of different lengths. Criteria and medians for high- and low-frequency words are presented in Table 1.

Lévy-Schoen, 1987). Actually, the same type of hypothesis might account for the tendencies noted above (although being non-significant) for intra-word regressions to be more likely with shorter skipped words, and closer launch sites since these might send the eyes further into the word, a case that favors the occurrence of intra-word regressions (see McConkie, Kerr, Reddix and Zola, 1988).

Skipped word frequency
The perceptibility of a word in parafoveal vision is a function of the frequency of occurrence of the word in the language (Inhoff and Rayner, 1986; Vitu, 1991). Therefore, the word identification explanation predicts that when words are skipped, regressions (and particularly regressions to the skipped word) are more likely if the skipped word is of lower, rather than higher, frequency. Fig. 6a, 6c and 6e support

Table 1

Criteria used to distinguish between high- and low-frequency 4- to 7-letter words, and median word frequency for both categories (in occurences per million)

	Low-frequency words		High-frequency words	
	Criterion	Median	Criterion	Median
3-letter words	≤589	195	≥1400	9489
4-letter words	≤592	183	≥1331	3567
5-letter words	≤158	65	≥266	392
6-letter words	≤49	14	≥108	251
7-letter words	≤49	12	≥108	282

this prediction, showing the expected pattern for 3-, 4- and 5- to 6-letter skipped words, and almost all prior saccade length intervals ($F(1, 3) = 9.46$, $p < 0.05$, $F(1, 3) = 18.57$, $p < 0.05$, $F(1, 3) = 12.87$, $p < 0.05$, respectively, for 3-, 4-, and 5- to 6-letter skipped words). In contrast, Fig. 6b, 6d and 6f indicate that the frequency of the skipped word has little or no effect on the likelihood of intra-word regressions ($F(1, 3) \leq 3.01$).

Analysis of the overall regression likelihood also shows more regressions following the skipping of low-frequency words, the effect being significant for 4- and 5- to 6-letter skipped words ($F(1, 3) = 17.14$, $p < 0.05$, $F(1, 3) = 15.04$, $p < 0.05$, respectively), but not for 3-letter skipped words ($F(1, 3) = 0.12$).

Summary

When a word is skipped during a progressive saccade, the likelihood of regressing back to it (here referred to as an inter-word regression) depends on the identifiability of that word (i.e., its length, frequency and retinal eccentricity) on the prior fixation as predicted by the word identification explanation, but not the eccentricity of the word on the following fixation. The effect of these variables on the likelihood of refixating a destination word (here referred to as an intra-word regression) is much smaller and different in nature. The distribution of regressions between inter- and intra-word regression categories also depends on factors that determine where the eyes land in the destination word.

Influence of origin word characteristics

In cases where no word was skipped, the reader's eyes sometimes regress to the word that was fixated during the previous fixation (see Fig. 2b). The question addressed here is whether the frequency of regressions to the origin word is also related to variables that influence the identifiability of that word: its length, and frequency, and the initial eye fixation position in the word.

Origin word length

Previous studies have shown that longer words presented in fovea are less likely to be correctly identified with a single eye fixation than shorter words (O'Regan, 1990; see also, Brysbaert et al., 1996; Vitu, 1991; Vitu, O'Regan and Mittau, 1990). The word identification hypothesis therefore predicts that longer origin words should cause more inter-word regressions than shorter words, at least when they receive a single eye fixation. In the present data, an initial analysis failed to find any relationship between the origin word length and the overall regression likelihood ($F(4, 12) = 0.44$). However, significant relationships were observed when a distinction was made between inter- and intra-word regressions, as shown in Fig. 7. Here, inter-word regressions are those that return the eyes to the origin word; intra-word regressions keep the eyes on the origin word. Fig. 7a indicates that the frequency of these inter-word regressions drops with prior saccade length ($F(3, 9) = 6.17$, $p < 0.05$), as shown by the (non-significant) trend in Fig. 3a, but that increased length of the origin word results in more regressions to it ($F(4, 12) = 4.13$, $p < 0.05$), as predicted by the word identification explanation. In contrast, origin word length appears to be inversely related to intra-word regression frequency in Fig. 7b, though neither this relationship nor the relationship

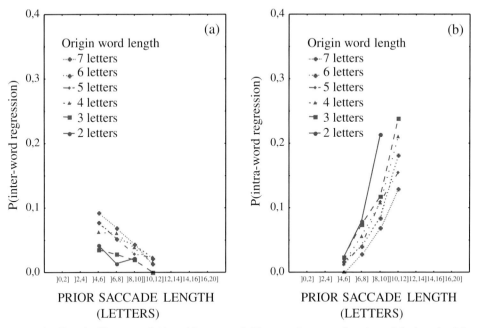

Fig. 7. Likelihood of inter-word (a) and intra- word (b) regressions as a function of the length of the prior saccade, for cases in which no word was skipped, and plotted separately for origin words of different lengths. Only cases where the origin word initially received a single fixation are included.

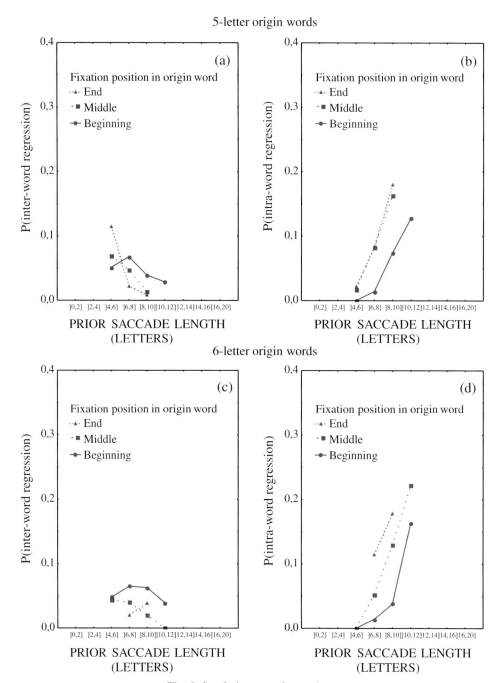

Fig. 8. See facing page for caption.

7-letter origin words

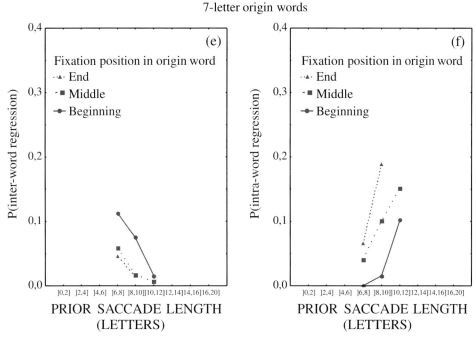

Fig. 8. Likelihood of inter-word (a, c, e) and intra-word (b, d, f) regressions as a function of the length of the prior saccade, for cases in which no word was skipped, and plotted separately for cases in which the initial fixation on the origin word was at its beginning, middle or end: (a, b) presenting data for 5-letter origin words, (c, d) for 6-letter origin words, and (e, f) for 7-letter origin words. 'Beginning' fixations were on the space before the word, or the first or second letter of 5- to 7-letter words. 'Middle' fixations corresponded to fixations on letter 3 for 5-letter words, letters 3 or 4 for 6-letter words, and letters 3, 4, or 5 for 7-letter words. 'End' fixations were on either of the final 2 letters of the word.

between saccade length and intra-word regression frequency were statistically significant ($F(4, 12) = 2.79$, $p < 0.10$ and $F(3, 9) = 2.31$, respectively). The interaction between prior saccade length and origin word length was not significant for either regression type.

Fixation location in origin word
On average, a word can be identified fastest (O'Regan and Jacobs, 1992) and with fewest refixations (McConkie, Kerr, Reddix, Zola and Jacobs, 1989; Nazir, O'Regan and Jacobs, 1991; O'Regan, 1990; O'Regan and Lévy-Schoen, 1987; Rayner and Fischer, 1996; Rayner, Sereno and Raney, 1996; Vitu et al., 1990) when the initial fixation is at its center, a phenomenon referred to as the optimal viewing position (OVP) effect. Thus, the word identification explanation predicts that an origin word should receive more regressions to it as the fixation location on it

moves further from its center. Fig. 8 shows the relation between saccade length and regression likelihood following fixations at the beginning, middle and end of origin words of different lengths, and plotting inter- and intra-word regressions separately. Fig. 8a, 8c and 8e present data for inter-word regressions which contradict the prediction just stated: inter-word regressions are most frequent following fixations at the beginning of the origin word, with reduced frequency for fixations at the center and end of the words. This trend was not statistically significant (analysis of variance included 5- to 7-letter words for prior saccade lengths ranging between 6 and 10 letters, yielding $F(2, 6) = 1.98$), and provides no support for the prediction. Intra-word refixations showed an opposite pattern with fixations at the end of the origin words producing the most regressions and those at the beginning producing the fewest. Again, these differences were not significant ($F(2, 6) = 1.78$).

Finally, fixation location in the origin word did not have a significant effect on the overall regression likelihood for saccade lengths between 6 and 10 letters.

Origin word frequency

Since higher-frequency words are more likely to be identified in a single fixation than are lower-frequency words (O'Regan, 1990; Vitu, 1991), the word identification explanation predicts that lower-frequency origin words should receive more inter-word regressions than higher-frequency words. Fig. 9a, 9c and 9e indicate that this prediction is supported for 6- and 7-letter words (for prior saccades ranging between 4 and 10 letters, and 6 and 8 letters, respectively), but not for 5-letter words. An analysis of variance involving prior saccade lengths ranging between 6 and 12 letters for 5- to 7-letter words, shows that the effect of word frequency is significant ($F(1, 3) = 16.51$, $p < 0.05$) and does not interact with either prior saccade length or origin word length ($F(2, 6) \leq 2.62$). Thus, the data support the prediction. Fig. 9b, 9d and 9f indicate that origin word frequency has no effect on the number of intra-word regressions on the destination word ($F(1, 3) = 1.97$). In the same way, the global regression likelihood revealed no clear effect of origin word frequency.

Summary

In cases where no word was skipped during the prior saccade, two variables influencing the perceptibility of the origin word, its length and frequency, had the expected effects on inter-word regressions (regressions taking the eyes back to the origin word). Longer and lower-frequency origin words were more likely to receive inter-word regressions. Of course, these two variables are highly intercorrelated and we did not try to determine whether they each make independent contributions to the regression likelihood. The third variable, the location of the fixation on the origin word, did not have the expected effect on inter-word regressions.

Discussion

As people read, they frequently make regressive eye movements. The analyses presented above are an attempt to describe the conditions under which these regressive movements occur and, more particularly, to determine whether their occurrence may be related to difficulty or failure in word identification. An earlier study of eye movements of 5th grade children during reading (Vitu et al., 1998) revealed a strong relationship between saccade length and regression frequency, plus a greater likelihood of making a regression following a saccade in which a word was skipped than one in which no word was skipped. These phenomena were replicated in adult reading data in the present study. In addition, a number of specific predictions were derived from the general principle that less perceptible words tend to stimulate regressions and to become the targets for regressions. With two exceptions, the data based on inter-word regression likelihood were compatible with these predictions, thus providing support for the underlying principle. The length, frequency and retinal eccentricity of a skipped word all affect the likelihood that the eyes will be drawn back to that word in the next saccade. Also, the length and frequency of the origin word, when no word is skipped, affects the frequency of regressing back to it. In contrast, there was no effect of the distance of the eyes with respect to the skipped word following skipping, thus failing to support one prediction made by the perceptibility or word identification explanation. There was also not a significant effect of the location at which the origin word was previously fixated, thus failing to support an other prediction; in fact, the data seem to show a pattern quite different than the one predicted. These observations are discussed further below.

Data based on regressions within the destination word (or intra-word regressions) are also compatible with predictions from the word identification explanation. These show that the likelihood of intra-word regressions does not vary much with factors that affect the perceptibility of a prior skipped word or origin word. Tendencies for an increase with shorter skipped or origin words and closer launch sites were present but not statistically significant, but an increase with longer prior saccades was significant. This latter result can be attributed to the fact that the position where the eyes land in the destination word is further from the beginning of the word, a condition which diminishes the perceptibility of the destination word, and favors the occurrence of intra-word regressions (McConkie et al., 1989; Nazir et al., 1991; O'Regan and Lévy-Schoen, 1987; Vitu, 1991; Vitu et al., 1990).

As noted above, only two results were found that contradict predictions from the word identification explanation. First, it is not true that more inter-word regressions to the origin word occur if that word has been fixated with a single fixation located toward the beginning or end, as compared to being fixated in the middle where identification should occur more readily (see McConkie et al., 1989; Nazir et al.,

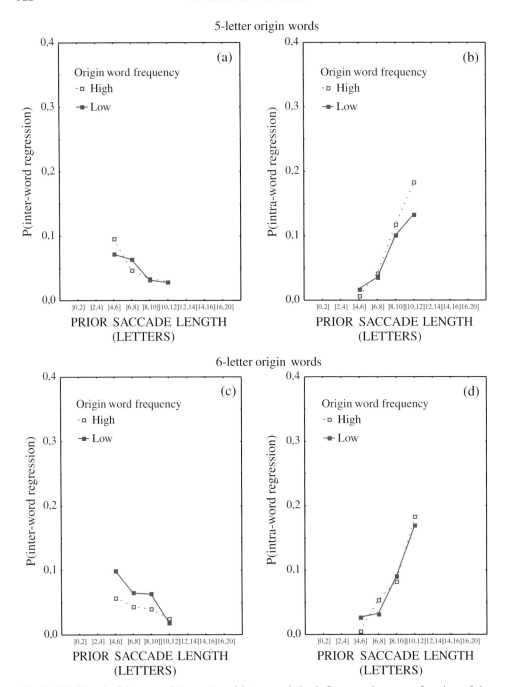

Fig. 9. Likelihood of inter-word (a, c, e) and intra-word (b, d, f) regressions as a function of the length of the prior saccade, for cases in which no word was skipped, and plotted separately for high- vs. low-frequency origin words (see Table 1): (a, b) presenting data for 5-letter origin words, (c, d) for 6-letter origin words, and (e, f) for 7-letter origin words. Only cases in which the origin word received a single fixation are included.

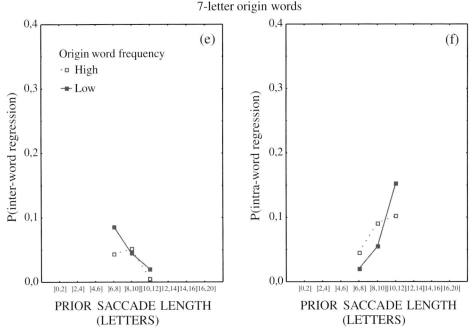

Fig. 9 (continued).

1991). The data indicate more inter-word regressions only to words that have received a single fixation toward their beginning. This may occur because, when the initial fixation on a word is toward its end, the prior fixation tends to be closer to that word than when the initial fixation is toward its beginning (see McConkie et al., 1988). Thus, the fixation on the word plus the prior fixation may give more visual information about the word in the former cases than in the latter. Our prediction may be faulty because we failed to take into account the location of the fixation prior to the first fixation in the quintuple used in the analyses of the current data.

The second result from the present study that contradicts predictions from the word identification explanation is the fact noted in word-skip cases that inter-word regression likelihood does not vary with the retinal eccentricity of the skipped word after skipping, while the visibility of the skipped word decreases the further the eyes land from the end of the skipped word. At present, we have no explanation for the present finding. One possibility might be that when reading a text, attention is mostly directed to the next words, enhancing processing of the information located to the right of fixation. Thus if a word located to the left of fixation needs to be processed further, an inter-word regression will have to be initiated, and this independently of the visibility of the word from the current eye location (see Chapter 9 for a discussion on that issue).

In exploring the basis for regressive saccades we have employed the concept of a word identification explanation: that regressions are, at least sometimes, induced and directed by problems in the identification of a given word. We have deliberately left this concept vague. It is possible that, on some occasions, regressions are induced by the actual failure to identify a given word that was skipped, previously fixated or currently fixated. Thus, the eyes are drawn to that word to provide the additional visual detail that is necessary in order for identification to occur. However, it is also possible that simply having encountered difficulties in identifying a given word might induce a regression to it. One possible basis for such an effect is that identification difficulty delays the successful identification of the word so that, at the time the saccade decision is made, the word has not yet been identified (see Schroyens, Vitu, Brysbaert and d'Ydewalle, 1999). As a result, that word competes more effectively as a target for the next saccade. However, after the time the saccade decision is made, identification of the word might occur. This would result in the eyes going to a word that has already been identified. Thus, we do not assume that regressions are necessarily taking the eyes to unidentified words (McConkie and Hogaboam, 1985).

We do not propose that word identification difficulties are the sole basis on which regressions are produced and directed. As noted above, semantic and syntactic complexities can also cause the eyes to regress (Frazier and Rayner, 1982; Rayner and Pollatsek, 1989). It is also possible that some regressions are 'corrective saccades' resulting from positioning error in oculomotor control (see Becker, 1989).

The fact that inter- and intra-word regressions behave differently in response to the experimental variables used in the above analyses supports the word-based nature of this aspect of saccade control during reading (Radach and McConkie, 1998; Vitu et al., 1998). The effect that these variables have on regression frequency depends on whether regressions to origin, skipped or destination words are being considered. This also argues that for many research purposes it is important to distinguish between inter- and intra-word regressions in data analyses, rather than assuming that all regressions are from a single population.

On the other hand, we wish to note that the word identification explanation is not the only possible explanation for several of the results that have been reported here. For example, the fact that longer skipped words produce more inter-word regressions to those words could be accounted for by a simple theory assuming random control of saccades. Since longer words occupy more space, more of the randomly generated saccades will land on them, thus resulting in more inter-word regressions to longer words. We have not yet carried out the modeling process that is necessary to insure that obtained results such as this are different than would be expected by chance. We have simply tested whether the data patterns obtained are compatible with predictions of the word identification explanation, rather than attempting to exclude other explanations.

Acknowledgements

The present study was conducted while Françoise Vitu was on sabbatical leave at the Beckman Institute, University of Illinois at Urbana-Champaign (from December 1996 to December 1997). It was supported by a NATO grant given to Françoise Vitu. It used data collected by Paul Kerr under grants # BNS 89-00320, and NICHHD 1-R01-HD28181 from National Science Foundation, with software developed by Gary S. Wolverton. The writing of the paper occurred while George W. McConkie was on sabbatical leave at Beijing Normal University in Beijing, China, partially supported by a Senior Scholar Grant from the Chiang Ching-kuo Foundation.

References

Andriessen, J.J. and DeVoogd, A.H. (1973). Analysis of eye movement patterns in silent reading. IPO Annual Progress Report, 8, 29–34.

Becker, W. (1989). Metrics. In: R.H. Wurzt and M.E. Goldberg (Eds.), The Neurobiology of Saccadic Eye Movements. Amsterdam: Elsevier, pp. 13–67.

Bouma, H. (1978). Visual search and reading: Eye movements and functional visual field: a tutorial review. In: J. Requin (Ed.), Attention and Performance VII. Hillsdale: Erlbaum, pp. 115–145.

Bouma, H. and DeVoogd, A.H. (1974). On the control of eye saccades in reading. Vision Research, 14, 273–284.

Brysbaert, M. and Vitu, F. (1998). Word skipping: implications for theories of eye movement control in reading. In: G. Underwood (Ed.), Eye Guidance in Reading and Scene Perception. Oxford: Elsevier, pp. 125–147.

Brysbaert, M., Vitu, F. and Schroyens, W. (1996). The right field visual advantage and the optimal viewing position effect: on the relation between foveal and parafoveal word recognition. Neuropsychologia, 10 (3), 385–395.

Buswell, G.T. (1920). An experimental study of the eye–voice span in reading. Supplementary Educational Monographs, 17, University of Chicago, Chicago.

Frazier, L. and Rayner, K. (1982). Making and correcting errors during sentence comprehension: eye movements in the analysis of structurally ambiguous sentences. Cognitive Psychology, 14, 178–210.

Hochberg, J. (1976). Toward a speech-plan eye-movement model of reading. In: R.A. Monty and J.W. Senders (Eds.), Eye Movements and Psychological Processes. Hillsdale, NJ: Erlbaum.

Inhoff, A.W. and Rayner, K. (1986). Parafoveal word processing during eye fixations in reading: effects of word frequency. Perception and Psychophysics, 40, 431–439.

Just, M.A. and Carpenter, P.A. (1980). A theory of reading: from eye fixations to comprehension. Psychological Review, 87, 329–354.

Kerr, P.W. (1992). Eye Movement Control During Reading. Doctoral Dissertation, University of Illinois at Urbana-Champaign.

Kuçera, H. and Francis, W.N. (1970). Computational Analysis of Present-Day American English. Providence, RI: Brown University Press.

Lesèvre, N. (1964). Les mouvements oculaires d'explanation. Etude électro-oculographique comparée d'enfants normauz et d'enfants dyslexiques. Doctoral dissertation, Paris.

McConkie, G.W. and Hogaboam, T.W. (1985). Eye position and word identification in reading.

In: R. Groner, G.W. McConkie and C. Menz (Eds.), Eye Movements and Human Information Processing. Amsterdam: North-Holland.

McConkie, G.W., Kerr, P.W., Reddix, M.D. and Zola, D. (1988). Eye movement control during reading, I. The location of initial eye fixations on words. Vision Research, 28 (10), 1107–1118.

McConkie, G.W., Kerr, P.W., Reddix, M.D., Zola, D. and Jacobs, A.M. (1989). Eye movement control during reading, II. Frequency of refixating a word. Perception and Psychophysics, 46, 245–253.

Nazir, T., O'Regan, J.K. and Jacobs, A.M. (1991). On words and their letters. Bulletin of the Psychonomic Society, 29, 171–174.

O'Regan, J.K. (1990). Eye movements and reading. In: E. Kowler (Ed.), Eye Movements and Their Role in Visual and Cognitive Processes. Amsterdam: Elsevier, pp. 395–453.

O'Regan, J.K. and Jacobs, A.M. (1992). Optimal viewing position effect in word recognition: a challenge to current theories. Journal of Experimental Psychology: Human Perception and Performance, 18 (1), 185–197.

O'Regan, J.K. and Lévy-Schoen, A. (1987). Eye movement strategy and tactics in word recognition and reading. In: M. Coltheart (Ed.), Attention and Performance XII: The Psychology of Reading. Hillsdale, NJ: Erlbaum, pp. 363–383.

Pollatsek, A. and Rayner, K. (1990). Eye movements and lexical access in reading. In: D.A. Balota, G.B. Flores d'Arcais and K. Rayner (Eds.), Comprehension Processes in Reading. Hillsdale, NJ: Erlbaum, pp. 143–163.

Radach, R. and McConkie, G.W. (1998). Determinants of fixation positions in words during reading. In: G. Underwood (Ed.), Eye Guidance in Reading and Scene Perception, Oxford: Elsevier, pp. 77–100.

Rayner, K. (1998). Eye movements in reading and information processing: 20 years of research. Psychological Bulletin, 124 (3), 372–422.

Rayner, K. and Fischer, M.H. (1996). Mindless reading revisited: eye movements during reading and scanning are different. Perception and Psychophysics, 58 (5), 734–747.

Rayner, K. and Pollatsek, S. (1989). The Psychology of Reading. London: Prentice-Hall.

Rayner, K., Sereno, S.C. and Raney, G.E. (1996). Eye movement control in reading: A comparison of two types of models. Journal of Experimental Psychology: Human Perception and Performance, 22 (5), 1188–1200.

Schroyens, W., Vitu, F., Brysbaert, M. and d'Ydewalle, G. (1999). Visual attention and eye movement control in reading: the case of parafoveal processing. Quarterly Journal of Experimental Psychology, 52A (4), 1021–1046.

Shebilske, W. (1975). Reading eye movements from an information-processing point of view. In: D. Massaro (Ed.), Understanding Language. London: Academic Press.

Shebilske, W.L. and Fisher, D.F. (1983). Eye movements and context effects during reading of extended discourse. In: K. Rayner (Ed.), Eye Movements in Reading: Perceptual and Language Processes. New York: Academic Press.

Taylor, E. (1971). The dynamic activity of reading: A model of the process. Research Information Bulletin No 9. New York: Educational Developmental Laboratories.

Vitu, F. (1991). The influence of parafoveal preprocessing and linguistic context on the optimal landing position effect. Perception and Psychophysics, 50, 58–75.

Vitu, F., McConkie, G.W. and Zola, D. (1998). About regressive saccades in reading and their relation to word identification. In: G. Underwood (Ed.), Eye Guidance in Reading and Scene Perception, Oxford: Elsevier, pp. 101–124.

Vitu, F., O'Regan, J.K. and Mittau, M. (1990). Optimal landing position in reading isolated words and continuous text. Perception and Psychophysics, 47 (6), 583–600.

CHAPTER 13

Planning Two-Saccade Sequences in Reading

Cécile Beauvillain, Dorine Vergilino and Tania Dukic
Université René Descartes

Abstract

The planning of two successive saccades in reading was investigated on four experiments in which eye movements were recorded in different paradigms: (1) target step during the primary saccade (Experiments 1 and 2), (2) target length change at different times during (Experiment 3), or after the primary saccade to the target (Experiment 4). The data reveal the existence of different mechanisms for the metrical control of inter- and intraword saccades. When the second saccade is directed to the next word, this saccade is recalculated in respect to the current position of the second word during the first fixation. Consequently, the eyes land left of the center of the second word. When the second word saccade is directed within the first word (i.e. a refixation saccade) this saccade is invariant with respect to the current eye position. The refixation saccade is found to be calculated on the target length information that was integrated before the primary saccade. This initially preprogrammed refixation saccade is modified on the basis of the new length information only for refixation saccades triggered more than 150 ms. The data demonstrate that the refixation saccade is not coded in retinocentric coordinates, as the interword saccade, but rather in motor space coordinates.

Reading as a Perceptual Process/A. Kennedy, R. Radach, D. Heller and J. Pynte (Editors)
© 2000 Elsevier Science Ltd. All rights reserved

Introduction

In reading or scanning a visual scene, continuous monitoring of saccadic performance is required to enable perceptual information uptake to occur with highly automated routines. The goal of this chapter is to explore one aspect of this skill that involves the control of successive saccades during reading. The question arises whether saccadic movements are executed as independent or interrelated commands. Saccades in reading can be stimulus-driven on a step-by-step basis in the sense that only one saccade is planned at a time. This would be predicted by the view that size and direction of goal-directed saccades are determined exclusively by the retinocentric coordinates of the current selected target. According to this view, only one saccade can be planned at a time, as the retinal location of the next target is not known until the preceding saccade is over. Alternatively, a sequence of successive saccades can be planned at a time. Subjects can preselect successive targets, plan the sequence of eye movements, and perform a self-paced timing of the scanning eye movements. The intended eye movements would therefore be conceived as invariant so that the amplitude of the preprogrammed saccade would be *predetermined* at the moment of the planning process on the basis of the visual information integrated at that time.

Evidence for the notion that saccades in reading are *guided* to the target selected during the current fixation is given by the initial saccade directed to a word. Most of the literature indicates that initial fixation locations within words are determined by the length of the to-be-fixated word (O'Regan, 1979; Rayner, 1979). The initial saccades are also influenced by visual factors such as the relative contrast of letters (Beauvillain, Doré and Baudouin, 1996). Although low-level visual information influences where the eyes initially land in a word, the orthographic properties of the initial letter cluster were found to also influence the initial landing (Beauvillain and Doré, 1998; Doré and Beauvillain, 1997; Hyönä, 1995). Thus, the metrics of such primary saccades to a target word seem under the control of the information obtained from the preceding fixation.

When a reader scans a word with two fixations, the primary saccade to the word is followed by a secondary intraword saccade which has the appearance of a guided saccade: it is directed towards the end of the word where information was difficult to extract from the initial fixation position. Yet, its latency is shorter than the interword saccade. Indeed, while the range of initial fixation duration is about 220–280 ms in the single fixation cases, it is about 180–240 ms in the two-fixation cases (Rayner, Sereno and Raney, 1996). Consequently, the manner in which new visual information integrated during the initial fixation may influence the metrics of intraword saccades is not obvious. Could it be that these saccades, including those directed to a target word, are preprogrammed as a package of two saccades? In other words, is an intraword saccade the second movement of a *predetermined* two-saccade sequence that is not elicited by the position of the initial fixation? The fact that the probability of refixating is higher for long words and quite high when the initial fixation location is further from the center of the word (McConkie, Kerr, Reddix, Zola and Jacobs, 1989; O'Regan, Lévy-Schoen, Pynte and Brugaillère, 1984) has been taken as an evidence for the programming of the refixation saccade during the initial fixation on a word. However, such responses are also compatible with a preprogrammed mode of operation and could result from the preselection of either one or two successive positions within the next word as a function of its length. Recently, Reichle, Pollatsek, Fisher and Rayner (1998) have proposed that the refixation saccade is planned automatically, but only at the onset of each initial fixation on a word. This program to refixate a word is subject to cancellation by the completion of the familiarity stage of the fixated word — the signal that causes the planning of the saccade to the next word.

Clear-cut evidence of planning is not easy to obtain in a free text reading situation. It presupposes the possibility of controlling the input stimuli and subject's intentions to some extent. One must, therefore, settle for evidence derived from situations with more constraints on the sequence of movements than are actually present in a text reading situation. We present here a series of experiments performed in the laboratory which investigate the two-saccade sequences in reading one or two linguistic stimuli with special reference to (a) the planning of such movements and (b) the integration of perceptual information across successive fixations. These experiments bear close resemblance to the 'double step' technique that has extensively investigated the simplest possible sequence, composed of two fixations and two saccades (Becker and Jürgens, 1979; Deubel, Wolf and Hauske, 1982). In the classical 'double step' technique, a target is flashed at an eccentric position and is then displaced to a second position while the subject is still preparing or executing the first saccade. When a subject plans an eye movement to a visual target, the stimulus on the retina is in the same location relative to the fovea as the goal of the eye movement planned to foveate the target. Thus no coordinate transformation is required for a simple visual target. However, if the retinal position of a target is displaced before an eye movement because of a displacement of the target or an intervening saccade, then the motor command to achieve the target is different from the earlier retinal location of the stimulus. In order to calculate the second saccade accurately, the saccadic system has to update it with the new eye position. All investigations based on the double step experiments have shown that the displacement is not perceived by the subject but is considered by the oculomotor system that programs and executes a correction saccade in order to capture the target.

One of the characteristics of these double-step studies was that eye movements were completely guided by the location of the single stimulus in the visual field. The question arises whether similar corrective mechanisms are involved in the generation of saccades triggered in a reading task situation when subjects scan a to-be-recognized word. The present experiments use the following paradigm. At various times during or after the primary saccade to a target letter string, the target is made to change its position or its length. Experiment 1 explores the saccadic response to different displacements of a single letter string during the primary saccade to it. We also varied the length of the letter string. The experiment demonstrates that the second saccade directed within the letter string, i.e. the refixation saccade, is invariant regardless to the target displacement. The amplitude of this refixation saccade was found to be only affected by the item length, irrespective of the initial fixation position. Experiment 2 used the same paradigm as Experiment 1 with two target words in order to see to what extent the second saccade, directed to the second word, corrects the induced error in initial landing position on the first word. While refixation saccades directed within the first word do not correct the error due to the displacement, thus replicating Experiment 1, it is found that saccades directed to the second word do correct the error and aim to a position left of the center of the second word. Clearly, when the second word is selected as the target, saccades are calculated on the basis of the retinal location of the second word during the fixation on the first word. These results reveal the existence of different mechanisms for the metrical control of interword and intraword saccades. Experiments 3 and 4 return to the refixation saccade and investigate the extent to which this saccade is calculated on the basis of visual characteristics of the letter string available before or after the primary saccade. The target letter string was made to change its length during the primary saccade to the target (Experiment 3) or at different times during or after the primary saccade (Experiment 4). Saccadic responses triggered less than 150 ms after the length change are calculated on the basis of the initial length information. An adjustment of the refixation saccade amplitude on the basis of the final length was found only for saccadic responses triggered more than 150 ms after the length change.

Experiment 1. Refixation saccades do not correct an initial fixation position error

For analyzing secondary refixation saccades within a letter string, Experiment 1 used a double-step paradigm in which the letter string that elicited the primary saccade was displaced during the primary saccade. The question arises whether the secondary saccades triggered after the initial fixation in reading are typical correction saccades, correcting an error produced by the saccade-triggered shift of the saccade goal. Two different types of corrective saccades may be predicted. First, the secondary saccade may be programmed in order to correct the exogenous error produced by the shift of the target during the primary saccade. Such a corrective mechanism should produce a second saccade directed to the intended landing position. However, landing at precise position for identifying an object is unlikely to be implemented in reading performance when subjects intentionally scan a to-be-recognized word. Second, readers may target a position for the second fixation in the second part of the word, where information was difficult to extract on the initial fixation. This makes sense, given that, once a fixation has occurred, the best place to refixate will be on the other side of the word. This was originally suggested by O'Regan (1990), who showed that imposed first fixation positions on one side of 11-letter words were followed by refixations in the other side of the word. According to such a corrective mechanism, the refixation saccade amplitude should be calculated as a function of the target displacement, to fixate a point halfway between the current fixation and the end of the letter string. This will cause an increase in the refixation saccade amplitude for an initial fixation located on the beginning of the letter string and a shortening of the refixation amplitude for initial fixation located in the middle of the word.

This experiment focused on small target steps within the range of typical first fixation positions observed in reading. During the primary saccade to a target letter string, displayed at 2°30 from the fixation point, the target letter string was displaced by 1 or 2 character-spaces, in the same direction (SD sequence) or opposite direction (OD sequence) of the primary saccade. 1- and 2-letter same direction displacements (1L or 2L SD) determined first fixation positions 1 or 2 character-spaces left of the intended landing position. 1- and 2-letter opposite direction displacements (1L or 2L OD) determined first fixation positions 1 or 2 character-spaces right of the intended landing position. No displacement occurred in the ND sequence. Subjects were instructed to read the target letter string and then to saccade to a cross displayed 2 character-spaces to the right of the target string. When the eyes left the target string, the target string disappeared and the cross was replaced by a comparison string. Subjects were asked to judge whether the second string was similar to the first one. Three different lengths of stimuli were used: 7-, 9- and 11-letter strings. To control the linguistic properties of the different length stimuli, nonsense letter strings were constructed sharing the same seven initial letters. These letter strings were orthographically legal in French. It was thus possible to keep the properties of the different length stimuli, sharing the same initial letters, constant by eliminating lexical influences that occur between different length words. This control allowed us to focus on the relation of specific perceptual variables to the metrical control of eye movements during recognition. Eight subjects participated in three blocks of 300 trials each.

Eye position was registered with a Bouis Oculometer system and sampled at 500 Hz. Absolute resolution of the eye tracker was 6 min of arc (Beauvillain and Beauvillain, 1995), and 1 character-space equaled 30′ of visual angle. Vision was binocular and head movements were restricted by a bite-board and a forehead rest.

Stimuli were displayed on a CRT screen (Hewlett Packard 1310 A; P15 phosphor) interfaced to a fast graphics system providing a frame frequency of 1000 Hz for stimulus presentation.

The displacement had an effect on the refixation frequency. The frequency of refixations was 38%, 37%, and 31% lower following an opposite direction displacement than in the no-displacement condition for 7-, 9- and 11-letter strings, respectively. A same direction displacement increased refixation frequency from 31%, 18% and 9%, for 7-, 9- and 11-letter strings, respectively. Thus, a position difference of one or two letters in the location at which the eyes land makes a substantial difference in the frequency of refixation. The letter string length also had an influence on refixation frequency: 62%, 80% and 89% in the no-displacement condition for 7-, 9- and 11-letter strings, respectively. The refixation frequency observed in the present study is higher than usually reported with words. This seems to be due to the use of nonsense letter strings.

The results of the first experiment indicate that secondary saccades triggered after the primary saccade to the target are not typical 'correction saccades', that is, saccades that correct fixation errors induced by the item displacement to target the intended landing position. Fig. 1 shows the distributions of first fixation position, refixation saccade amplitude and second fixation position for the different displacements made for 7-, 9- and 11-letter strings. Obviously, the distributions of refixation saccade amplitudes for the different displacements overlap. These data reveal that refixation saccade amplitude is uniform and is not modulated by the displacement conditions. Clearly, this saccadic behavior differs profoundly from saccadic responses observed in double-step experiments, with a single dot as the target, where a consecutive correction saccade is triggered, bringing the foveal line of sight to the target position. In our experiment, the only corrective saccades that target the intended landing position are regressive saccades in response to the opposite direction step. These regressive saccades represented 22% of responses. As a matter of fact, many saccadic responses triggered after an opposite direction displacement were progressive saccades directed towards the following cross. These responses represented 59%, 33% and 23% of the responses for 7-, 9- and 11-letter strings, respectively.

Another possibility is that the refixation saccade amplitude was calculated to produce a fixation halfway between the first fixation position and the end of the letter string. Such a corrective mechanism predicts that the further the center of the letter string the eye fixates, the larger should be the refixation saccade amplitude. To test this hypothesis, the data were partitioned on the basis of actual landing positions so that the amplitude could be compared for different actual landing positions. Fig. 2 represents the saccade amplitude distributions for actual landing positions located at 2, 3 and 4 letters from the center of the letter string. Specifically, it can be seen in this figure that the refixation amplitude is not calculated on the basis

First Fixation Position
Refixation Amplitude

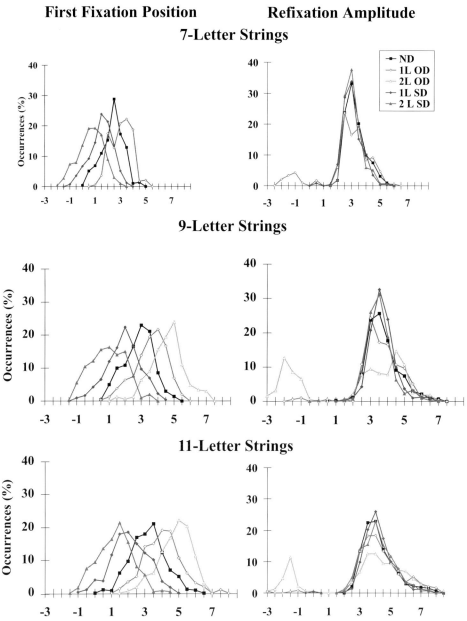

Fig. 1. Distributions of first fixation position (left) and refixation saccade amplitude (right), for displacement in opposite direction (OD) or same direction (SD) as the primary saccade. ND represents the no-displacement condition. The amplitude of the displacement was 1 or 2 letters. The data are presented for 7-, 9- and 11-letter strings. Distributions based on small sample sizes were not included. The first fixation position is plotted as a function of the percentage of fixations at each letter position. The refixation amplitude is plotted in character-spaces.

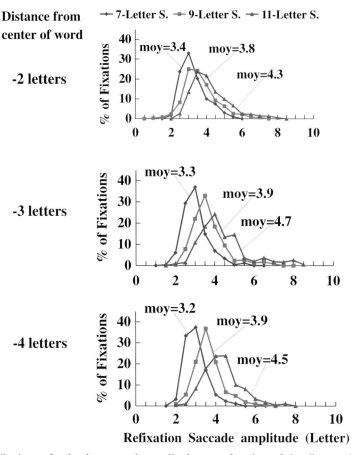

Fig. 2. Distributions of refixation saccade amplitudes as a function of the distance between first fixation position and the center of words, for 7-, 9- and 11-letter strings.

of the distance between the first fixation position and the string-ending boundary. The landing position appears to have no influence on the execution of the refixation saccade. Thus, the appropriate oculomotor response to a target displacement in a reading task is a refixation saccade with constant amplitude. This refixation saccade amplitude seems mainly computed on the basis of the string length.

These data are compatible with the hypothesis that the eyes are sent a specific distance, regardless of initial fixation location, with length having a constant influence on this distance. This predicts a perfect relation between the first and the second fixation position (i.e. slope = 1). As shown in Fig. 3, that plots second fixation positions as a function of first fixation positions for the different displacement conditions (Fig. 3a) and the no-displacement condition (Fig. 3b), the data are consistent with this prediction. It would have been possible to find the eyes

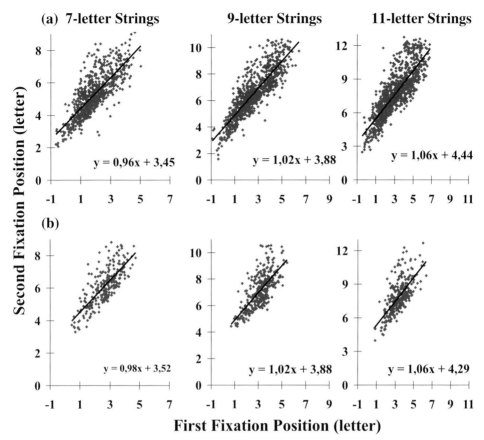

Fig. 3. Second fixation positions plotted as a function of first fixation positions for refixation saccades on 7-, 9- and 11-letter strings. Figures represent the data for the different displacement conditions (a) and the no-displacement condition (b).

always go to a precise target location in the second part of the item, indicating no relation between first and second fixation position (i.e. slope = 0). It would also have been possible to find that the eyes always go to the center of the configuration between the actual first fixation position and the item-ending boundary. In this latter case we would have obtained a slope of 0.5. Our data did not confirm these two last predictions. Rather, they show that the second fixation position strictly depends on the position of the first fixation. A perfect relationship is obtained between the launch site and the second fixation position as the slope is near to 1. This means that the eyes are simply sent a particular distance for each length, regardless of initial first fixation position.

An examination of the first fixation duration for the refixation cases revealed an effect of the displacement. The mean first fixation durations in the same direction

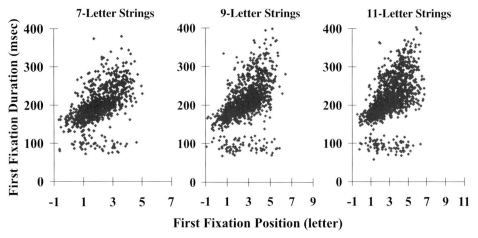

Fig. 4. First fixation durations plotted as a function of the first fixation positions for refixation saccades on 7-, 9- and 11-letter strings. The data include all the conditions.

of the primary saccade are significantly shorter (25 ms and 43 ms for 1 and 2 character-spaces displacement, respectively) and those in the opposite direction are significantly longer (13 ms and 23 ms for 1 and 2 character-spaces displacement, respectively) than in the no-displacement condition for the different lengths. The same effect has been observed by changing an isolated target position close to or after the end of the main saccade (Deubel, Wolf and Hauske, 1982). One possible functional explanation for this effect was proposed by Robinson (1973) who hypothesized that undershoots save processing time by keeping the target's neural image in the same hemisphere. Overshooting would require additional time because of hemispheric information transfer, leading to longer fixation. It can be seen from Fig. 4 that first fixation duration increases when the first fixation moves to the center of the word. This replicates data obtained by Vitu and O'Regan (1995) in a text reading situation. Conceivably, this phenomenon is in agreement with the undershooting strategy of the saccadic system.

Except for regressive saccadic responses obtained when the eye overshot the center of the item, our results show that secondary saccades do not respond to an error produced by the saccade-triggered shift of the saccade goal. On the other hand, there is no evidence in our data of either shortening or lengthening of refixation saccade amplitude, such as would be expected by a saccade guided to a selected target position between the current fixation and the letter string end. Rather, the eyes are sent a specific distance, regardless of initial fixation. It follows that refixation amplitude is not coded as a function of the position of the item on the retina. It seems to be mainly coded as a movement vector to acquire the stimulus. This movement vector depends on the stimulus length.

Experiment 2. The metrics of intra- and interword saccades

The previous experiment demonstrated that the refixation saccade is invariant with respect to a first fixation error caused by letter string displacement. This suggests that such saccades do not target a precise position within the second part of the letter string. Apparently, the metrics of these saccades seem to differ from those of initial saccades to a word, which are usually found to be guided towards the center of a to-be-fixated word. What happens with saccades directed towards a second word in a step paradigm? Do these saccades correct the error due to the displacement to target the center of the following word? This would show that the metrics of interword saccades differ from thoses of intraword saccades. Experiment 2 investigates whether the response of the saccadic system to an error induced by the displacement of a two-word sequence during the primary saccade to the first word differs for refixation saccades and for saccades directed to the next word. The displacement paradigm, as described in Experiment 1, was used with a sequence of two 7-letter words. During the primary saccade to the first word, the two-word sequence was displaced by one or two letters in the same or opposite direction of the primary saccade. Subjects were instructed to read the two words and then to saccade to a cross displayed two character-spaces right of the end of the second word. To discount any influence of the second word on the second saccade, parafoveal preview of the second word was withheld by replacing each letter of the second word with an X, up to the time the eye crossed the interword blank space. At that point, the letters of the second word were available. This experiment also examined an eventual influence of the initial fixation duration on the subsequent saccade programming. It is possible that the extent to which the initial fixation error is corrected depends on the time period that precedes the triggering of the following saccade. In order to examine this question with a large range of first fixation durations the frequency of the first word was manipulated. Two classes of high- and low-frequency nouns were selected as the first word. The second word was always an adjective. Seven subjects participated in two blocks of 300 trials each.

The refixation frequency on the first word was strongly affected by the displacement condition (Fig. 5). Replicating Experiment 1, we found that a large proportion of responses triggered after an opposite direction displacement were directed towards the second word, whereas responses triggered after a same direction displacement were refixation saccades. A slight effect of the frequency of the first word may be seen in this figure, low-frequency words being read more often with two fixations than high-frequency words.

Fig. 6 shows the distributions of first-fixation position in the first word (Fig. 6a), the amplitude of the secondary saccade (Fig. 6b), and secondary fixation position (Fig. 6c) on the word $n + 1$ (left) or in the word n (right). As no significant effect

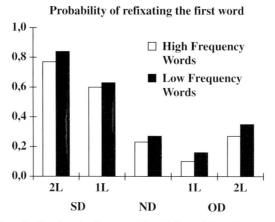

Fig. 5. Probability of refixating the first word for high- and low-frequency 7-letter words.

of the first word frequency was found on the amplitude of the secondary saccades, for either refixation saccades directed to the word n, or for saccades directed to the word $n + 1$, this figure presents the overall data combining high- and low-frequency words. It is evident from this figure that the saccadic response to a displacement of the two-word sequence differs for refixation saccades directed within the first word, and/or interword saccades directed to the second word. Replicating the data obtained in Experiment 1, the refixation saccade amplitude was invariant with respect to the first fixation position error. Except for regressive saccades observed after an opposite direction step, the progressive refixation saccades did not correct fixation errors induced by the displacement. Interestingly, saccadic performance is very different when the next word is selected as the target for the secondary saccade. Opposite direction displacements, leading to an initial fixation position further into the first word, produced shorter saccade amplitudes than in the no-displacement condition. Additionally, same direction displacements, leading to initial fixation position at the beginning of the first word, produced longer saccade amplitudes than in the no-displacement condition. This indicates that the secondary saccades directed to the second word correct the error induced by the two-word sequence displacement during the primary saccade, targeting the center of the second word. Clearly, the amplitude of these interword saccades is determined with respect to the actual position of the second word on the retina.

This different pattern of data for progressive refixations and saccades directed to the next word can be seen in Fig. 7, which plots second fixation positions as a function of first fixation positions. For refixations, the perfect relationship between first and second fixation position found in Experiment 1 with letter strings is replicated here with words (slope = 1). This strict dependence between second fixation and the prior fixation position (i.e. launch site) for refixation saccades is not observed

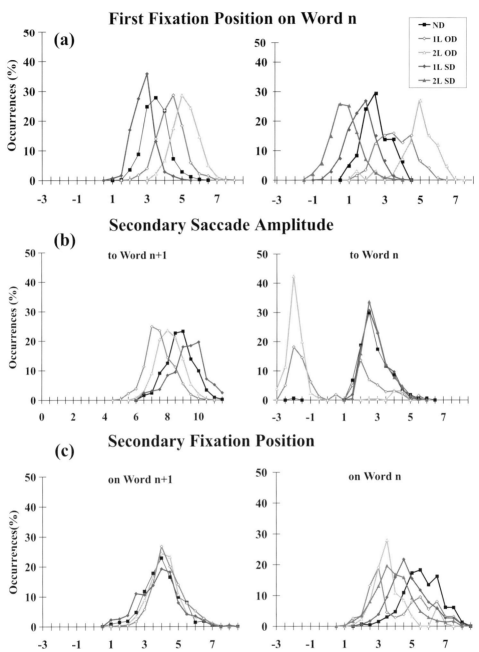

Fig. 6. Distributions of first fixation positions (top), refixation saccade amplitudes (middle), and secondary fixation positions (bottom) for second saccades directed to the word *n* + 1 (left) or to the word *n* (right) for displacement in opposite direction (OD) or same direction (SD) as the primary saccade. ND represents the no-displacement condition. The amplitude of the displacement was 1 or 2 letters. Distributions based on small sample sizes were not included. Fixation position is plotted as a function of the percentage of fixations at each letter position. Saccade amplitude is plotted in character-spaces.

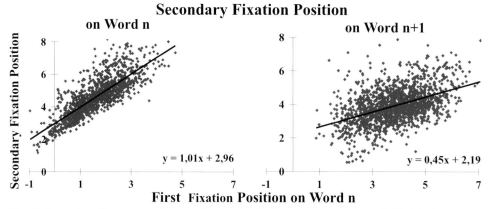

Fig. 7. Secondary fixation positions on the word n (left) or on the word $n + 1$ (right) plotted as a function of first fixation positions. Secondary fixation positions on the word $n + 1$ correspond to landing positions on the word $n + 1$.

with interword saccades. Indeed, for saccades directed to the next word, the actual data yielded a slope of 0.4. It is interesting that the relationship found for interword saccades is very similar to that obtained by McConkie, Kerr, Reddix and Zola (1988) in a text reading situation. McConkie et al. (1988) found a slope of 0.49 between prior fixation (i.e. launch site) in the preceding word and landing position on a word, showing that there is not a perfect relationship between these two variables.

An examination of first fixation durations of both single-fixation and two-fixation cases showed shorter fixation durations for saccades that undershot than for those which overshot the intended landing position in the word, replicating the data of Experiment 1 (Table 1). In other respects, mean fixation durations were found to be longer when the word was read with one than with two fixations. Specifically, when single fixations were made on the first word, there was a significant frequency effect on the duration of the single fixation. In the cases where two fixations occurred, word frequency did not significantly affect the first fixation duration but did influence the second fixation duration (see also O'Regan and Lévy-Schoen, 1987). This suggests that recognition of the word occurred during initial fixation on the first word only for the cases where the word was read with one single fixation. Interestingly, our data suggest that the ability of the saccadic system to correct the error induced by the displacement appears to be related to the selection of a new target for recognition. That is, the selection of a new target word for recognition determines a recalculation of the second movement and delivers the spatial coordinates of the intended target word. Additionally, this recalculation was found to be slightly more accurate for saccades following low-frequency than high-frequency first words. This effect reflects a general tendency of saccades directed to the next word to be more accurate following longer fixation durations (Fig. 8). This indi-

Table 1

Mean fixation duration (ms) for high frequency (HF) and low frequency (LF) for refixations and single fixations

Refixations		ND	1L SD	2L SD	1L OD	2L OD
First fixation	HF	231	206	187	201	–
	LF	229	211	187	223	–
Frequency effect		−2	5	0	22	
Second fixation	HF	139	171	198	136	–
	LF	153	185	213	156	–
Frequency effect		14 [a]	14 [a]	15 [d]	20 [a]	
Single fixations	HF	272	254	–	279	286
	LF	282	262	–	300	302
Frequency effect		10 [a]	8		21 [c]	16 [b]

Means based on small sample sizes were not included.
[a] $p < 0.05$, [b] $p < 0.025$, [c] $p < 0.025$, [d] $p < 0.005$.

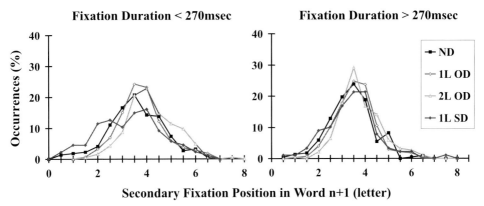

Fig. 8. Distributions of secondary fixation positions on the word $n + 1$ following short (<270 ms) and long (>270 ms) first fixation duration on word n, for no displacement (ND), one letter same direction displacement (1L SD) and one or two letters opposite direction displacement (1L OD or 2L OD) conditions. Secondary fixation positions on the word $n + 1$ correspond to landing positions on the word $n + 1$.

cates that the consistency of landing sites on the second word, as indicated by the standard deviations of landing site distributions, increases with fixation duration.

We can conclude from this experiment that the metrics of intra- and interword saccades differ. Interword saccades are calculated on the basis of the distance that separates the current fixation position in the first word and the center of the second word. These results, whilst illustrating no new principles, nevertheless add to the body of data on the metrics of interword saccades obtained in a text reading situation. For this reason, the method of adding an exogenous error seems to be an appropriate method for analyzing the saccadic control during reading. The ability of the saccadic system to correct a fixation error produced by the displacement only for interword saccades is an indication of a functional target location within the next word. Once a word-object has been selected as the target for a saccade, the location of the fixation on that word is determined on the basis of the actual retinal position of the target word. This would indeed be predicted by the view that the size and direction of goal-directed saccades are determined by the retinotopic coordinates of the current selected target. A surprising result from Experiments 1 and 2 is that intraword saccades are controlled by a different mechanism. These saccades do not target a precise target position, as found for interword saccades. Clearly, these saccades are not coded in retinotopic coordinates, as they are not calculated on the basis of the word image on the retina during the first fixation on the word. Rather, the eyes are sent a specific distance calculated on the basis of the item length. This would be predicted if these saccades are specified in a motor frame of reference, provided before the first fixation on the word, and memorized for a short period of time. The following experiments test this hypothesis.

Experiment 3. Planning of the refixation saccade begins before the initial fixation on a word

The previous experiments show that a refixation saccade is mainly coded as a movement whose amplitude primarily depends on the item length. The fact that a refixation saccade is invariant with respect to the actual landing position may be an indication that this saccade is the second movement of a two-saccade sequence planned before execution of the primary saccade to a target letter string. According to this hypothesis, this second movement would be preprogrammed at the same time as the primary saccade, based on the length of the to-be-fixated letter string. However, it may be predicted that this initial planning could be modified on the basis of the visual information integrated during the initial fixation on the word. Experiment 3 tried to test this hypothesis by having subjects read a letter string whose initial and final length required a modification of the refixation saccade amplitude. At the time of the primary saccade to the target letter string, the string was made to change its length. Two length changes were designed: 11 to 9 letters and 9 to 11 letters. Two control conditions were employed, with no length change. In order to test precisely the length influence without any lexical influence, 240 nonsense 9- and 11-letter strings were constructed that shared the same 9 initial letters. The target letter string was displaced during the primary saccade by half

Table 2

Mean refixation saccade amplitude for control and length change conditions reported in character-space

		Final length: 9 letters		11 letters	
	Initial length:	9 letters	11 letters	11 letters	9 letters
Refixation amplitude saccade	9-letter landing position	9/9	11/9 + 0.5	11/11 + 0.5	9/11
		3.15	3.44	3.92	3.59
	11-letter landing position	9/9 − 0.5	11/9	11/11	9/11 − 0.5
		2.98	3.21	3.70	3.61
	Mean	3.06	3.32 [a,c]	3.81	3.60 [b]

In the first row of the table, the 11-letter sequences and the 11- to 9-letter sequences are displaced by 0.5 character-space in the same direction to the primary saccade so that the initial first fixation corresponds to that obtained for a 9-letter sequence. In the second row of the table, the 9-letter sequences and the 9- to 11-letter sequences are displaced by 0.5 character-space in the opposite direction to the primary saccade so that the initial first fixation corresponds to that obtained for a 11-letter sequence.
Comparison with the control 9-letter conditions: [a] $p < 0.06$; [b] $p < 0.005$.
Comparison with the control 11-letter conditions: [c] $p < 0.005$.

a character-space in the same or opposite direction of the primary saccade to compare the refixation saccade amplitude with landing positions approximately similar for the length change and no length change control conditions. Five subjects participated in the experiment.

A global data analysis revealed a significant effect of the string length given before the primary saccade on the amplitude of the refixation saccade (Table 2). The mean amplitude of the refixation saccade in the 11- to 9-letter change was significantly different to that obtained for the 9-letter control sequences, and also to that obtained for the 11-letter control sequences. Thus, the mean refixation amplitude saccade was found to be intermediate (3.32) to that obtained in the control 9-letter (3.06) and 11-letter control conditions (3.81). This result suggests that the refixation saccade is determined by both the length information sampled before the completion of the primary saccade, and the new length information sampled after the completion of the primary saccade. However, the extent to which this refixation saccade is corrected depends on the required modification. In the 9- to 11-letter sequences the mean amplitude of the refixation saccade (3.60) was similar to that obtained in the control 11-letter condition, and was significantly different to that obtained in the control 9-letter condition. This shows that the refixation saccade had been corrected during the first fixation, on the basis of the length information

Opposite page: Fig. 9. Figures represent the data for 9- to 11-letter sequences and no length change conditions. (a) Histogram showing distributions of first fixation durations. (b–d) Distributions of refixation saccade amplitudes for first fixation durations less and more than 200 ms with no displacement of the letter string (b) when the control 11-letter sequences are displaced by 0.5 character-spaces in the same direction of the primary saccade so that the initial first fixation corresponds to that obtained for a 9-letter sequence (c) when the 9-letter sequences and the 9 to 11 letter sequences are displaced by 0.5 character-spaces in opposite direction to the primary saccade so that initial first fixations correspond to that obtained for a 11-letter sequence (d). Open symbols represent the control conditions, and filled squares the length change condition.

---

extracted at that time. The change introduced by the lengthening of the letter string (9 to 11 sequences) was fully compensated for by the correction, whereas the change introduced by shortening the letter string length (11 to 9 sequences) was not totally corrected.

How can we explain this different pattern of results between the two types of length change? Consider the consequence of the two types of length change for the oculomotor system. In the 11 to 9 sequences, the initial refixation saccade, planned on the basis of an 11-letter item, overshoots the saccade calculated on the basis of the final 9-letter item. Consequently, the length change requires a direction change of the initial preprogram. In the 9 to 11 sequences, the initial refixation saccade planned on the basis of a 9-letter item undershoots the saccade calculated for the final 11-letter item. For the 9 to 11 sequences, the correction of the planned movement only requires a lengthening of the movement. The undershooting strategy of the oculomotor system would lead to an increased frequency of correction saccades for our 9 to 11 sequences. Many studies have found that corrective saccades requiring only an increase of the metric were triggered faster than corrective saccades requiring a decrease or a direction change (Deubel et al., 1982; Henson, 1978; Hou and Fender, 1979). This outcome would predict that undershooting demands less processing time and thus leads to a higher frequency of correction saccades. Although no effect of the type of length change was found in our experiment on first fixation duration, the reprocessing time would be sufficient for increasing, but not for decreasing the amplitude of the impending saccade. In order to determine whether there is a relationship between the first fixation duration and the saccadic response, we partitioned the 9 to 11 sequence data on the basis of first fixation duration. Fig. 9a presents the histogram of first fixation durations for 9- to 11-letter sequences and no length change conditions.

Whereas most fixation durations were about 200 ms, duration was relatively variable and correlated with different saccadic responses. Amplitudes of refixation saccades for first fixation durations shorter than 200 ms were about 3 character-spaces and very similar to those obtained in 9-letter strings (Fig. 9b–d). These

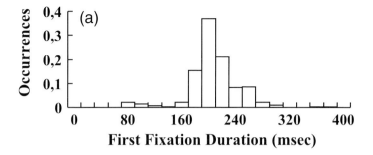

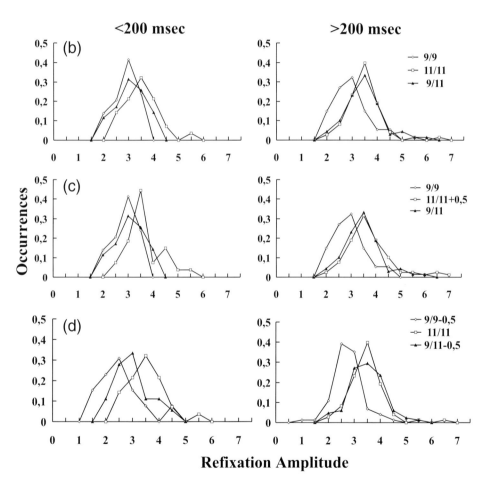

Refixation Amplitude

refixation saccades occurred too early to take final length into account. For this range of first fixation durations, the amplitude of the refixation saccade was computed on the visual information given before the primary saccade. For longer fixation durations, amplitudes were about 3.5 character-spaces and similar to those obtained in 11-letter strings. These saccades corrected an initially programmed movement on the basis of the final length information extracted during the first fixation. For long fixation durations, the processing time was sufficient for the saccadic system to lengthen the initial preprogrammed saccade.

These results support the hypothesis of a preprogramming of the refixation saccade amplitude, computed on the basis of the target item length available before execution of the primary saccade. While the primary saccade to a letter string target is programmed, the second refixation saccade is planned. These two successive saccades are computed on the basis of the visual information extracted from the to-be-fixated item. However, it also appears that the saccadic system can modify the initial motor program on the basis of the new length information extracted during the first fixation. When the modification requires a shortening of the initially programmed saccade, intermediate values of the refixation saccade were found. When it requires a lengthening of the initial program, the amplitude of the refixation saccade is found to depend on first fixation duration. For short fixation durations, initial length responses occur. For values of fixation duration greater than 200 ms, final length responses occur. Experiment 3 shows that the intrinsic variability in first fixation duration may influence saccadic responses.

Experiment 4. The processing time to adjust the refixation saccade amplitude

To measure precisely the time available for the second length to modify the refixation saccade planned to the initial length, the time of the length change may be varied by the experimenter. Experiment 4 changed the target length at various times during or after (50, 140 and 220 ms) the primary saccade to the target. This allows us to plot refixation saccade amplitude against a time variable (D) that measures the time from the length change to the refixation saccade initiation process. We used the same length changes as in the preceding experiment. Moreover, in order to reduce as far as possible the difference in the visual feedback between the two length change conditions, the target letter string was extinguished 30 ms before the length change and lit again with the length change. An abrupt length change in the 9- to 11-letter sequences involved an apparent motion at the end of the target letter string, that appeared to disappear with a blanking period lasting 30 ms. Six subjects participated in three blocks of 350 trials each.

As in the previous experiment, no effect of the length change was found on the mean first fixation duration. The mean amplitudes were about 3 character-spaces for 9-letter strings and 3.6 character-spaces for the 11-letter strings. Amplitude of the refixation saccades as a function of the interval between the length change and the refixation saccade onset is plotted in Fig. 10 (top: 11- to 9-letter sequences; bottom: 9- to 11-letter sequences).

For saccadic responses triggered less than 120 ms after the length change, the mean amplitudes were about 3 and 3.5 character-spaces for the 9- to 11-letter and the 11- to 9-letter sequences, respectively. This indicates that these saccadic responses were calculated on the basis of the initial length of the sequences. For larger intervals, of about 200 ms between the length change and the refixation saccadic responses, the amplitudes of the saccades were about 3.7 and 3.1 character-spaces for 9- to 11-letter and 11- to 9-letter sequences, respectively. These responses took full account of the final length. Intermediate refixation amplitudes were observed in the 9- to 11-letter sequences as well as in the 11- to 9-letter sequences for responses occurring within 150–200 ms after the length change.

It will be noted in Fig. 10 that we did not observe responses within 120–160 ms after the length change. Examining the histograms of fixation duration for the different times of the length change, we observed no responses within 120–160 ms when the length target was changed 140 ms after the primary saccade (Fig. 11). In this case, the saccadic reaction times split into two different populations located at different values of the fixation duration (Fig. 11a): (1) refixation saccades triggered about 80 ms after the length change; these refixation saccades occurred too early to take the final length into account and their amplitude corresponds to the initial length, in the 9- to 11-letter sequences as well as in the 11- to 9-letter sequences (Fig. 11b); (2) refixation saccades triggered more than 150 ms after the length change; the preparation of the refixation saccade in this case always follows the reappearance of the target. Interestingly, the amplitude of these refixation saccades only takes account of the final length in the 9 to 11 sequences (Fig. 11b). This indicates that saccadic responses triggered 150 ms after the length change only consider new visual information when the change requires a lengthening of the saccade amplitude. This replicates the different pattern of data obtained for the 9 to 11 and 11 to 9 sequences in Experiment 3, where the length change made during the primary saccade was not perceived by the subjects. This argues for a motor rather than a perceptual account to this difference. The saccadic system prefers to lengthen rather than to shorten an initially programmed saccade.

It is also of interest to examine whether the recalculation of the refixation saccade was mainly influenced by the item length, regardless of initial fixation position, as found in Experiment 1. It may be that a recalculation of the refixation saccade involves a saccade directed to a target location intermediate between the actual first fixation position and the item-ending boundary. To examine this, the relation between the first and second fixation position was plotted for refixation responses triggered before (Fig. 12 left) and after the transition region (Fig. 12 right). It can be seen that the slopes for saccadic responses computed before and after the transition region are identical. As in Experiment 1, a perfect linear relation is found between

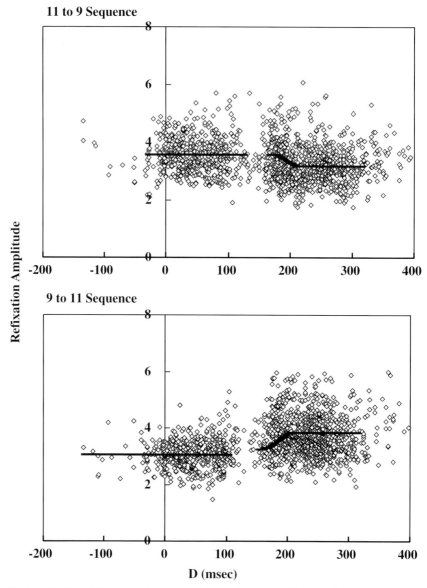

Fig. 10. Amplitude of the refixation saccade as a function of the delay between the length change and the triggering of the refixation saccade in the 11- to 9- and the 9- to 11-letter sequences. Negative values correspond to refixation saccades triggered before the length change, while positive values correspond to refixation saccades triggered after the length change.

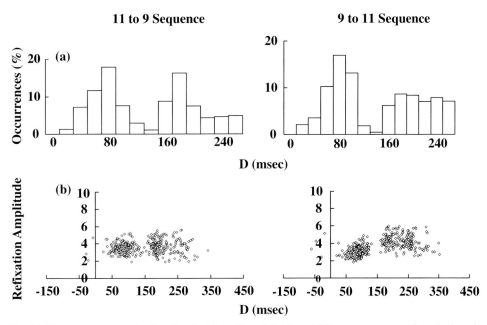

Fig. 11. Figures represent the data for the 11- to 9- and the 9- to 11-letter sequences when the length change occurs 140 ms after the primary saccade. (a) Histogram of refixation saccade latencies after the length change. (b) Amplitude of the refixation saccades as a function of the delay between the length change and the triggering of the refixation saccade. Negative values correspond to refixation saccades triggered before the length change while positive values correspond to refixation saccades triggered after the length change.

first and second fixation positions. The eyes are simply sent a particular distance for each length. The saccade amplitude is computed on the basis of length information, with first fixation position having no influence. Even when the refixation saccade is recomputed on the basis of final length, this saccade does not target a precise location between the actual first fixation and the item-ending boundary. Rather, the saccade amplitude computed on initial length is adjusted to the final length.

This final experiment describes the time course of the refixation saccade programming. It shows that for small time intervals from the length change to the refixation saccade initiation, initial length saccadic responses occur. A certain minimum time must elapse before any effect of the final length is manifest. The minimal reprocessing interval of the ongoing saccade amplitude is estimated within 150–200 ms. This interval includes the time needed to integrate the new length information and to adjust the initial program.

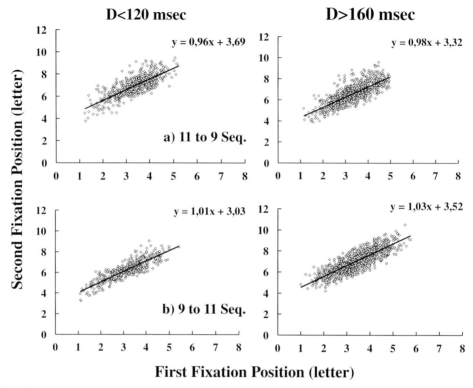

Fig. 12. Second fixation positions plotted as a function of first fixation positions for refixation saccades triggered less than 120 ms and more than 160 ms after the length change for the 11- to 9-letter sequences (a) and the 9- to 11-letter sequences (b).

Conclusion

The present experiments demonstrate the existence of different mechanisms for the metrical control of intra- and interword saccades. The intraword saccade was shown to remain invariant across changes in the retinal location of the item. The perfect relationship between the first and second fixation position, with first fixation position having no influence, is surprising (Experiment 1). This shows that, in preparation for a refixation saccade, the signal for the saccadic system is a command to move the eyes for a certain distance in the orbit. This is an indication that the refixation saccade is not coded in retinotopic but in motor space coordinates. These saccades are not directed to a precise position within the item. Interestingly, a different pattern was observed for saccades directed to the next word. When readers select the next word as the target for the subsequent saccade, the item shift during the first saccade causes a recalculation based on a new representation of the second movement and the amplitude of the saccade is modulated to target the center of the target word. Here, the size of this goal-directed saccade is mainly determined by the retinocentric coordinates of the current selected target (Experiment 2).

The hypothesis that is most consistent with the data obtained for refixation saccades is that these saccades are preprogrammed before the primary saccade, on the basis of length information acquired at that time. The fact that the properties of this refixation saccade remain invariant across changes in the value of the parameters suggests that these saccades have been preplanned before the initial fixation on the word. At the time a first saccade is planned, the second intended movement is also coded as a movement to acquire the complete information within the word. This initially preprogrammed refixation saccade is coded on the basis of the length of the to-be-fixated stimulus (Experiment 3). However, an adjustment of the initially preprogrammed refixation amplitude may take place during initial fixation depending on the new visual information extracted at that time. This modification of the initial program can be seen only for saccades triggered more than 150 ms after the length change (Experiment 4). Thus the motor movement to refixate the item is modulated as a function of the new length information. Interestingly, we found again that the adjustment of the initial preprogrammed refixation saccade is made, irrespective of the retinal position of the item during the first fixation. This shows that there is no coordinate transformation as the saccadic system does not update the saccade with the new eye position.

However, the initial representation of the intended movements planned by the reader may be subject to complete transformation. Our data show that a recalculation for a new representation of the second movement occurred when the item displacement during the primary saccade overshot the intended landing position, causing an initial fixation location at the center of the word. At this location, the first word can be recognized, and the following saccade is directed to the next word selected by the reader. These results clearly argue for the hypothesis that the selection of a new target word for the recognition system delivers the spatial coordinates of the intended word. Thus, when a refixation saccade has been preplanned within the first word, the selection of the next word cancels the program to refixate the current word. In this case, there is a transformation of motor space to retinotopic coordinates. However, the second saccade may have been preplanned to the second word. Then, the second movement is recalculated on the basis of the actual position in order to target the second word. Finally, the data of Experiments 1 and 2 indicate that the frequency of refixating a letter string is mainly a function of the location of the first fixation location on the word, with fewest refixations following a fixation at the center of the word. Our data show that undershoot and overshoot errors substantially affect the probability of refixating. Thus, with the method of inducing an artificial motor error in the initial first fixation, we replicated a phenomenon that occurs in normal reading (McConkie et al., 1989). As found by McConkie et al., a single letter difference in fixation location makes a sizable difference in the likelihood of refixating a word. At the same time, the frequency of making a refixation relates to, but does not directly indicate, the frequency of word identification failure. Indeed, Experiment 2 showed a significant but slight effect of word frequency on refixation frequency. A recent model of reading, the E-Z reader model (Reichle et al., 1998), has emphasized the rôle of familiarity of a word as the signal that lexical access is imminent and that a saccade should be planned to the subsequent word. Experiment 2 shows a trend in this direction, but it is small. The primary determinant of the probability of refixating is the location of the initial fixation.

An interesting aspect of the paradigm developed here is that it may serve as an empirical means for categorizing different types of saccade in reading. Obviously, the launch site distance and the length of the item are the primary determinant of where refixations go. However, interword saccades directed to a selected word-object are not found to be greatly determined by launch site distance. Only interword saccades with short fixation durations appeared to be affected by launch site distance. Nevertheless, in a text reading situation, launch site distance was shown to have a greater influence on landing position (McConkie et al., 1988; Rayner et al., 1996). It seems likely that this is due to the fact that perceptual variability is greater in a text reading situation. When engaged in a two-word sequence reading task, subjects may easily gain precise visual information about the target word location.

The present data hint at a dissociation between primary saccades to a word that are guided by the current visual information and refixation saccades that are planned and held in short-term memory. The notion of a pre-established organized plan has been previously proposed in target scanning (Zingale and Kowler, 1987), and in other situations requiring the execution of a motor plan, such as typing or handwriting (Viviani and Terzuolo, 1980, 1982). The important result of the Zingale and Kowler study which is relevant to the issue discussed here, is their demonstration that saccade sizes during the scanning of targets depended idiosyncratically on the length of the sequence and on the ordinal position of the movement within that sequence. Each subject produced a stable motor pattern which was preplanned before the first movement. It can be argued that sequences of saccades also constitute units of motor action. Motor action unit sequences could be memorized before execution and the role of visual information viewed as advisory, permitting correction in the plans during execution. (See Viviani, 1990, for a complete discussion on this point). Consistent with the proposal that preplanned refixation saccades are coded in motor space is the physiological finding that memory-linked activity has been found to be a motor or motor-planning signal (Andersen and Gnadt, 1989). When monkeys are required to perform a memorized double-movement task, a class of neurons has been found in the posterior parietal cortex that does not code the signal in sensory-related retinotopic coordinates. These cells have been labeled intended movement neurons as their responses represent the intent to make eye movements of a specific direction and amplitude.

The present study supports the notion that motor planning should be considered in reading, where most saccades are 'intentional' in the sense that they are internally triggered by the subject's goals and intentions. Thus, it makes sense that sequential dependencies between successive fixation positions and saccade sizes should be present in reading. Readers may plan and store in memory a sequence of saccadic movements. During the execution of the eye movement sequences, the necessity of correcting the initial plan may result from failure to identify the word. Otherwise, feedback information about the actual eye position provides the possibility of correcting errors. Further research is needed to investigate the actual basis for such a planning.

References

Andersen, A. and Gnadt, J.W. (1989). Posterior parietal cortex. In: R.H. Wurtz and M.E. Goldberg (Eds.), The Neurobiology of Saccadic Eye Movements. Amsterdam: Elsevier, pp. 315–335.

Beauvillain, C. and Beauvillain, P. (1995). Calibration of an eye movement system for use in reading. Behavior Research Methods, Instruments and Computers, 27 (3), 331–337.

Beauvillain, C. and Doré, K. (1998). Orthographic codes are used in integrating information from the parafovea by the saccadic computation system. Vision Research, 38 (1), 115–123.

Beauvillain, C., Doré, K. and Baudouin, V. (1996). The 'centre of gravity' of words: evidence for an effect of the word-initial letters. Vision Research, 36, 589–603.

Becker, W. and Jürgens, R. (1979). An analysis of the saccadic system by means of double step stimuli. Vision Research, 19, 967–983.

Deubel, H., Wolf, W. and Hauske, G. (1982). Corrective saccades: effect of shifting the saccade goal. Vision Research, 22, 353–364.

Doré, K. and Beauvillain, C. (1997). Latency dependence of word-initial letter integration by the saccadic system. Perception and Psychophysics, 59, 523–533.

Henson, D.B. (1978). Corrective saccades: effects of altering visual feedback. Vision Research, 18, 63–67.

Hou, R.L. and Fender, D.H. (1979). Processing of direction and magnitude by the saccadic eye movement system. Vision Research, 19, 1421–1426.

Hyönä, J. (1995). Do irregular letter combinations attract readers' attention? Evidence from fixation locations in words. Journal of Experimental Psychology: Human Perception and Performance, 21, 68–81.

McConkie, G.W., Kerr, P.W., Reddix, M.D. and Zola, D. (1988). Eye movement control during reading, I. The location of initial eye fixations on words. Vision Research, 28, 1107–1118.

McConkie, G.W., Kerr, P.W., Reddix, M.D., Zola, D. and Jacobs, A.M. (1989). Eye frequency control during reading, II. Frequency of refixation a word. Perception and Psychophysics, 46, 245–253.

O'Regan, J.K. (1979). Saccades size control in reading: evidence for the linguistic control hypothesis. Perception and Psychophysics, 25, 501–509.

O'Regan, J.K. (1990). Eye movements and reading. In: E. Kowler (Ed.), Eye Movements and Their Role in Visual and Cognitive Processes. Amsterdam: Elsevier, pp. 395–453.

O'Regan, J.K. and Lévy-Schoen, A. (1987). Eye movements strategy and tactics in word recognition and reading. In: M. Coltheart (Ed.), Attention and Performance XII: The Psychology of Reading. Hillsdale, NJ: Erlbaum, pp. 363–383.

O'Regan, J.K., Lévy-Schoen, A., Pynte, J. and Brugaillère, B. (1984). Convenient fixation location within isolated words of different length and structure. Journal of Experimental Psychology: Human Perception and Performance, 10, 250–257.

Rayner, K. (1979). Eye guidance in reading: fixations location within words. Perception, 8, 21–30.

Rayner, K., Sereno, S. and Raney, G.E. (1996). Eye movement control in reading: a comparison of two types of models. Journal of Experimental Psychology: Human Perception and Performance, 22, 1188–1200.

Reichle, E.D., Pollatsek, A., Fisher, D.L. and Rayner, K. (1998). Toward a model of eye movement control in reading. Psychological Review, 105, 125–157.

Robinson, D.A. (1973). Models of the saccadic eye movement control system. Kybernetika, 14, 71–83.

Vitu, F. and O'Regan, J.K. (1995). A challenge to current theories of eye movements in reading. In: J.M. Findlay, R. Walker and R.W. Kentridge (Eds.), Eye Movements Research: Mechanisms, Processes, and Applications. Amsterdam: North-Holland, pp. 381–393.

Viviani, P. (1990). Eye movements in visual search: cognitive, perceptual and motor control aspects. In: E. Kowler (Ed.), Eye Movements and Their Rôle in Visual and Cognitive Processes. Amsterdam: Elsevier, pp. 353–391.

Viviani, P. and Terzuolo, C. (1980). Space–time invariance in learned motor skills. In: G.E. Stelmach and J. Requin (Eds.), Tutorials in Motor Behavior. Amsterdam: North-Holland, pp. 525–533.

Viviani, P. and Terzuolo, C. (1982). On the relation between word-specific patterns and the central control model of typing: a reply to Gentner. Journal of Experimental Psychology: Human Perception and Performance, 8, 811–813.

Zingale, C.M. and Kowler, E. (1987). Planning sequences of saccades. Vision Research, 27, 1327–1341.

COMMENTARY ON SECTION 2

Attention, Information Processing, and Eye Movement Control

Heiner Deubel
Ludwig-Maximilians-University

J. Kevin O'Regan
Université René Descartes

and

Ralph Radach [1]
Technical University of Aachen

Ever since Morrison (1984) put forward an attention-based model, the basic idea that the movement of the eyes in reading is predominantly determined by moment-to-moment shifts in visual attention has been extremely influential. The Morrison model, and the models derived from it, postulate an intimate relation between the time course of lexical processing and the allocation of visual attention in reading. The assumed sequence of processing steps starts with attention allocated to the currently fixated word and linguistic analysis commencing. After a certain amount of lexical processing has occurred, disengagement and shift of attention to the next word in the direction of reading is allowed. The deployment of attention on the (parafoveal) word determines the signals for amplitude and timing of the next saccadic eye movement and, at the same time, allows for some preprocessing of this word. Then, after the saccadic programming time, the saccade occurs. In some cases, however, the processing of the parafoveal word may allow its complete identification *before* the saccade is actually initiated, which may result in the cancellation of the saccade program. Under this condition, it is assumed that attention shifts to the word beyond the next word

---

1 Since Ralph Radach provided extremely valuable support and comments during the course of writing, the first two authors decided to adopt him as a co-author of this paper.

Reading as a Perceptual Process/A. Kennedy, R. Radach, D. Heller and J. Pynte (Editors)
© 2000 Elsevier Science Ltd. All rights reserved

in the text, entailing the programming of a saccade that skips the first parafoveal word.

This 'attention-shift' theory has been through a number of revisions (brief summaries are provided in the chapters here by Inhoff, Radach, Starr and Greenberg, and Kennedy), but the latest version, the *E-Z Reader model*, is to be found in Reichle, Pollatsek, Fisher and Rayner (1998)[2]. This is a fairly comprehensive model of eye movement control in reading, able to predict saccadic behaviour quite accurately. Accordingly, the majority of the chapters of the present section on "Attention, Information Processing, and Eye Movement Control" relate their findings rather directly to this class of 'Sequential Attention Shift' models (hereafter, SAS model), with the aim of testing and discussing some of its basic assumptions. From the work presented in these chapters it turns out that some of the basic tenets of the model have to be questioned on the basis of new empirical findings. Among the most controversial aspects are the assumptions that saccades can be programmed independently of shifts of attention, and that lexical information in reading is processed strictly one word at a time. Also under question is the mechanism that is proposed for word skipping, and finally the general, fundamental claim that language processing (more specifically, lexical access) is the main factor driving eye movements. In this commentary, we will therefore discuss some of the basic properties of the SAS Model, together with some of the empirical findings of the various chapters, in the light of what can be derived from basic research (not necessarily in the domain of reading) on eye movement and attention control.

What is the nature of the coupling between attention and eye movement control?

Probably the most controversial aspect of the Reichle et al. (1998) version of the SAS model is the assumption that shifts of covert attention are decoupled from eye movement programming, in the sense that the programming of the saccade to the next word may be initiated while attention is still on the currently fixated word. This is made possible by the hypothesis that the two processes are driven by different cognitive events: While eye movements are programmed as soon as an initial lexical familiarity check of the currently fixated word is completed, the attention shift to the next word follows only after lexical access is achieved. According to Reichle et al., this assumption is necessary in order to explain findings that preview benefits decrease as the difficulty of foveal processing increases

---

2 Editors' note: An updated version, which also accounts for initial landing positions in words and refixations during reading, is presented by Rayner, Pollatsek and Reichle in the present volume.

(foveal-on-parafoveal modulations; e.g., Henderson and Ferreira, 1990), and also to explain 'spillover effects' in which the frequency of a word influences fixation durations on the following word (e.g., Rayner and Duffy, 1986).

The assumption that saccades can be programmed without an obligatory, preceding shift of attention is certainly in conflict with most of the more recent investigations on the relation of attention and saccade control. The question of how saccades and attention shifts are related has been tackled in quite a number of studies since the late seventies (Posner, 1980; Klein, 1980; Remington, 1980; Rizzolatti, 1983; Shepherd, Findlay and Hockey, 1986; Crawford and Müller, 1992; Reuter-Lorenz and Fendrich, 1992; Kowler, Anderson, Dosher and Blaser, 1995; Hoffman and Subramaniam, 1995; Deubel and Schneider, 1996; Stelmach, Campsall and Herdman, 1997). Of specific relevance for the task of reading are studies that used perceptual discrimination as the measure for attentional allocation. For example, Hoffman and Subramaniam (1995) and Kowler et al. (1995) used a dual task paradigm where participants had to saccade to a specified location and to identify a target letter. Perceptual performance was best when saccade target and target letter location were identical, compared to conditions with differing locations. The stimulus material in the experiments of Deubel and Schneider (1996) probably comes closest to a reading situation, in that they presented participants with a horizontal string of letters separated by blanks. In their dual-task paradigm a central cue indicated a specific item of the string as the target for the saccade. Before the onset of the eye movement, a discrimination target was briefly presented within the string of items. The results showed an extremely high degree of spatial selectivity: Discrimination performance was close to perfect if the saccade was directed to the critical item, but close to chance level when the saccade target was only one item to the left or right of the critical discrimination stimulus. Importantly, the data also showed that this object-specific coupling of saccade programming and object discrimination was indeed obligatory under conditions that would have been optimal for a decoupling. The only study arguing that saccades could be programmed independently of attention shifts is by Stelmach et al. (1997), who used a temporal order judgement as the indicator for attention allocation. However, their findings are somewhat difficult to interpret because of the kind of task used and the low number of participants (two, including one of the authors).

So, in general, the majority of recent studies argue for a tight, mandatory coupling of attention and eye movement control. This has led to the currently dominant view that the presaccadic shift of attention is equivalent to the *selection* of the peripheral item as the target of the saccade (e.g., Schneider, 1995), thus constituting the first step in the programming of a saccade. It seems that, from the viewpoint of basic research, one of the fundamental assumptions of the SAS model would have to be dismissed, namely, the proposal that attention can be deployed on the next word *before* the onset of the saccade, though only *after* the saccade programming is initiated. Clearly, experiments are urgently required better to determine the exact time course of attention shifts and saccade execution in different experimental situations. In defence of the SAS models, it may turn out that the results from basic research are not totally applicable to the reading situation. Indeed, a major difference between the laboratory tasks described above and the more 'natural' reading task is that, in the former, shifts of attention occur voluntarily according to instructions or visual cues, while in reading shifts of attention are endogenously controlled, unconscious and, to some degree, automatic (Reichle et al., 1998). A recent study by one of us (Deubel, Mokler, Fischer and Schneider, 1999) provides some evidence that truly automatic, involuntary saccades may be programmed without the involvement of attention. In these experiments, participants were instructed to perform an antisaccade task: upon the onset of a visual stimulus, they had to program a saccade *in the opposite direction* to the visual stimulus. The programming of antisaccades involves the suppression of a prepotent response, which is the reflexive saccade to the stimulus, and the reprogramming of a saccade to another, intended, location. Allocation of attention was measured in a secondary letter discrimination task. Moreover, participants were asked to indicate whether they felt that they had produced the required response or had made an erroneous (pro-)saccade to the stimulus. It turned out that in this situation, they indeed produced about 20% involuntary, erroneous prosaccades directed to the visual stimulus. The discrimination data showed that for the correct, *voluntary* antisaccades discrimination performance was best at the position of the saccade goal, confirming the earlier findings. For those trials in which an erroneous, *involuntary* prosaccade was made, however, discrimination performance was either very low at the saccade target position, indicating that attention may have remained at the fixation position, or it was better on the side where the subject was instructed to look than on the side where the subject actually looked. This was particularly pronounced in the cases where the participants did not perceive that they had made an error. Taken together, these findings suggest that the programming of *involuntary, reflexive* saccades may not require visual attention. Applied to reading, it is frequently proposed that the control of eye movements is based on an automatic, low level process that could, in the light of these new findings, very well work without the involvement of attention. Curiously, although this idea may be necessary to square the attention-shift models with basic data on attention and saccades, it is actually contrary to the fundamental rationale of the SAS model. This is because it suggests that a component of eye movements in reading would have to be preprogrammed independently of ongoing lexical processing (as in the strategy–tactics model of O'Regan and Lévy-Schoen, 1987, and O'Regan, 1992). Obviously, further experimental work on differences in attentional control in tasks involving voluntary vs. involuntary eye movements is urgently required.

Is attention in reading allocated to strictly one word at a time?

A basic tenet of the SAS model is that attention is limited to the currently fixated word, and processing occurs in a strictly word-by-word fashion, i.e., is not distributed over several words. This is in line with common spotlight models of visual attention (e.g., Treisman, 1969; Posner, 1980). From this perspective, when lexical access is completed, attention shifts and is allocated exclusively to the next word to be fixated. This is compatible with findings from most of the laboratory studies on the spatial relation of attentional deployment and saccade target selection discussed above which seem to show that, before saccadic eye movements, the capability for perceptual processing is virtually limited to the object that constitutes the saccade target (e.g., Deubel and Schneider, 1996). However, several papers in this section seriously challenge this view and present convincing evidence for processing of more than one item at a time in reading.

Kennedy (Chapter 8) describes two experiments showing that the fixation duration on a word is influenced by the length and the type-frequency of the initial letters of the next word. This demonstrates that some analysis of the word in the right peripheral visual field is being done while the eye is still processing the current word — in contradiction to the basic claim of attention-shift models, according to which processing on the next word only starts once attention has moved off the current word. Inhoff, Radach, Starr and Greenberg's contribution also stresses that a critical test of the attention-shift type models is the question of whether processing at the current fixation can be influenced by information in the word to the right of fixation. In their critical review of existing data on the question, they conclude that there is evidence for such an effect, certainly as concerns orthographic information in peripheral vision, and perhaps as concerns lexical or semantic information. The first experiment they report strengthens this assertion by showing, in a sentence-reading situation closer to normal reading than used in previous studies, that fixation and gaze duration on a word were affected by similarity and associatedness of the word in the sentence position. In a second experiment they test another question critical to the SAS position: whether, when a word is being processed, the word to the left of this word is also simultaneously being processed. The evidence clearly indicates that some information from a word to the left of a word undergoing current fixation is indeed extracted. Underwood, Binns and Walker's chapter has a similar purpose, namely to illustrate an influence of foveal processing on peripheral processing, and, conversely, whether there is an influence of peripheral processing on foveal processing. In two experiments they show, first, an effect of foveal-on-peripheral processing (as evidenced by effects on number of fixations and fixation duration on the to-be-fixated word) and, second (in line with Kennedy's data), evidence that the informativeness of a to-be-fixated word increases fixation duration on the currently fixated word. Although this latter effect is not modulated by the ease of processing of the foveated word, as might have been expected, taken together the two results argue for an account of reading in which visual processing is distributed over several words at a time, and not just limited to the currently fixated word.

The Chapter by Vitu and McConkie provides further data relevant to the question of word-by-word processing in reading. Their study looks at the properties of regressions, extending to adults an earlier study limited to fifth-grade readers. The probability of regressing to a word depends on the word's length and frequency, and (in the case where the word was previously skipped) on the eccentricity at which the skipped word was seen prior to the skip. Vitu and McConkie argue for a theory in which regressions to words, and particularly to skipped words, occur because these words have not been completely processed. However, they discuss two minor aspects of their data which may possibly pose problems to this view: the lack of an effect of eccentricity on regression probability, and the fact that, contrary to expectation, there are not more regressions to a word when the word has not been fixated near its middle. However, these problems may be overcome by postulating an asymmetry in the attentional window.

Thus, surveying the informative and carefully argued contributions in this section, it would appear that several authors would welcome a version of the SAS model in which the attentional window is not restricted to individual words, but might have a 'fuzzier' contour, encompassing more than the currently fixated word. Indeed, the question of whether, and to what extent, attention can be 'divided' among several items, channels, features etc. is probably as old as attention research itself. Clearly, there is ample evidence from basic research that, depending on the task, 'unattended' stimuli are nevertheless semantically processed. This has even led to the radical position of some theorists that *all* messages, attended or not, undergo semantic processing (e.g., Duncan, 1980; Van der Heijden, 1992), in parallel and without processing limits. In this context, it is less surprising to find this same controversy also reflected in discussions of the role of attention in reading. In our view, the bulk of evidence presented here demands that an account in terms of attention shifts, with processing restricted to a single individual word at a time, must be softened to allow for what Inhoff et al. here call a 'gradient of attention', which may include a number of words, each of which is weighted differently at a given moment during processing.

How can all this be squared with the evidence from the various laboratory studies discussed above which seem to show that, at least for the specific situation before a saccadic eye movement, processing is strictly limited to the saccade target (e.g., Hoffman and Subramaniam, 1995; Kowler et al., 1995; Deubel and Schneider, 1996)? Again, possible implications for the reading situation probably must be pursued with caution. First, in all of the studies cited above, items at positions neighbouring the target could be perceived above chance level, suggesting that some small amount of attention had actually been attributed to them. This aspect was further addressed by Kowler et al. (1995), who analysed their data on the basis of an 'attentional operating characteristic' and demonstrated that when the emphasis on the saccade task was relaxed, participants were indeed better able to identify items at other positions. Second, all the above studies analysed presaccadic attentional engagement toward *peripheral* items: none of them studied in parallel pre-saccadic perceptual performance at the fixation position. We have informal evidence from dual-task experiments, such as that of Deubel and Schneider (1996), that it is indeed the case that perceptual performance at the current fixation remains high until the onset of the saccade, even while attention is already deployed on the peripheral target. Finally, all the above studies are characterised by short-term stimulus presentations of the critical items to be identified and such short presentation times could act to prevent shifts of attention between several of the presented items, in contrast to the rather static stimulus conditions in situations such as reading.

What can be learned from basic research on saccade programming?

All the variants of the SAS model are couched within the classic framework of saccade programming, in which it is assumed that 'where' and 'when' decisions are made more or less independently, and that there is a phase of saccade 'program-ming' during which saccade characteristics are more or less impervious to new incoming information. These basic assumptions stem from various findings derived from double step experiments (e.g., Becker and Jürgens, 1979; Becker, 1991) — data which have allowed important insights into the basic mechanisms of saccade control. Several chapters in this section (and elsewhere in this volume) directly refer to these basic control mechanisms, and some raise the issue of whether these correctly predict the empirical findings in reading. It would be helpful, therefore, if we first sketch out here some of the current assumptions on the basic saccade control mechanisms.

In a typical double-step experiment, an initial horizontal displacement of a target, usually a small dot, initiates the programming of a primary saccade. Before the saccade is executed, a secondary displacement of the target occurs, either in the same direction as the first step or in the opposite direction. Depending on the timing, size and direction of this second target step, different effects on the saccadic behaviour can be observed — both the spatial end position and the latency of the saccade may be affected by the interfering target displacement, in characteristically different ways. Depending on its relative size and direction, the perturbing stimulus induces basically different effects, which led Ottes, Van Gisbergen and Eggermont (1984) to postulate two different 'modes': one, in which *averaging* responses occur, and the other, in which a *bistable* response pattern prevails. The findings may be summarised as follows:

Averaging can be observed when the two locations stimulated are on the same side of the retina and are not too far apart (e.g., at 10° and at 15° eccentricity). In this case, the *amplitude* of the response is modified in a characteristic way. It turns out that the amplitude can be modified by the sensory information from the second stimulus if it occurs as late as 70 ms before the saccadic reaction. This surprisingly short value indicates that the oculomotor system is prepared to take into account new visual information concerning *spatial properties* until the latest possible moment before the onset of the movement. If the target step occurs in an interval between approximately 70 and 180 ms before saccade onset, the saccade consistently lands *in between* the first and the final target location, suggesting that, rather than using one or the other target position, a spatial average of target eccentricity calculated within a particular temporal window before the saccade is taken. As the latency of the primary saccade increases, this leads to a systematic transition of the saccade end points, from positions close to the first stimulus location towards positions close to the second location. This data pattern was termed the 'Amplitude Transition Function' (ATF) by Becker and Jürgens (1979). A *bistable response* occurs when the presaccadic second target shift is very large with respect to the first step (e.g. 10° and 30°), or involves a change in saccade direction. Instead of being directed to a spatial average, the saccade now is directed to one location or the other, depending on the specific timing. Also, the occurrence of delayed responses including a single saccade is markedly increased, which is interpreted as the time needed for a cancellation of the old saccade program and the reprogramming of the targeting saccade (the *'reprocessing time'*, see Becker, 1991). So, only in this case is the timing of the primary saccade altered. Interestingly, saccade timing can be affected only until up to about 120 ms before saccade onset.

Finally, it is important to note here that Becker and Jürgens (1979) and others, have found evidence of the *parallel programming* of two successive saccades in different stages of the computation process. This was suggested essentially by the observation that the amplitude and/or latency of the second saccade of a two-saccade response to a double-step stimulus depends on the time between the second target step and the first response. Moreover, the latency of a secondary, corrective saccade turns out to be a function of the size of the error it corrects: large remaining errors tend to be corrected with very short saccade latencies. As a consequence, 'averaging' primary saccades in double-step paradigms are often followed by short-latency, secondary saccades directed to the final target position.

Some implications of these findings are of specific interest. First, it seems that the result of amplitude computation is independent of the absolute latency of the primary saccade to the first step, and, moreover, the effect of the target displacement can be observed until up to 240 ms after its occurrence (Deubel, Wolf and Hauske, 1984). This suggests that amplitude computation is a process running continuously, independent of the decision of triggering a saccade. Second, the latest point in time where saccade triggering is affected is earlier than the minimum modification time for saccade amplitude: that is, the decision to elicit a saccade is accomplished *before* the amplitude computation is finished. Taken together, these findings suggest that the process that computes *where* a saccade is going is essentially independent of and parallel to the process that decides *when* the movement should be elicited. While the process of amplitude computation shows the attributes of a machine-like, low-level process, saccade timing is much more vulnerable to instructions and expectations and exhibits considerable variability between participants.

Let us now consider some implications of the postulated saccadic mechanisms for the task of reading. A situation that can be closely linked to a double-step stimulus occurs in reading when a word is *skipped*. The SAS model postulates that word skipping takes place when the lexical processing of the first peripheral word (subsequently referred to as word $N + 1$) is completed very early during the fixation period on a given word N. It is then assumed that the ongoing preparation of the saccade aimed to this word is cancelled, and the saccade reprogrammed to the next word in the line (word $N + 2$). In the light of the research reviewed above, one would now expect one of two alternative observations. The first possibility (related to the *bistable response mode*) would be to find indication of a 'reprogramming time', reflected in a considerable inflation of fixation durations before words are skipped. The saccades should then land on, or near, the centre of either the first or the second word. We will argue below that the evidence on this point is equivocal. Alternatively, if the *averaging mode* is relevant, there should be evidence of something analogous to ATFs, both in terms of an amplitude transition from landing on word $N + 1$ to landing on word $N + 2$, and in terms of the very short secondary saccade latencies typical for many averaging responses. More specifically, one would necessarily expect that the probability of landing closer to word $N + 2$ should increase with longer fixation duration on word N and that there are many short fixations at the respective landing positions.

Given the fact that the averaging scenario occurs under experimental conditions close to reading (e.g., Findlay and Harris, 1984) and is at the core of current versions of the SAS model, it is quite surprising that, to the present, no study has specifically addressed the question of the existence or absence of ATFs in reading. However, looking at the problem from a different angle, Radach, Heller and Inhoff (1999) studied the occurrence of very short duration fixations during reading. In a sample of 24 participants of a sentence reading experiment they found that the occurrence of fixations in the range of 80 to 120 ms varied from 0.5 to 12%. Although saccade reprogramming is a very likely explanation for the occurrence of very short fixations, their extremely uneven distribution among individual readers raises doubts about the possible role of averaging responses as the default mechanism for *every* case of word skipping.

Of relevance to the question is the effect of fixation duration on saccade length in reading. Radach and Heller, in this section, provide an exhaustive classification of possible hypotheses on this matter, and review much of the available data. One conclusion is to confirm previous observations that the duration of a fixation increases when the preceding saccade is long; this is consistent with the idea that parafoveal preprocessing of a word facilitates its subsequent processing. In addition, they make the novel observation, however, that there is only a weak relationship between the duration of a fixation and the extent of the following saccade. In particular, they find no evidence that fixation durations are longer prior to the eye skipping a word (see also McConkie, Kerr and Dyre, 1994). Since this contrasts with studies reporting increased fixation durations before word-skipping (Pollatsek, Rayner and Balota, 1986; Reichle et al., 1998) it is clear that the question needs further investigation, but it can be concluded that at this point there is no clear empirical support for the presence of a mechanism similar to the *bistable response* in the double-step paradigm. This conflicts with the claim of SAS models that word skipping necessarily requires cancellation of a potential saccade to the next word and thereby involves a longer prior fixation duration. It could be that, depending on the local visual configuration, words are 'skipped' as part of a general scanning routine selecting words as fixation targets on the basis of their length and eccentricity (Reilly and O'Regan, 1998) and we shall return to this point later.

The picture is further complicated by the fact that Vonk, Radach and Van Rijn in this section demonstrate a small but reliable effect of cognitive processing on saccade size. In a review of the literature on the effects of local cognitive processing on the eye's landing site in reading, they initially show that evidence for such effects is scarce and to be found only in restricted conditions such as single sentence reading, where participants may be reading particularly carefully, and in cases where orthographic familiarity is strongly manipulated. When contextual constraint is well controlled and orthographic familiarity manipulated in a less extreme fashion (as in the experiment reported here), there is a weak, but systematic, 1/3rd-letter effect of a word's orthographic familiarity on landing position in the word. Vonk et al. interpret their data in terms of a gradual modification and refinement of the amplitude of the impending saccade, which takes place even *after* the final decision to elicit the saccade has occurred. This is obviously consistent with the assumption derived from the basic research discussed above that a decision to move the eyes is made *before* computation of saccade amplitude is finished.

In conclusion, the question of exactly what reading researchers can learn from current experimental findings on oculomotor control turns out to be quite difficult to answer. Some of the data presented in this section seem to indicate that certain basic assumptions (e.g., those predicting averaging responses) are not warranted by the empirical findings. The problem is the familiar one: that it is not clear to what extent results from rather artificial laboratory situations can be transferred to the task of reading. For example, the stimulus eccentricities and saccade sizes used in many studies of basic oculomotor properties are far larger than those normally involved in reading. Equally important, the saccades in these situations were obviously reflexive saccades triggered by external, transient stimulus changes. The underlying processes might be very different for endogenously controlled saccades on visually static reading material. Finally, it should be noted that systematic behavioural investigations of basic mechanisms of saccade programming, of the type carried out by Becker and Jürgens, have virtually ceased since the mid-eighties (see the review by Findlay and Walker, in press). We think that in order to improve models of reading, this type of research requires urgent resurrection, using stimuli and tasks more closely approaching the reading situation.

Viewed from the other side, perhaps models of the saccade control processes can be constructed which are more flexible than those postulated in the double-step paradigm, and which are more applicable to the reading situation. For example, an alternative approach to saccade control has been suggested recently by Clark (1998). Derived from the pre-motor theory of attention (Rizzolatti, 1983), Clark rejects the notion that saccades are 'programmed', and yet is able to account for classic phenomena like the double-step effects, the gap effect (Saslow, 1967), and the effect of saccade latency and predictability on saccade accuracy (e.g., Coëffé and O'Regan, 1987), using a simple, winner-take-all neural net, compatible with the known neurophysiology of the superior colliculus (see, e.g., Wurtz, 1996, for an introductory review). The model involves a spatiotopic saliency map where bottom-up visual factors and top-down cognitive processing interact to create regions of competing activity. The eyes make a saccade when a peripheral region of the saliency map becomes more active than the saliency of the currently fixated region. The time course and endpoint of the saccade are determined by the dynamics of the winner-take-all competition. This idea is quite different from most current models of eye movement control in reading: serial word-by-word allocation of attention is replaced with competition between (parallel) allocation of processing resources at the fixated location, and allocation of resources in the peripheral region. It would be interesting to investigate whether the effects of interaction between central and peripheral processing that have been observed by several of the papers in this section might be modelled in this way.

Whither models of eye movement control in reading?

We want to conclude the commentary by widening the discussion a little. One of the most persistent ideas underlying theories of eye movement guidance in reading has been the notion that eye movements should be tightly linked to ongoing linguistic processing. This has proved enticing to psycholinguists and has been a constant motivation for eye movement research over the last 20 years. An early manifestation of this idea was the notion of perceptual span control. Thus, the earliest of modern studies on eye movements in reading (e.g., McConkie and Rayner, 1975; O'Regan, 1979) were motivated by the idea that the distance the eyes move at each saccade might be determined, in a moment-to-moment fashion, by the amount of text material that is visible or being processed at each fixation. In one respect the SAS model is the heritage of the notion of perceptual span, being based on the idea that it is moment-to-moment processing that is determining the choice of the next word. However, in other respects the model departs quite substantially from the original notion, because rather than assuming that the eyes aim for some location at the edge of the perceptual span, the SAS model is concerned with how words are selected for fixation as a result of local processing *within* the span.

The 'processing difficulty hypothesis' of Hyönä and Pollatsek (Chapter 4, but see also Hyönä, 1995; Henderson and Ferreira, 1990) represents another variant of local processing, claiming that "the *perceptual span* (our italics) around the fixation from which useful information is picked up is narrowed down with increasing difficulty in parafoveal and foveal processing. Thus, when a word in foveal or parafoveal vision is low-frequency, less parafoveal processing will be done, which should then lead to a shorter forward saccade" (p. 77). The results of Hyönä and Pollatsek on reinspection patterns within complex words are very interesting both from the perspectives of word processing and eye movement control. However, their theoretical proposal marks a renaissance of ideas close to the classic notion of perceptual span control, which, although very appealing, has unfortunately been shown to be not in harmony with a substantial body of empirical evidence. First, there are studies that manipulated visual parameters, such as viewing distance (O'Regan, Lévy-Schoen and Jacobs, 1983), target-background similarity and letter visibility (Jacobs, 1986; Jacobs and O'Regan, 1987) using psychophysical methods. In these studies the concomitant changes in saccade extent or fixation duration to be expected from perceptual span control were not observed. Second, and more relevant to the particular hypothesis put forward by Hyönä and Pollatsek, it is not necessarily the case that a deterioration of parafoveal visual performance as a function of foveal processing load must take the form of a narrowing of the perceptual span or, to use another popular concept, of inducing 'tunnel vision'. For example, in a study using a cognitive load manipulation at a primary foveal task (memory comparison) and a secondary visual detection task, no evidence of tunnel vision was found, with a uniform performance decrease over a range of eccentricities (Van de Weijgert, 1993; see also Williams, 1988).

This suggests that in reading and visual search, it is possible for a viewer to invoke different overall strategies, not directly related to perceptual span, corre-sponding to more or less careful scanning. Following McConkie, Kerr, Reddix and Zola's (1988) excellent quantitative analyses of landing site distributions in reading, Reilly and O'Regan (1998) showed that a very good account of saccade behaviour could be given by supposing that at each saccade the eye attempts to move to the longest word in a peripheral window of about 20 characters to the right of the fixation point, but that it suffers from oculomotor aiming errors (centre of gravity effects or range effects) which make it deviate somewhat from the aimed-for location. This simple principle yields a good description of what the eye does in reading. But the question arises: Do the eyes move in this way 'intelligently', that is, because they wish to process each (longish) word sequentially? Or do the eyes move this way because they are using a 'dumb', oculomotor strategy unrelated to ongoing processing, but which 'looks intelligent' because on average it provides textual input to the visual system at a convenient rate?

The proponents of 'processing' models of eye guidance in reading opt for the 'intelligent' alternative. One of their arguments is that there exist data showing that in reading there are effects of word frequency on the probability of refixating or skipping a word. But they slip from noting that "cognitive variables appear to be *influencing* (our italics) gross decisions, such as which word to fixate (e.g. Do I refixate this word? Do I skip this word?)" to the claim that cognitive variables are the *main drivers* of eye movements in reading. It is now established beyond doubt that there are indeed effects of lexical factors on refixation and skipping probability (e.g., Rayner, Sereno and Raney, 1996; Brysbaert and Vitu, 1998). However, this does not mean that *the main driving force* behind eye movements is lexical processing: just as being able to avoid a puddle doesn't prevent walking from being primarily an autonomous rhythmic activity, in reading the existence of lexical-dependent skipping does not imply that the underlying strategy is driven by lexical processing. In fact, a number of indications seem to suggest that the driving force behind eye movements in reading is a 'move forward' strategy which is independent of sentence processing. First of all, as pointed out by Vonk et al. in this section (see also O'Regan, 1990; Brysbaert and Vitu, 1998), the effects of linguistic variables on refixation and skipping are relatively modest. Secondly, the Reilly and O'Regan simulation noted above actually gave better results when a mechanism for skipping high frequency words was excluded than when it was included. A stronger argument in favour of a 'dumb' eye movement strategy was given by the zzz-experiment of Vitu, O'Regan, Inhoff and Topolski (1995), and its replication by Rayner and Fischer (1996). In this experiment very similar distributions of landing sites and probabilities of word skipping were found in a task of scanning through lines of sequences of z's spaced out like words in normal text. Even though Rayner and Fischer (1996) claim that there are 'important differences' between normal reading and zzz-reading, and even though they claim their results show that "eye movements are *not* guided by a global strategy and local tactics, but by immediate processing demands" (p. 734), it is clear that the major portion of variability of the landing site and refixation probability distributions in their data is common to both normal and zzz-reading. It is true that there are effects related to lexical processing, but these merely modulate underlying effects that are common to both types of reading. It therefore remains questionable that cognitive processing is the driving force behind saccades in reading. On the contrary, as claimed by Vitu et al., it is possible that a 'dumb' strategy underlies reading, and that this is modulated by ongoing linguistic processing.

We will now turn to consider the question of landing position within words. A moment-to-moment processing account of saccade control in reading would suggest that if the eye lands too far from the optimal position for recognising a word (which is generally near the word's middle), then the most advantageous strategy would be to move fairly far to the other side of the word so as to maximise the amount of material within the word that could be encompassed. Indeed, examination of landing sites within words when two fixations are made shows this kind of behaviour (O'Regan and Lévy-Schoen, 1987 for isolated words, and Vitu and O'Regan, 1989 and Vitu et al., 1995 for reading). Similar data are also presented by Beauvillain, Vergilino and Dukic in this section. But the same question can be posed: Is this necessarily the result of 'intelligent', ongoing eye movement guidance, or is it the result of a 'dumb' strategy that has adapted to provide the visual processor with lexical material at an overall convenient rate? Analysis of landing sites for cases where the eye fixated a word twice were also done in the zzz-reading experiments, and again these show very similar patterns to refixations in normal reading. There are small differences of course — for example, Vitu and O'Regan (1989) found that the eye fixates further towards word beginnings and endings when making refixations in reading than when making refixations in zzz strings, and this effect is stronger when a word has received parafoveal preprocesssing prior to the eye landing upon it. But overall, the main underlying component of the eye's behaviour in refixating zzz-strings is strikingly similar to that for normal reading. An experiment by Nazir (1991) also suggests the presence of strong oculomotor components to within-word eye movement tactics: when the eye moves from fixating a target within a string of k's to an adjacent string, even though for processing there is no reason to do so, the eye tends to make a second stop in the string before leaving it. Beauvillain et al. in their chapter have taken the initial steps in investigating the oculomotor programming involved in such cases, and the extent to which linguistic processing can modulate this programming. They claim that the intra-word program is different from the inter-word program, whereas Radach and McConkie (1998) claim that both types of saccades can be explained from a unitary fixate-near-the-middle routine, with some oculomotor range error added.

Consider what happens when you ask a person to move their eyes smoothly along a straight line. It is well-known that the eyes cannot autonomously produce a smooth eye movement, but that they move in saccades. There is thus an underlying mechanism within the oculomotor system which, as attention moves smoothly along, transforms this into a series of saccades. Lévy-Schoen (1980) carried out an experiment whose outcome also argued in favour of a 'chunking' of saccadic exploration. She had readers read silently along with another reader who was reading the text out loud slowly. She found that the silent reader's eye movements consisted in repetitive refixations of each word, presumably unrelated to linguistic processing, resembling the backwards and forwards movements that an excited dog makes around its master when the master is walking too slowly. The fixation durations and saccade sizes had means and distributions very similar to those for normal reading: there were just more of them. The interpretation, again, is that the eye has its own dynamics. It does not like to sit still, and its motions are strongly governed by its own laws, not directly related to cognitive processes.

As we have discussed, basic oculomotor mechanisms of the kind advocated above have been incorporated in recent 'processing' models of eye movement control in reading. For example, Reichle et al. (1998) propose a low-level routine which programs a refixation that is *automatically* executed if it is not cancelled as a consequence of completing a lexical familiarity check on the target word. As Rayner et al. note, this 'dumb' default strategy is not very different from that proposed by O'Regan (1992). In a revision of the E-Z reader model, presented in this volume, they integrate into their processing-based framework the perceptuo-motor principles proposed by McConkie et al. to account for the distribution of saccade landing sites.

While in such local processing models oculomotor factors play an important role in the control of saccades, this is not the case for the control of fixation durations. Yet, even in very simple tasks such as that mentioned above of trying to move one's attention along a continuous line, the eye will tend to make fixations whose durations are similar to those observed in reading (i.e., in the 150–300-ms range). In the zzz-string reading, fixation durations were also in the same range as in normal reading, and more importantly, their dependence on the location fixated in the strings followed the same curves that apply to reading words. Thus, for example, when a single fixation is made in a string, the duration of the fixation obeys an upside-down U-shaped function, with the longest fixation occurring near the middle of the string (Rayner and Fischer, 1996). This is exactly what happens in normal reading (Vitu, McConkie, Kerr and O'Regan, in preparation; Vitu and O'Regan, 1995). It is, parenthetically, a rather peculiar effect: on processing grounds one might have expected that the closer one fixates to the optimal viewing position in a word, the shorter the duration of the fixation would have to be. This, and the fact that the effect occurs both for strings and words, suggests that it does not originate in lexical processing. However, in normal reading there is an effect on this curve of the word's frequency: fixation durations are somewhat longer for low-frequency words. This shows that linguistic factors are active. Our suggestion, however, is that these factors are essentially modulating influences operating on the basis of the underlying oculomotor strategy.

A similar point can be made concerning the durations of individual fixations when there are two in a word. The durations of these fixations obey a very interesting law (for isolated words: O'Regan and Lévy-Schoen, 1987; also in O'Regan, 1990; for words in reading: O'Regan, Vitu, Radach and Kerr, 1994): when the first fixation is near the beginning of a word or near the end of a word, it is short, and it is longer when it is near the middle of the word. The duration of the second fixation of two is short if the first is long, and long if the first is short. The sum of the two durations is approximately constant, independently of where the first fixation occurred in the word. This pattern strongly suggests that the processing of the word is spread over the two fixations[3]. Furthermore, the durations depend on lexical variables, being longer when the word is unpredictable and of low frequency. But again, further investigation shows that these patterns may be the consequence of a strategy that 'looks' intelligent but is, in fact, dumb, without requiring ongoing processing to actually determine eye movements in a moment-to-moment fashion. Thus, when experiments are performed using strings of characters, and in cases where no processing at all need be done, very similar curves are obtained (unpublished work cited in O'Regan, 1990; O'Regan, Vitu, Radach and Kerr, 1994). At the very least, our claim is that more work is necessary to distinguish between phenomena of eye guidance that really are intelligent, and those that just seem intelligent. In this work it will be important to keep in mind that because eye movement behaviour may be strongly modulated by linguistic factors, this does not necessarily imply that linguistic processing is the prime mover of the eyes: neither as concerns saccades nor as concerns fixation durations.

Conclusions

As incontestably demonstrated by the interest it has generated, the current version of SAS models (the E-Z reader model), is a remarkable achievement, indicating that our discipline has reached a state of maturity where theories are specific enough to become testable on a computational level (see Jacobs, this volume, for a detailed discussion). It is, however, noteworthy that, as demonstrated by the arguments presented here, the alternative notion that low-level oculomotor processes might be playing the dominant role in eye movement control during reading, remains a serious possibility. It certainly seems worthwhile giving such a predominantly low-level control theory the degree of formalisation and testability

---

3 Kennedy, in this section, suggests that similar trade-offs may occur over two successive *words*.

as has benefited the SAS model. Within such a theory, of course, room would have to be made for some degree of modulation of low-level oculomotor programs by ongoing linguistic processing. The existence of such cognitive modulation of eye movement parameters will naturally provide a theoretical base for the use of eye movements in psycholinguistic research. In fact it may turn out that it will be easier to extract the linguistically modulated component of eye movement behaviour within such a theory than within an attention-based framework[4]. This is because under the hypothesis of predominantly low-level visuomotor control, baseline variations in oculomotor parameters will be rather easily definable in terms of low-level parameters, and any deviations from these will be recognisable as linguistic effects. This is in contrast to the situation within an attention-based model, where eye movements are more inextricably intertwined with cognitive processing (see also Inhoff and Radach, 1998 and Murray, this volume, for discussions on the complexities of using oculomotor measures in psycholinguistic research).

Another important point arising from the argument we have developed here concerns the relation between eye movement control in reading and basic oculomotor research. It is clear that workers studying reading have in the past made use of principles derived from basic research on saccade generation. Examples of this are the analogy between the double-step studies and the SAS theories; the use of the concept of the saccadic range effect (Kapoula and Robinson, 1986) in McConkie et al.'s (1988) explanation of saccadic landing positions in reading; and O'Regan's (1990) use of the 'global' or 'centre of gravity' effect (Findlay, 1982; Ottes et al., 1984; Deubel et al., 1984) in his strategy–tactics theory. However, many of the principles that have been appealed to were based on experimental work using very simple stimuli and tasks quite unlike those found in normal reading. It would be very helpful if an effort could be made to extend the methods and approaches of basic research so as to be more applicable to the situation of normal reading, thereby rendering possible the establishment of functional explanations of reading behaviour via basic oculomotor principles.

References

Becker, W. (1991). Saccades. In: R.H.S. Carpenter (Ed.), Eye Movements, Vol. 8: Vision and Visual Dysfunction. Basingstoke, London: Macmillan Press.

Becker, W. and Jürgens, R. (1979). An analysis of the saccadic system by means of double-step stimuli. Vision Research, 19, 967–983.

---

4 We are using this more general term here because the argument made relates not only to sequential attention shift models, but also to the attentional gradient variant, proposed by Inhoff et al., this volume.

Brysbaert, M. and Vitu, F. (1998) Word skipping: Implications for theories of eye movement control in reading. In: G. Underwood (Ed.), Eye Guidance in Reading and Scene Perception. Amsterdam: Elsevier, pp. 125–148.

Clark, J.J. (1998). Spatial attention and latencies of saccadic eye movements. Vision Research, 39, 585–602.

Coëffé, C. and O'Regan, J.K. (1987). Reducing the influence of non-target stimuli on saccade accuracy: Predictability and latency effects. Vision Research, 27, 227–240.

Crawford, T.D. and Müller, H.J. (1992). Spatial and temporal effects of spatial attention on human saccadic eye movements. Vision Research, 32, 293–304.

Deubel, H., Mokler, A., Fischer, B. and Schneider, W.X. (1999). Reflexive saccades are not preceded by shifts of attention: Evidence from an antisaccade task. Paper presented at the 10th European Conference on Eye Movements, Utrecht, Sept. 23–25.

Deubel, H. and Schneider, W.X. (1996). Saccade target selection and object recognition: Evidence for a common attentional mechanism. Vision Research, 36, 1827–1837.

Deubel, H., Wolf, W. and Hauske, G. (1984). The evaluation of the oculomotor error signal. In: A.G. Gale and F. Johnson (Eds.), Theoretical and Applied Aspects of Eye Movement Research. Amsterdam: Elsevier, pp. 55–62.

Duncan, J. (1980). The locus of interference in the perception of simultaneous stimuli. Psychological Review, 87, 272–300.

Findlay, J.M. (1982). Global visual processing for saccadic eye movements. Vision Research, 22, 1033–1045.

Findlay, J.M. and Harris, L.R. (1984). Small saccades to double-stepped target moving in two dimensions. In: A.G. Gale and F. Johnson (Eds.), Theoretical and Applied Aspects of Eye Movement Research. Amsterdam: Elsevier, pp. 71–78.

Findlay, J.M. and Walker, R. (in press). A model of saccade generation based on parallel processing and competitive inhibition. Behavioral and Brain Sciences.

Henderson, J.M. and Ferreira, F. (1990). Effects of foveal processing difficulty on the perceptual span in reading: Implications for attention and eye movement control. Journal of Experimental Psychology: Learning, Memory, and Cognition, 16, 417–429.

Hoffman, J.E. and Subramaniam, B. (1995). The role of visual attention in saccadic eye movements. Perception and Psychophysics, 57, 787–795.

Hyönä, J. (1995). Do irregular letter combinations attract readers' attention? Evidence from fixation locations in words. Journal of Experimental Psychology: Human Perception and Performance, 21, 68–81.

Inhoff, A.W. and Radach, R. (1998). Definition and computation of oculomotor measures in the study of cognitive processes. In: G. Underwood (Ed.), Eye Guidance in Reading and Scene Perception. Oxford: Elsevier, pp. 77–100.

Jacobs, A.M. (1986). Eye-movement control in visual search: How direct is visual span control? Perception and Psychophysics, 39, 47–58.

Jacobs, A.M. and O'Regan, J.K. (1987). Spatial and/or temporal adjustments of scanning behavior to visibility changes. Acta Psychologica, 65, 133–146.

Kapoula, Z. and Robinson, D.A. (1986). Saccadic undershoot is not inevitable: Saccades can be accurate. Vision Research, 26 (5), 735–743.

Klein, R. (1980). Does oculomotor readiness mediate cognitive control of visual attention? In: R. Nickerson (Ed.), Attention and Performance, VIII. Hillsdale, NJ: Erlbaum, pp. 259–276.

Kowler, E., Anderson, E., Dosher, B. and Blaser, E. (1995). The role of attention in the programming of saccades. Vision Research, 35, 1897–1916.

Lévy-Schoen, A. (1980). La flexibilité des saccades et des fixations au cours de la lecture. L'Année Psychologique, 80, 121–136.

McConkie, G.W. and Rayner, K. (1975). The span of the effective stimulus during a fixation in reading. Perception and Psychophysics, 17, 578–586.

McConkie, G.W., Kerr, P.W. and Dyre, B.P. (1994). What are 'normal' eye movements during reading: Toward a mathematical description. In: J. Ygge and G. Lennerstrand (Eds.), Eye Movements in Reading. Oxford: Elsevier, pp. 315–327.

McConkie, G.W., Kerr, P.W., Reddix, M.D. and Zola, D. (1988). Eye movement control during reading: I. The location of initial eye fixation on words. Vision Research, 28, 1107–1118.

Morrison, R.E. (1984). Manipulation of stimulus onset delay in reading: Evidence for parallel programming of saccades. Journal of Experimental Psychology: Human Perception and Performance, 10, 667–682.

Nazir, T.A. (1991). On the role of refixations in letter strings: The influence of oculomotor factors. Perception and Psychophysics, 49, 373–389.

O'Regan, J.K. (1979). Saccade size control in reading: Evidence for the linguistic control hypothesis. Perception and Psychophysics, 25, 501–509.

O'Regan, J.K. (1990). Eye movements and reading. In: E. Kowler (Ed.), Eye Movements and their Role in Visual and Cognitive Processes (Vol. 4 of Reviews of Oculomotor Research). Amsterdam: Elsevier, pp. 395–453.

O'Regan, J.K. (1992). Optimal viewing position in words and the strategy–tactics theory of eye movements in reading. In: K. Rayner (Ed.), Eye Movements and Visual Cognition: Scene Perception and Reading. New York: Springer, pp. 333–354.

O'Regan, J.K. and Lévy-Schoen, A. (1987). Eye movement strategy and tactics in word recognition and reading. In: M. Coltheart (Ed.), Attention and Performance XII: The Psychology of Reading. Hillsdale, NJ: Erlbaum, pp. 363–383.

O'Regan, J.K., Lévy-Schoen, A. and Jacobs, A. (1983). The effect of visibility on eye movement parameters in reading. Perception and Psychophysics, 34, 457–464.

O'Regan, J.K., Vitu, F., Radach, R. and Kerr, P.W. (1994). Effects of local processing and oculomotor factors in eye movement guidance in reading. In: J. Ygge and G. Lennerstrand (Eds.), Eye Movements in Reading. Oxford: Pergamon Press, pp. 329–348.

Ottes, F.P., Van Gisbergen, J.A.M. and Eggermont, J.J. (1984). Metrics of saccade responses to visual double stimuli: Two different modes. Vision Research, 24, 1169–1179.

Pollatsek, A., Rayner, K. and Balota, D.A. (1986). Inferences about eye movement control from the perceptual span in reading. Perception and Psychophysics, 40, 123–130.

Posner, M.I. (1980). Orienting of attention. Quarterly Journal of Experimental Psychology, 32, 3–25.

Radach, R., Heller, D. and Inhoff, A.W. (1999). Occurrence and function of very short fixation durations in reading. In: W. Becker, H. Deubel and T. Mergner (Eds.), Current Oculomotor Research: Physiological and Psychological Aspects. New York: Plenum, pp. 321–331.

Radach, R. and McConkie, G.W. (1998). Determinants of fixation positions in words during reading. In: G. Underwood (Ed.), Eye Guidance in Reading and Scene Perception. Amsterdam: Elsevier, pp. 77–100.

Rayner, K. and Duffy, S.A. (1986). Lexical complexity and fixation times in reading: Effect of word frequency, verb complexity, and lexical ambiguity. Memory and Cognition, 14, 191–201.

Rayner, K. and Fischer, M.H. (1996). Mindless reading revisited: Eye movements during reading and scanning are different. Perception and Psychophysics, 58, 734–747.

Rayner, K., Sereno, S.C. and Raney, G.E. (1996). Eye movement control in reading: A comparison of two types of models. Journal of Experimental Psychology: Human Perception and Performance, 22, 1188–1200.

Reichle, E.D., Pollatsek, A., Fisher, D.L. and Rayner, K. (1998). Toward a model of eye movement control in reading. Psychological Review, 105, 125–157.

Reilly, R.G. and O'Regan, J.K. (1998). Eye movement control during reading: A simulation of some word-targetting strategies. Vision Research, 38, 303–317.

Remington, R.W. (1980). Attention and saccadic eye movements. Journal of Experimental Psychology: Human Perception and Performance, 6, 726–744.

Reuter-Lorenz, P.A. and Fendrich, R. (1992). Oculomotor readiness and covert orienting: Differences between central and peripheral cues. Perception and Psychophysics, 52, 336 344.

Rizzolatti, G. (1983). Mechanisms of selective attention in mammals. In: J.P. Ewart, R. Capranica and D.J. Ingle (Eds.). New York: Plenum, pp. 261–297.

Saslow, M.G. (1967). Effects of components of displacement step stimuli upon latency for saccadic eye movement. Journal of the Optical Society of America, 57, 1024–1029.

Schneider, W.X. (1995). VAM: A neuro-cognitive model for visual attention control of segmentation, object recognition and space-based motor actions. Visual Cognition, 2, 331–375.

Shepherd, M., Findlay, J.M. and Hockey, R.J. (1986). The relationship between eye movements and spatial attention. Quarterly Journal of Experimental Psychology, 38A, 475–491.

Stelmach, L.B., Campsall, J.M. and Herdman, C.M. (1997). Attentional and ocular eye movements. Journal of Experimental Psychology: Human Perception and Performance, 23, 823–844.

Treisman, A. (1969). Strategies and models of selective attention. Psychological Review, 76, 282–299.

Van der Heijden, A.H.C. (1992). Selective Attention in Vision. London: Routledge.

Van de Weijgert, E. (1993). Foveal load and peripheral task performance: Tunnel vision or general interference? In: D. Brogan, A. Gale and C. Carr (Eds.), Visual Search 2. London: Taylor and Francis.

Vitu, F., McConkie, G.W., Kerr, P.W. and O'Regan, J.K. (in preparation). About the relation between fixation durations and fixation positions in reading.

Vitu, F. and O'Regan, J.K. (1989). Le rôle du prétraitement périphérique dans la lecture de textes. Journal Med. Nucl. Biophys., 13, 359–366.

Vitu, F. and O'Regan, J.K. (1995). A challenge to current theories of eye movements during reading. In: J.M. Findlay, R.W. Kentridge and R. Walker (Eds.), Eye Movement Research: Mechanisms, Processes and Applications. Amsterdam: Elsevier, pp. 381–392.

Vitu, F., O'Regan, J.K., Inhoff, A.W. and Topolski, R. (1995). Mindless reading: Eye movement characteristcs are similar in scanning letter strings and reading texts. Perception and Psychophysics, 57, 352–364.

Williams, L.J. (1988). Tunnel vision or general interference? Cognitive load and attentional bias are both important. American Journal of Psychology, 101, 171–191.

Wurtz, R.H. (1996). Vision for the control of movement. Investigative Ophthalmology and Visual Science, 37, 2131–2145.

Phonology in Reading

Section Editor

Ralph Radach

CHAPTER 14

The Assembly of Phonology in Italian and English: Consonants and Vowels

Lucia Colombo
University of Padua

Abstract

This chapter is focussed on the nature of the assembly mechanism in reading. Several topics are discussed, but the main issue is related to whether independent representations and processes are involved in the construction of the phonology for consonants and vowels. The model proposed by Berent and Perfetti (1995), the two-cycles model, supporting the notion of a processing priority for consonants, is presented and discussed in the light of recent experimental data in Italian, showing a pattern that provides only partial support for the two-cycles model. In particular, the processing advantage for consonants as compared to vowels appearing in the backward masking paradigm in Berent and Perfetti's data can be attributed to the irregularity of vowels in the English language. Another factor that may affect the process of converting print into sound, and is important in Italian, is the ratio between consonants and vowels. Because there are fewer vowels than consonants in Italian, they belong to a smaller domain, and the phonological emergence of vowels is faster as compared to that of consonants, leading to their advantage in Italian. The implications of the different findings in Italian and English are discussed.

Reading as a Perceptual Process/A. Kennedy, R. Radach, D. Heller and J. Pynte (Editors)
© 2000 Elsevier Science Ltd. All rights reserved

Introduction

A highly debated issue in the literature on word recognition is how the computation of phonology influences the process of identifying words in reading. There are two important aspects to this issue. One is related to the question whether in identifying a word we need to compute its phonology. The second concerns the way the phonology of a word is computed. The two issues are obviously interrelated, as is apparent from a consideration of the models proposed in the literature. Among these, perhaps the most popular is the dual route model (Coltheart, 1978; Coltheart, Curtis, Atkins and Haller, 1993; Paap and Noel, 1991; Paap, Noel and Johansen, 1992) according to which reading is accomplished through the operation of two mechanisms, a lexical mechanism that retrieves the phonology of a word directly through the association of the orthographic pattern to its phonological correspondent stored in the lexicon, and an assembly mechanism, that operates by assembling the output of a process of conversion of spelling–sound correspondences. The two processes operate in parallel, but the lexical process is usually fast and for normal readers it is the lexical output that is used for computing the phonology of a word and programming its articulation. In particular, the assembly mechanism cannot produce a correct output for irregular words, and its output is usually too slow with respect to the lexical process for high frequency words, so that its effects can only be apparent for low frequency regular words and for nonwords (Monsell, Doyle and Haggard, 1989; Paap et al., 1992; Seidenberg, 1985; Seidenberg, Waters, Barnes and Tanenhaus, 1984). In the dual route framework the computation of phonology is seen as a horse race, or competition, between the two processing mechanisms, that are assumed to be independent, and the nature of these has been thoroughly debated (Brown and Besner, 1987; Brown, Lupker and Colombo, 1994; Carr and Pollatsek, 1985; Paap et al., 1992; Patterson and Coltheart, 1987; Seidenberg and McClelland, 1989; Van Orden, Pennington and Stone, 1990). In particular, it is the nature of the assembly process that has been object of much discussion and which will be considered in the present chapter.

Nature of the assembly mechanism

The assembly process is seen as a slow mechanism, that requires effort, or attentive resources, and is therefore subject to strategic control (Baluch and Besner, 1991; Paap and Noel, 1991). Evidence in favour of this claim is provided by the fact that naming low frequency irregular words is faster with a memory load of five digits, as compared to one digit, indicating that the assembly route has been disabled by the attentional requirements and therefore the lexical route no longer suffers from competition (Paap and Noel, 1991, but see Pexman and Lupker, 1995, and Bernstein and Carr, 1996). Also, naming exception words is faster when these words are in a pure list, as compared to when they are mixed with nonwords, indicating that the assembly route necessary for reading nonwords has been disabled in the pure list, where it produces an interfering output (Monsell, Patterson, Graham, Hughes and Milroy, 1992; Zevin and Balota, 2000; but see Lupker, Brown and Colombo, 1997). Moreover, semantic priming and frequency effects, that are taken to indicate contact with the lexicon, are eliminated or reduced when nonwords are added to a list (Baluch and Besner, 1991; Colombo and Tabossi, 1992; Tabossi and Laghi, 1992; Zevin and Balota, 2000). All these results together demonstrate that the assembly route is a slow, controlled, process that requires attentional resources and can be strategically disabled.

Other evidence, on the other hand, indicates that the phonology of words is computed very fast (Perfetti and Bell, 1991; Perfetti, Bell and Delaney, 1988; Perfetti, Zhang and Berent, 1992; Van Orden, 1987). Results from studies using the backward masking procedure, for example, show that when a target word is very briefly presented (around 30 ms) and masked by a nonword immediately followed by a pattern mask, there is a strong impairment in the recognition of the target word. This impairment is reduced when target and mask share orthographic or phonological characteristics. For example, if the target word (*rate*) is masked by a pseudohomophone (RAIT) and by a graphemic mask (RALT) both display a mask reduction effect, that is, a smaller impairment in accuracy with respect to a control condition in which the mask does not share any property with the target (BUSK). Moreover, the mask reduction effect is larger for the phonemic than for the graphemic mask (Naish, 1980; Perfetti and Bell, 1991; Perfetti et al., 1988). Similar evidence indicating very early phonological effects is found in priming studies (Ferrand and Grainger, 1992, 1993, 1994; Lukatela and Turvey, 1990).

The results of all these studies imply that the phonological representation of a word is activated after a very brief and incomplete presentation of a word, and that this activation grows so fast as to make apparent the effects of phonology, despite the fact that the orthographic analysis starts earlier.

The two-cycles model

In a recent review, Berent and Perfetti (1995) pointed out the contradiction in these views in the literature. On one hand, the assembly process is considered slow and controlled, and its output is only apparent for low frequency regular words and nonwords. On the other hand, it appears that the phonology of words and nonwords is activated rapidly upon very brief stimulus presentation. This contradiction is solved, according to Berent and Perfetti, within the framework of the model they propose, the two-cycles model.

There are several important characteristics of the two-cycles model that I will review here. The first important aspect to be stressed in this model relates to the structure of the assembled representation for English visual word recognition. Berent and Perfetti challenge the view that this representation is formed by a linear combination of phonemes, each of which is the result of the grapheme–phoneme association. The assembled representation is instead formed by two independent constituents, the structure for consonants and that for vowels, in agreement with autosegmental views of phonology (Archangeli, 1985; Clements and Keiser, 1983; McCarthy, 1989). The second important aspect of the two-cycles model is that the multiple levels of representation of the assembled structure correspond to different processes. That, is, the phonological computation of consonants and vowels is performed by two distinct processes whose nature and time course are different, because they depend on the characteristics of the English language. In English, which is a language with irregular spelling–sound correspondences, the irregularity is mainly due to the vowels: consonants are considered 'islands of reliability' (Brown and Besner, 1987; Carr and Pollatsek, 1985). The process that operates on consonants is therefore fast and automatic and produces an output that can place constraints on the word recognition process, such as mask reduction or priming effects, at very brief presentations. In contrast, the processing of vowels is slow and controlled, because the mapping between the vowel graphemes and the corresponding phonemes is not consistent. The two processes operate in two cycles with different time courses, corresponding to the nature of the operating processes and to the nature of the input to the processes. During the first cycle, very shortly after presentation, only consonants are processed, while the second cycle is devoted to the processing of vowels.

The evidence in favour of the two-cycles model presented by Berent and Perfetti (1995) is quite extensive. In a backward masking paradigm, with a spelling task, the presentation of a target word (*rake*) is facilitated when it is followed by a homophone mask (RAIK), and by a mask that preserves the consonants and not the vowels of the target (RIKK) at very brief presentations (15 ms for the target and 30 ms for the mask), as compared to a control condition (BLIN). Only at longer durations does a mask that preserves the vowels and not the consonants (RAIB) produce a mask reduction effect.

In a Stroop-type masking paradigm, where participants were required to name the colour of a word, at short durations greater interference (larger proportion of errors) was found when the mask preserved the consonants of the colour word (GRAHN, for the target *green*), indicating a greater interference of the colour word due to the better-assembled representation of the consonant mask compared to the vowel mask (GREAP). Further, in a concurrent task of digit recall within the backward masking paradigm, it was found that at brief durations performance was independent of load for the same-consonant condition, supporting the view that the computation of consonants is automatic. In contrast, at longer durations, the same-vowel mask produced a mask reduction effect only in the low-load, but not in the high-load condition, consistent with the idea that the computation of vowels is an attention-demanding process. Evidence for a rapid computation of phonology of consonants as compared to that of vowels was also found when the paradigm was priming rather than backward masking, and the masks preceded the target word to be named.

An important aspect of the two-cycles model is a prediction it makes about regularity effects. As the irregularities in English words mainly derive from vowels, the straightforward prediction is that during the first cycle, where only the consonants are computed, there should be no regularity effect. Indeed, in their experiments Berent and Perfetti showed that the regularity effects appear only at the longer durations, in concomitance with the advantage of the same vowel mask.

Thus, in the formulation of the two-cycles model it is possible to account for why there are contradictory statements in the literature about the nature and time course of the assembly process. Those results that show evidence that assembly is slow and attention-demanding, showing, for instance, regularity effects for low frequency words, are based on the output of the second cycle, that computes the phonology of vowels. In contrast, the studies showing evidence for a fast and automatic mechanism are based on paradigms that display the output of the second cycle, in which consonants are computed (see also Berent, 1997).

An even more important aspect of the two-cycles model is given by its implications for other languages, that is, its generality. Berent and Perfetti (1995) admit that, as far as the experimental and theoretical evidence indicates, the differences found in the computation of vowels and consonants may simply reflect the inconsistency in the English system of correspondence between orthography and phonology. On the other hand, they also consider the possibility that the characteristics of the English language, such as its orthographic depth, reflect linguistic phonological constraints on the language, like the fact that, in English, vowels are less distinct phonologically than consonants (Liberman, 1970). In the latter case, then, evidence for the segregation of consonants and vowels into different domains, and of two distinct computational mechanisms to process consonants and vowels, should generalize to other languages. We might therefore expect that, if the linguistic constraints are universal, the same pattern of results should obtain also in Italian, despite its different orthographic system.

Italian is a language with a very regular system of spelling–sound correspondences. The few variations in the phonological correspondence of graphemes are predictable. For instance, the consonant 'c' is realized as /c/ before /e/ and /i/ and as /k/ before /a/, /o/ and /u/. Moreover, these variations are mainly due to consonants, rather than vowels, but they are, as noted, context-dependent. If the segregation of consonants and vowels in different planes is a general linguistic constraint, then it should manifest itself also in Italian. But with what empirical consequences? Given that vowels are no more irregular than consonants, it may not be necessarily the case that, in Italian, processing consonants is faster than processing vowels. The advantage for consonants predicted on the basis of the two-cycles model might not become apparent.

Other considerations can be entertained, however. It has been claimed that consonants are more informative about the identity of words: for example, words can more easily be guessed when their vowels rather than their consonants are deleted (Adams, 1981). In the neuropsychological domain, spelling errors of two Italian patients showed a deficit in reporting vowels but not consonants (Cubelli, 1991). Although it is certainly not the most compelling interpretation of the latter data, it is possible to argue that consonants are more resistant to deterioration. On the basis of these considerations it could be argued that, assuming that a segregation of consonants and vowels occurs at some level, consonants are then processed faster than vowels, and therefore they should show this advantage somehow.

The Italian experiments

We performed a replication of some of the experiments reported by Berent and Perfetti (Colombo, Cubelli, Zorzi, Caporali and Rigo, submitted) with the aim of determining whether evidence can be found for the independent representation of consonants and vowels, and for a different time course in their processing. In summary, we tested the two-cycles model in Italian.

We carried out two experiments using the backward masking paradigm. In the first experiment, the task was to spell the target word, as in Berent and Perfetti's Experiment 1. In the second experiment, the task was to name the target word aloud. In both cases accuracy was the dependent variable. The target stimuli were two-syllable and three-syllable words with regular stress. Each target word was masked by four types of nonword mask. There was a mask preserving the consonants (VIRBO for *verbo*), a mask preserving the vowels (VERPO), a pseudohomophone mask (WERBO) and a control (VAGRI) that did not maintain either consonants or vowels, except for the initial phoneme. The same-consonant and same-vowel masks were orthographically similar to the target. In contrast, the pseudohomophone was less similar. Indeed, as Italian is regular in spelling–sound correspondences, we had to devise a way to construct nonwords that could be read like real words, but that did not correspond orthographically to real words. To this end, we substituted one grapheme in each word with a grapheme not present in the Italian alphabet, but rather commonly known, because present in many popular foreign words. These graphemes were 'y', 'w' and 'k', that are pronounced, respectively, like the Italian phonemes /i/, /v/ and /c/. [1] Therefore, *cane* (dog) became KANE, and *insetto* became YNSETTO. We tested these pseudohomophones in a separate pre-test naming experiment, where we verified that indeed accuracy was higher with these types of nonwords as compared to nonwords with the same foreign graphemes, but whose pronunciation did not correspond to real words.

There were four durations, referring to the interval between the onset of the target's presentation, and the onset of the mask, and between the mask's onset and the pattern mask's onset. They were as close as possible to those used in the original experiment by Berent and Perfetti. In the first duration, each target word was presented for 16 ms, followed by the mask, that was substituted by a pattern mask after 33 ms. The remaining durations were, respectively for the target and the mask, 33/33, 50/33 and 50/67 ms.

As all the masks, except the control, shared most of the graphemes and phonemes with the target word, a mask reduction effect was expected, that is, an increase in accuracy for the experimental conditions, as compared to the control condition, as found in numerous experiments by Perfetti and collaborators (Perfetti and Bell, 1991; Perfetti et al., 1988; Perfetti and Zhang, 1995).

As noted in the former section, on the basis of the empirical results obtained by Berent and Perfetti (1995), and in view of the theoretical considerations discussed above, in such a replication of Berent and Perfetti's experiment an advantage for the consonant preserving mask with respect to the vowel preserving mask might be expected. Alternatively, if the main constraint on the phonological realization of the target words is the regularity of the spelling–sound correspondence, given that the phonological realization of vowels in Italian is regular, no difference would be predicted between the same-consonant and the same-vowel mask conditions, but just a mask reduction effect of both with respect to the control condition. Moreover, it was particularly interesting to see whether the pseudohomophone mask would yield a mask reduction effect, as found in English.

The unexpected result was instead an advantage in the vowel-preserving condition with respect to the consonant-preserving condition, even at very short durations (see Fig. 1), although both showed a mask reduction effect compared to the control condition. Also interesting was the advantage for the pseudohomophone mask at these short durations, indicating a very early phonological activation, despite the graphemic dissimilarity. [2] At longer durations the difference between the same-consonant and the same-vowel mask disappeared, although the mask reduction effect

---

1 As noted above, the grapheme 'c' is pronounced /k/ when followed by the vowels /a/, /o/, /u/.

2 It should be noted that the graphemic dissimilarity of the pseudohomophone mask presumably produced a disadvantage at the orthographic level. Therefore the obtained advantage can only be attributed to the phonological level.

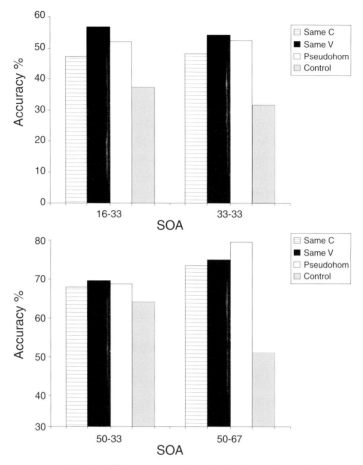

Fig. 1. The accuracy rate for the different types of masks in the spelling task (Experiment 1, from Colombo, Cubelli, Zorzi, Caporali and Rigo, submitted).

persisted. Similar results were obtained in the second experiment, where the naming task was used.

What could explain the complete reversal of the consonant advantage in the Italian experiments? The interpretation proposed starts from a consideration of the consonant–vowel ratio in the Italian phonological system, as compared to the English one. The Italian phonemes are formed by 26 consonants, and only 7 vowels (Nespor, 1993). In other classifications, in which are included the geminates, the number of consonant phonemes rises to 40 (Bortolini, Degan, Minnaja, Paccagnella and Zilli, 1977; Busa, Croatto-Martinolli, Croatto, Tagliavini and Zampolli, 1962). In the English phonological system, in contrast, there is a much more even ratio between consonants and vowels: 24 to 20 (Oxford Psycholinguistic Database,

Quinlan, 1993). If the computation of the phonology for consonants and vowels is a process that is somehow sensitive to the relative size of the two types of phonemes, then an influence of this factor is expected to show under specific conditions. In particular, the vowel–consonant ratio would not have an effect in English, because the ratio is even, but it would in Italian, because the vowels are relatively few, as compared to consonants, and therefore their computation is facilitated. We will see in the next section how the operation of this factor can be described more precisely.

In English, therefore, given that the number of consonants and vowels is similar, the only effect would be that due to the irregularity of the spelling–sound correspondence for vowels, producing an advantage for the same-consonant condition. In Italian, in contrast, given its phonological regularity for both consonants and vowels, the only visible effect would be due to the vowel–consonant ratio.

The results of the two Italian experiments converge in suggesting that during word identification an assembled code is formed very rapidly. This code is based on two independent representations for consonants and vowels, and these representations are separately influenced by the characteristics of the language in which the words are presented. In both experiments, however, the computation of a phonological code was somehow required by the task. Naming requires the formation of a phonological code, by definition. As regards spelling, although in principle it may be true that participants might have converted the orthographic input code directly into the corresponding orthographic output code, in our view it is rather unlikely that they did so. Indeed, it is very implausible that the scarcely specified orthographic code derived under degraded conditions of presentation, such as those used in the backward masking paradigm (or any masking paradigm, for that matter) could be used as a basis for the construction for the orthographic output representation. Rather, it is more likely that from the degraded representation a phonological code is derived, that helps to maintain the activated word unit in memory until all the operations necessary to spell it are performed (Hawkins, Reicher, Rogers and Peterson, 1976).

In conclusion, both the spelling and the naming task require the construction of a phonological representation. This phonological representation is presumably an output of the assembly mechanism, rather than of the lexically addressed process. But if the task does not *require* the construction of a phonological code, or at least, not to the same extent that the naming task does, for instance, if a lexical decision is made on the target word under the same conditions of masking as before, we might expect a change in the pattern of results. First, there is evidence to suggest that different strategies can be adopted on the basis of the task requirements (Hawkins et al., 1976; Pugh, Rexer and Katz, 1994). Second, there is evidence that lexical decision can be carried out solely on the basis of an orthographic analysis (Pugh et al., 1994; Waters and Seidenberg, 1985). In fact, some computational models are based on this assumption (Grainger and Jacobs, 1996; Plaut, 1997).

If lexical decision can indeed be made exclusively on the basis of an orthographic code we might expect no mask reduction effect for the pseudohomophone. And if the advantage of vowels versus the consonants (or vice versa) is a reflection of the assembly process, it should no longer be obtained. In a third experiment (Colombo et al., submitted) the backward paradigm was used with a lexical decision task. As in the first experiment, there were four durations, and participants were required to decide if the target was a word or a nonword. The results showed a different pattern from that found in the first two experiments. At the very brief duration (16/33) there was a mask reduction effect of about the same size for both the same-consonant and the same-vowel mask, but not for the pseudohomophone mask. At such an interval, the evidence that was found in the naming and spelling task for the operation of an assembly mechanism (i.e., the mask reduction effect for the pseudohomophone mask, coupled with the same-vowel mask advantage versus the same-consonant mask) was no longer present, indicating that, presumably, lexical decision is performed on the basis of the orthographic code derived from the visual presentation. At longer durations, the mask reduction effect for the same-consonant and the same-vowel mask was maintained, and was accompanied by a parallel effect for the pseudohomophone mask. At longer durations, therefore, a phonological code is formed and can also influence lexical decision.

The segregation of consonants and vowels

The results of both the Italian and the English data seem to converge on one of the main assumptions of the two-cycles model, that is, the assumption that consonants and vowels are assigned to different domains (planes or levels) of representation, on the basis of a process that segregates the two types of graphemes at some point during the processing of the word. It is important now to make some speculations on how this process occurs and why.

Let us assume that a pre-categorization of letters as consonants or as vowels is a mandatory aspect of the process of parsing the letter string. An important aspect to consider is why this segregation process would occur, and to what end. Such a pre-categorization could be conceived of as a process that occurs whenever a phonological sequence must be derived from the letter string, and whose aim, therefore, would be somehow connected to the *formation of the assembled code*. We may conceive of an alternative possibility, however. That is, this process might occur at an orthographic level, and its output might be used *in order to identify each letter*. I will consider first the latter hypothesis.

Let us assume that a mechanism parses the visual string, and the input to this mechanism can be formed by several perceptual indicators as to whether the letter is a consonant or a vowel. For instance, evidence may accumulate about whether a letter is a consonant or a vowel on the basis of its global shape and its position within the word. Distributional constraints might help in this task. For instance, knowledge that an initial letter in Italian is likely to be a consonant, and a final letter is likely to be a vowel. Or the knowledge about the fact that the most likely word structure is formed by CVCV, or CVCVCV. Therefore, in some positions either a consonant, or a vowel, is more likely.

This evidence may not be sufficient for the identification of the letter, but can constitute a sufficient basis for its (at least provisional) categorization as a consonant or as a vowel. In an interactive activation framework, evidence about the nature of the categorization would come also from higher levels of representation, such as the word level (Grainger and Jacobs, 1996; McClelland and Rumelhart, 1981). That is, all words sharing, for instance, an 'n' in third position (band, land, sand) will send activation back to the letter level to the letter 'n'. This may, in turn, bias the decision that the letter is a consonant. Such a probabilistic decision on the nature of the letter may be similar to that used in lexical decision for establishing whether a letter string is a word or not, on the basis of a global familiarity value (Grainger and Jacobs, 1996).

Once the assignment of a letter to the domain of consonants or vowels has been performed, on the basis of the pre-categorization process, the letter's definitive identification occurs *within each domain*. At the orthographic level, the two domains are of equivalent size in English and in Italian. In the English alphabet, vowel graphemes are five and consonant graphemes are twenty in number. In Italian, there are five vowel graphemes and sixteen consonant graphemes. This fact leads to the prediction that the identification of a letter will have similar time courses in the two languages, as far as the vowel–consonant ratio is concerned. According to this description, the vowel–consonant ratio, operating during the orthographic analysis of the string, could not produce an advantage in the identification of vowels in Italian, without producing a parallel advantage in English. Therefore, the potential explanation of the function of the categorization process, in terms of a contribution to the letters' identification procedure, must be ruled out.

Another reason why this conceptualization must be rejected is that it leads to the prediction that an advantage for vowels in Italian should be found independently of whether the task requires the assembly of the phonology of the word, or simply its identification on the basis of whatever sources are available. This is because it assumes that the locus of the vowel advantage is the process that identifies letters orthographically. Why should the output of the orthographic analysis not be detected by the lexical decision task? However, this prediction is not consistent with the results obtained in the lexical decision task, where the size of the mask reduction effect was the same for consonants and vowels. The vowel advantage in Italian, therefore, cannot be attributed to the process of identifying the abstract orthographic letter representation, because in this case we should expect it in lexical decision as well.

Let us consider now the alternative interpretation of the segregation process, and its function, suggesting that this process is contingent on, or is a requirement of, the assembly process. According to this view, the segregation into consonant and vowel domains is performed during the construction of the orthographic code from which the corresponding phonological code will be activated. As Berent and Perfetti note, the appropriate phonological correspondence of a grapheme in English is often obtained by considering the word or sub-word context. For example, the correct pronunciation of the vowel *a* in many English words depends on whether it is followed by a consonant and there is a final *e*. Therefore "to achieve the mapping of the *a* grapheme unit it is necessary to determine whether the graphemes in its environment are consonants or vowels" (Berent and Perfetti, 1995, p. 157). Once identified as a consonant or as a vowel, the appropriate phoneme can emerge and become part of the phonological representation to be assembled. It is at this stage that the different phonological factors intrinsic to a language may show their influence. The phonological correspondence of each letter is activated with a mainly consistent mapping function, for regular languages like Italian, while for English multiple phonemes may be activated for each grapheme. This process, therefore, has different time courses for consonants and vowels, because the selection, or the emergence of the appropriate phoneme, is slowed down by the inconsistency of vowels.

Considering the different vowel–consonant ratio in the phonological systems of the two languages, the computation of a phoneme would have different time courses, depending on whether it is a consonant or a vowel, in Italian and English. That is, in Italian the computation of a phoneme is a very fast process in the small vowel domain, while it takes longer in the larger size consonant domain. In English, in contrast, the time course of the phonemic computation is similar for consonants and vowels, because the relative domains have similar sizes.

The frequency of consonants and vowels

A different interpretative approach to the data might be considered, suggesting that the differential advantages of consonants and vowels may be not due to their pre-categorization into distinct domains. This approach is grounded on the consideration of the possible influence of the relative frequency of the different phonemes. If we consider the distributional frequency of the different phonemes in Italian, we can see that the seven vowels have a very high percentage of frequency. In a recent study it has been found that the percentage of frequency of the seven vowels is 47.04% of all the phonemes (from a corpus of 12519 spoken words), while the percentage of frequency for the 40 consonants (including geminates) is 52.96% (Panzeri and Foscarini, 1998). In particular, the vowels /a/, /e/, /o/ and

/i/ account for 40.13% of the total frequency, with the vowels /a/ and /e/ rising to, respectively, 10.86 and 10.7. This leads to the possibility that the advantage of vowels in Italian may be simply a reflection of their greater relative frequency.[3]

The phonology for more frequent phonemes might emerge more quickly as compared to the phonology for less frequent ones. Under this interpretation, the vowel advantage would not require the assumption of a representational distinction between consonants and vowels, and of the process of pre-categorization of the phonemes into separate domains.

If this interpretation were correct, however, we should expect that the greater frequency of occurrence of vowels should lead to a vowel advantage also in lexical decision. This objection is based on the notion that the great relative frequency of vowel phonemes corresponds to a high degree to similar values in the vowel graphemes. Even if lexical decision is made predominantly on an orthographic basis, the same frequency-based vowel advantage effect would be expected with this task as well.

It is therefore likely that the frequency differences between consonants and vowels is not responsible for the vowel advantage in Italian. However, it is certainly important to investigate whether and how letter frequencies may influence word processing under the conditions used in the present experiments, and in particular how it affects the processing of consonants and vowels.

Two cycles or one?

In describing the two-cycles model as proposed by Berent and Perfetti (1995) we pointed out that it is based on two main assumptions. One is relative to the distinct representations for consonants and vowels, and leads to the process of segregation of the letters into different domains. The second, related, assumption refers to the consequent separation of the processes devoted to each domain, each with a different temporal course. The fast process, in the first cycle, computes the phonology of the letters whose phonological correspondence have a consistent mapping function, while the slow process, in the second cycle, computes the phonology for the inconsistent vowels.

Considering the English and Italian data together, the first assumption seems to be supported. The advantage for the same-consonant mask, on one hand, and for the same-vowel mask, on the other hand, can be explained in the framework of two different factors that both affect the operation of spelling–sound conversion, and both imply the segregation of consonants and vowels at an early stage.

---

3 I wish to thank Albrecht Inhoff for suggesting to me this possibility.

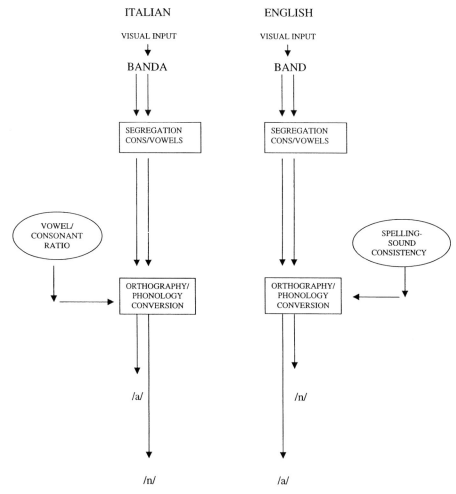

Fig. 2. A model of how different factors can affect the process of converting print into sound in Italian and English.

As regards the second assumption, the evidence also suggests that there are two processes of a different nature that compute the phonology of consonants and vowels. The different properties of each language, namely, spelling–sound consistency for English, and vowel–consonant ratio for Italian, both act on the same process, that is, the construction of the assembled code, although the effects on the computation of phonology for consonants and vowels are opposite in the two languages. Fig. 2 displays a possible model of how the process goes for two words, one Italian and one English, that are orthographically similar, 'banda' and 'band'. The orthographic representation of a word is the input to the process that segregates, or labels, the graphemes as consonants and vowels. The time course is similar for the two languages, as the figure shows. The output of this process is taken as input by the assembly process, during which the phonological realization of each phoneme is computed. During this process the language-specific factors operate, namely, spelling–sound consistency and vowel–consonant ratio. The relative time courses for a vowel or a consonant in the two languages are indicated by the different length of the lines: the vowel emerges earlier than the consonant in Italian, and vice versa in English.

As is apparent from the figure, the process of categorization of graphemes as consonants or vowels does not imply, by itself, differential phonological computations for English and Italian. As noted above, at the orthographic level the two languages have similar characteristics as far as the vowel–consonant ratio is concerned. The differential advantage of consonants and vowels arises, as Berent and Perfetti also claim, during the phonological computation. However, the fact that the computation of the phonology for consonants and vowels has different time courses in the two languages is not an intrinsic property of the system, dependent on the categorization of consonants and vowels into different domains. For instance, we might conceive of a language that has both regular spelling–sound correspondences, and an even vowel–consonant ratio. In this case, we would not expect any differential advantage for either consonants or vowels, despite the assumption of their distinct representations. The two factors, the spelling–sound consistency for English, and the vowel–consonant ratio for Italian, reflect the different properties of the two languages, and are, in turn, reflected in the computational characteristics for consonants and vowels in the two languages. The nature of the processes that emerges from the data reflects therefore the characteristics of the language. As Berent and Perfetti argue, it may be the case that "the differences in the speed and automaticity of assembling consonants and vowels merely reflects the differences in the consistency of grapheme to phoneme mapping in the English orthography", and not "the linguistic constituency structure of the assembled code".

The question then becomes whether the evidence for two cycles, or two qualitatively different processes, is a matter contingent on the specific languages, or a more general characteristic of the reading process, dependent on the linguistic constraints of a Universal Grammar. In this context it is important to consider whether Berent and Perfetti's arguments in favour of two distinct processes are compelling, and whether alternative views are possible.

The conceptualization used by Berent and Perfetti is grounded in a very extensively shared view of the literature on attentional processes, that is, the idea that attention can be viewed as the allocation of resources from a central system of limited capacity (Norman and Bobrow, 1975; Posner and Snyder, 1975). It is generally assumed that processes that require attentive resources will be fast and accurate when more capacity is devoted to them, and also that they are under intentional control. In contrast, automatic processes do not require any resources, or very few, and are not under intentional control. This logic is the same as that applied to distinguish the two mechanisms underlying the naming process according to the dual route theory, namely, the lexical route and the assembly route (Paap and Noel, 1991; Paap et al., 1992).

More recent conceptualizations of automaticity, however, have stressed the fact that the processes that are automatic, and those that are under attentional control, may belong to the same continuum and are not necessarily qualitatively distinct (Cohen, Dunbar and McClelland, 1990; MacLeod, 1991). Accordingly, it may be a single process, and not two, which is responsible for the differential effects found in the data. Namely, this single process is one of converting graphemic units into phonological units, and the output of this process differs depending on what factor influences its operation.

There is, in fact, evidence coming from simulations that one process is able to capture the differential effect for consonants and vowels in English. In a connectionist model proposed by Zorzi, Houghton and Butterworth (1998), the dual process model, the assemby of phonology is computed by a network formed by an orthographic and a phonological layer. This network is able to produce a consistency effect, namely longer latencies (simulated by a larger number of cycles) for the final decision on the pronunciation of words with multiple phonological mappings for their component units. The model is able to simulate with a single process the longer latencies for vowels, compared to consonants, due to the vowels inconsistency. Moreover, a distinct representation for consonants and vowels is an important aspect of the model. The function of this labelling of graphemes as consonants or vowels in the model is to allow the alignment of the orthographic to the phonological level. Thus, this model, including both the representational assumption of distinct representational formats for consonants and vowels, and a single process devoted to the computation of phonology, is able to simulate both the consistency effect and the consonant advantage. The model's characteristics may reflect the computational properties of the human mind, or just simulate the effects obtained on human participants. But it shows that it is not necessary to posit the existence of two processes, or cycles, to explain the consonant advantage obtained in English. Different effects may be obtained by a single process.

Are consonants more informative?

I noted above that in principle there are reasons to assume that, independently of the computational system used to convert print into sound, consonants might have been expected to show an advantage also in Italian. This advantage would be grounded on factors that may, or may not, be reflected in the orthography-to-phonology conversion system. For example, the redundancy of vowels is very large, compared to the redundancy of consonants, which implies that the latter's informativeness about the words' identity is greater. In an experiment conducted in English (Miller and Friedman, 1957) it was found that the removal of vowels in short texts presented visually did not affect, or affected very little, the reconstruction accuracy rate with respect to the normal condition. That is, participants were able to reconstruct a text easily after the removal of its vowels. I do not know of similar evidence for Italian, but given its characteristics it is likely that the same phenomenon would be found. Moreover, in priming experiments conducted in French, in which the visual prime was formed by either the consonants or the vowels of the target word, it was found that there was no priming effect for the vowel primes, whereas there was a significant priming effect for the consonant primes (D. Zagar, pers. commun., 1998).

This fragmentary evidence suggests that consonants might provide greater information about the identity of words. This effect in English is confused with the factor of phonological inconsistency of vowels, leading to an advantage for consonants in any case. But if the greater amount of information provided by the consonants holds for Italian as well, then one might expect it to emerge somehow.

One reason why it did not in the present experiments may be that the advantage for vowels in Italian substantially reflects the process of converting print into sounds, the assembly process, rather than the process of identifying words, at least at the very early stages of processing, that is, at very short durations, in particular with the naming and spelling tasks. This is supported by the fact that presumably the backward masking paradigm favours phonological recoding (see Verstaen, Humphreys, Olson and D'Ydewalle, 1995 for arguments supporting this view). Therefore, at short durations only the effects operating during the assembly process are apparent (i.e., the same-vowel mask advantage). In contrast, longer durations (where same-vowel and same-consonant masks had the same effect) would be more likely to reflect the process of identifying words.

Perhaps, then, the results in the lexical decision task might be given a different interpretation. The fact that there is no differential advantage for the same-vowel mask with respect to the same-consonant mask might reflect an increase in the level of accuracy for the same-consonant mask in this task, where the primary function is the identification of a word, as compared to the spelling and naming tasks, due to the greater informativeness value of consonants. Obviously, further experimentation is needed on the issue of the relative informative value of consonants and vowels, related presumably also to their redundancy.

Conclusions

In this chapter I have reviewed some recent experimental data in English and in Italian, with the purpose of examining a very important theoretical issue, the contribution of consonants and vowels to the assembly of a phonological representation, in the first place, and also to word identification, to some extent. The conceptualization proposed by Berent and Perfetti (1995) to explain differential effects found for consonants and vowels is very interesting, and can explain both the English and the Italian data, after considering language-specific differences. Several alternative interpretations of the different effects are possible, as we have seen, that can account for both English and Italian data to different extents. Only further empirical and theoretical explorations will be able to disentangle the different issues, and to offer a complete and more secure view of the facts.

Acknowledgements

This paper is based on a talk I have given at the Sixth European Workshop on Language Comprehension, held in Marseille, April 1998. I wish to thank Alan Kennedy and Wayne Murray for their kind invitation. I also wish to thank Roberto Cubelli and Marco Zorzi for helpful discussions.

References

Adams, M.J. (1981). What good is orthographic redundancy? In: O.S.L. Singer and H. Tzeng (Eds.), Perception of Print: Reading Research in Experimental Psychology. Hillsdale, NJ: Erlbaum.

Archangeli, D. (1985). Yokuts harmony: evidence for coplanar representation in nonlinear phonology. Linguistic Inquiry, 16, 335–372.

Baluch, B. and Besner, D. (1991). Visual word recognition: evidence for strategic control of lexical and nonlexical routines in oral reading. Journal of Experimental Psychology: Learning, Memory and Cognition, 17, 644–652.

Berent, I. (1997). Phonological priming in the lexical decision task: Regularity effects are not necessary evidence for assembly. Journal of Experimental Psychology: Human Perception and Performance, 23 (6), 1727–1742.

Berent, I. and Perfetti, C.A. (1995). A rose is a reez: the two-cycles model of phonology assembly in reading English. Psychological Review, 102, 146–184.

Bernstein, S.E. and Carr, T.H. (1996). Dual route theories of spelling to pronunciation: what can be learned from concurrent task performance? Journal of Experimental Psychology: Learning, Memory and Cognition, 22, 86–116.

Bortolini, U., Degan, F., Minnaja, C., Paccagnella, L. and Zilli, G. (1977). Statistics for a stochastic model of spoken Italian. Proceedings of the Twelfth International Congress of Linguists, pp. 580–586.

Brown, P. and Besner, D. (1987). The assembly of phonology in oral reading: a new model. In: M. Coltheart (Ed.), Attention and Performance XII. Hillsdale, NJ: Erlbaum, pp. 471–489.

Brown, P., Lupker, S.J. and Colombo, L. (1994). Interacting sources of information in word naming: a study of individual differences. Journal of Experimental Psychology: Human

Perception and Performance, 20 (3), 537–554.

Busa, R., Croatto-Martinolli, C., Croatto, L., Tagliavini, C. and Zampolli, A. (1962). Una ricerca statistica sulla composizione fonologica della lingua italiana parlata, eseguita con un sistema IBM a schede perforate. Proceedings of the 12th International Speech and Voice Therapy Conference, pp. 542–562.

Carr, T.H. and Pollatsek, A. (1985). Recognizing printed words: a look at current models. In: D. Besner, T.G. Waller and G.E. MacKinnon (Eds.), Reading Research: Advances in Theory and Practice, Vol. 5. San Diego, CA: Academic Press, pp. 1–82.

Clements, G.N. and Keiser, S.J. (1983). CV phonology: LI Monography Series, No. 9. Cambridge, MA: MIT Press.

Cohen, J.D., Dunbar, K. and McClelland, J.L. (1990). On the control of automatic processes: a parallel distributed processing account of the Stroop effect. Psychological Review, 97 (3), 332–361.

Colombo, L., Cubelli, R., Zorzi, M., Caporali, A. and Rigo, E. (submitted for publication). The status of consonants and vowels in phonological assembly: testing the two-cycles model with Italian.

Colombo, L. and Tabossi, P. (1992). Strategies and stress assignment: evidence from a shallow orthography. In: R. Frost and L. Katz (Eds.), Orthography, Phonology, Morphology, and Meaning. Amsterdam: Elsevier, pp. 319–340.

Coltheart, M. (1978). Lexical access in simple reading tasks. In: G. Underwood (Ed.), Strategies of Information Processing. London: Academic Press, pp. 151–216.

Coltheart, M., Curtis, B., Atkins, P. and Haller, M. (1993). Models of reading aloud: dual-route and parallel-distributed-processing approaches. Psychological Review, 100, 589–608.

Cubelli, R. (1991). A selective deficit for writing vowels in acquired dysgraphia. Nature, 353, 258–260.

Ferrand, L. and Grainger, J. (1992). Phonology and orthography in visual word recognition: evidence from masked nonword priming. Quarterly Journal of Experimental Psychology, 45A, 353–372.

Ferrand, L. and Grainger, J. (1993). The time course of orthographic and phonological code activation in the early phases of visual word recognition. Bulletin of the Psychonomic Society, 31, 119–122.

Ferrand, L. and Grainger, J. (1994). Effects of orthography are independent of phonology in masked form priming. Quarterly Journal of Experimental Psychology, 47A, 365–382.

Grainger, J. and Jacobs, A.M. (1996). Orthographic processing in visual word recognition: a multiple read-out model. Psychological Review, 103, 518–565.

Hawkins, H., Reicher, M., Rogers, M. and Peterson, L. (1976). Flexible coding in word recognition. Journal of Experimental Psychology: Human Perception and Performance, 2, 380–385.

Liberman, A.M. (1970). The grammar of speech and language. Cognitive Psychology, 1, 301–323.

Lukatela, G. and Turvey, M.T. (1990). Automatic and pre-lexical computation of phonology in visual word identification. European Journal of Cognitive Psychology, 2, 325–343.

Lupker, S.J., Brown, P. and Colombo, L. (1997). Strategic control in a naming task: changing routes or changing deadlines? Journal of Experimental Psychology: Learning, Memory and Cognition, 23, 570–590.

MacLeod, C.M. (1991). Half a century of research on the Stroop effect: an integrative review. Psychological Bulletin, 109, 163–203.

McCarthy, J.J. (1989). Linear order in phonological representation. Linguistic Inquiry, 20, 71–99.

McClelland, J.L. and Rumelhart, D.E. (1981). An interactive activation model of context effects in letter perception, part I. An account of basic findings. Psychological Review, 88, 375–405.

Miller, G.A. and Friedman, E.A. (1957). The reconstruction of mutilated English texts. Information and Control, I, 38–55.

Monsell, S., Doyle, M.C. and Haggard, P.N. (1989). Effects of frequency on word recognition tasks: where are they? Journal of Experimental Psychology: General, 118, 43–71.

Monsell, S., Patterson, K.E., Graham, A., Hughes, C.H. and Milroy, R. (1992). Lexical and sublexical translation of spelling to sound: strategic anticipation of lexical status. Journal of Experimental Psychology: Learning, Memory, and Cognition, 18, 452–467.

Naish, P. (1980). The effects of graphemic and phonemic similarity between targets and masks in a backward visual masking paradigm. Quarterly Journal of Psychology, 32, 57–68.

Nespor, M. (1993). Fonologia. Bologna: Il Mulino.

Norman, D.A. and Bobrow, D.J. (1975). On data-limited and resource-limited processes. Cognitive Psychology, 7, 44–64.

Paap, K.R. and Noel, R.W. (1991). Dual-route models of print to sound: still a good horse race. Psychological Research, 53, 13–24.

Paap, K., Noel, R.W. and Johansen, L.S. (1992). Dual-route models of print to sound: red herrings and real horses. In: R. Frost and L. Katz (Eds.), Orthography, Phonology, Morphology and Meaning. Amsterdam: North-Holland.

Panzeri, M. and Foscarini, V. (1998). Distribuzione degli elementi fonologici nell'italiano parlato. Unpublished thesis.

Patterson, K.E. and Coltheart, V. (1987). Phonological processes in reading: a tutorial review. In: M. Coltheart (Ed.), Attention and Performance XII: The Psychology of Reading. Hillsdale, NJ: Erlbaum, pp. 421–447.

Perfetti, C.A. and Bell, L.C. (1991). Phonemic activation during the first 40 ms of word identification: evidence from backward masking and masked priming. Journal of Memory and Language, 30, 473–485.

Perfetti, C.A., Bell, L.C. and Delaney, S.M. (1988). Automatic (prelexical) phonemic activation in silent word reading: evidence from backward masking. Journal of Memory and Language, 27, 59–70.

Perfetti, C.A. and Zhang, S. (1995). Very early phonological activation in Chinese reading. Journal of Experimental Psychology: Learning, Memory, and Cognition, 21, 24–33.

Perfetti, C.A., Zhang, S. and Berent, I. (1992). Reading in English and Chinese: evidence for a 'universal' phonological principle. In: R. Frost and L. Katz (Eds.), Orthography, Phonology, Morphology, and Meaning. Amsterdam: Elsevier, pp. 319–340.

Pexman, P.M. and Lupker, S.J. (1995). Effects of memory load in a word naming task: five failures to replicate. Memory and Cognition, 23, 581–595.

Plaut, D.C. (1997). Structure and function in the lexical system: insights from distributed models of word reading and lexical decision. Language and Cognitive Processes, 12, 767–808.

Posner, M.I. and Snyder, C.R.R. (1975). Facilitation and inhibition in the processing of signals. In: P.M.A. Rabbit and S. Dornic (Eds.), Attention and Performance V. New York: Academic Press.

Pugh, K.R., Rexer, K. and Katz, L. (1994). Evidence for flexible coding in visual word recognition. Journal of Experimental Psychology: Human Perception and Performance, 20, 807–825.

Quinlan, P.T. (1993). The Oxford Psycholinguistic Database. London: Oxford University Press.

Seidenberg, M.S. (1985). The time-course of phonological code activation in two writing systems. Cognition, 19, 1–30.

Seidenberg, M.S. and McClelland, J.L. (1989). A distributed, developmental model of word recognition and naming. Psychological Review, 96, 523–568.

Seidenberg, M.S., Waters, G.S., Barnes, M.A. and Tanenhaus, M.K. (1984). When does irregular spelling or pronunciation influence word recognition? Journal of Verbal Learning and Verbal Behavior, 23, 383–404.

Tabossi, P. and Laghi, L. (1992). Semantic priming in the pronunciation of words in two writing systems: Italian and English. Memory and Cognition, 20, 315–328.

Van Orden, G.C. (1987). A ROWS is a ROSE: spelling, sound, and reading. Memory and Cognition, 15, 181–198.

Van Orden, G.C., Pennington, B.F. and Stone, G.O. (1990). Word identification in reading and the promise of subsymbolic psycholinguistics. Psychological Review, 97, 488–522.

Verstaen, A., Humphreys, G.W., Olson, A. and D'Ydewalle, G. (1995). Are phonemic effects in backward masking evidence for automatic prelexical phonemic activation in visual word recognition? Journal of Memory and Language, 34, 335–356.

Waters, G.S. and Seidenberg, M.S. (1985). Spelling–sound effects in reading. Time course and decision criteria. Memory and Cognition, 13, 557–572.

Zevin, J.D. and Balota, D.A. (2000). Priming and attentional control of lexical and sublexical pathways during naming. Journal of Experimental Psychology: Learning, Memory and Cognition, 26, 121–135.

Zorzi, M., Houghton, G. and Butterworth, B. (1998). Two routes or one in reading aloud? A connectionist dual-process model. Journal of Experimental Psychology: Human Perception and Performance, 24, 1131–1161.

CHAPTER 15

Phonological Coding in Word Perception and Reading

Alexander Pollatsek, Keith Rayner and Hye-Won Lee
University of Massachusetts

Abstract

The work presented here indicates that phonological coding is an important component of the silent reading process in two languages, English and Chinese, that have often been thought to have orthographies that discourage phonological coding in going from print to meaning. The research indicates that phonological codes are extracted early in the reading process, even before a word is fixated in text. Moreover, they are involved in accessing the meanings of words. Accompanying work on phonological coding suggests that (a) phonological codes may be closer in form to the acoustic speech stream than an abstract representation of phonemes, (b) that they are not necessarily formed sequentially from left-to-right, and (c) that the pattern of information accrual may depend on the language involved.

Reading as a Perceptual Process/A. Kennedy, R. Radach, D. Heller and J. Pynte (Editors)
© 2000 Elsevier Science Ltd. All rights reserved

The role of phonological coding in skilled reading has been quite contentious in cognitive psychology and in education. Over the course of years, various positions have been staked out, running from the position of Smith (1971) that phonological coding is irrelevant in the transcription from print to meaning in skilled reading, to the position of Van Orden (1987) that the primary access from print to meaning is by phonological coding and that direct contact between orthographic information and the access of meaning only occurs during a secondary, 'verification', process.

In cognitive psychology, however, there appears to be fairly general agreement that phonological coding plays a significant part in reading by aiding short-term memory, which in turn is presumably crucial in constructing the meaning of phrases, clauses, and sentences. Thus, we take the arena of debate in cognitive psychology to be the role that phonological coding plays in accessing the meaning of a word. We will argue that the truth is close to the second position: that phonological coding enters into the identification process early (i.e., even before a word is fixated) and that this occurs in a variety of orthographies including Chinese. In addition, we will speculate a bit on the nature of this code.

Plausibility arguments

One possible reason that people have such differing opinions on the role of phonological coding is that they start out with plausibility arguments that perhaps seem more compelling to them than any set of experiments (which can always be explained away by positing that the procedures or materials were flawed in some way). As a result, it might be profitable to explore some of these arguments to determine whether any are really compelling.

Arguments against sound coding being important in word identification

There appear to be two primary arguments for why it does not make much sense that a phonological code is an important intermediary in getting to the meaning of a word: (1) sound coding is slow; (2) many orthographies code imperfectly for sound — there is either little or no representation of the sound of a word (e.g., Chinese) or the orthographic code is highly irregular (e.g., English). As a result of these two arguments, sound coding is either thought to be irrelevant for accessing meaning, or at best, a secondary 'backup' coding system that may play a role only for quite low-frequency words.

Although there is merit to both arguments, we find neither compelling. First, the argument that sound coding is slow appears to presume that the sound code is something like 'inner speech', which takes something like 150 ms per syllable.

Given an average of something like two syllables per word, this translates to something like 150–160 words per minute. This is admittedly a bit slower than normal silent reading rates, which are approximately 300 words per minute for standard nontechnical prose. However, this discrepancy does not seem like a compelling argument against sound coding. This is especially true, given that the traditional measure of the rate of inner speech is assessed from a task such as 'counting from 1 to 100 in your head' or a short-term memory task with conscious rehearsal. Thus, 150 ms per syllable may be a lower bound on the rate of producing a phonological code, if some part of the traditional estimate of the rate of inner speech is slowing down the code enough to allow 'hearing' the code in one's head or converting it to a motor code. In addition, the phonological code may be a 'shorthand' record of the material being read in which certain phonemes, syllables, or even words may be omitted.

This argument, however, raises the question of whether a phonological code needs to be serial, in the sense that it needs to be accessed over time. That is, if it is indeed a code that is used as an intermediary in the perception of speech, one could argue that there must be some sequential component to it. This is not strictly necessary, however, as there could be a 'front end' in the speech perception system that turns the raw speech stream into something like an ordered abstract string of phonemes (or other possible phonological units) which then makes contact in parallel with the phonological code that we are interested in.

The second argument against phonological coding generally goes something like this. If skilled readers can read an orthography like Chinese at rates approximating those of skilled readers of alphabetic languages, it indicates that a strict grapheme-to-phoneme (GPC) routine is certainly not necessary to read fluently. Moreover, since English contains so many irregularities, using such a system would not be particularly helpful in English either. A person making this argument might concede that sound coding would make more sense with regular orthographies such as Spanish, Italian, and Finnish, but then claim that there is no compelling reason to believe that these languages are read any faster than irregular languages, and thus that it is most parsimonious to posit that the role of sound coding is minor in all languages. A variant of this position is that the role of sound coding is minor except in alphabetic languages with regular orthographies.

Arguments for the plausibility of sound coding

There are essentially three major arguments in favor of a central role for phonology in decoding printed words. The first is that language is primarily oral. This is true first in the sense that we are biologically programmed to speak and understand spoken language, whereas writing is a relatively recent cultural invention. It is also true in the sense that people in literate cultures learn to speak and decode spoken language before they learn to read and write; hence it seems natural that they should construe the reading task as mapping the written language on the spoken language. Moreover, people for whom spoken language does not exist or is impoverished, such as the deaf or speaking impaired, rarely learn to read very fluently.

The second argument is related to the first. It starts with the observation made above that obtaining sound codes appears to be important in reading for short-term memory purposes. If so, then it would make sense that coding for sound is an important goal and an integral part of the word decoding process. This argument, of course, does not imply that sound coding necessarily occurs before access of meaning. However, for alphabetic languages where prelexical coding is possible, it strongly suggests that there is no rationale in terms of system design to make phonological coding purely subsequent to access of meaning.

The third argument, which we think is rarely made, is that the idea of 'direct look-up' of a word's meaning by an orthographic string of indefinite length may be unrealistic. That is, the assumption that 'normal' word identification is a fluent matching process between an alphabetic string and a sequence of letters in a mental 'lexicon' presupposes that such matching is possible. However, it is not clear that humans are either equipped to learn relatively long sequences of arbitrary symbols well or to recognize them fluently. A related problem is how the ordinal position of a letter in the visual array is extracted. Many of the popular 'direct look-up' models of visual word recognition tacitly assume that the ordinal position of a letter in a word is encoded without error, but this seems like an extremely unrealistic assumption. It is possible that this objection can be overcome by using a 'front end' in the visual domain consisting of hidden units that encode the orthographic regularities of the language. Nonetheless, it is good to keep in mind that a direct look-up process assumes that one can easily form and use mental representations of sequences of letters, and it is not necessarily clear that this can be done, especially for longer words. The alternate possibility that we favor is that humans are biologically programmed to encode sequences of speech sounds and that the sound code is the 'glue' that holds the mental representation of a word together (Share, 1999).

Phonological coding in reading

The above arguments can help to set the parameters of the debate but clearly can not resolve them, especially because we are in such basic ignorance about how visual pattern recognition takes place. As a result, the bulk of the remainder of the chapter will present several lines of research that appear to converge on the conclusion that phonological coding is ubiquitous in accessing the meanings of words in reading. This research involves both normal reading of text and word identification paradigms. Because of space limitations, we cannot present a comprehensive discussion of the literature. Instead, we will focus on presenting our contributions to the literature on sound coding. We begin with a discussion of research in English.

We think that the proper focus of a discussion of phonological coding is whether it is involved in the access of meaning rather than whether it is involved in 'lexical access'. One reason for this preference is that the research focusing on the latter issue has almost exclusively relied on the lexical decision task. In addition to the lexical decision judgment being unecological (people typically assume that strings of letters in text are meaningful, they rarely find reason to make such judgments), there is currently considerable controversy about whether the lexical decision task does tap pure 'lexical access', if such a state does indeed exist. That being said, there is no task that codes purely for accessing the meaning of a word either. However, the two tasks we primarily rely on quite plausibly tap understanding of the meaning of a word in some sense. The first is the time that readers spend on a word in text (primarily *gaze duration*) and the second is the semantic judgment task (i.e., deciding whether two words are semantically related). A third task, which is less plausibly related to extracting meaning, is word naming; however, we will argue that the patterns of data from this paradigm are quite similar to those from silent reading of text.

Phonological coding in reading English

Preview and priming effects
We have employed two closely related paradigms (the boundary paradigm and the fast-priming paradigm) to study the earliest stages of word encoding in reading text. They involve making changes in the text display as a sentence is being read for comprehension. Both involve a key target word which fits into the sentence that is being read. In the *boundary* paradigm (Rayner, 1975), there is a parafoveal preview that occupies the target location before the reader crosses an invisible boundary and fixates the target word (see Fig. 1a). The display change is made while the reader is in mid-saccade, and thus the reader is unaware of the display change. Moreover, the reader is unaware of the identity of the preview word. Thus, this paradigm is as close as you can get to normal reading consistent with manipulating something of interest.

In the conditions of primary interest, the preview was either identical to the target word *surf*, a homophone of it (*serf*) or an orthographic control word that shared as many letters with the target word in the same positions as the homophone (*self*). The key finding (Pollatsek, Lesch, Morris and Rayner, 1992) was that reading was faster when the preview was the homophone preview than when it was the orthographic control preview: *first fixation durations* were 20 ms shorter and *gaze durations* were 14 ms shorter.[1] A second experiment (Pollatsek et al., 1992) examined phonological coding in the parafovea by displaying a single word in the parafovea which readers then fixated and named (see Fig. 1b). Here, the dependent variable was naming latency, and there was a 19-ms advantage for the homophone preview over the orthographic control preview.[2] Thus, two different paradigms using quite different dependent measures indicate that phonological codes are extracted from a word that has yet to be fixated and influence the speed at which it is processed. In both paradigms, however, processing was more efficient for identical previews than for homophone previews, indicating that the reader had extracted more than the phonological code from the preview word.

Similar manipulations were employed in the *fast priming* paradigm to assess the nature of coding early in a fixation in silent reading. In this paradigm (Sereno and Rayner, 1992), there are two display changes. The stimulus originally in the target word location is a meaningless letter string (to prevent extraction of parafoveal information). When the reader crosses a boundary, the stimulus in the target word location changes to the *prime* word (see Fig. 2). The prime is then displayed for the first *n* ms of the initial fixation on the target word location and then is replaced by the target word. (The *prime duration*, the time between when the fixation begins and the second display change is made, is a key manipulation in this paradigm.) As with the preview experiments, the reader is unaware of the first display change; however, the second display change is often visible as a flicker and, for longer durations, the reader can identify the prime word a fraction of the time. Thus, this paradigm is somewhat less like normal reading than the preview experiments described above (although we think it is still more like normal reading than most of the paradigms used to study reading).

Again, the critical comparison is between the homophone prime and the orthographic control prime (which we will call *phonological priming*), although we will discuss two other types of primes shortly. Table 1 presents the results from four

---

1 The *first fixation duration* is the duration of the first or only fixation on a word on the first pass through the text. The *gaze duration* is the sum of all fixation durations on a word on the first pass through the text. *First pass* means that there were no preceding fixations on the target word or to the right of it. In both cases, the mean fixation duration is conditional on the word being fixated: that is, when the target word is skipped on the first pass, that trial is not included in either the first fixation duration or gaze duration calculation.

2 The naming experiment (Experiment 1 of Pollatsek et al., 1992) actually had a bit more complex design, as the homophone previews and orthographic control previews were for different targets, although the homophones and orthographic controls were matched in similarity to the targets. Each was compared to the identical preview, and there was a 9-ms difference for the homophone previews and a 28-ms difference for the orthographic controls, resulting in a 19-ms phonological preview effect.

(a) Parafoveal Preview in Reading (Boundary)

```
      *    |
```
The rough serf crashed incessantly.　　　　　　　　　**(Fixation n-1)**

```
         |    *
```
The rough surf crashed incessantly.　　　　　　　　　**(Fixation n)**

Other possible previews: surf, self, loan

(b) Parafoveal Preview in Naming

```
                                    *
```
Subject fixates cross　　　　　　　　　　　**+**

```
                                    *
```
Fixation 1　　　　　　　　　　　　　　　　　　**beach (preview)**

```
                                          *
```
Fixation 2　　　　　　　　　　　　　　　　　　**beech   (target)**

Other possible previews: beech, bench, fluid

Fig. 1. Illustrations of two parafoveal preview paradigms. (a) In the *boundary* paradigm, an invisible 'boundary' (whose position is indicated by the vertical line above the line of text) determines when the display change takes place. As the first line indicates, when the position of the eye (indicated by the asterisk above the line of text) is to the left of the boundary, the *preview* word (*serf* in the example) is displayed in the target word location. As the second line indicates, the first time the eye crosses the boundary, the preview word is replaced by the target word. In the illustration, the preview word is a homophone of the target word, but other words could be previews, such as an orthographic control word, an orthographically different word, or the target word itself. (b) The logic of the naming paradigm is similar. As the first line indicates, a central cross is initially fixated. When the experimenter is assured that the cross is fixated, a preview word appears about 2° to the right of fixation (line 2). The target word is then fixated (line 3), and during the saccade to that location, the preview word is changed to the target word. As with the boundary paradigm, various previews can be used.

separate experiments, run on different subjects (and in one case with a different monitor; Rayner, Sereno, Lesch and Pollatsek, 1995). Nonetheless, the results are surprisingly consistent. As seen in Table 1, phonological priming does not occur at all prime durations. Instead, it appears to surface at nominal prime durations of about 30 ms and then disappears when the nominal prime duration approaches

Fast Priming in Reading

```
        *   |
```
The rough cxsl crashed incessantly.   **(Fixation n-1)**

```
          |   *
```
The rough serf crashed incessantly.   **(Fixation n: Prime)**

```
          |   *
```
The rough surf crashed incessantly.   **(Fixation n: Target)**

Other possible primes: surf, self, loan

Fig. 2. Illustration of the fast-priming paradigm in reading. As with the boundary paradigm (see Fig. 1a), before an invisible boundary is crossed, a preview string is in the target location (line 1). However, in this case the preview string is a random string of letters. When the boundary is crossed, the preview string is changed to the prime (line 2). The prime is then left on until a predetermined time after the beginning of the initial fixation on the target word location. Within 6 ms of this time, the prime word is changed to the target word (line 3). As with the preview experiments, the nature of the prime can be manipulated.

40 ms.[3] Our best construal of this pattern is: (a) that the phonological code of the prime at shorter prime durations is not yet fully developed enough for the homophone to prime better than its control; and (b) that subjects are sometimes aware of the prime on at least some trials at longer prime durations, and thus there may be inhibitory effects that neutralize the priming effects.

Three other points are worth noting about the fast priming experiments. The first is that an *orthographic priming* effect (the difference between a prime that is orthographically similar to the target with one that is very different from the target) is obtained at all prime durations and appears to be a more or less constant value within each experiment. The second is that there is also a *semantic priming* effect, which also appears within a narrow time window. What is especially worth noting is that it appears no earlier than the phonological priming effect and possibly later when they were directly compared (H.-W. Lee, Rayner and Pollatsek, 1999). The third is the effect of frequency and/or lexicality of the prime on the homophone priming effect. Note that the homophone priming effect in Experiment 2 of Lee, Binder, Kim, Pollatsek and Rayner (1999) was smaller than in the other experiments presented in Table 1. This is because the frequency of the prime was manipulated and half the words had low-frequency primes. In fact, the priming

---

3 The Rayner et al. (1995) data contradict the generalization somewhat, because there was no phonological priming at 30 ms. However, this experiment was done with an older monitor and with a less satisfactory font; hence extraction of codes from the prime may have taken longer in this experiment.

Table 1

Results from fast priming experiments

Nominal prime duration [a]	Phonological priming experiment [b]			
	Rayner et al. (1995)	Y.-A. Lee et al. (1999) Expt. 1	Y.-A. Lee et al. (1999) Expt. 2	H.-W. Lee et al. (1999)
24 ms	2 ms	–	–	–
29–30 ms	1 ms	–	–	41 ms
32 ms	–	–	16 ms	31 ms
35–36 ms	30 ms	30 ms	–	45 ms
38 ms	–	–	−2 ms	−5 ms
41–42 ms	–	−20 ms	–	5 ms

	Orthographic priming experiment [c]			
	Rayner et al. (1995)	Y.-A. Lee et al. (1999) Expt. 1	Y.-A. Lee et al. (1999) Expt. 2	H.-W. Lee et al. (1999)
24 ms	26 ms	–	–	–
29–30 ms	37 ms	–	–	35 ms
32 ms	–	–	39 ms	57 ms
35–36 ms	39 ms	30 ms	–	57 ms
38 ms	–	–	37 ms	61 ms
41–42 ms	–	33 ms	–	59 ms

	Semantic priming experiment [d]	
	Sereno and Rayner (1992)	H.-W. Lee et al. (1999)
24 ms	2 ms	–
29–30 ms	1 ms	5 ms
32 ms	–	37 ms
35–36 ms	30 ms	12 ms
38 ms	–	13 ms
41–42 ms	–	13 ms

[a] The actual prime duration equals the nominal prime duration plus a random component ranging from 0 to 6 ms to repaint the screen. Hence the actual mean prime duration is equal to the nominal prime duration plus 3 ms.

[b] Difference in gaze duration between orthographic control prime and homophone prime.

[c] Difference in gaze duration between an orthographically dissimilar condition and an orthographically similar condition. In all experiments besides H.-W. Lee et al. (1999), the latter was the orthographic control for the homophones.

[d] Difference in gaze duration between semantic control prime and semantically related prime.

effect for the high-frequency primes was quite similar to the priming effects in the other experiments (41 ms) but was actually −8 ms for the low-frequency primes. Y.-A. Lee et al. (1999) also investigated phonological priming effects for pseudohomophone primes (all the data in Table 1 are for word homophone primes). There was no consistent evidence for phonological priming obtained from pseudohomophones: 6 and −11 ms priming effects in Experiment 1 and 6 and −11 ms in Experiment 2 at the shorter and longer prime durations, respectively. (Rayner et al., 1995, however, found a marginally significant pseudohomophone priming effect at the same prime duration on which they found a homophone priming effect.)

It is clear that much still needs to be learned about the fast priming paradigm. Nonetheless, we think that several points from the fast-priming research are clear. The first is that phonological codes are activated relatively early in a fixation and guide the identification of a word in reading. These results, together with those from the preview experiments, indicate that phonological coding appears to be a natural part of the early stages of word encoding in reading: occurring both before a word is fixated and during the first 30 ms or so when it is fixated. The second is that phonological coding occurs at least as rapidly as semantic coding during a fixation. Moreover, so far, there is only negative evidence for a purely semantic or morphemic preview effect in reading (Rayner and Pollatsek, 1989; Rayner, 1998). Thus, phonological coding appears to be occurring well in advance of semantic coding. This temporal priority does not necessarily mean that there is a causal link whereby phonological codes activate semantic codes, but does indicate that at least some phonological coding is pre-semantic. The third is that the (at best weak) phonological priming effect from pseudohomophones and low-frequency words indicates that lexical activation is involved in early phonological coding. This could either be due to a 'direct look-up' of the phonological code from the lexical entry or to a more complex interactive process, whereby early phonological coding feeds into the orthographic lexicon (or its equivalent in a distributed representation) and then gets excitatory feedback in the case of high-frequency words.

Semantic judgment tasks

The categorical judgment paradigm is commonly cited to document the important role of phonological coding in obtaining the meaning of a word (Van Orden, 1987). In this paradigm, a category label (e.g., *flower*) is given, followed by a *probe* word; the task is to judge whether the probe word denotes an exemplar of the category. Of critical importance are trials on which the probe word is a homophone of a category exemplar (e.g., *rows*). The critical finding is that there are massive interference effects for these trials compared to trials on which the probe word is an orthographic control (e.g., *robs*): in many experiments, there are error rate differences of 10% or greater and response time differences of 100 ms or more. These results appear to argue strongly and directly that sound coding is employed to access the meanings of words. That is, if meaning were solely accessed by a visual and/or orthographic coding scheme, there would be no reason to expect that a homophone would access the meaning of the category word any more than the control word.

There are two primary concerns with the paradigm. The first (Jared and Seidenberg, 1991) is that the effect only appears to occur for low-frequency words when *broad* categories (e.g., living thing) are used. This suggests that at least part of the effect may be due to the category 'priming' the homophone. However, it is worth pointing out that, even if this effect occurred only for 'primed' words, there would still be a phonological component, as the observed phenomenon is a difference between the homophone and the orthographic control. The second concern (Taft, 1991) is that the orthographic controls employed in these experiments are not real controls as the homophones are putatively more orthographically similar to the exemplars than are the controls. (The latter criticism could also be extended to the above reading experiments.) Neither criticism is particularly easy to refute as the notions of 'priming' and 'orthographic similarity' are both fairly vague.

Before returning to these criticisms, it will be helpful to introduce another type of manipulation that has been used to get at the nature of the phonological coding causing the interference in this paradigm. Van Orden, Johnston and Hale (1988) introduced pseudohomophones into the judgment task (e.g., subjects were asked whether *sute* was an article of clothing). Quite surprisingly, they found an interference effect roughly comparable to that when homophones were used, suggesting that the phonological coding process involved was largely without guidance from any kind of orthographic lexical information.

Lesch and Pollatsek (1998) explored the issue in a somewhat different way, using a slightly different task: a *semantic relatedness judgment* on two simultaneously presented words. One motivation for changing the task from category judgment to semantic relatedness was that there were a relatively limited number of target words and many were difficult to place in a natural semantic category. Lesch and Pollatsek included homophone foils (e.g., *beech–sand* with a control of *bench–sand*) and obtained effects similar to that obtained in the categorical judgment task (error rate differences of 10% and significant RT differences that varied from 50 to 100 ms) in three experiments. Of greater interest were *false homophone* stimuli (e.g., *pillow–bead* with a control of *pillow–bend*). These were dubbed 'false homophones' because *bead* could be a homophone of *bed*: the body *-ead* can be pronounced the same way as the body in *bed* (e.g., as in *dead*), but it just happens to be pronounced differently for *bead*. The interesting finding was that there was a reduced, but significant, interference effect for these false homophones: in Experiments 1 and 2, there were significant RT effects (about 40–50 ms) but no error rate differences, and in Experiment 3, there was a significant 5% difference in error rates, but little RT difference.

In sum, the findings of Van Orden et al. (1988) and of Lesch and Pollatsek (1998) both indicate that the phonological code that is causing the interference is not merely looked up in the following sequence: letter string → orthographic lexicon → phonological code → semantic interference. If that were the case, non-words would not produce any interference — nor would false homophones, whose lexical entry does not yield the appropriate phonological code.

In addition, the experiments of Lesch and Pollatsek (1998) allow for a test of whether the main interference effect is merely due to uncontrolled differences in orthographic similarity. The argument that Taft (1991) raised against the homophone experiments is that the homophones are more orthographically similar to the correct target words than are the controls. For example, Taft would argue that if the target word was *beech*, then the homophone *beach* is more similar to it than is the control *bench*. There are various components of the argument, but the most subtle is that the letter combinations *-ee-* and *-ea-* are likely to be extremely orthographically similar because they can represent the same sound. On some level, that appears to be conceding that the 'orthographic' code is actually phonological. However, one can argue that this correlation between orthographic and phonological similarity is a function of the learning history of the organism, but that no phonological code is actually accessed at the time of encoding the word *beach* during the experiment.

We think that the difference between the false homophones and the true homophones in the Lesch and Pollatsek (1998) experiments, however, indicates that the whole interference effect cannot be explained even by this kind of orthographic similarity. That is, by Taft's argument, *cowl* (false homophone of *coal*) and *coil* should be as orthographically different as *rein* (homophone of *rain*) and *ruin*, and so the interference effects should be of equal sizes for the two classes of characters. Instead, there was virtually no interference effect in the error rates in Experiments 1 and 2 for the false homophones, but a 10% difference for the true homophones. We recently conducted new analyses on the stimuli of Experiments 1 and 2 on well-matched pairs of homophones (16 pairs in Experiment 1 and 20 pairs in Experiment 2) and found differences in the error rates that were virtually identical to those in the full analysis. (These differences for these purified lists were significant in both experiments.) Thus, what is relevant is not only what the orthographic pattern *could* sound like, but what it *actually* sounds like.

A second piece of evidence against Taft's hypothesis is the frequency effect found in the phonological fast priming effect. That is, if the difference between the homophones and their orthographic controls is merely that the homophones are more orthographically similar to the targets than are the controls, then the frequency of the prime should have little influence on the size of this putative orthographic similarity effect. In fact, one could think of arguments why more rapid access of a competing lexical entry (in the case of the high-frequency homophone primes) should produce more interference and hence less priming. (It should be noted that the frequency of the target had no effect on the size of the phonological priming effect.) In addition, if the phonological fast priming effect was truly an orthographic effect, the temporal pattern seems wrong. That is, the pattern of orthographic priming appears to be largely independent of prime duration, whereas the phonological priming effect is essentially zero at smaller prime durations and then becomes approximately equal to the orthographic priming effect at nominal prime durations of about 30–36 ms.

To summarize, the above data from preview and fast priming experiments in English indicate that phonological codes are extracted early in reading and appear to be extracted at least as early as semantic codes. The results from the categorical and semantic relatedness tasks indicate that phonological codes are not only extracted rapidly, but are functional in accessing the meaning of a word. Moreover, the differences observed between homophones and their orthographic controls are not plausibly due to uncontrolled differences in orthographic similarity to the targets between these two classes of stimuli. We have not dealt with the other criticism of the homophone interference effect — that it may be restricted to situations in which the word is 'primed'. However, the phonological effects observed in the preview and fast priming techniques are certainly not due to semantic priming of the target words. The sentence frames were set up so that these words were not predictable from sentence context. We will return to this issue in the next section.

Phonological coding in reading Chinese

In this section, we discuss some of our recent research investigating phonological coding in reading Chinese characters. Chinese is of interest in the current context for two main reasons. The first, indicated earlier, is that it has often been thought that it is extremely unlikely for phonological coding to be of any importance in decoding Chinese characters because the orthography is not alphabetic. The second is that, unlike in English, orthographic and phonological similarity can be easily unconfounded. That is, in English, most homophones are orthographically and visually similar to each other as well as sounding alike; in contrast, homophones in Chinese can often have no orthographic or visual similarity. Our results indicate, however, that contrary to the intuition that phonological coding should be unimportant in Chinese, it appears to occur early in decoding Chinese characters. Moreover, there are phonological effects observed in Chinese that are extremely unlikely to be due to uncontrolled effects of orthographic similarity.

Parafoveal preview effects
We conducted three experiments investigating parafoveal preview effects in Chinese (Pollatsek, Tan and Rayner, 1999). They all used the same single word naming paradigm as the one discussed above in Pollatsek et al. (1992). A single Chinese

character appeared almost five degrees to the right of fixation. (However, the character was larger than normal print.) The subject rapidly moved his or her eyes to fixate the character and named it. As in the parafoveal preview naming study in English, the subjects were unable to identify the preview stimulus. [4] The logic was similar to the parafoveal preview studies in English; a brief description of Chinese orthography, however, is probably necessary to explain the design.

First, a character in Chinese represents both a syllable and a morpheme. The average Chinese word is two characters long; however, the single characters employed in the experiment were also words. [5] Second, there are two types of characters, *unified* and *compound*. Unified characters have no recognizable subunits, whereas compound characters have two components (usually written side-by-side) called *radicals*. Moreover, for most (but not all) compound characters, the two radicals have different functions. One of the radicals is a *phonetic radical* and the other is a *semantic radical*. The semantic radical usually gives a clue as to the meaning of the word and the phonetic radical gives a clue as to the sound of the word. Most phonetic radicals can occur in isolation as unified characters; however, about two-thirds of the time, the compound character is pronounced differently from the phonetic radical. Thus, the phonetic radical is an unreliable guide to the pronunciation of a character. The semantic radical can also have a different meaning from the compound character it is in; however, it is a more reliable indicator of the semantics than the phonological radical is of the pronunciation.

About 85% of the characters in common use in Chinese are compound characters consisting of a semantic and phonological radical (Perfetti and Tan, 1999; Zhu, 1988); we used only characters of this form as targets in the experiments. A major reason for using compound characters (besides their frequency in the language) was that orthographic similarity can be varied easily. The orthographically similar characters shared a radical (the phonetic radical in the case of the phonological preview targets and the semantic radical in the case of the semantic preview targets of Experiment 2). A preview stimulus that was orthographically dissimilar to the target shared neither radical and had no visual similarity to the target beyond the fact that they are both compound characters. Note that it is possible, however, to have non-homophones sharing a phonetic radical and to have semantically unrelated

---

4 Due to limitations of our software, the Chinese characters were fairly large (larger than would be normal for text). Thus, the eccentricity of the characters was larger than for the typical parafoveal preview naming study in English. The actual value of the eccentricity was determined by pilot work, in which the character was moved in as close as it could to the initial fixation point consistent with it not being identified.

5 The basic unit in Chinese is the morpheme, as fluent Chinese (including linguists) can disagree where word boundaries should be placed.

words sharing a semantic radical because of the inconsistency of both types of radicals.

There was clear evidence of phonological involvement in identifying Chinese characters. First, consider the phonological preview data. In all three experiments, target characters preceded by a homophone preview were named 20–30 ms faster than the control stimuli (the differences were significant in all three experiments). This is most notable in terms of the orthographically dissimilar homophone previews, which shared no orthographic features with the targets. The one somewhat odd feature of the data is that in Experiment 1 (but not in Experiments 2 and 3), the homophone previews also produced higher error rates than did the control previews. We do not understand why the error pattern was different in Experiment 1, but it is important to note that homophony of the preview still had a significant influence on processing even there. In addition, there was no benefit from preview characters that shared the initial phoneme with the target, so that it is unlikely that the homophone preview benefit is due to facilitating the motor programming for naming

The data from Experiments 2 and 3 indicated that orthographic similarity, by itself, also produced a significant preview benefit: previews that shared a phonetic radical but were non-homophones and previews that shared a semantic radical but were semantically unrelated also produced a significant preview benefit. The evidence for semantic preview effects was more equivocal, however, as there was a preview benefit from synonyms in only one of the three conditions using synonyms in the study.

In sum, the preview data from compound Chinese characters appear to be roughly equivalent to those obtained in parafoveal naming experiments in English. First, in both languages, there appears to be significant preview benefit when there is homophony. Second, in Chinese as in English (e.g., Pollatsek et al., 1992; Rayner, McConkie and Ehrlich, 1978), there appears to be significant preview benefit when there is orthographic similarity. Moreover, in Chinese, these two manipulations can be unconfounded, so that it appears that either effect can occur in the absence of the other. Third, in English, as mentioned earlier, there is no benefit when the preview is only semantically (or morphologically) similar to the target. The data above suggest that there may be a semantic preview benefit effect in Chinese and thus that Chinese may be processed differently from English. As the semantic preview effect in Chinese was somewhat ephemeral, however, it needs to be confirmed in order to conclude that there is any significant difference in the pattern of preview benefit between the two orthographies.

The problem with the above experiments in Chinese, of course, is that the task was naming, so that phonological involvement may merely be driven by the requirement to produce a vocal response. In English, however, the preview effects obtained in reading (both orthographic and phonological) have been pretty much the same as in naming. (Note the similarity of the sizes of the phonological effects in the naming and reading experiments of Pollatsek et al., 1992, discussed earlier.) Moreover, another lab has, in fact, reported a phonological preview effect in reading Chinese (Liu and Inhoff, 1996). In this experiment, subjects read Chinese sentences for meaning, and previews could either be orthographically similar or homophones. A significant preview benefit occurred for both types of preview (compared to dissimilar previews). However, the phonological preview effect surfaced somewhat later than the orthographic effect — only on the fixation after the target character. This suggests that the phonological information from the preview may be affecting processing somewhat later than the orthographic processing in Chinese. However, it is good to keep in mind that characters are not necessarily words in Chinese.

Semantic judgment

Another study also indicates that phonology is involved in accessing the meaning of Chinese words (Xu, Pollatsek and Potter, 1999). This was a semantic judgment task similar to that of Lesch and Pollatsek (1998), except that the stimuli were presented sequentially. That is, two Chinese words were presented sequentially, and the participants were asked to judge whether the second *probe* word was semantically related to the first. (The probe word was always a single compound character.) As in the Van Orden paradigm, the trials of primary importance were those in which the probe word was a homophone and/or orthographically similar to a word related to the first word. In Experiment 1, orthographic similarity (phonetic radical overlap) and homophony were factorially varied. Thus, the distractor probe stimulus could be either a homophone of a word semantically related to the first word, orthographically similar to a word semantically related to the first word, neither, or both. (There were obviously also trials on which the probe word was semantically related to the first word.)

The first finding of interest in Experiment 1 was that there was a significant homophone interference effect. The error rate difference was bigger when the homophones were orthographically related, but there was still a significant homo-phone interference effect even when there was no orthographic similarity. Second, there was also a large effect of orthographic similarity, which appeared to be larger than the homophone effect. This suggests (as do the Liu and Inhoff results) that orthographic coding may play a somewhat larger role in Chinese relative to phonological coding than in English.

Experiment 2 eliminated all distractors that were orthographically similar to true semantic associates to determine whether the homophone effect observed in Experiment 1 might have been an artifact of slow processing induced by these kinds of orthographic confusions. In fact, the homophone interference effect was about the same size (5%) as that observed in Experiment 1 for the orthographically dissimilar homophones. The second finding of interest in Experiment 2 was that there was no homophone effect for words which were homophones except that they differed in 'tone'.[6] Thus, it appears that, in Chinese, the phonological codes have to be exactly the same to produce interference.

Summary of results

In both English and Chinese, the data indicate that phonological coding is an integral component of printed word recognition in reading. In both languages, there is evidence that phonological codes are extracted from a word before it is fixated, which facilitates the processing of the word when it is later fixated. These data cover both reading (Pollatsek et al., 1992, Experiment 2; Liu and Inhoff, 1996) and naming (Pollatsek et al., 1992, Experiment 1; Pollatsek et al., in press). Moreover, the fast priming data in English (H.-W. Lee et al., 1999; Y.-A. Lee et al., 1999; Rayner et al., 1995) suggest that phonological codes are extracted early in a fixation as well. The semantic judgment data in both English and Chinese also indicate that phonological coding is a key component of extracting the meaning of a word. The convergence of results from all these tasks makes it unlikely that phonological coding is some sort of epiphenomenon in the reading task. Because these two languages are, for reasons indicated earlier, likely to be the languages most problematic for phonological coding to be important, it seems likely that phonological coding is important in decoding all written languages.

There are two loose ends, however, that are somewhat puzzling. The first is that the fast priming data seem to indicate that early extraction of phonological codes is largely post-lexical, as there was little phonological priming from pseudowords or low-frequency words. In contrast, the data from the semantic judgment tasks (Lesch and Pollatsek, 1998; Van Orden et al., 1988) suggest a strong prelexical component to the phonological code subserving identification of word meanings. In addition, a parafoveal preview study employing a lexical decision task (Henderson, Dixon, Petersen, Twilley and Ferreira, 1995) found greater preview benefit for phonologically regular words than for phonologically irregular words, again suggesting

---

6 Chinese is a tonal language in that different fundamental frequency (F0) contours indicate different tones for otherwise identical phonemes. Chinese Mandarin dialect has four major tones (four different F0 contours). The same consonant–vowel pairs with different tones specify completely different lexical items. Characters that share the same consonants and vowels but different tones are mostly semantically unrelated, although sometimes they may share the same phonetic radical. Tone in Chinese has some resemblance to intonation in English, although intonation in English rarely carries lexical information.

that prelexical phonology enters into word identification early in processing.[7] The second is the slightly peculiar involvement of phonological coding in the Chinese preview studies. In one of the naming studies (Pollatsek et al., 1992), a phonological preview seemed to increase errors. Why this would happen is not clear. In addition, in the reading study (Liu and Inhoff, 1996), the facilitative effect of a phonological preview surfaced only after the character had been fixated (even though the information had been extracted before the character was fixated). These phenomena in the Chinese preview studies, as well as the apparently larger orthographic interference effects in the semantic judgment task, suggest that phonology may play a somewhat smaller part in Chinese word recognition than in English word recognition. However, cross-orthographic and cross-language comparisons are hazardous, because it would be hard to equate orthographic similarity or confusability across the two languages.

The homophonic reading paradigm

It is probably also worth discussing a paradigm in which data have been obtained that are apparently at variance with the conclusion that phonological codes are activated early in the reading process (Chapter 17; Daneman and Reingold, 1993; Daneman, Reingold and Davidson, 1995). In this paradigm, people silently read text while their eye movements are monitored, but certain target words in the text are altered. There are essentially three conditions of interest. In one, the target word is unaltered (e.g., ... a funny vain little man ...), whereas in the other two, it is changed either to a homophone (e.g., *vein*) or to an orthographic control word (e.g., *vine*). (Individual subjects, of course, only see one of the three versions for each target word.) The key question of interest is how 'first-pass' measures of reading on the target words (which presumably tap early processing of the word) differ among the three conditions.

The findings of Daneman and coworkers are as follows: (a) there are significant differences between the correct homophone and wrong homophone conditions on gaze duration; and (b) there are no significant differences between the wrong homophone and orthographic control conditions in any of their studies (although most find some advantage for the wrong homophone condition). In contrast, they

---

7 It is worth noting that Pollatsek et al. (in press) also observed a 'regularity effect' in Chinese. As mentioned earlier, the phonetic radical has a pronunciation in isolation. Thus, in 'regular' characters, the pronunciation of the character is identical to the radical in isolation, whereas for irregular characters, the pronunciation of the radical in isolation and the pronunciation of the character differ. The regularity effect observed was about 15 ms, and unlike the roughly analogous regularity effect in English, it was not smaller for high-frequency characters.

find large differences between the wrong homophone and orthographic control conditions in later 'second pass' measures. From these findings, they argue that sound coding only occurs late in the reading process (i.e., after the meaning of the word has been initially encoded).

Space precludes a full discussion of the issue, so we will just confine ourselves to a few remarks. The first is that the presence of these 'errors' in the text makes this a somewhat unnatural reading task. Given that the instructions are vague (to avoid having readers dwell on the errors), it is not clear how they are in fact treated. However, it is reasonable to assume that the reading process is changed either because the reader has to engage in problem solving to figure out what word 'should have been there' or because subjects might suspect they will be asked memory questions about the changed words (or both). One feature that makes us suspect that this is not normal reading is that the target words were fixated virtually all the time (even if unchanged), which is not the usual case in normal reading for words as short as many of these target words were.

The second remark is that the pattern described above has not always been observed in this paradigm. Rayner, Pollatsek and Binder (1998) found a different pattern when the target words were predictable from prior sentence context, consistent with a model that posits an early role for phonology. They found, for these predictable target words, that first fixation durations and single fixation durations (when readers made only one fixation on the word) on the wrong homophones were virtually the same as those on the correct word when the wrong homophone was orthographically similar to the correct one. In contrast, for these same targets, first fixation durations on the wrong homophones were shorter than for the orthographic controls. (Moreover, on about half the trials there was no evidence at any later point in the sentence of any 'double take' for having read the wrong homophone.) These data, for the predictable, orthographically similar, homophones are more in line with an early phonology model such as a verification model in which the sound code is accessed first, followed by a 'spelling check' against the orthographic representation. That is, the sentence predictability creates an expectation of a word to come, and if it 'sounds like a match', early processing is not disrupted, whereas if it does not sound like a match, early processing is disrupted. The putative later verification process takes some additional time, and because the homophones here are close orthographic matches, detection of a mismatch should be relatively slow and, in this case, it is too slow to affect first fixation times (although it did affect gaze duration times).

When the predictable homophones were less orthographically similar, Rayner et al. (1998) did find differences on first fixation duration between the right and wrong homophones, but also found significant differences between the wrong homophones and the orthographic controls. This pattern of data is also consistent with the early phonology view above. That is, when the homophones are less orthographically similar, the process of detecting a mismatch in the spelling check stage should be quicker. Thus, it is reasonable to think that the wrong homophone could be detected more rapidly than when it is orthographically similar to the correct one, and thus that the verification process is plausibly fast enough to affect first fixation durations. Admittedly, this pattern of data is ambiguous and it could easily be reconciled with a late phonology view as well.

Thus the Rayner et al. (1998) data with predictable target words are consistent with an early phonology view and all the other findings summarized in this chapter. Now we turn to the third point, which is how to interpret this paradigm when the target words are not predictable from sentence context, which was usually the case in the work of Daneman and coworkers. Rayner et al. (1998) also included a low predictability condition and got the same ambiguous pattern as that described in the prior paragraph: correct homophones yielded shorter fixations than wrong homophones and wrong homophones yielded shorter fixations than orthographic controls. (This pattern is thus somewhat different from that observed by Daneman and coworkers.)

More generally, the results from the homophone reading paradigm have been inconsistent: some data appear to support an early phonology view and other data appear to support a late phonology view and most of it (including the data in Chapter 17) is consistent with either. For example, Jared, Levy and Rayner (1999) reported results of three eye movement experiments which were consistent with both views, and suggested that reading ability, the amount of contextual constraint, and word frequency of the homophone all influenced the pattern of results. Jared et al. also reported three proofreading experiments, which Daneman and Stainton (1991) used to argue (contrary to the eye movement experiments of Daneman and colleagues) for the early involvement of phonological codes in reading, which likewise demonstrated that the pattern of data depends on a number of factors.

It is important to note that the homophone reading paradigm is not tapping the speed of word identification, but instead the process by which the identified meaning or meanings activated by a letter string are judged as being anomalous with the sentence context. We think that the latter process is likely to be complex, especially in the low predictability condition because no word is expected in this condition. Thus, the process being studied is not whether the orthographic string matches an expected meaning (as in the high predictability condition), but instead, is a process of encoding the meaning or meanings activated by the target string and then deciding how well they fit with the prior context. Moreover, the decision 'does not fit with the prior context' has to be decisive and rapid to be able to cause the eye movement system significant 'early' trouble (i.e., at the time the target word is fixated).

But this is a complex situation that is difficult to analyze. Consider the example given above of 'the funny vain little man'. When the reader encounters *vein* or *vine* in this context, neither word seems blatantly anomalous until the next word or two of text is decoded (and there is little in the prior text as well to make either of them particularly anomalous). One can get ratings to get the 'degree of anomaly', but that is a conscious, reflective, judgment and may not reflect how anomaly is detected 'on-line'. (In addition, participants may be subtly biased by the homophony to rate the homophone as less anomalous than it really is, so that the homophones rated as equally anomalous may be more anomalous.) Moreover, the task of deciding 'anomaly here!' is not really comparable for the homophone and the spelling control. That is, according to an early phonology view, both meanings of the wrong homophone are accessed (the one that fits in with the passage and the one that does not), and thus it might actually be faster, in some cases, to detect that the wrong homophone (e.g., *vein*) is 'wrong' than to detect that the orthographic control (e.g., *vine*) is 'wrong' because the meaning of the homophone consistent with the target word *vain* has also been accessed and serves as a signal that 'something is wrong'.

We should note in this regard that there is excellent corroborative evidence that both meanings of homophones are accessed in normal reading (Chapter 16; Folk, 1999). Although there are several lines of evidence for this assertion (see Morris and Folk in Chapter 16), space limitations allow only a brief description of one. Morris and Folk included sentences in which the sentence prior to a low-frequency homophone, such as *thyme*, was consistent with both *thyme* and its much higher frequency mate, *time*. Quite remarkably, readers regressed back to *thyme* as much in this situation (when later context made clear that the 'herb' meaning was intended) as with homographic homophones (Duffy, Morris and Rayner, 1988) such as *calf* (when later context made clear the 'body part' meaning was intended). These data (and other aspects of the Morris and Folk data) only make sense if the reader first encoded the sound of the word and often encoded the higher-frequency meaning, even when the orthography of the higher-frequency meaning was inconsistent with the word actually presented in the text. That is, these data indicate that encoding of meaning often went through the sound code without an 'orthography check', even with no prior biasing context.

This raises the question of why the Morris and Folk data are so consistent with an early phonology model, even though they came from a paradigm that involved reading text with no display changes (as did the data of Daneman and coworkers). Daneman and Reingold (Chapter 17) appear to conclude that the key difference is that they used extended passages, whereas Morris and Folk used single sentences and our homophonic reading experiments used short passages. It strikes us as being implausible that sound coding is used for word encoding only in short passages or single sentences, as extended passages supply readers with greater context than one or two sentences, and thus would be likely to encourage more use of 'top-down' information for word identification and thus careful examination of the orthography would be less likely. Instead, we think it is more plausible that the presence of the relatively frequent misspellings in the homophone reading task often caused readers to engage in a problem solving task, and thus to examine the orthography more closely than is normal in silent reading.

The nature of phonological coding

The discussion of the plausibility of phonological coding at the beginning of this chapter suggested certain questions about the nature of phonological coding. That is, if one grants that the above data have indicated that phonological coding plays an important part in extracting the meaning of words in reading, the question remains as to what kind of beast this phonological code is. Below we discuss two questions about the phonological code used in silent reading. The first is whether the code extracted is close to an acoustic code (i.e., is in a form similar to that of the acoustic wave form of the speech signal) or is a relatively abstract phonological code (i.e., similar to a sequence of abstract phonemes).

Is the phonological code 'abstract' or acoustic?

One experiment (Birch, Pollatsek and Kingston, 1998) attempted to assess this issue using *acoustic pseudohomophones* (henceforth *acoustic PHs*). That is, acoustic PHs are non-words that are homophones (or very near homophones) at the acoustic level (e.g., *racts* is an acoustic PH of *racks*), but are not homophones at an abstract phonemic level. (In this case, the *t* in *racts* is represented at an abstract phonetic level, but is lost in the speech stream.) Birch et al. had subjects make two kinds of judgments on these acoustic PHs and 'real' PHs (i.e., the normal type of pseudohomophone that is a homophone at both acoustic and abstract levels of representation). In one experiment, subjects had to judge whether the letter strings (all non-words) 'sounded like real words', and in the other experiment, they had to judge whether the letter strings were real words (i.e., a lexical decision task). In the 'sounds like' task, subjects were not given feedback, because a key question was whether they would categorize acoustic PHs as real words or not.

The findings from the two tasks were somewhat different. In the 'sounds like' task, there appeared to be a substantial difference between the acoustic PHs and the 'real' PHs; subjects classified the acoustic PHs as real words much less frequently than the 'real' PH controls. However, they did judge the acoustic PHs to sound like real words more than their orthographic controls. (Because of the high error rates, RT differences were hard to interpret.) In the lexical decision task, phonological involvement was assessed by the *pseudohomophone interference effect*, the difficulty subjects had in classifying a PH as a non-word, relative to an orthographic control. In fact, there were roughly equal interference effects for the two types of PHs, suggesting that the phonological code producing the pseudohomophone interference effect in the lexical decision task was a surface acoustic code rather than an abstract phonological code.

The Birch et al. (1998) data indicate that the phonological code used may be task dependent. Birch et al. concluded that tasks that require introspection about the sound code, such as the 'sounds like' task, may involve an abstract phonological code as well as a surface level phonological code, whereas tasks, such as lexical decision, which are faster and are likely to discourage conscious phonological coding, mainly involve acoustic phonological codes. On the basis of these data, they speculated that the lexical decision task is more like silent reading and that the phonological code employed in silent reading is more likely to be a surface acoustic code. Needless to say, this conclusion is highly speculative. First, lexical decision is not reading. Second, because the key data in the sounds like task were errors and those in the lexical decision task were RTs, it is a bit difficult to compare the two experiments. Third, it was quite difficult to equate the acoustic PHs and 'real' PHs exactly on their orthographic similarity to real words. Nonetheless, the data are interesting and suggest a distinction that can be explored in future research.

Is the phonological code developed in stages?

At the outset of this chapter, we raised the question of whether a phonological code was a code that extends in time (analogous to a speech signal). We will return to this question below, but this question, in turn, raises another question: is the phonological code constructed in a sequential fashion? The classic proposal for how a phonological code is constructed sequentially is that it is put together left-to-right by applying a series of grapheme-to-phoneme conversion (GPC) rules (Coltheart, 1978). An interesting alternative, recently proposed by Berent and Perfetti (1995) is that consonants are the essential 'backbone' of the phonological code and are developed first, with vowels being added in a later stage.

Berent and Perfetti's evidence for this comes from a backward masking paradigm in which there is a briefly presented target followed by an even more briefly presented masking letter string, which is then followed by a pattern mask that masks the masking letter string (Berent and Perfetti, 1995; see Chapter 14 for a more complete description of this paradigm). The involvement of phonological coding in this paradigm is indexed by a reduction in masking. That is, earlier work by Perfetti, Bell and Delaney (1988) indicated that a homophone masked the target word less than an orthographic control word did. (It is worth noting that people can rarely report the masking stimulus, and hence this result is not plausibly due to identifying the masking stimulus and then guessing the target.) The interesting finding of Berent and Perfetti was that for brief target durations, masks that preserved consonants of targets (e.g., *reez* as a mask of *rose*) were as effective as actual homophones (e.g., *roze* as a mask of *rose*). In contrast, at longer target durations, the homophone masks produced higher target identification rates than did the masks that agreed with the targets only on the consonant sounds. As indicated above, they concluded from these data that only consonants may be specified in the initial stages of phonological code formation and that vowels are fully specified later.

We (Lee, Rayner and Pollatsek, in press) were interested in testing this hypothesis in a paradigm closer to silent reading, so we used a variant of the fast priming technique described earlier. In this paradigm, the prime contained a missing letter (which was replaced by a hyphen). For example, either *w-lk* or *wa-k* was a prime for *walk*, or *pl-n* or *p-an* was a prime for *plan*. As in the other fast priming studies, the task was to read a sentence for meaning and the gaze duration on the target word was the major dependent variable. Analogous to Berent and Perfetti, at the short prime duration (30 ms), the prime with the vowel missing was a significantly better prime than the one with the consonant missing, whereas at the longer prime duration (60 ms), both primes were equally effective. (Note that the missing vowels and consonants were each equally often in the second and third letter position.) Thus, in English, it appears that consonant information is utilized in constructing a phonological code more rapidly than vowel information.

There is a body of evidence (see Chapter 14), however, that indicates that the pattern in the masking paradigm is quite different for Italian than for English, with no early advantage for consonant information (and in fact an indication that the pattern in Italian is the opposite of that in English). This suggests that there is no structural constraint in the phonological processing system that requires that a consonantal scaffolding be created before vowel information is incorporated into the phonological code. Instead, it suggests that the pattern may be determined by idiosyncracies of the orthographic and phonological systems of a particular language. In this case, (a) English has many more vowel sounds than Italian, and (b) the orthographic system for representing vowels in English is the most irregular part of the orthography, whereas the orthographic representation of vowels in Italian is about as regular as for consonants.

This pattern of results suggests the following argument about how the phonological code is constructed in alphabetic languages. The pattern in English indicates that consonantal representations in the phonological code tend to be formed first (as consonants are 'islands of regularity' in the grapheme to phoneme conversion). Thus, it appears that a completely serial left-to-right GPC conversion is not what occurs (at least in English). Instead, the pattern suggests either a parallel-interactive system (such as posited by a typical interactive PDP model) in which the consonantal information accrues first, or a type of GPC system that does not work in a strictly serial left-to-right fashion. The Italian data are certainly consistent with a parallel account in which the phonological information accrues at different rates in the two languages consistent with the 'consistency' of the local transformations. The Italian data could also be consistent with a serial account, but one in which the sequence of operations is not predetermined. In either case, the data seem to be arguing for the significance of local regularities, whether they be implemented as GPCs or by incorporating units functionally equivalent to bigrams, trigrams and the like (e.g., Plaut, McClelland, Seidenberg and Patterson, 1996; see Columbo, in Chapter 14, for an excellent discussion of this issue).

This leads us to one of the questions raised at the outset of the chapter: is the phonological code something that is sequential in time? The above discussion suggests that it is not necessarily formed in that manner from print, so that there does not need to be anything fundamentally 'sequential' in the code. Of course, this code must be attached to sequential components as one can presumably use it to 'play back' conscious inner speech. Moreover, if this code is also involved in the perception of spoken speech, then it must be interfaced with components that are sequential in time. The finding that the phonological code involved in the lexical decision task is not completely abstract and may be largely 'acoustic' suggests that there may in fact be a common code involved in speech perception and reading.

Summary

The work presented here indicates that phonological coding is an important component of the silent reading process in two languages, English and Chinese, that have often been thought to have orthographies that discourage phonological coding in going from print to meaning. The research indicates that phonological codes are extracted early in the reading process — even before word is fixated in text. Moreover, they are involved in accessing the meanings of words. Accompanying work on phonological coding suggests that (a) phonological codes may be closer in form to the acoustic speech stream than an abstract representation of phonemes, and (b) that they are not necessarily formed sequentially from left-to-right, and that the pattern of information accrual may depend on the language involved.

Acknowledgements

Preparation of this chapter was supported by Grant HD26765 from the National Institute of Health. The second author was also supported by a Research Scientist Award from the National Institute of Mental Health (MH01255).

References

Berent, I. and Perfetti, C.A. (1995). A rose is a reez: the two-cycles model of phonology assembly in reading English. Psychological Review, 102, 146–184.

Birch, S., Pollatsek, A. and Kingston, J. (1998). The nature of the sound codes accessed by visual language. Journal of Memory and Language, 38, 70–93.

Coltheart, M. (1978). Lexical access in simple reading tasks. In: G. Underwood (Ed.), Strategies of Information Processing. London: Academic Press, pp. 151–216.

Daneman, M. and Reingold, E. (1993). What eye fixations tell us about phonological recoding during reading. Canadian Journal of Experimental Psychology, 47, 153–178.

Daneman, M., Reingold, E.M. and Davidson, M. (1995). Time course of phonological activation during reading: evidence from eye fixations. Journal of Experimental Psychology: Learning, Memory, and Cognition, 21, 884–898.

Daneman, M. and Stainton, M. (1991). Phonological recoding in silent reading. Journal of Experimental Psychology: Learning, Memory, and Cognition, 17, 618–632.

Duffy, S.A., Morris, R.K. and Rayner, K. (1988). Lexical ambiguity and fixation times in reading. Journal of Memory and Language, 27, 429–446.

Folk, J.R. (1999). Phonological codes are used to access the lexicon during silent reading. Journals of Experimental Psychology: Learning, Memory and Cognition, 25, 892–906.

Henderson, J.M., Dixon, P., Petersen, A., Twilley, L.C. and Ferreira, F.C. (1995). Evidence for the use of phonological representations during transsaccadic word recognition. Journal of Experimental Psychology: Human Perception and Performance, 21, 82–97.

Jared, D., Levy, B.A. and Rayner, K. (1999). The role of phonology in the activation of word meanings during reading: evidence from proofreading and eye movements. Journal of Experimental Psychology: General, 128, 219–264.

Jared, D. and Seidenberg, M.S. (1991). Does word identification in reading proceed from spelling to sound to meaning? Journal of Experimental Psychology: General, 120, 358–394.

Lee, H., Rayner, K. and Pollatsek, A. (1999). The time course of phonological, semantic, and orthographic coding in reading: evidence from the fast priming technique. Psychonomic Bulletin and Review, 6, 624–634.

Lee, H., Rayner, K. and Pollatsek, A. (in press). The relative contribution of consonants and vowels in word recognition in reading.

Lee, Y.A., Binder, K.S., Kim, J., Pollatsek, A. and Rayner, K.(1999). Activation of phonological codes during eye fixations in reading. Journal of Experimental Psychology: Human Perception and Performance, 25, 948–964.

Lesch, M.F. and Pollatsek, A. (1998). Evidence for the use of assembled phonology in accessing the meaning of printed words. Journal of Experimental Psychology: Learning, Memory, and Cognition, 24, 573–592.

Liu, W. and Inhoff, A.W. (1996). Eye movements and the use of graphemic and phonological character information during the reading of Chinese sentences. Paper presented at the 37th Annual Meeting of the Psychonomic Society.

Perfetti, C.A., Bell, L.C. and Delaney, S.M. (1988). Automatic (prelexical) phonetic activation in silent word reading: evidence from backward masking. Journal of Memory and Language, 27, 59–70.

Perfetti, C.A. and Tan, L.H. (1999). The constituency model of Chinese word identification. In: J. Wang, A. Inhoff and H.C. Chen (Eds.), Reading Chinese Script: A Cognitive Analysis. Mahwah, NJ: Lawrence Erlbaum, pp. 115–134.

Plaut, D.C., McClelland, J.L., Seidenberg, M.S. and Patterson, K. (1996). Understanding normal and impaired word reading: computational principles in quasi-regular domains. Psychological Review, 103, 56–115.

Pollatsek, A., Lesch, M., Morris, R.M. and Rayner, K. (1992). Phonological codes are used in integrating information across saccades in word identification and reading. Journal of Experimental Psychology: Human Perception and Performance, 18, 148–162.

Pollatsek, A., Tan, L.H. and Rayner, K. (in press). The role of phonological codes in integrating information across saccadic eye movements in Chinese character identification. Journal of Experimental Psychology: Human Perception and Performance.

Rayner, K. (1975). The perceptual span and peripheral cues in reading. Cognitive Psychology, 7, 65–81.

Rayner, K. (1998). Eye movements in reading and information processing: 20 years of research. Psychological Bulletin, 124, 372–422.

Rayner, K., McConkie, G.W. and Ehrlich, S.F. (1978). Eye movements and integrating information across fixations. Journal of Experimental Psychology: Human Perception and Performance, 4, 529–544.

Rayner, K. and Pollatsek, A. (1989). The Psychology of Reading. Englewood Cliffs, NJ: Prentice-Hall.

Rayner, K., Pollatsek, A. and Binder, K. (1998). Phonological codes and eye movements in reading. Journal of Experimental Psychology: Learning, Memory, and Cognition, 24, 476–497.

Rayner, K., Sereno, S.C., Lesch, M.F. and Pollatsek, A. (1995). Phonological codes are automatically activated during reading: evidence from an eye movement priming paradigm. Psychological Science, 6, 26–30.

Sereno, S.C. and Rayner, K. (1992). Fast priming during eye fixations in reading. Journal of Experimental Psychology: Human Perception and Performance, 18, 173–184.

Share, D. (1999). Phonological recoding and orthographic learning: a direct test of the self-teaching hypothesis. Journal of Experimental Child Psychology, 72, 95–129.

Smith, F. (1971). Understanding Reading: A Psycholinguistic Analysis of Reading and Learning to Read. New York, NY: Holt, Rinehart and Winston.

Taft, M. (1991). Reading and the Mental Lexicon. Hove: Lawrence Erlbaum.

Van Orden, G.C. (1987). A ROWS is a ROSE: spelling, sound, and reading. Memory and Cognition, 15, 181–198.

Van Orden, G.C., Johnston, J.C. and Hale, B.L. (1988). Word identification in reading proceeds from spelling to sound to meaning. Journal of Experimental Psychology: Learning, Memory, and Cognition, 14, 371–386.

Xu, Y., Pollatsek, A. and Potter, M. (1999). The activation of phonology during silent Chinese word reading. Journal of Experimental Psychology: Learning, Memory and Cognition, 25, 838–857.

Zhu, X. (1988). Analysis of the cueing function of the phonetic in modern Chinese. In: Proceedings of the Symposium on the Chinese Language and Character. Beijing: Guang Ming Daily Press (in Chinese).

CHAPTER 16

Phonology is Used to Access Word Meaning during Silent Reading: Evidence from Lexical Ambiguity Resolution

Robin K. Morris
University of South Carolina

and

Jocelyn R. Folk
Kent State University

Abstract

This chapter reviews a series of eye movement studies that address the role of phonological information in accessing word meaning during silent reading by examining the role of phonological information in lexical ambiguity resolution. The data converge on a model of skilled silent reading in which phonological information is active early in word processing, and is involved in activating word meaning. The fact that effects of phonological information persist even when activation of that information is not to the readers' benefit, and that these effects persist even for high frequency words lead us to conclude that phonological coding is an integral part of early word processing in silent reading.

Reading as a Perceptual Process/A. Kennedy, R. Radach, D. Heller and J. Pynte (Editors)
© 2000 Elsevier Science Ltd. All rights reserved

Introduction

While there is considerable data documenting a role for phonological information
in skilled silent reading (e.g., Coltheart, Patterson and Leahy, 1994; Folk, 1999;
Folk and Morris, 1995; Inhoff and Topolski, 1994; Jared and Seidenberg, 1991;
Lesch and Pollatsek, 1993, 1998; Lukatela and Turvey, 1991; Pollatsek, Lesch,
Morris and Rayner, 1992; Rayner, Pollatsek and Binder, 1998; Rayner, Sereno,
Lesch and Pollatsek, 1995; Van Orden, 1987; Van Orden, Johnston and Hale, 1988)
there is also considerable debate concerning the nature of that role. Much of this
debate is centered on whether or not phonological codes are involved in accessing
the meaning of words in skilled silent reading.

Some researchers argue that phonological information is an obligatory part of
meaning activation (e.g., Lukatela and Turvey, 1991; Van Orden, 1987; Van Orden
et al., 1988). Others, however, assert that meaning activation occurs primarily via
orthography, with little or no role for phonology (e.g., Jared and Seidenberg, 1991;
Seidenberg, 1985a,b; Waters and Seidenberg, 1985). This latter position is usually
cast in terms of a dual-route model of word recognition. According to such models,
there is a 'direct' orthographic route that is the dominant route used in activating
word meaning, and a slower 'indirect' phonological route (e.g., Coltheart, Curtis,
Atkins and Haller, 1993; Jared and Seidenberg, 1991).

The phonological route is described as 'indirect' because it involves the extra
step of converting orthography to phonology, and then accessing meaning. Because
the phonological route is portrayed as the 'less direct' route, it is thought to
influence meaning activation only in cases in which word processing is protracted,
as when the perceptual input is degraded or a low frequency word is encountered
(see Pollatsek, Rayner and Lee, this volume, for plausibility arguments against the
'slow' phonology hypothesis).

Two possible phonological routes to meaning have been proposed: (1) an addressed phonological route that goes from orthography to a lexical look-up of stored
phonological forms to meaning; and (2) an assembled phonological route that relies
on the sublexical translation of graphemes to phonemes based on a reader's knowledge of grapheme to phoneme correspondences (e.g., Coltheart, 1978). In either
case, the phonological route is said to be slower than the orthographic route because
it involves the extra step of converting visual input to sound on the way to meaning.
Thus, meaning activation is said to occur primarily via orthography.

In this chapter, we review data from our own lab that addresses questions
concerning the timing of availability of phonological information in reading as well
as the role that phonological information plays in word processing in skilled silent
reading. To address these questions, we examined the influence of phonological
information on the process of resolving lexical ambiguity. Our data indicate that: (1)
phonological codes are active early in word recognition in reading; (2) phonological

codes are involved in activating word meaning; (3) phonological effects are not limited to cases in which word processing is slow.

Lexical ambiguity is quite common in natural spoken language and in text. Readers frequently encounter words with more than one possible interpretation. *Pitchers* may hold liquid or throw balls. *Balls* may be social events at which people dance or spherical toys that may be hit with a bat. A *bat* may be a flying mammal or a wooden club. A *club* may be a thick stick for hitting things or a place where people go to socialize, and so forth. When encountering a visual word form, a reader may have to resolve multiple types of lexical ambiguity, especially when there is no prior context to aid the reader. There is *lexical-semantic* ambiguity in which there are at least two possible meanings associated with a single visual word form (e.g., bat). A reader may also have to resolve *syntactic-category* ambiguity in which the visual word form belongs to multiple syntactic categories (e.g., duck), or *phonological* ambiguity in which the visual word form has multiple pronunciations (e.g., sewer). Some words such as 'sewer' are potentially ambiguous at multiple levels — not only are there two phonological forms associated with a single visual form (i.e., phonological ambiguity), but there are also two meanings associated with one visual form (i.e., lexical–semantic ambiguity). In addition, words that have distinct visual forms, such as the heterographic word pair 'soul/sole', may create ambiguity. The two visual word forms (sole and soul) share a common phonological form. If word meaning is activated from the phonological form, then heterographs may create ambiguity for the reader, even though the visual form can logically differentiate between the two word meanings. Faced with any or all of these circumstances, the reader must resolve the ambiguity and arrive at a single contextually appropriate meaning for the word in order to comprehend the intended meaning of the text successfully. The prevalence of lexical ambiguities in language processing warrants the study of ambiguity processing in its own right. However, it also provides a fertile field for harvesting a greater understanding of word processing more generally.

There is widespread agreement that orthographic, phonological, syntactic category, and meaning information are relevant to word processing in reading. However, it is less clear when and how each type of information is utilized. By looking at the relative influence of each type of information in lexical ambiguity resolution, we hope to shed some light on questions of how and when this information is used in the reading of both ambiguous and unambiguous words. Our particular interest is in using this information to address questions regarding the early involvement of phonological processing in arriving at word meaning in skilled silent reading. We will use the findings from the lexical–semantic ambiguity literature as the base from which to build our case.

Resolution of lexical–semantic ambiguity

There have been a number of eye movement studies that have examined lexical–semantic ambiguity resolution in reading. A fairly consistent pattern of results has emerged demonstrating that multiple word meanings are activated and meaning is resolved within the readers' initial processing time on the ambiguous word (e.g., Binder and Morris, 1995; Dopkins, Morris and Rayner, 1992; Duffy, Morris and Rayner, 1988; Folk and Morris, 1995; Rayner and Duffy, 1986; Rayner, Pacht and Duffy, 1994; Sereno, 1995). Initial processing time in these studies has been accessed by looking at first fixation duration and at gaze duration on the target word. The typical finding is that the pattern of effects is consistent across the two measures, and thus reporting both measures is redundant. We will follow this convention and report first fixation duration only if it is inconsistent with gaze duration. In addition, the meaning dominance of the word and the context in which the word occurs have been shown to influence the resolution process (e.g., Binder and Morris, 1995; Dopkins et al., 1992; Duffy et al., 1988; Folk and Morris, 1995; Rayner et al., 1994). Meaning dominance refers to the extent to which one meaning is more likely to occur than another: *balanced words* are words with relatively equally likely interpretations, and *biased words* have one interpretation that is much more likely than the other(s). Likelihood in these studies is typically operationally defined as the probability that a particular meaning is given as the first associative response to the word presented in isolation. This is taken as an indication of which meaning the reader is most familiar with. While we recognize that many words have more than two possible meanings, item selection for experimental purposes is often restricted to words with two meanings, or words for which the additional meanings are very infrequent.

One of the earliest papers to demonstrate both meaning dominance and sentence context effects on lexical–semantic ambiguity resolution in reading was Duffy et al. (1988). In this experiment readers encountered homophonic ambiguous words such as 'port' (a place where ships dock, or an alcoholic beverage) that have multiple meanings associated with one spelling and pronunciation. Half of the ambiguous words were biased and half were balanced. Processing time on the ambiguous word (underlined in the example below) was compared to processing time on an unambiguous control word (in parentheses in the example below) that was matched in length and word frequency (Francis and Kuçera, 1982) to the ambiguous word. Half of the participants saw the sentence context with the ambiguous word and half saw the same sentence frame with the unambiguous control word. Sentence contexts were written so that the disambiguating contextual information could appear either before or after the ambiguous word as in the biased word example below. The context always supported the subordinate interpretation for the biased ambiguous words.

Table 1

Mean gaze duration (in milliseconds) on ambiguous words and control words in Duffy et al. (1988)

	Context Before		Context After	
	Biased	Balanced	Biased	Balanced
Ambiguous	276	264	261	279
Control	255	264	259	261
Ambiguity effect	+21	0	+2	+18

Context Before:

(1) When she finally served it to her guests, the <u>port</u> (<u>soup</u>) was a great success.

Context After:

(2) Last night the <u>port</u> (<u>soup</u>) was a great success when she finally served it to her guests.

For our present purposes, of major interest are the immediate effects on processing caused by the lexical ambiguity of the target words. First consider the situation in which the context preceding the ambiguous word was neutral (see sentence 2 above). Duffy et al. found that readers spent more initial processing time on the balanced ambiguous words than on the biased ambiguous words or the unambiguous control words (see the Context After conditions in Table 1). This seems most naturally explained by assuming that two equally likely meanings become available close together in time and compete for selection. In contrast, when there is a dominant meaning, as in the case of the biased words, that meaning presumably becomes available first, so that readers select it before the less likely meaning can effectively compete. We refer to this difference in the pattern of initial processing time between balanced and biased words as the *meaning dominance effect*.

Further evidence in support of this interpretation comes from looking at processing time on the disambiguating contextual information. When subsequent disambiguating information supported the subordinate interpretation of the ambiguous word, readers spent more time on that region than if the region followed an unambiguous control word. This increased processing time is thought to reflect the fact that readers had originally selected the dominant interpretation of the biased ambiguous word and now had to reanalyze their choice.

The pattern was quite different, however, when the prior context was biased toward one interpretation (the subordinate meaning) of the ambiguous (see sentence 1 above). In this case, there was no initial processing difficulty on the balanced ambiguous word (see the Context Before conditions in Table 1). However, for the biased ambiguous words, the initial processing time on that word was inflated relative to either a balanced word or a length and frequency matched unambiguous control, presumably because the subordinate meaning became available close together in time with the dominant interpretation due to an effect of context. This effect has been termed the subordinate bias effect (Rayner et al., 1994). These findings indicate that meaning activation is influenced by contextual information. In the case of the balanced ambiguous words, the context boosts the activation of the context appropriate meaning, so that it is available for selection prior to the alternative meaning, eliminating the initial competition for selection between the two equally likely meanings. The same effect would be predicted if the context inappropriate interpretation were inhibited. However, existing evidence supports the activation account. For example, when readers are presented with paragraphs containing two instances of a balanced ambiguous word, and the context appropriate interpretation changes from first to second encounter, there is no initial processing time cost associated with the meaning switch (Binder and Morris, 1995). If the context inappropriate meaning of the word was inhibited at the first encounter, it should have been more difficult to access that meaning later in the passage and it was not. In addition, the activation account is the more parsimonious explanation in that it can also account for the biased word effects. For the biased ambiguous words, the context apparently boosts the activation of the subordinate interpretation enough that it competes with the dominant interpretation for selection.

Subsequent studies have yielded similar patterns of data with effects of similar magnitude (e.g., Binder and Morris, 1995; Dopkins et al., 1992; Folk and Morris, 1995; Rayner et al., 1994). Thus, the Duffy et al. (1988) data provide a representative baseline from which to measure the effects of other forms of lexical ambiguity on the process of arriving at a single word meaning.

Is phonological information available prior to meaning resolution?

One way to test whether phonological information is available during the process of meaning resolution is to examine how readers process words that are phonologically ambiguous in addition to being ambiguous with respect to their meaning. For example, each pronunciation of the word 'tear' is associated with a unique meaning; pronounced as /tir/ it means a liquid that pours from the eyes, while its alternative pronunciation /tɛr/ means a rip or a hole. Previous work examining the processing of phonologically ambiguous words focused on phonology's role in working memory processes and error recovery during reading (Carpenter and Daneman, 1981; Daneman and Carpenter, 1983). However, Folk and Morris (1995) were also interested in the role of phonology in meaning resolution. Thus, they compared ambiguity resolution for heterophonic homographs such as 'tear' to the established pattern of results discussed above for lexical–semantic ambiguity resolution in reading homophonic homographs (e.g., ruler). They reasoned that if there was an impact of phonological ambiguity on lexical processing, above and beyond effects that could be attributed to meaning resolution, that phonological information had to be available prior to meaning resolution during silent reading.

Folk and Morris (1995) embedded both ambiguous heterophones and ambiguous homophones in sentences. All ambiguous words selected for inclusion in this study had at least two semantically distinct noun interpretations. If there was a possible verb interpretation it had to be semantically consistent with one of the noun interpretations. Each ambiguous condition in this experiment was paired with a control condition in which the ambiguous word was replaced with an unambiguous control word that was matched in length and frequency with the ambiguous word. The context preceding the ambiguous word was consistent with the less likely interpretation of that word, as in the following example sentences:

Homophone:
(1) They asked the powerful <u>ruler</u> (<u>witch</u>) to help them when the war began.

Heterophone:
(2) Jim caught his sleeve on a branch causing a <u>tear</u> (<u>hole</u>) in his new shirt.

If phonological information is available prior to meaning resolution then readers should have greater initial processing difficulty with heterophonic ambiguous words than with homophonic ambiguous words because there are two sources of ambiguity to be resolved in the former case. If, on the other hand, phonological information is accessed only after meaning is resolved there should be no cost associated with the added phonological ambiguity of the heterophones because only the pronunciation associated with the selected meaning would be activated.

The ambiguous homophones showed the typical ambiguity effect, replicating Duffy et al. (1988). However, the processing time on the heterophones was longer than on the ambiguous homophones. The phonological ambiguity effect was 40 ms, much greater than the size of the effect of lexical–semantic ambiguity alone (see Table 2). The data from this experiment demonstrate that the addition of phonological ambiguity to lexical–semantic ambiguity is costly. This cost could

Table 2

Mean gaze duration (in milliseconds) on biased ambiguous target words and control words with Context Before (from Folk and Morris, 1995)

	Homophones (ruler)	Heterophones (tear)
Ambiguous	323	358
Control	297	318
Ambiguity effect	+26	+40

arise from phonological activation prior to meaning activation or from phonological activation that results from meaning activation.

Is phonological activation epiphenomenal to meaning activation?

It is also possible to account for the heterophone ambiguity effect in Table 2 without positing phonologically driven activation of meaning if the phonological information associated with a meaning of a word is activated only after that meaning is activated. Even in that case, there would be two meanings and two pronunciations activated, resulting in two sources of ambiguity to resolve, creating extra processing costs.

If activation of phonological information only occurs after the activation of meaning, then the dominant interpretation of a heterophone and its pronunciation should be available prior to the subordinate interpretation and its pronunciation when the context follows a biased ambiguous heterophone. If so, readers should easily be able to select the dominant meaning of the word. Thus, readers should show little or no evidence of processing difficulty on this word, just as when they encounter biased ambiguous homophones in neutral context. In contrast, if the presence of multiple phonological representations creates interference even in this context, this would indicate that resolving the phonological code is an integral part of the process of resolving the meaning.

Folk and Morris (1995) conducted a second experiment in which the context that disambiguated to the subordinate interpretation appeared after the biased ambiguous words. This experiment included the same target words and controls as the previous experiment:

Homophone:
(3) They looked for the <u>ruler</u> (<u>witch</u>) and asked her to help as the war began.

Heterophone:
(4) There was a <u>tear</u> (<u>hole</u>) in Jim's new shirt after he caught his sleeve on a branch.

Remember that the standard result (replicated many times) for biased homophonic ambiguous words under these conditions is that there is no initial processing time difference between the ambiguous word and an unambiguous control. This indicates that for homophones, the dominant interpretation is available first and there is no competition.

Folk and Morris similarly observed that in these neutral context conditions, the ambiguity effect for the homophones goes away (see Table 3). That is, for the homophonic ambiguous words, initial processing cost was reduced from 26 ms (Table 2) to −7 ms (Table 3) with the shift in context. In contrast, for the heterophonic ambiguous words, the cost doubled from 40 ms to 81 ms,

Table 3

Mean gaze duration (in milliseconds) on biased ambiguous target words and control words with Context After (from Folk and Morris, 1995)

	Homophone (ruler)	Heterophone (tear)
Ambiguous	342	389
Control	349	308
Ambiguity effect	−7	+81

demonstrating initial activation of multiple phonological codes and a unique cost associated with this additional source of ambiguity.

The fact that there is such a striking contrast between the effects of meaning dominance and context on heterophones compared to ambiguous homophones indicates that activation of phonological information is not epiphenomenal to the activation of word meaning. We would like to argue on the basis of these data that activation of phonological information *precedes* activation of meaning. This position would be strengthened by data showing that lexical–semantic and phonological ambiguity resolution were differentially affected by a common lexical factor, as opposed to a contextual factor. The factor that we chose to investigate is syntactic category membership.

Phonological ambiguity across syntactic category — a further test of early activation

Some lexically ambiguous words have meanings that differ with respect to syntactic category membership. For example, the word 'duck' can mean a type of bird (a noun) or the act of lowering oneself (a verb). In many cases, the two interpretations are semantically unrelated, as was the case for the homophones used in the previous studies. But they differ in that one interpretation is a member of the noun category and the other is a verb, whereas in the previous studies both interpretations were of the same syntactic category (nouns, in all of the research discussed thus far).

O'Seaghdha (1989, 1997) argued that the process of syntactic category assignment precedes assignment of meaning. We reasoned that if syntactic category disambiguation can modulate semantic resolution, then prior context that is structurally unambiguous should reduce or eliminate the subordinate bias effect when the two interpretations of the biased ambiguous word are members of different syntactic categories. To test this, biased ambiguous homophones that had a dominant verb interpretation and a less likely noun interpretation were read in structurally unambiguous sentences. The noun and verb interpretations were also not semantically related. The intended meaning was always the less likely meaning of the word, and that was always the noun interpretation. Processing time on the noun–verb ambiguous word did not differ from an unambiguous control when it appeared in structurally unambiguous context (Morris and Folk, 1995). The presence of unambiguous structural information appeared to dictate the syntactic category assignment of the target word and thus to eliminate the lexical–semantic ambiguity effect. This suggests that syntactic category information was available prior to meaning resolution.

Unambiguous syntactic context eliminated the subordinate bias effect when the two meanings of the word do not share a common syntactic category. Therefore, if the phonological code is accessed only via the meaning of the word, we would expect that the phonological ambiguity effect would also be eliminated when the possible interpretations of the heterophone come from different syntactic categories. In order to test this, we placed heterophones whose meanings were in different syntactic categories in structurally unambiguous sentences like the following and compared processing time on these words to syntactic category ambiguous homophones (i.e., ambiguous words with a single pronunciation) and to unambiguous controls.

Homophone:

(1) Mike saw the <u>duck</u> (sheep) drink from the pond this morning.

Heterophone:

(2) John knew that the <u>sow</u> (pig) rolled in the mud to stay cool.

As expected, the lexical semantic ambiguity effect was eliminated when the syntactic context unambiguously indicated the noun interpretation. In contrast, the phonological ambiguity effect persisted, even when the two pronunciations differed in syntactic category membership and the context was structurally unambiguous (see Table 4). We take this as evidence that the activation of phonological information precedes the resolution of syntactic category or lexical–semantic ambiguity. However, there was roughly a 20-ms reduction in the magnitude of the ambiguity effect when meanings came from different syntactic categories, compared to when they came from the same syntactic category (Table 4 compared to Table 2). This

Table 4

Mean gaze duration on syntactic category ambiguous words and unambiguous controls

	Homophonic semantic + syntactic category ambiguity (duck)	Heterophonic semantic + syntactic category ambiguity (sow)
Ambiguous	272	290
Control	271	273
Ambiguity effect	+1	+17

was true for both ambiguity types (homophones and heterophones). Since meaning ambiguity is the common denominator in these two cases, we attribute the reduction in effect size to the attenuation of lexical–semantic ambiguity and not to changes in phonological ambiguity resolution.

Does phonological information mediate access to meaning?

While the previous studies are consistent with the claim that phonological information is active prior to meaning resolution, and that phonological activation is qualitatively different from meaning activation, they do not provide direct evidence that word meaning is accessed via phonology. Folk (1999) conducted a more direct test of phonologically mediated access to meaning by examining gaze duration on heterographic homophones (henceforth, heterographs). Heterographs are words that share a common name but that have different meanings that are represented by different spellings, such as the words 'soul' and 'sole' in the following sentences:

(1) Todd believed that his <u>soul</u> would go to heaven after he died.
(2) Julie noticed that the <u>sole</u> of her shoe had a hole in it.

Other studies have examined the processing of heterographs during silent reading. However, in those studies reading time on the contextually inappropriate spelling of a heterograph such as 'He wore <u>blew</u> jeans' was compared to processing time on the context appropriate spelling 'blue' or on an orthographic control word such as 'blow' (e.g., Daneman and Reingold, 1993; Daneman, Reingold and Davidson, 1995; Rayner et al., 1998). In contrast, readers in Folk's study always saw the contextually appropriate spelling of a balanced heterograph or an unambiguous length and frequency matched control word embedded in a sentence. Thus, there were no misspellings and no semantic anomalies in the text. The heterographs were balanced in that the two spellings had roughly equivalent word frequencies. Contextual information related to the meaning of the word appeared either before or after the heterograph.

In silent reading, heterographs are only ambiguous if meaning is activated via the phonological code. If meaning is activated via phonology, then multiple meanings should be active when one spelling of a heterograph is encountered in print. That is, when the spelling s-o-u-l is encountered, both the 'spirit' meaning associated with that spelling and the 'bottom of a shoe or foot' meaning associated with the alternative spelling s-o-l-e should be active via their common phonological code /sol/. Thus, readers should show a similar pattern of effects in initial processing time on a balanced heterograph as they did when reading a balanced ambiguous homograph in which both meanings share a common spelling, such as 'bank' — both word types are ambiguous with respect to their intended meaning. On the other hand, if

Table 5

Mean gaze duration (in milliseconds) on balanced heterographs (from Folk, 1999)

	Context After	Context Before
Heterograph	283	296
Control	263	306
Ambiguity effect	+20	−10

meaning is activated directly from the orthographic representation, then only a single meaning should be activated when a heterograph is encountered, since there is only one meaning associated with each spelling. If that is the case, initial processing time on the heterographs should mimic that of the unambiguous controls.

The studies involving heterograph errors have produced ambiguous results (see Daneman and Reingold, this volume, or Pollatsek, Rayner and Lee, this volume, for extensive discussion of this issue). In contrast, the results from Folk (1999) in which there were no secondary tasks, no semantic anomalies, and no spelling errors, were quite straightforward. When readers encountered a balanced heterograph and the prior context was neutral with respect to the meanings associated with the word name, reading times on the heterograph were longer than on an unambiguous control word (see the Context After conditions in Table 5). This ambiguity effect indicates that multiple meanings were active when one spelling of a heterograph was encountered. These effects were attenuated when prior context supported the meaning of the word that was associated with the spelling that occurred in print (see the Context Before conditions in Table 5), indicating that context influences the order in which the meanings of a heterograph are accessed. These reading patterns on the heterographs are similar in both pattern and magnitude to those observed for ambiguous homographs in Duffy et al. (1988) and subsequent lexical ambiguity studies (e.g., Binder and Morris, 1995). The fact that the heterographs were processed as if they were ambiguous homographic homophones indicates the meanings of the word were activated via phonology. If word meaning was only activated directly from the orthographic input, then there should not have been any ambiguity effects associated with the heterographs.

Is the phonological route slow?

The heterograph ambiguity effect clearly demonstrates phonologically mediated access to meaning. However, a further question remains. Is phonological information only involved in meaning activation when word processing is slow, as predicted by

Table 6

Mean gaze duration (in milliseconds) on high and low frequency balanced heterographs with context after (from Folk, 1999)

	High frequency	Low frequency
Heterograph	260	305
Control	245	280
Ambiguity effect	+15	+25

some dual-route models of reading (e.g., Jared and Seidenberg, 1991)? To address this question, Folk manipulated the frequency of the balanced heterographs. Half of the balanced word pairs selected for the experiment consisted of two relatively low frequency words and half were relatively high frequency word pairs. If the phonological route is the 'slow' route to meaning, then we would expect to see ambiguity effects associated with the low frequency heterographs but not with the high frequency heterographs when the related context occurs after the target word.

The results presented in Table 6 are the data from the Context After condition in Table 5 broken down by the frequency of the word pair. There are ambiguity effects associated with both the high and low frequency heterographs. The high frequency heterographs are read more quickly than the low frequency heterographs, and, not surprisingly, show a numerically smaller ambiguity effect. However, we believe that these results provide compelling evidence that word meaning was activated via phonology, even for words that are highly familiar. The fact that there is an ambiguity effect even when the heterograph pair consists of two relatively high frequency words is clear evidence that phonology is used to activate word meaning, and it argues against the idea that phonological processing is slow (see also Lesch and Pollatsek, 1993, 1998).

Does orthography matter?

We do not mean to suggest that readers do not attend to orthographic information. Clearly, a reader cannot develop a phonological representation without some processing of the visual input. The extent to which that orthographic analysis results in a 'complete' orthographic representation remains an open question, as discussed in the chapter by Pollatsek, Rayner, and Lee in this volume, and does not bear directly on the interpretation of Folk's findings. Folk's data indicate that, even though readers accessed multiple meanings of the balanced heterograph in the presence of unambiguous orthographic information, they selected the meaning that matched the presented orthography. That is, when prior context was neutral, there were no inflated re-analysis effects associated with the subsequent disambiguating region, indicating that readers did initially select the correct interpretation. This is in contrast with the finding from the lexical–semantic literature in which there is typically inflated processing time associated with the disambiguating region following a balanced homograph (Duffy et al., 1988). With homographs such as 'pitcher', the orthography does not indicate which of the two meanings is intended, only the subsequent context does that. So, some of the time readers initially select a meaning that turns out to be incompatible with the subsequent context (Duffy et al., 1988). This re-analysis difference between heterographs and homographs indicates that readers did make use of the orthographic information to resolve the ambiguity that arose from the phonologically driven multiple activation of word meaning for the heterographs, under these specific circumstances.

It should be noted, however, that Folk (1999) found that the presence of unambiguous orthographic information did not always result in readers initially selecting the orthographically correct meaning. Rather, orthography played a lesser role in meaning resolution than did other factors such as frequency and meaning dominance. This was evident in the reading patterns for the biased heterographs. In the case of biased heterographs, even when the visual word form correctly indicated that the less frequent meaning of the word was intended, there was evidence that readers may have initially selected the meaning associated with the more frequent spelling. Under those circumstances, readers made more regressions to the heterograph and spent more total time on it than on the unambiguous homograph control, suggesting that they had initially selected the meaning that was inconsistent with the orthography. That meaning also turned out to be inconsistent with the subsequent context, prompting increased re-reading. In this case both word frequency and meaning dominance favored the meaning which was inconsistent with the spelling. Apparently orthography's initial influence was not strong enough to overcome the activation advantage of the dominant (high frequency) meaning over the subordinate (low frequency) meaning. In the case of the balanced heterographs, on the other hand, both meanings were relatively equal in frequency. The balanced word data demonstrates a role for orthography early when the frequency of the spellings and meanings is equated, but the biased word data suggests that orthography's constraint may not be enough to overcome conflicting support from frequency and meaning dominance.

Is access to phonological representations ordered by meaning dominance?

The meaning dominance effects observed in lexical ambiguity resolution are thought to reflect competition between two or more activated candidates for word meaning, that is, competition at the level of meaning resolution. The effects observed in Folk and Morris (1995) stand out from the other ambiguity resolution data that we have discussed in that the heterophones fail to show the standard meaning dominance effect.

In the case of a biased ambiguous homophone like 'bank', there is typically a roughly 20-ms cost associated with the initial processing of the ambiguous word compared to an unambiguous control when the ambiguous word is read in context that supports the subordinate interpretation. As argued above, this cost is due to competition between the two meanings. The context favoring the non-dominant meaning has boosted its activation level to be comparable to that of the dominant meaning. Heterophones like 'sewer' elicited an even larger (40 ms) cost (see Table 2). The added processing cost for the heterophones is most likely a result of an added competition between possible phonological codes. In contrast, when the context prior to ambiguous homophones such as 'bank' is uninformative with respect to meaning resolution, the initial processing **cost** goes from roughly 20 ms to no difference with the shift in context (see Rayner and Morris, 1991 for a review; see also Table 1). This elimination of the ambiguity effect is attributable to meaning dominance. The dominant interpretation is available for selection prior to the subordinate, and it is only when the reader encounters subsequent context consistent with the subordinate interpretation that there is any measurable processing difficulty. However, for the heterophones the cost doubles, increasing from 40 ms to 81 ms (Folk and Morris, 1995; see Tables 2 and 3). The effect of prior context on phonological ambiguity resolution was qualitatively different from that observed for meaning resolution alone. If the phonological information were activated via meaning activation, it should have been vulnerable to similar effects of meaning dominance, and it was not. The lack of meaning dominance effects for the heterophones supports our general conclusion that there is phonological activation prior to meaning activation, and that phonological information can mediate access to meaning. This early phonological activation could be activation of addressed form level lexical phonology or grapheme-to-phoneme correspondence assembled phonology. We have no basis for making such a distinction based on these data (however, see Lesch and Pollatsek, 1998).

We have argued that the ambiguity effects observed for the heterographs (Folk, 1999) and the heterophones (Folk and Morris, 1995) are the result of phonological involvement in accessing word meaning. So, why are there meaning dominance effects for the heterographs (e.g., sole/soul) that are comparable to those observed for homographs (e.g., bank), but not for the heterophones (e.g., wind)? This is most likely because the spelling of a word activates the phonological code, which in turn activates meaning. In the case of the heterographs, the spelling activates a single phonological representation, which in turn, activates all of the meanings associated with that name. As a result there are multiple meanings competing for selection, but there is no phonological ambiguity. The same is true for the homographic ambiguous words (e.g., bank). That is, there is activation of multiple meanings from a common phonological code. Thus, one would expect comparable meaning dominance effects for the two word types because the ambiguity effects are arising solely from meaning ambiguity. However, in the case of heterophones, processing is much different, because the spelling activates two phonological representations. Thus, there is ambiguity in the system at two levels, the phonological level prior to meaning activation, and the level of meaning. Because initial processing difficulty is found on the heterophones even in those cases where meaning dominance eliminates the ambiguity effect for homophones, one has to conclude that the availability of phonological information is not frequency ordered. The phonological activation preceded meaning activation and was not affected by the relative dominance of the meanings.

Is activation of the phonological code obligatory on the way to accessing meaning?

The answer to this question is clearly 'yes' in the sense that there is ample data which indicates that healthy skilled silent readers, even in cases in which use of phonological information complicates the meaning resolution process, seem unable to avoid phonological activation (e.g., Folk, 1999; Folk and Morris, 1995; Van Orden, 1987). In this chapter, we reported data from several silent reading experiments in which phonology was initially active, even though that activation was costly to readers in terms of slowing reading times. In the heterophone studies, we found that multiple phonological codes were active initially even when the heterophone had one highly likely meaning and no context at that point to contradict the selection of the dominant meaning (see Table 3). The initial activation of the multiple phonological codes resulted in a substantial processing time cost to the reader. In comparison, there was no cost when there was a word with multiple meanings, but only a single pronunciation. This cost associated with phonological ambiguity persisted even when the two interpretations were from different syntactic categories and the prior sentence structure dictated a priori that only one interpretation was acceptable (see Table 4). Perhaps even more striking is the finding that when readers encounter a heterograph like 'soul', the meaning of 'sole' is also activated. That is, lexical–semantic ambiguity is present that would not be there if readers accessed the meaning of the word directly from the visual input (see Table 5). Even though the orthography of the heterograph clearly indicated which meaning was intended, phonology was still used to activate meaning. This was true even for heterograph pairs that were both high frequency words.

However, the answer to the question of whether phonological information is obligatory on the way to accessing meaning is clearly 'no' in the sense that there are data from the neuropsychological literature which suggest that access to meaning can occur without access to phonology. There are numerous documented cases of patients who are no longer able to access phonological information about a written word, but who can still access the meaning of that word (e.g., Hanley and McDonell, 1997; Miceli, Benvegnu, Capasso and Caramazza, 1997; Rapp, Benzing and Caramazza, 1997; Shelton and Weinrach, 1997). For example, Shelton and Weinrach (1997) reported the performance of patient EA who is impaired in tasks that require the derivation of phonology from orthography, such as in a non-word reading task. However, EA performed well on several single-word comprehension tasks, such as matching a written noun to a picture in the presence of semantic distracters. Based on data such as this, it was concluded that EA had impaired access to the phonology of written words with intact comprehension of written words. However, it should be noted that the intact written comprehension that patients such as EA display is comprehension of single words given unlimited time. It is not clear that these patients could successfully read in the normal sense of comprehending words in sentences with no processing impairment. The loss of phonological processing capability is clearly not without cost to reading performance in these patients.

Another reading population that might lend support to the idea that reading does not obligatorily involve access to sound-based coding is the population of profoundly deaf readers. In contrast to the neuropsychological patients, who have apparently lost access to the phonological information associated with visual word forms, these people have never experienced sound and therefore have no basis for phonological activation from visual word form. Treiman and Hirsh-Pasek (1983) compared the reading performance of 14 congenitally, profoundly deaf adult readers to that of 14 hearing readers. The deaf readers did not have the same difficulty with homophonic words and tongue twisters that hearing readers did, suggesting that the deaf readers are not using a sound-based code in reading. However, the same caveat is appropriate with respect to deaf readers as with the neuropsychological patients mentioned previously. Although many profoundly deaf individuals do learn to read, they do not read very well (Conrad, 1977). In fact, Treiman and Hirsh-Pasek estimate that only about 25% of the population of congenitally deaf readers read well enough to be classified as functionally literate. Thus, we would argue that the lack of phonological processing capability, whether it was lost or never was acquired, severely compromises reading performance.

Taken together these data indicate that under normal circumstances, phonological information mediates access to meaning in skilled silent reading. However, the patient data demonstrates that the phonological route is not the only route to meaning, and that word meaning can be accessed directly from orthographic input. It seems likely that both orthography and phonology contribute to accessing word meaning during skilled silent reading (e.g., Coltheart et al., 1994; Folk, 1999; Van

Orden, Pennington and Stone, 1990), but it is difficult to argue in the face of these data that meaning activation primarily occurs via orthography, with little or no role for phonology. Rather, our data indicate that, in skilled silent reading, phonological information plays a dominant role in accessing meaning, and this is not limited to cases in which word processing is slow.

It is not necessary to posit a dual route model of word processing in reading to accommodate these data. For instance, it is possible that the orthographic and phonological information contribute to lexical activation continuously as those representations develop. Initially, incomplete orthographic and phonological analyses would result in activation of a neighborhood of lexical candidates that arise from visual or phonological similarity to the partially analyzed input. Under this view, the orthographic analysis and phonological analysis are not independent processing streams racing to produce a definitive 'answer'. Rather, these are two sources of information contributing to activation of lexical candidates within a single lexicon. This could also be instantiated in a distributed processing model that does not assume discrete lexical representations. Our data do not distinguish between these different styles of word processing models. However, whichever model one adopts, it must account for the prevalence of phonological effects in word processing in skilled silent reading.

References

Binder, K.S. and Morris, R.K. (1995). Eye movements and lexical ambiguity resolution: Effects of prior encounter and discourse topic. Journal of Experimental Psychology: Learning, Memory, and Cognition, 21, 1186–1196.

Carpenter, P.A. and Daneman, M. (1981). Lexical retrieval and error recovery in reading: A model based on eye fixations. Journal of Verbal Learning and Verbal Behavior, 20, 137–160.

Coltheart, M. (1978). Lexical access in simple reading tasks. In: G. Underwood (Ed.), Strategies of Information Processing. San Diego, CA: Academic Press, pp. 151–216.

Coltheart, M., Curtis, B., Atkins, P. and Haller, M. (1993). Models of reading aloud: Dual-route and parallel-distributed-processing approaches. Psychological Review, 100, 589–608.

Coltheart, V., Patterson, K. and Leahy, J. (1994). When a ROWS is a ROSE: Phonological effects in written word comprehension. Quarterly Journal of Experimental Psychology, 47A, 917–955.

Conrad, R. (1977). The reading ability of deaf school-leavers. British Journal of Educational Psychology, 47, 138–148.

Daneman, M. and Carpenter, P.A. (1983). Individual differences in integrating information between and within sentences. Journal of Experimental Psychology: Learning, Memory and Cognition, 9, 561–584.

Daneman, M. and Reingold, E. (1993). What eye fixations tell us about phonological recoding during reading. Canadian Journal of Experimental Psychology, 47, 153–178.

Daneman, M., Reingold, E. and Davidson, M. (1995). Time course of phonological activation during reading: Evidence from eye fixations. Journal of Experimental Psychology: Learning, Memory and Cognition, 21, 884–898.

Dopkins, S., Morris, R.K. and Rayner, K. (1992). Lexical ambiguity and eye fixations in reading: A test of competing models of lexical ambiguity resolution. Journal of Memory and Language, 31, 461–476.

Duffy, S.A., Morris, R.K. and Rayner, K. (1988). Lexical ambiguity and fixation times in reading. Journal of Memory and Language, 27, 429–446.

Folk, J.R. (1999). Phonological codes are used to access the lexicon during silent reading. Journal of Experimental Psychology: Learning, Memory, and Cognition, 25, 892–906.

Folk, J.R. and Morris, R.K. (1995). The use of multiple lexical codes in reading: Evidence from eye movements, naming time, and oral reading. Journal of Experimental Psychology: Learning, Memory, and Cognition, 21, 1412–1429.

Francis, W.N. and Kuçera, H. (1982). Frequency Analysis of English Usage: Lexicon and Grammar. Boston: Houghton Mifflin.

Hanley, J.R. and McDonell, V. (1997). Are reading and spelling phonologically mediated? Evidence from a patient with a speech production impairment. Cognitive Neuropsychology, 14, 3–33.

Inhoff, A.W. and Topolski, R. (1994). Use of phonological codes during eye fixations in reading and in on-line and delayed naming tasks. Journal of Memory and Language, 33, 689–713.

Jared, D. and Seidenberg, M.S. (1991). Does word identification proceed from spelling to sound to meaning? Journal of Experimental Psychology: General, 120 (4), 358–394.

Lesch, M.F. and Pollatsek, A. (1993). Automatic access of semantic information by phonological codes in visual word recognition. Journal of Experimental Psychology: Learning, Memory, and Cognition, 19, 285–294.

Lesch, M.F. and Pollatsek, A. (1998). Evidence for the use of assembled phonology in accessing the meaning of printed words. Journal of Experimental Psychology: Learning, Memory, and Cognition, 24, 573–592.

Lukatela, G. and Turvey, M.T. (1991). Phonological access of the lexicon: Evidence from associative priming with pseudohomophones. Journal of Experimental Psychology: Human Perception and Performance, 17, 951–966.

Miceli, G., Benvegnu, B., Capasso, R. and Caramazza, A. (1997). The independence of phonological and orthographic lexical forms. Cognitive Neuropsychology, 14, 35–69.

Morris, R.K. and Folk, J.R. (1995). Semantic ambiguity across syntactic category. Poster presented at the Annual Meeting of the Psychonomic Society, Los Angeles.

O'Seaghdha, P.G. (1989). The dependence of lexical relatedness effects on syntactic connectedness. Journal of Experimental Psychology: Learning, Memory and Cognition, 15, 73–87.

O'Seaghdha, P.G. (1997). Conjoint and dissociable effects of syntactic and semantic context. Journal of Experimental Psychology: Learning, Memory, and Cognition, 23, 807–828.

Pollatsek, A., Lesch, M.F., Morris, R.K. and Rayner, K. (1992). Phonological codes are used in integrating information across saccades in word identification and reading. Journal of Experimental Psychology: Human Perception and Performance, 18, 148–162.

Rapp, B., Benzing, L. and Caramazza, A. (1997). The autonomy of lexical orthography. Cognitive Neuropsychology, 14, 71–104.

Rayner, K. and Duffy, S.A. (1986). Lexical complexity and fixation times in reading: Effects of word frequency, verb complexity, and lexical ambiguity. Memory and Cognition, 14, 191–201.

Rayner, K. and Morris, R.K. (1991). Comprehension processes in reading ambiguous sentences: Reflections from eye movements. In: G.B. Simpson (Ed.), Understanding Word and Sentence. Advances in Psychology (No. 77). Elsevier Science Publishers: North Holland, pp. 175–198.

Rayner, K., Pacht, J.M. and Duffy, S.A. (1994). Effects of prior encounter and global discourse bias on the processing of lexically ambiguous words: Evidence from eye fixations. Journal of Memory and Language, 33, 527–544.

Rayner, K., Pollatsek, A. and Binder, K.S. (1998). Phonological codes and eye movements in reading. Journal of Experimental Psychology: Learning, Memory and Cognition, 24, 476–497.

Rayner, K., Sereno, S.C., Lesch, M.F. and Pollatsek, A. (1995). Phonological codes are automatically activated during reading: Evidence from an eye movement priming paradigm. Psychological Science, 6, 26–32.

Seidenberg, M.S. (1985a). The time course of information activation and utilization in visual word recognition. In: D. Besner, T.G. Waller and E.M. MacKinnon (Eds.), Reading Research: Advances in Theory and Practice (Vol. 5). San Diego, CA: Academic Press, pp. 199–252.

Seidenberg, M.S. (1985b). The time course of phonological code activation in two writing systems. Cognition, 19, 1–30.

Sereno, S.C. (1995). The resolution of lexical ambiguity: Evidence from an eye movement priming paradigm. Journal of Experimental Psychology: Learning, Memory, and Cognition, 21, 582–595.

Shelton, J.R. and Weinrach, M. (1997). Further evidence of a dissociation between output phonological and orthographic lexicons: A case study. Cognitive Neuropsychology, 14, 105–129.

Treiman, R. and Hirsh-Pasek, K. (1983). Silent reading: Insights from second generation deaf readers. Cognitive Psychology, 15, 39–65.

Van Orden, G.C. (1987). A ROWS is a ROSE: Spelling, sound, and reading. Memory and Cognition, 15, 181–198.

Van Orden, G.C., Johnston, J.C. and Hale, B.L. (1988). Word identification in reading proceeds from spelling to sound to meaning. Journal of Experimental Psychology: Learning, Memory, and Cognition, 14, 371–386.

Van Orden, G.C., Pennington, B.F. and Stone, G.O. (1990). Word identification in reading and the promise of subsymbolic psycholinguistics. Psychological Review, 97, 488–522.

Waters, G.S. and Seidenberg, M.S. (1985). Spelling–sound effects in reading: Time-course and decision criteria. Memory and Cognition, 13, 557–572.

CHAPTER 17

Do Readers Use Phonological Codes to Activate Word Meanings? Evidence from Eye Movements

Meredyth Daneman and Eyal M. Reingold
University of Toronto

Abstract

Do readers use phonological codes to activate word meanings during natural silent reading? Many researchers have been arguing for the early involvement of phonology in activating word meanings. However, the evidence has depended largely on tasks that required readers to make some response in addition to reading (e.g., lexical decisions, proofreading). For example, when asked to proofread text for errors, readers have been less likely to detect homophonic errors (e.g., *He wore blew jeans*) than nonhomophonic errors (e.g., *He wore blow jeans*), a finding that has been taken as evidence that phonology is used to access word meanings. Although such findings are consistent with phonologically mediated lexical access, they do not provide conclusive evidence. There is always the concern that the secondary task may have changed the nature of the reading process itself, making the results less generalizable to natural reading. Furthermore, because the phonological involvement has been inferred from a slow secondary response rather than from reading itself, the findings are equivocal with respect to the time course of the phonological activation. Our research avoided these pitfalls. Readers were not asked to proofread for errors. They simply read for comprehension, and their eye movements were monitored for evidence of spontaneous disruptions when encountering homophonic errors (e.g., *blew*) versus orthographic control errors (e.g., *blow*). The evidence strongly suggests that readers use orthographic codes to access word meanings, with phonological codes playing a more restricted role in the accessing of meanings for low-frequency words. In this chapter we describe our research and we respond to a recent article by Rayner, Pollatsek and Binder (1998) which challenges our conclusions.

Reading as a Perceptual Process/A. Kennedy, R. Radach, D. Heller and J. Pynte (Editors)
© 2000 Elsevier Science Ltd. All rights reserved

In 1993, Daneman and Reingold claimed to have provided evidence from eye movement data that skilled adult readers use orthographic codes rather than phonological codes to activate word meanings (see also Daneman, Reingold and Davidson, 1995). Evidence for the *early* involvement of phonology in activating word meanings had depended largely on paradigms that required readers to make some response in addition to reading (e.g., making semantic judgments about words and sentences, proofreading text for inconsistent words) and so there was always the concern that the secondary task requirement had changed the nature of the reading process itself. The significance of Daneman and Reingold's claims is that they were based on a task that demanded nothing other than normal reading for comprehension. However, a recent study by Rayner et al. (1998) has challenged the Daneman and Reingold (1993) and Daneman et al. (1995) claims. Using a variant of the Daneman and Reingold eye-movement monitoring task, Rayner et al. (1998) interpreted their data as evidence for the early and dominant involvement of phonology in accessing word meanings. In this chapter we critically evaluate the position of Rayner et al. (1998) in the context of new data that replicate and extend our earlier findings.

The background

Many proponents of phonologically mediated lexical access have drawn on evidence from tasks showing homophone confusion effects. [1] One such task is lexical decision in which subjects judge whether a given letter string is a word. A typical finding is that subjects take more time to reject pseudohomophone foils, such as *brane*, than control foils, such as *brene* (Coltheart, Davelaar, Jonasson and Besner, 1977; Rubenstein, Lewis and Rubenstein, 1971). A common explanation for the effect is that the pseudohomophone *brane* activates the phonological representation /breɪn/, which in turn activates the lexical entry for the word *brain*. The activation of a lexical entry makes *brane* more difficult to classify as a nonword. Another task showing homophone confusions to single words is the semantic categorization task of Van Orden (1987). In this task, subjects are presented a category name (e.g., type of food) followed by a target word (e.g., *meet, melt*), and their task is to decide whether or not the target word is a member of the category. The typical finding is that subjects make more false categorization responses to *meet* which sounds like the genuine category member, *meat*, than they do to *melt* which is orthographically similar to *meat* but does not sound like it (Van Orden, 1987; Van Orden, Johnston

---

1 Although see also Pollatsek, Lesch, Morris and Rayner (1992) and Rayner, Sereno, Lesch and Pollatsek (1995) who use homophone preview/priming paradigms to argue for the early involvement of phonological codes in word identification and lexical access. The homophone preview paradigm will be discussed later.

and Hale, 1988). Homophone confusions have also been demonstrated in tasks that require readers to make semantic decisions about an entire sentence rather than an isolated word. The typical finding is that readers make more false-positive semantic acceptability decisions to incorrect sentences that sound correct (e.g., *She has blond hare*) than to incorrect sentences that do not sound correct (e.g., *She has blond harm*) (Coltheart, Avons and Trollope, 1990; Coltheart, Laxon, Rickard and Elton, 1988; Treiman, Freyd and Baron, 1983). And finally, homophonic confusions are not restricted to tasks that involve decisions to lists of unrelated words or simple sentences; they have been demonstrated for realistic, everyday prose as well (Daneman and Stainton, 1991; see also Van Orden, 1991). Daneman and Stainton (1991) had subjects proofread a lengthy and complex prose passage containing inconsistent words that were or were not homophones of consistent ones. Phonology was implicated by the finding that readers were less likely to detect homophonic errors (e.g., *One night a week they would meat* ...) than nonhomophonic orthographic control errors (e.g., *One night a week they would moat* ...). The finding that homophonic words are commonly misinterpreted as their sound-alike mates has been taken as evidence for phonology playing an early and dominant role in accessing word meanings.

Although demonstrations of homophone confusions are consistent with phonologically mediated lexical access, they do not provide conclusive evidence for early phonological influences. Because the demonstrations of homophone confusions have all relied on paradigms that required readers to make some response in addition to reading (e.g., lexical decisions, semantic decisions, proofreading), there is always the concern that the secondary task may have changed the nature of the reading process itself, making the results less generalizable to natural reading situations. Furthermore, because the phonological involvement has been inferred from the often slow secondary response rather than from reading itself, the findings are equivocal with respect to the time course of the phonological activation. Phonological interference could have resulted from the delayed effect of phonological codes that were not involved in the initial activation of word meanings. Consequently, it would be preferable to look for evidence of phonological involvement from an on-line reading measure (see also Van Orden, 1991).

The Daneman and Reingold studies

Daneman and Reingold (1993)

In Daneman and Reingold (1993), we looked for evidence of phonologically mediated lexical access in the most natural or typical of reading situations possible, reading for comprehension and enjoyment. Participants read the same 1100-word text (called *Russell Wood*) used in the Daneman and Stainton (1991) proofreading study. However, they were not told that inconsistent words had been introduced into the text, nor were they given explicit instructions to proofread for the inconsistent words as they read; they were simply asked to read for comprehension and their eye fixations were recorded to examine whether phonological involvement was spontaneously revealed in the moment-to-moment computational processes of regular reading. Previous research has shown that readers gaze longer at words that are inconsistent with previously read information (Carpenter and Daneman, 1981; Frazier and Rayner, 1982; Just and Carpenter, 1980) and frequently make regressive fixations as they attempt to resolve the inconsistencies (Carpenter and Daneman, 1981). Thus, any additional time spent fixating an inconsistent word (e.g., ... *One night a week they would meat* ... or ... *One night a week they would moat* ...) relative to the consistent one (e.g., ... *One night a week they would meet* ...) could be attributed to the processes involved in inconsistency detection and recovery. If phonological codes are used to activate word meanings as the Daneman and Stainton (1991) proofreading data would have us believe, then readers should frequently fail to detect homophone errors, showing no additional processing time when first encountering *meat* relative to processing time spent when first encountering the contextually appropriate *meet*. On the other hand, if orthographic codes are used to activate word meanings, then readers should have no difficulty detecting homophone errors, showing as much disruption when initially encountering the homophone error *meat* as the orthographic control error *moat*.

The Daneman and Reingold (1993) eye fixation data suggested that readers use orthographic codes rather than phonological codes to activate the meanings of words during natural silent reading. Contrary to the results of Daneman and Stainton (1991) from their secondary proofreading task, Daneman and Reingold (1993) found no evidence that homophony interfered with the initial detection of homophone errors. In fact, first pass gaze durations showed that not only did the homophone errors cause more disruptions than the contextually correct homophones when first encountered (Experiments 1 and 2), but these homophone errors were as disruptive as the orthographic control errors (Experiment 2), suggesting that they were detected as easily. This lack of phonological interference in the early detection of homophonic errors was taken as evidence against those models that assume that phonological sources of activation invariably precede lexical access (Daneman and Stainton, 1991; Van Orden, 1987). Instead, the results suggested that readers bypass phonology, using the orthographic representations for *meat* and *moat* as a direct route to their contextually inconsistent meanings, 'edible flesh' and 'trench', respectively. The Daneman and Reingold (1993) eye-fixation data also revealed that the orthographic similarity between the homophone impostor and its mate did not affect the detectability of homophone errors; readers were as likely to detect orthographically similar same-length homophone impostors (e.g. *meat* posing as *meet*) as they were to detect less orthographically similar different-length homophone impostors (e.g., *wade* posing as *weighed*).

Whereas the initial detection data of Daneman and Reingold (1993) did not provide evidence for the early engagement of phonological processes in activating a word's meaning, the post-detection data provided some evidence for the delayed involvement of phonology in the error recovery processes. We found that homophony facilitated the error recovery processes that are initiated after an inconsistency is detected. The regressive eye fixations showed that readers spent less time rereading phrases containing homophonic errors (e.g., *One night a week they would meat . . .*) relative to phrases containing the orthographically matched nonhomophonic errors (e.g., *One night a week they would moat . . .*), presumably because for those cases in which readers had successfully detected the inconsistent impostor word (*meat*), they could exploit the shared phonology (e.g., /mit/) as a route to recovering the correct alternative (*meet*). These data suggested that phonology has its influence after lexical access.

Daneman, Reingold and Davidson (1995)

In Daneman et al. (1995), we provided evidence for the reliability of the Daneman and Reingold (1993) findings. In Experiment 1, participants read one of two new texts, and their eye movements were monitored for evidence of spontaneous disruptions when encountering homophonic and nonhomophonic error words. In one text (called *Black Queen*), all the homophone errors were low-frequency words relative to their contextually correct mates (e.g., *meat* substituted for *meet*; *rein* substituted for *rain*). In the other text (called *Desjardins*) all the homophone errors were high-frequency words relative to their contextually correct mates (e.g., *meet* substituted for *meat*; *rain* substituted for *rein*). As in the Daneman and Reingold (1993) study, we found that homophony did not interfere with the initial detection of homophone errors. First pass gaze durations showed that not only did homophone errors cause more disruption than correct homophones (Experiments 1A and 1B), but these homophone errors were as disruptive as the orthographic control errors (Experiment 1B), suggesting that orthography rather than phonology is used to activate word meanings. The only possible hint of an early influence of phonology came in the Black Queen text which contained the lower-frequency homophone errors; although the data showed no statistical support for any effect of relative word frequency on the initial detection of homophone errors, there was a hint (albeit a nonsignificant one) that the lower-frequency homophone errors were less disruptive than their orthographic controls (Experiment 1B), an issue that will be addressed in the present study. There was, of course, a delayed involvement of phonology in the error recovery process: Experiment 1 replicated the Daneman and Reingold (1993) finding that homophony facilitated error recovery by showing that readers spent less time in regressive fixations to homophone errors than to orthographic control errors.

The Daneman et al. (1995) study also exposed the dangers of using a secondary proofreading response to make inferences about the time course of phonological activation during reading. In Experiment 2, participants read the original Daneman and Reingold (1993) Russell Wood text, but this time they were given explicit instructions to proofread for inconsistent words as they read. By collecting eye movement data in conjunction with an explicit proofreading task, we showed that overt proofreading responses are unreliable indices of error detection because even when readers failed to make an overt error detection response, their eye fixations revealed that they were disrupted by an error. Taken alone, the proofreading data would have led to the conclusion that phonology is used to activate word meanings because they showed that readers were less likely to make an overt detection response in the presence of homophonic errors than in the presence of orthographic control errors. However, the eye fixations revealed the same degree of disruption when readers first encountered homophonic errors as when they encountered orthographic control errors, leading to the conclusion that orthography rather than phonology is used to activate word meanings.

Our model

We believe that the on-line eye fixation data from our inconsistency detection paradigm provide compelling evidence concerning the time course of phonological activation during natural silent reading. With the possible exception of low-fre-quency words (Daneman et al., 1995, Experiment 1B), we take our data to be inconsistent with a theory of lexical access in which phonological codes play an early and/or dominant role (e.g. Daneman and Stainton, 1991; Inhoff and Topolski, 1994; Perfetti, Bell and Delaney, 1988; Pollatsek et al., 1992; Rayner et al., 1995; Van Orden, 1987; Van Orden, Pennington and Stone, 1990). Rather, the data are consistent with a theory in which orthographic codes play the dominant role in activating word meanings (see also Coltheart, 1978; McCusker, Hillinger and Bias, 1981; McCutchen and Perfetti, 1982). Our model is depicted in Fig. 1. The figure highlights the main pathways of activation involved in accessing words meanings and detecting semantic inconsistencies in the kinds of low-constraint texts used in Daneman and Reingold (1993) and Daneman et al. (1995). Because most of our target words were not predictable from the preceding context, we believe that bottom-up sources of activation played the major role; later we will describe how the model can be extended to account for top-down sources of activation in the highly predictable contexts used by Rayner et al. (1998). As seen in Fig. 1, the predominant route from print to meaning is via the orthographic representation;

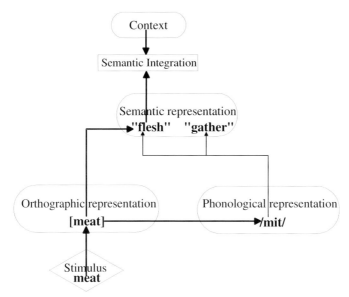

Fig. 1. A model of meaning activation and inconsistency detection consistent with the findings of Daneman and Reingold (1993) and Daneman et al. (1995). Note that arrows depict the direction of activation and stronger activation pathways are depicted by thicker links.

the printed stimulus *meat* activates the orthographic representation *[meat]* which in turn activates the semantic interpretation 'edible flesh.' The error word *meat* will be detected if the reader fails to integrate 'edible flesh' with the preceding context '*One night a week they would . . .* ' Although orthography plays the dominant role in lexical access, our model leaves open the possibility of phonologically mediated lexical access. As seen in Fig. 1, the orthographic representation *[meat]* also activates the phonological representation */mit/* which can activate the semantic representations 'flesh' and 'gather'; if the latter meaning is selected, semantic integration will succeed and the error word *meat* will go undetected. However, word meaning is less likely to be activated by the phonological representation than by the orthographic representation because activation from phonology is considerably weaker and/or delayed.

The Rayner, Pollatsek, and Binder critique and our response

Using a variant of our eye-movement inconsistency detection paradigm, Rayner et al. (1998) have reported a pattern of data that is inconsistent with our pattern in several ways, and they have interpreted their data as evidence for the early involvement of phonology in accessing word meanings. We will first describe their

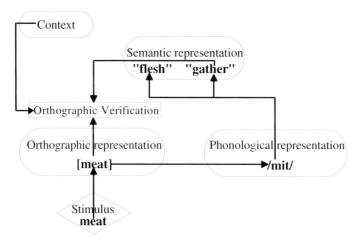

Fig. 2. The verification model of meaning activation and inconsistency detection proposed by Rayner et al. (1998).

model of lexical access and inconsistency detection and the predictions derived from the model. Then we will describe their main findings and critically evaluate their interpretation of these findings. Finally we will present new data from a norming study and a replication study to support our position.

Rayner, Pollatsek, and Binder's model

Rayner et al. (1998) appeal to the verification model of lexical access (see also Van Orden, 1987) to make their predictions and to explain their results. The verification model is depicted in Fig. 2.[2] According to the verification model, the phonological representation is activated immediately and used exclusively to gain access to a word's semantic representation, with the orthographic representation playing a post-activation verification role. As seen in Fig. 2, when the reader encounters the printed word *meat*, its phonological representation */mit/* is immediately activated from the orthographic features, and it is the phonological representation that activates candidate lexical entries such as 'flesh' and 'gather'. However, before an activated lexical entry can be selected, it must pass a verification test or spelling check. The orthographic representation associated with the most active candidate

---

2 Rayner et al. (1998) do not provide as detailed an account of the verification model in their paper as we provide here. However, we believe that it is important to articulate their model and its predictions clearly if we are to critically evaluate their study, and we believe that our rendition of the model is entirely consistent with the model that they appear to be using to make their predictions and to explain their results. Our rendition is also consistent with the verification model described by Van Orden (1987).

is retrieved from memory and compared with the orthographic representation of the word being read. If a match occurs, the lexical entry is selected; if not, the verification process is repeated on the next most active candidate lexical entry. According to this model, the printed homophone *meat* may sometimes be mistaken for *meet* if the false candidate *meet* were made available to the orthographic verification procedure and the mismatch in spelling slipped by undetected. According to Rayner et al. (1998), two factors influence the likelihood of detecting a spelling error when the false candidate of a homophone undergoes orthographic verification. The first factor is the orthographic similarity of the homophone to its mate; the greater the orthographic similarity of the homophones, the harder it should be to detect the mismatch (e.g., the error word *meat* would be harder to detect than the error word *chute* because *meat* is more orthographically similar to *meet* than *chute* is to *shoot*). The second factor that influences orthographic verification is the predictability of the correct target word from the prior context; if the prior context strongly predicts a target word, top-down or expectancy-driven reading may lead to a relaxation or abortion of the verification process, allowing a mismatch to go undetected. Rayner et al. (1998) tested these predictions by manipulating orthographic similarity and contextual constraint. Orthographically similar homophone pairs shared the same first two letters (e.g., *meat–meet*) or the same first letter (e.g., *rain–rein*); orthographically dissimilar pairs did not share the same first letter (e.g., *chute–shoot*; *right–write*). In the high-constraint passages, the correct homophone target was highly predictable from the preceding context ($M = 0.86$); in the low-constraint passages, the correct homophone target was not predictable ($M = 0.03$). Whereas Rayner et al. (1998) argue that their data "appear to be compatible with" (p. 492) the verification model, we will argue that their high-constraint data are compatible but their low-constraint data are not.

Before describing the results of Rayner et al. (1998), it is worth highlighting an important difference between their model and ours with respect to the locus at which an error/inconsistency is detected. For the most part, Rayner et al. (1998) appear to be assigning error detection to the orthographic verification process rather than to the processes that attempt to integrate an activated word meaning with the preceding context as we do in our model. This locus is logically possible in the case of detecting homophonic errors (e.g., *meat* posing for *meet*); the phonology /mit/ activates the false candidate *meet* which is made available to the orthographic verification procedure and the mismatch in spelling between the retrieved orthography *[meet]* and the actual orthography of the printed word *[meat]* is successfully detected. However, an orthographic control error (such as *moat* posing for *meet*) cannot be detected by orthographic verification; in this case the phonological code /mot/ would have activated the semantic representation 'trench' and because its associated orthographic representation *[moat]* matches the actual printed orthography *moat*, there is no mismatch to be detected. The only way to detect that the word *moat* is erroneous is to notice that the activated meaning 'trench' is inconsistent with the preceding context. Interestingly, Rayner et al. (1998) do not seem to have appreciated that their model calls for two different mechanisms for detecting homophonic versus nonhomophonic errors, or if they have, they do not make it explicit in their paper. A by-product of their emphasis on orthographic verification rather than semantic integration as the locus of error detection is that they favour first fixation durations as the most sensitive measures of early processing. Because we emphasize semantic integration and inconsistency detection, we favour gaze duration (the sum of all fixations on a word prior to moving to another word) because gaze duration has been shown to better reflect both meaning retrieval and semantic integration than does first fixation duration (Carpenter and Daneman, 1981; Inhoff, 1984; Just and Carpenter, 1987).

Rayner, Pollatsek, and Binder's data and our response

Strongest support for phonologically mediated lexical access came from Rayner et al.'s (1998) *high-constraint texts*. As the verification model (Fig. 2) predicts, homophony interfered with the initial detection of homophone errors particularly if they were orthographically similar to their mates. In the orthographically similar condition (e.g., *meat*, *meet*), first fixation durations showed that homophone errors behaved the same as contextually correct homophones (Experiments 1, 2, 3), and both were less disruptive than were the orthographic control errors (Experiments 2 and 3). In the orthographically dissimilar condition (e.g., *chute*, *shoot*), first fixation durations showed that homophone errors were more disruptive than contextually correct homophones, but less disruptive than orthographic errors. These data are consistent with Rayner et al.'s (1998) verification model (Fig. 2) because the model predicts that homophone errors should be especially difficult to detect if the contextually correct homophone is highly predictable and similar in spelling to the homophone error.

It is when we come to Rayner et al.'s (1998) data for low-constraint texts (the texts more like ours) that the verification model runs into trouble. When the correct target word was not predictable, fixation durations showed a pattern similar to that for orthographically dissimilar homophones in high-constraint text. Regardless of the orthographic similarity condition, first fixation durations showed that homophone errors were more disruptive than contextually correct homophones but less disruptive than orthographic control errors (Experiment 3). The finding of a difference in fixation durations for incorrect homophones and correct homophones is consistent with Rayner et al.'s (1998) model which predicts that homophone errors should be more easily detected in low-constraint contexts than in high-constraint contexts because the orthographic verification check is more efficient when the target word is not predictable. However, the model cannot account for the finding that orthographic similarity between the homophone error and its contextually correct mate did not affect the detectability of homophone errors.

Rayner et al. (1998) recognize that the lack of an orthographic similarity effect is a problem for a verification model such as theirs. They attempt to accommodate the finding within the framework of their model by arguing that "under low constraint conditions, the bottom-up verification process works more efficiently with no top-down expectation process to abort it, and thus it operates rapidly enough to affect first fixation durations even when the homophones are orthographically similar." (p. 492). This explanation is of course totally unsatisfactory. The only way it could work is if the orthographic verification process were so efficient that it succeeded in detecting all homophone errors, and then there should have been no difference in the degree of disruption for homophone errors versus orthographic control errors. Although that was the pattern we found in our experiments, it was not the pattern found in the experiment of Rayner et al. (1998); first fixation durations for homophone errors were shorter than for orthographic errors, suggesting that some of the homophone errors had slipped by the orthographic verification process undetected. As long as some homophone errors were not being detected, there should have been a higher probability that they were the orthographically similar ones. It would appear that Rayner et al. (1998) are not entirely convinced by their own argument because immediately after making it they say "Although this is possible, it seems strange that there appeared to be no modulation of the size of the effect as a function of orthographic similarity" (p. 492).

The next attempt of Rayner et al. (1998) to deal with the lack of an orthographic similarity effect in low-constraint texts is even more puzzling. Instead of abandoning their orthographic verification model, they seem to be proposing a second model for lexical access and error detection in low-constraint conditions. Issues of parsimony aside, we will argue that this model cannot co-exist with their orthographic verification model because the two are logically incompatible. Rayner et al. (1998) argue that the low-constraint condition "may not be particularly diagnostic because the initial detection of anomaly may be largely based on the degree of anomaly of the actual words to the preceding context rather than to any orthographic or phonological similarity to the correct homophone" (p. 492). In other words, because they could not find an effect of orthographic similarity for low-constraint texts, they want to argue that phonological identity and orthographic similarity are important factors in error detection in high-constraint texts, whereas semantic inconsistency is the locus of error detection in low-constraint texts. Of course, we have argued all along that semantic inconsistency detection is the mechanism for detecting all error words in this paradigm. [3] However, Rayner et al. (1998) still want to maintain the phonological route to meaning activation and so they propose that homophony has two opposing effects on error detection in low-constraint texts: "(a) activation of a semantic code that is a good continuation, which delays (or possibly aborts) judgments that the word does not make sense in context, but (b) activation of a semantic code that is a 'model' of good continuation that makes detection of the meaning of the wrong homophone easier and faster" (Rayner et al., 1998, p. 495). We have no problems with mechanism (a); after all, the paradigm was designed to investigate the possibility that homophony might lead to the activation of the false but contextually consistent meaning, making the homophone error word difficult to detect. However, we are puzzled by their proposal of mechanism (b), the idea that phonological activation of both homophone meanings results in homophone errors being more inconsistent and hence easier to detect. This proposal is puzzling on empirical grounds because it predicts that homophone errors will be more conspicuous than orthographic errors, a pattern neither they nor we have found. Of course, by suggesting that "under certain circumstances, mechanisms (a) and (b) may be equally potent" (p. 495) Rayner et al. (1998) give themselves a way to account for the lack of difference between homophone errors and control errors we obtained in our experiments; however, trade-off explanations of null effects are complex and not particularly satisfying. In any case, there is reason to dismiss Rayner et al.'s (1998) proposal for low-constraint texts on logical grounds because it is incompatible with their verification model for high-constraint texts. As illustrated earlier (see Fig. 2), according to the verification model, context only has its effect at the orthographic verification phase which is *after* phonology has activated meaning. Consequently, mechanisms (a) and (b) should be equally possible in the high-constraint condition as in the low-constraint condition. And yet Rayner et al. (1998) invoke these two mechanisms for detecting semantic inconsistencies in conditions of low contextual constraint only, and we find this troublesome.

In the final analysis, Rayner et al. (1998) seem willing to ignore the low-constraint data and to base their strong claims for the phonological activation of word meaning on the data from high-constraint texts alone. We see two problems with this decision. First, words that are as highly predictable as Rayner et al.'s (1998) high-constraint words probably represent a small proportion of the content words that occur in natural complex prose; consequently, we think it unwise to assume

---

3 And Rayner et al.'s (1998) own data demonstrated that inconsistency detection is the mechanism for detecting error words in this paradigm. Remember that their first attempt to investigate error detection in low-constraint texts (Experiment 2) was a failure; there was no difference in first pass times for correct homophones, homophone errors, and orthographic control errors, precisely because the error words were consistent with the prior context when first encountered and only became inconsistent later in the sentence.

that the way readers process highly predictable words will generalize to the way they process most content words in natural texts. Second, even though Rayner et al.'s (1998) high-constraint data are consistent with phonologically mediated access and post-access verification, there is an equally plausible account of the findings of Rayner et al. that does not involve the use of phonological codes to activate meaning. This account is depicted in Figs. 3 and 4, and is an extension of our model for low-constraint texts depicted in Fig. 1.

Our alternative model for high-constraint text

Whereas our model for low-constraint texts emphasized bottom-up sources of activation (from print to orthography to meaning), the model in Figs. 3 and 4 includes top-down influences as well (see also McClelland, 1987). Fig. 3 illustrates the model for the homophone error *meat*; Fig. 4 illustrates the model for the orthographic control error *moat*. As seen in the top panel of Fig. 3, if the context for *meet* is highly constrained, it will begin to activate the semantic representation 'gather' and the semantic representation will itself activate the corresponding phonological representation /*mit*/ and orthographic representation [*meet*] before the reader has even fixated the printed word *meat*. When the reader does fixate the printed word (Fig. 3, bottom panel), the phonological representation /*mit*/ and semantic representation 'gather' will receive further activation. The combination of top-down activation by the preceding context and bottom-up activation by the printed word may be enough to select the phonological representation /*mit*/ and semantic representation 'gather,' allowing the homophone error *meat* to go unnoticed (see also Jared and Seidenberg, 1991). According to this model, it is meaning that first activates phonology and not phonology that first activates meaning. Fig. 4 illustrates why it is easier to detect the orthographic control error *moat* than the homophone error *meat* in highly constrained text. The first phase of activation before the printed word is encountered is of course identical for *moat* as for *meat*, with the semantic representation 'gather' and the phonological representation /*mit*/ receiving activation before the error word is encountered (Fig. 4; top panel). However, once the printed word *moat* is fixated, the contribution of bottom-up activation will be more diffuse because there will be bottom-up activation of an additional phonological representation /*mot*/ (Fig. 4; bottom panel). Consequently, there will be less convergence of activation on /*mit*/ and 'gather' than there was in the case of the printed word *meat*, and hence less of a probability that the orthographic control error *moat* goes undetected. We think that the model depicted in Figs. 3 and 4 provides a plausible account of the homophone interference effect found in Rayner et al.'s high-constraint texts without invoking exclusive bottom-up activation of meaning by phonology. The model is consistent with our model for processing words in the more natural low-constraint texts.

Before fixating 'meat'

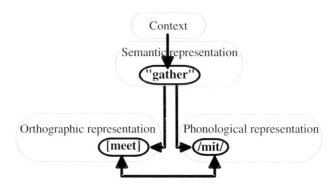

While fixating 'meat'

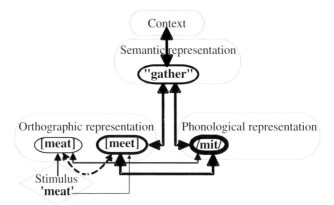

Fig. 3. A model of meaning activation in highly predictable texts, as it applies to the homophone error *meat*. Bidirectional arrows depict activation in two directions. Dotted lines represent inhibitory processes.

Rayner et al.'s concerns about our research

So far we have focused on Rayner et al.'s (1998) interpretation of their findings and our concerns about their interpretation. Next we will briefly mention two issues they raise about *our* experiments and our response to these issues. Rayner et al. (1998) raise the issue of how to characterize the degree of contextual constraint in our experimental passages. Given that degree of contextual constraint had a large effect on the pattern of results in their study, it is difficult to compare the results from the two laboratories without having some idea about the contextual constraint levels in our texts. As Rayner et al. (1998) point out, it would appear that many of our correct

Before fixating 'moat'

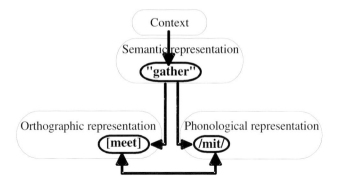

While fixating 'moat'

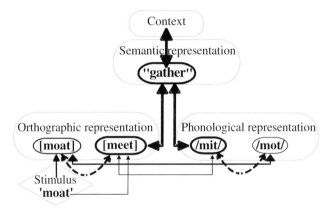

Fig. 4. A model of meaning activation in highly predictable texts, as it applies to the orthographic error *moat*. Bidirectional arrows depict activation in two directions. Dotted lines represent inhibitory processes.

homophones were not predictable from the preceding context, making our natural texts more like their carefully constructed low-constraint passages. However, as they also point out, some of our correct homophones were highly predictable from the preceding context, and so a direct comparison across laboratories becomes tricky. Rayner et al. (1998) also question whether our homophone errors and our orthographic control errors are equally inconsistent with the preceding context. Whereas Rayner et al. (1998) tried to equate degree of inconsistency by collecting formal ratings for the two kinds of errors in their low-constraint passages, our assessment of degree of semantic inconsistency for our two kinds of errors was an informal one. As Rayner et al. (1998) point out, "the immediacy of detecting that the actual word does not fit (and hence the degree to which it would affect early measures of processing such as first fixation duration and gaze duration) would depend on the degree to which it was anomalous with the prior context" (p. 495). If our homophone errors were more inconsistent than our control errors, this could have accounted for why they were detected easily and immediately.

The norming study

Our first step was to conduct a formal evaluation of these issues in a norming study. We used procedures similar to those used by Rayner et al. (1998) to obtain contextual constraint estimates and semantic consistency ratings for the three experimental texts we have used: the *Russell Wood* text used in Daneman and Reingold (1993) and in Experiment 2 of Daneman et al. (1995), and the *Black Queen* and *Desjardins* texts used in Experiments 1A and 1B of Daneman et al. (1995). For each of the three texts, contextual constraint scores were obtained by having three separate groups of 20 University of Toronto undergraduate students perform a modified cloze task in which they were presented the text up to but not including the target word, and they were asked to guess what the next word would be. For each of the three texts, semantic consistency scores were obtained by presenting three new groups of 30 undergraduate students with the text up to and including the target word and their task was to rate on a scale of 1 to 7 how well the target word fit into the preceding context. (A rating of 1 meant that the word was totally inconsistent with the context, whereas a rating of 7 meant that the word was consistent and a good continuation of the passage.) For the semantic consistency ratings for each of the three texts, each rater provided ratings for one third of the correct target words, one third of the homophone errors, and one third of the orthographic control errors. The contextual constraint scores (expressed as the proportion of completions with the correct homophone) and the semantic consistency ratings (1–7) for our three texts are provided in Table 1.

There are several points to note from the norming data in Table 1. First, the contextual constraint scores show that all three of our texts can be considered low-constraint texts when compared to the passages used by Rayner et al. (1998). However, it is also interesting to note that the average predictability of correct homophone target words in the Black Queen text was higher (0.28) than in the Russell Wood (0.04) and Desjardins (0.08) texts, and there was also a wider range of predictability scores for correct target words in the Black Queen text (scores ranged from 0.00 to 1.00, SD = 0.33). The Black Queen text was the text that showed a hint of a phonological effect in Daneman et al. (1995, Experiment 1B). We had attributed the weak phonological effect to the fact that the homophone errors in the Black Queen text were lower-frequency words than the homophone errors in the Desjardins text. However, it is possible that the weak effect was due to the

Table 1

Contextual constraint scores (in a proportion) and semantic consistency ratings (1–7) from norming study

Text	Contextual consistency ratings		Semantic consistency ratings					
			Correct word		Homophone error		Orthographic error	
	Mean	SD	Mean	SD	Mean	SD	Mean	SD
Russell Wood	0.04	0.06	6.74	0.60	1.53	0.85	1.34	0.52
Desjardins	0.08	0.13	6.82	0.27	1.55	0.23	1.36	0.27
Black Queen	0.28	0.33	6.78	0.25	1.51	0.26	1.10	0.10

presence of some highly predictable target words in the Black Queen text. This is an issue we explore in the replication study reported next. And finally, the semantic consistency scores show that our results were unlikely to have been contaminated by differences in semantic inconsistency between homophone errors and orthographic control errors. As seen in Table 1, our homophone errors were not judged to be more inconsistent with the preceding context than were our orthographic control errors; if anything there were judged to be a little less inconsistent. Consequently, it was not a failure to equate for semantic inconsistency that produced our pattern of results in which homophone errors were as easy to detect as orthographic control errors. What the norms in Table 1 show is that at least two of our texts, Russell Wood and Desjardins, are comparable to the Rayner et al. (1998) low-constraint passages in terms of degree of contextual constraint and degree of semantic inconsistency. This means that neither contextual constraint nor semantic inconsistency can explain why we found no evidence for early phonological involvement in accessing word meanings in our low-constraint texts whereas they found some evidence for early phonological involvement.

The replication study

In addition to collecting norms, we also ran another experiment in which we attempted a replication of the experiment with the Desjardins and Black Queen texts (Experiment 1B, Daneman et al., 1995). In the original Daneman et al. study there were only 15 participants who read the Desjardins text and 15 participants who read the Black Queen text. By collecting eye movement data from a further 18 participants on the Black Queen text, the replication allowed us to see whether the previous hint of a phonological effect for the Black Queen text was a real effect and also whether differences in the probability of detecting the homophone errors in the Black Queen text were correlated with differences in the degree to which their correct homophone mates were constrained by the preceding context. In addition, by collecting eye movement data from a further 18 participants on the Desjardins text, the replication experiment allowed us to see whether we could once again find the pattern of homophone errors being detected as easily as control errors in the low-constraint Desjardins text, the pattern that has been challenged by Rayner et al. (1998).

The materials for our replication experiment were identical to those for Experiment 1B in Daneman et al. (1995), so we will describe them only briefly here. The experimental manipulation involved 30 homophone word pairs with asymmetric word frequencies (e.g., *hair–hare*; *meet–meat*, *peer–pier*, and *rain–rein*). The mean Kuçera and Francis (1967) frequency count for the higher-frequency member of the pair (e.g., *hair*, *meet*, *peer*, and *rain*) was 336 occurrences per million (Mdn = 162, SD = 520); the mean frequency count for the lower frequency member of the pair (e.g., *hare*, *meat*, *pier*, and *rein*) was 43 occurrences per million (Mdn = 14, SD = 85). [4] Although the members of a homophone pair differed in frequency, they were orthographically similar to one another in that each member of the pair was spelled with the same initial letter and was the same length as the other. The orthographic control word for each homophone pair shared the same consonant sounds as the correct word and its homophone mate but differed only in the vowel sound (e.g., *moat* for *meet–meat* and *ruin* for *rain–rein*). Because the controls were matched for orthographic similarity rather than for frequency, we used the same orthographic control for both members of a homophone pair. The 30 lower-frequency homophones all appeared in (or were edited into) the short story *The Desjardins* by Duncan Campbell Scott (1988); the 30 higher-frequency homophones all appeared in (or were edited into) the short story *The Black Queen* by Barry Callaghan (1988). Participants read a version of the Desjardins or Black Queen text in which 10 of the target words appeared in their correct form, 10 as homophone errors, and 10 as orthographic control errors. Counterbalancing was accomplished by creating three versions of each text; a target word appeared in a different form (correct word, homophone error, and orthographic error) in each version. In the original Daneman et al. (1995) study, 15 participants read the Desjardins text and 15 participants read the Black Queen text. In the replication study, we had 18 participants read Desjardins and another 18 read the Black Queen. Participants in both studies were students at the University of Toronto.

The procedure for the replication study was similar to that for the original Experiment 1B of Daneman et al. (1995). Participants were told that they would

---

4 Note that our frequency manipulation involved a manipulation of the relative word frequency of the text word and the error replacement rather than a manipulation of their absolute frequency. Even our lower-frequency homophones were sufficiently common that readers would be likely to know their meaning and spelling (e.g., *meat–meat* and *rain–rein*, but not *pigeon–pidgin* or *bridal–bridle* as in Jared and Seidenberg, 1991).

be presented a short story on successive screens of a computer monitor. They were instructed to read the story silently at their own pace, making sure they understood it well enough to answer questions about its content later. The text was presented in black (brightness $= 4$ cd/m^2) on a white background (brightness $= 68$ cd/m^2). Proportional spaced fonts were used with an average of 2.2 characters per degree of visual angle and an average of 10 lines per screen. Displays were generated using an S3 VGA card and a 17″ ViewSonic 17PS monitor. At the 60-cm viewing distance the display subtended a visual angle of 30° horizontally and 22.5° vertically. When participants finished reading a screen they pressed a button to proceed to the next screen. In the original Daneman et al. (1995) study, eye fixations were recorded by an Iscan (Model RK-416) video-based eye tracking system. In the present replication study, the eye tracker employed was the SR Research Ltd. EyeLink system. This system has high spatial resolution (0.005°), and a sampling rate of 250 Hz (4 ms temporal resolution). The EyeLink headband has three cameras, allowing the simultaneous tracking of both eyes and of head position for head-motion compensation. By default, only the participant's dominant eye was tracked in our study. The EyeLink system uses an Ethernet link between the eye tracker and display computers for real-time saccade and gaze position data transfer. The system also performs saccade and blink detection on-line. In the present study, the configurable acceleration and velocity thresholds were set to detect saccades of 0.5° or greater. A 9-point calibration was performed at the start of the experiment, followed by a 9-point calibration accuracy test. Calibration was repeated if any point was in error by more than 1°, or if the average error for all points was greater than 0.5°.

The eye fixation results of the replication study are presented in Table 2. As discussed earlier, our preferred measure of initial meaning retrieval and semantic integration/inconsistency detection is gaze duration on the target word (the sum of all fixations on the target word prior to moving to another word); however, first fixation duration on the target word (the duration of the first fixation on the target word independent of the number of fixations on that word) and single fixation duration on the target word (the fixation duration when only one fixation is made on the word) are also presented in Table 2 because these are measures analyzed in Rayner et al. (1998). In addition to these three measures which are sensitive to early processes, total time on the target word (the sum of all fixations on the target word, including regressions) is presented as a measure that is sensitive to the later processes of error recovery as well. The corresponding data from Experiment 1B of Daneman et al. (1995) are also provided in Table 2 for comparison purposes,[5] as are the combined data for the original and replication studies.

---

5 Note that single fixation durations were not reported in Daneman et al. (1995).

Table 2

Mean reading times (in milliseconds) in the replication experiment, Daneman et al.'s (1995) Experiment 1B, and averaged across the two experiments

	Replication			Daneman et al. (1995)			Combined		
	Correct word	Hom. error	Orthog. error	Correct word	Hom. error	Orthog. error	Correct word	Hom. error	Orthog. error
n:	(18)	(18)	(18)	(15)	(15)	(15)	(33)	(33)	(33)
Desjardins									
Gaze duration	280	314	319	288	339	334	284	325	326
First fixation duration	232	240	247	247	269	276	238	253	260
Single fixation duration	235	253	254	250	283	281	242	267	267
Total time	346	532	591	341	592	721	343	559	650
Black Queen									
Gaze duration	252	299	332	250	294	330	251	296	331
First fixation duration	219	236	237	228	235	257	223	235	246
Single fixation duration	223	242	234	230	241	270	226	241	250
Total time	296	477	579	266	523	637	282	498	605

Hom. error = homophone error; orthog. error = orthographic control error.

As Table 2 shows, the eye fixation data from the new study closely replicated the eye fixation data from the original Daneman et al. (1995) Experiment 1B. Indeed, across-experiment statistical analyses showed no main effect of Experiment (original vs. replication) and no interactions between Experiment and any of the experimental manipulations (all $ps > 0.05$), so we will focus our discussion on the results averaged across the two experiments.

Take first the results for the Desjardins text. Remember, this is the text in which the correct words were the lower-frequency homophones (e.g., *meat, rein*), and the homophone errors were the higher-frequency homophones (e.g., *meet* substituted for *meat*; *hair* substituted for *hare*). It is also a text that was judged to have low contextual constraint in our norming study (the mean predictability of the correct homophone target words was 0.08). And it is the text that showed clear evidence for the orthographic route to meaning access in Experiment 1B of Daneman et al. (1995). In that experiment, the Desjardins text showed no evidence for the early engagement of phonological processes in meaning retrieval because homophone errors were as disruptive as orthographic control errors when initially encountered. However, there was evidence for the delayed involvement of phonology in error recovery in that readers spent less time regressing to homophone errors than control errors. This pattern of early orthographic influences and later phonological influences was closely replicated in the new study.

If we look at the results averaged across all 33 participants who read the

Desjardins text, the gaze durations in Table 2 show that readers initially took 41 ms longer to process a homophone error than its contextually correct mate ($t(32) = 3.53$, $p < 0.003$) and they took 42 ms longer to process an orthographic control error than the contextually correct word ($t(32) = 4.38$, $p < 0.001$). However, there was no significant difference in initial processing time for homophone versus orthographic control errors ($t(32) = 0.08$, $p > 0.90$). This lack of difference in initial processing time for homophone versus orthographic control errors was also observed in first fixation durations ($t(32) = 0.99$, $p > 0.30$) and single fixation durations ($t(32) = 0.03$, $p > 0.95$). The lack of difference suggests that homophone errors were detected as easily as orthographic control errors, and so orthography rather than phonology was used to activate word meanings. We did find evidence for a delayed involvement of phonological codes when we examined total time on the target words, a measure that includes later regressions to the target word. As Table 2 shows, readers spent 216 ms longer reading and rereading a homophone error than its contextually correct mate, and they spent 307 ms longer reading and rereading an orthographic control error than the correct word; however, now the time spent on homophone errors was significantly less than on the orthographic errors (all p-values <0.01), presumably because for those cases in which readers had successfully detected the inconsistent imposter word (e.g., *meat* substituted for *meet*) they could capitalize on the shared phonology (/*mit*/) as a route to recovering the correct alternative (*meet*). The finding of a delayed involvement of phonology in error recovery is noncontentious because Rayner et al. (1998) found it too. However, the finding that homophone errors were as disruptive as orthographic control errors for the low-constraint Desjardins text is inconsistent with Rayner et al.'s finding for low-constraint texts, because Rayner et al. (1998) reported a pattern in which homophone errors were less disruptive than orthographic control errors. Nevertheless, the pattern of results for our Desjardins text is entirely consistent with the pattern of results for our other low-constraint text, Russell Wood (Daneman and Reingold, 1993, Experiment 2; Daneman et al., 1995, Experiment 2) and so we continue to argue that the orthographic route is the dominant route to meaning retrieval when words are not highly predictable as is the case for most content words in natural complex prose.

The results for the Black Queen text differed somewhat from those for Desjardins. Remember, Black Queen is the text in which the correct words were the higher-frequency homophones (e.g., *meet*, *rain*), and the homophone errors were the lower-frequency homophones (e.g., *meat* substituted for *meet*; *hare* substituted for *hair*). It is also the text that was judged to be higher in contextual constraint than the Desjardins and Russell Wood texts; the mean predictability of the correct homophone target words was 0.28 in Black Queen. Although a mean contextual constraint score of 0.28 is much lower than the 0.86 mean predictability in Rayner et al.'s (1998) high-constraint texts, the predictability scores for some of the words in the Black Queen were high (0.80–1.00) and there was a wide range of predictability scores across the 30 target words (0.00–1.00, SD = 0.33). In the Daneman et al. (1995) Experiment 1B, the results for the 15 participants who read the Black Queen text showed a hint (albeit a nonsignificant one) of an early phonological influence in that the homophone errors were less disruptive than their orthographic controls. We had attributed the weak phonological effect to the fact that the homophone errors in the Black Queen were words of lower frequency than the homophone errors in the Desjardins text. However, the results of the norming study suggest that the weak effect could be due to the presence of some highly predictable target words in the Black Queen text. By running a replication study with a further 18 participants, we could see whether the nonsignificant trend with 15 participants is indeed real and reliable. We could also examine the effect of contextual constraint by computing the correlation between a target word's predictability and the degree to which the homophone impostor error was likely to be detected.

As Table 2 shows, the replication study produced a similar pattern of results to the original Daneman et al. (1995) Experiment 1B in that there was a nonsignificant trend of homophone errors being less disruptive than orthographic errors when initially encountered. When statistical analyses were computed for all 33 readers of the Black Queen text, this effect was significant for the gaze duration measure. As the gaze durations in Table 2 show, readers initially took 45 ms longer to process a homophone error than its contextually correct mate ($t(32) = 3.35$, $p < 0.003$) and they took 80 ms longer to process an orthographic error than the correct word ($t(32) = 6.53$, $p < 0.001$). Moreover, the 35 ms less spent in initial gaze durations on homophone errors than orthographic errors was also significant ($t(32) = 3.01$, $p < 0.006$).[6] This finding suggests that homophone errors were less disruptive than orthographic errors, and hence detected less easily, a finding consistent with the view that phonology was used to activate some of the word meanings. One explanation for why there was an early phonological effect in the Black Queen text but not in the Desjardins text is that phonology may be more likely to be implicated in the processing of low-frequency words (Jared and Seidenberg, 1991), and the homophone errors were words of lower frequency in the Black Queen text than in the Desjardins text. A second possibility is that the phonological effect may have been due to the presence of some highly predictable homophone target words in the Black Queen text. If predictability of the correct homophone was related to the likelihood of an impostor homophone being missed rather than detected, then we should expect a correlation between the degree of predictability of a correct homophone and the disruptiveness of the homophone error, such that the higher the

---

6 The trend was there for first fixation durations and single fixation durations but the differences were not statistically significant, for both cases $p > 0.10$.

predictability of the correct homophone the less disruptive the error. To test this hypothesis, we computed the correlation between the contextual constraint score for each of the 30 target words in the Black Queen text and the disruptiveness of the homophone error relative to the orthographic control error (i.e., orthographic error gaze duration minus homophone error gaze duration), averaged across the 33 participants who read Black Queen. This correlation was 0.47, $p < 0.008$, and suggested that the more predictable a target homophone, the more disruptive was the orthographic error relative to the homophone error. This finding is consistent with the findings of Rayner et al. (1998) to the extent that it shows that homophone interference effects (failure to detect homophone impostors) are more likely to occur when words are highly predictable. Presumably, Rayner et al. (1998) would argue that the finding is consistent with their verification model (depicted in Fig. 2) in which there is a bottom-up activation of meaning by phonology. However, as discussed earlier, we believe that an equally plausible alternative is the top-down model (depicted in Figs. 3 and 4) in which context activates (primes) the phonology before the printed word is even fixated. The advantage of this top-down account is that it is entirely consistent with our bottom-up model (depicted in Fig. 1) for processing words in the more natural low-constraint texts.

Concluding remarks

Rayner et al.'s (1998) article made us recognize the importance of taking the contextual predictability of a word into consideration when interpreting our data from the inconsistency detection paradigm. The data from our texts with low target word predictability (Russell Wood: Daneman and Reingold, 1993; Desjardins: Daneman et al., 1995, replication experiment) have consistently shown homophone errors to be as disruptive as orthographic errors, thus providing strong evidence that orthography rather than phonology is used to activate word meanings. However, these data are inconsistent with the data from Rayner et al.'s texts with low target word predictability. The data from our text that had a greater range of target word predictability (Black Queen: Daneman et al., 1995, replication experiment) are consistent with the view that phonology may be involved in activating word meanings, because they showed a pattern in which homophone errors were less disruptive than orthographic control errors, particularly if the correct homophones were highly predictable from the preceding context. These data are consistent with the data from Rayner et al.'s (1998) texts with high target word predictability, but we provide a different model to account for them.

We believe that our results for low-constraint text are best accommodated by the model depicted in Fig. 1. According to this model, when a word is not highly predictable from the preceding context, as is the case for most content words in everyday texts, the dominant route from print to meaning is via the orthographic representation. However, the model leaves open the possibility of phonologically mediated lexical access, as may be the case when word recognition is slowed down by an unfamiliar or low-frequency word. A nice feature of our model is that it can be extended to account for top-down sources of activation in highly predictable contexts, as depicted in Figs. 3 and 4. According to the model depicted in Figs. 3 and 4, the homophone effects found by us and Rayner et al. (1998) for highly predictable words are a result of meaning activating phonology and not phonology activating meaning as Rayner et al. (1998) advocate in their verification model depicted in Fig. 2. However, we should stress that most content words are not highly predictable from their preceding context, and so top-down effects play a relatively small role in reading natural text. We certainly see no reason for invoking the verification model to account for the homophone effects found in the case of highly predictable words. The verification model does not account for our low-constraint data and it does not account for the low-constraint data of Rayner et al. (1998) either.

But how do we account for the contradictory findings for low-constraint text, for the fact that Rayner et al. (1998) did find evidence for the early involvement of phonology in meaning retrieval when target words had low predictability, whereas we have repeatedly not found such evidence?[7] A recent paper by Jared, Levy and Rayner (1999) may provide some answers to this puzzle. Jared et al. (1999) used a very similar eye movement inconsistency detection task to ours, but they also examined whether factors such as reading skill and word frequency could account for the contradictory across-lab findings for low-constraint texts. Their results suggested that both factors may have played a role. Essentially, Jared et

---

7 Pollatsek et al.'s (1992)'s parafoveal previewing task is another on-line that has yielded data inconsistent with ours. In this chapter we have focused on research that has looked for evidence of phonological involvement during reading by showing homophone interference effects. However, there have also been some on-line studies that have looked for evidence of phonological involvement by showing homophone facilitation effects in preview or priming paradigms (e.g., Pollatsek et al., 1992; Rayner et al., 1995). For example, in the study of Pollatsek et al. (1992), processing of a target word (e.g., *beech*) was facilitated if a homophone of that target word (e.g., *beach*) had been presented as a preview in the parafovea more so than if a visually similar control (e.g., *bench*) had been presented as a preview in the parafovea. The Pollatsek et al. data are inconsistent with our data because they suggested that phonological codes are activated very early in the word identification process, even before the word in question is foveally fixated. Interestingly, however, the advantage of a homophone preview over a visually similar preview was only statistically reliable for the first fixation on the target word but not for the gaze duration on the target word (see Pollatsek et al., 1992, Experiment 2). We believe that even if the preview paradigm has provided evidence for very early (nonlexical) involvement of phonology in the word encoding process, it has not provided evidence for the involvement of phonological codes in the subsequent process of accessing a word's meaning.

al. (1999) closely replicated our pattern of findings for good readers and for high-frequency words. Across three experiments, Jared et al.'s good readers showed the same pattern of data that we have continued to find; good readers were as disrupted by homophone errors as by orthographic control errors, suggesting that they used the orthographic route to retrieving word meanings. Jared et al.'s pattern of data for poor readers was similar to Rayner et al.'s (1998) data; poor readers were less disrupted by homophone errors than by orthographic errors, suggesting that they used the phonological route to meaning. Jared et al. also found an effect, albeit a less consistent one, for word frequency, such that lower-frequency words showed some evidence for phonological effects whereas higher-frequency words did not. Jared et al. (1999) suggested that "Daneman and colleagues may have tested primarily good readers using higher frequency words whereas Rayner et al. may have included readers with a wider range of abilities and used more lower frequency words" (p. 253). Thus, it would appear that factors such as predictability, word frequency, and reading skill may all have an effect on the extent to which phonology is implicated in activating a word's meaning.

In any event, we believe that there is now considerable evidence against the strong early phonology position. Our findings, together with Jared et al.'s findings for good readers and high-frequency words, make a compelling case against any model that gives phonology an early and exclusive role in gaining access to a word's semantic representation.

Acknowledgements

Preparation of this paper was supported by grants to Meredyth Daneman and Eyal Reingold from the Natural Science and Engineering Research Council of Canada. We thank Robin Morris and Sandy Pollatsek for their reviews of the chapter. Correspondence should be addressed either to Meredyth Daneman, Department of Psychology, University of Toronto, Mississauga, Ontario, Canada, L5L 1C6 (E-mail: daneman@psych.utoronto.ca) or to Eyal Reingold, University of Toronto, Department of Psychology, 100 St. George Street, Toronto, Ontario, Canada, M5S 3G3 (E-mail: reingold@psych.toronto.edu).

References

Callaghan, B. (1988). The black queen. In: M. Atwood and R. Weaver (Eds.), The Oxford Book of Canadian Short Stories. London: Oxford University Press, pp. 305–307.
Carpenter, P.A. and Daneman, M. (1981). Lexical retrieval and error recovery in reading: a model based on eye fixations. Journal of Verbal Learning and Verbal Behavior, 20, 137–160.

Coltheart, M. (1978). Lexical access in simple reading tasks. In: G. Underwood (Ed.), Strategies in Information Processing. London: Academic Press, pp. 151–216.

Coltheart, M., Davelaar, E., Jonasson, J.T. and Besner, D. (1977). Access to the internal lexicon. In: S. Dornic (Ed.), Attention and Performance VI. New York: Academic Press, pp. 534–555.

Coltheart, V., Avons, S.E. and Trollope, J. (1990). Articulatory suppression and phonological codes in reading for meaning. Quarterly Journal of Experimental Psychology, 42A, 375–399.

Coltheart, V., Laxon, V., Rickard, M. and Elton, C. (1988). Phonological recoding in reading for meaning by adults and children. Journal of Experimental Psychology: Learning, Memory, and Cognition, 14, 387–397.

Daneman, M. and Reingold, E.M. (1993). What eye fixations tell us about phonological recoding during reading. Canadian Journal of Experimental Psychology, 47, 153–178.

Daneman, M., Reingold, E.M. and Davidson, M. (1995). Time course of phonological activation during reading: Evidence from eye fixations. Journal of Experimental Psychology: Learning, Memory, and Cognition, 21, 884–898.

Daneman, M. and Stainton, M. (1991). Phonological recoding in silent reading. Journal of Experimental Psychology: Learning, Memory, and Cognition, 17, 618–632.

Frazier, L. and Rayner, K. (1982). Making and correcting errors during sentence comprehension: eye movements in the analysis of structurally ambiguous sentences. Cognitive Psychology, 14, 178–210.

Inhoff, A.W. (1984). The stages of word processing during eye fixations in the reading of prose. Journal of Verbal Learning and Verbal Behavior, 23, 612–624.

Inhoff, A.W. and Topolski, R. (1994). Use of phonological codes during eye fixations in reading and in on-line and delayed naming tasks. Journal of Memory and Language, 33, 689–713.

Jared, D., Levy, B.A. and Rayner, K. (1999). The role of phonology in the activation of word meanings during reading: evidence from proofreading and eye movements. Journal of Experimental Psychology: General, 128, 219–264.

Jared, D. and Seidenberg, M.S. (1991). Does word identification proceed from spelling to sound to meaning? Journal of Experimental Psychology: General, 120, 358–394.

Just, M.A. and Carpenter, P.A. (1980). A theory of reading: from eye fixations to comprehension. Psychological Review, 4, 329–354.

Just, M.A. and Carpenter, P.A. (1987). Psychology of Reading and Language Comprehension. Newton, MA: Allyn and Bacon.

Kuçera, H. and Francis, W.N. (1967). Computational Analysis of Present-day American English. Providence, RI: Brown University Press.

McClelland, J.L. (1987). The case for interactionism in language processing. In: M. Coltheart (Ed.), Attention and Performance XII: The Psychology of Reading. Hove: Erlbaum, pp. 3–36.

McCusker, L.X., Hillinger, M.L. and Bias, R.G. (1981). Phonological recoding and reading. Psychological Bulletin, 89, 217–245.

McCutchen, D. and Perfetti, C.A. (1982). The visual tongue-twister effect: phonological activation in silent reading. Journal of Verbal Learning and Verbal Behavior, 21, 672–687.

Perfetti, C.A., Bell, L.C. and Delaney, S.M. (1988). Automatic (prelexical) phonological activation in silent word reading: evidence from backward masking. Journal of Memory and Language, 27, 59–70.

Pollatsek, A., Lesch, M., Morris, R.K. and Rayner, K. (1992). Phonological codes are used in integrating information across saccades in word identification and reading. Journal of Experimental Psychology: Human Perception and Performance, 18, 148–162.

Rayner, K., Pollatsek, A. and Binder, K.S. (1998). Phonological codes and eye movements in reading. Journal of Experimental Psychology: Learning, Memory, and Cognition, 24, 476–497.

Rayner, K., Sereno, S.C., Lesch, M.F. and Pollatsek, A. (1995). Phonological coldes are automatically activated during reading: evidence from an eye movement priming paradigm. Psychological Science, 6, 26–30.

Rubenstein, H., Lewis S.S. and Rubenstein, M.A. (1971). Evidence for phonemic recoding in visual word recognition. Journal of Verbal Learning and Verbal Behaviour, 10, 645–657.

Scott, D.C. (1988). The Desjardins. In: M. Atwood and R. Weaver (Eds.), The Oxford Book of Canadian Short Stories. London: Oxford University Press, pp. 24–28.

Treiman, R., Freyd, J. and Baron, J. (1983). Phonological recoding and use of spelling-sound rules in reading sentences. Journal of Verbal Learning and Verbal Behavior, 22, 682–700.

Van Orden, G.C. (1987). A ROWS is a ROSE: spelling, sound and reading. Memory and Cognition, 15, 181–198.

Van Orden, G.C. (1991). Phonological mediation is fundamental to reading. In: D. Besner and G.W. Humphreys (Eds.), Basic Processes in Reading: Visual Word Recognition. Hillsdale, NJ: Erlbaum, pp. 77–103.

Van Orden, G.C., Johnston, J.C. and Hale, B.L. (1988). Word identification in reading proceeds from spelling to sound to meaning. Journal of Experimental Psychology: Learning, Memory, and Cognition, 14, 371–386.

Van Orden, G.C., Pennington, B.F. and Stone, G.O. (1990). Word identification in reading and the promise of subsymbolic psycholinguistics. Psychological Review, 97, 488–522.

COMMENTARY ON SECTION 3

Dual Routes from Print to Speech and Dual Routes from Print to Meaning: Some Theoretical Issues

Max Coltheart
Macquarie University

Are we *ever* going to understand the role of phonology in reading? Will we *ever* know whether Paul Kolers was right ("Reading does not need to proceed by the reader's forming auditory representations of printed words" Kolers, 1970), or whether instead Eleanor Gibson was right ("The heart of [reading skill] is surely the process of decoding the written symbols to speech" Gibson, 1970)? Even though cognitive psychologists were already investigating this topic a century ago, and though it has been very extensively investigated over the past three decades, we still do not know the answer to such questions. So the reading researcher might be excused a certain despondency. All that is needed to dispel this despondency, however, is to compare current work on reading — for example, the four chapters on phonology and reading in this volume — to chapters in comparable books on reading published in the 1970s: books such as *Basic Studies in Reading* (Levin and Williams, 1970), *The Psychology of Reading* (Gibson and Levin, 1975), or *Theoretical Models and Processes of Reading* (Singer and Ruddell, 1970). Any such comparison makes it plain that we know much more now than we did then. For example, in the early seventies work on phonology and reading was almost exclusively devoted to English; now it is standard practice to consider the role of phonology in the reading of other alphabetically written languages (as Colombo's chapter in this volume considers Italian) and also in the reading of languages written in nonalphabetic scripts (as the chapter by Pollatsek and colleagues in this volume considers Chinese). We also now have a good understanding of how readers' strategies can modulate the role played by phonology, an issue also dealt with in Colombo's chapter, and in much current work (see e.g. Rastle and Coltheart, 1999b). Many other such examples can be drawn from current work on reading.

This is not to say that we now know everything we need to know about phonology and reading. On the contrary, there has been a recent rapid expansion

Reading as a Perceptual Process/A. Kennedy, R. Radach, D. Heller and J. Pynte (Editors)
© 2000 Elsevier Science Ltd. All rights reserved

of interest in this issue, which would not have happened if all of the problems had been solved; and opinions still differ greatly as to what the correct answer is to the fundamental Kolers–Gibson question. Current opinion as to what is the most plausible functional architecture for a model of reading also varies, and this is a question which is taken up, in one way or another, by all four of the chapters on phonology and reading in this volume.

Colombo begins her chapter by noting that amongst models for analysing phonological influences on reading "perhaps the most popular is the dual-route model (Coltheart, 1978; Coltheart, Curtis, Atkins and Haller, 1993; Paap and Noel, 1991; Paap, Noel and Johnson, 1992)", and Morris and Folk also begin their chapter with some discussion of the dual-route model. Here it is important to appreciate that there are two different dual-route models of reading. One is a model of how readers generate phonology from print: I will refer to this as the DR-P model. The other is a model of how readers access meaning from print: I will refer to this as the DR-M model. Colombo is concerned with the DR-P model, which she defines as follows: "reading is accomplished through the operation of two mechanisms, the lexical mechanism that retrieves the phonology of a word directly through the association of the orthographic pattern to its phonological correspondent stored in the lexicon, and the assembly mechanism, that operates by assembling the output of a process of conversion of spelling-sound correspondences". Morris and Folk, on the other hand, are concerned with the DR-M model, which they define as follows: "there is a 'direct' orthographic route that is the dominant route used in activating meaning, and a slower 'indirect' phonological route." Daneman and Reingold are also concerned with the DR-M model rather than the DR-P model, and their fig. 1 is indeed a diagram exactly of the DR-M model.

The reason why it is critical to appreciate the distinction between these two dual-route models is that the two models, DR-P and DR-M, are logically independent of each other. It is a perfectly coherent theoretical stance to advocate a dual-route theory of reading comprehension whilst rejecting a dual-route theory of reading aloud. It is equally coherent to reject a dual-route theory of reading comprehension whilst advocating a dual-route theory of reading aloud. Some authors clearly appreciate this distinction: "There are two versions of the dual-route model, and they should not be confused. The first one involves two possible routes for generating a phonological code, while the second involves two possible routes to accessing meaning. These issues are almost orthogonal" (Frost, 1998, p. 86). Other authors, however, overlook the distinction. Consider, for example, the following passage (Lukatela and Turvey, 1998, pp. 1059–1060), in which I have represented the material about DR-P in bold and the material about DR-M in italics so as to make it clear which parts of this passage are actually about which model:

"The most influential theory of visual word recognition is the dual-route theory (Coltheart, 1978; *see fig. 2*). Assuming a storehouse of word representations (**an**

internal lexicon, *a semantic memory*), there are two paths to this storehouse from the internal site at which a viewed word's letter code is formed. One path goes directly to this storehouse (albeit via one or more recodings of the graphic information). The other path is more involved, incorporating a transformation in the modality of the code. **On this path, the letter or orthographic code is converted by rules to a phoneme code** (that is, a code involving abstract representations of the sounds of speech), and then this phoneme code is used to access the storehouse. Of the two paths, *the direct, nonphonological path* will generally be the faster."

Note also the confusion here between the terms 'internal lexicon' (which means a store of orthographic or phonological word forms) and 'semantic memory' (which means a store of word meanings). In this passage, these terms are mistakenly treated as synonymous, and are represented by the single generic term 'storehouse', making much of the passage ambiguous: if 'storehouse' is taken to mean 'lexicon', then what is being discussed is DR-P, whereas if 'storehouse' is taken to mean 'semantic system', then what is being discussed is DR-M. It is possible that Morris and Folk have also overlooked this distinction, since, when they discuss the DR-M model, they reference the paper by Coltheart et al. (1993), a paper which is about the DR-P model.

This distinction is directly relevant to all of the four chapters on phonology and reading. So what I plan to do in this commentary is to make the distinction as clear as I can by describing both of the models, and then to consider the relationship of each of the two models to the work discussed in the four chapters.

Dual-route models of reading aloud and dual-route models of reading comprehension

The DR-P model

The core architecture of this model is shown in Fig. 1. This diagram embodies the distinction between a lexical and a non-lexical route for reading aloud; thati what makes it a dual-route model. But the DR-P model is generic, in the sense that is that various different specific versions of it can be created by making various specific theoretical commitments.

One such commitment in this diagram is that the nonlexical route uses grapheme-phoneme correspondences and applies these serially left-to-right across the input string (Coltheart and Rastle, 1994; Rastle and Coltheart, 1999b). An alternative commitment re the nonlexical route is to propose that it operates not in one single serial pass across the input string, but in two stages: an initial and fast stage in which the consonants are translated into their phonemes, and a later and slower stage in which the vowels are translated into their phonemes. That is the two-cycles model

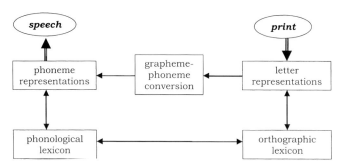

Fig. 1. The DR-P model: a dual-route model of reading aloud.

of Berent and Perfetti (1995). Both models are DR-P models; they differ not in the architecture of the model, but only in what specific theoretical commitment has been made re how one component of this architecture (the nonlexical route) operates.

Another such commitment in the diagram is represented by the fact that the arrows of the model's lexical route are double-headed. This represents a commitment to interactive rather than purely feed-forward processing in the lexical route, a commitment deriving from the IAC (interactive activation and competition) model of McClelland and Rumelhart (1981). These authors exploited this property of their model to give a plausible account of the word superiority effect in forced-choice tachistoscopic letter recognition. If instead one wished the processing by the lexical route to be purely feedforward rather than interactive, that would be a different model than the one shown in Fig. 1; but it would still be a DR-P model.

A third commitment which I will make is to cascaded rather than thresholded processing. In thresholded processing, one stage of a model completes its job entirely before passing on any information to the next stage (as in logogen models; Morton, 1979). In cascaded processing, as soon as there is any activation at all at one level, this is passed on to subsequent levels. The justification for this commitment seems strong: there is evidence that the orthographic neighbours of a nonword affect its reading aloud (for review, see Andrews, 1997), and since no unit in the orthographic lexicon reaches threshold when a nonword is presented, a thresholded version of the DR-P model would not allow any activation of the phoneme level from the lexical route when the stimulus is a nonword.

If one is engaged in converting a verbal model into a computational model, specific theoretical commitments like these have to be made, since decisions have to be made as to what program code to write. The three commitments here were made when converting the DR-P model into a specific computational model, the DRC model (Coltheart et al., 1993; Coltheart, Rastle, Perry, Langdon and Ziegler, in press; Rastle and Coltheart, 1999a,b). I will be discussing below their implications for subsequent chapters.

The DR-M model

As noted above, fig. 1 in Chapter 17 is a diagram of the DR-M model. However, in relation to this diagram it is worth considering a valuable point made by Morris and Folk in Chapter 16: "two possible phonological routes to meaning have been proposed: (1) an addressed phonological route that goes from orthography to a lexical look-up of stored phonological forms to meaning; and (2) an assembled phonological route that relies on the sublexical translation of graphemes to phonemes based on a reader's knowledge of grapheme to phoneme correspondences." Coltheart (1980) argued for the existence of route (2) from orthography via phonology to meaning as follows. If you are asked whether the printed nonword PHOCKS sounds exactly like the name of an animal, you can respond correctly. The conversion of the orthographic form PHOCKS to the phonological form /foks/ is required as part of this process, and it cannot be done by Morris and Folk's route (1), because there is no orthographic entry for PHOCKS in the lexicon to be addressed. Hence being able to carry out this task requires that route (2) exists. But if the only route from print to phonology used sublexical translation of graphemes to phonemes, then we would not be able to read exception words aloud, since they violate the rules of such translation. Hence there must be an addressed route from print to phonology too.

This does not mean, however, that this addressed route is a route from print to phonology and then from phonology to meaning. It could be a route that goes from print to meaning to phonology. That would suffice for the reading aloud of exception words. However, if this is what the addressed route is like, people with profound impairments of the semantic system would not be able to read exception words aloud. But exactly this pattern of reading performance has been reported in a number of such cases (e.g., Cipolotti and Warrington, 1995; Lambon Ralph, Ellis and Franklin, 1995; Schwartz, Saffran and Marin, 1980). Since it is possible to read exception words aloud without accessing their meanings, there must be an addressed phonological route that goes from orthography to a lexical lookup of stored phonological forms, bypassing semantics: that route is Morris and Folk's route (1).

Fig. 1 of Daneman and Reingold has Morris and Folk's route (1), but needs also their route (2) to be a complete representation of the DR-M model. Contrast this with the model diagram of Taft and Van Graan (1998); this is a diagram of a DR-M model which is identical to that of Daneman and Reingold except that it has not only a route (1) but also a route (2), which consists, in Daneman and Reingold's terms, of a pathway from stimulus to a grapheme–phoneme conversion system which in turn feeds into the component labelled phonological representation in the Daneman–Reingold figure. That is the route that allows us to judge that the printed nonword PHOCKS sounds exactly like the name of an animal. So to draw an appropriate diagram of the DR-M model we must at a minimum make this addition to the Daneman–Reingold figure. That is obviously only a minor amendment.

Opposite page: Fig. 2. The DR-M model: a dual-route model of reading comprehension. DR-M (a) assumes no distinction between input and output lexicons. DR-M (b) does make that distinction.

But there is also a much more major theoretical issue that needs contemplation here. Consider the component in the Daneman–Reingold figure labelled phonological representation. Is this used both for recognizing and for producing spoken words? Or are there two separate phonological representation systems, one needed for recognizing spoken words (e.g. when performing the auditory lexical decision task) and the other needed for producing spoken words (e.g. when naming pictures)?

Both ideas have been proposed. In the models of Allport and Funnell (1982), Friedman (1996), Plaut, McClelland, Seidenberg and Patterson (1996) and Seidenberg and McClelland (1989), there is a single phonological system. In contrast, the models of Ellis and Young (1988), Harris and Coltheart (1986), Morton (1980); Patterson and Shewell (1987) and Shallice (1988) all posit two separate phonological systems: a phonological input lexicon and a phonological output lexicon. Since this issue is so fundamental with respect to modelling the human language processing system, it has attracted a certain amount of investigation (e.g. Behrmann and Bub, 1992; Coltheart and Funnell, 1987; Weekes and Coltheart, 1996). Unfortunately, nothing conclusive has emerged from such research, and so as yet we have no empirical basis upon which to choose between these two very different theories.

Hence Fig. 2 shows two DR-M models, one (Fig. 2a) which assumes no distinction between input and output lexicons, and another (Fig. 2b) which assumes separate input and output lexicons.[1] I will consider from here on only the simpler of these two models (Fig. 2a, which makes no distinction between input and output lexicons), whilst emphasizing that future work might yield data which supports the more complex model, over the simpler one.

The independence of DRC-P and DRC-M models

The DR-M models described above are also, of course, DR-P models, since they contain not only pathways from print to meaning but also pathways from print to speech. But DR-M and DR-P models are logically independent, so it is easy to make these models into DR-M but not DR-P models or vice versa, as follows (the argument applies to both DR-M models, but only the one without separate input and output lexicons will be considered here).

---

1 Neither model has lexical and nonlexical procedures for spelling. These are easy enough to add (see e.g. Patterson and Shewell, 1987) but are not considered here since this chapter is just concerned with reading.

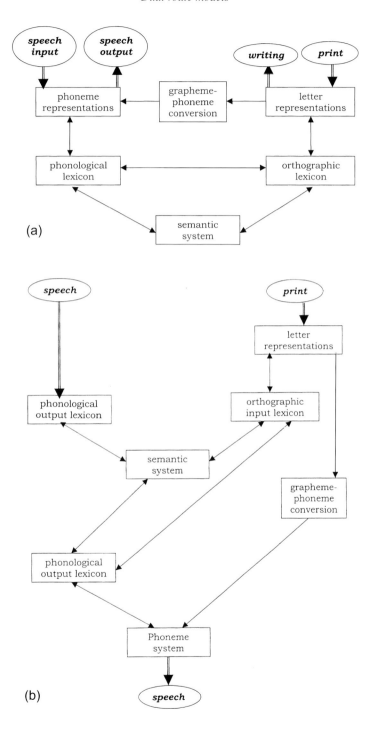

(a)

(b)

One could propose that the Fig. 2a model is correct *except* that the pathway from orthographic lexicon to semantics does not exist: reading comprehension is purely phonologically mediated. Now we have a DR-P model which is not a DR-M model. Or one could propose that the Fig. 2a model is correct *except* that words and nonwords use the same pathway from orthography to phonology when being read aloud (as in analogy models of reading aloud), so the separate grapheme–phoneme pathway does not exist. Now we have a DR-M model which is not a DR-P model.

Having offered a rationale for the particular DR-M and DR-P model represented in Fig. 2a, I will now go on to consider how this particular model relates to the work described in the preceding four chapters.

Issues in dual-route modelling of reading

Strategy effects in reading aloud

Colombo's chapter deals solely with reading aloud and does not directly address issues concerning the role of phonology in reading comprehension. One issue she is concerned with is the ability of readers strategically to control the operation of the nonlexical route: she suggests that this route is "a slow, controlled process that requires attentional resources and can be strategically disabled". If by 'disabled' Colombo means 'turned off completely', then there is evidence against this view. Coltheart, Woollams, Kinoshita and Perry (1999) studied Stroop colour-naming when the colour-bearing stimuli were words all semantically unrelated to colour. Colour-naming latencies were longer when none of the phonemes of the colour-bearing word matched any phonemes of the colour name than when the word and the colour name had one phoneme in common. This effect was larger when the matching phoneme was the initial phoneme than when it was the final phoneme, indicating that at least part of the phoneme activation arising from the printed word was being contributed by the serially operating left-to-right nonlexical reading route. This activation is irrelevant to the task of colour naming, and is in fact harmful, since even in the condition where one phoneme of a word matches one phoneme of the colour name, the rest of the word's phonemes conflict with the colour name. Hence if subjects could turn the nonlexical route off completely, they should do so here. This result therefore suggests that skilled readers cannot completely switch off the nonlexical route.

However, the term 'strategically disabled' could be construed to mean 'turned down' rather than 'completely turned off'. Whether the two routes for reading aloud can be strategically adjusted was investigated by Coltheart and Rastle (1994). They measured the size of the regularity advantage in reading aloud under two conditions: (a) when filler items were all exception words: this should lead subjects to emphasize the lexical route more than the nonlexical route, since the lexical route is needed for reading exception words, and hence the regularity effect should be small or zero here; and (b) when filler items were all nonwords: this should lead subjects to emphasize the nonlexical route more than the lexical route, since the nonlexical route is needed for reading nonwords, and hence the regularity effect should be maximal here, since it is the contribution of the nonlexical route that is responsible for the regularity effect.

No evidence for strategic variation of the routes was obtained in this experiment: the regularity effect was the same in the two conditions.

This experiment is typical of studies which seek to obtain evidence of strategy effects in reading aloud. Nevertheless, it contains a subtle flaw. Rastle and Coltheart (1999b) showed that the size of the regularity effect depends upon where in an exception word the irregular grapheme–phoneme correspondence is. When it is in the first position, the effect is large; when it is in the second position, the effect is significantly smaller but still significantly greater than zero; when it is in the third position there is no effect. This is because the nonlexical route is operating from left to right (as is also shown by the Stroop study of Coltheart et al. (1999) referred to above), and by the time this route has got to the third grapheme–phoneme correspondence the lexical route has generated enough phonemic activation to allow an exception word to be uttered.

Now, many of the exception-word fillers used by Coltheart and Rastle (1994) were exceptional in the third or later positions. Such words will not be troubled by the operation of the nonlexical route; hence they will not induce readers to deemphasize that route, even if such strategic deemphasis is possible. What *will* be particularly troubled by the nonlexical route are exception words with *first-position* irregularities. So Rastle and Coltheart (1999b) studied naming latencies for regular words and nonwords under two filler conditions: (a) fillers are exception words with first-position irregularities; (b) fillers are exception words with third-position irregularities. If strategic control of the routes is possible, one might expect the lexical route to be stronger than the nonlexical route in condition (a), compared to condition (b).

There are two possible ways in which this could happen: readers might turn up the lexical route in condition (a) relative to condition (b), or they might turn down the nonlexical route in condition (a) relative to condition (b). These possibilities can be distinguished, since they have different consequences for the regular word targets. If the lexical route is turned up in condition (a), then the regular words will be faster in condition (a) than in condition (b). If the nonlexical route is turned down in condition (a), then the regular words and the nonwords will be slower in condition (a) than in condition (b). And, of course, if readers cannot strategically vary either route, the two conditions will not differ. What Rastle and Coltheart (1999b) actually found was that the regular words (and the nonwords) were slower in condition (a) than in condition (b). This supports Colombo's view that the nonlexical route can be strategically disabled (as long as we take 'disabled' to mean 'turned down' rather than 'turned off'). It also shows that one must be careful in choosing the fillers in strategy experiments of this kind: simply using exception words vs. nonwords is not enough.

The two-cycles model of phonological recoding

Colombo also discusses the two-cycles model of Berent and Perfetti (1995), according to which there are two processes involved in the assembly of phonology from print, both processes being parallel processes. There is a fast process which is applied in parallel to all the consonants in the input string, translating them into their phonemes, and a slower process that is applied in parallel to all the vowels, translating them into their phonemes. This idea of how the assembly process operates is clearly completely at variance with the idea discussed above that assembly is a serial left-to-right process. Evidence for the latter conception has already been described: the effect of position of irregularity on the regularity effect in reading aloud, the effect of position of irregularity in filler stimuli on strategy effects in reading aloud, and the effect of position of phoneme overlap on Stroop colour naming. All of these findings are inconsistent with the two-cycles model.

A direct adjudication between the two ideas is possible using the Stroop data of Coltheart et al. (1999), who showed that colour naming was significantly faster when printed word and colour name shared their last phoneme than when there was no phoneme overlap. In two types of stimuli (when the colour was red or green) this last phoneme was a consonant; in the third type (when the colour was blue) it was a vowel. If the assembly of phonology from print is slower when the phoneme is a vowel than when it is a consonant, then whether the last phoneme overlaps with the colour name or not will have less effect when that phoneme is a vowel than when it is a consonant. No such effect was observed by Coltheart et al. (1999): colour did not interact with the size of this effect, which was in fact numerically larger when the colour was blue than when it was red or green. That result is inconsistent with the two-cycles model.

What reasons, then, did Berent and Perfetti have for proposing such a model? They did so on the basis of a backward masking experiment in which a target word was briefly presented and was followed by a brief backward mask. The mask was either a pseudohomophone of the target (rake RAIK), had the same vowels as the target but one different consonant (rake RAIB), had the same consonants as the target but one different vowel (RIKK), or was completely different (rake BLIN). At the shortest target durations, accuracy of target report was higher with the consonant-preserving mask than with the vowel-preserving mask, which Berent and Perfetti took as evidence for the two-cycles model.

However, in the stimuli used by Berent and Perfetti in this experiment, there is a perfect confounding between mask type and position of phoneme at which mask and target differed. In almost every vowel-preserving mask, mask and target differed only at the third phoneme; in almost every consonant-preserving mask, mask and target differed only at the second phoneme. Now, according to the serial theory of assembly of phonology, at the offset of the briefly presented target the left-to-right assembly process will only have dealt with the first one or two letters in the target. So, whilst all of the phonemes of the target will have received a little activation via the lexical route, the first one or two phonemes will also have received some additional activation from the nonlexical route. When a backward mask is presented that shares all but one of the phonemes of the target, and therefore boosts their activations, it is plausible to argue that the more weakly activated phonemes would benefit more from this boost (this argument is due to Perry, 1997, p. 73). Since the third phoneme of the target will have been more weakly active at target offset than the second, a mask which contains that third phoneme will be more beneficial than a mask which contains the second. Masks which Berent and Perfetti referred to as 'consonant-preserving' almost always contained the third phoneme of the target; and masks which Berent and Perfetti referred to as 'vowel-preserving' almost always contained the second phoneme of the target.

Thus because of the confounding between mask type and position of phoneme mismatch in these materials, it is possible to give a plausible account of their results in terms of an assembly process that is a single serial left-to-right process, rather than a pair of parallel processes (i.e. the two-cycles model). Since the serial account is also consistent with various other findings concerning the regularity effect, the Stroop effect and the onset effect, whereas the two-cycles model is not, it seems clear that we should favour the serial model over the two-cycles model.

This confounding of mask type with mismatch position may also be important for the replication of the Berent–Perfetti work in Italian, described in Colombo's chapter. In the example of a consonant-preserving mask she gives, VIRBO–*verbo*, the mismatch is at position 2; in the example of a vowel-preserving mask she gives, VERPO–*verbo*, the mismatch is at position 4. If we assume that this was true in general for the Italian materials, then there is a confounding here, but it is in the opposite direction to the confounding present in the Berent–Perfetti materials. And Colombo reports that in the Italian experiment "The unexpected result was instead an advantage in the vowel preserving condition with respect to the consonant preserving condition." Since the Italian and English experiments confounded mask type with mismatch position in opposite ways and found opposite effects of mask type, this is very strong evidence indeed that the effects here cannot be explained by the two-cycles model but can be explained by a model in which the nonlexical assembly of phonology from orthography is carried out by a process that is serial and left-to-right.

Fast and early phonology

Chapter 15, of Pollatsek et al., is mainly concerned not with how phonology is computed from print in reading aloud experiments, but what roles phonology plays when meaning is being accessed from print — that is, their work has to do with DR-M rather than DR-P. They begin their chapter by suggesting two primary arguments which might be made against any view that phonology is important for reading comprehension: "(1) sound coding is slow; (2) many orthographies code imperfectly for sound — there is either little or no representation of the sound of a word (e.g. Chinese) or the orthographic code is highly irregular (e.g. English)."

Considering these arguments in relation to the DRC-M model (Fig. 2a) indicates that the term 'sound coding' might be taken to describe either of two different processing routes. It might mean:

(a) Pathway X: letter representations $\rightarrow$ grapheme–phoneme conversion $\rightarrow$
                phoneme representations $\rightarrow$ phonological lexicon

or it might mean:

(b) Pathway Y: letter representations $\rightarrow$ orthographic lexicon $\rightarrow$ phonological
               lexicon.

There's good reason to believe that pathway X is slow, and clearly it will fail for the irregular words of English, and equally clearly fail for all words of Chinese, since there is no method by which phonemes can be mapped from sublexical elements of a Chinese printed word. But there is no reason to believe that pathway Y is slow. In English, it will work just as well for irregular words as for regular words, and it is just as feasible for Chinese as it is for English as long as we replace 'letter representations' by some more general term such as 'orthographic representation'. So when we are considering a role for phonology in reading comprehension that depends upon pathway Y, differences between regular and irregular words, and differences between alphabetic and ideographic orthographies, are not relevant.

To show the involvement of pathway X in reading comprehension, it is necessary to use pseudohomophones: letter strings such as SUTE, which are absent from the orthographic lexicon but whose phonology is present in the phonological lexicon. If pathway X is so slow, then one might expect it to have no influence on reading comprehension tasks, and so there should be no effects of pseudohomophony in reading comprehension experiments. However, Van Orden, Johnston and Hale (1988) observed such an effect: a high false alarm rate with trials such as AN ARTICLE OF CLOTHING–*sute* in a semantic categorization experiment. Pollatsek and colleagues confess to be somewhat puzzled by this result, given that they observed little priming from nonwords in their fast priming studies, which led them to conclude that pathway X is slow.

The solution to this puzzle is to note that effects such as that of Van Orden et al. are obtained when the response is NO. In semantic categorization tasks, NO responses are much slower than YES responses (perhaps because they are made by a response deadline, or perhaps because they are made after the completion of an exhaustive serial search). That allows time for the slow pathway X to achieve semantic activation and influence performance, even if it cannot do so when the correct response is YES, because the access to meaning via pathway Y and via the direct pathway from orthographic lexicon to meaning is too fast. Arguments of this kind re YES and NO were initially applied to the lexical decision task by Coltheart, Davelaar, Jonasson and Besner (1977) but apply equally to the semantic categorization task.

This distinction between pathways X and Y in DR-M models is of rather general importance. Imagine an experiment in which a target word is preceded by a briefly presented masked prime which is a pseudohomophone of the target (e.g. *horce*– HORSE) or a control (e.g. *horke*–HORSE); the task might be, for example, semantic categorization (animate/inanimate). Suppose the YES response to the target is faster in the pseudohomophone condition than the control condition. Because the primes are not words, it is tempting to take such a result as evidence that prelexical phonological recoding is a precursor of visual word recognition. That is, the prime *horce* is converted to phonology not by looking up its orthographic representation (since it does not have one) but by some nonlexical means. Then this prelexically obtained phonological representation is used to activate the semantic representation for 'horse', and perhaps also to activate the orthographic representation HORSE. These activations are the source of priming when the following target is in fact HORSE. Here a thoroughly phonological theory of reading comprehension is constructed on the basis of the view that the occurrence of *horce*–HORSE priming must mean that letter strings are prelexically phonologically recoded and that subsequent access to semantic or orthographic word representations is achieved solely by use of this code.

Consideration of Fig. 2a shows why this view is mistaken. Provided that interactive (rather than just feedforward) activation is allowed, and that activation can rise gradually over time (rather than instantaneously reaching its maximum value), activation of the orthographic representation HORSE by the pseudohomophone prime *horce* can be post-lexical, rather than having to be necessarily prelexical as assumed by the view being criticized here. The pathway that permits such post-lexical activation is:

Pathway Z: letter representations → grapheme–phoneme conversion phoneme representations → phonological lexicon → orthographic lexicon.

This way for *horce* to activate the orthographic representation of HORSE, and thus to cause priming, is *postlexical*, even though the prime *horce* is a nonword, because the activation can only occur *after* the entry in the phonological lexicon for 'horse' has been activated.

Conclusion

This discussion of the roles of phonology in reading aloud and reading comprehension has been organized around dual-route conceptions since all four of the chapters being commented upon make use of such conceptions. I have tried to show, firstly, why it is necessary to distinguish clearly between the dual-route approach to the explanation of reading aloud and the dual-route approach to the explanation of reading comprehension and, secondly, how even this is not sufficient: explicit commitment to specific rather than generic forms of dual-route model (e.g. commitment to one or other of Fig. 2a or Fig. 2b) is also necessary. Terms such as 'pre-lexical' or 'non-lexical' have a precise meaning, and precise empirical consequences, only after such specific commitments have been explicitly made. I have done this in the hope of making even clearer the relationship between dual-route conceptions of reading and the results discussed in the preceding four chapters.

References

Allport, D.A. and Funnell, E. (1982). Components of the mental lexicon. Philosophical Transactions Royal Society London, B295, 397–410.

Andrews, S. (1997). The effect of orthographic similarity on lexical retrieval — resolving neighborhood conflicts. Psychonomic Bulletin and Review, 4, 439–461.

Behrmann, M. and Bub, D. (1992). Surface dyslexia and dysgraphia: dual routes, single lexicon. Cognitive Neuropsychology, 9, 209–251.

Berent, I. and Perfetti, C.A. (1995). A rose is a reez — the two-cycles model of phonology assembly in reading English. Psychological Review, 102, 146–184.

Cipolotti, L. and Warrington, E.K. (1995). Semantic memory and reading abilities: a case report. Journal of the International Neuropsychological Society, 1, 104–110.

Coltheart, M. (1978) Lexical access in simple reading tasks. In: G. Underwood (Ed.), Strategies of Information Processing. London: Academic Press.

Coltheart, M. (1980) Reading phonological recoding, and deep dyslexia. In: M. Coltheart, K. Patterson and J.C. Marshall (Eds.), Deep Dyslexia. London: Routledge and Kegan Paul.

Coltheart, M., Curtis, B., Atkins, P. and Haller, M. (1993). Models of reading aloud: dual-route and parallel-distributed-processing approaches. Psychological Review, 100, 589–608.

Coltheart, M., Davelaar, E., Jonasson, J.T. and Besner, D. (1977) Access to the internal lexicon. In: S. Dornic (Ed.), Attention and Performance VI. Hillsdale, NJ: Lawrence Erlbaum Associates, 1977.

Coltheart, M. and Funnell, E. (1987) Reading and writing: one lexicon or two? In: D.A. Allport, D.G. MacKay, W. Prinz and E. Scheerer (Eds.), Language Perception and Production: Shared Mechanisms in Listening, Reading and Writing. London: Academic Press.

Coltheart, M. and Rastle, K. (1994). A left-to-right serial process in reading aloud. Journal of Experimental Psychology: Human Perception and Performance, 20, 1197–1211.

Coltheart, M., Rastle, K., Perry, C., Langdon, R. and Ziegler, J. (in press). DRC: a dual route cascaded model of visual word recognition and reading aloud. Psychological Review.

Coltheart, M., Woollams, A., Kinoshita, S. and Perry, C. (1999). A position-sensitive Stroop effect: further evidence for a left-to-right component in print-to-speech conversion. Psychonomic Bulletin and Review, 6, 456–463.

Ellis, A.W. and Young, A. (1988). Human Cognitive Neuropsychology. London: Lawrence Erlbaum Associates (2nd ed. 1996).

Friedman, R. (1996). Phonological text alexia: poor pseudoword reading plus difficulty reading functors in text. Cognitive Neuropsychology, 13, 869–886.

Frost, R. (1998). Toward a strong phonological theory of visual word recognition — true issues and false trails. Psychological Bulletin, 123, 71–99.

Gibson, E. (1970). The ontogeny of reading. American Psychologist, 25, 136–143.

Gibson, E. and Levin, H. (1975). The Psychology of Reading. Cambridge, MA: MIT Press.

Harris, M. and Coltheart, M. (1986). Language Processing in Children and Adults. London: Routledge and Kegan Paul.

Kolers, P. (1970) Three stages of reading. In: H. Levin and J.P. Williams (Eds.), Basic Studies in Reading. New York, NY: Basic Books.

Lambon Ralph, M.A., Ellis, A.W. and Franklin, S. (1995). Semantic loss without surface dyslexia. Neurocase, 1, 363–369.

Levin, H. and Williams, J.P. (Eds.) (1970). Basic Studies in Reading. New York, NY: Basic Books.

Lukatela, G. and Turvey, M. (1998). Reading in two alphabets. American Psychologist, 53, 1057–1072.

McClelland, J.L. and Rumelhart, D.E. (1981). An interactive activation model of context effects in letter perception, Part I. An account of basic findings. Psychological Review, 88, 375–407.

Morton, J. (1979). Some experiments on facilitation in word and picture recognition and their relevance for the evolution of a theoretical position. In: P.A. Kolers, M.E. Wrolstad and H. Bouma (Eds.), The Processing of Visual Language I. New York, NY: Plenum Press.

Morton, J. (1980), The logogen model and orthographic structure. In: U. Frith (Ed.), Cognitive Approaches to Spelling. London: Academic Press

Paap, K.R. and Noel, R.W. (1991). Dual route models of print to sound: still a good horse race. Psychological Research, 53, 13–24.

Patterson, K. and Shewell, C. (1987). Speak and spell: dissociations and word-class effects. In: M. Coltheart, R. Job and G. Sartori (Eds.), The Cognitive Neuropsychology of Language. London: Lawrence Erlbaum Associates, pp. 273–294.

Perry, C. (1997) A Computational and Experimental Investigation of Visual Word Recognition and Naming. Unpublished PhD Thesis, Swinburne University of Technology.

Plaut, D.C., McClelland, J.L., Seidenberg, M.S. and Patterson, K.E. (1996). Understanding normal and impaired word reading: computational principles in quasi-regular domains. Psychological Review, 103, 56–115.

Rastle, K. and Coltheart, M. (1999a). Lexical and nonlexical phonological priming in reading aloud. Journal of Experimental Psychology: Human Perception and Performance, 25, 461–481.

Rastle, K. and Coltheart, M. (1999b). Serial and strategic effects in reading aloud. Journal of Experimental Psychology: Human Perception and Performance, 25, 482–503.

Schwartz, M.F., Saffran, M. and Marin, O.S. (1980). Dissociations of language function in dementia: A case study. Brain and Language, 10, 249–262.

Seidenberg, M.S. and McClelland, J.L. (1989). A distributed, developmental model of word recognition and naming. Psychological Review, 96, 523–568.

Shallice, T. (1988). From Neuropsychology to Mental Function. Cambridge: Cambridge University Press.

Singer, H. and Ruddell, R.B. (Eds.) (1970) Theoretical Models and Processes of Reading. Newark, DE: International Reading Association.

Taft, M. and Van Graan, F. (1998). Lack of phonological mediation in a semantic categorization task. Journal of Memory and Language, 38, 203–224.

Van Orden, G.C., Johnston, J.C. and Hale, B. (1988). Word identification in reading proceeds from spelling to sound to meaning. Journal of Experimental Psychology: Learning, Memory and Cognition, 14, 371–386.

Weekes, B. and Coltheart, M. (1996). Surface dyslexia and surface dysgraphia: treatment studies and their theoretical implications. Cognitive Neuropsychology, 13, 277–315.

Syntax and Discourse Processing

Section Editor

Joël Pynte

CHAPTER 18

Modifier Attachment in Dutch: Testing Aspects of Construal Theory

Don C. Mitchell
University of Exeter

Marc Brysbaert
Universiteit Gent

Stefan Grondelaers
Katholieke Universiteit Leuven

and

Piet Swanepoel
Universiteit van Suid-Afrika, Pretoria

Abstract

When a relative clause is attached to a complex head of the type NP1-of-NP2, the preferred attachment (to NP1 or NP2) has been found to differ across languages. In English the relative clause is preferentially attached to NP2. However, in many other languages investigated so far there is a clear preference for attachment to NP1. One interpretation of this language difference is that comprehension preferences are affected in a complex and indirect way by the availability in a language of more than one genitive form (e.g. in English the Saxon as well as the Norman form). This idea has been used as a basis for explaining attachment differences in Construal theory, as well as in other influential approaches. In the present chapter, we investigate the proposal by carrying out a detailed analysis of reading data for Dutch sentences that have a felicitous Saxon genitive alternative, and by looking at off-line questionnaire data for Afrikaans, which like English has a frequently-used Saxon genitive form. Both sets of data argue against the proposal that cross-linguistic attachment differences can be explained in terms

Reading as a Perceptual Process/A. Kennedy, R. Radach, D. Heller and J. Pynte (Editors)
© 2000 Elsevier Science Ltd. All rights reserved

of the availability of alternative syntactic devices for expressing possessive relations. This leaves several accounts (including Construal theory) without a satisfactory explanation of cross-linguistic attachment differences.

Introduction

Theories of human parsing aim to identify the procedures people use to compute the relationships between the different constituents they hear or read. Some of these relationships concern links between verbs and their arguments (a combination that determines 'who did what to whom'). Others connect modifiers and qualifiers to their heads (e.g. adjectives, prepositional phrases and relative clauses to appropriate noun phrases and adverbial phrases, and clauses to the relevant verbs).

The present chapter is concerned with parsing operations of the second kind. In particular, we are concerned with the procedures which are used to link modifiers to appropriate noun heads. In the past, the bulk of the work on this topic has centred on the resolution of relative-clause attachment ambiguities of the kind illustrated in sentence (1).

(1) "Someone shot the servant of the actress who was on the balcony."

In materials of this kind, first examined by Cuetos and Mitchell (1988), the relative clause ('who was on the balcony') can be attached to either one of the two noun phrases ('the servant' or 'the actress', hereafter referred to as NP1 and NP2, respectively). A full syntactic analysis of the sentence requires that the relative clause (RC) be attached to one or other of the sites. Contrary to the predictions of all theories at the time, Cuetos and Mitchell (1988) found that the preferred attachment (to NP1 or NP2) varied according to the language under scrutiny. Questionnaire data indicated that English readers tended to resolve the ambiguity by attaching the relative clause to NP2, whereas with Spanish readers both questionnaire and on-line data revealed a bias in favour of NP1 attachment. Subsequent research in a variety of languages has yielded overwhelming evidence that such cross-linguistic variation is a robust phenomenon, and there have been numerous attempts to provide persuasive theoretical explanations for this variation. The present chapter focuses on one particular approach (dubbed the Gricean account), and our main aim is to establish that this framework comprehensively fails to provide an adequate explanation of cross-linguistic differences.

Relative-clause attachment

Before launching into a description of the Gricean account, it would be useful to provide a very brief review of the facts that have been established about relative-clause attachment (RC attachment) since the initial Cuetos/Mitchell study. In doing this we focus upon variation across language, leaving aside the substantial evidence for attachment variation within languages (for reviews covering these issues see Frazier and Clifton, 1996; Gilboy, Sopena, Clifton and Frazier, 1995; Hemforth, Konieczny and Scheepers, 2000).

The original Spanish and English findings have been corroborated by several different researchers using a variety of experimental techniques ranging from questionnaire and sentence completion studies to subject-paced reading and eye-tracking experiments. Where RC modifiers follow complex noun phrases (NPs) of the form NP1-of-NP2 (or NP1-de-NP2), studies using English predominantly confirm that NP2 attachment is preferred (Carreiras and Clifton, 1999; Corley, 1996; Fernandez, 1999; Frazier and Clifton, 1996; Henstra, 1996). Occasionally, the NP2 bias is not statistically reliable (e.g. Carreiras and Clifton, 1993), but where this has happened, the use of more refined experimental techniques has substantiated the finding (Carreiras and Clifton, 1999). With comparable materials, the Spanish NP1 bias has also been replicated frequently (Carreiras, 1992; Carreiras and Clifton, 1993, 1999; Cuetos, Mitchell and Corley, 1996; Igoa, Carreiras and Meseguer, 1998; Thornton, MacDonald and Gil, 1999).

Similar investigations have been extended to a number of other languages, with the majority showing an NP1 bias. These include French (Frenck-Mestre and Pynte, 2000, Chapter 21; Mitchell, Cuetos and Zagar, 1990; Pynte and Frenck-Mestre, 1996; Zagar, Pynte and Rativeau, 1997), German (Hemforth, Konieczny and Scheepers, 2000), Dutch (Brysbaert and Mitchell, 1996), Russian (V. Kempe and R. Radach, pers. commun., 1993) and Thai (V. Robertson, pers. commun., 1996). As the evidence accumulates, it seems likely that Italian also falls into this category (see Chapter 21). However, this is a language in which the facts are hotly contested (e.g. Baccino, De Vincenzi and Job, 2000; De Vincenzi and Job, 1993, 1995; Frenck-Mestre and Pynte, 2000; Pynte and Frenck-Mestre, 1996). In contrast with this range of documentation for languages showing NP1 preference, there is emerging evidence of further NP2-favouring languages, such as Brazilian Portuguese (Miyamoto, 1998) as well as Swedish, Norwegian and Romanian (Ehrlich, Fernández, Fodor, Stenshoel and Vinereanu, 1999). Finally, in Japanese, the complex noun phrase is headed by NP2 and questionnaire data indicate that it is this second potential host which is the preferred final attachment site (Kamide, 1998; Kamide and Mitchell, 1997). Bearing in mind that it is a head-final language, this bias corresponds most closely with the pattern associated with NP1 preference in head-initial languages.

Numerous different theoretical proposals have been put forward to account for this cross-linguistic variation. It is beyond the scope of this chapter to provide a comprehensive review of this work (for broad overviews of the topic see Cuetos et al., 1996 and Mitchell and Brysbaert, 1998). Instead, we focus upon one particular proposal which has attracted relatively wide-ranging support. This is the suggestion that the cross-linguistic differences can be traced back indirectly to cross-linguistic variation in the syntactic devices available for expressing genitive relationships.

The Gricean account

The argument was first set out by Frazier (1990, p. 324), and has since been further elaborated within Construal theory (Frazier and Clifton, 1996), where it is given the task of explaining all cross-linguistic differences in RC attachment. The same basic idea has also been adopted and extended by others (e.g. De Vincenzi and Job, 1993, 1995; Thornton et al., 1999). The starting point is the observation that some languages (like Spanish and French) have just one genitive form that can be used for expressing possessive relationships whereas others (e.g. English, Dutch, and German) have two or more such forms. In English, the two versions are the so-called Norman form (e.g. 'the servant of the actress') and the Saxon form ('the actress's servant'). (The labels obviously identify the historical sources of influence on the English language.) Spanish, French and at least some other Romance languages allow the use of just the Norman form (e.g. 'el Craido de la actriz' in Spanish). It follows from this that in some languages there is just one way of setting out a complex NP followed by a nominal modifier such as a relative clause. In others there are two or more. Interestingly, as Frazier (1990) first pointed out, the non-Norman form is typically unambiguous, as illustrated in English by sentence (2).

(2) "Someone shot the actress's servant who was on the balcony."

Here, the use of the Saxon genitive ensures that the sentence is unambiguous, conveying definitively that it is the 'servant' who was on the balcony.

Given this set of observations, Frazier (1990) went on to develop an explanation of attachment biases based on Gricean principles (cf. Grice, 1975). Assuming that speakers and writers follow Grice's Maxim of Clarity, she argued that English speakers would use the Saxon form to be unambiguous in communicating RC attachment to 'servant' (or its equivalent), leaving the Norman form predominantly to signal attachment to 'actress'. Playing by the same rules, a listener or reader would be forced to interpret the relative clause in sentence (2) as modifying 'servant', but would correspondingly interpret the technically ambiguous Norman form (in sentence (1)) as tacitly conveying the message that the relative clause should be interpreted as being attached to 'actress' (i.e. to NP2). Frazier (1990) argued that this would introduce a tendency to favour an NP2-attached interpretation of the original ambiguous sentence. In Spanish, however, the Norman structure would not be available for special-purpose use in this way (because there is no alternative device for conveying attachment to the higher NP, 'the servant'). It follows that the pressure towards NP2 attachment would not materialise here. To explain the fact that there was an NP1 bias in Spanish (rather than no bias at all) Frazier (1990) postulated a new discourse-based influence which she referred to as 'relativized relevance' (a principle which states that the parser should " ... preferentially construe a phrase as being relevant to the main assertion of the current sentence", p. 321).

So, to summarise, Frazier's (1990) proposal is that in all languages featuring the RC-attachment ambiguity, there is a broad tendency to favour NP1 attachment (as a result of relativised relevance (RR)). However, in certain languages this is countermanded by a more powerful Gricean tendency to attach the relative clause to NP2. The languages in which RR works alone are those with a single-genitive form. Those in which the Gricean influences dominate are languages with two or more genitive forms in which the non-Norman structure is unambiguous. For the rest of the chapter this broad proposal will be referred to as the 'Gricean hypothesis' or the 'Gricean argument'. It is this proposal that is held up as providing an explanation of cross-linguistic differences in RC attachment (De Vincenzi and Job, 1993, 1995; Frazier and Clifton, 1996; Thornton et al., 1999).

The Gricean argument may be applied at several different levels of analysis. It can either be implemented at the level of entire languages or, alternatively, it can be assumed that the pressures in favour of NP2 attachment operate differentially over different classes of sentences within individual languages. In its simplest form, the Gricean effects can be characterised as being triggered by a simple switch which determines the RC-attachment preferences in different languages. If the language has just a single-genitive form, the switch is 'off' and the attachment is driven by discourse influences (e.g. relativised relevance), resulting in an NP1-attachment bias. If the language has more than one form (in particular, an unambiguous non-Norman form), then the switch is 'on', causing the Gricean influences to override the discourse effects so that NP2 attachment ends up prevailing. In more complex versions of the model, the simple on/off switch may be replaced by a sliding parameter varying between minimum and maximum values (say, 0 and 1). On such accounts the zero-setting would apply to single-genitive languages, but other languages may be assigned a variety of non-zero values depending on the degree of specialisation of the different genitive forms. In within-language versions of the Gricean hypothesis the parameter might be set at different levels for different classes of sentence or it might even be set on the basis of the lexical characteristics of an individual word in the complex NP. A coarse-grained version of the model might apply if the usage of non-Norman genitive forms varies across different classes of noun phrases. For example, if non-Norman genitive forms are more acceptable when the second noun within the NP complex represents a human, then the parameter might be set at a high level for all sentences in which a human noun appears in the NP2 slot. A proposal of this kind might result in a range of different settings within an individual language, with parameter values varying across different classes of NP complex. At the fine-grained extreme the parameter might be set dynamically according to the lexical properties of each individual noun in the NP complex. That is, the parameter value might be set high if the particular noun in the NP2 slot can readily be expressed in the alternative genitive form, whereas for less flexible nouns the setting would be lower. As an illustration of this suggestion, the parameter value would be high in examples like sentence (1) above, because the noun 'actress' readily takes a Saxon genitive (as in sentence (2)). However, where the Saxon form is questionable (e.g. 'the road's left' instead of 'the left of the road'), then the Gricean parameter would be set close to zero. This version of the proposal may be characterised as showing the workings of what Chuck Clifton (pers. commun.) has dubbed the 'smart Gricean reasoner'. In the remainder of the chapter, we shall examine each of these possibilities at some length.

Before proceeding to consider the individual versions of the Gricean hypothesis it is worth asking whether there is any empirical evidence that speakers behave in the expected way in different languages. In languages which have only the Norman genitive form, do speakers actually use sentences like (1) irrespective of whether they are trying to convey that it is the 'servant' or the 'actress' who was on the balcony? In languages, like English, where there is more than one form, do they genuinely tend to use the Norman form (1) to communicate that it was the 'actress' who was on the balcony and the Saxon form (2) to convey that it was the 'servant' who was in that location? In the accounts described above, this is just a matter of speculation. However a recent study by Viñas, Oria-Merino, Heydel and Sáinz (1999) offers explicit empirical evidence on this issue. These authors had subjects read a short description of a situation and then required them to construct a sentence to describe the situation. Typical situations were described as follows.

(3a) "There is a milkman and he has got a cousin. The cousin has been to Argentina and Mary argued with him." (This scenario corresponds with NP1 or high-attachment in sentence structure (1).)

(3b) "There is a milkman and he has got a cousin. The milkman has been to Argentina and Mary argued with him." (Corresponding with NP2 or low-attachment in structure (1).)

After reading a description, subjects were required to rephrase the description by completing a sentence fragment like:

(4) "Mary argued with . . . that had been to Argentina."

This study can be viewed as providing an explicit test of the productive component of the Gricean hypothesis. In constructing sentences to describe the different scenarios, do writers or speakers genuinely make differential use of the genitive forms available in their language?

Viñas et al. (1999) tested monolinguals in Spanish, English and German. Their results provided a certain amount of support for the Gricean claims, but the overall picture was rather less clearcut than might have been expected on the basic account sketched out above.

In Spanish about 89% of the people chose the Norman form for the description given in (3a) and for (3b) the corresponding figure was approximately 97%. That is, following Gricean expectations they converted *both* kinds of situations into Spanish equivalents of structure (1).

For (3a) they were assuming the NP1 interpretation of (4), whereas for (3b) they were adopting the NP2 reading. They only had one useful structure so they used it to describe both competing situations. (On the 5% of trials when they *did not* do this, they provided incomplete responses like "Mary argued with the milkman that had been to Argentina.".)

In English (and even more so in German) the situation was much more complex. In English about 87% of the people used that Saxon form (2) for situation (3a) as in sentence (5):

(5) "Mary argued with the milkman's cousin that had been to Argentina."

Only about 4% of subjects used the Norman genitive form in this condition.

This is more or less as predicted. However, an unexpected finding was that 39% also used the Saxon form (5) to describe (3b), even though it is impossible for this to work (the relative clause cannot be interpreted as modifying 'milkman' in English). A rather higher percentage (45%) used the more appropriate Norman form.

In summary, it seems that although there is some tendency to make differential use of the alternative genitive forms for specific communicative purposes, the evidence suggests that the actual usage of the different forms is somewhat unsystematic and it seems unlikely that this behaviour would provide a secure basis for listeners and readers to carry out 'Gricean calculations' in their interpretations of RC-attachment ambiguities.

As with the question of productive usage, however, this is an empirical question and the rest of the chapter is devoted to a consideration of the question of whether readers and listeners show signs of exploiting productive patterns in resolving attachment ambiguities, and hence whether the Gricean account can provide a convincing explanation of cross-linguistic differences.

We start with the basic version of the hypothesis: essentially the claim that Gricean influences are either switched on or off in any given language. This proposal was quickly shown to be incapable of accounting for the data. As

Brysbaert and Mitchell (1996) spelt out, Dutch meets all of the conditions for the Gricean switch to be 'on', and so the proposal wrongly predicts that Dutch should be an NP2-biased language. More specifically, Dutch has three genitive forms: a Norman form ('de hoed van vader' [the hat of father]), a Saxon form ('vaders hoed' [father's hat]), and an antecedent + possessive pronoun form ('vader zijn hoed' [father his hat]). The two non-Norman forms are unambiguous in exactly the same way as the English Saxon form is (for details see Brysbaert and Mitchell, 1996, pp. 684–687). Despite this, numerous on- and off-line studies have confirmed that there is an NP1-attachment bias in Dutch. Nor does it seem that Dutch is an isolated exception to an otherwise solid rule. It turns out that German has a range of genitive forms similar to those in Dutch, which means that according to the Gricean prediction it should be an NP2-favouring language. In fact, in the case of the RC modifiers under examination here, the existing evidence suggests that NP1 is the preferred attachment site (e.g. Hemforth, Konieczny and Scheepers, 1994, 2000). There is also an equivalent failure of the Gricean prediction for the Japanese language (Kamide, 1998, pp. 251–252). Although the head-final order of Japanese makes it misleading to use the present NP1/NP2 terminology to refer to the competing attachment sites, like the languages just considered, Japanese has an ambiguous genitive form and a second, unambiguous form which forces attachment to the host which is in the high phrase-marker position in the ambiguous form. Following the logic of the Gricean argument it turns out that Japanese RC attachment should be biased in favour of low attachment. In fact, both off- and on-line evidence suggests that it is high attachment that eventually dominates (cf. Kamide, 1998; Kamide and Mitchell, 1997).

In all of the cases outlined above the shortcomings of the simple switch version of the Gricean account were connected with the fact that the hypothesis makes incorrect predictions for languages with more than one genitive form. Recently, Miyamoto (1998) has claimed that the proposal is equally unsuccessful in dealing with a language which, like Spanish, only has a single Norman genitive form. Following the arguments set out above, the Gricean prediction would be that all such languages should show an NP1 preference. However, Miyamoto (1998) has presented evidence that Brazilian Portuguese favours NP2 attachment, at least in an off-line study.

To sum up the argument so far, the simple switch version of the Gricean hypothesis is clearly inadequate. While it might be argued that it makes the correct predictions for English, Spanish and French, it mispredicts the bias for the majority of the languages that have so far been examined in relation to this issue. In view of this evidence, it is somewhat surprising to note that versions of the Gricean argument are still being championed in recent papers (e.g. Thornton et al., 1999). A possible defence for this move is to claim that Gricean effects are not the *only* influence on cross-linguistic RC-attachment differences, and that the variability identified above derives from some further source. However, this raises questions about this unspecified explanation of cross-linguistic differences, and it also begs the question of whether the simple Gricean account makes any useful contribution to explaining the phenomena. If there were data from enough languages to put Gricean switch values into a regression analysis to predict RC attachment, the indications from the findings to date are that the Gricean variable would account for close to 0% of the variation, and it is not easy to see any case for retaining such an uninformative factor in any explanatory account.

If it is granted that the simple switch version of the Gricean account is not viable, then an obvious alternative might be the use of a sliding Gricean parameter, rather than an on/off switch. As indicated above, this proposal is based on the assumption that the Gricean effect does not necessarily come into play at full strength for all languages with more than one genitive forms, but is instead weighted at a value between zero and one depending (say) upon the proportion of nouns in the languages that permit the use of the non-Norman form. Assuming that the final attachment preference is determined by a weighted combination of a discourse-based NP1 bias (presumably fixed for all languages) and a language-related Gricean effect, it might be possible to explain some of the inconsistencies encountered in the all-or-none account. As spelt out by Brysbaert and Mitchell (1996, pp. 686–687), the use of the non-Norman form is much more restricted in Dutch than it is in English. Within the framework of the 'sliding parameter' proposal, this might be represented as a lower Gricean parameter value for Dutch. Assuming that the Gricean effect is proportional to the parameter value, the result might be that for Dutch the Gricean influence in favour of NP2 attachment is not strong enough to outweigh the universal discourse-based bias in favour of NP1 attachment, resulting in an overall NP1 bias.

While such an account clearly has the capacity to deal with patterns of data which undermine the simpler Gricean model, it is still incapable of accounting for findings that are already available. It seems reasonable to assume that the parameter setting is reduced to its minimum value for all languages in which there is but one genitive form (implying that the Gricean effects are simply inactive in such languages). However, the implication of this is that all such languages should display the same attachment preferences. This being the case, there needs to be some unrelated explanation for the finding by Miyamoto (1998) that Brazilian Portuguese apparently shows an NP2 bias. In the next few paragraphs, we highlight further shortcomings of the account. If the sliding parameter is set on the basis of the scope of usage for non-Norman genitive forms then (we will argue) the Gricean parameter should at least be of the same magnitude for Afrikaans as for English (and both languages should have a higher parameter than Dutch; see above). It follows that Afrikaans should show an NP2 bias, and that this bias should minimally be of the same strength as that found in English. In fact, it turns out that Afrikaans shows an NP1 bias which is almost identical to that found in Dutch.

Evidence from Afrikaans

As Brysbaert and Mitchell (1996) pointed out, the reason why the Gricean parameter might be lower for Dutch than for English is that the scope of usage of the non-Norman Dutch genitive forms is much more restricted than that for comparable English forms. Of the two Dutch non-Norman forms, the Saxon form is essentially restricted to human nouns and proper nouns (e.g. 'Amsterdams haven' [Amsterdam's port]). In fact, current usage is even more restricted, being more or less confined to proper nouns and family relations (Haeseryn, Romijn, Geerts, de Rooij and van den Toorn, 1997: 163). The second non-Norman form (the possessive pronoun form) (e.g. 'de actrice haar zoon' [the actress her son]) is also more or less restricted to human nouns and largely confined to informal settings (Haeseryn et al., 1997, p. 297, 822; Koelmans, 1975). If these linguistic considerations lead to the Gricean parameter being set lower in Dutch than in English, then presumably, within this conceptual framework, a language which makes more liberal use of non-Norman forms than English would have to be assigned a *higher* parameter value.

Afrikaans appears to be just such a language. It features a non-Norman genitive form that, according to current grammars, seems to be used more widely than the Saxon genitive form in English. We base the next section of our discussion on Donaldson's (1993) English grammar of Afrikaans. With respect to possession, Donaldson (1993, pp. 98–99) writes:

"The particle se, historically an unemphatic form of sy[n] [his], fulfils a role in Afrikaans very similar to that of apostrophe s (or s apostrophe) in English, but its functions are even wider, e.g. *die kind se toontjie* [the child's toe], *die kinders se toontjies* [the children's toes], *Suid-Afrika se hoofstad* [South Africa's capital] ... Just as a double Anglo-Saxon genitive is possible in English, so is a double se construction in Afrikaans, e.g.
Ons bure se vriende se seun
[our neighbours' friends' son]
...
As in colloquial English, the possessive can be tacked on to the end of a clause or phrase that further qualifies the noun to which it refers, e.g.
Dit was die vrou wat so pas hier was se kind.
[It was the lady who was just here's child.]
...
Both the previous examples may be possible in spoken English — although some speakers may not even agree with that — but in Afrikaans they are permissible in both speech and writing, even where such constructions are not at all possible even in spoken English ... Periphrastic

forms with van 'of' are not as common in Afrikaans as in English ... There are rules in English which determine which nouns can take 's: it is not usual, for example, to use it with inanimate objects, e.g. 'that building's roof' is better said 'the roof of that building', but 'that dog's tail' is quite acceptable. This distinction does not exist in Afrikaans, thus *die gebou se dak* and *die hond se stert*."

The remainder of Donaldson's text continues to list examples of uses of the Saxon genitive form in Afrikaans that are more common and/or acceptable than in English, thus giving the impression that, if anything, Afrikaans has a more flexible way of disambiguating ambiguous Norman genitive forms than English (corpus data are, of course, needed to verify whether this principled freedom is indeed reflected in the actual use of the language, but there are no a priori reasons to doubt this). What apparently has happened is that the ancient antecedent + possessive pronoun genitive form has become much more common in Afrikaans than in Dutch (probably due to the major interactions with the English-speaking population of South Africa; for an in-depth discussion of these interactions, see Ponelis, 1998).

The foregoing analysis suggests that the sliding Gricean parameter should be set higher for Afrikaans than for English (which in turn is higher than the setting for Dutch, as already spelt out). It follows that pressures in favour of NP2 attachment should be stronger in Afrikaans than in English, which implies in turn that the attachment bias should be more marked NP2-favouring than it is in English.

To test attachment preferences in Afrikaans and to compare them with previous data (in particular Cuetos and Mitchell, 1988; and Brysbaert and Mitchell, 1996), one of the authors (PS) translated the Cuetos and Mitchell (1988) questionnaire in Afrikaans and administered it to 87 students of the University of South Africa at Pretoria. All participants were native speakers Afrikaans. There were 24 test sentences, interspersed with 26 filler sentences representing a variety of other, unrelated kinds of ambiguity. Of the 24 test sentences, 11 were examples in which both of the potential attachment sites were human nouns (e.g. 'die bediende van die aktrise' [the servant of the actress]), whereas in the remaining 13 sentences the first noun was non-human and the second noun was human (e.g. 'die boek van die meisie' [the book of the girl]). This slight imbalance was an unintended feature of the original Cuetos/Mitchell questionnaire and was retained to keep the comparison as close as possible. The order of the sentences was also the same as in the previous English, Spanish, and Dutch questionnaires. As in the earlier studies, each sentence was followed by a question designed to tap the reader's preferred attachment of the ambiguous relative clause, as in: "Iemand het geskiet op die bediende van die aktrise wat op die balkon was." [Someone shot the servant of the actress who was on the balcony.] [Who was on the balcony? ...]

The following table shows the most important results (percentage NP2 attachment):

	Human/human	Non-human/human
English (C&M)	61	32
Spanish (C&M)	28	22
Dutch (B&M)	44	33
Afrikaans	45	41

The non-human/human value for the English test should be treated with scepticism. The sentences in this category used the relative pronoun 'that' which almost certainly introduced a bias in favour of the non-human NP1. Had this been replaced by 'who' the bias would have been reversed. So, it is doubtful that the attachment is genuinely ambiguous in this condition.

No formal statistical test is needed to establish that Afrikaans fails to confirm the predictions of the 'sliding parameter' account. Not only does the NP2-attachment bias fail to exceed that for English. There is no bias in that direction at all. In fact, on the contrary, there was evidence for a reliable NP1 preference (analysis by subjects: $t = 3.96$, df $= 86$, $p < 0.01$; analysis by materials $t = 2.02$, df $= 23$, $p < 0.06$, two-tailed). There was no reliable difference between both head types either ($F_1(1, 86) = 2.36$, $p > 0.10$; $F_2(1, 22) < 1$).

In short, although Dutch, English and Afrikaans are plausibly placed at progressive points on a scale of usage for non-Norman forms, there is no evidence that the 'Gricean reasoner' capitalises on these differences as predicted in the 'sliding parameter' version of the model.

Next we turn to the possibility that the Gricean parameter is set, not for each language as a whole, but is allowed instead to take numerous different settings depending upon different classes of NP complex (i.e. the proposal we referred to earlier as Clifton's 'smart' Gricean account).

Evidence from Dutch

Preliminary questionnaire

A detailed investigation of the potential of the 'smart' Gricean account of cross-linguistic differences depends upon precise information about the acceptability of competing forms of the genitive materials under examination. The present questionnaire set out to establish these facts for the 36 basic genitive noun phrases used in Experiment I, below.

To recap on the general linguistic facts, Dutch has three different ways of linking noun phrases in genitive structures: the Norman genitive, the Saxon genitive, and the antecedent with possessive pronoun form. A modifier following the NP complex can be attached to either of the two potential heads within the Norman genitive. In the two other forms it can only be attached to one. On the basis of grammatical considerations we know that the last two genitive forms are not equally acceptable for all types of constructions. However, given that the acceptability may be influenced by cultural influences, it seems important to conduct an explicit test of the acceptability of the different genitive forms, in addition to relying on the rules and conventions set out in grammar books.

Method

Participants. Participants were 116 first-year students attending the University of Leuven. All were native Dutch speakers. They were tested at the beginning of a practical course in small groups. They had not previously participated in any similar studies.

Questionnaire. The items of the questionnaire consisted of the main clauses of the 36 sentences subsequently used in the experiment. Six versions of each were compiled (4a–4f): two with the Norman genitive form, two with the Saxon genitive form, and two with the possessive pronoun form. There were two versions of each genitive form: one in which both noun phrases had the same gender marking (e.g. both non-neuter), and one in which the genders differed (e.g. one NP neuter and the other non-neuter). Singular non-neuter Dutch nouns take the definite article 'de' and the relative pronoun 'die'; singular neuter nouns take the definite article 'het' and the relative pronoun 'dat'. As will be described below, we wanted to use this grammatical feature to try to disambiguate the relative clause from the very first word on. A Latin-square design was used to ensure that each participant saw only one version of a sentence. In addition, in order to avoid sequence effects, the sentences were ordered according to six different randomisations (i.e. a total of 36 different questionnaires were used, each with a different random permutation of 6 sentences according to (4a), 6 according to (4b), and so on).

(4a) "De gangsters schoten op de zoon van de actrice."
(4b) "De gangsters schoten op het zoontje van de actrice."
(4c) "De gangsters schoten op de actrices zoon."
(4d) "De gangsters schoten op de actrices zoontje."
(4e) "De gangsters schoten op de actrice haar zoon."
(4f) "De gangsters schoten op de actrice haar zoontje."

The instructions to the participants were as follows (translated from Dutch): "The Dutch grammar formulates rules to which the Dutch language adheres in general. Because these rules form the common part, it is possible that some sentences which are in principle correct, do not conform to our feelings. On the other hand, it is also possible that sentences which according to the rules are wrong, seem right to us. This questionnaire tries to get insight in this language feeling. Therefore, we ask you to indicate for each of the following sentences to what extent the sentence sounds correct to you. Use a digit between 1 and 5 with the following meaning: 1 = completely unacceptable; 2 = rather unacceptable; 3 = neutral; 4 = rather acceptable; 5 = completely acceptable). Write the digit after the sentence. Try to follow your first impression and do not look back at sentences you've already finished. Good luck and thanks for your cooperation."

Results and discussion

Acceptability judgements were averaged as a function of head type, similarity of the gender of the two nouns, and genitive form (see Table 1).

ANOVAs indicated that for the Norman form, there was a reliable difference between the head types (p_1, $p_2 < 0.01$), due to the lower scores for the h/nh head types. For the Saxon forms, there were reliable main effects for head type (p_1, $p_2 < 0.01$) and gender equivalence (p_1, $p_2 < 0.01$). The effect of head type was mainly caused by the h/nh heads, which were less acceptable. The effect of gender equivalence was due to the fact that the Saxon genitive form was more or less unacceptable when the genders of the two nouns did not agree, probably because in the Saxon genitive form, the article is implicitly taken to refer to both nouns, which causes confusion when the articles of the two nouns do not agree. Finally, there was also a significant main effect of head type for the possessive pronoun genitives (p_1, $p_2 < 0.01$), again due to h/nh head type.

All in all, notwithstanding our caution, the findings agree quite well with what might have been expected on the basis of official statements about the grammar. The non-Norman genitive forms are only acceptable if they refer to human nouns.

Table 1

Acceptability of the various genitive forms as a function of head type (human/human [the son of the actress], non-human/human [the book of the girl], or human/non-human [the owner of the house]), gender equivalence of the nouns, and genitive form (1 = completely unacceptable; 5 = completely acceptable)

	Norman	Saxon	Possessive pronoun
Human/human			
Same	4.8	2.6	3.5
Different	4.8	1.9	3.4
Non-human/human			
Same	4.8	2.2	3.2
Different	4.7	1.8	3.4
Human/non-human			
Same	4.5	1.7	1.7
Different	4.5	1.3	1.7

In the other cases, the Saxon form is less acceptable than the possessive pronoun form and this is particularly true when the genders of the two nouns differ.

Eye-tracking experiment

The 'smart' Gricean account assumes that the Gricean parameter is set either for different classes of NP complexes (coarse version) or on the basis of individual lexical items occupying the NP2 slot (fine-grained version). Given the variation over different NP classes in their potential for expression in alternative genitive forms (as confirmed in the pretest), the model predicts corresponding variation in RC-attachment bias over the different classes of NP complex. In particular, NP1-attachment preferences should be strengthened for the h/nh head types where alternatives to Saxon genitives are least acceptable.

For the purposes of the fine-grained version of the model, attachment bias might be expected to vary on a sentence-by-sentence basis. Specifically, the sentences with the least acceptable alternatives to the Saxon forms should show the strongest preference for NP1 over NP2 attachment.

Method

Participants. The participants were 48 students from the University of Leuven. They were paid or received course credits for participating in the experiment. All were native Dutch speakers and had normal or corrected to normal vision. Before the sentence reading experiment, each student had taken part in at least one other experiment with the eye-tracking device, so that they had some experience with the equipment. None of the participants was aware of the research hypothesis.

Stimulus materials. The test sentences consisted of 36 groups of 4 sentences which allowed an orthogonal variation of (i) eventual resolution of the sentence in favour of attachment to the first or the second noun phrase in the complex head, and (ii) whether or not the attachment site was first signalled by the gender of the relative pronoun or at a point a word or two later in the relative clause. Twelve of the 36 groups of sentences had complex heads of the type human/human (e.g. 'the son of the actress'), 12 other groups were of the type non-human/human (e.g. 'the book of the girl'), and 12 of the type human/non-human (e.g. 'the main character of the film'). All sentences were constructed in such a way that the disambiguation of the relative clause started as early as possible in the clause (i.e. within the first two or three words after the relative pronoun when this was not unambiguous by itself).

The relative clauses always contained two subclauses connected by a conjunction. The first subclause disambiguated the attachment (e.g. 'the son of the actress who had his arm in a cast ... '), the second one could be attached to the first noun as well as to the second noun (e.g. ' … and who was sitting on a bank.'). In practice, this meant that if the first subclause disambiguated towards NP1, the second subclause was attached to NP1 as well, whereas the second subclause was attached to NP2, when the first part disambiguated towards NP2. The second part of the relative clause was added because previous research, reported by Brysbaert and Mitchell (1996), showed that observers tend to re-read the whole sentence if they encountered a processing problem near the end of the sentence. This made it difficult to distinguish between immediate effects and re-analysis effects.

Test sentences were combined with 156 filler sentences, which were either first sentences of Dutch novels and detective stories ($n = 48$) or sentences that addressed other unrelated questions ($n = 108$). Twenty-five of the filler sentences were followed by a question that addressed the content of the sentence and that could be answered by 'yes' or 'no' (e.g. (translated) 'In front of the gate of Mariabronn Abbey near the road stood a chestnut tree.'; question 'Was there a road in front of the gate of the abbey?'). The purpose of the questions was to encourage the participants to read the sentences for comprehension. Mean number of mistakes on these questions was moderate: 3.8 out of 25.

Procedure. Observers were seated at a distance of 120 cm from a $21''$ CRT monitor, with the line of sight of the right eye orthogonal to the central screen position. The head was immobilised by means of a head rest and a bite bar with dental impression compound. Eye movements were monitored with a Generation-V dual-Purkinje-image eye-tracker (as described in Crane and Steele, 1985) which has a spatial accuracy of 1 min of arc. Only the right eye was tracked, although viewing was binocular. Horizontal and vertical eye position was sampled every millisecond.

The experiment was carried out in three phases, each of which started with a calibration procedure. In this procedure the observer fixated a series of diagonally aligned calibration points which were presented one at a time in a self-paced manner. After successful completion of the calibration routine, a calibration check was run. This check consisted of five '+' signs aligned on the 12th line of the 80×25 character space of a screen presented in text mode. The plus signs were placed on character positions 10, 25, 50, 65, and 70. The observer had to fixate each sign and press on a button (as in the normal calibration routine). Upon pressing the button, the observer got feedback about the eye position calculated by the eye-tracker. This was done by displaying a '×' sign. Ideally, the '×' sign had to fall on the '+' sign. A deviation of maximally two letter positions left or right and one letter position up or down was allowed, however.

As soon as the calibration check had been successfully completed, the sentences were presented one at a time on a self-paced basis. In order to initiate a trial, participants had to look at the beginning of line 8 where the rank number of the trial was displayed. This ensured us that observers always started reading at the beginning of the sentence. Sentences were presented on the 10th text line if they were one-line sentences and on the 10th and the 13th line if they were two-line sentences. Participants were asked to read the sentences in order to understand the content. They were told not to learn the sentences by heart, just to read them. At the end of the session, a new calibration check was run to ensure that the observer's head had not moved. The observer had to remain motionless during the whole experimental session, which lasted between 8 and 20 min depending on the reading speed of the participant.

The first experimental session consisted of 15 practice sentences, all of which were first sentences of novels. They were presented to introduce the calibration checks and the task to the participants (the calibration procedure was already known from previous experiments). The second and the third session contained 96 sentences. The sentences were obtained by making a random permutation of the 36 test sentences and the 156 filler sentences and by dividing the sequence in two halves. Every participant got a different randomisation and saw only one of the four possible combinations of a test sentence (according to a Latin-square design). Where filler items were followed by questions, the initial sentence was removed from the screen and the question was presented on the 16th text line. The participant had to indicate his/her answer by pressing a button with the right (yes) or the left (no) hand. In the event of a mistake, feedback was given in the form of a message saying 'Wrong!'.

Results

Table 2 shows a latency measure for several different regions of the experimental sentences. The regions were defined as follows: (r1) the phrases constituting the head of the main clause (i.e. the subject and the verb of the main clause); (r2) NP1 of the complex head; (r3) NP2; (r4) the relative pronoun; (r5) the phrases constituting the disambiguating part of the relative clause; and (r6) the phrases constituting the neutral part of the relative clause (i.e. the part that could be attached to NP1 as well as to NP2; see above). A further distinction was made when the observers started re-reading the sentence. This re-reading time began from the moment when the observer returned from region 6 to the main clause.

The latency measure used here is the cumulative region reading time (CRRT), which is defined as the sum of fixations between the moment when the eyes cross the front border of the region and the moment when they cross the back border. This variable differs from first-pass reading time (FPRT) because regressions arising from a region are added to the CRRT of that region but not to the FPRT. CRRT is preferred to FPRT in parsing studies because readers often respond to processing difficulty not by dwelling on the text in the vicinity of the problem but rather by making a quick regression to earlier material. The FPRT measure fails to take account of the costs associated with response sequences of this kind. For further

Table 2

Cumulative region reading times (CRRTs) in milliseconds in different regions of the test sentences (see text for definitions of CRRTs and sentence regions)

	r1 begin	r2 NP1	r3 NP2	r4 rel. pronoun	r5 disam.	r6 remain.	r7 re-read.
Human/human							
D-1	706	405	640	122	1231	1046	510
D-2	712	487	549	132	1217	1105	578
I 1	697	422	507	99	1049	987	391
I-2	731	492	532	110	1175	1103	647
Non-human/human							
D-1	695	496	528	114	894	1166	416
D-2	611	505	561	156	964	1217	550
I-1	673	587	564	163	1035	1147	477
I-2	678	477	576	121	980	1199	520
Human/non-human							
D-1	706	589	564	118	982	1216	475
D-2	686	570	588	95	1062	1229	709
I-1	681	545	534	115	922	1195	492
I-2	719	585	514	109	1124	1283	548
Average							
NP1	693	507	556	122	1019	1126	460
NP2	690	519	554	121	1087	1189	592

Latency values are tabulated by head type (human/human, non-human/human or human/non-human), by point of disambiguation (immediately on the pronoun (I) or delayed (D)), and by the host site of the attachment forced in the disambiguation region (NP1 or NP2).

methodological discussion of these issues see Brysbaert and Mitchell (1996), Konieczny, Hemforth and Scheepers (1994) and Liversedge and Pickering (1995).

Analyses of variance yielded only two effects that were reliable both for F_1 and F_2. These were the main effects of attachment site ($F_1(1, 47) = 11.95$, $MS_e = 123607$, $p < 0.01$; $F_2(1, 24) = 8.62$, $MS_e = 44291$, $p < 0.01$) and region ($F_1(6, 282) = 134.89$, $MS_e = 529444$, $p < 0.01$; $F_2(6, 144) = 129.92$, $MS_e = 137554$, $p < 0.01$). The interaction between attachment site and region was reliable by participants ($F_1(6, 282) = 3.90$, $MS_e = 97946$, $p < 0.01$) but only approached significance by materials ($F_2(6, 144) = 2.12$, $MS_e = 45179$, $p < 0.06$).

Analyses of variance for each separate region produced just one effect that was reliable both for F_1 and F_2. This was the main effect of attachment site in region 6 (i.e. the second part of the relative clause; $F_1(1, 47) = 7.37$, $MS_e = 778903$,

$p < 0.01$; $F_2(1, 24) = 6.07$, $MS_e = 24842$, $p < 0.03$). Attachment site was also reliable across participants for region 5 (i.e. the disambiguating part of the relative clause) and region 7 (i.e. re-reading time) but only approached significance in the analysis by materials (region 5: $F_1(1, 47) = 5.58$, $MS_e = 118921$, $p < 0.03$; $F_2(1, 24) = 3.15$, $MS_e = 54715$, $p < 0.09$; region 7: $F_1(1, 47) = 6.67$, $MS_e = 372133$, $p < 0.02$; $F_2(1, 24) = 3.04$, $MS_e = 206592$, $p < 0.10$). It is noteworthy that there was no difference in reading pattern between the sentences with an ambiguous relative pronoun and the sentences with a disambiguating pronoun (i.e. one that pointed to an NP with a corresponding gender). This agrees with other studies we have been doing and which show that the gender information of the relative pronoun is rarely used to disambiguate RC attachment in Dutch, not even in off-line questionnaire studies.

In order to determine whether materials with acceptable non-Norman genitive forms went against the general NP1-attachment preference (as predicted by the Gricean hypothesis), we carried out a series of correlations between rating scores and a measure of NP2-attachment penalty. If this penalty is reduced (or reversed) in sentences with more acceptable non-Norman forms, then there should be a negative correlation between these measures. In line with the analyses above, the measure we chose for 'NP2-attachment penalty' was the mean CRRT measure for regions 5 through 7 for sentences disambiguated in favour of NP2 attachment minus the corresponding mean latency for sentences disambiguated in favour of NP1 attachment.

The results showed that none of the correlations approached significance. In the delayed condition there was a small, and clearly unreliable negative correlation between the measure of NP2 penalty and Saxon genitive acceptability ($r = -0.05$, $n = 36$, $p > 0.5$). In the immediate condition the corresponding statistic was slightly positive, but still completely unreliable ($r = 0.03$, $n = 36$, $p > 0.5$). For the acceptability ratings of possessive forms the corresponding figures were $r = 0.01$ ($n = 36$, $p > 0.5$), and $r = -0.07$ ($n = 36$, $p > 0.5$).

Given that neither acceptability measure alone produced a reliable correlation with NP2 penalty, the two measures would not be expected to do so in combination. This was confirmed by regression analysis indicating that even when both acceptability measures were used as independent variable they failed to explain a significant proportion of the variance of the penalty measure ($F(2, 33) = 0.08$, $R^2 = 0.001$, for the delayed condition and $F(2, 33) = 0.23$, $R^2 = 0.014$, for the immediate condition.

The general lack of a relation between the acceptability measures and NP2 penalty is shown clearly in the scatterplots provided in Figs. 1 and 2.

To avoid basing our case against the Gricean proposal merely on the failure to reject the null hypothesis (that there is no correlation), we next focused our attention on the six sentences with the most acceptable Saxon forms (i.e. those with ratings above 3; essentially the extreme right-hand examples in Fig. 1). These

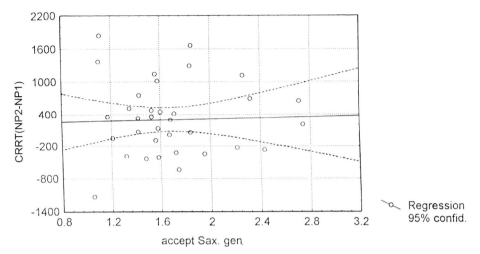

Fig. 1. Scatterplot for the immediate disambiguation condition indicating how the penalty for forcing NP2 attachment varies as a function of the rated acceptability of the Saxon genitive alternative to the complex NP host. The penalty measure is based on the cumulative region reading time (CRRT) summed over analysis regions 5–7 and is defined as the difference in milliseconds between the figure for sentences disambiguated in favour of NP2 and that for sentences disambiguated in favour of NP1. Points above zero in the *y*-axis therefore represent the individual sentences which showed an NP1-attachment preference. The *x*-axis acceptability score for each sentence comes from earlier ratings of the corresponding materials (as summarised in the middle column of Table 1).

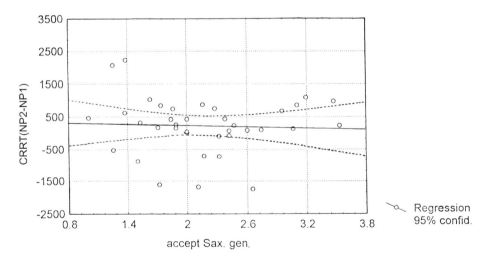

Fig. 2. Scatterplot equivalent to that in Fig. 1, but for the delayed disambiguation condition.

Table 3

CRRT by region for the 'best' sentences

	r1 begin	r2 NP1	r3 NP2	r4 rel. pronoun	r5 disam.	r6 remain.	r7 re-read.
D-1	821	459	648	88	1189	1092	344
D-2	786	579	518	148	1300	1228	762

sentences also had ratings above 3 on the acceptability scale for the possessive pronoun genitive form. According to the Gricean hypothesis these materials should be most prone to NP2-attachment preference.

Table 3 gives the mean results for these six sentences.

Like the rest of the data these sentences clearly showed no sign of an NP2 preference. (In fact, a material analysis indicated that, contrary to the prediction of Gricean proposals, there was a reliable NP1 preference in a planned comparison over the last three regions: $F_2(1, 5) = 16.8$, $MS_e = 26246$, $p < 0.01$. No subject analysis could be carried out because of the unequal distribution of conditions over individuals.)

Discussion

Overall, results show no sign at all that a Gricean mechanism plays a role in influencing RC-attachment preferences. The evidence for NP1 attachment was no more marked in the human/non-human condition (where alternative genitive forms are least available and Gricean pressures toward NP2 attachment least influential) than it was in the other conditions where Gricean effects would have been expected to play a role. More critically, a detailed sentence-by-sentence analysis showed no sign at all that attachment preferences are correlated with the judged acceptability of alternative genitive forms.

These findings argue emphatically against interpreting cross-linguistic differences in RC-attachment preferences in terms of differences in the availability of alternatives to the Norman genitive across different languages. Proposals of this kind fail to account for the data when the putative Gricean shift is triggered by the mere existence of alternative genitive forms in the language (as previously demonstrated by Brysbaert and Mitchell, 1996). They are also incapable of accounting for the data if the Gricean shift is assumed to be initiated by the availability of an alternative form for the sentence currently under consideration (i.e. the position we earlier dubbed the 'smart' version of the Gricean model). Perhaps the most telling evidence against the proposal is that NP2 attachment fails to show up, even in the materials which would be expected to show the Gricean effects at their strongest (i.e. the sentences with the most acceptable alternative forms).

Conclusion

We have examined the Gricean hypothesis in every guise we can imagine and we conclude that in all variants without exception the proposal is consistently found wanting. Whether the Gricean effects are assumed to operate as simple switches or sliding parameters applying to languages as a whole, or implemented differently for different subclasses of materials within individual languages, we have not succeeded in finding any version of the hypothesis which succeeds in accounting for variation in RC-attachment bias in different conditions. We therefore conclude that the time has come to move on and resume the search for more productive suggestions concerning the mechanisms underlying cross-linguistic variation in RC attachment.

References

Baccino, T., De Vincenzi, M. and Job, R. (2000). Cross-linguistic studies of the late closure strategy: French and Italian. In: M. De Vincenzi and V. Lombardi (Eds.), Cross-linguistic Perspective on Language Processing. Dordrecht: Kluwer.

Brysbaert, M. and Mitchell, D.C. (1996). Modifier attachment in sentence processing: evidence from Dutch. Quarterly Journal of Experimental Psychology, 49A, 664–695.

Carreiras, M. (1992). Estrategias de análisis sintáctico en el procesamiento de frases: cierre temprano versus cierre tardío. Cognitiva, 4, 3–27.

Carreiras, M. and Clifton, C. (1993). Relative clause interpretation preferences in Spanish and English. Language and Speech, 36, 353–372.

Carreiras, M. and Clifton, C. (1999). Another word on parsing relative clauses: eye-tracking evidence from Spanish and English. Memory and Cognition, 27, 826–833.

Corley, M.M.B. (1996). The Role of Statistics in Human Sentence Processing. Unpubl. PhD Thesis, University of Exeter.

Crane, H.D. and Steele, C.M. (1985). Generation-V Dual-Purkinje-Image-Eyetracker. Applied Optics, 24, 525–537.

Cuetos, F. and Mitchell, D.C. (1988). Cross-linguistic differences in parsing: restrictions on the use of the Late Closure strategy in Spanish. Cognition, 30, 73–105.

Cuetos, F., Mitchell, D.C. and Corley, M.M.B. (1996). Parsing in different languages. In: M. Carreiras, J. Garcia-Albea and N. Sabastian-Galles (Eds.), Language Processing in Spanish. Hillsdale, NJ: Erlbaum, pp. 145–187.

De Vincenzi, M. and Job, R. (1993). Some observations on the universality of the late-closure strategy. Journal of Psycholinguistic Research, 22, 189–206.

De Vincenzi, M. and Job, R. (1995). An investigation of late closure: the role of syntax, thematic structure and pragmatics in initial and final interpretation. Journal of Experimental Psychology: Learning, Memory and Cognition, 21, 1303–1321.

Donaldson, B.C. (1993). A Grammar of Afrikaans. Berlin: Mouton de Gruyter.

Ehrlich, K., Fernández, E., Fodor, J.D., Stenshoel, E. and Vinereanu, M. (1999). Low attachment of relative clauses: new data from Swedish, Norwegian and Romanian. Poster presented at the 12th Annual CUNY Conference on Human Sentence Processing. CUNY, New York, March 18–20.

Fernandez, E.M. (1999). Processing strategies in second language acquisition: some preliminary results. In: E. Klein and G. Martohardjono (Eds.) The Development of Second Language Grammers: A Generation Approach. Amsterdam: John Bergamms Publishing Co., pp. 127–239.

Frazier, L. (1990). Parsing modifiers: special purpose routines in the human sentence processing mechanism? In: D.A. Balota, G.B. Flores d'Arcais and K. Rayner (Eds.), Comprehension Processes in Reading. Hillsdale, NJ: Erlbaum, pp. 303–330.

Frazier, L. and Clifton, C. (1996). Construal. Boston, MA: MIT Press.

Frenck-Mestre, C. and Pynte, J. (2000). In: M. De Vincenzi and V. Lombardi (Eds.), Cross-linguistic Perspective on Language Processing. Dordrecht: Kluwer, pp. 199–148.

Gilboy, E., Sopena, J.M., Clifton, C. and Frazier, L. (1995). Argument structure and association preferences in Spanish and English complex NPs. Cognition, 54, 131–167.

Grice, H.P. (1975). Logic and conversation. In: P. Cole and J. Morgan (Eds.), Syntax and Semantics, Vol. 3: Speech Acts. New York: Academic Press, pp. 41–58.

Haeseryn, W., Romijn, K., Geerts, G., de Rooij, J. and van den Toorn, M.C. (1997). Algemene Nederlandse Spraakkunst (2nd ed.). Groningen: Martinus Nijhoff; and Deurne: Wolters Plantyn.

Hemforth, B., Konieczny, L. and Scheepers, C. (1994). Principle-based and probabilistic approaches to human parsing: how universal is the human language processor? In: H. Trost (Ed.), Tagungsband KONVENS '94. Berlin: Springer, pp. 161–170.

Hemforth, B., Konieczny, L. and Scheepers, C. (2000). Syntactic attachment and anaphor resolution: two sides of relative clause attachment. In: M. Crocker, M. Pickering and C. Clifton (Eds.), Architectures and Mechanisms for Language Processing. Cambridge, UK: Cambridge University Press.

Henstra, J. (1996). Relative clause attachment in English: eye-tracking versus self-paced reading. Poster presented at AMLaP-96, Turino, September 20–21.

Igoa, M.J., Carreiras, M. and Meseguer, E. (1998). A study on late closure in Spanish: priciple-grounded vs. frequency-based accounts of attachment preferences. Quarterly Journal of Experimental Psychology, 51A, 561–592.

Kamide, Y. (1998). The Role of Argument Structure Requirements and Recency Constraints in Human Sentence Processing. Unpubl. PhD Thesis, University of Exeter.

Kamide, Y. and Mitchell, D.C. (1997). Relative clause attachment: non-determinism in Japanese parsing. Journal of Psycholinguistic Research, 26, 247–254.

Koelmans, L. (1975). Jan z'n boek en de pregenitieven. De nieuwe Taalgids, 68, 433–445.

Konieczny, L., Hemforth, B. and Scheepers, C. (1994). Reanalysis vs. internal repairs: nonmonotonic processes in sentence perception. In: B. Hemforth, L. Konieczny, C. Scheepers and G. Strube (Eds.), First Analysis, Reanalysis, and Repair. IIG-Berichte 8/94, pp. 1–22.

Liversedge, S.P. and Pickering, M.J. (1995). Investigations into analyses of eye movements during reading. 8th European Conference on Eye Movements, Derby, 6–9 September.

Mitchell, D.C. and Brysbaert, M. (1998). Challenges to recent theories of cross-linguistic variation in parsing: evidence from Dutch. Syntax and Semantics, 31, 313–335.

Mitchell, D.C., Cuetos, F. and Zagar, D. (1990). Reading in different languages: is there a universal mechanism for parsing sentences? In: D. Balota, G.B. Flores d'Arcais and K. Rayner (Eds.), Comprehension Processes in Reading. Hillsdale, NJ: Erlbaum, pp. 285–302.

Miyamoto, E.T. (1998). A low attachment preference in Brazilian Portuguese relative clauses. Paper presented at the AMPaP-98 Meeting held in Freiburg im Breisgau, 24–26 September.

Ponelis, F.A. (1998). Standaardafrikaans en die Afrikaanse taalfamilie. Annale van die Universiteit van Stellenbosch, 1998/1.

Pynte, J. and Frenck-Mestre, C. (1996). Evidence for early-closure attachments on first-pass reading times in French: a replication. Poster presented at AMLaP-96, Turino, September 20–21.

Thornton, R., MacDonald, M.C. and Gil, M. (1999). Pragmatic constraint on the interpretation of complex noun phrases in Spanish and English. Journal of Experimental Psychology: Learning, Memory and Cognition, 25, 1347–1365.

Viñas, G., Oria-Merino, L., Heydel, M. and Sáinz, J.(1999). Resolución de ambiguedades de adjunción: evidencia procedente de la producción de oraciones en Español, Aleman e Ingles. Poster presented at the 4th Symposium on Psycholinguistics held in Miraflores de la Sierra, Madrid, April 21–24.

Zagar, D., Pynte, J. and Rativeau, S. (1997). Evidence for early closure attachment on first-pass reading times in French. Quarterly Journal of Experimental Psychology, 50A, 421–438.

CHAPTER 19

Modifier Attachment in German: Relative Clauses and Prepositional Phrases

Lars Konieczny
Freiburg University and Saarland University

and

Barbara Hemforth
Freiburg University

Abstract

In this chapter, we present new results from an eye-tracking experiment on NP1–NP2-modifier attachment in German. We will focus on attachment preferences across modifier types, namely relative clauses (RCs) and semantically highly comparable prepositional phrases (PPs), showing that different preferences hold for these two types of constructions. Whereas PP attachment follows recency-based principles, resulting in low attachment, RCs are preferentially attached high. These data provide an on-line confirmation of results from various questionnaire studies presented in Hemforth, Konieczny and Scheepers (in press; see also Hemforth, Konieczny and Scheepers, 1994). Furthermore, the effects for RCs and PPs showed up most clearly either in regression-sensitive (regression path durations) and regression-insensitive (first-pass reading times) measures, respectively. To provide the means for analysing the re-reading process, we established a new measure (*load contribution*).

Reading as a Perceptual Process/A. Kennedy, R. Radach, D. Heller and J. Pynte (Editors)
© 2000 Elsevier Science Ltd. All rights reserved

Introduction

Modifier attachment has become one of the central topics in psycholinguistic research on sentence processing, in particular when questions about crosslinguistic comparisons of parsing preferences are concerned (see Mitchell, 1994, for an overview). Modifiers, and especially relative clauses in sentences like (1), have been shown to be preferentially attached to a non-recent host in many languages (such as Spanish: Cuetos and Mitchell, 1988; French: Zagar, Pynte and Rativeau, 1997; Dutch: Brysbaert and Mitchell, 1996; and German: Hemforth, Konieczny and Scheepers, in press).

(1) The daughter of the teacher who lived in France.

In all of these languages (and several others) the relative clause is preferentially attached to the first NP (the daughter) [1], contradicting any kind of recency-based principles like *late closure* (Frazier, 1987), *most recent head attachment* (Konieczny, Hemforth, Scheepers and Strube, 1997), or *recency* (Gibson, 1998). There is considerable debate as to whether the data from the different languages reflect the initial parsing stage (Frazier, 1990; De Vincenzi and Job, 1993, 1995; Pynte and Frenck-Mestre, 1996). With the possible exception of Italian (De Vincenzi and Job, 1993, 1995), no evidence for an early recency-based preference has yet been empirically substantiated in any high attaching language. Like Frenck-Mestre and Pynte (see Chapter 21), we will present eye-tracking data which supposedly reflect early processing stages.

Eye-tracking has been used in sentence processing research for a considerable time. Data analysis has mostly made use of a restricted set of measures, notably first fixation duration (i.e., the time spent on the very first fixation on a region), first pass reading time (i.e., the time spent on a region from when it is first encountered from the left until it is left on either side), and total reading time (i.e., the sum of all fixations on a region). Now that more and more labs use the eye-tracking technique, it has become clear that more information can be extracted from the stream of fixations. In particular, it has been argued that the time spent on a critical disambiguating region does not necessarily reflect parsing difficulty. Readers sometimes notice very quickly that something went wrong while reading a sentence and look back at earlier regions without spending too much time at the point where they notice their mistake. Therefore, we will use regression sensitive measures to give a detailed picture of the parsing process. We also raise the question of whether differences obtained for different modifiers can be attributed to oculomotoric reasons

---

1 However, this preference is modulated by the existence of various thematic assigners separating the potential hosts. If a more recent host-NP is part of a thematic PP, for instance, it becomes a more likely attachment site for RCs (Gilboy et al., 1995).

induced by the obligatory comma before RCs, rather than higher level cognitive processing. In particular, we will examine where people tend to go back to, and how long they stay there, while re-reading portions of the sentence.

Relative clauses and prepositional phrases

Before going into the details of the experiment, let us briefly describe what we know from questionnaire experiments on RC attachment and PP attachment in German. Participants in these questionnaires read sentences like (2a,b). They were then asked to indicate the preferred host for the modifier, i.e., whether they thought it was the daughter or the teacher who came from France.

(2a) The daughter of the teacher who was from France met a friend.
(2b) The daughter of the teacher from France met a friend.

The questionnaire data usually show a clear interaction of modifier type and preferred host: RCs are preferentially attached to the first NP (the daughter) and PPs are preferentially attached to the second NP (the teacher).

How can this interaction be explained? Whereas the NP2-attachment preference for PPs is easily compatible with the classical late closure principle, as well as other variants of a recency or locality principle, the NP1-attachment preference for RCs is not. However, it is clear that some recency based principle applies to modifier attachment in German, it just does not apply to relative clauses in this particular kind of construction. Thus, the results rule out any account that gives a general solution for modifier attachment within a language. As we stated elsewhere (Hemforth et al., in press; Konieczny and Hemforth, 1996), we do not take this as evidence that universal recency based principles are not at work in sentence processing. On the contrary, we still consider recency as one of the major principles governing syntactic attachment preferences. RC attachment, however, is not only syntactic in nature. Whenever a relative pronoun is involved in ambiguity resolution, both syntactic *and* anaphoric processes influence the attachment preference (*attachment-binding dualism*). Whereas syntactic attachment is guided by recency, anaphoric binding will be influenced by the salience of available discourse entities. Given that salience is furthermore affected by focus, thematic assignment, topic etc., binding will generally be high (i.e. to N1, which is closer to the main predicate and receives a thematic role from the verb), but will be modulated by intervening thematic assigners, like prepositions, which may raise the salience of lower sites. The interaction of the two processes is conceived of as a race: whichever process succeeds earlier will win and determine the initial interpretation.

Languages differ with respect to a pronoun's effectiveness as an anaphoric cue. English, for instance, permits the omission of the pronoun in reduced relative clauses, whereas other languages, like German, require an overt pronoun. English thus exhibits a much weaker over-all N1 attraction for RCs (Cuetos and Mitchell, 1988).

We should hasten to add that there are other possible explanations of modifier specific preference patterns. One of the most interesting candidates is the prosody-based 'same size sister'-principle (Fodor, 1998). Roughly speaking, this principle says that modifiers are attached such that a prosodically balanced structure results from the attachment. As a consequence, short modifiers are preferentially attached to NP2, whereas longer modifiers should preferentially be attached to NP1. Since the PPs in our experiments were shorter than the respective RCs, this principle may render an alternative account of these data. However, recent results on RCs and PPs controlled for length suggest that this is not generally the case (Walter, Hemforth, Konieczny and Seelig, 1999).

The question we will try to answer in this chapter is whether the preferences we have found for RCs and PPs in questionnaire experiments reflect *initial* parsing strategies. If recency works for modifiers initially, irrespective of their particular type, we should not find a modifier by attachment interaction in eye-tracking measures reflecting early parsing stages.

The experiment

Materials

The experimental sentences were manipulated according to a 2×2 within-subjects design with the factors modifier (RC vs. PP), and attachment (N1/high vs. N2/low). See example (3) for a sample set. The order of the sentences was randomized. For each experimental condition, three sentences were presented, resulting in 12 target sentences per subject. The materials were rotated such that every sentence from every set was presented to an equal number of participants. In addition to the target sentences there were 76 filler sentences.

(3a) PP (high)
      Die Köchin der vegetarischen Vorspeise mit dem exklusiven Restaurant war sehr bekannt.
      The cook (fem) of the vegetarian starter (fem) with the exclusive restaurant was very well known.
(3b) PP (low)
      Die vegetarische Vorspeise der Köchin mit dem exklusiven Restaurant war sehr bekannt.
      The vegetarian starter (fem) of the cook (fem) with the exclusive restaurant was very well known.

(3c) RC (high)

Die Köchin der vegetarischen Vorspeise, die ein exklusives Restaurant besaß, war sehr bekannt.

The cook (fem) of the vegetarian starter (fem) who owned an exclusive restaurant was very well known.

(3d) RC (low)

Die vegetarische Vorspeise der Köchin, die ein exklusives Restaurant besaß, war sehr bekannt.

The vegetarian starter (fem) of the cook (fem) who owned an exclusive restaurant was very well known.

Participants

Twenty-four undergraduate students (native speakers of German) from the University of Freiburg were paid to participate in the study. All of them had normal, uncorrected vision and they were all naive concerning the purpose of the study. During an experimental session of approximately 40 min, each of the participants had to read 88 isolated sentences and yes–no questions while their eye movements were monitored.

Procedure

Prior to the experiment, participants were familiarized with the procedure and were instructed to read the sentences at normal speed. They were then fitted to a headrest to prevent head movements during reading. This was followed by a calibration procedure and a warm-up block of 4 filler sentences. The experiment consisted of 4 blocks. Each block was initiated by a brief calibration procedure and contained 21 sentences — 2 filler sentences followed by 19 randomly mixed target and filler sentences. Before each sentence, the subject had to fixate a cross on the screen which indicated the position of the first character in the sentence. When the participants had finished reading the sentence, they pressed a button, and the sentence was erased from the screen. Each sentence of the experiment was followed by a simple yes/no-question which the subject was to answer by pressing one of two buttons (left-hand button: 'yes', right-hand button: 'no'). They answered with a high degree of accuracy (93%) and equally well across conditions.

Apparatus

The participants' eye movements were monitored by a Generation 5.5 Dual Purkinje Image Eyetracker. Viewing was binocular, but eye movements were recorded only from the right eye. The eyetracker was connected to an Intel Pentium 60-based computer, which controlled the stimulus presentation and stored the output from the eyetracker. The sampling rate for data collection was 1 kHz. The sentences were presented on a 20-inch color monitor, beginning at the 6th column of the 80×24 character matrix of the display. Participants were seated 83 cm from the face of the screen, so that 3 letters equaled about 1 degree of visual angle. External distractions and light reflections were screened off by a black tube and the room was slightly darkened.

Reading time measures

The data were summarized for the region containing the entire modifier (RC or PP). First-pass reading times (FPRTs), regression-path durations (RPDs), and *load contributions* were computed as dependent measures. First-pass reading time (Table 1) is the amount of time a reader spends on a region for the first time during normal left to right reading (i.e., if the region has been skipped before first reading, FPRT amounts to zero). Regression-path durations (RPDs) (Table 2) sum up all durations of fixations in the regression path, i.e., in the set of contiguous fixations starting with the first fixation on a region and including all fixations up to a forward saccade past the region under consideration. As with FPRTs, only a region which has not been skipped before can produce an RPD value different from zero. Regression-path durations have been demonstrated to be more sensitive to garden-pathing than first-pass reading times in certain circumstances (see Konieczny, 1996; Konieczny et al., 1997). The *load contribution* measure

Table 1

Length corrected first pass reading times on the modifier

	PP	RC
High	485	457
Low	293	580

Table 2

Length corrected regression path durations on the modifier

	PP	RC
High	675	471
Low	640	741

(LCs, see Konieczny, 1996) is a two-place function that calculates the amount of time spent on a certain region *A* in (or during the duration of) the regression path of a subsequent region *B*. For instance, given the regression path of the modifier (RPmod) in the present experiment, we were interested in the total reading time (TRT) spent on NP1 and NP2 (Tables 3 and 4). The load contribution of N1 to the processing of the modifier is thus:

We also calculated load contributions of the modifier itself, a measure that includes the first pass reading times as well as second pass times which result from refixations following re-reading of previous regions of the sentence (Table 5).

Data analysis

Four participants had to be excluded from the data analysis because of too many track-losses and/or too many erroneous fixations. Therefore, the data of only 20 participants entered the analyses.

For first pass reading times, regression path durations, and load contributions of the modifier, extreme values and FPRTs and RPDs smaller than 200 ms were

Table 3

Load contribution of NP1 to RPmod

	PP	RC
High	263	54
Low	78	46

Table 4

Load contribution of NP2 to RPmod

	PP	RC
High	322	106
Low	275	240

Table 5

Length corrected load contribution of modifier (PP or RC) to RPmod

	PP	RC
High	639	454
Low	505	634

calculated based on the interquartile technique and replaced following the procedure suggested by Winer (1962, see also Boland et al., 1990; Altmann, Garnham and Dennis, 1992). Eight percent of the FPRT and RPDs were affected by this procedure. Load contributions of the first and the second NP only entered the analyses if there was a regression from the modifier to an earlier region. If a complete design cell was empty for a given subject, its mean was estimated using the Winer procedure. Fourty-nine percent of these measures were affected. Therefore, these data should be treated with caution.

Regression analyses on the first and second NP showed a mean length effect of 36 ms per character. Accordingly, FPRTs, RPDs, and load contributions of the modifier were adjusted by subtracting 36 ms for each character. The adjusted data were then submitted to a 2×2 design including the factors modifier type (RC vs. PP) and attachment (high vs. low).

Results

For first pass reading times, a reliable modifier effect could be established for the length adjusted data, but only by participants: longer fixation durations were found for RCs compared to PPs (RCs: 519 ms, PPs: 389 ms, $F1[1, 19] = 8.79$, $p < 0.01$, $F2[1, 11] = 2.17$, n.s.). The interaction between modifier type and attachment site was also statistically reliable in the subject-analysis ($F1[1, 19] = 10.53$, $p < 0.01$) and approached significance in the item analysis ($F2[1, 11] = 3.85$, $p < 0.08$). This interaction resulted from increased reading times for high attached PPs compared to low attached PPs ($F1[1, 19] = 5.95$, $p < 0.03$, $F2[1, 11] = 7.17$, $p < 0.03$) and from marginally increased reading times for low attached RCs compared to high attached RCs in the subject analysis only ($F1[1, 19] = 4.00$, $p < 0.07$, $F2[1, 11] = 0.77$, n.s.).

No modifier effect was found for RPDs. However, the interaction between modifier type and attachment site was again reliable by participants ($F1[1, 19] = 6.66$, $p < 0.02$), and marginally reliable by items ($F2[1, 11] = 3.57$, $p < 0.09$). In this measure, there was no reliable difference between high and low attached PPs. However, RPDs for low attached RCs were reliably increased compared to RPDs for high attached RCs ($F1[1, 19] = 12.31$, $p < 0.01$, $F2[1, 11] = 5.54$, $p < 0.04$).

Looking at the amount of time spent on the modifier before a region to its right was encountered (load contribution of the modifier, lc(mod, mod)) again showed a reliable interaction of modifier type and attachment site ($F1[1, 19] = 7.94$, $p < 0.02$). This was due to a marginal low attachment preference for PPs ($F1[1, 19] = 3.51$, $p < 0.08$). Load contributions for low attached RCs were only numerically larger compared to high attached RCs ($F1[1, 19] = 2.81$, $p < 0.12$).

Load contributions of the first and second NP have to be treated with some caution because of missing data which had to be replaced. However, these measures do give a more detailed answer to the question of why attachment preferences for the different modifier types show up reliably in different measures.

For load contributions of the first NP (lc(N1, mod)) a main effect of modifier type ($F1[1, 19] = 40.27$, $p < 0.01$; $F2[1, 11] = 9.81$, $p < 0.01$), a main effect of attachment site ($F1[1, 19] = 23.69$, $p < 0.01$; $F2[1, 11] = 3.54$, $p < 0.9$) as well as an interaction of these factors ($F1[1, 19] = 15.57$, $p < 0.01$; $F2[1, 11] = 16.43$, $p < 0.01$) was found. These effects result from the fact that participants refixated the first NP, particularly in the case of a high attached PP (PP high vs. PP low: $F1[1, 19] = 22.15$, $p < 0.01$, $F2[1, 11] = 14.09$, $p < 0.01$).

On the second NP, load contributions showed a main effect of modifier type ($F1[1, 19] = 19.18$, $p < 0.01$; $F2[1, 11] = 2.98$, $p < 0.12$) and an interaction of modifier type and attachment site ($F1[1, 19] = 6.12$, $p < 0.03$; $F2[1, 11] = 2.99$, $p < 0.12$), but only by participants. NP2 was refixated longer in the case of a PP modifier (PPs: 299 ms, RCs: 179 ms). After reading a low attached RC, NP2 was refixated longer than after a high attached RC ($F1[1, 19] = 4.87$, $p < 0.05$; $F2[1, 11] = 9.81$, $p < 0.01$; $F2[1, 11] = 6.57$, $p < 0.03$). No reliable attachment preference could be established for PP modifiers.

Discussion

As in earlier questionnaire experiments, these data establish an interaction between modifier type and attachment site in this eye-tracking experiment. The low attachment preference found for PP modifiers and the high attachment preference found for RC modifiers is obviously no late preference, but shows up very early, i.e., as soon as the attachment is disambiguated towards one or the other site.

Although the general picture is very clear, it is interesting to see that attachment preferences for PPs and RCs show up differently in the reading times measures we looked at. The low attachment preference for PPs can be seen most clearly in local measures such as first pass reading times, and disappears in regression path durations. The high attachment preference for RCs, on the other hand, was found most clearly for regression path durations.

Load contributions of the first and second NP give a more detailed picture of what is going on so that these differences can be explained. When reading a modifying PP, participants are obviously more willing to look back to earlier regions even if no reanalysis is necessary, as is the case for low attached PPs. This is particularly so for the local NP whereas NP1 is mostly refixated if the PP has to be attached to this site. After reading a modifying RC, participants very rarely look back to NP1. They refixate NP2 in particular if they have to attach the RC to this dispreferred site.

It has been suggested that commas influence reading at the level of oculo-motor behavior (Hill and Murray, see Chapter 22) and block regressive saccades

(Konieczny, Hemforth and Scheepers, 2000). This would account for reduced re-reading times for RCs. However, we do find differential effects on re-reading the second NP, indicating that regions preceding the comma are still cognitively available.

Two possible explanations suggest themselves for these differential patterns: the first may be that unforced rechecking is done locally. Only if reanalysis is necessary are more distant regions refixated. Therefore, participants refixate NP1 as the dispreferred host for PP attachment, whereas they do not recheck NP1 attachment for RCs when it is preferred anyway. The general modifier effect for load contributions, however, points to another solution: participants seem to be more willing to refixate earlier regions after reading a modifying PP than after reading a RC. The sentence boundary before the relative clause seems to block regressions. Only when a regression seems necessary, as for low attaching RCs, is this boundary crossed. This would be highly compatible with data from different kinds of ambiguity where a similar clause boundary effect could be established (Konieczny et al., 2000).

References

Altmann, G.T., Garnham, A. and Dennis, Y. (1992). Avoiding the garden path: Eye movements in context. Journal of Memory and Language, 31, 685–712.

Boland, J.E., Tanenhaus, M.K. and Garnsey, S.M. (1990). Evidence for the immediate use of verb control information in sentence processing. Journal of Memory and Language, 29, 413–432.

Brysbaert, M. and Mitchell, D. (1996). Modifier attachment in sentence parsing: Evidence from Dutch. Quarterly Journal of Experimental Psychology, 49A, 664–695.

Cuetos, F. and Mitchell, D. (1988). Cross linguistic differences in parsing: Restrictions on the issue of the late closure strategy in Spanish. Cognition, 30, 73–105.

De Vincenzi, M. and Job, R. (1993). Some observations on the universality of the late closure strategy: Evidence from Italian. Journal of Psycholinguistic Research, 22, 189–206.

De Vincenzi, M. and Job, R. (1995). An investigation of late closure: The role of syntax, thematic structure and pragmatics in initial and final interpretation. Journal of Experimental Psychology: Learning, Memory, and Cognition, 21 (5), 1303–1321.

Fodor, J. (1998). Learning to parse. Journal of Psycholinguistic Research, 21 (5), 1303–1321.

Frazier, L. (1987). Sentence processing: A tutorial review. In: M. Coltheart (Ed.), The Psychology of Reading. Attention and Performance XII. Hove: Erlbaum, pp. 559–586.

Frazier, L. (1990). Parsing modifiers: Special purpose routines in the human sentence processing mechanism. In: D.A. Balota, G.B.F. D'Arcais and K. Rayner (Eds.), Comprehension Processes in Reading. Hillsdale, NJ: Erlbaum, pp. 303–331.

Gibson, E. (1998). Linguistic complexity: Locality of syntactic dependencies. Cognition, 68, 1–76.

Gilboy, E., Sopena, J., Frazier, L. and Clifton, C. (1995). Argument structure and associated preferences in Spanish and English complex NPs. Cognition, 54, 131–167.

Hemforth, B., Konieczny, L. and Scheepers, C. (1994). Probabilistic or universal approaches to sentence processing: How universal is the human language processor? In: H. Trost (Ed.), KONVENS'94, October. Berlin: Springer, pp. 161–170.

Hemforth, B., Konieczny, L. and Scheepers, C. (2000). Syntactic attachment and anaphor resolution: two sides of relative clause attachment. Cambridge: Cambridge University Press.

Konieczny, L. (1996). Human sentence processing: A semantics-oriented parsing approach. IIG-Bericht Nr. 3/96. Freiburg: Universität Freiburg, Institut für Informatik und Gesellschaft.

Konieczny, L. and Hemforth, B. (1996). SOUL: A principled model of human sentence processing. Workshop on Computational Psycholinguistics at the NIAS, Wassenaar, Juli 1996.

Konieczny, L., Hemforth, B. and Scheepers, C. (2000). Head position and clause boundary effects in reanalysis. In: B. Hemforth and L. Konieczny (Eds.), German Sentence Processing. Dordrecht: Kluwer, pp. 247–278.

Konieczny, L., Hemforth, B., Scheepers, C. and Strube, G. (1997). The role of lexical heads in parsing: Evidence from German. Language and Cognitive Processes, 12, 307–348.

Mitchell, D.C. (1994). Sentence parsing. In: M.A. Gernsbacher (Ed.), Handbook of Psycholinguistics. San Diego: Academic Press, pp. 375–410.

Pynte, J. and Frenck-Mestre, C. (1996). Evidence for early-closure attachments on first-pass reading times in French: A replication. Poster presented at the 2nd Conference on Architectures and Mechanisms for Language Processing in Turino, Italy, September 1996.

Walter, M., Hemforth, B., Konieczny, L. and Seelig, H. (1999). Same size sisters in German? Poster presented at the 12th CUNY Conference on Human Sentence Processing, New York, March 1999.

Winer, B.J. (1962). Statistical Principles in Experimental Design. New York: McGraw-Hill.

Zagar, D., Pynte, J. and Rativeau, S. (1997). Evidence for early closure attachment on first-pass reading times in French. Quarterly Journal of Experimental Psychology, 50a, 421–438.

CHAPTER 20

Decoupling Syntactic Parsing from Visual Inspection: The Case of Relative Clause Attachment in French

Joël Pynte
CNRS and University of Provence

and

Saveria Colonna
CNRS and University of Provence

Abstract

Three eye-tracking experiments were conducted in order to further examine French readers' attachment preferences for N1-of-N2-Relative clause (RC) constructions. Experiment 1 manipulated the relative lexical frequency of N1 and N2. Disambiguation was provided by an adjective located within the RC, whose gender agreed either with N1 or N2. First-fixation durations recorded at that point were found to be shorter when gender forced attachment to the lower-frequency noun. The aim of Experiments 2 and 3 was to examine attachment preferences in the case of a short RC (e.g. the relative pronoun followed by an intransitive verb). A general preference for low attachment was found in this case. A tentative explanation, likely to account for both frequency and length effects, is presented, based on the assumption that syntactic parsing can be decoupled from visual inspection in expert reading.

Reading as a Perceptual Process/A. Kennedy, R. Radach, D. Heller and J. Pynte (Editors)
© 2000 Elsevier Science Ltd. All rights reserved

Introduction

Over the past 30 years, a great deal of research has been devoted to uncovering a set of (cognitively motivated) general parsing principles, likely to apply to a variety of linguistic constructions, without the need to refer to detailed linguistic information (Bever, 1970; Kimbal, 1973; Frazier, 1978, 1987). A well-known example of such a principle is Frazier's late-closure principle, which states that incoming words, whatever their precise syntactic status, are preferentially attached into the clause or phrase currently being processed. This is illustrated by sentences (1), (2) and (3) below, whose (a) version has been shown to be easier to comprehend than the (b) version (see Frazier, 1979).

(1a) "Though George kept on reading the story Sue bothered him."
(1b) "Though George kept on reading the story still bothered him."
(2a) "Without her contributions the funds are inadequate."
(2b) "Without her contributions would be very inadequate."
(3a) "Mary kissed John and his brother when she left."
(3b) "Mary kissed John and his brother started to laugh."

Although the late-closure principle seems to successfully account for these examples, as well as a number of other syntactic constructions (basically the relations between a main verb and its various arguments within a single clause; for a review see Frazier and Clifton, 1996), it can hardly be considered as 'general'. Sentences like (4), in particular, have proved difficult to deal with in this framework. According to the late-closure principle, the relative clause beginning with 'who . . . ' should be attached to the second noun phrase (N2) in the N1-of-N2 construction (the actress, not her servant, was on the balcony).

(4)   "Someone shot the servant of the actress who was on the balcony with her husband."

In contrast to this prediction, Cuetos and Mitchell (1988) presented evidence from questionnaire studies and self-paced reading studies that suggested that native Spanish readers prefer to interpret the relative clause in Spanish sentences like (4) as modifying the first NP (62% N1 choice in their Experiment 1). British readers on the other hand preferred to have the relative clause modify N2 (37% choice of N1 in sentences with the relative pronoun who), as predicted by the late-closure principle. Since the seminal work of Cuetos and Mitchell (1988), the processing of relative clauses with complex heads has been the focus of intense theoretical and empirical debate, and there is now an extensive literature on this matter, showing that the preference for N1 vs. N2 modification varies both cross-linguistically (Brysbaert and Mitchell, 1996; De Vincenzi and Job, 1993, 1995; Hemforth, Konieczny and Scheepers, 1997; Zagar, Pynte and Rativeau, 1997) and, within a given language, as a function of certain syntactic and semantic aspects of the constructions studied. For example, in a questionnaire experiment conducted in Spanish and English, Gilboy, Sopena, Clifton and Frazier (1995) showed that in both languages, attachment preferences depend on the particular details of the complex NP 'hosting' the relative clause. Among the main factors identified were the type of preposition relating N1 and N2 (if this preposition is a theta-assigner, that is likely to assign a semantic role to the following noun phrase, then N2, not N1, will be chosen as the host of the relative clause), and referentiality (absence of a determiner in front of N2 makes it less attractive as a relative-clause host).

Moreover, attachment preferences have been found to vary as a function of the moment when the measure is made during the comprehension process, suggesting that different factors may be at work at different processing steps. For example, in a series of experiments conducted in Italian with sentences such as (5), De Vincenzi and Job (1993, 1995) observed a high-attachment preference (i.e. an attachment to N1) in a questionnaire experiment (presumably assessing the final interpretation given to the sentence), and an apparent on-line low-attachment preference (i.e. an attachment to N2) in a self-paced reading experiment, with shorter reading times recorded on the disambiguating past participle when its gender forced low attachment. A similar pattern of results was found by Baccino, De Vincenzi and Job (1996) with French translations of De Vincenzi and Job's Italian sentences (Example 6), with, again, a preference for the high-attachment interpretation in a questionnaire experiment (the senator's girlfriend killed herself), and a tendency for attaching low at the moment when the disambiguating word was encountered in a self-paced reading experiment (longer reading times for the feminine version).

(5) "Il cronista intervisto l'amica del senatore che si è ucciso(a) ieri notte."
(6) "Le journaliste interrogeait l'amie du sénateur qui s'était suicidé(e) hier soir." (The reporter interviewed the girlfriend of the senator who killed him/herself yesterday night.)
(7) "Un journaliste aborda l'avocat de la chanteuse qui semblait plus confiant(e) que de raison." (A journalist approached the barrister (male) of the singer (female) who seemed more confident (masculine/feminine) than s/he ought to.)

However, in a study using similar stimulus sentences (see Example 7), Zagar, Pynte and Rativeau (1997) did not find any evidence of on-line low-attachment preference. On the contrary, they found a clear preference for attaching to N1 for both off- and on-line measures. In a sentence completion experiment, the majority of completions was in favour of high attachment (the barrister was confident), and again a high-attachment preference was found at the disambiguating point in an eye-tracking experiment (shorter first-pass gazes on the disambiguating adjective when its gender forced attachment to N1).

The primary aim of the series of experiments reported in this chapter was to try to explain the discrepancy between Baccino et al.'s and Zagar et al.'s results for on-line measures (low attachment for Baccino et al., high attachment for Zagar et al.). A first possible explanation can probably be looked for in the composition of the experimental lists in Baccino et al.'s experiment, and in particular in the fact that the N1-of-N2 constructions were mixed with N1-with-N2 constructions (the preposition 'with' in the structure N1-with-N2-RC has been shown to lead to an N2 preference, due to N2 being theta-marked; see Frazier and Clifton, 1996), which could have produced syntax setting effects (Frenck-Mestre and Pynte, 2000; Pynte and Frenck-Mestre, 1996). We are not going to discuss this point further here. In this chapter, we shall focus instead on the properties of the stimulus sentences used in each study. Two possible sources of difference will be investigated, namely the relative frequency of N1 and N2 (Experiment 1), and the length of the relative clause (Experiment 2).

A secondary aim of the present study was to further investigate the time course of attachment decisions for N1-of-N2-RC constructions in French. More precisely, we were interested in finding out whether different attachment preferences can be observed at different processing steps, as suggested by De Vincenzi and Job and Baccino et al.'s studies. The fact that no difference was observed between on-line and off-line measures in Zagar et al.'s study, together with the fact that the observed initial attachment was at odds with the preferred interpretation of the sentence in Baccino et al.'s (as indicated by the questionnaire experiment), suggest that there might be something special in Baccino et al.'s sentences that triggered a temporary low-attachment preference. This hypothesis will be considered in Experiment 1. The alternative view, namely that there might be something special in Zagar et al.'s stimulus sentences that triggered an on-line high-attachment preference will be considered in Experiment 2. Finally, the nature of the bias at work in this type of construction (if any) will be discussed in the General discussion section. Given the extreme diversity of the results reported in the literature, one can indeed wonder whether an approach in terms of general parsing principles can be maintained. An alternative approach has been to consider that attachment preferences are dependent on interpretation processes (see Frazier and Clifton, 1996) and are thus likely to vary as a function of detailed syntactic, semantic and pragmatic factors. In an attempt to escape this controversy, we will try here to discuss in detail the possible time course of attachment decisions for N1-of-N2-RC constructions.

Experiment 1: the relative frequency of N1 and N2

One difference between the stimulus sentences used in Baccino et al.'s and in Zagar et al.'s experiments relates to the relative frequency of N1 and N2. In Baccino et al.'s sentences (like in the Italian sentences they were translated from, see De Vincenzi and Job, 1993, 1995), N1 was most of the time a high-frequency noun like 'son', 'father', 'friend', etc., whereas N2 was a less frequent word (usually referring to a profession like 'senator', 'tailor', 'director', etc.). In contrast, the frequency of N1 and N2 was equalised in Zagar et al.'s experiment. This difference in lexical frequency between N1 and N2 may have introduced a bias in Baccino et al.'s experiment. For example, participants may have been led to consider that the discourse entity referred to by the lower-frequency word was more important or more salient, and thus more likely to be the subject of a subsequent predication. The role of discourse salience in attachment decisions was investigated by Schafer, Carter, Clifton and Frazier (1996) in an experiment conducted in the auditory modality that manipulated the pitch accent carried by different noun phrases. The results indicated that accented phrases are indeed more likely to attract relative clauses. According to Schafer et al., this result demonstrates the importance of focus or discourse salience in attachment decisions. The same argument seems to be applicable to word frequency: it is possible to argue that low-frequency words are more salient than high-frequency ones, just as accented words are more salient than unaccented ones.

The aim of Experiment 1 was to determine whether the relative frequency of N1 and N2 can, indeed, have influenced attachment preferences in Baccino et al.'s experiment. The sentences were similar to (6) above. Two conditions were compared, namely a condition in which the noun of N1 was low frequency (and the noun of N2 was high frequency), and a condition in which the noun of N2 was low frequency (and the noun of N1 was high frequency). We were expecting the relative clause to be 'attracted' by N1 (high attachment) in the low-frequency-N1 condition, and by N2 (low attachment) in the low-frequency-N2 condition.

Method

Participants
Twenty-four students from the University of Provence volunteered for the study. All were native French speakers. They had normal, uncorrected vision and were unaware of the purpose of the experiment.

Materials
Forty experimental sentences (see examples in 8a and 8b) mixed with 42 fillers were presented.

(8a) "Il parle à l'époux de la servante qui semble dépressif(ve) depuis peu."
(8b) "Il parle au mari de la soubrette qui semble dépressif(ve) depuis peu." (He is talking to the husband of the maid who has recently seemed depressed (masc/fem).)

Each sentence could be presented in four versions, defined by crossing two experimental factors, namely type of disambiguation (forcing either attachment to N1 or to N2), and the relative frequency of N1 and N2. In one condition (low-frequency N1), N1 was a low-frequency word and N2 a high-frequency word, whereas in the second condition (low-frequency N2), it was the other way around. As can be seen from Example (8), 'husband' was translated either by 'époux', an old-fashioned and low-frequency word, or by 'mari', which is much more frequent. Similarly, 'maid' was translated either by 'servante', or by 'soubrette', which is also quite old-fashioned in French. The mean frequencies were 17, 288, 19, and 164 per million for low-frequency N1s, high-frequency N1s, low-frequency N2s, and high-frequency N2s, respectively. Disambiguation was provided by an adjective located within the relative clause, whose gender agreed either with N1 or N2.

Apparatus
Eye movements were recorded with a standard Dr. Bouis oculometer device. The sentences were displayed on a monitor interfaced with a PC computer. They were shown on a single line in normal upper-case and lower-case letters. Participants viewed the display binocularly, and the horizontal displacement of they right eye was sampled every 5 ms. The apparatus was calibrated using an array of five numbers spaced evenly across the display screen. Eye-movement data were analysed off-line. The overall accuracy of the system was approximately plus or minus one character. Participants were seated 60 cm from the screen, where 3.25 character spaces subtended one degree of visual angle.

Task and procedure
Each participant sat with his or her head fixed by means of a dental-composition bite-bar, with the index finger of each hand on a response button. Before each presentation, a fixation point appeared two character positions to the left of the location where the first character of the sentence would be displayed. The participant triggered the presentation of the stimulus sentence by looking at this fixation point. After having read a sentence, participants performed an acceptability judgement (was the sentence acceptable? Yes/no answer by pressing one of two buttons located under their left and right index fingers). Some of the filler sentences comprised a slight syntactic anomaly (example: 'la journée qu'ils sont partis en pique-nique était ensoleillée': 'the day that they went to picnic was sunny'). Calibration of the eye-movement system took place every each four sentences. The sentences were counterbalanced so that each participant read an equal number of late- and early-closure sentences with either a low-frequency N1 or a low-frequency N2. The same participant never read more than one of the four versions of each sentence, which were obtained by crossing the type of attachment (attachment to N1 or N2) and frequency (low-frequency N1 or N2) factors.

Results and discussion

For analysis purposes, the sentences were considered to contain five zones (separated by slashes in Example 8c): an initial zone (Zone 1) up to and including the first verb (plus the following preposition if any); Zone 2 containing the N1-of-N2 phrase; Zone 3 containing the locally ambiguous part of the relative clause; Zone 4 (critical zone) containing the disambiguating materials; and the final zone containing the remaining words. In order to track the precise moment when disambiguation occurred, the critical zone was restricted to nine characters around the last letter of the adjective (i.e. four letters on the left and four letters on the right).

(8c) "Il parle à /l'époux de la servante /qui semble dépr/essif dep/uis peu./"

Separate analyses of variance were carried out for each zone, using a 2 (low-frequency N1 vs. low-frequency N2) by 2 (high vs. low attachment) factorial design. Both factors were within subjects. In order to distinguish on-line from final-interpretation preferences, two measures were analysed, namely first-fixation duration and total time (the sum of all fixations recorded in a zone). Any 'on-line' preference for attaching the ambiguous relative clause either to N1 or N2 should lead to a difference in first-fixation durations at the disambiguating point (i.e. Zone 4), whereas the preferred final interpretation should show up at the end of the sentence (e.g. Zone 5), presumably on total times.

The mean duration of the first fixation recorded in each zone is presented in Fig. 1 (gender in favour of high attachment for the top panel and gender in favour of

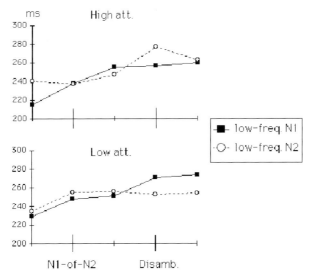

Fig. 1. First-fixation durations per zone as a function of the relative frequency of N1 and N2 for the high-attachment (top panel) and the low-attachment (bottom panel) conditions.

low attachment for the bottom panel). As can be seen from this figure, first fixations in the disambiguating zone were shorter when the gender of the adjective forced attachment to the lower-frequency noun, that is to N1 for the low-frequency-N1 condition and to N2 for the low-frequency-N2 condition. The interaction between attachment and frequency was significant for the critical zone (257 ms vs. 271 ms, and 277 ms vs. 253 ms, for high vs. low attachment, and for the low-frequency-N1 and the low-frequency-N2 conditions, respectively, $F_1(1, 20) = 7.08$, $p < 0.025$ and $F_2(1, 36) = 6.02$, $p < 0.025$). No other significant effect showed up for this measure (all Fs less than or close to 1).

The pattern of results was very different as far as total times are concerned (see Fig. 2). For this measure, no interactions between frequency and attachment were found (all Fs less than or close to 1). However, a main effect of frequency was found at the disambiguating point, with shorter total times for the low-frequency-N1 condition than for the low-frequency-N2 condition ($F_1(1, 20) = 7.82$, $p < 0.025$; $F_2(1, 36) = 11.45$, $p < 0.0025$). Moreover, a marginally significant main effect of attachment was found at the end of the sentence (Zone 5), with shorter total times for high attachment as compared to low attachment ($F_1(1, 20) = 3.12$, $p < 0.10$; $F_2(1, 36) = 7.48$, $p < 0.025$). Interestingly, a difference in favour of high attachment was found for both the low-frequency-N1 and the low-frequency-N2 conditions (461 ms vs. 544 ms, and 557 ms vs. 588 ms, respectively).

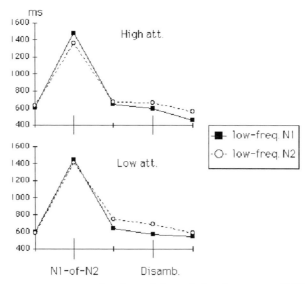

Fig. 2. Total times per zone as a function of the relative frequency of N1 and N2 for the high-attachment (top panel) and the low-attachment (bottom panel) conditions.

Overall, the pattern of results found in this experiment is consistent with the notion that attachment preference is likely to vary over time during the reading of a locally ambiguous sentence, and suggests that word frequency, or some related factor, can influence initial decisions. As indicated above, a possible interpretation can probably be looked for in terms of focus, or discourse salience. For example, the reader may wonder why the word 'soubrette' was used in Sentence (8b), instead of the more frequent 'servante'. As a consequence, 'soubrette' could become the focus of the sentence, and attract the relative clause for this reason. In this view, the observed preference for initially attaching to the lower-frequency noun would thus be the consequence of some discourse-dependent process. However, it should be noted that, in the low-frequency-N2 condition, this initial decision apparently went against the preferred interpretation (since a high-attachment preference showed up at the end of the sentence, irrespective of the relative frequency of N1 and N2). This suggests that the mechanism responsible for the initial N2 attachment in this condition possibly took place at a moment when the final interpretation was not decided yet, that is, at the parsing level, prior to semantic interpretation. This possibility will be further discussed in the General discussion section.

Experiment 2: the length of the relative clause

Another difference between the two sets of sentences relates to the fact that the relative clause was longer in Zagar et al.'s experiment than in Baccino et al.'s. This could be an important factor if one goes along with the recent proposal by Fodor (1998) that the parser has a tendency to equalise the length of sister constituents. She wrote: " . . . A constituent likes to have a sister of its own size . . . A preference for balanced weight is familiar from work on prosodic phrasing. I suggest, therefore, that prosodic processing occurs in parallel with syntactic processing (even in reading) . . . Height of attachment ambiguities are resolved by the prosodically motivated same-size-sister constraint . . . ." In this second experiment, the relative clause only comprised the relative pronoun and an intransitive verb. If Fodor is right, then we should expect a tendency to attach low in such a situation, in contrast with Zagar et al.'s results.

Method

Participants
Twenty-four students from the University of Provence volunteered for the study. None had participated in Experiment 1. All were native French speakers. They had normal, uncorrected vision and were unaware of the purpose of the experiment.

Materials

Twenty-four experimental sentences such as (9a) below were used. N1 and N2 frequencies were matched. The relative clause only comprised two words, namely the relative pronoun and an intransitive verb. Its mean length was 10.71 characters. Each experiment sentence could be presented in four versions obtained by varying the number of N1, N2 and of the last verb (see Example 9a). For half the cases the number of the verb agreed with N1, and for the other half, it agreed with N2, thus forcing either high or low attachment. Experimental sentences were embedded in three-line paragraphs and were displayed in the middle of the second line of text (with linguistic materials located on both sides). The visual inspection of the relative clause was thus probably included in a sequence of eye movements developed at the line level. Each participant was presented with a given paragraph only once. Four experimental lists were prepared so that to balance experimental sentences with versions across participants.

(9a) "Il connait la(les) frere(s) de la (des) fille(s) qui entre(nt)." (He knows the brother(s) of the girl(s) who is (are) entering).

Apparatus and procedure

The same apparatus and calibration procedure as in Experiment 1 were used (one calibration every two paragraphs). After having read a given paragraph, participants made a semantic acceptability judgement concerning this paragraph by pressing one of two buttons. It should be noted that no answer was required on the test sentence itself.

Results

For analysis purposes, the sentences were considered to contain three zones (separated by slashes in Example 9b): an initial zone up to and including the first verb, the N1-of-N2 phrase, and the relative clause. Separate analyses of variance were carried out for each zone, with type of attachment (the number of the verb forced either high or low attachment) as the main factor. Given that the relative clause only comprised two words, we are not dealing here with 'disambiguation' but simply with processing difficulty. Any preference for attaching the relative clause either high or low should show up in the reading times recorded on the last zone.

(9b) "Il connait /le frere des filles /qui entre."

The mean duration of the first fixation recorded in each zone is indicated in Fig. 3, and the mean total time per zone in Fig. 4. A low-attachment preference was found on this latter measure, with shorter total times recorded on the relative clause when the number of the verb forced low attachment (841 ms vs. 950 ms for the low- and high-attachment conditions, respectively, $F_1(1, 20) = 6.50$, $p < 0.025$

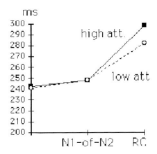

Fig. 3. First-fixation durations per zone as a function of type of attachment (Experiment 2).

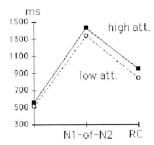

Fig. 4. Total times per zone as a function of type of attachment (Experiment 2).

and $F_2(1, 20) = 9.93$, $p < 0.01$). No effect was found on first-fixation durations. The difference visible in Fig. 3 for Zone 3 was not significant in the subject analysis (282 ms vs. 298 ms; $F_1(1, 20) = 1.23$, $F_2(1, 20) = 5.15$, $p < 0.05$). This is not surprising given that first fixations were often located on the relative pronoun, that is at a position where the attachment could hardly be decided (but see the General discussion section). However, a significant difference showed up on first-pass gazes (Kennedy, Murray, Jennings and Reid, 1989) recorded on the relative clause (shorter durations in the N2-attachment case as compared to the N1-attachment case, 563 vs. 679 ms, respectively, $F_1(1, 20) = 7.32$, $p < 0.025$ and $F_2(1, 20) = 7.58$, $p < 0.025$). Before further discussing these results, let us first determine whether the length of the relative clause was indeed the determining factor.

Control experiment

In this control experiment, the same experimental sentences as in Experiment 2 were used. However, the relative clause was made longer (31.71 characters on average, as compared to 10.71 in Experiment 2) by adding a prepositional phrase at the end of each of Experiment-2 sentence (see Example 10a). Sentences were presented in isolation and were mixed with 20 filler sentences. Each trial was terminated by an acceptability judgement (yes/no answer) as in Experiment 1.

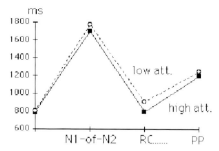

Fig. 5. Total times per zone as a function of type of attachment (control experiment).

(10a) "Il connait le frere des filles qui entre dans la cour."
(10b) "Il connait /le frere des filles /qui entre /dans la cour." (He knows the
      brother of the girls who is entering the courtyard.)

For analysis purposes, the sentences were considered to contain four zones (separated by slashes in Example 10b), namely the same three zones as in Experiment 2,
plus an additional zone corresponding to the prepositional phrase. Separate analyses
of variance were carried out for each zone, with type of attachment as the main
factor. As in Experiment 2, any preference for attaching the relative clause either
high or low should show up in the reading times recorded on the relative clause
(e.g. third and/or fourth zones). No effect was apparent on first-fixation durations
or first-pass gazes (all Fs less than or close to 1). A preference for high attachment
was found, on total gaze however (the sum of all fixations made in a zone, see
Fig. 5), with shorter durations recorded on the third zone when the number of
the verb forced high attachment (791 vs. 908 ms; $F_1(1, 20) = 8.30$, $p < 0.025$;
$F_2(1, 20) = 6.71$, $p < 0.01$). No effect was found on any of the other zones (all Fs
less than or close to 1).

Overall, the results of Experiment 2, together with the results of this control
experiment are consistent with Fodor's (1998) proposal that high attachment is due
to a tendency to equalise the length of sister constituents, and can thus only be
observed if the relative clause is relatively long. Note, however, that this kind of
interpretation raises serious questions concerning the time course of attachment
decisions. It is unclear, for example, how the reader knows that the relative clause
is long (or short) before having read the prepositional phrase (or reached the end
of the sentence). Or must we consider that the same-size-sister constraint applies
once visual inspection is completed, as could be suggested by the lack of effect on
first-pass gazes in the control experiment? These questions are further examined in
the next section.

General discussion

The primary aim of this study was to further investigate attachment preferences in the case of N1-of-N2-RC constructions, and more specifically to account for the discrepancy found in French for on-line measures, with one study providing evidence for an initial low attachment (Baccino et al., 1996) and another one providing evidence for high attachment for both on-line and off-line measures (Zagar et al., 1997). Both factors that we manipulated, namely the relative frequency of N1 and N2 (Experiment 1) and the length of the relative clause (Experiment 2) seemed to exert some influence, and can apparently account for part of this discrepancy.

The nature of the mechanisms that might be involved in each case remains to be specified, however. As far as the length effect found in Experiment 2 is concerned, an account in terms of general parsing strategies, in accordance with Fodor's same-size-sister constraint, seems possible. However, as noted above, it is not clear how this constraint could operate on-line during the visual inspection process (how can the reader know the length of the relative clause before having read it?). A similar problem arose concerning the frequency effect found in Experiment 1. The notion of focus, that was called for in the context of this experiment, clearly relates to the semantic interpretation level. In this view, one would thus expect attachment to the focused word to be favoured by interpretation processes. How can we explain, in this case, that the final interpretation of the sentence (as indexed by the reading times recorded at the end of the sentence) sometimes favoured the opposite attachment? (an overall N1 preference was apparent at the end of sentences, irrespective of the frequency of N1 and N2). In this section, we try to deal with these questions in a unitary manner, by assuming some kind of decoupling between visual inspection and psycholinguistic processing.

Let us first consider the effect of the length of the relative clause. Hereafter, we are going to assume that, in fluent reading, visual inspection is usually ahead of syntactic processing. As a consequence, a certain number of words would sometimes be left unstructured (or given an underspecified description; Marcus and Hindle, 1990; Sturt and Crocker, 1996) for a certain period of time. For example, in the case of a sentence like (9), the eye could find itself inspecting the relative clause at a moment when the N1-of-N2 construction is not totally built up yet (see Fig. 6). If the relative clause is short, then its processing may happen to be completed at a moment when the N1-of-N2 construction is not available as a possible attachment site, and this could explain why attaching high is difficult in this case (for further elaboration of this notion see Pynte, 1998). In order to illustrate this point, we briefly describe below how a parser based on this principle would deal with an N1-of-N2-RC construction (the parser was implemented in LISP, using a simple categorial grammar, see Steedman, 1991). The process is illustrated in Fig. 7 (for

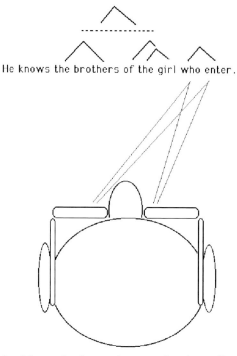

Fig. 6. The visual-inspection/syntactic-processing decoupling assumption.

the sake of simplicity, nouns have been replaced by the letter N and verbs by the letter V).

The first determiner and the first noun immediately combine in order to produce a noun phrase, but this noun phrase cannot combine with the following preposition. The preposition cannot combine with the following determiner either, and visual inspection goes on, until the second noun is reached and combines with the determiner, forming a second noun phrase. Now, the preposition can combine with this second noun phrase, but meanwhile visual inspection goes on, and the relative pronoun combines with the following verb in parallel. At this point, we are in the situation described in Fig. 6: the N1-of-N2 construction needs one more processing step in order to be completed, and is thus unable to host the relative clause. In fact, the implemented version of the parser happened to combine the relative clause with the preceding prepositional phrase, which is more like a low attachment.

Now let us consider the case of a long relative clause by adding a prepositional phrase to Sentence (9). Not surprisingly, we obtain exactly the same result, with the prepositional phrase at the end of the sentence being left unattached (Fig. 8). In order to allow the final prepositional phrase to incorporate into the relative clause, it is possible, for example, to prevent the verb from immediately combining with

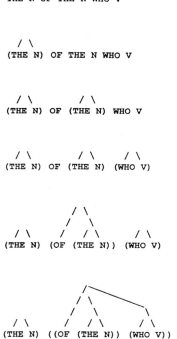

Fig. 7. The time course of attachment decisions for short relative clauses.

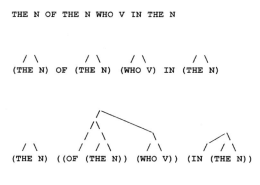

Fig. 8. The time course of attachment decisions for long relative clauses.

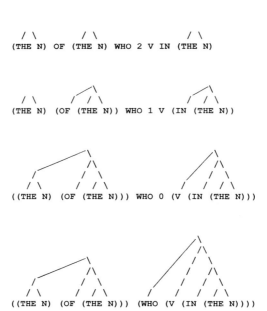

Fig. 9. Synchronising processes: the delay trick.

the relative pronoun by imposing a delay to the parser. For example, in Fig. 9, it will take three processing steps before the relative pronoun will be allowed to combine [1], and the N1-of-N2 construction will thus get a chance to build up before the relative clause is completed, and ready for attachment. The consequence will be an attachment to the whole complex noun phrase. This solution may sound unrealistic: how can the reader determine the right value for the delay before having read the whole relative clause? Apparently we are facing here the same kind of paradox as the one already encountered about Fodor's same-size-sister constraint. A possible answer to this, in line with Fodor's proposal, would be to assume that the delay is set up as a function of what the reader feels the length of a such and such a constituent should be for the sentence to be well balanced (or as a function of the reader's knowledge concerning the usual length of relative clauses in the language). [2]

Now, what about the effect of word frequency? In Fig. 10, we have been

---

1 It is assumed that all the delays are decremented at each processing step, and that two words separated by a delay are allowed to combine as soon as the delay reaches the zero value.

2 In order to account for the short RC case it is necessary to assume that the delay is reset to zero as soon as the end of the sentence is reached.

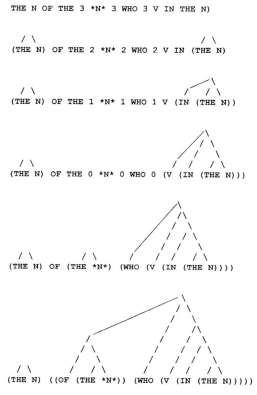

Fig. 10. The low-frequency-N2 case.

assuming that low-frequency words are not immediately available for syntactic processing, either because of difficulties encountered during word recognition, or difficulties recovering the grammatical information associated with the word. For example, it will take here three processing steps before N2 can combine with its neighbours, and the N1-of-N2 construction will not be ready in time for becoming a possible attachment site for the relative clause, in spite of the delay introduced after the relative pronoun. This could explain why a low-attachment preference was observed in Experiment 1 for the low-frequency-N2 condition. Interestingly, the same values do not produce the same effect when applied to N1. As can be seen in Fig. 11, the N1-of-N2 construction now builds up in parallel with the relative clause, and will be ready in time for hosting it. Again, this result is consistent with the results of Experiment 1, and more precisely, with the high-attachment preference found for the low-frequency-N1 condition.

Note, we are not arguing here that the human sentence parser actually works in this way. The goal of the present discussion was to determine, in a very tentative way, whether decoupling visual inspection from syntactic processing could, in

```
THE 3 *N* 3 OF THE N WHO 3 V IN THE N
```

```
                    / \                      / \
THE 2 *N* 2 OF (THE N)  WHO 2 V IN (THE N)
```

```
                  /\                      /\
                / / \                   / / \
THE 1 *N* 1 (OF (THE N))  WHO 1 V (IN (THE N))
```

```
                                        \
                                      / /  \
                /\                  / /  / \
              / / \               / /  / / \
THE 0 *N* 0 (OF (THE N))  WHO 0 (V (IN (THE N)))
```

```
                                        \
                                      / /
                                    / /  \
           /              \       / /  / \
         /              / / \   / /  / / \
       / \            /  / \  / /  / / / \
((THE *N*)  (OF (THE N)))  (WHO (V (IN (THE N))))
```

Fig. 11. The low-frequency-N1 case.

principle, account for a few puzzling results concerning relative clause attachment preferences in French. As to whether the assumptions we have been doing are realistic, given what we know concerning eye-movement control in reading, is an independent question.

References

Frazier, L. (1979). On comprehending sentences: Syntactic parsing strategies. Bloomington, IN: Indiana University Linguistics Club.

Baccino, T., De Vincenzi, M. and Job, R. (1996). Cross-Linguistic Studies of the Late-Closure Strategy: French and Italian. Paper presented at AMLaP'96, Torino, September.

Bever, T.G. (1970). The cognitive basis for linguistic structures. In: J.R. Hayes (Ed.), Cognition and the Development of Language. New York: Wiley, 279–352.

Brysbaert, M. and Mitchell, D.C. (1996). Modifier attachment in sentence parsing: evidence from Dutch. Quarterly Journal of Experimental Psychology, 49A, 664–695.

Cuetos, F. and Mitchell, D.C. (1988). Cross-linguistic differences in parsing: restrictions on the use of the Late Closure strategy in Spanish. Cognition, 30, 73–105.

De Vincenzi, M. and Job, R. (1993). Some observations on the universality of the late-closure strategy. Journal of Psycholinguistic Research, 22, 189–206.

De Vincenzi, M. and Job, R. (1995). An investigation of late-closure: the role of syntax, thematic structure, and pragmatics in initial and final interpretation. Journal of Experimental Psychology: Learning, Memory, and Cognition, 21, 1303–1321.

Fodor, J.D. (1998). Learning to parse? Journal of Psycholinguistic Research, 27, 285–319.

Frazier, L. (1987). Sentence processing: a tutorial review. In: M. Coltheart (Ed.), Attention and Performance XII. Hillsdale, NJ: Lawrence Erlbaum Associates.

Frazier, L. and Clifton, C. (1996). Construal. Cambridge, MA: MIT Press.

Frenck-Mestre, C. and Pynte, J. (2000). In: M. De Vincenzi and V. Lombardi (Eds.), Cross-linguistic Perspective on Language Processing. Dordrecht: Kluwer, pp. 199–148.

Gilboy, E., Sopena, J.M., Clifton, C. and Frazier, L. (1995). Argument structure and association preferences in Spanish and English complex NPs. Cognition, 54, 131–167.

Hemforth, B., Konicczny, L. and Scheepers, C. (1997). A principled model of modifier attachment. Paper presented at the 10th Annual CUNY Conference on Human Sentence Processing, Santa Monica, CA.

Kennedy, A., Murray, W.S., Jennings, F. and Reid, C. (1989). Parsing complements: comments on the generality of the principle of minimal attachment. Language and Cognitive Processes, 4, 51–76.

Kimbal, J. (1973). Seven principles of surface structure parsing. Cognition, 2, 15–47.

Marcus, M. and Hindle, D. (1990). Description theory and intonation boundaries. In: G.T. Altmann (Ed.), Cognitive Models of Speech Processing: Psycholinguistic and Computational Perspectives. Cambridge, MA: MIT Press.

Pynte, J. (1998). The time-course of attachment decisions: evidence from French. Syntax and Semantics, 31, 227–245.

Pynte, J. and Frenck-Mestre, C. (1996). Early-closure attachment in French: a replication. Poster presented at AMLaP'96, Torino, September.

Schafer, A., Carter, J., Clifton, C. and Frazier, L. (1996). Focus in relative clause construal. Language and Cognitive Processes, 11, 135–163.

Steedman, M. (1991). Structure and intonation. Language, 67, 260–296.

Sturt, P. and Crocker, M.W. (1996). Monotonic syntactic processing: a cross-linguistic study of attachment and reanalysis. Language and Cognitive Processes, 11, 449–494.

Zagar, D., Pynte, J. and Rativeau, S. (1997). Evidence of Early-closure attachment on first-pass reading times in French. Quarterly Journal of Experimental Psychology, 50A, 421–438.

CHAPTER 21

'Romancing' Syntactic Ambiguity: Why the French and the Italians don't See Eye to Eye

Cheryl Frenck-Mestre and Joël Pynte
CNRS and University of Provence

Abstract

In this chapter we examined the preferred attachment, in Italian, of a subject relative clause to a preceding complex NP (N1-of-N2-RC) using the recording of eye movements. Our data do not support the hypothesis that Italian readers show a systematic preference to attach the RC low, to N2, in contrast to data reported previously. Moreover, the data provide clear evidence that the resolution of this particular ambiguity will vary, even within a language, depending upon characteristics of the complex NP. The data are discussed in relation to previous findings in Italian and in French, and more generally, in relation to recent empirical findings and theoretical accounts.

Reading as a Perceptual Process/A. Kennedy, R. Radach, D. Heller and J. Pynte (Editors)
© 2000 Elsevier Science Ltd. All rights reserved

Introduction

As highlighted by linguists, despite a common ancestry, French and Italian differ in many significant ways. One example is provided by auxiliary selection. While both languages offer a choice of auxiliary in perfect tenses ('être' and 'avoir' in French, 'essere' and 'avere' in Italian), in contrast to English (which only offers 'to have'), the choice of auxiliary is much more constrained and clear cut in modern French than in modern Italian (cf. Burzio, 1986; Sorace, 1993). In cases such as this, where distinct grammatical differences exist between the two languages, one could quite logically predict French and Italian speakers to differ in their approach to understanding their respective languages. This prediction of distinct processing in French and Italian is not so obvious in instances where the two languages offer identical grammatical rules. As we will argue, however, differences in processing across these and other linguistically close languages can be accounted for just as readily as processing differences across more distant cousins, depending upon the type of structure that is studied.

The structure under question in the present study, a complex noun phrase followed by a relative clause, as illustrated in (1), has in fact sparked a great deal of interest (see reviews by Cuetos, Mitchell and Corley, 1996; Frazier and Clifton, 1996; Frenck-Mestre and Pynte, 2000; Hemforth, Konieczny and Scheepers, 2000) and is also the subject of several papers in the present volume (cf. Konieczny and Hemforth, this volume; Mitchell, Brysbaert, Grondelaers and Swanepoel, this volume; Pynte and Colonna, this volume).

(1) Jean saw the daughter of the baker who was crossing the street.

The ambiguity of this structure concerns the attachment of the relative clause; two hosts are in principle available, i.e., both the first and the second noun within the complex NP. Various factors have been shown to influence readers' preference for one or the other potential host. Segmentation of the complex NP is one of these. For example, whereas Spanish readers have repeatedly been shown to prefer to attach the RC 'high' to the head of the complex NP for N1-'of'-N2 sentences (Carreiras and Clifton, 1993, 1999; Cuetos and Mitchell, 1988; Gilboy, Sopena, Clifton and Frazier, 1995), they reportedly drop this preference when the complex NP is segmented (on a computer display) into the head and the modifying NP (e.g., 'the X' 'of the Y'; Gilboy and Sopena, 1996; but see Carreiras and Clifton, 1999).

The nature of the preposition within the complex NP has also been shown to play a substantial role in subjects' preference to attach the RC to one or the other possible host sites, as was first demonstrated by Gilboy et al. (1995). When the preposition has semantic content, as in 'with' or 'near' (e.g., 'the house near the corner'), both on-line and off-line studies show a systematic preference for N2 as the host of the RC, in all languages studied to date: Spanish (Gilboy et al., 1995; Cuetos et al., 1996), English (Gilboy et al., 1995), French (Frenck-Mestre and Pynte, 2000;

Zagar, Pynte and Rativeau, 1997) and Italian (De Vincenzi and Job, 1993, 1995). Such a systematic bias is not apparent, however, when the preposition is 'of' or its equivalent in other languages. In German, Spanish, French and Dutch, readers show a preference to attach the RC to N1 when the preposition is 'of' as illustrated in (2a–2d). This has been shown both off-line, in questionnaire studies (Brysbaert and Mitchell, 1996; Cuetos and Mitchell, 1988; Gilboy et al., 1995; Mitchell, Cuetos and Zagar, 1990; Hemforth, Konieczny and Scheepers, 2000) and on-line, via the recording of eye movements during reading and of self-paced reading times (Brysbaert and Mitchell, 1996; Carreiras and Clifton, 1999; Frenck-Mestre, 1997; Frenck-Mestre and Pynte, 2000; Hemforth et al., 2000; Zagar, Pynte and Rativeau, 1997). However, for the same preposition, an initial N2 preference has been reported in published studies of Italian (De Vincenzi and Job, 1993, 1995), English (Carreiras and Clifton, 1993, 1999; Cuetos and Mitchell, 1988; Gilboy et al., 1995), Japanese (Kamide and Mitchell, 1997) and indeed, most recently, French (Baccino, De Vincenzi and Job, 2000).

(2a) [Die Tochter der Lehrerin] die aus Deutschland kam, traf John.
(2b) Andrés estuvo cenando con [la sobrina del portero] que conocimos el verano pasado.
(2c) Jacques regardait [le fils de la gitane] qui quittait la carvane.
(2d) De gangsters schoten op [de zoon van die actrice] die op het balkon zat.

Several models have been forwarded to account for the processing of this particular structure (and that of modifier attachment in general). Among the most recent are the 'recency/predicate proximity' model (Gibson, Pearlmutter, Canseco-Gonzalez and Hickock, 1996), the 'construal' hypothesis (Frazier and Clifton, 1996; Gilboy et al., 1995) and the 'syntactic attachment/anaphor resolution' proposal (Hemforth et al., 2000; Konieczny and Hemforth, this volume). In all of these proposals, the cross-linguistic variation noted above for RC attachment is accounted for on the basis of competing principles of one flavour or another (cf. Mitchell et al., this volume, for a discussion of one of these principles). None of these recent models attributes RC attachment to a single, recency-based syntactic attachment principle such as 'late closure' (Frazier and Fodor, 1978) or 'most recent head attachment' (Konieczny, Hemforth, Sheepers and Strube, 1997). Indeed, the accumulative evidence from the various languages studied so far renders highly implausible any syntactically determined universal account of RC attachment. It can be noted, indeed, that even within a given language, considerable variation in attachment preferences for the same structure has been reported, as we will outline below. Despite this, there are those who continue to advocate the idea of a strictly syntactic, universal account as concerns the resolution of this ambiguity (cf. Baccino et al., 2000; De Vincenzi and Job, 1993, 1995), namely a 'late closure' strategy (Frazier and Fodor, 1978). The latter argument is based upon results obtained in Italian (De

Vincenzi and Job, 1993, 1995), and more recently in French (Baccino et al., 2000). A brief review of these results should help to set the scene.

De Vincenzi and colleagues (De Vincenzi and Job, 1993, 1995; Baccino et al., 2000) reportedly show an initial preference for N2 as the host of a subject relative clause (that is, in which the head of the RC is the subject) in both Italian and in French. This initial 'N2 preference' was found for reading times on the disambiguating segment in a self-paced reading task; reading times were shorter when grammatical information provided by this segment necessitated N2 attachment of the RC than when it implied N1 attachment. However, this initial 'late closure preference' was apparently rapidly reversed, as revealed by the results of a comprehension task (readers were asked to indicate, immediately after reading a sentence, which of the two NPs was the subject of the relative clause). Comprehension of the structure N1-of-N2-RC was significantly better in Italian (De Vincenzi and Job, 1993, 1995) as well as in French (Baccino et al., 2000) when N1 was the host of the RC than when N2 was. De Vincenzi and colleagues interpret this pattern of results as the result of a two-stage process. According to these authors, modifier attachment is initially driven by the 'late closure principle' (Frazier and Fodor, 1978) according to which, if grammatically permissible, the human parser will attach incoming elements into the clause or phrase currently being processed. At this initial stage, semantic and thematic considerations are not taken into account. The subsequent reversal of preference is explained, by De Vincenzi and colleagues, by the application of Frazier's (1990) 'Relativized Relevance Principle' which asserts that, other things being equal, adjuncts are preferably construed as being relevant to the main assertion of the sentence. Informed readers will recognise Frazier and colleagues' original garden path theory in these proposals. Indeed, De Vincenzi and colleagues directly reject recent modifications of the garden path theory, formulated by Frazier and Clifton (1996), which stipulate that 'non-primary relationships' such as clausal modifiers are 'construed' rather than being governed by strictly syntactic principles, such as late closure (see also Gilboy et al., 1995). In this framework, the 'construal hypothesis' applies immediately in the case of relative clauses, rather than in a second stage as suggested by De Vincenzi and colleagues (and by the garden path model). Hence, unless N2 is in some way put into focus (or 'theta-marked,' for example by the preceding preposition), N1 will be the last discourse entity in focus and should be construed as the host of the RC (due to the relevance principle). Note that Frazier and Clifton have argued that an immediate 'N1 preference' should be observed for the ambiguity in question in all languages which have only one manner of expressing genetive relationships, as is the case, for example, in Italian, French and Spanish (but see Mitchell et al., this volume, for an alternative viewpoint). The construal hypothesis is at odds with the data reported by De Vincenzi and colleagues, which may partially explain these authors' reluctance to abandon the original garden path model.

It is worth noting that the results reported by De Vincenzi and colleagues were obtained across languages (Baccino et al., 2000; De Vincenzi and Job, 1995) and, apparently, across studies (De Vincenzi and Job, 1993, 1995), with the same set of materials (and task). Without wishing to get bogged down in endless arguments over items, this point is not trivial in the present case. In fact, we will argue that a different set of materials should lead to quite different results from those obtained in Italian, and in French, by De Vincenzi and colleagues.

Let us consider, first, the case of French. In four separate eye movement experiments, an 'N1 preference' was found in this language for the structure N1-de-N2-RC (Frenck-Mestre, 1997; Frenck-Mestre and Pynte, 2000; Pynte and Colonna, this volume; Zagar et al., 1997). Moreover, these studies have clearly shown that non-syntactic factors can influence RC attachment (Frenck-Mestre and Pynte, 2000; Pynte and Colonna, this volume). The immediate 'N1 preference' was originally demonstrated on-line by Zagar et al. (1997), who showed that French readers process subject relative clauses faster when the RC is attached, on grammatical grounds, to N1 than to N2. The effect was later replicated by Frenck-Mestre (1997), again with grammatical disambiguation as provided by number agreement between the subordinate verb and N1 or N2. In both of these studies, the frequency of the two noun phrases was either balanced (Zagar et al.) or completely neutralised (Frenck-Mestre). Examples of the sentences used in these experiments are given in (3) and (4), below.

(3a) Un officiel repoussa l'entraîneur de la sprinteuse qui paraissait plus mal-heureux (N1) que les autres.

(3b) Un officiel repoussa l'entraîneur de la sprinteuse qui paraissait plus mal-heureuse (N2) que les autres.

(4a) Jean connait la gouvernante des filles qui revient de Paris en avion (N1).

(4b) Jean connait les filles de la gouvernante qui revient de Paris en avion (N2).

The results from these two studies alone, showing a clear preference to attach the modifier high in French, cast some doubt on the validity of De Vincenzi and colleagues' claim for a linguistically universal late closure strategy for this ambiguity. The claim for a syntactically driven, linguistically universal strategy as concerns modifier attachment is also questioned by the fact that non-syntactic factors can reverse attachment preference. The latter was demonstrated in French by both Frenck-Mestre and Pynte (2000; Pynte and Frenck-Mestre, 1996) and by Pynte and Colonna (this volume). In the former study, it was clear that French readers can be induced to abandon their 'N1 attachment preference' when processing the structure N1-de-N2-RC, simply by having them first process sentences for which N1 attachment is strongly dispreferred (e.g., N1-with-N2-RC). The implications of this result will be discussed at greater length below. More recently, Pynte and Colonna (this volume) further demonstrated that French readers do not systematically adopt an 'N1 strategy' when attaching a subject relative clause to the preceding ('N1-de-N2') complex NP. In a first experiment, these authors found that attachment preference was influenced by the length of the relative clause. When the RC was short (e.g., 'qui entre/entrent', i.e. 'who enter/enters') French readers preferred to attach this constituent to N2 rather than to N1. In a second experiment, Pynte and Colonna found that the characteristics of the complex NP determined RC attachment. When N1 was of lower frequency than N2, French readers preferred to attach the RC to N1. However, when N1 was of higher frequency than N2, attachment preference was for N2. Considered as a whole, the results of the four studies reported above paint a coherent yet complex picture of modifier attachment (see Hemforth et al., 2000; Konieczny and Hemforth, this volume, for discussions of factors affecting modifier attachment in German).

The initial finding of an on-line preference to attach the RC high in French (Zagar et al., 1997; Frenck-Mestre, 1997) must be reinterpreted in view of the results of subsequent studies (Frenck-Mestre and Pynte, 2000; Pynte and Colonna, this volume) which clearly demonstrate that this preference is influenced, and quite possible driven, by non-syntactic factors. Indeed, the influence of non-syntactic factors on RC attachment has been shown for languages other than French. As stated above, Gilboy and Sopena (1996) recently demonstrated, in a self-paced reading task, that whereas Spanish readers prefer to attach the RC to N1 when the complex NP is presented as a single segment (see also Carreiras and Clifton, 1993; Cuetos and Mitchell, 1988; Gilboy et al., 1995) these readers drop their 'N1 preference' when the complex NP is presented in two segments (but see Carreiras and Clifton, 1999). Gilboy and Sopena attribute their results to prosodic processing (see Gilboy and Sopena for further elaboration of this argument, specific to the Spanish language). A somewhat similar proposal was recently forwarded by J.D. Fodor (1998). Fodor suggests that prosodic processing occurs in parallel with syntactic processing, with attachment ambiguities such as the one inherent in N1-Prep-N2-RC being influenced by prosodic factors. That is, if the RC is short and N2 is too, then low attachment should occur as these constituents are similar in prosodic weight. When the RC is relatively long, then it should modify the entire complex NP (thus favouring attachment to the head of the complex NP) as the two constituents, again, will have roughly equal prosodic weight. This proposal is supported by the results of Pynte and Colonna's first experiment, showing that low RC attachment is preferred when the RC consists of only a relative pronoun and a verb. The prior observation of an N1 attachment preference in French (Zagar et al., 1997; Frenck-Mestre, 1997; Frenck-Mestre and Pynte, 2000) was found for sentences where the RC consisted of several words, as illustrated in examples (3) and (4).

Consider, now, the results reported in Italian (De Vincenzi and Job, 1993, 1995) and more recently in French (Baccino et al., 2000) as concerns the attachment of a subject relative clause to a preceding complex NP. As stated earlier, the set of sentence materials used in Italian (provided in the appendix of De Vincenzi and

Job, 1995, exp. 1) was translated for the purposes of the French (Baccino et al., 2000) study. While this guarantees clean comparisons across languages, as the same structure is compared, it also means that any idiosyncrasies of the original Italian sentences were also present in the French sentences. We already pointed to one factor, linked to the sentence set, which may have influenced the pattern of results obtained by De Vincenzi and colleagues, such being the mixing of prepositions ('di' and 'con') within a list (cf. Frenck-Mestre and Pynte, 2000). As outlined above, the type of preposition within the complex NP is of particular importance (cf. Frazier and Clifton, 1996; Gilboy et al., 1995). When the preposition in the complex NP has lexical content (such as 'with', 'on', 'above', etc.), there is a systematic bias across languages (Italian, French, English and Spanish) to attach the RC to N2. In fact, De Vincenzi and colleagues have never directly shown an 'N2 attachment preference' for the structure N1-'of'-N2-RC in the absence of sentences which strongly bias for N2 attachment (i.e. N1-'with'-N2). Another important factor to consider, as highlighted by Pynte and Colonna (this volume), is the relative frequency of the two noun phrases within the complex NP. A quick check of the De Vincenzi and Job (1995, experiment 1) and Baccino et al. (2000) materials reveals an imbalance: for the N1-di-N2-RC sentences, N2 was less frequent than N1 for more than half of the sentences and was relatively equal in frequency to N1 in the remaining sentences. This frequency imbalance is suggested, moreover, in the data reported by De Vincenzi and Job (1995) and by Baccino et al. (2000). Mean reading times were numerically longer for N2 than for N1 in both studies for the 'N1-di-N2' sentences. As no direct statistical comparison was made in these studies between N1 and N2 reading times, any post-hoc conclusions we might put forward are of course limited. Nonetheless, given the results obtained by Pynte and Colonna, it is quite reasonable to assume that differences in frequency for the two noun phrases, and notably the overall lower frequency of N2, could have influenced processing, thus prompting Italian readers to attach the RC to N2 (De Vincenzi and Job, 1993, 1995). Moreover, it is plausible that the same pattern of results should be found for these materials when translated into another language, i.e. French (Baccino et al., 2000).

The present study was an attempt to get to the heart of what may drive French and Italian native speakers (not to mention English, German, Dutch, Spanish and Japanese speakers, among others, cf. Mitchell et al., this volume) to lean towards one or another possible solution of the ambiguity inherent in the N1-Prep-N2-RC structure. As is evident in our way of posing the question, our underlying belief is that RC attachment is not the product of strictly syntactic considerations, and that there is not necessarily a universal strategy applied even in close languages. However, neither of these beliefs precludes the understanding of the factors that influence processing or the reason for the seemingly inconsistent results across studies, even within a given language.

We chose to conduct our study in Italian for several reasons. First, the study is a direct extension of previous work (Frenck-Mestre and Pynte, 2000), which stated the need for further work in Italian to confirm the De Vincenzi and Job (1993, 1995) data showing an 'N2 attachment preference' for the structure N1-di-N2-RC. In our previous study, we stressed that the mixing of prepositions within an experimental session, i.e. 'di' ('of') and 'con' ('with'), could have influenced readers to adopt an 'N2 strategy'. The present study thus consistently used 'N1-di-N2-RC' experimental sentences. If the 'N2 preference' observed by De Vincenzi and Job was a by-product of mixing prepositions, then testing the 'N1-di-N2' sentences independently should at least weaken the N2 preference. Another reason for conducting the study in Italian was to further test the hypothesis (Pynte and Colonna, this volume) that RC attachment following a complex NP will depend upon characteristics of the latter. If N2 is more salient than N1 (because of frequency or other reasons), an N2 attachment preference should be found. Conversely, if N1 is the more salient of the two NPs, than an N1 attachment preference should be found. In view of the characteristics of the De Vincenzi and Job (1995) materials, an N2 preference could thus be predicted for their sentences, although for reasons different than those forwarded by De Vincenzi and colleagues. A third aim of the study was to compare processing for the De Vincenzi and Job (1995) sentences with that for the Frenck-Mestre and Pynte (2000; Pynte and Frenck-Mestre, 1996) sentences translated into Italian. Frenck-Mestre and Pynte have clearly shown an 'N1 preference' for their materials in French when viewed in unbiased conditions. If this preference is due, as claimed by Frenck-Mestre and Pynte, to 'construal' and/or, as suggested by Pynte and Colonna, to characteristics of the complex NP, then testing these materials in Italian should produce the same 'N1 preference' as was obtained in French. However, if a 'universal late closure strategy' is initially applied, as suggested by De Vincenzi and colleagues, then an 'N2 preference' should be observed for these sentences in Italian. These hypotheses were tested via the recording of eye movements during the reading of single sentences. Two sets of Italian sentences were examined: the eight 'N1-of-N2-RC' sentences employed by De Vincenzi and Job (1995) and the sixteen 'N1-of-N2-RC' sentences used by Frenck-Mestre and Pynte, translated into Italian (by a native speaker).

Method

Subjects

Eighteen native Italian speakers, including men and women aged 19 to 24, participated in the experiment in exchange for a small fee. All subjects were recruited from a six-week summer French course for foreign students at the Université de Provence. None of the subjects was proficient in the French language, as attested

by their score on a placement test for the summer course, and none had lived
in France or a French speaking country for more than six weeks at any time. At
the time of participation, subjects had been living in France for a mean of three
weeks.

Materials

All materials were presented in Italian. Twenty-four experimental sentences were
presented along with 48 fillers. Experimental sentences were of the structure: NP
VERB NP1-of-NP2 RC. The two nouns of the complex NP were always opposite
in gender, and sentence disambiguation as concerns attachment of the RC was
provided by gender agreement between NP1 or NP2 and a constituent in the RC.
Sixteen of the experimental sentences were translated from the French materials
used in Frenck-Mestre and Pynte (2000) and were disambiguated by gender
marking on the adjective in the RC, as illustrated in example (5a). The other eight
sentences were taken from De Vincenzi and Job (1995) and were disambiguated
by gender marking on the past participle, illustrated in example (6a). All sentences
were seen in two conditions, defined by the attachment of the RC (N1 versus N2).
For both N1 and N2 attachment of the relative, half were feminine disambiguations
and half were masculine disambiguations. There was thus no difference in length
of the disambiguating region. Two lists were created such that a given subject saw
each sentence in only one condition.

(5a) Gianni osserva il ragioniere de Caterina che sembra più pensieroso(a) del
     normale.
(6a) Patrizia conosceva la segretaria del direttore che era svenuto(a) alla festa.

Procedure

A single block of 76 sentences, comprised of the 24 experimental sentences and 48
fillers, preceded by 4 warm-up sentences, was presented to participants. Sentences
were presented on a single line of a CRT screen linked to a PC. Participants were
seated with their head restrained by means of a chin rest and bite-bar, 60 cm away
from the CRT screen, such that 3.25 character spaces subtended 1 degree of visual
angle. Horizontal eye movements were sampled from the right eye every 5 ms by
means of a Dr. Bouis oculometer. Calibration of the system was performed every
four sentences by means of an array of five digits spaced evenly across the CRT
screen. Participants were instructed that they could take breaks between calibrations
but that they should avoid all movement while reading. The analysis of data was
performed off-line and all trials contaminated by head movements were discarded.
The session took approximately 25 min.

Results

Independent analyses were performed on each of four sentence segments, corresponding to: the beginning of the sentence, the complex NP, the head of the relative clause, and the disambiguating word. The final region of the sentence was not considered as it often consisted of a function word followed by a single content word and thus corresponded roughly to the final word of the sentence. The regions of analysis are illustrated in (5b) and (6b), below. Two reading measures were examined: first pass gaze duration (i.e. all fixations within a region coming from the left of that region, from the first fixation until the eye left the region to the left or right) and total reading times (i.e. all fixations within a region). Means are presented in Table 1 as a function of Region (Beginning, Complex NP, Head of RC, Disambiguating word), Disambiguation (N1 vs. N2 attachment) and Sentence origin (Frenck-Mestre and Pynte, 2000 vs. De Vincenzi and Job, 1995).

> (5b) Gianni osserva / il ragioniere de Caterina / che sembra più / pensieroso(a) / del normale.
> (6b) Patrizia conosceva / la segretaria del direttore / che era / svenuto(a) / alla festa.

At the beginning of the sentence, reading times did not differ as a function of experimental factors. As is clear in Table 1, neither measure of reading time was notably affected by subsequent Attachment of the relative clause ($F1$ and $F2 < 1$ for both gaze duration and total reading times) or by Sentence origin ($F1$ and $F2 < 1$ for both gaze duration and total reading times).

At the complex NP, the analysis of gaze durations failed to show significant effects of either Sentence origin ($F1$ and $F2 < 1$) or subsequent Attachment of the RC ($F1$ and $F2 < 1$). This was equally true of the pattern of total reading times: Sentence origin ($F1 < 1$, $F2(1, 20) = 2.07$, ns), Attachment ($F1$ and $F2 < 1$). Moreover, the main effect of the position of the noun phrase within the complex NP, i.e. either the first or second NP, was not significant in either the analysis of gaze durations or total reading times ($F1$ and $F2 < 1$, for both reading measures). However, this factor significantly interacted with Sentence origin, both in the analysis of gaze durations ($F1(1, 16) = 22.97$, $p < 0.001$; $F2(1, 20) = 17.50$, $p < 0.001$) and in the analysis of total reading times ($F1(1, 16) = 31.78$, $p < 0.001$; $F2(1, 20) = 22.22$, $p < 0.001$). For the Frenck-Mestre and Pynte sentences, mean first pass gaze durations were longer for the first than for the second noun phrase of the complex NP (553 vs. 456 ms, respectively; $F1(1, 16) = 14.35$, $p < 0.001$; $F2(1, 14) = 8.20$, $p < 0.01$), whereas for the De Vincenzi and Job sentences mean first pass gaze durations were longer for the second than for the first noun phrase of the complex NP (568 vs. 441 ms, respectively; $F1(16) = 16.64$, $p < 0.001$; $F2(1, 6) = 11.60$, $p < 0.01$).

Table 1

Mean reading times as a function of sentence origin, sentence region and RC attachment

| | Sentence region | | | | |
| | Region 1 | Region 2 | | Region 3 | Region 4 |
		NP1	NP2		
De Vincenzi and Job sentences					
Attachment					
N1 attachment					
Gaze	876	431	574	341	372
Total	1152	804	1033	530	674
N2 attachment					
Gaze	883	451	562	393	380
Total	1189	780	970	603	625
Frenck-Mestre and Pynte sentences					
Attachment					
N1 attachment					
Gaze	897	564	468	485	444
Total	1159	907	643	690	646
N2 attachment					
Gaze	878	542	443	485	446
Total	1147	929	727	792	736

The same pattern was true for total reading times: Frenck-Mestre and Pynte, 918 vs. 685 ms for NP1 and NP2, respectively ($F1(1, 16) = 32.03$, $p < 0.001$; $F2(1, 14) = 16.27$, $p < 0.001$), De Vincenzi and Job, 792 vs. 1002 ms for NP1 and NP2, respectively ($F1(1, 16) = 6.56$, $p < 0.02$; $F2(1, 6) = 10.05$, $p < 0.02$).

At the head of the relative clause, the factor Sentence origin was significant in the analysis of gaze durations ($F1(1, 16) = 43.88$, $p < 0.001$; $F2(1, 20) = 27.57$, $p < 0.001$). Reading times were longer for the Frenck-Mestre and Pynte sentences than for the De Vincenzi and Job sentences (485 and 367 ms, respectively), undoubtedly due to the difference in length at this region for the two sentence sets. No other effects were significant in the analysis of gaze durations (Attachment: $F1(1, 16) = 2.46$, $p < 0.13$; $F2(1, 20) = 1.82$, ns; Attachment × Sentence origin $F1 < 1$; $F2(1, 20) = 1.61$, ns). The analysis of total reading times revealed effects of Sentence origin ($F1(1, 16) = 6.98$, $p < 0.02$; $F2(1, 20) = 7.75$, $p < 0.01$) and of Attachment ($F1(1, 16) = 12.93$, $p < 0.01$; $F2(1, 20) = 8.72$, $p < 0.01$). Total reading times were longer for the Frenck-Mestre and Pynte sentences than the De Vincenzi and Job sentences (741 vs. 566 ms, respectively) and following N2 than

N1 attachment of the relative clause (697 vs. 610 ms, respectively). No other effects were significant.

At the disambiguating region, the analysis of gaze durations revealed only a main effect of Sentence origin ($F1(1, 16) = 8.54$, $p < 0.01$; $F2(1, 20) = 7.12$, $p < 0.01$), due to reading times being longer for the Frenck-Mestre and Pynte than for the De Vincenzi and Job sentences at this region (445 vs. 372 ms, respectively). The effect of Attachment was not significant ($F1$ and $F2 < 1$), nor did this factor interact with Sentence origin ($F1$ and $F2 < 1$). Quite a different pattern of results was found for total reading times. The analysis of total reading times failed to show significant main effects of either Sentence origin ($F1(1, 16) = 1.32$, ns; $F2 < 1$) or of Relative clause attachment ($F1$ and $F2 < 1$). However, these factors produced a significant interaction in the subject analysis ($F1(1, 16) = 6.16$, $p < 0.02$; $F2(1, 20) = 2.01$, ns). Total reading times tended to be faster following N1 than N2 attachment of the relative clause for the Frenck-Mestre and Pynte sentences (646 vs. 736 ms, respectively, $F1(1, 16) = 3.14$, $p < 0.09$; $F2(1, 14) = 2.01$, ns). For the De Vincenzi and Job sentences, total reading times did not vary significantly as a function of relative clause attachment ($F1(1, 16) = 1.02$, ns; $F2(1, 6) = 2.16$, ns) although there was a numerical difference in favour of N2 attachment (674 vs. 625 ms for N1 and N2 attachment, respectively).

Discussion

The most striking result to emerge from this study is the difference in processing observed for the two sentence sets. This difference in processing was found, moreover, at critical regions of the sentence: at the complex NP and at the disambiguating region. For the De Vincenzi and Job sentences, reading times were significantly longer at the second than at the first noun of the complex NP. Downstream from the complex NP at the disambiguating word of the RC, no significant differences as a function of attachment were found for these sentences (although a slight numerical difference was found in favour of N2 attachment). The mirror image of these results was found for the Frenck-Mestre and Pynte sentences. Processing was significantly longer for the first than the second noun of the complex NP. Downstream from this region at the disambiguating region of the RC, the trend was for shorter processing following N1 than N2 attachment of the relative clause for these sentences.

These results have several implications. First, it can be noted that our data do not replicate data previously reported for Italian, despite our using precisely the same ('N1-di-N2-RC') materials. That is, no clear 'N2 attachment preference' was found for the De Vincenzi and Job sentences. This challenges these authors' claim for the immediate application of late closure for this structure. In fact, however, as mentioned earlier, it is not entirely clear that an 'N2 preference' has indeed been shown for these sentences in prior studies. De Vincenzi and Job (1993, 1995) concluded in favour of an 'N2 preference' for the present set of sentences on the basis of results obtained for both these 'N1-of-N2' sentences and another set of 'N1-with-N2' sentences combined. That is, an 'overall N2 preference' was obtained, but no statistical test was provided for the effect of RC attachment for the 'N1-of-N2' sentences as a separate set (this is also true of the French data, reported by Baccino et al., 2000). The results of the present study suggest, in line with the arguments forwarded by Frenck-Mestre and Pynte (2000), that the N2 preference reported by De Vincenzi and Job does not hold for the 'N1-of-N2-RC' sentences, processed independently.

The absence of a clear N2 preference for the De Vincenzi and Job sentence set also somewhat undermines the argument in the introduction, suggesting that the N2 preference observed previously in Italian may have resulted from frequency differences between N1 and N2 (Pynte and Colonna, this volume). Our data show, indeed, that processing was longer for N2, which was less frequent than N1. However, this did not then lead to a statistically reliable preference for N2 as the host for the relative clause. It is, in fact, possible that the weak trend we found for N2 attachment for these sentences would have been reliable, had a larger set of sentences been available. However, it is also quite likely that the frequency difference between N1 and N2 in the De Vincenzi and Job set may have been too small to produce an N2 preference on its own. Pynte and Colonna employed nouns which differed dramatically in frequency, thus prompting readers to 'focus' more on the lower frequency noun and later attach the RC to this focused element. It is plausible, in fact, that two factors were at play in the De Vincenzi and Job study: prepositions were mixed within a list, and N2 was lower overall in frequency. The combined effect of these two factors may have produced the N2 attachment preference observed by De Vincenzi and Job, but which was absent in the present study. Conjecture is indeed open. As things stand, however, our results do not provide any support for the strong claim offered by De Vincenzi and colleagues that modifier attachment is governed by strictly syntactic principles and independent of factors such as those examined here.

The results obtained for the Frenck-Mestre and Pynte sentences translated into Italian also question the validity of a 'late closure' strategy for this particular structure. For these sentences, a healthy trend towards 'N1 attachment' of the RC was found on total reading times. This is in line with the results obtained previously for their French translations. Note, however, that the effect reported here for Italian is weaker than that reported in prior studies for French, in which a clear and statistically reliable N1 attachment preference was found on first pass reading times. The exact reason for the difference across studies remains to be clarified. Quite interestingly, Baccino et al. (2000) have recently suggested that, were the sentences used by Frenck-Mestre and Pynte (2000) to be presented in Italian, the same 'N1 preference' found in French would be obtained. Baccino et al. argue, in fact, that the linguistic construction underlying the Frenck-Mestre and Pynte sentences is different from that underlying the De Vincenzi and Job sentences, and, moreover, that the Frenck-Mestre and Pynte sentences bias towards an N1 interpretation. If the latter were true, it would indeed be embarrassing for our own argument. An example of the Frenck-Mestre and Pynte sentences is given again in (7) and translated in (8).

(7)   Giorgio accusa l'amistratore de Nadia che sembra meno indiscreto/indiscreto del solito.

(8)   George accused the administrator of Nadine who seemed less discrete than before.

Baccino et al. argue that the use of a proper noun in the second noun position, illustrated above, renders N2 attachment difficult. This is based on their intuition that readers will first attempt to interpret the RC as a restrictive clause, rather than as an appositive. As Baccino et al. correctly state, restrictive relative clauses cannot attach to a proper noun. In this light, N1 attachment of the RC would be mandated. However, the French language in no way necessitates the use of a comma to indicate an appositive relative clause. Moreover, as Hill and Murray (this volume) point out, there is scant direct empirical evidence that punctuation plays a critical role in parsing. This means, then, that there simply is no hard evidence that readers should initially interpret the Frenck-Mestre and Pynte sentences as containing restrictive rather than appositive clauses. What is more, the argument forwarded by Baccino et al. seemingly undercuts their own proposal that modifier attachment is governed by strictly syntactic considerations. The interpretation of a relative clause as being restrictive rather than appositive is most certainly a referential process. Finally, Baccino et al.'s argument does not explain why three independent studies have shown an 'N1 preference' in French where both noun phrases were common nouns (Frenck-Mestre, 1997; Pynte and Colonna, this volume; Zagar et al., 1997).

To conclude, we have (again) shown that many factors play an important role in the resolution of the ambiguity inherent in the attachment of a relative clause modifier to a preceding complex noun phrase. While the experiment reported here focused primarily on two related languages, Italian and French, it is our contention that the results provide important information for the more general issue of modifier attachment and the processes that guide it. No single, syntactic strategy is apparently able to account for the entirety of data already accumulated for this particular structure, even within a given language. This does not detract from the hypothesis that linguistically universal processes may be at play. Simply, as suggested here and elsewhere (cf. Frazier and Clifton, 1996; Fodor, 1998;

Frenck-Mestre and Pynte, 2000; Konieczny and Hemforth, this volume; Mitchell et al., this volume) they need not be syntactic in the present case.

References

Baccino, T., De Vincenzi, M. and Job, R. (2000). Cross-linguistic studies of the late closure strategy: French and Italian. In: M. De Vincenzi and R. Job (Eds.), Cross-linguistic Perspectives on Language Processing. Kluwer Academic Press.

Brysbaert, M. and Mitchell, D.C. (1996). Modifier attachment in sentence processing: evidence from Dutch. Quarterly Journal of Experimental Psychology, 49A, 664–695.

Burzio, L. (1986). Italian Syntax. A Government Binding Approach. Dordrecht: Reidel.

Carreiras, M. and Clifton, C. (1993). Relative clause interpretation preferences in Spanish and English. Language and Speech, 36, 353–372.

Carreiras, M. and Clifton, C. (1999). Another word on parsing relative clauses: eye-tracking evidence from Spanish and English. Memory and Cognition, 27, 826–833.

Cuetos, F. and Mitchell, D.C. (1988). Cross-linguistic differences in parsing: Restrictions on the late-closure strategy in Spanish. Cognition, 30, 73–105.

Cuetos, F., Mitchell, D.C. and Corley, M. (1996). Parsing in different languages. In: M. Carreiras, J. Garcia-Albea and N. Sebastien-Galles (Eds.), Language Processing in Spanish. Mahwah, NJ: LEA.

De Vincenzi, M. and Job, R. (1993). Some observations on the universality of the late closure strategy. Journal of Psycholinguistic Research, 22, 189–206.

De Vincenzi, M. and Job, R. (1995). An investigation of late closure: The role of syntax, thematic structure and pragmatics in initial and final interpretations. Journal of Experimental Psychology: Learning, Memory and Cognition, 21, 1303–1321.

Fodor, J.D. (1998). Learning to parse? Journal of Psycholinguistic Research, 27, 285–319.

Frazier, L. (1990). Parsing modifiers: Special purpose routines in HSPM? In: D.A. Balota, G.B. Flores d'Arcais and K. Rayner (Eds.), Comprehension Processes in Reading. Hillsdale, NJ: LEA.

Frazier, L. and Clifton, C. (1996). Construal. Cambridge, MA: MIT Press.

Frazier, L. and Fodor, J.D. (1978). The sausage machine: A new two-staged parsing model. Cognition, 6, 291–326.

Frenck-Mestre, C. (1997). Examining second language reading: An on-line look. In: A. Sorace, C. Heycock and R. Shillock (Eds.), Proceedings of the GALA '97 Conference on Language Acquisition. Edinburgh: Human Communication Research Centre.

Frenck-Mestre, C. and Pynte, J. (2000). Resolving syntactic ambiguity: Cross-linguistic differences? In: M. De Vincenzi and R. Job (Eds.), Cross-linguistic Perspectives on Language Processing. Kluwer Academic Press.

Gibson, E., Pearlmutter, N., Canseco-Gonzales, E. and Hickok, G. (1996). Cross-linguistic attachment preferences: evidence from English and Spanish. Cognition, 59, 23–59.

Gilboy, E. and Sopena, J.M. (1996). Segmentation effects in processing complex noun pronouns with relative clauses. In: M. Carreiras, J. Garcia-Albea and N. Sebastien-Galles (Eds.), Language Processing in Spanish. Mahwah, NJ: LEA.

Gilboy, E., Sopena, J.M., Clifton, C. and Frazier, L. (1995). Argument structure and association preferences in Spanish and English complex NPs. Cognition, 54, 131–167.

Hemforth, B., Konieczny, L. and Scheepers, C. (2000). Syntactic attachment and anaphor resolution: two sides of relative clause attachment. In: M. Crocker, M. Pickering and C. Clifton (Eds.), Architectures and Mechanisms for Language Processing. Cambridge, UK: Cambridge University Press.

Hill, R.L. and Murray, W.S. (this volume). Commas and spaces: Effects of punctuation on eye movements and sentence parsing.

Kamide, Y. and Mitchell, D.C. (1997). Relative clause attachment: Non-determinism in Japanese parsing. Journal of Psycholinguistic Research, 26, 247–254.

Konieczny, L., Hemforth, B., Sheepers, C. and Strube, G. (1997). The role of lexical heads in parsing: Evidence from German. Language and Cognitive Processes, 12, 307–348.

Konieczny, L. and Hemforth, B. (this volume). Attachment and binding: Evidence from eyetracking experiments.

Mitchell, D.C., Cuetos, F. and Zagar, D. (1990). Reading in different languages: is there a universal mechanism for parsing sentences? In: D. Balota, G.B. Flores d'Arcais and K. Rayner (Eds.), Comprehension Processes in Reading. Hillsdale, NJ: Erlbaum, pp. 285–302.

Mitchell, D.C., Brysbaert, M., Grondelaers, S. and Swanepoel, P. (this volume). Modifier attachment in Dutch: Testing aspects of Construal theory.

Pynte, J. and Colonna, S. (this volume). Decoupling syntactic parsing from visual inspection: The case of relative clauses.

Pynte, J. and Frenck-Mestre, C. (1996). Evidence for early closure attachments on first pass reading times in French: A replication. AMLAP'96, Torino, Italy, 21–22 Sept.

Sorace, A. (1993). Incomplete vs. divergent representations of unaccusativity in non-native grammars of Italian. Second Language Research, 9, 22–47.

Zagar, D., Pynte, J. and Rativeau, S. (1997). Evidence for early closure attachment on first-pass reading times in French. Quarterly Journal of Experimental Psychology, 50A, 421–438.

CHAPTER 22

Commas and Spaces: Effects of Punctuation on Eye Movements and Sentence Parsing

Robin L. Hill and Wayne S. Murray
University of Dundee

Abstract

While it has been widely assumed that punctuation may play a critical role in reading, there has been relatively little direct empirical investigation of its effects on the process in general or eye movements in particular. Most research on sentence parsing has either avoided the use of punctuation or simply assumed that it necessarily serves a disambiguating role. There has been little or no consideration of how 'disambiguation' might occur or of the precise nature of the effects that punctuation might have on the reading process. Previous work using self-paced reading (Hill and Murray, 1997a,b) has in fact shown that simplistic assumptions related to the disambiguating effect of punctuation cannot be supported. These studies demonstrated that while punctuation plays a potent disambiguating role in some structures, the effect is by no means universal. It remained unclear, however, whether these conclusions could be generalised to a more natural reading situation and whether eye-movement patterns while reading punctuated text provide an insight into the underlying parsing mechanisms.

In this chapter we discuss more recent studies which have extended this work by monitoring subjects' eye movements while reading exemplars of three types of locally ambiguous items with and without inserted punctuation. In order to control for simple oculomotor effects related to the additional spacing associated with punctuation, the studies also included a condition with equivalent spacing but without punctuation. The results show potent effects of punctuation on the first-pass processing of two structures (early-closure and reduced relative-clause constructions), but not in the 'preferred' versions of either of these and not in sentences containing prepositional phrase ambiguities. Punctuation also exerted

Reading as a Perceptual Process/A. Kennedy, R. Radach, D. Heller and J. Pynte (Editors)
© 2000 Elsevier Science Ltd. All rights reserved

effects on local processing difficulty, suggesting that it cues parsing decisions at particular points in a sentence. Frequently, inserted punctuation increased processing time on sections of a sentence immediately preceding a comma, while facilitating the processing which followed. The focus of this chapter, however, is on the effects of punctuation on eye-movement parameters in punctuated and unpunctuated sentences, the ways in which these differ from unpunctuated sentences with equivalent spacing and the extent to which they reflect the processing consequences of punctuation and spacing. It was found that punctuation and increased spacing between words had similar effects on the pattern of eye movements with increases in saccade extent of more than the added character space, but this similarity was not mirrored in equivalent effects on reading time and disambiguation. Punctuation therefore appears to convey information related to structure that is more potent than the simple 'chunking' of text, but this effect is limited to particular structural conditions. The results also suggest a dissociation between some eye-movement parameters and their consequences for underlying sentence processing.

Neglected marks

comma] *the least of the marks of punctuation, and therefore a type of something small and insignificant.*

This lowly entry in Dr. Samuel Johnson's historical 1755 work 'A Dictionary of the English Language' continues to epitomise the general consensus concerning punctuation today. The near-absence of research into punctuation is oddly conspicuous to say the least: in linguistics, work on punctuation is almost negligible (Nunberg, 1990); in automated natural language processing, punctuation is typically deleted before any parsing is initiated, or simply ignored (Jones, 1994); and in psycholinguistics, conclusions about the effect of punctuation on sentence comprehension appear to be largely intuitive and undocumented. Investigators have repeatedly assumed that punctuation prevents many forms of reading difficulty. Frazier and Rayner (1982, p. 185), for example, state "We should emphasize that none of the sentences used in the experiment contained commas", reasoning that commas would often be used to disambiguate sentences in normal prose. Similarly, " . . . , if a string is locally disambiguated (e.g. by punctuation or by clear prosodic effects) then by definition there will be only one permissible analysis of the input and we would expect perceivers to construct that analysis." (Frazier, 1987, p. 563) and "Sentence-level processes include syntactic parsing processes. Using surface markers, word class, word position, and *punctuation*, these processes organise the words of sentences into a syntactic structure." (Haberlandt, 1994; p. 2, emphasis added). However, while punctuation is certainly an integral part of normal prose, there is a paucity of empirical evidence supporting these sorts of claims about processing facilitation.

Punctuation is a relatively recent development in language and was initially provided for rhetorical guidance (Scholes and Willis, 1990). It was only in the 17th century that grammarians started to advocate a syntactic role for punctuation in the English language. This has left us with two functionally distinct schools of thought. The *elocutionary* branch maintains that punctuation essentially encodes prosodic instructions, such as 'breathe here', in writing, whereas the *syntactical* approach claims that its purpose is to guide grammatical construction in a similar manner to other orthography. In practice, these approaches often coincide, but conflicts between grammar and prosody can occur. For example, a single comma must not be used between a subject and a predicate even when a pause in delivery would be acceptable (Chafe, 1988): *The man over there in the corner, is obviously drunk.* And so we have a dispute over the importance and usage of punctuation even before empirical work is begun. This chapter will begin to redress this linguistic injustice by reviewing some findings concerning the role of punctuation in sentence parsing, derived both from our own work and from a small number of other studies that have introduced punctuated versions of experimental items (invariably with the assumption that this will provide effective disambiguation). However, one dimension of punctuation that has been *entirely* neglected is the psychophysical/visual aspect. There is no extant literature which links the use of punctuation with eye-movement parameters such as saccade size and landing position within a word and we know nothing of the extent of any relationship between such factors and the processing consequences of inserted punctuation. To what extent is it possible to divorce any psychophysical effects of punctuation on eye-movement patterns from their processing repercussions? In order to address this question, we consider the consequences of strategically inserting commas or double spaces into a series of ambiguous, garden-path structures, as well as their unambiguous counterparts.

Why commas in particular?

There are a variety of sound reasons for considering commas before other punctuation marks. From a frequency perspective, commas are the most commonly encountered form of punctuation (Francis and Kuçera, 1982; Johansson and Hofland, 1989) and they also produce the most controversy over purpose, style and (mis)usage (Quirk, Greenbaum, Leech and Svartvik, 1985). As sentence-internal features they ought to produce clear on-line effects and, in support of the wide-ranging intuitions held by writers, readers and psycholinguists, it seems reasonable to have high expectations for their potential effect on sentence parsing. In addition, the little psycholinguistic research that does exist on punctuation tends to involve commas (e.g. Adams, Clifton and Mitchell, 1998; Clifton, 1993; Mitchell, 1986; Pickering and Traxler, 1998).

Why spaces at all?

Some questions about the general visibility of commas need to be raised. Since they are quite small symbols of uncertain lexical significance that are always tagged on to the end of a word, visual acuity for commas is likely to be relatively diminished. And, as they are not letters, it seems safe to assume that they cannot directly affect the recognition of the lexical item to which they are attached. Advocates of a perceptually minimalist approach might therefore maintain that commas are transparent objects to the human sentence processor which are simply ignored. If this were true, the insertion of commas should have no noticeable effect on reading. A slightly less extreme hypothesis is that the result of inserting a comma into a sentence is, in real terms, just the equivalent of stretching inter-word spacing. Alternatively, commas may actually provide a unique source of syntactic information that directly and specifically influences language processing. In other words, the question is whether commas indirectly influence processing by physically 'chunking' the text at a low perceptual level or whether they convey a special meaning and relevance.

Increasing the spacing at phrasal boundaries has previously been shown to enhance the readability of text, particularly for less competent readers (Bever, Jandreau, Burwell, Kaplan and Zaenen, 1990; Jandreau, Muncer and Bever, 1986). Kennedy, Murray, Jennings and Reid (1989) also demonstrated that spatial features, such as line breaks, can cue clausal segmentation. In order to answer the question of whether commas carry *unique* syntactic information, it is therefore necessary to consider whether their effects differ from the sort of perceptual segmentation that might be achieved with spacing alone. For this reason, we included an experimental condition containing double spaces rather than commas. This mirrors the comma condition in terms of amount of spacing between words and the exact physical location of lexical items.

So far as basic eye movements are concerned, there are two obvious possibilities. Either additional spacing will have no effect, with saccade length extended and the maintenance of a preferred landing position (Rayner, 1979) close to the 'convenient' or 'optimal' viewing position (O'Regan, 1992; O'Regan and Lévy-Schoen, 1987), or saccade size will be unaffected, resulting in a leftward shift in landing position. Such sub-optimal landing will presumably result in some form of processing inhibition, reflected in either longer fixation durations or corrective refixations.

Commas in sentence processing

As suggested above, there are strong grounds for assuming that punctuation can alleviate certain processing difficulties, and, indeed, many investigators have *assumed* exactly that. This section briefly reviews the published literature relevant to this question together with the findings from a number of studies in our laboratory (Hill, 1996; Hill and Murray, 1997a,b, 1998a,b).

Closure ambiguities

Reading problems associated with early closure sentences, such as *After the Martians invaded the town was evacuated*, are well documented and notoriously difficult to avoid. It appears to be the case that plausibility influences the degree of commitment to a late-closure analysis and influences ease of recovery when this turns out to be incorrect, but does not prevent an incorrect structural analysis in the first place (Pickering and Traxler, 1998). Manipulations of animacy (Clifton, 1993) show a similar pattern of results. In principle, from a 'constraint-satisfaction' viewpoint (e.g. MacDonald, 1996; Trueswell and Tanenhaus, 1994), it should be possible to find circumstances under which the weight of evidence in support of an early-closure analysis precludes garden-pathing, but to date there appears to be no study showing this in the absence of appropriate punctuation. However, in common with the assumptions of the constraint-satisfaction view, that information from a variety of sources may constrain the emerging analysis, a number of investigators have *assumed* that commas provide effective disambiguation in this structure (e.g. Adams, Clifton and Mitchell, 1998; Clifton, 1993; Mitchell, 1986; Pickering and Traxler, 1998). But while the results from these studies certainly show 'facilitation' in the processing of early-closure items with inserted punctuation, none of the studies included a 'preferred' late-closure alternative for comparison. We therefore remain uncertain about whether the commas provided *complete disambiguation* or merely aided the correct analysis. Whichever is the case, it appears uncontroversial to suggest that, in the absence of at least very strong cues, everyone is garden-pathed in early-closure items and nearly everyone assumes that an appropriately placed comma would help. The point of early closure seems an appropriate and expected place to mark with a comma. If this assumption is correct and we can demonstrate that commas *eliminate* processing difficulties in such a strong garden-path, this clearly provides serious support for the argument that punctuation can convey critical syntactic information. In order to do this, however, we need to consider not only the processing of punctuated and unpunctuated early-closure items, but also their late-closure counterparts.

Relative-clause ambiguities

Like closure ambiguities, reduced relatives are also generally held to promote very strong garden-paths. This is especially true in 'unforgiving' structures, such as *The farmer sold the pigs fattened them up*, where the second noun phrase (NP) is potentially a direct object. There have been a large number of studies examining a range of factors which might influence the processing of this ambiguity. But while some have claimed effects of factors such as context, verb structure, etc., on its resolution (e.g. MacDonald, 1994; Spivey-Knowlton and Tanenhaus, 1998; Trueswell, Tanenhaus and Garnsey, 1994), others have denied the existence of such effects (e.g. Clifton and Ferreira, 1989; Murray and Liversedge, 1994; Patterson, Liversedge and Underwood, 1999). Wherever the truth may eventually be found to lie, it again seems uncontroversial to claim that this, especially in sentences where the initial verb is followed by a potential direct object, presents a very robust garden-path. However, unlike early closure, it is not immediately intuitively obvious that punctuation would necessarily help. But, rather than resolving this ambiguity by expanding the relative clause into its unreduced form, a similar effect might be obtained by physically 'chopping' the sentence into its primary constituents. Delineating the clausal boundaries with commas is just such a possible (and non-radical) mechanism of textual segmentation. While contextual and other factors *might* influence the processing of this structure, it seems pretty clear that if manipulations of this sort are to have any hope of success, they must be robust (and probably compound). But if a couple of humble commas can alleviate this kind of processing difficulty, irrespective of other factors, then punctuation must surely have a rapid and dominant influence on parsing.

Prepositional phrase ambiguities

The final traditionally problematic sentence structure to be considered here involves prepositional phrase (PP) attachment. In sentences, such as *Alan observed the girl with the binoculars*, the principle of minimal attachment (Frazier, 1987) maintains that the PP *'with the binoculars'* will be attached high, to the verb phrase (VP), and taken as describing the instrument used for observation. While the binoculars could legitimately belong to the girl rather than to Alan, this is argued to create a more complex phrase structure involving the insertion of an additional node in the second NP. Simplicity (minimal attachment) dictates that the initial structural preference will always favour the VP attachment and that this preference should prevail even when plausibility or other factors ought to provide an advantage to the NP analysis (for example, if the PP were *'with the short skirt'* and/or the reader had a broader contextual awareness, such as knowing Alan's habits or something about the number of girls in the vicinity). However, this default attachment is by no means uncontested (e.g. Frenck-Mestre and Pynte, 1997; Taraban and McClelland, 1988, 1990) and certain caveats are placed on it in later versions of the 'garden-path' approach (Frazier and Clifton, 1996), but this is generally construed to be a 'soft' or easily resolved ambiguity in any case. As such, commas might readily provide a mechanism for steering the parser towards the correct (or, indeed, incorrect) attachment in this sort of sentence.

Interestingly, Pynte and Prieur (1996) found that prosodic breaks could influence attachment decisions in spoken sentences containing this sort of PP ambiguity in French. However, their experiments included a prosodic break (marked in the example below with a '#') immediately after the verb. A comma at the equivalent location would be ungrammatical (Quirk et al., 1985): *The spies inform # the guards # of the conspiracy*. Consequently, in our reading studies, commas were used to partition the PP, rather than to segment the second NP.

Processing findings

We investigated the influence of the comma on the reading of these three 'classic' garden-path, locally ambiguous, sentence structures: early- vs. late-closure ambiguities; reduced vs. unreduced relative-clause ambiguities; and high vs. low prepositional phrase attachment ambiguities. The general findings were consistent across both 'cumulative' self-paced reading (Kennedy and Murray, 1984) and eye-movement studies, and these are briefly reported below.

Examples of the experimental items can be seen in Table 1. These show where the optional commas were placed. Some of the experiments actually used slightly shorter ending regions than those in the example sentences, but in all cases this was irrelevant to the key structures being examined. Throughout this section, any mean times quoted will refer to an eye-movement experiment using the full-length items but reflect a consistent pattern of results found across all experiments, including those using self-paced reading.

Closure ambiguity

As well as testing whether a comma successfully indicates the point of early closure, the effect of placing a comma at the 'preferred' late-closure boundary was also examined in these studies. As predicted, a comma after the verb in an

Table 1

Examples of experimental items (early/late closure, reduced/unreduced relative and noun/verb phrase attaching prepositional phrase sentences), with the location of the optionally inserted commas

EC	Once the dog stopped scratching(,) the nice vet laughed out loud before sitting down.
LC	Once the dog stopped scratching the nice vet(,) he laughed out loud before sitting down.
RR	The critic(,) played the music(,) listened very attentively before saying no.
UR	The critic(,) who was played the music(,) listened very attentively before saying no.
NP	The vet injected the cat(,) with the collar(,) before leaving for a rather late lunch.
VP	The vet injected the cat(,) with the needle(,) before leaving for a rather late lunch.

early-closure sentence had a dramatic effect on reading time. This led to marginal delays on the verb when it carried a comma, with an increase in inspection time of 36 ms (mean 313 ms when punctuated vs. 267 ms when unpunctuated), but this paid off in the long run with first-pass reading times [1] an average of 82 ms faster (231 ms vs. 313 ms) on the second verb and each of the two subsequent words. Second-pass reading times were also considerably shorter in the presence of a comma, suggesting a reduced need for reinspection. Not surprisingly, these combined to produce shorter overall times for the punctuated sentences. These times, however, were still marginally slower than average reading times for the late-closure sentences. It appears, therefore, that appropriate punctuation does indeed greatly reduce, if not entirely eliminate, garden-path effects in early-closure sentences.

For late-closure sentences, there was a (non-significant) tendency to slow down on arrival at the comma, together with a reciprocal increase in speed immediately following it. This effectively balanced the reading times and resulted in no overall differences in either first- or second-pass reading time between the punctuated and unpunctuated [2] versions. The additional 'cue' in this case had no effective processing consequence.

Reduced relative ambiguity
Punctuated relative-clause sentences used a pair of commas to mark the relative clause, as shown in Table 1. As with the early-closure items, punctuated reduced relatives showed significantly faster first-pass reading times at the point of disambiguation (i.e. on the second verb), as well as lower second-pass and overall reading times. Commas therefore exert a substantial effect on the processing of a second class of 'difficult' garden-path sentences. Again, there was a tendency for longer reading times upon initially encountering a comma, but this coincided with shorter times immediately following it. Reading time in the critical second verb region, following a comma, was not significantly greater than in this region of the unambiguous unreduced relatives. While the presence of commas benefited the processing of reduced relatives immensely, the overall effect on the unreduced items was negligible: there was a mean difference of only 3 ms in total reading time between punctuated and unpunctuated unreduced relatives as compared to an average benefit of 240 ms in reduced items.

---

1 The first-pass reading time measure used here is 'total pass per word' as defined in Kennedy, Murray, Jennings and Reid (1989).

2 We use the term 'punctuated' only to refer to the presence or absence of commas. All experimental items and fillers had sentence-terminating punctuation marks.

Prepositional phrase attachment

Punctuated versions of the prepositional phrase sentences used a pair of commas to 'parenthesise' or nest the three-word prepositional phrase (see Table 1). While unpunctuated items produced clear garden-path effects, with sentences containing NP-attaching prepositional phrases provoking longer reading times than those with VP-attachment, punctuation did not provide a miracle cure (or much effect at all) in this structure. What commas did do, however, was to 'bring on' the garden-path phenomenon at an earlier point. The presence of commas prompted longer first-pass reading times while reading the NP-attaching PP itself, but not on the words that followed it; the unpunctuated items only showed slower times on the region following the PP.

This was the only substantial difference found between 'cumulative' self-paced reading and the eye-movement studies (pace the conclusions of Ferreira and Henderson, 1991). Under the less naturalistic reading conditions of the self-paced experiments, the delay indicative of a garden-path effect materialised over the three words following the PP in both the punctuated and unpunctuated versions. The eye-movement experiments also showed that punctuation significantly reduced second-pass reading time in the NP-attaching sentences. So it seems that commas have a different kind of processing consequence in this type of garden-path sentence, as compared to either early closure or reduced relatives. Commas prompted an earlier identification of the problem, but did not allow it to be avoided. In fact, first-pass reading was marginally longer overall in the presence of commas, but this combined with reduced second-pass reading to show no overall effect. The pattern of results suggests that while punctuation does not stop small, localised, regressions, it does suppress the need for more global re-reading. This speculation will be examined in greater depth when the pattern of eye movements are discussed below.

As was the case with the versions of the other structures predicted to be non-problematic, a comma produced only a small delay when encountered in the VP minimally attaching sentences, but resulted in slightly accelerated subsequent reading times. Again, punctuation neither facilitated nor inhibited the 'default' attachment preference.

Processing summary

This body of evidence undoubtedly indicates that Dr. Johnson greatly maligned the worth of a comma: it might be small but it is far from insignificant. Strategic placement of punctuation can ease the processing of two very difficult sentence structures. However, there is perhaps room for some debate regarding the question of whether reading problems were completely obliterated, and therefore grounds for restraint before declaring the punctuated versions as truly unambiguous. It is unclear whether commas successfully prevent any difficulty arising by guiding the parser in its initial structural analysis, or if they only aided recovery and reanalysis after the mistake in parsing was detected, albeit extremely rapidly. While punctuation had no effect on the total reading time of sentences containing NP-attaching prepositional phrases and therefore provided no obvious benefit, it did change the way that the sentences were processed.

Perhaps the most unexpected finding was the lack of any overall processing effect with the non-garden-path structures. It seems surprising that the addition of a strong constraint in late-closure sentences does nothing and that using a pair of commas to highlight a relative clause or a prepositional phrase can be a redundant exercise. At certain key structural points, commas can have remarkable consequences for reading and yet at others they appear to be totally superfluous.

A sensible conclusion to draw is that commas can fragment sentences into smaller components of syntactic significance, but whether this translates into a processing advantage is entirely structure-dependent.

Spacing and processing

So far we have considered only the 'segmentation' provided by commas, but, as suggested above, other visual factors, such as spacing or line breaks, can provide cues to segmentation. The effects obtained, however, appear to be considerably less robust than those found with punctuation. In the eye-movement experiments where spacing was manipulated, strategic double spacing was added at the same locations as the inserted commas (see Table 1). Given the use of a mono-pitch font for the screen display, this resulted in exactly the same inter-word spacing as obtained in the punctuated conditions.

The results showed that strategic double spacing reduced first-pass reading time slightly, but the effects were marginal, at best, and never nearly as strong as those associated with the presence of a comma. At the most, it could be claimed that physically chunked text like this occupies a middle ground somewhere in-between the results found for punctuated and unpunctuated ambiguous sentences. However, there was no influence of double spacing on second-pass reading time and no clear overall evidence of any processing advantage accruing from stretched phrasal boundaries.

Punctuating the pattern of eye movements

From the evidence discussed so far, it is clear that punctuation can influence reading time and the ease with which certain sentence structures are processed. But the results also suggest that the *way* in which sentences are processed is fundamentally altered by punctuation; it is not simply a facilitatory effect involving faster reading and shorter fixations.

We also need to consider certain basic questions related to the influence of commas on eye movements, whether or not their presence results in any processing gain. Are commas treated as the equivalent of an additional character in a word? In other words, is a five-letter word followed by a comma treated as a six-letter lexical object? Is the saccade size out of a word simply increased by a single character as a result of leaping over a comma? And, are any of these possible effects specific to the punctuation or merely attributable to words being further apart (i.e. double spacing)? Whether commas effectively lengthen a word or just the space between words, or indeed neither, will have strong implications for how we interpret and understand punctuation, along with the role it plays in language processing. Understanding these eye-movement parameters also allows us to interpret more accurately the nature of the reading time differences that are (and those that are not) prompted by punctuation.

One of the eye-movement experiments was therefore designed to investigate the effects of punctuation and spacing on the pattern of number of fixations, landing position and saccade size on surrounding words.

Method

Participants
The eye movements of 36 native English speakers, all with good eyesight and reading skills, were recorded. Subjects were paid for their participation.

Materials and design
There were 24 sets of experimental items constructed for each of the three sentence types: early/late closure, reduced/unreduced relatives and NP/VP attaching prepositional phrases, as shown in Table 1. Each set comprised six versions of a sentence, varying along two dimensions: structure ('garden-pathing' vs. 'preferred' or unambiguous) and punctuation (without commas, with commas and with double spacing). For example, one set of closure items was:

```
While the janitor was cleaning the old clock chimed loudly in the dusty hallway.
While the janitor was cleaning the old clock it chimed loudly in the dusty hallway.
While the janitor was cleaning, the old clock chimed loudly in the dusty hallway.
While the janitor was cleaning the old clock, it chimed loudly in the dusty hallway.
While the janitor was cleaning the old clock chimed loudly in the dusty hallway.
While the janitor was cleaning the old clock it chimed loudly in the dusty hallway.
```

For the prepositional phrase sentences, the alternative noun pairs were matched for word length, and for word frequency of Kuçera and Francis (1967).

The various versions of the experimental sentences were assigned to one of six different counterbalanced lists, such that each list contained four items of each type for each of the three sentence structures and no list contained more than one version of the same base structure. This gave a total of 72 experimental items in each list and these were intermixed with 94 filler items or comprehension-testing questions. One third of all fillers contained commas while another third contained randomly placed double spaces in order to inhibit any strategic response to their presence.

Procedure

Sentences were presented on a high-resolution monochrome monitor and were displayed in a mono-pitch font along a single line. The sentences were actually organised into pairs with participants reading the first sentence and then pressing a button to reveal the second, which overwrote the first. The second sentence was a contextually related filler sentence 75% of the time and a comprehension-testing question in the remaining quarter of the trials. Questions required a *yes* or *no* decision via a button press.

Throughout the experiment, participants' head movements were constrained by the use of a dental composition bite-bar and chin-rest while their eye movements were monitored using a 'Dr. Bouis' infrared pupil-centre computation device, sampled with a 12 bit A-D at 5 ms intervals. Data were stored for off-line analysis. Calibration of the equipment was carried out at the beginning of the experiment and after every four sentence pairs. The calibration and clustering algorithms employed statistical procedures to maximise resolution for each participant on each trial. This provided a resolution of better than one character space.

After completing the experiment, participants were administered a questionnaire to probe their awareness of the punctuation that they had encountered, as well as whether they thought any sentences were ungrammatical or failed to make sense.

Results and discussion

The three primary sentence structures will be discussed individually. In each case the critical analyses are centred on the optionally punctuated words; these are emphasised in italics in the examples below and will be referred to as Position 1 and Position 2. The location of the commas was consistent across the examples for each structure.

Prepositional phrase attachment:

NP: The natives stalked the *soldiers(,)* from the *fort(,)* before launching a fast and furious attack.

VP: The natives stalked the *soldiers(,)* from the *rear(,)* before launching a fast and furious attack.

It should be remembered here that there were no overall temporal gains or penalties from the inclusion of commas in the prepositional phrase sentences. As such, any punctuation (or spacing) induced modulation of the pattern of eye

Table 2

The number of fixations made on the initial reading of the word at Positions 1 and 2 in prepositional phrase sentences

	Position 1:				Position 2:			
	No comma	Comma	Space	Mean	No comma	Comma	Space	Mean
Verb phrase	0.91	1.06**	1.01	0.99	1.01	1.13**	1.02*	1.05
Noun phrase	1.00	1.07**	1.02	1.03	0.98	1.16**	1.14*	1.09
Mean	0.96	1.07**	1.02		1.00	1.15**	1.08*	

** indicates a significant difference at the 1% level (based on analysis by subjects).
* indicates a significant difference at the 5% level (based on analysis by subjects).

movements suggests some dissociation between processing and eye-movement control.

Gaze duration [3] was 31 ms longer at Position 1 (257 ms vs. 226 ms) and 37 ms longer at Position 2 (270 ms vs. 233 ms) when the words were followed by a comma rather than unpunctuated, irrespective of structure ($F_1(1, 30) = 8.900$, $p < 0.01$; $F_2(1, 18) = 8.532$, $p < 0.01$ and $F_1(1, 30) = 5.392$, $p < 0.05$; $F_2(1, 18) = 7.503$, $p < 0.01$). There was a similar effect of double spacing, but only at Position 2 (mean 260 ms; difference 27 ms) ($F_1(1, 30) = 4.272$, $p < 0.05$; $F_2(1, 18) = 5.712$, $p < 0.05$). Although average gaze duration preceding double spacing was shorter than in the punctuated condition, there was no significant difference between them.

This pattern of results was not attributable to modulation of the duration of either the first or last fixation falling on the word. This suggests that the gaze effect was principally driven by an increase in the number of fixations, perhaps because the comma acts as an extra character pulling the eye away from the optimal viewing position on the word. Table 2 shows that the number of fixations made reflects the significant pattern found in gaze durations, right down to the lack of a difference between punctuation and spacing at Position 2, supporting the suggestion that the comma might encourage an error in landing position resulting in the need to make a corrective refixation. This was not the case, however. An analysis of landing position on the words at Positions 1 and 2 showed that the initial fixation landed at the same character position irrespective of whether the word was followed by a comma or not: there was no pull to the right. It appears that a comma is not treated as the equivalent of a letter character in determining the initial saccade size into a word; if anything, the tendency is for spacing to pull slightly more to the right (but

---

3 Gaze duration is defined here as the duration of the first fixation on a word plus all subsequent fixation durations until the eye leaves the word, either to the left or the right, i.e. the period spent reading the word for the first time.

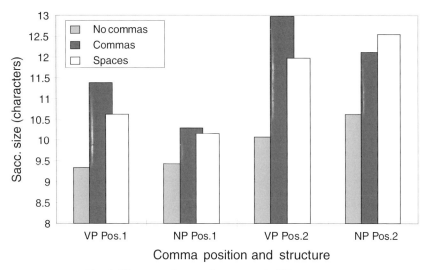

Fig. 1. First saccade over the comma in PP sentences.

non-significantly). So commas do not influence the initial landing position but are effectively holding the reader for longer on the word.

Does this then have any implications for the saccade size over the comma? We might expect to find an increase in saccade size arising from the need to jump over the comma or extra space if the reader is targeting the same initial landing position in the subsequent word. However, it should also be borne in mind that the extra refixations in the presence of commas are likely to result in a (small) rightward shift in launch position, so saccade size may actually be reduced because of this. However, Fig. 1 shows that increases in saccade size of more than the extra character space are common. In the case of VP-attaching sentences at Position 2, the average saccade length is in fact extended by almost three characters in the presence of a comma. As the figure shows, saccades associated with double spacing between words were also extended by a similar amount. Remember, of course, that these changes in the pattern of eye movements are not associated with any sentence-processing consequences.

This leaves us with the question of whether the additional fixations on the word before the comma resulted in a rightward shift of launch position, as might be expected, or whether the 'reinspections' in fact moved the eye back to the left and the increased saccade size is a consequence of this. Table 3 shows that average launch position in the comma and space conditions was in fact slightly to the right of launch position when there was no comma (the figures represent distance from the *end* of this word, so -1 is the final character, -2 the second last, etc.). At Position 1, the effect of punctuation was significant overall ($F_1(2, 60) = 6.374$, $p < 0.005$;

Table 3

The mean launch position measured from the end of the word at Positions 1 and 2 in the prepositional phrase sentences before a rightward inter-word saccade

	No comma	Comma	Space
Position 1	−5.42	−4.95	−4.39
Position 2	−6.61	−6.14	−5.76

$F_2(2, 36) = 5.195$, $p < 0.05$) with a reliable difference between the no-comma and double-space conditions, ($F_1(1, 30) = 14.705$, $p < 0.001$; $F_2(1, 18) = 14.988$, $p < 0.01$), but no other contrast achieved statistical significance. The trend at Position 2 was not statistically reliable. Thus, overall, there is a tendency, albeit a small one, for changes in launch position that might be expected to lead to shorter, not longer, saccades.

However, when we consider landing position in the following word, there is a very clear rightward shift (note that this is landing position in the word irrespective of the amount of preceding space). Landing position was 0.92 character-spaces further into the subsequent word after a comma at Position 1 ($F_1(1, 30) = 14.705$, $p < 0.001$; $F_2(1, 18) = 14.988$, $p < 0.01$) and 0.66 character-spaces further right after a comma at Position 2 ($F_1(1, 30) = 7.560$, $p < 0.01$; $F_2(1, 18) = 8.677$, $p < 0.01$). An extra space at both Positions 1 and 2 produced similar results (1.03 and 0.77 character-spaces, respectively) ($F_1(1, 30) = 19.767$, $p < 0.001$; $F_2(1, 18) = 17.274$, $p < 0.001$ and $F_1(1, 30) = 8.624$, $p < 0.01$; $F_2(1, 18) = 15.435$, $p < 0.01$). There were no significant differences in landing position between the comma and spacing conditions. Fixations *are* therefore falling further to the right following commas and spaces, and to a roughly equivalent degree.

Overall, the pattern of eye movements shows some 'hesitation' on the word preceding the comma or double spacing and this is associated with a slightly higher probability of refixating the word. The subsequent saccade, however, is extended by more than the extra character space occupied by the comma or double spacing and lands roughly a full character further into the following word. Since these effects are equivalent at Positions 1 and 2, do not vary between commas and spacing, and are not, in any case, clearly associated with processing effects at either location, it seems clear that they must represent an oculomotor phenomenon largely divorced from on-line processing difficulty. The ability to saccade further into the subsequent word is presumably a consequence of greater uptake of parafoveal information when the inspection time on the preceding word is extended. In common with the proposals of Kennedy (1998) and Murray (1998), this suggests that processing can be distributed across more than one word object at the same time, with increased durations at one location offset by faster subsequent reading. What these results demonstrate, however, is that extended inspection time is not always a direct consequence of processing 'difficulty'.

Relative-clause sentences:

RR: The *actress(,)* sent the *flowers(,)* was very pleased at receiving them.
UR: The *actress(,)* who was sent the *flowers(,)* was very pleased at receiving them.

Gaze durations were again longer on the punctuated words at Positions 1 (mean 312 ms vs. 279 ms; difference 33 ms) and 2 (mean 262 ms vs. 235 ms; difference 27 ms) irrespective of structure ($F_1(1, 30) = 9.715$, $p < 0.01$; $F_2(1, 18) = 8.090$, $p < 0.05$ and $F_1(1, 30) = 5.388$, $p < 0.05$; $F_2(1, 18) = 4.710$, $p < 0.05$). Extra spaces did not, however, produce the same effect as punctuation on gaze duration with this structure. At Position 1, the difference between the unpunctuated and the double-space condition was -8 ms (mean 279 ms vs. 271 ms) and at Position 2, the difference was 9 ms (mean 235 ms vs. 244 ms). Neither difference was statistically reliable and there was no interaction with structure.

Table 4 shows that while there was a tendency for punctuated words to induce a greater number of fixations at Position 1, this was not statistically reliable and there was also no difference in the number of fixations in the no-comma and spacing conditions. This may be related to the fact that Position 1 was only the second word of the relative-clause sentences and this was preceded only by a determiner, and consequently did not engage more normal reading dynamics. In contrast, the increase in fixation rate at Position 2 was statistically reliable. There was also a structural effect on the number of fixations at Position 2, but this seems likely to be related to the fact that unreduced relative sentences were two words longer by this point. There was, however, no interaction here between the effects of punctuation and structure.

As with the prepositional phrase items, variation in the number of fixations on the word preceding the comma tended to produce some movement in launch position

Table 4

The number of fixations made on the initial reading of the word at Positions 1 and 2 in the relative-clause sentences

	Position 1:				Position 2:			
	No comma	Comma	Space	Mean	No comma	Comma	Space	Mean
Reduced relatives	1.25	1.28	1.29	1.27	0.90	1.06**	0.96	0.97*
Unreduced relatives	1.26	1.39	1.15	1.27	0.998	1.155**	1.058	1.070*
Mean	1.26	1.34	1.22		0.950	1.108**	1.010	

** indicates a significant difference at the 1% level (based on analysis by subjects).
* indicates a significant difference at the 5% level (based on analysis by subjects).

Table 5

The mean launch position measured from the end of the word at Positions 1 and 2 in the relative-clause sentences before a rightward inter-word saccade

	No comma	Comma	Space
Position 1	−4.59	−5.14	−4.29
Position 2	−5.28	−5.11	−5.00

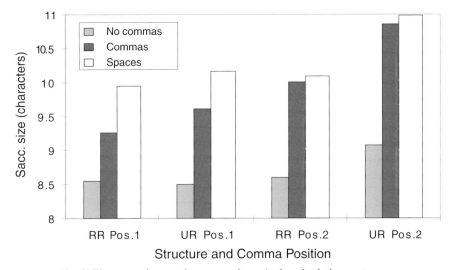

Fig. 2. First saccade over the comma in un/reduced relative sentences.

(see Table 5). However, in this case, the effects were very small and none achieved statistical significance. Nonetheless, the saccade length data shown in Fig. 2, again demonstrate a stretching in the presence of a comma or an extra space. While this effect is relatively modest at Position 1, only slightly exceeding the added character space, it is more substantial later in the sentence at a point where it would be expected that more normal reading dynamics are engaged.

Landing positions were, however, once again further to the right following a comma or double space, even at Position 1, as Table 6 shows. Commas and spaces had equivalent effects on subsequent landing position and there were no interactions with structure.

Overall, with the possible exception of some of the results at Position 1, the pattern of findings with relative-clause sentences matches those from the prepositional phrases. The inspection of words preceding commas appears to be extended. This is followed by a saccade into the subsequent word which is increased

Table 6

The character position of the first fixation on the text immediately after Positions 1 and 2 in the relative-clause sentences

	Position 1:				Position 2:			
	No comma	Comma	Space	Mean	No comma	Comma	Space	Mean
Reduced relatives	3.54	4.08*	4.39**	4.00	3.54	4.01**	4.29***	3.95
Unreduced relatives	3.83	4.63*	4.32**	4.26	3.57	4.63**	4.82***	4.34
Mean	3.68	4.36*	4.36**		3.56	4.32**	4.56***	

*** indicates a significant difference at the 0.1% level (based on analysis by subjects).
** indicates a significant difference at the 1% level (based on analysis by subjects).
* indicates a significant difference at the 5% level (based on analysis by subjects).

in size by more than the added space and which results in a more rightward landing position in that word. The same effect occurs with double spacing. Again, this appears to reflect oculomotor processes largely divorced from any processing consequences of the commas or spaces, since the effect occurs equivalently with both manipulations and also shows up in the unambiguous unreduced relatives.

Closure sentences:

EC: While the janitor was *cleaning(,)* the old *clock* chimed loudly in the dusty hallway.

LC: While the janitor was *cleaning* the old *clock(,)* it chimed loudly in the dusty hallway.

Gaze duration was 46 ms longer, on average, when a comma marked the point of early closure at Position 1 (313 ms vs. 267 ms; $F_1(1, 30) = 6.433$, $p < 0.05$; $F_2(1, 18) = 8.951$, $p < 0.01$). An extra space increased the reading time by a non-significant 14 ms (mean 281 ms) and this was reliably smaller than the increase generated by a comma ($F_1(1, 30) = 4.906$, $p < 0.05$; $F_2(1, 18) = 5.333$, $p < 0.05$). Although a comma at Position 2 resulted in a mean gaze duration of 235 ms rather than the unpunctuated gaze of 210 ms, this difference was statistically unreliable, as were the comparisons with the duration of 233 ms for the spacing condition. Table 7 shows that this pattern is also consistent with the number of fixations made.

Again, the data in Table 8 show a small trend for launch position to move slightly to the right following the extra fixations in comma and double-space conditions, but as with the relative-clause sentences, this modest trend did not achieve statistical significance.

However, despite the comparatively moderate effects of commas and spacing on gaze on the critical words, Fig. 3 shows that the expected pattern of exaggerated

Table 7

The number of fixations made on the initial reading of the word at Positions 1 and 2 in the closure sentences

	Position 1:				Position 2:			
	No comma	Comma	Space	Mean	No comma	Comma	Space	Mean
Early closure	1.18	1.30*	1.16	1.21	0.92	0.97	0.93	0.94
Late closure	1.12	1.22*	1.12	1.15	0.93	1.01	1.00	0.98
Mean	1.15	1.26*	1.14		0.92	0.99	0.96	

* indicates a significant difference at the 5% level (based on analysis by subjects).

Table 8

The mean launch position measured from the end of the word at Positions 1 and 2 in the closure sentences before a rightward inter-word saccade

	No comma	Comma	Space
Position 1	−5.34	−5.31	−5.27
Position 2	−5.25	−4.91	−5.10

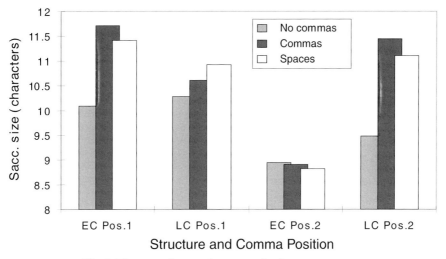

Fig. 3. First saccade over the comma in closure sentences.

saccade size for both commas and spaces was nonetheless obtained. This then translated into a rightwards shift in landing position immediately following a comma or space, although the spacing effect in late closure was only marginally significant. A comma at Position 1 increased the next rightwards landing position by an average of 0.76 characters ($F_1(1, 30) = 5.350$, $p < 0.05$; $F_2(1, 18) = 6.332$, $p < 0.05$) while an extra space stretched it by 0.64 characters ($F_1(1, 30) = 5.501$, $p < 0.05$; $F_2(1, 18) = 7.429$, $p < 0.05$). For Position 2 the comma effect was 1.40 characters ($F_1(1, 30) = 7.725$, $p < 0.01$; $F_2(1, 18) = 9.381$, $p < 0.01$) and 0.67 characters following double spacing ($F_1(1, 30) = 3.017$, $p < 0.1$; $F_2(1, 18) = 2.981$, $p < 0.1$). Again, these effects are divorced from processing difficulty, since this varied dramatically between commas and spaces and there was no apparent effect on processing of inserted commas or spaces at Position 2.

Eye-movement summary

There is little doubt that commas have a profound influence on eye-movement patterns. Perhaps because they are small orthographic features tucked away at the ends of words, they do not influence saccades *into* the words to which they are attached. However, they appear to be a powerful weapon at close range, holding the eye longer on a word to which they are attached. This increase in reading times on punctuated words does not mean that the eyes are simply locked in place for longer. There was no evidence of a consistent effect on fixation duration. Rather, the pattern of longer gaze durations was paralleled by the number of fixations made. This might suggest some high-level process, sensitive to punctuation, directly and rapidly interfering with the normal flow and programming of saccades, causing small inter-word refixations. This is the type of interpretation favoured by Rayner, Kambe and Duffy (2000). They found a remarkably similar pattern of eye movements associated with words that either did and did not end a clause, in a situation where clause ending was marked by a comma. However, since very similar effects were also found here with double spacing and the effects appear to be relatively independent of processing load, a simpler, low-level, interpretation seems more plausible.

It is not clear from these data what that interpretation may be, but it appears to be related either to segmentation or word spacing or both. The spacing interpretation, at a simple oculomotor level, is that the extra gap is apparent in the pattern of low spatial frequency 'blobs' in the periphery and that an atypical gap disrupts smooth reading dynamics, with some 'hesitation' before the jump. The extra inspection time at this point allows additional processing of the information falling to the right of fixation and a larger saccade is therefore programmed. A slightly higher-level interpretation suggests that text is normally processed in 'chunks' with delineation of these usually marked with increased spacing. Normal dynamics therefore apply within segments, but not necessarily between them. This pattern is then applied regardless of the actual load associated with processing the 'chunk'. That is, it is a 'chunk wrap up' effect, only loosely coupled to processing load. The end of a chunk is a good place to 'take stock' in case there is any processing lagging behind the current point of regard, but nothing is lost if this is not true, since there is still the possibility of information uptake from the periphery. Clearly, of course, the answer might also involve a combination of these possibilities, but what seems clear is that it is not an effect critically related to local processing load in any particular instance.

Whatever the reason for it, longer times spent fixating punctuated words appear to allow increased parafoveal processing of subsequent words to occur. This, in turn, allows larger jumps into the following text. And these extended saccades are not compensated for by longer fixations on landing; if anything, there is a trend for shorter durations to follow. The processing of the words preceding and following a comma appears to be distributed across fixations, with longer times in one location offset by shorter ones in the other.

Although the extra-space condition did not produce an exact replication of the punctuation effects, there were more similarities than differences as concerns the pattern of fixations and saccades on the words surrounding the punctuation. Whereas spacing is much more similar to the unpunctuated condition in processing terms, it is clearly closer to the punctuated condition so far as local eye-movement patterns are concerned.

Conclusions

The simple conclusion is that commas are complicated little things. Their strongest feature seems to be their ability to enhance the awareness of constituent structure and phrasal boundaries, both physically, in terms of eye movements, and mentally, in terms of processing. One result of this is that structural effects are much more immediate and therefore any problems are sorted out earlier (but not necessarily with any overall processing advantage). Even though there was still a garden-path effect in the non-minimally attaching NP + PP items, the problem was identified and resolved at its source, with the added benefit of reducing the need to reread the sentence: smaller, localised delays and regressions minimised the requirement for larger, more global ones.

Commas do exert a large influence on processing when they are syntactically informative and are primarily used as evidence *against* 'preferred' or 'default' structures. When they coincide with boundaries in the 'preferred' structure, they are more or less redundant from a processing point of view; small trade-offs with slower reading before the comma are balanced by faster reading afterwards. These findings seem to be independent of the reader's awareness of the punctuation. The results from the questionnaires suggest that readers have little awareness of when they encountered commas or the frequency or appropriateness of their occurrence in their prior reading. This, coupled with the lack of formal rules covering usage and the inconsistency of personal writing-style in general, suggests that punctuation affects basic sentence parsing processes rather than processing 'strategies'.

Consistent effects of commas on the distribution of eye movements and eye-movement patterns were found, *irrespective of processing consequences*. Commas did not influence the initial fixation on a punctuated word, either in terms of landing position or first-fixation duration, but they did extend reading times on the word, as a whole, along with the number of fixations made on the word. As such, adding a comma does not seem to be the equivalent of increasing the letter-count of the word. Saccade length and landing position into the subsequent text were stretched, however. For movements into a word, following commas appear to be transparent, while for internal movements or movements out of the word they become extremely tangible indeed. Although an extra space did not produce similar processing effects, it *did* have a similar effect on many eye-movement parameters regardless of processing implications.

Both commas and spaces therefore have an effect on the segmentation of text. Their presence produces a consistent effect on eye movements although their processing repercussions are considerably more variable. However, as commas are capable of preventing the need for major reanalysis, either eliminating garden-path effects or enabling a rapid repair, they are definitely doing more than just physically segmenting text or activating some low-level oculomotor function. Although the fragmentation, with commas, of sentences into their primary components did not facilitate overall reading times in the 'preferred' and unambiguous sentence structures examined here, it is something that may indeed prove important in longer or more complex sentences where memory load and clarity may become more of an issue. In general terms, however, it is clear that punctuation does not provide 'just another cue' to the correct structural analysis of a sentence. It does not appear to be the case that it adds to the weight of evidence which already exists in favour of a particular analysis, as might be suggested from a 'constraint satisfaction' viewpoint. Rather, punctuation, while not 'invisible' at a low level of analysis, appears to be completely redundant in a preferred or unambiguous structure. In contrast, where it can provide a critical 'cue', it does so with sufficient force to effectively block an incorrect parse.

Importantly, for those investigators using eye movements to investigate 'processing difficulty' at various points within a sentence, there is a clear warning from these results. Some factors which clearly do perturb local eye-movement patterns, such as punctuation and spacing, do not necessarily have equivalent effects on 'processing difficulty'. Local effects, although highly robust, may reflect oculomotor perturbations with little or no longer-term processing consequence. As demonstrated here, the selection of a larger analysis region often provides a more accurate reflection of on-going processing load. While there is certainly a close coupling between eye movements and on-going sentence processing, this coupling appears to retain some flexibility, with effects potentially distributed across a number of words and with more than one word being processed (perhaps simultaneously) while the eye rests in one location.

References

Adams, B.C., Clifton, C. and Mitchell, D.C. (1998). Lexical guidance in sentence processing? Psychonomic Bulletin and Review, 5, 265–270.

Bever, T.G., Jandreau, S., Burwell, R., Kaplan, R. and Zaenen, A. (1990). Spacing printed text to isolate major phrases improves readability. Visible Language, 25, 74–87.

Chafe, W. (1988). Punctuation and the prosody of written language. Written Communication, 5, 395–426.

Clifton, C. (1993). Thematic roles in sentence parsing. Special Issue: Reading and Language Processing. Canadian Journal of Experimental Psychology, 47, 222–246.

Clifton, C. and Ferreira, F. (1989). Ambiguity in context. Special Issue: Parsing and Interpretation. Language and Cognitive Processes, 4, Si77–Si103.

Ferreira, F. and Henderson, J.M. (1991). Recovery from misanalyses of garden-path sentences. Journal of Memory and Language, 30, 725–745.

Francis, W.N. and Kuçera, H. (1982). Frequency analysis of English usage: lexicon and grammar. Boston, MA: Houghton Mifflin.

Frazier, L. (1987). Sentence processing: a tutorial review. In: M. Coltheart (Ed.), Attention and Performance 12: The Psychology of Reading. Hove, England: Erlbaum, pp. 559–586.

Frazier, L. and Clifton, C. (1996). Construal. Cambridge, MA: MIT Press.

Frazier, L. and Rayner, K. (1982). Making and correcting errors during sentence comprehension: eye movements in the analysis of structurally ambiguous sentences. Cognitive Psychology, 14, 178–210.

Frenck-Mestre, C. and Pynte, J. (1997). Syntactic ambiguity resolution while reading in second and native languages. Quarterly Journal of Experimental Psychology: Human Experimental Psychology, 50a, 119–148.

Haberlandt, K. (1994). Methods in reading research. In: M.A. Gernsbacker (Ed.), Handbook of Psycholinguistics. San Diego, CA: Academic Press, pp. 1–31.

Hill, R.L. (1996). A Comma in Parsing: A Study into the Influence of Punctuation (Commas) on Contextually Isolated 'Garden-Path' Sentences. Unpubl. M.Philos. Thesis, University of Dundee.

Hill, R.L. and Murray, W.S. (1997a). Punctuated parsing: signposts along the garden path. Poster presented at the CUNY Conference on Human Sentence Processing, Santa Monica, CA.

Hill, R.L. and Murray, W.S. (1997b). Marking the true path: commas as critical cues in parsing. Poster presented at the Architectures and Mechanisms for Language Processing Conference, Edinburgh.

Hill, R.L. and Murray, W.S. (1998a). Commas and spaces: the point of punctuation. Poster presented at the CUNY Conference on Human Sentence Processing, New Brunswick, NJ.

Hill, R.L. and Murray, W.S. (1998b). The dissociation of processing and eye-movement patterns: evidence from punctuation. Poster presented at the Architectures and Mechanisms for Language Processing Conference, Freiburg, Germany.

Jandreau, S.M., Muncer, S.J. and Bever, T.G. (1986). Improving the readability of text with automatic phrase-sensitive formatting. British Journal of Educational Technology, 17, 128–133.

Johansson, S. and Hofland, K. (1989). Frequency Analysis of English Vocabulary and Grammar. Based on the LOB Corpus, Vol. 1. Tag Frequencies and Word Frequencies. Oxford: Clarendon Press.

Jones, B.E.M. (1994). Can punctuation help parsing? Aquilex-II Working Paper 29, Cambridge University Computer Laboratory.

Kennedy, A. (1998) The influence of parafoveal words on foveal inspection time: evidence for a processing trade-off. In: G. Underwood (Ed.), Eye Guidance in Reading and Scene Perception. Oxford: Elsevier, pp. 149–180.

Kennedy, A. and Murray, W.S. (1984). Inspection times for words in syntactically ambiguous sentences under three presentation conditions. Journal of Experimental Psychology: Human Perception and Performance, 10, 833–849.

Kennedy, A., Murray, W.S., Jennings, F. and Reid, C. (1989). Parsing complements: comments on the generality of the principle of minimal attachment. Language and Cognitive Processes, 4, 51–76.

Kučera, H. and Francis, W.N. (1967). Computational analysis of present-day American English. Providence, RI: Brown University Press.

MacDonald, M.C. (1994). Probabilistic constraints and syntactic ambiguity resolution. Language and Cognitive Processes, 9, 147–149.

MacDonald, M.C. (1996). Representation and activation in syntactic processing. In: T. Inui and J.L. McClelland (Eds.), Attention and Performance 16: Information Integration in Perception and Communication. Cambridge, MA: MIT Press, pp. 433–456.

Mitchell, D.C. (1986). On-line parsing of structurally ambiguous sentences: evidence against the use of lookahead. Unpublished manuscript.

Murray, W.S. (1998). Parafoveal pragmatics. In: G. Underwood (Ed.), Eye Guidance in Reading and Scene Perception. Oxford: Elsevier, pp. 181–199.

Murray, W.S. and Liversedge, S.P. (1994). Referential context effects on syntactic processing. In: C. Clifton, L. Frazier and K. Rayner (Eds.), Perspectives on Sentence Processing. Hillsdale, NJ: Erlbaum, pp. 359–388.

Nunberg, G. (1990). The Linguistics of Punctuation (Vol. 18). Stanford, CA: Center for the Study of Language and Information.

O'Regan, J.K. (1992). Optimal viewing position in words and the strategy-tactics theory of eye movements in reading. In: K. Rayner (Ed.), Eye Movements and Visual Cognition: Scene Perception and Reading. New York: Springer, pp. 333–354.

O'Regan, J.K. and Lévy-Schoen, A. (1987). Eye-movement strategy and tactics in word recognition and reading. In: M. Coltheart (Ed.), Attention and Performance 12: The Psychology of Reading. Hove, England: Erlbaum, pp. 363–383.

Patterson, K.B., Liversedge, S.P. and Underwood, G. (1999). The influence of focus operators on syntactic processing of short relative clause sentences. Quarterly Journal of Experimental Psychology: Human Experimental Psychology, 52A, 717–737.

Pickering, M.J. and Traxler, M.J. (1998). Plausibility and recovery from garden paths: an eye-tracking study. Journal of Experimental Psychology: Learning, Memory and Cognition, 24, 940–961.

Pynte, J. and Prieur, B. (1996). Prosodic breaks and attachment decisions in sentence parsing. Language and Cognitive Processes, 11, 165–191.

Quirk, R., Greenbaum, S., Leech, G. and Svartvik, J. (1985). A Comprehensive Grammar of the English Language. London: Longman.

Rayner, K. (1979). Eye guidance in reading: Fixation locations in words. Perception, 8, 21–30.

Rayner, K., Kambe, G.A. and Duffy, S.A. (2000). The effect of clause wrap-up on eye movements during reading. Quarterly Journal of Experimental Psychology (in press).

Scholes, R.J. and Willis, B.J. (1990). Prosodic and syntactic functions of punctuation: a contribution to the study of orality and literacy. Interchange, 21, 13–20.

Spivey-Knowlton, M.J. and Tanenhaus, M.K. (1998). Syntactic ambiguity resolution in discourse: modeling the effects of referential context and lexical frequency. Journal of Experimental Psychology, Learning, Memory and Cognition, 24, 1521–1543.

Taraban, R. and McClelland, J.L. (1988). Constituent attachment and thematic role assignment in sentence processing: influences of content-based expectations. Journal of Memory and Language, 27, 597–632.

Taraban, R. and McClelland, J.L. (1990). Parsing and comprehension: a multiple-constraint view. In: D.A. Balota, G.B. Flores d'Arcais and K. Rayner (Eds.), Comprehension Processes in Reading. Hillsdale, NJ: Erlbaum, pp. 231–263.

Trueswell, J.C. and Tanenhaus, M.K. (1994). Toward a lexicalist framework of constraint-based syntactic ambiguity resolution. In: C. Clifton, L. Frazier and K. Rayner (Eds.), Perspectives on Sentence Processing. Hillsdale, NJ: Erlbaum, pp. 155–179.

Trueswell, J.C., Tanenhaus, M.K. and Garnsey, S.M. (1994). Semantic influences on parsing: Use of thematic role information in syntactic ambiguity resolution. Journal of Memory and Language, 33, 285–318.

CHAPTER 23

Effects of the Focus Particle *Only* and Intrinsic Contrast on Comprehension of Reduced Relative Clauses

Charles Clifton Jr. and Jeannine Bock
University of Massachusetts

and

Janina Radó
Massachusetts Institute of Technology

Abstract

A focus particle like *only* can affect the interpretation of sentences in various ways. Ni, Crain and Shankweiler (1996) have proposed that it can directly affect syntactic parsing decisions by establishing discourse conditions that affect referential possibilities. Ni et al. demonstrated that using *only* in a sentence like *Only students furnished answers received high marks* largely eliminated the normal garden-path normally observed in such sentences when they contain a definite NP subject. Ni et al. claimed that *only* establishes a requirement for selection from a contrast set and that the relative clause after *students* satisfies this requirement. The present paper reports two experiments that attempted but largely failed to replicate the Ni et al. finding, using their materials and techniques similar or identical to theirs, and a third eyetracking experiment that tested a novel implication of the Ni et al. claims. This third experiment used subject nouns that had an intrinsic contrast that could satisfy the requirements of *only* without a postnominal modified (e.g., *Only bachelors ... .* [as implicitly opposed to married men]) and found, contrary to predictions, that such high-contrast nouns actually increased the effect of *only* in reducing garden-pathing, compared to low-contrast nouns. While we are not certain of the reasons for the discrepancies between our results and the results of Ni et al., we believe that the bulk of the data can best be understood in terms of how *only* affects recovery from an initial syntactic misanalysis.

Reading as a Perceptual Process/A. Kennedy, R. Radach, D. Heller and J. Pynte (Editors)
© 2000 Elsevier Science Ltd. All rights reserved

Readers and listeners have to construct the meanings of sentences in ways that are constrained by the syntactic structures in which the words occur and the semantic requirements of these structures. We and our colleagues (Ferreira and Clifton, 1986; Frazier, 1979, 1987; Frazier and Clifton, 1996; Frazier and Rayner, 1982; Rayner, Carlson and Frazier, 1983) have emphasized how syntax constrains semantics and how, therefore, computing the syntax of a sentence is a crucial task for the human language processor. We argue that since syntactic structures are required for semantic interpretation, it would be efficient and effective for a language comprehension system to create a syntactic structure as quickly as possible in order to permit semantic interpretation and evaluation to begin. Our data provide some support of a depth-first (Frazier, 1995) processing hypothesis, in which a reader/listener develops a single analysis to the point of semantic interpretation rather than considering several incomplete analyses in parallel.

We have entertained various hypotheses about how semantic interpretation can feed back onto syntactic analyses. For instance, Frazier (1990) developed the possibility that some systems for computing semantic interpretation can communicate freely with systems for computing syntactic structures, constrained only by the requirement that each distinct system can perform computations only on representations of a form to which it has access. From this perspective, no architectural constraints force syntactic representations to be computed before semantic representations are created; however, if the system that creates semantic representations interprets syntactic structures, then the structures must be built before the semantic system can operate.

Others have argued for different views of the syntax–semantics interface. One claim that contrasts in an interesting fashion with the analysis we have advanced is the 'referential theory' of Crain and Steedman (1985), as developed in Ni, Crain and Shankweiler (1996). This theory proposes that semantic factors, not syntactic factors, guide the processor's initial choice among analyses. We will concentrate primarily on the claims this theory makes about how a 'focus operator' such as *only* is used in constructing a representation of a sentence.

Referential theory

All psycholinguists know that sentences like the garden-path sentence of Bever (1970) in (1) are difficult to comprehend. A reader or listener takes the initial verb as the main verb of the sentence and has great difficulty arriving at the required relative clause analysis. Experimental demonstrations of this fact abound (e.g., Frazier and Rayner, 1982). On the other hand, some psycholinguists have pointed out that sentences superficially like (1), such as that in (2), are easy to comprehend as relative clauses when they occur in appropriate contexts.

(1) The horse raced past the barn fell.
(2) A person presented with *the evidence examined by the lawyer* may interpret ... (Ferreira and Clifton, 1986, quoted by MacDonald, Pearlmutter and Seidenberg, 1994, p. 678).

Crain and Steedman (1985) proposed a 'referential theory of sentence processing' to account for some of the variability in difficulty of comprehending relative clause constructions, among a variety of other effects. In their model, the parser constructs all syntactic analyses of a fragment, choosing which analysis to pursue on semantic/pragmatic grounds, namely, whichever analysis violates the fewest presuppositions or requires the fewest additions to the evolving discourse model. They assumed that a restrictive relative clause felicitously modifies a definite noun phrase only if it is used to identify a subset from an already established context set. In the absence of a context set, only the main clause interpretation of, say, 'The horse raced past the barn ... ' will be felicitous. This is not because the main clause analysis is syntactically preferred, but because a relative clause can be used to modify a definite noun phrase only if the discourse context contains multiple possible referents of the head noun from which the relative clause permits selection. If this discourse presupposition is not met, the reader/listener must accommodate it by adding possibly contrasting entities to the discourse context, a process which is costly and therefore to be avoided.

There is good reason to doubt the validity of this assumption about the discourse requirements of relative clauses, and hence reason to doubt the validity of the Crain and Steedman analysis (cf. Clifton and Ferreira, 1989). It is not at all clear that relative clauses are predominantly, or even commonly, used in the way Crain and Steedman assume that they must be used. Fox and Thompson (1990) present a careful pragmatic analysis of the actual use of relative clauses in a corpus of spoken English. Their analysis of 414 relative clauses (all at least arguably restrictive) indicated that while all relative clauses were 'grounded', in the sense of being linked to given referents in the discourse, the linkage took a variety of forms. A common use was as a 'file-establishing' relative clause, which introduces a new entity into the discourse. In their example (4), ... *the uh heater thing we put in I think was a hundred ... dollars*, the relative clause *we put in* is linked by the word *we* to the conversational participants (who are necessarily represented in the discourse model). Another way of grounding is called 'proposition-linking'. An example is the relative clause *who isn't a Catholic* from Fox and Thompson's example (6): ... *The mother's sister is a real bigot. Y'know and she hates anyone who isn't a Catholic*. Here, the relative clause is grounded through the frame provided by the word *bigot*.

Fox and Thompson explicitly distinguish between two functions of the relative clauses they collected, namely, "provid[ing] a characterization of a New Head

NP referent, not previously known to the hearer," and "help[ing] to identify a Given Head NP referent, previously known to the hearer" (pp. 301–302). Crain and Steedman's analysis claims that only (a subset of) the latter use of relative clauses is felicitous when the relative clause is used to modify a definite NP. Fox and Thompson's data suggest that this claim may be too strong. They provided explicit statistics on 382 relative clauses with nonhuman head nouns. They were able to categorize the communicative function of 228 of these: 141 (62%) were used as 'identifying' and 87 (38%) as 'characterizing'. Including the 154 relative clauses whose function could not be securely determined (but were presumably not used as 'identifying') only these 141 (37% of the total) met the criterion of selecting from a set of discourse entities. If all of these relative clauses modified definite NPs, only the 'identifying' usage should be possible according to Crain and Steedman. Unfortunately for the purposes of this analysis, Fox and Thompson did not provide a breakdown by NP definiteness. They did note that 85% of subject NPs modified by a relative clause were definite and that only 43% of all subject NP relative clauses were used as 'identifying' (and that 28% of object NPs modified by a relative clause were definite, with 25% of all object NP relative clauses being 'identifying'), suggesting that at least a substantial number of definite NPs had relative clauses that were not used to identify a specific referent.

Existing evidence about referential theory and relative clauses

The claim of Crain and Steedman (1985) has led to a substantial amount of research about whether providing an appropriate discourse context can eliminate the normal dispreference for the relative clause reading. This research, for the most part, can be described as 'inconclusive' (see Clifton and Ferreira, 1989, and Steedman and Altmann, 1989 for reviews of the early research; see Murray and Liversedge, 1994, Rayner, Garrod and Perfetti, 1992, Spivey-Knowlton, Trueswell and Tanenhaus, 1993, and Trueswell and Tanenhaus, 1991, for more recent research). A cautious conclusion is that the reduced relative clause garden path is difficult, but perhaps not impossible, to eliminate by manipulating context.

One line of research, however, provides dramatic support for the referential theory and its account of relative clause comprehension difficulty. Ni et al. (1996) investigated the effect of *only* on the ease of understanding sentences with a temporary ambiguity between a main clause and a relative clause analysis. *Only* requires a contrast set. For example, in the context of a discussion of horses at Kathy's farm, a speaker might felicitously utter *Only the horse raced past the barn fell*. This utterance partitions the set of horses at Kathy's farm into the horse that was raced past the barn and the other horses (the contrast set).

Since *only* requires a contrast set, Ni et al. reason that an ambiguous relative clause/main clause should preferentially be interpreted as a relative clause, thereby providing the information needed to set up a contrast set. The relative clause permits reference to one particular entity or set of entities, allowing the remaining entities denoted by the head of the relative clause to constitute the contrast set. Hence (3a) should show evidence of a garden path in the disambiguating region (*received*) but (3b) with *only* should not.

(3) (a) The students furnished answers before the exam received high marks.
    (b) Only students furnished answers before the exam received high marks.

Ni et al. (1996) presented a series of four experiments, two examining relative clause structures like (3) and two examining prepositional phrase structures (*The man painted the doors with large brushes/cracks*). The first relative clause experiment used a word-by-word grammaticality judgment task, and the second measured eye movements while subjects read sentences for comprehension. Each included unambiguous control sentences like those in (4), and the first experiment also included sentences where an adjective preceded the first noun (e.g., *The/Only dishonest students . . .*).

(4) (a) The hunters bitten by the ticks worried about getting Lyme disease.
    (b) Only hunters bitten by the ticks worried about getting Lyme disease.

The results were quite clear. The presence of *only* immediately before the noun largely (in the grammaticality judgment experiment) or totally (in the eyetracking experiment) eliminated any evidence of disruption in the region of the sentence that disambiguated toward the relative clause interpretation (the region beginning with *received* in (3)). First-pass eye fixation durations were not lengthened in sentences with *only* like (3b) or (4), while they were in (3a). In the grammaticality judgment study, while sentences like (3b) were read somewhat more slowly and rejected more often in the disambiguating region than unambiguous sentences like (4), they were read much faster and rejected much less often than sentences without *only* like (3a). Adding an adjective before the noun (*Only dishonest students . . .*) restored disruption comparable to that observed with the definite determiner of (3a). Ni et al. (1996, p. 300) interpret their results as showing that "a potential garden path was averted" by the contrast requirements of *only*. They conclude that *only* creates a focus on one specific instance or set of the entities denoted by the following noun so that some message can be asserted of the focused element. In doing this, *only* presupposes a set of items, the contrast set, of which the message cannot be asserted. In order to create this distinction between the focused element and the contrast set, the noun must be modified. Instances of the noun to which the modification applies fall into the focused set, and the remainder into the contrast set. An adjective satisfies this need for modification, but if no modification is present, a postnominal modifier is required. Interpreting the ambiguous phrase *furnished answers ...* as a relative clause satisfies this semantic requirement, leading to the relative clause being the preferred analysis and eliminating any garden-path effects.

Evaluation of the evidence, and implications for garden-path theory

We accept the basic claim that *only* requires a contrast set and that its presence in an ambiguous relative clause sentence might facilitate processing of the sentence. We are less sure whether the facilitatory effects of *only* arise from the particular mechanism offered by the referential theory, viz. parallel syntactic analysis of both the main clause and relative clause structures followed by rapid selection of the relative clause analysis to satisfy *only*'s need for a contrast set.

Van Gompel et al. (Chapter 24) provide evidence that *only* in fact has rather gentle effects on parsing decisions that are similar to the relative clause attachment decisions under discussion. Van Gompel et al. use the focus properties of *only* to bias the interpretation of prepositional phrase modifiers in sentences like *The hunter killed only the poacher with the rifle*. Without *only*, these sentences are biased toward a verb modification (or verb argument) interpretation in which the hunter is using the rifle to kill something (Rayner, Carlson and Frazier, 1983) and against the interpretation in which the phrase modifies the noun. Using *only* as the determiner reduces the bias to the 50% range and equates the two interpretations in plausibility. However, it falls far short of forcing the decision to interpret the prepositional phrase as modifying the noun.

Frazier and Clifton (1996, chapter 4) presented evidence that is directly germane to the question of whether phrases with semantic requirements of contrast sets affect the interpretation of relative clauses. Their experiment measured the time to read sentences like (5), which contain a relative clause *who has/have teeth* (bracketed for convenience in (5)) that (apart from number) could modify either *the only one* or *Sam's employees*.

(5) (a) Matt met the only one of Sam's employees [who has teeth] who drives a pickup truck.
    (b) Matt met the only one of Sam's employees [who have teeth] who drives a pickup truck.

The *only one of ...* phrases of these sentences require a contrast set to be explicitly designated by material in the sentence. This requirement is met in (5a), where the number of the relative clause immediately following *employees* (bracketed in (5)) makes it appropriate as a modifier of *the only one*. The corresponding relative clause of (5b), however, does not satisfy this requirement, but must be taken as modifying *employees*. Sentences like (5a) were read more quickly in the region of this relative clause, and following, than sentences like (5b), while there were no differences between otherwise-similar control sentences.

This case contrasts with the materials used by Ni, Crain and Shankweiler (1996) in several ways. First, (5) does not involve an ambiguity that results in a severe garden path. The effect of temporarily violating the semantic requirement of *the only one* is actually quite modest, involving the choice of two possible heads for a relative clause. Second, (5) does require the specification of a contrast set in the sentence, a specification met by the relative clause. The sentences used by Ni, Crain and Shankweiler (1996) do not actually have such a requirement. It would be perfectly reasonable if (3b) had continued *Only students furnished answers, not teachers* . . . It is not clear, in fact, that the analysis underlying the Ni et al. experiments actually would have to predict a preference for the relative clause analysis.

The experiments to be reported in the final section of this chapter explore this line of reasoning, with rather surprising results. However, first consider the implications of the findings of Ni et al. taken at face value. By themselves, they pose a severe challenge to the depth-first parsing theory sketched at the beginning of this chapter. The disappearance of garden-pathing in sentences like (3b) is difficult to reconcile with the claim that the main clause analysis is first computed on the basis of its structural simplicity and then revised, however quickly, to a reduced relative clause analysis. The implications become even more challenging when one takes into account as yet unpublished results reported by Ni and his colleagues (Crain, Ni, Shankweiler, Conway and Braze, 1996). These researchers followed up the challenge of Frazier (1995) and showed not only that garden-pathing (as indexed by first-pass reading time in an eyetracking experiment) disappears in sentences like (3b), but that severe disruption seems to appear in similar sentences that are resolved as normally preferred main-clause sentences. Taken at face value, it appears that a sentence beginning as *Only N V* will be analyzed, for presumably semantic reasons, as a complex NP modified by a relative clause, and taken as a simple main clause only with difficulty.

There are reasons, however, to question whether the data should be taken at face value. Paterson, Liversedge and Underwood (1999) report an eyetracking experiment using sentences similar to those used by Ni et al. (3a), and find that the focus particle *only* does not by any means eliminate garden-pathing. While *only* reduced the amount of time spent re-reading after a sentence was disambiguated in favor of the relative clause interpretation, it did not affect first-past reading times. However, the sentences of Paterson et al. were uniformly 'short,' in the sense that they began with a subject NP, a verb, and immediately following that a second NP. An example is *Only actors refused an audition received an apology within the week.* Paterson et al. prefer to restrict their conclusions to such sentences, noting that Ni et al. used some sentences that contained a prepositional phrase after the initial verb or its direct object, prior to the disambiguating verb.

In addition, several eyetracking experiments have been conducted in our laboratory studying sentences containing *the* vs. *only* and having a temporary ambiguity between a main clause vs. a reduced relative clause reading or between a sentence complement vs. a relative clause reading (Clifton and Frazier, 1995; Clifton, 2000). Our main goal was the same as that of Crain et al. (1996), to determine whether garden-pathing would be observed in main clause versions of these when *only* was used, as it should be if *only* biases the parser to seek a postnominal modifier. These experiments have uniformly failed to find any effects of the presence of the focus particle *only* on early measures of reading speed, regardless of whether the sentence was resolved in favor of a reduced relative or a main clause (or complement clause) interpretation. All effects were limited to measures of re-reading effects, as was the case in Paterson et al. (1999). We took this to suggest that *only* affects semantic integration processes, not initial parsing decisions.

Attempted replications of the Ni et al. experiments

Because of the clear implications of the Ni et al. results for our favored theory, we decided to attempt close replications of Experiments 1 and 2 of Ni et al. (1996). Weijia Ni kindly provided us with the full sets of materials used in these experiments, including filler items. We conducted two experiments, the first an incremental grammaticality judgment study like Experiment 1 of Ni et al. (1996), and the second a self-paced reading version of their eyetracking Experiment 2. We used self-paced reading methodology because of its greater ease, and because of our beliefs that major garden-path effects such as those observed in (3a) are easily demonstrated using self-paced reading and their disappearance should be equally easily observed (cf. Clifton, Speer and Abney, 1991; Ferreira and Clifton, 1986; Speer and Clifton, 1998).

Experiment 1: incremental grammaticality judgment

Experiment 1 was conducted as much like Experiment 1 of Ni et al. as possible, using all 32 of their ambiguous items (as in (3)), all 16 of their unambiguous control items (as in (4)), and all 92 of their filler sentences. The experimental items varied in whether they began with *the* or *only* and in whether or not they contained a prenominal adjective (to provide the necessary contrast set and remove the need for a prenominal modifier). The only differences were that (1) each of our subjects received an independent randomization of the materials, (2) different instructions had to be used (the original instructions not being available to us), including a brief pretest in which Ss completed a written 10-item grammaticality judgment questionnaire as practice, and (3) 48 University of Massachusetts undergraduate students, rather than the 32 undergraduate subjects of Ni et al. were used. Our subjects thus read a total of 140 sentences in a self-paced word-by-word fashion, pulling a trigger with their right hand to indicate that the sentence continued to be acceptable and a trigger with their left hand to indicate when the sentence had become ungrammatical. The time to make each response was measured, and the presentation of a sentence terminated with a response of 'ungrammatical'.

The numbers of 'reject' responses and the reaction times of 'accept' responses were cumulated and averaged (respectively) over the same six analysis regions used by Ni et al. (1996). Sentence (3b) is reproduced below, for convenience, with analysis regions marked by / and numbered. Region 1 was the subject NP, Region 2 the first verb, Region 3 the remainder of the first VP apart from the last word, Region 4 the last word of the VP, Region 5 the next two words (either an auxiliary verb plus the main verb, or the main verb plus the next word), and Region 6 the remainder of the sentence except for the sentence-final word, which was eliminated.[1] Region 5 was the disambiguating region, since it grammatically forced the preceding material to be a complex NP.

(3b) Only students $_1$/ furnished $_2$/ answers before the $_3$/ exam $_4$/ received high $_5$/ $_6$/ marks./

The results of this analysis appear in Fig. 1 and 2. Fig. 1 presents the cumulative percentages of sentences rejected,[2] word by word, and Fig. 2 presents the reaction times of responses continuing to accept the sentences. They can be compared to figs. 2 and 1 of Ni et al. (1996), respectively. Consider first the top panel of Fig. 1, the ambiguous sentences. No differences were significant before Region 5. More ambiguous sentences were rejected in Region 5, the disambiguating region,

---

1 It was impossible to apply these definitions precisely. As Ni et al.'s Appendix makes clear, several sentences ended with the two-word critical Region 5 and others (like 3b) had only one word following Region 5; in both these cases, no Region 6 is possible. Still others had only one word after the initial verb, meaning that no Region 3 could be identified. In all these cases, 'dummy' regions were defined (indicated in (3b) by the double //), yielding no data for the sentences involved.

2 Ni et al. do not actually specify that they presented the cumulative proportion of rejections ('errors') as opposed to the conditional proportions of rejections of a sentence at a given region, and it is not clear whether their statistical analyses involve cumulative proportions (which make analyses of successive regions nonindependent) or individual region conditional proportions. Since their fiig. 2 shows proportions that, apart from a few early points, are monotonically increasing (as cumulative proportions must be), and since their plotted proportions are generally similar to our cumulative proportions and quite different from our conditional proportions, we follow the normal convention for incremental grammaticality data of presenting cumulative proportions of rejections and statistically analyzing the proportions of rejections in each region, conditional upon the sentence being accepted up to that region (Boland and Boehm-Jernigan, 1998).

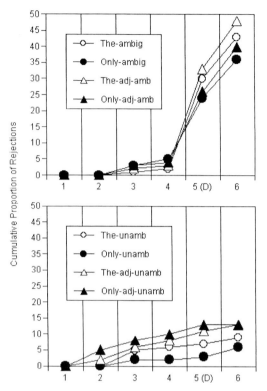

Fig. 1. Cumulative proportions of rejecting sentences as ungrammatical, Experiment 1. Top panel: temporarily ambiguous sentences. Bottom panel: unambiguous sentences.

for sentences beginning with *the* than sentences beginning with *only* (30.7% vs. 22.7% conditional percentage of rejection; $F_1(1, 47) = 12.11$, $p < 0.01$). This difference is similar to the difference reported by Ni et al. (38% vs. 26% cumulative frequency of rejection, estimated from their figure; Ni et al. do not present the conditional percentages which we analyzed, but our cumulative frequencies are quite similar, 32 vs. 25%). This difference could be taken as evidence that *only* reduces garden-pathing via the referential mechanism posited by Ni et al., or it could simply be taken as evidence that *only* does require a contrast set, which provides one justification for a relative clause modifier and presumably facilitates its interpretation.

   Evidence relevant to deciding this issue comes from a crucial difference between the two sets of results. Ni et al. found that the effect of *only* was much larger in sentences without adjectives (36 vs. 19% rejection without vs. with *only* when no adjective was present; 40 vs 34% when one was present). We observed the effect of *only* both without (30 vs. 24%) and with (33 vs. 26%) an adjective, a difference

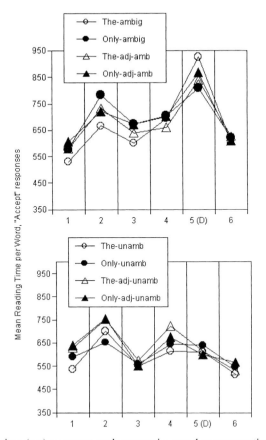

Fig. 2. Mean reaction time (ms) to accept each successive word as grammatical, Experiment 1. Top panel: temporarily ambiguous sentences. Bottom panel: unambiguous sentences.

essentially identical to the difference Ni et al. observed when an adjective was present. Ni et al. reported a significant interaction between *only* and adjective presence, reflecting the dramatic reduction in difficulty in the no-adjective *only* case; the interaction in our data had an $F < 1$.

In Region 6, more sentences with adjectives were rejected than sentences without adjectives (28.2% vs. 20.1% conditional percentage of rejection; $F_1(1, 46) = 6.34$, $p < 0.02$).[3] The conditional (as opposed to cumulative) effect of *only* became nonsignificant. As was the case in Region 5, no other effects approached significance in either region, and the critical interaction had an $F < 1$.

_____

3 The df are 46 because one subject had no observations in Region 6, having rejected all sentences earlier.

Comparison of these data with the data from the lower panel of Fig. 1 (unambiguous sentences) makes it clear that all of the ambiguous sentences were rejected far more often than any unambiguous sentences, by a factor of 3 in the closest case and a factor of 6 (36% vs. 6%) in the case of most interest, the *only NP* condition. Ni et al. also reported lower rejection rates for unambiguous than ambiguous sentences. Since this difference held for sentences with *only*, one might conclude that Ni et al. did observe some garden-pathing in the ambiguous *only* condition (as indeed Ni et al. suggest they may have done, on a minority of trials). However, this conclusion requires a comparison across unmatched ambiguous and unambiguous sentences, and it appears to us that the theoretically crucial point is whether or not *only* has its effect via the mechanisms posited by referential theory, not whether or not its effectiveness is 100%.

The data from the unambiguous conditions are of some interest in themselves. Readers were more likely to reject sentences with adjectives than sentences without adjectives (significant conditional probabilities in Region 2, 3.6% vs. 0.5%, $F_1(1, 47) = 8.29$, $p < 0.01$, marginally significant in Region 5, 2.8% vs. 1.1%, $F_1(1, 47) = 3.64$, $p < 0.07$, and nonsignificant elsewhere). Further, they were more likely to reject sentences with *only* than sentences with *the* in Region 2 (2.9% vs. 1.3%, $F_1(1, 47) = 4.86$, $p < 0.04$). While the interaction between *the*/*only* and adjective presence was nonsignificant ($F_1(1, 47) = 3.13$, $0.05 < p < 0.10$), examination of the data shows that the effect of *only* was limited to sentences with adjectives. No other differences were significant. Examination of the sentences (Ni, Crain and Shankweiler, 1996, Appendix) suggests that some of the adjectives may have been less than highly plausible, especially with *only*, although Ni et al. did not obtain our finding of a greater likelihood of rejecting unambiguous sentences with adjectives than without adjectives.

Fig. 2 presents the grammaticality judgment time data. We will concentrate exclusively on the disambiguating Region 5, where Ni et al. obtained their interesting effects. Judgement times were slow in all four ambiguous conditions, as had been observed by Ni et al. The fastest mean time for an ambiguous sentence in Region 5 was 810 ms; the slowest mean time for an unambiguous control sentence in this region was 639 ms. An analysis of variance of the Region 5 data indicated a highly significant effect of ambiguity (861 vs. 615 ms; $F_1(1, 47) = 62.11$, $p < 0.001$). In contrast to the Ni et al. data, the three-way interaction of ambiguity, *the*/*only*, and adjective presence was significant ($F_1(1, 47) = 6.95$, $p < 0.02$; standard error of a difference between two means $= 35.9$ ms). This reflects a significant two-way interaction between *the* vs. *only* and presence vs. absence of an adjective in the ambiguous but not the unambiguous sentences. Ambiguous sentences with *only* but no adjective were judged quickly (810 ms), comparable to sentences with adjectives (839 and 867 ms), while ambiguous sentences with *the* but no adjective were judged quite slowly (926 ms). In contrast, Ni et al. found that ambiguous sentences with adjectives were judged somewhat more slowly than sentences with *the* but no adjective, while all these sentences were judged much more slowly than sentences with *only* but no adjective. These latter sentences were not noticeably slowed in the disambiguating region, compared to the previous region, while all other sentences were.

Our data again indicate that the presence of *only* (or, oddly, the presence of an adjective) may speed the time to judge an ambiguous sentence in the disambiguating region. However, our data do not contain the evidence reported by Ni et al. that *only* without an adjective dramatically speeds judgement. Once again, it seems reasonable to conclude that *only* may have reduced the magnitude of the garden-pathing effect, but hardly that it eliminated the effect.

Experiment 2: self-paced reading

Experiment 2 was similar to Experiment 2 of Ni et al., apart from (1) its use of self-paced word-by-word reading methodology, (2) its use of individually randomized presentation orders, and (3) its use of 20 University of Massachusetts undergraduates instead of 22 undergraduate students from the population available to Ni et al. Thus, our subjects read 24 temporarily ambiguous and 16 unambiguous sentences together with 60 fillers, just as in Ni et al. The presentation of a sentence began by displaying underscores where each letter would appear. Pulling a key with the right index finger brought up the first word; each successive pull replaced the previous word with the underscores and made the next word appear. The time each word was displayed was recorded. Ten of the unambiguous sentences, and 50 of the fillers, were followed by two-choice questions that the subjects answered by pulling a response key. Only the conditions without adjectives were examined in Experiment 2.

The reading time data were analyzed by computing the mean reading time per word in each of the regions used by Ni et al. (described earlier in Experiment 1). These mean times appear in Fig. 3. The top panel presents the residual reading times (after subtracting the time predicted on the basis of linear regressions relating reading time to analysis region length, based on all 100 sentences in the experiment; Ferreira and Clifton, 1986; cf. Trueswell, Tanenhaus and Garnsey, 1994); the bottom panel presents unadjusted reading times. We will emphasize the former measure and present statistics based on it, since Ni et al. used it, but since we do not think that it should be presented as the only measure of reading time, we also present the unadjusted times.

Analyses of variance were conducted on each region, with the factors *the* vs. *only* and ambiguity. Region 1 indicated slower reading time for phrases including *only* than ones with *the* ($F_1(1, 19) = 13.83$, $p < 0.01$). A similar effect was observed in Region 2 ($F_1(1, 19) = 4.94$, $p < .05$). By Region 3, only the effect of ambiguity

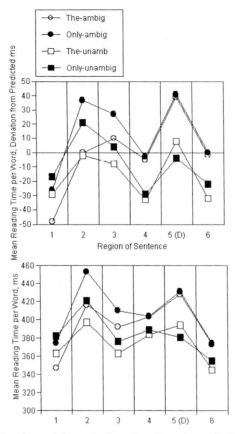

Fig. 3. Mean time to read each word, by analysis region, Experiment 2. Top panel: residual reading times (difference in ms from time predicted as linear function of word length). Bottom panel: uncorrected times, ms.

approached significance; unambiguous sentences were read faster than ambiguous ones ($F_1(1, 19) = 3.85$, $p < 0.07$), as Ni et al. also observed. This advantage for unambiguous sentences became significant by Region 4 (where it disappeared in Ni et al.), and remained significant through Region 6 ($F_1(1, 19) = 702$, 14.53, and 9.18, respectively; all $p < 0.01$). No other F value exceeded 1.05 in Regions 4–6, including the interaction F that was highly significant in Region 5 for Ni et al.

Since this interaction was critical for Ni et al.'s argument that garden-pathing would be observed with *the* but not with *only*, our data do not support their interpretation that *only* can avert garden-pathing. *Only* was difficult to process in the early regions, but this difficulty did not guide our readers' understanding of the sentences. There was a substantial effect of ambiguity, independent of *only*, which could be taken as evidence for garden-pathing, except that it appeared two regions before the disambiguating region and was very strong one region before the disambiguating region. The other putative evidence for garden-pathing, increase in reading times from the region before the disambiguating region to the disambiguating region, was present (and highly significant in an analysis treating Region 4 vs. Region 5 as a factor; $F_1(1, 19) = 17.43$, $p < 0.001$), but was present in both the ambiguous and the unambiguous sentences.

The design of Ni ct al. (1996), replicated here, used different and unrelated sentences in the ambiguous and the unambiguous conditions. Thus, comparing ambiguous and unambiguous sentences in Region 4 or Region 5 involves comparing totally different words in totally different sentences. Given the great dependence of reading time on lexical factors, such a comparison is very problematic. Ni et al. used residual reading times to correct for differences in length, but the correction provided by this measure is far from perfect (especially, perhaps, for word-by-word self-paced reading data, where we have found that correlation between word length and reading time tends to be quite low), and it does not correct for any other incidental lexical differences apart from length. In addition, it is puzzling that Ni et al. did not find fast reading times for their unambiguous sentences in their Experiment 2, given that they (and we) found fast judgment times in Experiment 1 and that we found a similar effect in Experiment 2's reading times.

It is informative to look at the uncorrected mean per-word reading times (bottom panel of Fig. 3). These show basically the same pattern as the residual reading times, except that the effect of ambiguity became nonsignificant in Region 4 ($F_1(1, 19) = 2.53$, $p > 0.12$), but remained fully significant in Regions 5 and 6. Unfortunately for the interpretation of the data, the interaction between Region 4 vs. 5 and ambiguity did not reach significance ($F_1(1, 19) = 2.77$, $p > 0.11$). If this interaction had been significant, the increase in reading time from Region 4 to Region 5 for ambiguous sentences (significant in itself; $F_1(1, 19) = 4.09$, $p < 0.05$) combined with the lack of any such increase for unambiguous sentences could have been taken as clear evidence for garden-pathing.

Conclusions

Experiment 1 demonstrated clear disruption when an ambiguous string was resolved in favor of a relative clause interpretation. Experiment 2 provided less convincing evidence of such disruption, presumably because of the sensitivity of word-by-word self-paced reading to lexical factors and the experimental design which required comparing unrelated word strings. Experiment 1 found some evidence that *only*, with or without an adjective, may have increased the acceptability of a sentence with a relative clause; Experiment 2 did not. Neither experiment, however, provided any evidence that the focus particle *only* made a reduced relative clause interpretation the preferred interpretation, as claimed by Ni et al.

Experiments on intrinsic contrast

To this point, we have presented some evidence that the focus particle *only* may slightly mitigate the difficulty of interpreting a postnominal modifier. We suggested that any effect it has is probably a matter of speeding revision of an initial erroneous analysis, not guiding the parser's initial choices. However, the evidence that we (and others, most notably Paterson et al., 1999) have provided is nearly all negative. We simply fail to find any sign of the dramatic effects reported by Ni et al. (1996).

How *are* the requirements of *only* satisfied? What factors *do* encourage readers to take an ambiguous string of words following an NP as a modifier? One interesting possibility [4] requires examining how much a noun can satisfy *only*'s requirement for a contrast set intrinsically, without relying on a modifier. Consider words like *actress*, *conservative*, and *winner* on the one hand, and words like *boxer*, *magician*, and *pirate* on the other. Each word from the former set has a clear lexical or conceptual contrast; *actress* contrasts with *actor*, *conservative* with *liberal*, etc. The words in the latter set lack any such specific contrast. If one is not a boxer, one could be a wrestler, or a professor, or a lover, or whatever. Now consider using such 'high-contrast' and 'low-contrast' words with the focus particle *only*. The phrase *Only conservatives* invites the implicit contrast set *liberals*; it focuses conservatives in contrast with liberals. Such a phrase seems to need no modification to define a contrast set. However, the phrase *Only boxers* might benefit from a modifier that partitions the set of boxers into a focused set and a contrast set. It could get by without one, contrasting the set of boxers with the set of individuals who are not boxers. But this contrast is not particularly salient, and it is plausible that *only* plus a low-contrast noun would invite postnominal modification.

This line of thought, together with the assumption that the contrast requirements of *only* guide the initial analysis of a temporarily ambiguous postnominal phrase, suggests that whatever advantage *only* confers on postnominal modifiers might be limited to low-contrast nouns. A high-contrast noun would presumably satisfy *only*'s contrast requirements, eliminating the need to analyze the postnominal material as a modifier. Quite different outcomes would be possible, however, if the

---

4 This possibility was originally brought to our attention by Mike Tanenhaus, in a review of Clifton and Frazier, 1995. We thank him for the suggestion. The same opposition was independently used in Radó (1996, 1997) to investigate how the parser constructs contrast sets for contrastively focused items in Hungarian. Radó found evidence for rapid use of focus information by the parser: while the interpretation of low contrast elements required immediate use of discourse context, as indicated by the need to have an explicit sentence topic, there was no corresponding need to have a topic in sentences with high contrast items. This was taken to suggest that the contrast supplied by the lexical content of high contrast items was sufficient for at least the initial interpretation of the focused element.

effect of *only* is actually to facilitate recovery from a garden-path. [5] We suspect that readers and listeners generally expect the contrast set of *only* to come from the discourse (*Jack and Jill went up the hill. Only Jack came down.*). We also suspect that when the discourse context does not provide a contrast set, a listener may expect the speaker to provide one after the sentence (*Only Jack came down the hill. Jill didn't.*). Attempts at within-sentence construction of a contrast set may only be made when other factors encourage it. The presence of a high-contrast noun may be one factor that at least raises the possibility of specifying a contrast set within the sentence, and as such may encourage revising the postnominal material as a relative clause modifier that specifies one particular contrast set. This position predicts that recovery from a garden path would actually be easiest in the *only* high-contrast noun condition.

Normative study

We initially identified high- and low-contrast nouns by having 35 University of Massachusetts undergraduates complete a questionnaire containing phrases like *If you're not a conservative, you're a . . .* and *If you're not a pirate, you're a . . .* Two randomizations of each of two forms were prepared. Each form contained 100 such items. There were 140 words (or lexicalized phrases such as *social workers*) in all; 60 appeared on both forms, and 80 appeared on just one form. These latter included contrasting pairs like *liberal* and *conservative*; we did not want a subject to see both members of such a pair.

All the completions were tabulated, and sixteen high-contrast items were chosen. An item was classed as a high-contrast noun if at least 50% of all responses to frames containing it were the same lexically or at least conceptually (e.g., while *newcomer* received seventeen lexically-different responses, nearly all involved the concept of an established individual, e.g., *oldtimer, veteran, old face, senior,* and *regular*). The mean percentage of conceptually-same completions for the sixteen selected items was 79%. A sentence was then constructed for this high-contrast item, and the norms were searched for a low-contrast noun that made equally good sense in the sentence. A noun was accepted as low contrast if no single concept represented a majority of completions (e.g., *pirate* elicited *soldier, thief, prisoner, miser, Peter Pan, captain, robber, normal person,* etc.). Unfortunately, suitable low-contrast nouns were found for only six of the sixteen experimental sentences. The experimenters were forced to rely on their intuitions to select low-contrast nouns that made the remaining ten sentences sensible. All nouns appear in Appendix A; full materials are available from the first author.

---

5 We thank Lyn Frazier for encouraging the development of this idea.

Experiment 3: eyetracking while reading

As indicated above, two highly plausible sentences containing a relative clause modifying the subject NP were made up for each pair of items, as illustrated in Table 1. Each sentence could occur in eight distinct versions, defined by the factorial combination of high vs. low contrast, *the* vs. *only*, and temporarily ambiguous vs. unambiguous. Sentences were made unambiguous by being unreduced, thus

Table 1

Illustration of sentences used in Experiment 3

	Sentence 1
High contrast, the, ambiguous	The bachelors warned of the perils of marriage had cold feet before their weddings.
High contrast, only, ambiguous	Only bachelors warned of the perils of marriage had cold feet before their weddings.
High contrast, the, unambiguous	The bachelors who were warned of the perils of marriage had cold feet before their weddings.
High contrast, only, unambiguous	Only bachelors who were warned of the perils of marriage had cold feet before their weddings.
Low contrast, the, ambiguous	The social workers warned of the perils of marriage had cold feet before their weddings.
Low contrast, only, ambiguous	Only social workers warned of the perils of marriage had cold feet before their weddings.
Low contrast, the, unambiguous	The social workers who were warned of the perils of marriage had cold feet before their weddings.
Low contrast, only, unambiguous	Only social workers who were warned of the perils of marriage had cold feet before their weddings.
	Sentence 2
High contrast, the, ambiguous	The bachelors refused child support accused the agency of discrimination.
High contrast, only, ambiguous	Only bachelors refused child support accused the agency of discrimination.
High contrast, the, unambiguous	The bachelors who were refused child support accused the agency of discrimination.
High contrast, only, unambiguous	Only bachelors who were refused child support accused the agency of discrimination.
Low contrast, the, ambiguous	The social workers refused child support accused the agency of discrimination.
Low contrast, only, ambiguous	Only social workers who were refused child support accused the agency of discrimination.
Low contrast, the, unambiguous	The social workers who were refused child support accused the agency of discrimination.
Low contrast, only, unambiguous	Only social workers who were refused child support accused the agency of discrimination.

containing *who were*. The resulting 32 sets of sentences were combined with 64 filler sentences of a variety of forms (including several sentences beginning with *Only N* but not continuing with a postnominal modifier). Twenty-four of the experimental sentences, and 36 of the filler sentences, were followed by a two-choice or true–false question. Sixteen of the experimental sentence questions queried the roles involved in the relative clause (e.g., [Some] bachelors/social workers warned someone of the perils; true or false?), while the remaining questions asked about a variety of aspects of the sentences they followed.

Thirty-two members of the University of Massachusetts community were tested in individual 40-min sessions using a Fourward Technologies DPI Eyetracker. Following initial calibration and an 8-item practice list, each subject received an individually randomized presentation of the 96 sentences in the experimental list. Each trial began with a calibration check, followed by the presentation of the sentence on an 80-character wide VGA display (of which at most 72 characters were used). The subject's eye fixations were recorded from the presentation of the sentence until s/he pressed a key to terminate the sentence. A question, if there was one, appeared immediately afterwards, with its two possible answers on the right and the left of the screen, and the subject pressed one of two corresponding keys.

The resulting eyetracking data were scored in a variety of ways, as is conventional in analyzing such data (Rayner, Sereno, Morris, Schmauder and Clifton, 1989). Each experimental sentence was divided into six regions. Region 1 was the subject NP, Region 2 was the *who were* phrase that appeared in the unambiguous versions (a null region in the ambiguous versions), Region 3 was the ambiguous region except for the last word or two, which was scored as Region 4 if it appeared at the beginning of the second line of text (so that no analysis regions would wrap across two lines), Region 5 was the first few words of the disambiguating region (as needed to provide at least eight characters or go to the end of the first line), and Region 6 was the remainder of the sentence. We will present first pass times, 'go-past' times, and second pass times. We view the first two measures as most sensitive to early processes of sentence comprehension, and the third measure as primarily sensitive to processes of recovering from initial processing difficulty. First pass times are the sum of all fixation durations from first entering the region to first leaving it, ignoring trials on which the region was skipped. 'Go-past' times (otherwise known as regression path duration; Konieczny, Hemforth, Scheepers and Strube, 1997; Liversedge, Paterson and Pickering, 1998) are the sum of all fixation durations from first entering a region to first going past it to the right, again ignoring skipped regions. Second pass times are defined here as the sum of all fixation durations in a region after the eye has first gone past the region to the right and then returned to the region; failures to return are counted as zero durations. In all cases, we will present reading times in milliseconds, not corrected for length of region.

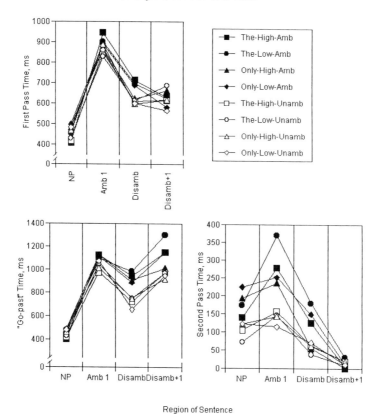

Fig. 4. Means of eyetracking measures for each analysis region, Experiment 3. Top left panel: first pass times. Bottom left panel: go-past times (regression path durations). Bottom right panel: second pass times. All times in ms.

The mean first pass times appear in Fig. 4, top panel (eliminating times from the *who were* region of the unambiguous sentences, and from Region 4 which was present only when the ambiguous region included one or two words at the beginning of the second line). The data from the disambiguating region appear in the top left panel of Fig. 5 as well. Clear disruption of reading can be seen in the disambiguating region of temporarily ambiguous sentences relative to unambiguous controls, *except* in one case: ambiguous high-contrast noun sentences with *only*. The mean reading time for this condition, 623 ms, did not differ from the four unambiguous conditions (599 to 614 ms). This finding is perplexing for several reasons. First, the condition that seems to have been facilitated by *only* was the condition with *high*-contrast nouns, not the condition with low-contrast nouns that should have benefitted if *only* guides initial parsing decisions. The condition with a high-contrast noun, by the logic laid out above, should have acted like Ni et al.'s

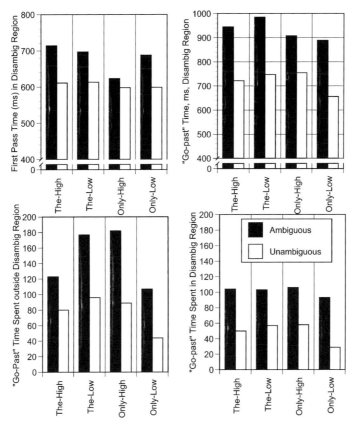

Fig. 5. Means of eyetracking measures for disambiguating region (or predisambiguating regions). Top left: first pass times. Top right: total go-past times. Bottom left: go-past time spent outside disambiguating region (sum of durations fixating in regions prior to disambiguating region from first entering disambiguating region to first going past disambiguating region). Bottom right: go-past time spent inside disambiguating region (sum of durations fixating disambiguating region from first entering disambiguating region to first going past disambiguating region). All times in ms.

Experiment 1 adjective condition. The phrase *Only bachelors*, with a high-contrast noun, invites construction of the contrast set of married men, just as adding the adjective in *Only dishonest students* invites the construction of the contrast set of honest students. In each case, following the Ni et al. logic, a reader should not need a postnominal modifier to create a contrast set for a high-contrast noun. Yet this is just the condition in which an ambiguous postnominal phrase seems to be read most easily as a modifying relative clause.

The second perplexing aspect of the data is that the main effect of ambiguity is the only significant effect in an analysis of variance conducted on the first pass time data. Reading time in the disambiguating region was 680 ms for the ambiguous condition, 606 ms for the unambiguous condition ($F_1(1, 31) = 11.50$; $F_2(1, 31) = 15.84$, $p < 0.01$). Each individual contrast between an unambiguous condition and its control was significant, except for the high-contrast *only* sentences (SE of a difference $= 38$ ms). The only other effect that approached significance was the main effect of *only* vs. *the*; sentences with *only* were read faster, 627 vs. 659 ms ($F_1(1, 31) = 3.10$, $p < 0.10$; $F_2(1, 31) = 2.58$, $p < 0.12$). The interactions that would support a differential facilitation of high-contrast *only* ambiguous sentences in no case had an F larger than 1.2.

Some insight into the data can be gathered by examining 'go-past' times (panel 2 of Fig. 4 and panels 2–4 of Fig. 5). These times are longer than first pass times to the extent that the eye regressed out of the disambiguating region rather than lingering in it and then going past. Regressions from the disambiguating region were rather infrequent (9% of the time in the *only* low-contrast condition, 14 to 18% of the time in the other conditions). However, re-reading was long enough when regressions did occur to indicate substantial disruption in the disambiguating region for *all* temporarily ambiguous conditions. Mean overall go-past time (the sum of all fixations from first entering a region to first going past it) was 932 ms in the disambiguating region for temporarily ambiguous items and 720 ms for unambiguous controls ($F_1(1, 31) = 30.23$; $F_2(1, 31) = 23.35$, $p < 0.01$). Times were longer in the ambiguous than in the unambiguous condition for each individual condition (SE of a difference $= 67$ ms; smallest difference $= 154$ ms, in the high-contrast *only* condition). While the first pass times taken by themselves would (apart from statistical nonsignificance) lead one to conclude that *only* eliminated garden-pathing for high-contrast nouns, the go-past times clearly indicated that disruption was still present in this condition. As suggested by Liversedge et al. (1998), this pattern of results may simply reflect different patterns of recovering from a misanalysis in the high-contrast *only* condition than in the other conditions: rather than letting the eyes linger in the disambiguating region while the repair is effected, the reader moves his or her eyes back to an earlier region to revise the analysis.

The time taken to go past the disambiguating region, after first entering it, can be broken down into two components: the time spent re-reading material that precedes the disambiguating region, and the time spent re-reading the disambiguating region itself after having regressed out of it (see Chapter 19 for discussion of such an analysis). Panels 3 and 4 of Fig. 5 present these data. In both cases (as in all other measures reported here), only trials on which the disambiguating region was fixated were included. However, trials on which the reader did not regress out of the disambiguating region were included in the analyses, contributing 0 ms fixation durations. The measure of panel 3, go-past time before the disambiguating region, was longer for ambiguous than for unambiguous sentences, 148 vs. 78 ms ($F_1(1, 31) = 9.86$, $F_2(1, 31) = 8.33$, $p < 0.01$). No other effect or interaction

approached significance apart from the interaction of *only* vs. *the* and high vs. low
($F_1(1, 31) = 5.44$, $p < 0.03$; $F_2(1, 31) = 2.83$, $p < 0.11$). The *only*–high and *the*–
low conditions resulted in relatively long times to re-read the pre-disambiguating
regions before going past the disambiguating region. The measure of panel 4, time
spent in the disambiguating region after regressing from it and before going past it,
also was longer for ambiguous than for unambiguous sentences ($F_1(1, 31) = 7.62$,
$p < 0.01$; $F_2(1, 31) = 5.48$, $p < 0.03$). In this case, no other effect or interaction
approached significance.

Inspection of the third panel of Fig. 4, second pass times, sheds a little light
on these data. Consider the initial NP and ambiguous regions as well as the disambiguating region. Second pass reading time (which includes the outside-region
'go-past' times just discussed, plus re-reading times that occurred after the eye had
gone beyond the disambiguating region) was longer in the sentence-initial NP for
ambiguous than for unambiguous sentences (284 vs. 140 ms; $F_1(1, 31) = 26.34$;
$F_2(1, 31) = 24.28$, $p < 0.01$). In addition, second pass times were longer for
sentences with *only* than for sentences with *the* (166 vs. 123 ms; $F_1(1, 31) = 8.62$;
$F_2(1, 31) = 9.03$, $p < 0.01$). While no interaction with ambiguity was significant,
examination of the data from the ambiguous sentences alone indicated significantly
longer second pass times in the sentence-initial NP for *only* than for *the* (209 vs.
156 ms; $F_1(1, 31) = 4.17$; $F_2(1, 31) = 4.44$, $p < 0.05$). The interaction with
contrast had an $F < 1$.

Second pass times in the ambiguous region seemed to show a different pattern.
Again, second pass times were longer for ambiguous than unambiguous sentences
(284 vs. 140 ms; $F_1(1, 31) = 26.55$; $F_2(1, 31) = 21.50$, $p < 0.01$). But here,
second pass times were nonsignificantly shorter for *only* than for *the* (244 vs. 324
ms; $F_1(1, 31) = 3.01$, $p < 0.10$; $F_2(1, 31) = 1.75$, $p < 0.20$), whereas they had
been longer for *only* in the NP region.

In the disambiguating region, second pass times were longer for ambiguous than
for unambiguous sentences (128 vs. 58 ms; $F_1(1, 31) = 13.94$, $F_2(1, 31) = 9.93$,
$p < 0.01$). In addition, the main effect of high vs. low contrast approached significance, and its interaction with ambiguity was fully significant ($F_1(1, 31) = 6.61$,
$p < 0.02$; $F_2(1, 31) = 5.25$, $p < 0.03$). Sentences with low-contrast initial nouns
were re-read longer in the disambiguating region than sentences with high-contrast
initial nouns, at least for ambiguous sentences (166 vs. 89 ms) but not for unambiguous controls (54 vs. 62 ms). Further, the interaction between ambiguity and *the*
vs. *only* approached significance ($F_1(1, 31) = 3.48$, $p < 0.08$; $F_2(1, 31) = 3.33$,
$p < 0.08$). Re-reading was longer for *the* than for *only*, but only for ambiguous
sentences (150 vs. 105 ms), not for unambiguous ones (54 vs. 63 ms).

In summary, while the traditional first-pass measure did not indicate any disruption of reading for temporarily ambiguous sentences in the *only*–high-contrast
condition, the other measures did indicate substantial disruption. It would not be

legitimate to conclude that the focus particle *only* eliminated garden-pathing in this condition. While the resolving power of the go-past and second-pass measures was not sufficient to specify precisely what the eye did in recovering from disambigua-tion in the *only*–high condition, these measures do suggest that re-reading of the initial NP containing *only* was substantial, more than when the initial NP contained *the*, and that the opposite may have occurred in the ambiguous region. Further, these measures indicate that the eye spent extra time in the disambiguating region after having regressed out of it but before going past it, and that still more time was spent re-reading this region after having gone past it, especially for the low-contrast and the *the* conditions.

Post-hoc sentence completion norms

The data that have been presented suggest, on balance, that the focus particle *only* did not eliminate garden-pathing but may have affected the course of recovery from a misanalysis. Having a high-contrast initial noun, such as *winner*, simi-larly speeded repair. The two interacted in a peculiar way, quite different from what was expected if *only* guided the analysis of the postnominal material, in influencing whether the eye would linger in the disambiguating region follow-ing a temporary ambiguity or whether it would quickly regress out to an earlier region.

It is very clear that the prediction based on Ni et al. (1996) that garden-pathing would be eliminated only in the low-contrast–*only* condition, was mistaken. This prediction was founded on the analysis advocated by Ni et al. that the phrase *Only N* with a low-contrast noun would lead a reader to expect that a postnominal modifier would be present to produce a contrast set. We conducted a final questionnaire study to assess this analysis, by presenting readers with the beginning of a sentence and having them complete it. Twenty University of Massachusetts undergraduates were given fragments of each of the ambiguous sentences used in the eyetracking experiment. Each subject saw 32 sentence fragments. Half of the fragments had the determiner *the* and half had the focus particle *only*. Orthogonally, half the fragments had a high-contrast noun and half a low-contrast noun, and half continued with the verb used in the experiment (e.g., *Only bachelors warned* . . .) while half contained just the determiner and the noun (*Only bachelors* . . .).

The most illuminating result was the frequency with which our subjects provided a postnominal modifier in their completion. The analysis of Ni et al. (1996) claims that this should be the preferred, even obligatory, completion of an *Only N* phrase, at least for a low-contrast noun. However, of the 640 possible completions in our experiment, precisely *one* contained a postnominal modifier.

This result certainly casts doubt on the analysis of relative clause usage that underlies the Ni et al. proposal. It buttresses the results of Fox and Thompson

(1990) described earlier in showing that it is no longer reasonable to analyze relative clauses solely in terms of how they select from among existing sets of discourse entities or how they create contrast sets of entities. These are certainly possible uses of relative clauses, but not uses that are so dominant that they form the basis of the initial decisions made by the parser in assigning structure to an ambiguous string of words.

Conclusions

Ni et al. (1996) provided dramatic support for the 'referential theory' first advanced by Crain and Steedman (1985). Their evidence indicated that the long-observed difficulty of reduced relative clauses, such as *The horse raced past the barn fell*, could be modulated and even totally eliminated by subtle semantic factors, such as whether the focus particle *only* and an adjective preceded the initial noun. Extensions of their results, reported by Crain et al. (1996), even indicated that the normally preferred main clause resolution of these sentences could be made to be a disruptive 'garden-path' sentence by the presence of *only*.

The present results give reason to question the results of Ni, Crain and their colleagues. Two attempts to replicate some of the Ni et al. experiments, using their materials and their filler items, failed quite notably. This failure to replicate is reinforced by the failure of Paterson et al. (1999) to obtain the Ni et al. results with the particular materials they used. The present Experiment 3 can also be seen as a failure to obtain the Ni et al. effects. Evidence of reading disruption was present in all ambiguous conditions, as long as one is willing to look beyond first pass reading times.

Some psycholinguists may take the lack of evidence of disruption of first pass reading times in the high-contrast–*only* condition to favor the Ni et al. position. After all, they might argue, the debate is about initial sentence analyses, and first pass reading times have been the measure of choice for identifying initial sentence analysis effects. This argument is unfortunately too simplistic. Showing that some manipulation creates a first pass (or even first fixation) effect actually provides evidence about how quickly a misanalysis is noticed and how quickly its revision begins. If disruption begins during the first pass reading of a disambiguating region, it is reasonable to conclude that some commitment was made earlier to an inappropriate analysis. Disruption that appears only later in the sentence, after the eye has gone past the disambiguating region, can too easily be ascribed to processes of deciding among alternative computed analyses or of integrating the interpretations of different phrases of the sentence.

Quickly observed disruption does not have to take the form of long first pass times (cf. Liversedge et al., 1998). First pass times (or, more conventionally, gaze durations) on individual words may well be the measure of choice in analyzing the process of lexical access and it may well be that the process of identifying individual words controls the normal process of moving the eyes forward through a text (Chapter 27). However, the disruption that we seem to be observing in our garden-path sentences goes beyond the boundaries of normal eye movement control. Such disruptions can result in long first pass times, but they can also take the form of rapid regressions from the disambiguating region followed by the search for information to resolve the conflict between the presumed initial interpretation and the disambiguation. The various versions of the go-past (regression path analysis) measure are designed to reflect such regression and search (cf. Chapter 19 for further discussion). The fact that this measure demonstrated disruption in all conditions of the present experiment indicates that our readers were in fact garden-pathed, regardless of the presence of *only*.

We doubt that the focus particle *only* sets up a requirement for a contrast set that overrides the parser's normal reluctance to analyze a verb as beginning a postnominal modifier. We believe that the readers in the experiments we reported here initially favored the main clause analysis of the temporarily ambiguous verb that followed the subject and were disrupted in their reading when this analysis proved to be incorrect. However, we also believe that the focus particle *only* facilitated recovery from the main clause analysis. The requirement for a set contrasting with the noun that *only* focuses can be met by modifying the noun, which does provide the reader with a reason for analyzing the material that follows the noun as a modifying relative clause.

Having a subject noun with a clear intrinsic contrast set (as our high-contrast nouns did) also seemed to facilitate eventually arriving at a relative clause interpretation of the temporarily ambiguous material. This may seem strange. After all, if the noun provides an intrinsic contrast set, the relative clause is not needed for that purpose (just as it was not needed in Ni et al.'s analysis when the noun had a prenominal modifier). One possible account was suggested in the introduction to Experiment 3. This account suggests that, when the contrast set required by *only* is not provided by the discourse context, a reader may be reluctant to create one before the end of the sentence. Material after the sentence may provide the needed discourse context. However, when other factors within the sentence encourage creation of a contrast set, the reader may be more willing to create one. The presence of a high-contrast noun after *only* is one such factor. Once the possibility of creating a contrast set has been raised, the reader may be more willing to create others, including the one created by interpreting the material following the noun as a modifying relative clause. Forming contrast sets is certainly one function of a relative clause, and invoking this function does allow the reader to assign a coherent and eventually successful analysis to the misanalyzed material.

This account is speculative, to be sure. We must acknowledge that our experimental sentences were made up with high-contrast nouns in mind, and low-contrast nouns were selected to match them in plausibility. However, there may be subtle differences, not involving contrast, between our high- and low-contrast sentences that we have not been able to identify. Even in this case, we are left with the puzzle of identifying the difference that would make our high-contrast nouns prefer to have a postnominal modifier. Further, we must admit that our present data do not let us determine with certainty just what interpretation our readers eventually came to. They may have taken *Only bachelors warned of the perils of marriage* to contrast either with bachelors who were not warned of the perils of marriage, or to contrast with nonbachelors plus unwarned bachelors (or they may not have fully specified the contrast set).

Pulling back slightly from our focus on *only* and postnominal modifiers, we can note that the general topic with which we are dealing is an extremely important one: how does the human sentence processor integrate the syntactic and semantic requirements of its grammar? The original garden-path theory gave one relatively simple answer: the processor first computes syntactic structures and then interprets them, and difficulties of interpretation (or perhaps the availability of tempting alternative thematic role assignments; Rayner, Carlson and Frazier, 1983) trigger a process of reanalysis. The referential theory of Crain and Steedman (1985) gave another simple answer: semantics provides the basis for choosing among alternative analyses. Various current lines of research suggest that both these positions are too simple, or at least that they are underspecified. To take just one instance, Konieczny and Hemforth (Chapter 19) analyze the contrast among pronouns, relative clauses, and prepositional phrases, suggesting that considerations of a preference for a local syntactic attachment site and preferences for satisfying semantic and discourse requirements play different roles in analyzing the different types of phrases (cf. also Chapter 18). We submit that the analysis of processing at the syntax–semantics interface will prove to be rich and interesting, and hope that the research reported here (and other approaches described in Clifton and Frazier, in prep. and Frazier, 1999, 2000) helps to advance the analysis.

Appendix A

High- and low-contrast noun pairs used in Experiment 3 (high contrast first): bachelors/social workers; children/players; conservatives/managers; democrats/staff people; employers/accountants; guests/relatives; winners/boxers; amateurs/biologists; freshmen/athletes; newcomers/housewives; nurses/engineers; rabbis/bankers; strangers/residents; teachers/researchers; undergraduates/translators; vegetarians/nutritionists.

Acknowledgements

The research reported in this chapter was supported in part by Grant HD-18708 to the University of Massachusetts. Author Radó is now at the University of Tuebingin, Tuebingin, Germany. We would like to thank Jennifer Boltuch, Vanessa Castagna, Anthony Luneau, Katie McSheehy, Julie Moore, and Janira Vazquez for their assistance in collecting the data reported here, and Lyn Frazier for her comments on an earlier version of the chapter. Copies of the materials used in Experiment 3 are available from the first author at cec@psych.umass.edu.

References

Bever, T.G. (1970). The cognitive basis for linguistic structures. In: J.R. Hayes (Ed.), Cognition and the Development of Language. New York: Wiley, pp. 279–352.

Boland, J.E. and Boehm-Jernigan, H. (1998). Lexical constraints and prepositional phrase attachment. Journal of Memory and Language, 39, 684–719.

Clifton, C., Jr. (2000). Evaluating models of sentence processing. In: M. Crocker, M. Pickering and J.C. Clifton (Eds.), Architecture and Mechanisms of Language Processing. Cambridge: Cambridge University Press.

Clifton, C., Jr. and Ferreira, F. (1989). Ambiguity in context. Language and Cognitive Processes, 4, 77–104.

Clifton, C., Jr. and Frazier, L. (1995). Crossover: Garden-paths in syntactically simple sentences? Unpublished paper, University of Massachusetts.

Clifton, C., Jr. and Frazier, L. (in prep.). Processing 'd-linked' phrases.

Clifton, C., Jr., Speer, S. and Abney, S. (1991). Parsing arguments: Phrase structure and argument structure as determinants of initial parsing decisions. Journal of Memory and Language, 30, 251–271.

Crain, S., Ni, W., Shankweiler, Conway, L. and Braze, D. (1996). Meaning, memory and modularity. Paper presented at the NELS 26 Sentence Processing Workshop, Cambridge, MA.

Crain, S. and Steedman, M. (1985). On not being led up the garden path: The use of context by the psychological parser. In: D. Dowty, L. Kartunnen and A. Zwicky (Eds.), Natural Language Parsing. Cambridge: Cambridge University Press, pp. 320–358.

Ferreira, F. and Clifton, C., Jr. (1986). The independence of syntactic processing. Journal of Memory and Language, 25, 348–368.

Fox, B.A. and Thompson, S.A. (1990). A discourse explanation of the grammar of relative clauses in English conversation. Language, 66, 297–316.

Frazier, L. (1979). On Comprehending Sentences: Syntactic Parsing Strategies. Bloomington, IN: Indiana University Linguistics Club.

Frazier, L. (1987). Sentence processing: a tutorial review. In: M. Coltheart (Ed.), Attention and Performance. Hillsdale, NJ: Lawrence Erlbaum Associates, pp. 559–586.

Frazier, L. (1990). Exploring the architecture of the language system. In: G. Altmann (Ed.), Cognitive Models of Speech Processing: Psycholinguistic and Computational Perspectives. Cambridge, MA: MIT Press, pp. 409–433.

Frazier, L. (1995). Constraint satisfaction as a theory of sentence processing. Journal of Psycholinguistic Research, 24, 437–468.

Frazier, L. (1999). On Sentence Interpretation. Dordrecht: Kluwer.

Frazier, L. (2000). Minimal lowering. In: M. Crocker, M. Pickering and C. Clifton Jr. (Eds.), Architecture and Mechanisms of Language Processing. Cambridge: Cambridge University Press, pp. 303–323.

Frazier, L. and Clifton, C., Jr. (1996). Construal. Cambridge, MA: MIT Press.

Frazier, L. and Rayner, K. (1982). Making and correcting errors during sentence comprehension: eye movements in the analysis of structurally ambiguous sentences. Cognitive Psychology, 14, 178–210.

Konieczny, L., Hemforth, B., Scheepers, C. and Strube, G. (1997). The role of lexical heads in parsing: evidence from German. Language and Cognitive Processes, 12, 307–348.

Liversedge, S.P., Paterson, K.B. and Pickering, M.J. (1998). Eye movements and measures of reading time. In: G. Underwood (Ed.), Eye Guidance While Reading and Watching Dynamic Scenes. Oxford: Elsevier, pp. 55–75.

MacDonald, M.C., Pearlmutter, N.J. and Seidenberg, M.S. (1994). Lexical nature of syntactic ambiguity resolution. Psychological Review, 101, 676–703.

Murray, W.S. and Liversedge, S.P. (1994). Referential context effects on syntactic processing. In: C. Clifton, L. Frazier and K. Rayner (Eds.), Perspectives on Sentence Processing. Hillsdale, NJ: Lawrence Erlbaum Associates.

Ni, W., Crain, S. and Shankweiler, D. (1996). Sidestepping garden paths: assessing the contributions of syntax, semantics and plausibility in resolving ambiguities. Language and Cognitive Processes, 11, 283–334.

Paterson, K.B., Liversedge, S.P. and Underwood, G. (1999). The influence of focus operators on syntactic processing of short relative clause sentences. Quarterly Journal of Experimental Psychology, 52A, 717–737.

Radó, J. (1996). Focus interpretation: limitations on the use of context. Paper presented at the Ninth Annual CUNY Conference on Human Sentence Processing, New York, March 21–23, 1996.

Radó, J. (1997). Processing Hungarian: The Role of Topic and Focus in Language Comprehension. Unpublished PhD dissertation, University of Massachusetts.

Rayner, K., Carlson, M. and Frazier, L. (1983). The interaction of syntax and semantics during sentence processing: eye movements in the analysis of semantically biased sentences. Journal of Verbal Learning and Verbal Behavior, 22, 358–374.

Rayner, K., Garrod, S. and Perfetti, C. (1992). Discourse influences during parsing are delayed. Cognition, 45, 109–139.

Rayner, K., Sereno, S., Morris, R., Schmauder, R. and Clifton, C.J. (1989). Eye movements and on-line language comprehension processes. Language and Cognitive Processes, 4, 21–50.

Speer, S. and Clifton, C., Jr. (1998). Plausibility and argument structure in sentence comprehension. Memory and Cognition, 26, 965–979.

Spivey-Knowlton, M.J., Trueswell, J.C. and Tanenhaus, M.K. (1993). Context effects in syntactic ambiguity resolution: discourse and semantic influences in parsing reduced relative clauses. Canadian Journal of Experimental Psychology, 47, 276–309.

Steedman, M.J. and Altmann, G.T.M. (1989). Ambiguity in context: a reply. Language and Cognitive Processes, 4, 77–105.

Trueswell, J.C. and Tanenhaus, M. (1991). Tense, temporal context and syntactic ambiguity resolution. Language and Cognitive Processes, 6, 303–338.

Trueswell, J.C., Tanenhaus, M.K. and Garnsey, S.M. (1994). Semantic influences on parsing: Use of thematic role information in syntactic disambiguation. Journal of Memory and Language, 33, 285–318.

CHAPTER 24

Unrestricted Race: A New Model of Syntactic Ambiguity Resolution

Roger P.G. van Gompel
University of Glasgow

Martin J. Pickering
University of Glasgow

and

Matthew J. Traxler
Florida State University and University of Glasgow

Abstract

In this chapter, we focus on a previously ignored aspect of sentence processing theories: is processing difficulty caused by reanalysis or competition? According to two-stage theories (e.g., Frazier, 1979; Rayner, Carlson and Frazier, 1983), reanalysis should occur when an initially adopted reading is inappropriate. In contrast, current constraint-based theories (e.g., MacDonald, 1994; McRae, Spivey-Knowlton and Tanenhaus, 1998) claim that processing difficulty is due to a competition between two or more syntactic analyses that are about equally activated. We review a number of eye-tracking experiments investigating this issue. No competition was observed in any of the experiments, thus ruling out current constraint-based theories. In fact, the opposite pattern emerged: sentences that should have produced processing difficulty according to constraint-based theories were actually easier to process than sentences that should not have produced difficulty. The data also turn out to be problematic for two-stage theories, as non-syntactic information appears to be employed before the point of reanalysis. The data provide evidence for a new model of syntactic ambiguity resolution (cf. Traxler, Pickering and Clifton, 1998; Van Gompel, Pickering and Traxler, 1999), the unrestricted race model. In this model, processing difficulty is due to reanalysis, but multiple sources of information can determine which analysis is initially adopted.

Reading as a Perceptual Process/A. Kennedy, R. Radach, D. Heller and J. Pynte (Editors)
© 2000 Elsevier Science Ltd. All rights reserved

Introduction: Two-stage versus constraint-based theories

Current sentence processing theories can roughly be divided into two fundamentally different classes which make very different claims about the architecture of the language processor. One class of theories are what we will call the two-stage theories. The garden-path theory, initially proposed by Frazier (1979; see also Ferreira and Clifton, 1986; Frazier, 1987; Rayner, Carlson and Frazier, 1983), has been the most influential of these theories, but there are other theories which are very similar in their basic assumptions, although they differ in many details (e.g., Abney, 1989; Crocker, 1995; Inoue and Fodor, 1995; Pickering, 1994; Pritchett, 1992). Many of the basic ideas of these theories date back from Bever (1970) and Kimball (1973), and they are strongly influenced by the modularity hypothesis (Fodor, 1983; Forster, 1979). One of the basic assumptions that two-stage theories make is that some potentially useful sources of information are initially ignored in sentence processing, because the sentence processor is informationally encapsulated. In the garden-path theory, for example, only information about syntactic tree structures can be used initially, and all other sources of information, such as thematic roles, discourse context, semantic plausibility and lexical frequency, are ignored during this initial stage. Other theories assume that information such as thematic roles (e.g., Pritchett, 1992; Abney, 1989) is used initially. By virtue of the fact that some sources of information are used later than others, all these models share the assumption that the processor works in two stages. In the first stage, the processor adopts one analysis on the basis of a restricted range of information. In the second stage, other sources of information are employed. If the initial analysis of an ambiguous syntactic structure is incorrect, another analysis is pursued. This reanalysis process causes processing disruption (a garden-path effect).

The second class of theories are the constraint-based theories, which are descended from older interactive theories (e.g., Marslen-Wilson, 1975; Taraban and McClelland, 1988; Tyler and Marslen-Wilson, 1977). Since the early 1990s, constraint-based theories have become the dominant type of account of sentence processing. Recently, these models have been worked out in more detail, so that it is possible to derive some predictions from them (e.g., MacDonald, Pearlmutter and Seidenberg, 1994; McRae, Spivey-Knowlton and Tanenhaus, 1998; Tabor, Juliano and Tanenhaus, 1997). All constraint-based theories stipulate that the processor works in a single stage and that it can employ all sources of information immediately. Because all relevant information can be employed immediately, there should be no reason to predict differences between on-line preferences while people are reading a sentence, and off-line preferences such as measured by sentence fragment completion studies. Constraint-based theories assume a parallel processor: different possible analyses of an ambiguous syntactic structure are activated simultaneously by the various sources of information and compete with each other until a certain threshold level is reached (e.g., McRae et al., 1998). When one analysis receives more support than the others, little competition occurs between the analyses, resulting in little processing difficulty. But when one or more alternative analyses are about equally activated, there is a strong competition between the analyses, which should lead to processing difficulty.

Constraint-based theories usually claim that this process of competition is exactly the same as in lexical processing (e.g., MacDonald et al., 1994). A number of studies on lexical ambiguity resolution observed that ambiguous words for which both meanings were equally high in frequency (balanced words) were read more slowly than their unambiguous controls, whereas ambiguous words that had a frequency bias toward one meaning (biased words) were read as fast as unambiguous control words (e.g., Duffy, Morris and Rayner, 1988; Rayner and Duffy, 1986; Rayner and Frazier, 1989). This can be interpreted as evidence for a process of competition between two meanings of a balanced ambiguous word. Similarly, when biased words were put in preceding contexts favouring the low frequency meaning, reading times were slower than when they were put in a context favouring the high frequency meaning (e.g., Dopkins, Morris and Rayner, 1992; Duffy et al., 1988; Rayner and Frazier, 1989; Rayner, Pacht and Duffy, 1994; Sereno, Pacht and Rayner, 1992). This is also consistent with a competition process between two alternative meanings. Therefore, if syntactic ambiguity resolution is indeed similar to lexical ambiguity resolution, competition effects should obtain in syntactic ambiguities as well.

On the other hand, some proponents of two-stage sentence processing theories claim that syntactic and lexical ambiguity resolution are fundamentally different (e.g., Frazier, 1989; Rayner and Morris, 1991; Traxler et al., 1998; Van Gompel et al., 1999). Competition may arise in lexical ambiguity resolution, but by virtue of its serial architecture, it cannot arise in syntactic ambiguity resolution.

The unrestricted race model

In Van Gompel et al. (1999; cf. Traxler et al., 1998) we proposed an alternative to current sentence processing models, the unrestricted race model, which we will describe in more detail here. This model combines properties of both constraint-based and two-stage models, but is different from both. As in constraint-based theories, there is no restriction on the sources of information that can provide support for the different analyses of an ambiguous structure; hence it is *unrestricted*. In the model, the alternative structures of a syntactic ambiguity are engaged in a race, with the structure that is constructed fastest being adopted. The more sources of information support a syntactic analysis and the stronger this support is, the more likely this analysis will be constructed first. The model claims that when the various sources of information strongly favour one analysis over its alternative (a biased ambiguity), this analysis will nearly always be adopted. In contrast, when two analyses are about equally preferred (a balanced ambiguity), each analysis will be adopted about half the time. A weak bias, however, might lead to one analysis being adopted most, but not all of the time. This is one way the unrestricted race model can account for gradations in garden-path effects (e.g., Garnsey, Pearlmutter, Myers and Lotocky, 1997; Trueswell, Tanenhaus and Kello, 1993; Trueswell, Tanenhaus and Garnsey, 1994; but see conclusions for further discussion of how graded garden-path effects may arise). In contrast to constraint-based theories, only one analysis is constructed at a time. Because only a single analysis is available at any time, reanalysis may sometimes be necessary if information following the initial analysis is inconsistent with it. Thus, the unrestricted race model is a two-stage reanalysis model.

The model assumes that the parser is strictly incremental. As it encounters each word, it checks whether the syntactic structure built so far is consistent with the new information provided by the word. If it is inconsistent with this information, reanalysis takes place, resulting in processing difficulty. There are logical restrictions on what information can be used first. Consider (1):

(1) While the guests were eating plates were brought in.

The verb *to eat* permits (at least) two analyses, corresponding to the transitive and intransitive uses of the verb. On the correct analysis in (1), *eating* is intransitive. However, the transitive analysis is initially preferred, at least for verbs which have a more frequent transitive than intransitive use (e.g., Clifton, 1993; Ferreira and Henderson, 1990; Frazier and Rayner, 1982; Pickering and Traxler, 1998). The semantic implausibility of *eating plates* in fact rules out this analysis in (1). However, because syntactic analysis is a prerequisite for semantic analysis, the processor cannot employ plausibility information immediately. The processor first needs to construct the direct object analysis before it can determine that it results in an implausible analysis. Thus, if the implausibility of the transitive analysis is sufficiently strong, reanalysis is predicted at *plates*, which is consistent with experimental evidence (Pickering and Traxler, 1998). Although semantic plausibility information can be used extremely rapidly, it cannot prevent a garden path occurring. Thus, the prediction that syntactic processing precedes semantic processing naturally falls out of the architecture of the model. It is not a property that has to be stipulated independently in the way informational encapsulation is in Fodor (1983).

Research suggests that there are similar restrictions on the use of other sources of information. For example, Traxler and Pickering (1996) investigated sentences such as (2):

(2a) I recognised she and her family would be unhappy here.

(Incongruent case marking)

(2b) I recognised you and your family would be unhappy here.
        (Congruent case marking)

The verb *recognised* can occur with a sentence complement, as in the ultimately correct analysis in (2), or with a direct object (as in *I recognised her*). The case marking of *she* in (2a) makes the direct object analysis impossible, whereas the case of *you* is ambiguous between a direct object and a subject analysis. Traxler et al. observed that readers experienced more difficulty in the region *she and her family* in (2a) than in *you and your family* in (2b). This suggests that this case is analogous to (1). As in (1), there is an initial preference to analyse the following noun phrase of the verb (*recognised*) as its direct object rather than as the subject of the following clause, at least for transitive biased verbs. Analogous to the use of semantic plausibility information, we assume that the processor first needs to construct the direct object analysis before it can assess that the case marking of *she* is inconsistent with it. Hence, reanalysis has to take place in (2a), resulting in processing difficulty compared to (2b).

The unrestricted race model claims that the use of non-syntactic information depends on where this information becomes available. If it occurs in the sentence at or after the point where the ambiguity arises, as in (1) and (2), it cannot be employed during the initial parse. But conversely, it predicts that non-syntactic information that precedes the point of ambiguity can be employed immediately. In the latter case, our claim is similar to that of current constraint-based theories. As an example of such a case, we will now consider (3):

(3) The hunter saw two poachers hiding behind the bushes.
       He killed the poacher with the rifle.

In the second sentence in (3), the prepositional phrase *with the rifle* is ambiguous between VP attachment (as in *killed with the rifle*) and NP attachment (as in *the poacher with the rifle*). In the absence of a context, such sentences normally demonstrate a preference for VP attachment (Britt, 1994; Britt, Perfetti, Garrod and Rayner, 1992; Clifton, Speer and Abney, 1991; Ni, Crain and Shankweiler, 1996; Rayner et al., 1983; Spivey-Knowlton and Sedivy, 1995; though cf. Taraban and McClelland, 1988). In (3), the preceding context sentence supports the NP attachment analysis. Because there are two poachers in the context, the second sentence is more felicitous if the prepositional phrase selects one of the two poachers — in other words, if the NP attachment analysis is adopted (cf. Crain and Steedman, 1985; Altmann and Steedman, 1988). Crucially, this discourse information can be used at *the poacher*, before the point where the ambiguity arises (at *with*), and therefore the unrestricted race model predicts that it will be used initially.

The claims that the unrestricted race model makes differ from both the garden-path theory (e.g., Frazier, 1979, 1987) and referential theory (e.g., Altmann and Steedman, 1988; Crain and Steedman, 1985). The garden-path theory claims that discourse information is completely ignored during initial processing and that readers always adopt VP attachment first, regardless of context. According to referential theory, the processor's initial decision is merely based on discourse information and therefore it should override any structural preferences. The unrestricted race model predicts that the initial analysis is based on both discourse information and a preference for VP attachment. Which analysis is adopted depends on the strength of both sources of information.

We think that current research supports the position of the unrestricted race model. For example, Britt (1994) showed that discourse information neutralised the VP attachment preference in verbs with an optional prepositional phrase, but did not override it. When the prepositional phrase was obligatory, there was no effect of context. This suggests that contextual neutralisation depends on the strength of the VP attachment preference. Furthermore, Britt et al. (1992) showed that contextual neutralisation occurred for VP/NP attachment ambiguities such as (3), but that context did not have a neutralising effect for reduced relative clause ambiguities (see, e.g., Bever, 1970; Rayner et al., 1983), which are more strongly biased towards one analysis. Both results are somewhat difficult to reconcile with referential and garden-path theory. According to referential theory, contextual information should always override (rather than neutralise) a bias that occurs when a sentence is presented in the absence of a context. This override should occur independently of whether a phrase is obligatory or not, and independently of the particular structure used. The garden-path theory claims that context should never neutralise or override a structural bias (but see Clifton and Ferreira, 1989). Because the unrestricted race model predicts that the strength of both syntactic and non-syntactic information determines whether neutralisation, override or neither takes place, the results are more consistent with this model. However, they are also consistent with current constraint-based theories (e.g., MacDonald et al., 1994; Spivey-Knowlton and Sedivy, 1995; Spivey-Knowlton, Trueswell and Tanenhaus, 1993), which make the same predictions.

As we shall see, the unrestricted race model makes different predictions from both two-stage and constraint-based theories with respect to when processing difficulty occurs. In order to test these new predictions and to contrast them with predictions from current two-stage and constraint-based theories, we conducted a number of experiments, which we will describe below. These experiments investigated a previously neglected issue: the question of whether processing difficulty is caused by competition or reanalysis.

Reanalysis or competition? Shedding new light on sentence processing theories

To date, a great deal of research on syntactic ambiguity resolution has attempted to distinguish between two-stage and constraint-based theories by investigating whether non-syntactic information can be employed immediately or not. Unfortunately, it hasn't reached a very clear conclusion, as proponents of both types of models usually claim that the data are compatible with their model. A number of studies have suggested that non-syntactic information such as lexical frequency information (Trueswell et al., 1993; Trueswell, 1996), discourse information (Altmann and Steedman, 1988; Altmann, Garnham and Dennis, 1992) and semantic information (Trueswell et al., 1994) can be employed extremely rapidly, which appears inconsistent with two-stage theories. However, proponents of two-stage theories have claimed that reanalysis can occur extremely rapidly when non-syntactic information is very strong, and that current methodologies such as self-paced reading or even eye-tracking may not be sensitive enough to detect garden-path effects in such cases (e.g., Clifton and Ferreira, 1989). Similarly, proponents of constraint-based theories respond to findings that non-syntactic information does not guide initial processing (e.g., Ferreira and Henderson, 1990; Ferreira and Clifton, 1986; Mitchell, 1987; Mitchell, Corley and Garnham, 1992; Rayner, Garrod and Perfetti, 1992) by claiming that the manipulation of non-syntactic information was not strong enough.

For this reason, we decided to focus on a currently neglected aspect of sentence processing theories: whether reanalysis or competition causes processing difficulty in syntactic ambiguity resolution. This question is a very important one, because, as we have described in the introduction, it discriminates between two fundamentally different architectures and distinguishes between the two main approaches in syntactic processing. Furthermore, it addresses the question of whether syntactic and lexical ambiguity resolution show the same characteristics, or whether they are completely different. Therefore, it is perhaps surprising that there has been very little research to investigate competition versus reanalysis and that the few studies which did claim to provide evidence for one or the other are in fact equivocal on a closer inspection.

Some of the first researchers who claimed to have found evidence for reanalysis were Rayner et al. (1983). They tested sentences such as (4), which are syntactically ambiguous between VP and NP attachment:

(4a) The spy saw the cop with a revolver but the cop didn't see him.

(NP attachment)

(4b) The spy saw the cop with the binoculars but the cop didn't see him.

(VP attachment)

Sentences like (4a) were semantically disambiguated towards NP attachment, whereas sentences like (4b) involved VP attachment (although many items were in fact semantically ambiguous). Rayner et a!. observed that (4a) took longer to read than (4b) and took this as evidence for a reanalysis process in (4a). They claimed that the processor initially pursued the structurally simpler VP attachment analysis (as in *see with the binoculars*) in both sentences. Because this analysis resulted in an implausible analysis in (4a), reanalysis had to take place, which caused the longer reading times compared to (4b), where no such reanalysis was necessary.

However, these results can easily be accounted for in a constraint-based frame-work assuming competition (cf. Spivey-Knowlton and Sedivy, 1995). Because the VP attachment analysis is preferred (presumably due to frequency information) but plausibility supports the alternative NP attachment analysis (as in *the cop with a revolver*), a process of competition arises in (4a) but not in (4b) where both sources of information are consistent.

More recently, proponents of constraint-based theories have claimed to have found evidence for competition. For example, MacDonald (1994) tested sentences such as (5) which are temporally ambiguous between a main clause analysis (as in *The ruthless dictator fought in the coup ten years ago*) and a reduced relative clause (as in the ultimately correct analysis in [5]).

(5a) The ruthless dictator captured in the coup was hated throughout the country.

                                    (Good reduced relative constraint)

(5b) The ruthless dictator fought in the coup was hated throughout the country.

                                    (Bad reduced relative constraint)

She compared them with unambiguous base-line conditions that included *that was* after *dictator* and observed that the reading time difference between the ambiguous condition and the unambiguous control was greater for (5a) than (5b) in the region consisting of *captured/fought in the coup*. She attributed this difference to a competition process in (5a). In (5) the main clause analysis is activated because it occurs most frequently or is least complex. In (5a), however, *captured in the coup* is barely consistent with the main clause analysis and supports the reduced relative alternative. Hence, MacDonald claimed that this led to competition between the two analyses. No such competition occurred in (5b), because *fought in the coup* is compatible with the main clause analysis.

Although MacDonald's data were consistent with a competition mechanism and thus with constraint-based theories, they can also be explained in a two-stage framework. This approach predicts that readers initially adopt the main clause analysis because this is the preferred analysis, but subsequently have to revise this analysis in (5a), because *in the coup* makes this analysis highly unlikely. In (5b), reanalysis does not occur until *was hated*.

The same argument applies for an experiment by McRae et al. (1998), in which sentences such as (6) and their unambiguous controls (disambiguated by *that was*) were tested.

(6a) The crook arrested by the detective was guilty of taking bribes.

                                    (Implausible main clause)

(6b) The cop arrested by the detective was guilty of taking bribes.

(Plausible main clause)

In (6a) the reduced relative is plausible and the main clause analysis is not, whereas it is the other way around in (6b). McRae et al. observed an interaction between sentence type (6a) and (6b) and ambiguity (ambiguous vs. unambiguous sentences) in the ambiguous region *arrested by*. In (6a) this region was much more difficult to read than in its unambiguous control, whereas this difference was less pronounced in (6b). This is consistent with competition: in (6a), the main clause, which is activated because it is structurally simple or highly frequent, competes with the plausibility of the reduced relative and the information provided by *by*, which support the reduced relative clause analysis; whereas in (6b) both the preference for a main clause and plausibility support the main clause analysis and only *by* supports the alternative. Thus, competition should be less here, and their reading-time data was consistent with this prediction.

Indeed, the reading times mirrored findings from a sentence completion task. Sentence fragments up to and including *by* were nearly always completed as a main clause in (6b), but in (6a) completions as a main and reduced relative were about equally frequent. McRae et al. took the reading time results in combination with the completion data as evidence for competition and as support for their con-straint-based simulation. They went on to claim that the results are inconsistent with the garden-path model and with two-stage models in general. They supported this claim by building simulations of the garden-path model using the same competition model but with the modification that all constraints except the main clause bias were delayed. These garden-path simulations made less accurate predictions than the constraint-based simulation in which all constraints were used simultaneously.

However, the assumption that two-stage theories incorporate competition is incorrect; instead, they employ reanalysis. Hence, the simulations do not show that constraint-based models predict processing performance better than two-stage models. They merely show that in a competition architecture, immediate use of all information gives a more accurate prediction of processing than when some information is delayed. In fact, a two-stage processor can straightforwardly account for the data. On such an account, the main clause analysis is preferred and initially adopted in both (6a) and (6b). In (6a), the analysis becomes unlikely when the region *arrested by* is encountered, because the main clause analysis is implausible and because the *by*-phrase usually indicates a reduced relative analysis. Hence, reanalysis ensues and processing difficulty arises. In (6b), *arrested* is consistent with a main clause analysis and therefore no reanalysis should take place at this point. *By* can trigger reanalysis in the region *arrested by*, but McRae et al.'s completion data indicated that this constraint alone is not very strong, as about half of their participants completed (6b) as a main clause after *arrested by* ... .

This suggests that reanalysis did not always occur in this region in (6b), whereas reanalysis was much more frequent in (6a) (in which main clause completions were much less frequent). Thus, both reanalysis and competition theory predict that processing difficulty in the region *arrested by* should be less in (6b) than in (6a), and McRae et al.'s results can be accounted for by either theory.

Relative clause attachment experiments: Evidence against constraint-based theories and the garden-path model

Thus, the aforementioned studies do not allow us to distinguish between reanalysis and competition. In order to resolve this debate, we need a case where reanalysis and competition frameworks make different predictions. Such a case occurs in globally ambiguous structures in which two analyses are roughly equally preferred. Competition frameworks predict that such globally ambiguous sentences should be more difficult to process than sentences that are disambiguated. In a globally ambiguous sentence, more than one syntactic structure remains activated through-out the sentence and therefore competition should occur between the analyses, which ought to produce difficulty. But when a sentence is disambiguated, only one analysis remains activated and therefore no such competition should arise. In contrast, according to reanalysis frameworks, globally ambiguous sentences should never be more difficult than disambiguated sentences, because reanalysis should never occur for globally ambiguous sentences. Because the unrestricted race model is also a reanalysis model, it also predicts that ambiguous struc-tures can never be more difficult than disambiguated structures. But in contrast to other two-stage models, it claims that non-syntactic information can be em-ployed initially. This leads, as we shall see, to different predictions in a number of cases.

Traxler et al. (1998) (experiments 1 and 3) tested the predictions of the various theories in two eye-tracking experiments that used relative clause attachment ambiguities such as (7–8). (Three other conditions, which we will not discuss here, were included in the experiment that tested sentences like [7].)

(7a) The son of the driver that had the moustache was pretty cool.

(Ambiguous)

(7b) The car of the driver that had the moustache was pretty cool.

(NP2 attachment)

(7c) The driver of the car that had the moustache was pretty cool.

(NP1 attachment)

(8a) The steak with the sauce that was tasty didn't win a prize.

(Ambiguous)

(8b) The steak with the sauce that was runny didn't win a prize.

(NP2 attachment)

(8c) The steak with the sauce that was tough didn't win a prize.

(NP1 attachment)

All these sentences are syntactically ambiguous, in that the relative clause can be attached to the first noun phrase (NP1) or the second noun phrase (NP2) of the sentence. Each item had three conditions: a globally ambiguous condition (version a), a condition that was semantically disambiguated toward NP2 attachment (version b) and a condition semantically disambiguated toward NP1 attachment (version c). This plausibility manipulation was checked by off-line pretests.

Further off-line pretests were conducted to determine whether there was a preference for either NP1 or NP2 attachment. As we shall see, this is important to derive predictions from some of the models. Participants had to indicate which noun phrase they thought that the relative clause modified. This is a commonly used methodology to asses the bias in syntactically ambiguous sentences (e.g., Cuetos and Mitchell, 1988; Frazier and Clifton, 1996; Gilboy, Sopena, Clifton and Frazier, 1995; Hemforth, Konieczny and Scheepers, 2000). There was a clear bias toward NP2 attachment in sentences such as (8), with the preposition *with*. Participants indicated that the relative clause attached to NP2 81% of the time. The bias was much less pronounced in sentences such as (7), with the preposition *of*. Attachment to NP2 was chosen only 68% of the time. Because the plausibility norms indicated that the plausibility of the attachment sites did not differ, these percentages reflected the bias in the materials before the point where plausibility was manipulated (at *moustache* in [7] and *tasty/runny/tough* in [8]).

Constraint-based theories predict that the globally ambiguous condition (7a) should be more difficult to read than the disambiguated conditions (7b) and (7c). In (7a), the semantic plausibility constraint does not favour one analysis over the other, and neither is there a strong non-semantic preference that biases one analysis over the other. Therefore, competition should emerge in (7a). They predict fairly similar difficulty for (7b) and (7c), as the difference in preference (68% vs. 32%) was relatively small. If there is a difference, NP2 attachment should be easier than NP1 attachment, because the off-line pretest indicated that NP2 attachment is somewhat preferred.

In constraint-based theories, the degree of processing difficulty depends on the bias of the materials, as measured by the off-line pretests. These pretests indicated that the bias for NP2 was much stronger in (8) than in (7). Thus, the predictions for (8) are different. Little competition is predicted in the ambiguous condition (8a), because the non-semantic NP2 preference information activates one analysis much more than the other. If the bias is strong enough, the ambiguous condition should be no more difficult than the NP2 attachment condition (8b), in which both plausibility information and the bias for NP2 attachment favour the same analysis. Condition (8c) should be most difficult: there should be a competition between the preference for NP2 and plausibility information which disambiguates toward NP1.

The predictions of two-stage models are different. According to the garden-path model (Frazier, 1979, 1987; Rayner et al., 1983) the principle of late closure causes the processor to make an initial attachment to NP2 in both (7) and (8). It should not matter whether there is an off-line preference for NP2 attachment or not. When NP2 attachment is implausible, reanalysis should occur. This predicts reanalysis in (7c) and (8c), but no reanalysis should occur in the other conditions, because the initially adopted NP2 attachment is plausible.

Recently, Frazier and Clifton (1996) have presented a new theory of syntactic ambiguity resolution: construal. According to construal theory, syntactic relation-ships can be divided into two different types: primary and non-primary relations. Primary relations include the subject and predicate of a finite clause, and com-plements and obligatory constituents of primary relations. Other relations are non-primary. For primary relations, the processor behaves as in the garden-path model, with only one analysis being pursued at a time. In contrast, construal applies to non-primary relations: they are associated in the currently active theta domain (the entire extended maximal projection of the most recent theta assigner), which can contain more than one possible attachment site. The processor then decides which site in the active theta domain to attach the non-primary relation to, on the basis of both syntactic and non-syntactic information.

Relative clauses constitute non-primary relations. In (8), the active theta domain for the relative clause attachment is *with* + NP2 (i.e., *with the sauce*), because *with* assigns a theta role to NP2. Hence, only NP2 is available as attachment site and therefore NP2 attachment should always be initially adopted in (8), just as in garden-path theory. The predictions are different for (7). Here, the active theta domain is the NP1 + *of* + NP2 complex (i.e., *the son of the driver*), because the preposition *of* does not assign a theta role to NP2. Construal stipulates that the relative clause is associated to this complex. At this point, both syntactic and non-syntactic information can be used to attach the relative clause to one of the NPs. Because plausibility information can be employed at this stage, the processor should somehow select the most plausible analysis. Construal does not make clear what mechanism is used. One possibility is that plausibility information guides attachment to the most plausible NP without resulting in processing cost in any of the three conditions. Another possibility is that the most plausible analysis is selected after a process of competition, as in constraint-based theories. This would make the ambiguous condition more difficult to read than the disambiguated conditions. And finally, the processor may slow down whenever one analysis is implausible before it adopts the alternative. Thus, construal does not make any predictions about how the ambiguous condition is processed.

Finally, the unrestricted race model predicts that the degree of processing difficulty depends on how often the initial analysis has to be revised. The more often reanalysis is required, the greater processing difficulty for a particular structure should be. When a structure is strongly biased, the processor will adopt the preferred analysis in nearly all cases. For example, NP2 attachment will nearly always be adopted in (8). When subsequent information is inconsistent with the preferred analysis, as in (8c), reanalysis will nearly always have to occur and the average processing difficulty should be great. In contrast, when subsequent information is inconsistent with the dispreferred analysis, as in (8b), little or no processing difficulty is predicted, because the dispreferred analysis is hardly ever adopted initially and therefore reanalysis should seldom occur. Reanalysis should never occur in a globally ambiguous sentence (where both analyses are plausible), because the initial analysis is appropriate regardless of which analysis was adopted.

The model makes different predictions for balanced ambiguities. In such ambiguities, each analysis will be adopted half the time. Given that there is only a slight preference in (7) (68% in the off-line test), the model predicts that reanalysis will occur in both (7b) and (7c). In (7b) reanalysis will occur on some trials because the implausible NP1 attachment was adopted initially, whereas in (7c) reanalysis will occur on some trials because NP2 attachment was adopted. Both conditions should produce more difficulty than the ambiguous condition (7a), in which the initial analysis is plausible regardless of which analysis was initially adopted. If the slight NP2 attachment preference is sufficiently strong, condition (7c) may also be more difficult than (7b), because reanalysis may occur somewhat more often in (7c) than in (7b).

Traxler et al. (1998) conducted two eye-tracking studies to test the predictions of the theories for (7) and (8). For the biased structure in (8), readers experienced more difficulty in the NP1 attachment condition than in the ambiguous and NP2 attachment condition, which did not differ from each other. The earliest point at which this pattern occurred was in first-pass regressions out of a short region immediately following the disambiguating noun (in this case, *didn't win*). (Throughout this chapter, first-pass regression is defined as the percentage of times leaving a region to the left before going past it.) This is consistent with other studies employing semantic disambiguation in our laboratory (Pickering and Traxler, 1998). (Unlike many studies, our critical regions contain a single word.) The same pattern also obtained in total time on the critical noun (e.g., *tasty*, *runny*, *tough*). (Total time is defined as the sum of all fixations in a region.)

The results from the experiment testing sentences such as (7) were very different. Total times on the critical word (*moustache*) were shorter in the ambiguous conditions than both disambiguated conditions, which did not differ from each other. This result provides strong evidence against competition-based frameworks. A competition mechanism predicts that the ambiguous condition should be more difficult to read than the disambiguated conditions, but the opposite was the case. In order to provide a more rigorous test of the competition mechanism, the items that were most balanced (ranging between 35% and 60% NP2 preference) were analysed separately. Competition frameworks predict that the competition between the two analyses in the ambiguous condition should be strongest for these items. However, the pattern of results for these items was exactly the same as for the entire set of items.

The results also provide evidence against the garden-path model, because late closure predicts that the NP1 attachment conditions should be more difficult to read than the ambiguous and NP2 attachment condition in both (7) and (8). Although this occurred in (8), it did not occur in (7). Reading times for the NP2 attachment condition in (7b) were longer than for the ambiguous condition, indicating that readers sometimes reanalysed an initially adopted NP1 attachment in condition (7b). Thus, we can conclude that late closure did not always apply.

The different pattern of results for (7) and (8) might be consistent with construal theory. As NP2 is the only NP in the active theta domain in (8), NP2 attachment should always apply. This is consistent with the results: NP2 attachment is easier than NP1 attachment and as easy as the globally ambiguous sentence. In (7), both NP1 and NP2 are in the active theta domain, which is consistent with the finding that the disambiguated conditions did not differ in the eye-tracking study. Furthermore, if one assumes that processing difficulty occurs whenever one attachment site is implausible, one can account for the finding that the disambiguated conditions were harder to read than the ambiguous condition.

The unrestricted race theory's proposals regarding the mechanisms that are employed in syntactic ambiguity resolution are also consistent with the results. In particular, it predicts different patterns of results for biased and balanced syntactic ambiguities. In a biased ambiguity such as (8), readers should nearly always adopt NP2 attachment initially, which should result in reanalysis in (8c), but not in (8a) and (8b). This was borne out by the data. In balanced ambiguities, the unrestricted race model predicts that readers should initially adopt each analysis half the time. This pattern of results was obtained for sentences such as (7). Both (7b) and (7c) were more difficult to read than the ambiguous condition (7a). This indicates that reanalysis took place on a considerable number of occasions in both disambiguated conditions, whereas reanalysis was never required in the ambiguous condition. This pattern of results provides strong support for the unrestricted race model.

The data from sentences (7) are crucial for the reanalysis/competition issue. However, the results from these sentences were obtained in total times, a relatively late measure of processing difficulty. Therefore, we conducted two further experiments on this kind of relative clause attachment ambiguity in order to determine whether the results can be obtained in earlier measures.

In the first experiment, we used sentences such as (9) (Traxler et al., 1998;

experiment 2). They are very similar to (7), but the relative pronoun is *who* rather than *that* and the sentences are disambiguated by the gender of a reflexive pronoun (*himself/herself*). In the second experiment (Van Gompel, Pickering, Liversedge and Traxler, 1999) we used sentences such as (10), which are disambiguated by the plausibility of a verb rather than a noun. As in the previous experiments, plausibility norms were obtained which confirmed this plausibility manipulation.

(9a) The brother of the colonel who shot himself on the balcony had been very depressed.

(Ambiguous)

(9b) The daughter of the colonel who shot himself on the balcony had been very depressed.

(NP2 attachment)

(9c) The daughter of the colonel who shot herself on the balcony had been very depressed.

(NP1 attachment)

(10a) The advisor of the mayor that had been driven to the meeting had a lot of problems.

(Ambiguous)

(10b) The village of the mayor that had been driven to the meeting had a lot of problems.

(NP2 attachment)

(10c) The mayor of the village that had been driven to the meeting had a lot of problems.

(NP1 attachment)

We conducted off-line preference pretests to determine whether the materials were biased. The ambiguous condition (9a) produced 70% NP2 attachment in the off-line test. The ambiguity in (10) was more balanced, with participants choosing NP2 attachment on 51% of the trials. The reliability of the latter result was confirmed by a completion task (e.g., Garnsey et al., 1997; McRae et al., 1998; Trueswell et al., 1993) in which participants had to complete sentence fragments after *that had been* ... . Of all relative clause completions, 56% were attached to NP2, which is very similar to the results from the off-line preference pretest. The reason for the difference in preference between (9) and (10) is not entirely clear. It may reflect random differences between the materials (there was also some variability within each set of materials), differences in off-line attachment preferences due to the relative pronoun (*who* vs. *that*), or subtle differences in the likelihood of particular NPs taking a relative clause modifier. Currently, no theory provides a satisfactory account of why there should be a difference in preference. Note, however, that the difference in results for (9) and (10) does not disprove constraint-based theories, construal or the unrestricted race model, as all these theories are underspecified with respect to what preferences should obtain in relative clause ambiguities such as (9) and (10).

The earliest effects for the sentences (9) and (10) obtained in first-pass regressions out of the region following the critical word (*on the balcony* and *to the meeting*), indicating that processing difficulty occurred soon after reading the disambiguating word. In (9), more regressions from this region occurred when the relative clause had to be NP1 attached (9c) than when the sentence was globally ambiguous (9a). The number of regressions in the NP2 attachment condition (9b) was also greater than in the ambiguous condition, but this result was only significant by items. A similar pattern occurred in total times on the critical region (*himself/herself*). These results are again consistent with the unrestricted race model, which predicts that the ambiguous condition should be easiest to read. The absence of a significant difference between the NP2 attachment condition and the ambiguous condition is compatible with the model. The 70% NP2 attachment preference suggests that the ambiguity in (9) was not perfectly balanced. Therefore, when the relative clause was disambiguated towards NP2 attachment, readers may have had to reanalyse in only a few instances, so that the difference between the NP2 attachment and ambiguous condition became impossible to detect. The direction of the means suggests that this was indeed the case.

Because the ambiguity in (10) is more balanced, the unrestricted race model predicts that the difference between the NP2 attachment and the ambiguous condition should be clearer. This was indeed the case. The percentage of regressions out of the post-critical region (i.e., *to the meeting*) in the ambiguous condition was less than in the disambiguated conditions. The disambiguated conditions did not differ. The same pattern was obtained in regression path times for this region. (Regression path time is defined as the sum of all fixations in and outside the region from first entering the region until first going past it; cf. Brysbaert and Mitchell, 1996; Duffy et al., 1988; Konieczny, Hemforth, Scheepers and Strube, 1997.) This replicates the pattern found for sentences like (7) in early measures of processing difficulty. Total reading times on the critical word (*driven*) showed the same result. Clearly, this pattern provides very strong support for the unrestricted race theory.

On the other hand, the results from (9) and (10) cannot be reconciled with competition-based frameworks such as current constraint-based theories. Such theories claim that globally ambiguous sentences should be slower than disambiguated sentences, because competition should arise when two syntactic analyses are about equally favoured by the various sources of information, but not when plausibility supports only one analysis.

Experiments on VP/NP attachment ambiguities: Problems for construal theory and referential theory

The results from the relative clause attachment ambiguities are consistent with the unrestricted race model, but they are also consistent with construal theory, as this theory does not specify what mechanism is used to resolve syntactic ambiguities involving non-primary relations such as relative clauses. Hence, the finding of a reanalysis effect can be reconciled with the model. Construal theory stipulates that primary relations are processed in a fundamentally different way from non-primary relations.

One case where construal does not apply is in sentences such as (11):

(11a) The hunter killed the dangerous poacher with the rifle not long after sunset.

(Ambiguous)

(11b) The hunter killed the dangerous leopard with the rifle not long after sunset.

(VP attachment)

(11c) The hunter killed the dangerous leopard with the scars not long after sunset.

(NP attachment)

Van Gompel et al. (1999) tested the processing of sentences like these. Such *VP/NP attachment ambiguities* have been investigated by other researchers (Britt, 1994; Britt et al., 1992; Clifton et al., 1991; Ni et al., 1996; Rayner et al., 1983; Spivey-Knowlton and Sedivy, 1995; Taraban and McClelland, 1988), but the comparison of all three conditions has not been conducted before. In these sentences, the prepositional phrase *with the rifle/scars* can be syntactically attached to either the verb (*killed*) or the object NP (*the dangerous poacher/leopard*). Construal theory predicts that the phrase will be initially attached to the verb, because this instantiates a primary relation, whereas attachment to the NP does not (Frazier and Clifton, 1996: p. 45). Thus, it predicts that VP attachment will always be adopted initially, and therefore that reanalysis should never occur when this analysis is plausible, as in (11b). The VP attachment condition should be no more difficult than the ambiguous condition (11a). Only the NP attachment condition (11c) should be difficult, because the initially adopted verb attachment has to be revised.

In fact, for this kind of ambiguities, construal theory makes exactly the same predictions as garden-path theory, although for different reasons. In garden-path theory, VP attachment is initially adopted because minimal attachment applies, rather than because primary relations are preferred to non-primary relations. Importantly, both construal theory and garden-path theory claim that non-syntactic constraints cannot be used initially to resolve ambiguities involving primary relations. In their second experiment, Van Gompel et al. (1999) tested this claim using sentences such as (12):

(12a) The hunter killed only the poacher with the rifle not long after sunset.

(Ambiguous)

(12b) The hunter killed only the leopard with the rifle not long after sunset.
                                                                    (VP attachment)

(12c) The hunter killed only the leopard with the scars not long after sunset.
                                                                    (NP attachment)

According to Ni et al. (1996), *only* functions as a form of discourse information (see also Paterson, Liversedge and Underwood, 1999). Ni et al. explained the discourse effects of *only* in the context of referential theory (Crain and Steedman, 1985; Altmann and Steedman, 1988). According to referential theory, readers initially adopt the analysis that has fewest unsupported presuppositions. In (11), the VP attachment analysis involves a simple noun phrase (e.g., *the dangerous leopard*), which requires the processor to postulate the existence of a single dangerous leopard, whereas the NP attachment analysis involves a complex noun phrase (e.g., *the dangerous leopard with the scars*) which requires the postulation of a set of dangerous leopards. Because only a single leopard is mentioned in (11), postulating one leopard requires fewest unsupported presuppositions, and therefore the VP attachment analysis will be adopted.

Ni et al. argued that the situation is different in (12). In these sentences, *only* precedes the object NP. They claim that, in such a case, readers assume more than one poacher or leopard. As a result, the processor analyses the prepositional phrase as a modifier, resulting in NP attachment. This should result in the VP attachment condition (12b) being more difficult than the ambiguous condition (12a) and NP attachment condition (12c), because reanalysis of the initially adopted NP attachment should only take place in (12b). Clearly, these predictions contrast with those from construal and garden-path theory, which stipulate that discourse information cannot be employed initially and that (11) and (12) are processed similarly.

The predictions of the unrestricted race theory depend on the bias in (11) and (12). In order to establish the preference in these sentences, we conducted an off-line preference pretest on the ambiguous conditions (11a) and (12a) and a completion study on all conditions. In the off-line preference study, readers indicated that they took the prepositional phrase as VP attached 78% of the time in sentences like (11), and 55% of the time in sentences like (12). The completions showed similar results: 93% VP attachment in (11) and 40% VP attachment in (12). Although there was a numerical difference between the off-line data and the completions, both indicated that the items in (11) were VP attachment biased, and that the items in (12) were roughly balanced. On the basis of these results, the unrestricted race model predicts that the NP attachment condition in (11c) should be difficult and that the ambiguous and VP attachment conditions should produce little or no difficulty. Because (12) is a balanced ambiguity, both disambiguated conditions should be difficult to read as compared with the ambiguous condition. Thus, the predictions of the unrestricted race model contrast with construal, garden-path theory and referential theory. They also contrast with constraint-based theories, which claim that processing difficulty arises due to a competition process. According to these theories, the ambiguous condition in a balanced ambiguity such as (12) should be more difficult than its disambiguated counterparts.

Two eye-tracking experiments using sets of materials like (11) and (12) were conducted (Van Gompel et al., 1999). For both sets of materials, the earliest effects arose in first-pass regressions and regression path times for the post-critical region (i.e., *not long after*). This showed that the basic eye-movement patterns are similar for biased and balanced ambiguities and indicated that the processing of balanced ambiguities such as (12) is no more delayed than that of frequently investigated biased ambiguities such as (11).

The results from (11) showed that VP attachment was easier than NP attachment, as reflected in first-pass regressions and regression path times for the post-critical region (e.g., *not long after*), and total times on the critical noun (e.g., *rifle/scars*) and the region preceding it (*with the*). This pattern is consistent with the pattern observed in previous research on this type of ambiguity. Additionally, the experiment provided data about the processing of an ambiguous condition, which had not been investigated before. Both first-pass regressions and regression path times for the post-critical region, and total times on the critical noun and the region preceding it indicated that the ambiguous condition was easier than the NP attachment condition, and did not differ from the VP attachment condition. This result is consistent with the predictions of the unrestricted race model for biased ambiguities, but it is also consistent with other models.

The results from (12) are crucial in distinguishing between the theories. First-pass regressions and regression path times for the post-critical region, and total times in the region *with the* revealed that both the VP and NP attachment condition were more difficult to read than the ambiguous condition. The disambiguated conditions did not differ. This result is evidence against construal theory and the garden-path theory, which claim that VP attachment is always initially adopted, so reanalysis should never be required in the VP attachment condition. However, the VP attachment condition was more difficult to read than the ambiguous condition. This finding is incompatible with Frazier (1995), who claimed that there is no evidence for processing difficulty when a structure is disambiguated toward an analysis that is favoured by minimal attachment or late closure. The NP attachment condition was also more difficult than the ambiguous condition. This provides evidence against Ni et al.'s version of referential theory, which claims that NP attachment should always be initially adopted when the direct object noun phrase is preceded by *only*. As a result, reanalysis should never be necessary in the NP attachment condition. Finally, the predictions of competition frameworks such as current constraint-based theories were once more disconfirmed. Contrary to their predictions, the ambiguous condition was easiest to read. This conclusion was corroborated by a correlation analysis. According to competition models, the more balanced an ambiguity is, the stronger the competition process. However, there was no correlation between the strength of the preference for an analysis (as assessed by both the off-line preference and completion study) and the number of regressions from the post-critical region of the ambiguous condition.

The results from (12) can be naturally explained by the unrestricted race model. Because (12) is a closely balanced ambiguity, VP and NP attachment should be adopted initially about equally often. This was borne out by the fact that the disambiguated conditions did not differ: in both conditions reanalysis should take place about half the time. The model explains why both were more difficult to read than the ambiguous condition, in which the initial analysis was always appropriate.

Conclusions

The results from the experiments reported above are clear. Using different structures and disambiguations, we have consistently found that sentences containing global, balanced syntactic ambiguities are easier to read than balanced syntactic ambiguities which are subsequently disambiguated. These results cannot be explained by frameworks that incorporate a competition mechanism for syntactic ambiguity resolution. A competition mechanism predicts that balanced globally ambiguous conditions should be more difficult because the constraints do not favour one analysis over the other. An ambiguous condition can never be faster than a disambiguated condition. Thus, these results provide evidence against current constraint-based theories (e.g., MacDonald, 1994; MacDonald et al., 1994; McRae et al., 1998; Spivey-Knowlton and Sedivy, 1995; Trueswell et al., 1993, 1994), which do assume such a mechanism.

As mentioned before, studies on lexical ambiguity resolution suggest that lexical ambiguity resolution proceeds through a process of competition. A number of studies (e.g., Duffy et al., 1988; Rayner and Duffy, 1986; Rayner and Frazier, 1989) have shown that balanced (in terms of frequency of the meanings) ambiguous words in a neutral context are more difficult to read than unambiguous controls. Our findings of reanalysis in syntactic ambiguity resolution suggest that the mechanisms in syntactic ambiguity resolution are fundamentally different from those in lexical ambiguity resolution. This distinction between lexical and syntactic processing is inconsistent with lexically oriented parsing theories, such as most current constraint-based theories (e.g., MacDonald et al., 1994; Trueswell, 1996; Trueswell et al., 1993). It supports the alternative claim (e.g., Frazier, 1989; Rayner and Morris, 1991; Traxler et al., 1998; Van Gompel et al., 1999) that lexical and syntactic ambiguity resolution are different.

However, the results from our experiments did not support the predictions of the garden-path theory. Both (7) and (12) showed that readers are sometimes garden-pathed on the structurally simplest analysis. The late closure principle was disconfirmed by the finding that relative clause attachment to NP2 in (7b) was more difficult than the globally ambiguous condition, and the minimal attachment principle was disconfirmed because the VP attachment condition in (12b) was also more difficult than its globally ambiguous counterpart. In both cases, the garden path theory predicts that the structurally simplest analysis is always chosen initially, so reanalysis should never occur.

The results from the relative clause attachment ambiguities were consistent with construal theory. However, the results from the VP/NP attachment ambiguity were not. Construal theory predicts that in sentences such as (11) and (12) VP attachment should always be adopted because it constitutes a primary relation, and NP attachment does not. The VP attachment condition in (12b) should be no more difficult than the ambiguous condition, but it was.

This leaves us with only one surviving account, the unrestricted race model. This model combines properties of constraint-based theories and traditional two-stage theories. As in constraint-based theories, non-structural information can be used initially. Although it is difficult to make comparisons between experiments using different materials, some of the experiments reported in this chapter suggest that non-structural information such as thematic information associated with different prepositions (*with* and *of*) can be employed in the initial stage of processing. When a relative clause had to be attached to a NP1 + *with* + NP2 complex, a NP2 attachment preference occurred, but the NP2 preference was much less pronounced when a relative clause had to be attached to a NP1 + *of* + NP2 complex. The experiments on VP/NP attachment ambiguities suggested that discourse information associated with *only* can be used initially. When the direct object NP is not preceded by *only*, a VP attachment preference occurred, but when it was, there was no clear preference for either VP or NP attachment.

In line with two-stage theories, the unrestricted race model stipulates that processing difficulty is caused by reanalysis, not by a competition process between two or more analyses. When subsequent information is inconsistent with a previously adopted analysis, reanalysis occurs. This prediction was supported by the finding that sentences containing global, balanced syntactic ambiguities are easier to read than balanced syntactic ambiguities which are subsequently disambiguated.

We think that the unrestricted race model can account for many findings in the literature that have been taken as support for constraint-based theories. We have mentioned in the introduction that reanalysis models can readily account for data that seemed to support a competition mechanism (MacDonald, 1994; McRae et al., 1998). The unrestricted race model can also account for recent findings that garden-path effects range on a continuum (e.g., Garnsey et al., 1997; Trueswell et al., 1993, 1994). For example, in a recent study, Garnsey et al. (1997) investigated structures such as (13).

(13a) The art critic wrote the interview had been a complete disaster.
(Direct object biasing verb)

(13b) The bank guard confessed the robbery had been his own idea.
(Subject biasing verb)

In these sentences the noun phrases *the interview* and *the robbery* are temporarily ambiguous between a direct object of the preceding verb (*wrote/confessed*) and the subject of the following clause. In (13a), the verb *wrote* is biased toward the direct object analysis, whereas in (13b) the verb *confessed* is biased towards the subject analysis. Garnsey et al. showed that first-pass reading times in the disambiguating region *had been* differed from an unambiguous control sentence in (13a), but not in (13b). Furthermore, the degree of difficulty in the disambiguating region was correlated with the strength of the preference for the direct object or subject analysis. For example, they observed that difficulty in the disambiguating region increased in sentences with subject biased verbs as the verb's likelihood of being used with direct objects increased, indicating that garden-path effects ranged on a continuum. Garnsey et al. took this as support for constraint-based theories and claimed that the results were incompatible with serial lexical guidance models (e.g., Ford, Bresnan and Kaplan, 1982). They argued that in such models, readers should always initially adopt the subject analysis in subject-biased verbs. They claimed that the strength of this bias should not matter in these models, because the processor always adopts the preferred verb frame. However, these are not the claims that the unrestricted race model makes. The unrestricted race model can readily account for the findings. Because lexical preference information is used initially, it determines the number of times that each analysis was initially adopted (contrary to the kind of serial lexical guidance model Garnsey et al. describe). The more often reanalysis is required, the more difficult, on average, a sentence will be. Hence, in sentences with very strong subject biasing verbs the subject analysis will be adopted more frequently than in sentences with a somewhat weaker subject bias. Consequently, reanalysis in the disambiguating region should occur less often when the subject bias is strong than when it is weak. Similarly, it predicts the subject analysis should be adopted more often in (13b) than (13a), explaining the pattern Garnsey et al. obtained for these sentences.

In a very similar study which investigated sentences such as (14), Pickering, Traxler and Crocker (in press) obtained seemingly different results.

(14a) The athlete realised his goals somehow would be out of reach.
(Plausible direct object)

(14b) The athlete realised his shoes somehow would be out of reach.
(Implausible direct object)

They contrasted sentences with a plausible direct object such as (14a) with sentences that had an implausible direct object such as (14b). The verb in these sentences always biased the following NP towards a subject of the following clause. Nevertheless, they observed that reading the noun *shoes* in (14b) was more difficult than *goals* in (14a). This can be taken as evidence that the lexical frequency bias of the verb does not determine initial preferences. Considered in this way, the results are in conflict with the results from the Garnsey et al. experiment, as was indeed argued by Pickering et al. (in press).

Clearly, the idea that lexical preferences are not initially employed by the processor is incompatible with the unrestricted race model. We would like to suggest two possible explanations here to account for the Pickering et al. results in the unrestricted race model. In the first explanation, there is no structural preference for the direct object analysis (as in constraint-based theories). However, even though only the verb bias is initially used, readers may still adopt the dispreferred direct object reading in a minority of cases. Indeed, a completion study using sentence fragments up to and including the determiner (*his* in [14]) produced 70% subject competions. Hence, even though the direct object reading was dispreferred, readers may still initially have adopted this analysis in 30% of the cases, resulting in reanalysis on a minority of trials. Because both the direct object and the subject analysis were plausible in (14a), reanalysis never occurred and it was therefore easier to read than (14b). Thus, the unrestricted race model suggests an interesting explanation for these findings.

An alternative explanation is that lexical preferences are used immediately, but that other information is also brought to bear. Pickering et al. (in press) proposed an *informativity* account to explain their data (see also Chater, Crocker and Pickering, 1998). According to this model, readers' choice of initial analysis pays attention to lexical preferences and other sources of information that suggest which analysis is most likely to be correct. However, they are not driven exclusively by these preferences. The argument is that it is not necessarily most efficient to initially adopt the analysis most likely to be correct. It may also be useful to pay attention to how *testable* an analysis is. The critical question is whether subsequent information is likely to provide good evidence about whether the analysis was correct or not. After *realised*, the processor can adopt the object or the subject analysis. If the processor adopts the object analysis, it will then encounter one of two types of noun. If it encounters a word like *goals*, *ambitions* or *dreams* (or very few others), there is a good chance this analysis will be correct. If it encounters *shoes*, *house*, *friend* (or almost anything else), it will know this analysis cannot be correct. Hence this analysis is highly testable. But if it adopts the subject analysis, any noun is possible as the subject of the new clause, but none is particularly likely. Hence, the analysis is much less testable. The argument is that it makes more sense to adopt the testable object analysis, and see whether the following noun confirms or disconfirms this analysis, than to adopt the less testable subject analysis. However, Pickering et al. argue that it would not be efficient to ignore frequency information entirely, and therefore propose the informativity model, whereby the processor pays attention to both frequency and testability in determining which analysis to pursue.

According to this explanation, the testability of the object analysis is much greater than the testability of the subject analysis, and this difference in testability is much greater than the frequency difference in favour of the subject analysis. Consequently, the processor adopts the object analysis initially, hence explaining the difficulty of (14b) compared with (14a). This implies that lexical preferences still have some influence, but that they can be outweighed by structural preferences.

The focus of this chapter has been to explain gradations in processing difficulty by the proportion of times readers have to revise their initially adopted analysis. However, it is important to stress that this is almost certainly not the only factor involved in explaining such gradations. There is some, although somewhat limited, evidence that the processing cost of adopting an initial analysis may affect degree of difficulty (e.g., Gibson, 1998; Holmes, Kennedy and Murray, 1987). Even when a structure is unambiguous, structures may differ in the processing cost associated with accessing them or with integrating them into the previously built structure.

Another factor that may affect degree of difficulty is that some reanalyses are harder than others. For example, Sturt, Pickering and Crocker (1999) found that reanalysing the direct object as part of a sentence complement of a verb, as in (15a), is easier than reanalysing it as a subordinate clause as in (15b):

(15a) The Australian woman saw the famous doctor had been drinking quite a lot.

(Sentence complement)

(15b) Before the woman visited the famous doctor had been drinking quite a lot.

(Subordinate clause)

A corpus analysis showed that the preference to take a following noun phrase as a direct object rather than the subject of a following clause was equally strong for both *saw* and *visited*. Nevertheless, sentences such as (15b) were more difficult to read than sentences such as (15a). This supports the idea that structures can differ in their degree of reanalysis difficulty (see also Ferreira and Henderson, 1991; Gorrell, 1995; Pritchett, 1988, 1992; Sturt and Crocker, 1996).

Clearly, it is important to develop theories as to how reanalysis proceeds (see, e.g., Fodor and Ferreira, 1998; Inoue and Fodor, 1995; Ferreira and Henderson, 1991; Fodor and Inoue, 1994; Sturt and Crocker, 1996). Similarly, we think it is crucial to our understanding of sentence processing to devise theories that provide principled accounts of how initial preferences arise, rather than deriving predictions from completions or off-line preference studies. Once we have coherent theories of such processes, we believe that they can be incorporated into the unrestricted race model. We hope that future research will take us closer to this goal.

Acknowledgements

Roger van Gompel acknowledges an ESRC Postgraduate Studentship and a University of Glasgow Postgraduate Studentship. Martin Pickering acknowledges support of ESRC Research Grant no. R000234542. We would like to thank Chuck Clifton for helpful discussions, and Wayne Murray for comments on an earlier draft of this chapter.

References

Abney, S.P. (1989). A computational model of human parsing. Journal of Psycholinguistic Research, 18, 129–144.

Altmann, G.T.M., Garnham, A. and Dennis, Y.I.L. (1992). Avoiding the garden path: Eye movements in context. Journal of Memory and Language, 31, 685–712.

Altmann, G.T.M. and Steedman, M.J. (1988). Interaction with context during human sentence processing. Cognition, 30, 191–238.

Bever, T.G. (1970). The cognitive basis for linguistic structures. In: J.R. Hayes (Ed.), Cognition and the Development of Language. New York: Wiley, pp. 279–362.

Britt, M.A. (1994). The interaction of referential ambiguity and argument structure in the parsing of prepositional phrases. Journal of Memory and Language, 33, 251–283.

Britt, M.A., Perfetti, C.A., Garrod, S.C. and Rayner, K. (1992). Parsing in context: Context effects and their limits. Journal of Memory and Language, 31, 293–314.

Brysbaert, M. and Mitchell, D.C. (1996). Modifier attachment in sentence parsing: Evidence from Dutch. Quarterly Journal of Experimental Psychology, 49A, 664–695.

Chater, N., Crocker, M.W. and Pickering, M.J. (1998). The rational analysis of inquiry: The case of parsing. In: M. Oaksford and N. Chater (Eds.), Rational Models of Cognition. Oxford: Oxford University Press, pp. 441–469.

Clifton, C. (1993). Thematic roles in sentence parsing. Canadian Journal of Experimental Psychology, 47, 222–246.

Clifton, C. and Ferreira (1989). Ambiguity in context. Language and Cognitive Processes, 4, SI 77–103.

Clifton, C., Speer, S. and Abney, S.P. (1991). Parsing arguments: Phrase structure and argument structure as determinants of initial parsing decisions. Journal of Memory and Language, 30, 251–271.

Crain, S. and Steedman, M.J. (1985). On not being led up the garden-path: The use of context by the psychological processor. In: D. Dowty, L. Kartunnen and A. Zwicky (Eds.), Natural Language Parsing. Cambridge: Cambridge University Press, pp. 320–358.

Crocker, M.W. (1995). Computational Psycholinguistics: An Interdisciplinary Approach to the Study of Language. Dordrecht: Kluwer.

Cuetos, F. and Mitchell, D.C. (1988). Cross-linguistic differences in parsing: Restrictions on the use of the late closure strategy in Spanish. Cognition, 30, 73–105.

Dopkins, S., Morris, R.K. and Rayner, K. (1992). Lexical ambiguity and eye fixations in reading: A test of competing models of lexical ambiguity resolution. Journal of Memory and Language, 31, 461–476.

Duffy, S.A., Morris, R.K. and Rayner, K. (1988). Lexical ambiguity and fixation times in reading. Journal of Memory and Language, 27, 429–446.

Ferreira, F. and Clifton, C. (1986). The independence of syntactic processing. Journal of Memory and Language, 25, 348–368.

Ferreira, F. and Henderson, J.M. (1990). Use of verb information in syntactic parsing: Evidence from eye movements and word-by-word self-paced reading. Journal of Experimental Psychology: Learning, Memory, and Cognition, 16, 555–568.

Ferreira, F. and Henderson, J.M. (1991). Recovery from misanalyses of garden-path sentences. Journal of Memory and Language, 30, 725–745.

Fodor, J.A. (1983). The Modularity of Mind. Cambridge, MA: MIT Press.

Fodor, F.D. and Ferreira, F. (1998). Reanalysis in Sentence Processing. Dordrecht: Kluwer.

Fodor, J.D. and Inoue, A. (1994). The diagnosis and cure of garden paths. Journal of Psycholinguistic Research, 23, 407–434.

Ford, M., Bresnan, J. and Kaplan, R.M. (1982). A competence-based theory of syntactic closure. In: J. Bresnan (Ed.), The Mental Representation of Grammatical Relations. Cambridge, MA: MIT Press, pp. 727–796.

Forster, K. (1979). Levels of processing and the structure of the language processor. In: W.E. Cooper and E.C.T. Walker (Eds.), Sentence Processing: Psycholinguistic Studies Presentend to Merrill Garrett. Hillsdale, NJ: Erlbaum, pp. 27–81.

Frazier, L. (1979). On comprehending sentences: Syntactic parsing strategies. Ph.D. dissertation, University of Connecticut. Bloomington, IN: Indiana University Linguistics Club.

Frazier, L. (1987). Sentence processing: A tutorial review. In: M. Coltheart (Ed.), Attention and Performance XII. Hillsdale, NJ: Erlbaum, pp. 559–586.

Frazier, L. (1989). Against lexical generation of syntax. In: W.D. Marslen-Wilson (Ed.), Lexical Representation and Process. Cambridge, MA: MIT Press, pp. 529–561.

Frazier, L. (1995). Constraint satisfaction as a theory of sentence processing. Journal of Psycholinguistic Research, 24, 437–468.

Frazier, L. and Clifton, C. (1996). Construal. Cambridge, MA: MIT Press.

Frazier, L. and Rayner, K. (1982). Making and correcting errors during sentence comprehension: Eye movements in the analysis of structurally ambiguous sentences. Cognitive Psychology, 14, 178–210.

Garnsey, S.M., Pearlmutter, N.J., Myers, E. and Lotocky, M.A. (1997). The contributions of verb bias and plausibility to the comprehension of temporarily ambiguous sentences. Journal of Memory and Language, 37, 58–93.

Gibson, E. (1998). Linguistic complexity: Locality of syntactic dependencies. Cognition, 68, 1–76.

Gilboy, E., Sopena, J.-M., Clifton, C. and Frazier, L. (1995). Argument structure and association preferences in Spanish and English complex NPs. Cognition, 54, 131–167.

Gorrell, P. (1995). Syntax and Parsing. Cambridge: Cambridge University Press.

Hemforth, B., Konieczny, L. and Scheepers, C. (2000). Syntactic attachment and anaphor resolution: Two sides of relative clause attachment. In: M.W. Crocker, M.J. Pickering and C. Clifton (Eds.), Architectures and Mechanisms for Language Processing. Cambridge: Cambridge University Press, pp. 259–281.

Holmes, V.M., Kennedy, A. and Murray, W.S. (1987). Syntactic structure and the garden path. Quarterly Journal of Experimental Psychology, 39A, 277–293.

Holmes, V.H., Stowe, L. and Cupples, L. (1989). Lexical expectations in parsing complement-verb sentences. Journal of Memory and Language, 28, 668–689.

Inoue, A. and Fodor, J.A. (1995). Information-paced parsing of Japanese. In: R. Mazuka and N. Nagai (Eds.), Japanese Sentence Processing. Hillsdale, NJ: Erlbaum, pp. 9–63.

Kimball, J. (1973). Seven principles of surface structure parsing in natural language. Cognition, 8, 15–47.

Konieczny, L., Hemforth, B., Scheepers, C. and Strube, G. (1997). The role of lexical heads in parsing: Evidence from German. Language and Cognitive Processes, 12, 307–348.

MacDonald, M.C. (1994). Probabilistic constraints and syntactic ambiguity resolution. Language and Cognitive Processes, 9, 157–201.

MacDonald, M.C., Pearlmutter, N.J. and Seidenberg, M.S. (1994). The lexical nature of syntactic ambiguity resolution. Psychological Review, 101, 676–703.

Marslen-Wilson, W.D. (1975). Sentence perception as an interactive parallel process. Science, 189, 226–228.

McRae, K., Spivey-Knowlton, M.J. and Tanenhaus, M.K. (1998). Modeling the influence of thematic fit (and other constraints) in on-line sentence comprehension. Journal of Memory and Language, 38, 283–312.

Mitchell, D.C. (1987). Lexical guidance in human parsing: Locus and processing characteristics. In: M. Coltheart (Ed.), Attention and Performance XII. Hillsdale, NJ: Erlbaum, pp. 601–618.

Mitchell, D.C., Corley, M.M.B. and Garnham, A. (1992). Effects of context in human sentence parsing: Evidence against a discourse-based proposal mechanism. Journal of Experimental Psychology: Learning, Memory, and Cognition, 18, 69–88.

Ni, W., Crain, S. and Shankweiler, D. (1996). Sidestepping garden paths: Assessing the contributions of syntax, semantics and plausibility in resolving ambiguities. Language and Cognitive Processes, 11, 283–334.

Paterson, K.B., Liversedge, S.P. and Underwood, G. (1999). The influence of focus operators on syntactic processing of 'short' relative clause sentences. Quarterly Journal of Experimental Psychology, 51A, 717–737.

Pickering, M.J. (1994). Processing local and unbounded dependencies: A unified account. Journal of Psycholinguistic Research, 23, 323–352.

Pickering, M.J. and Traxler, M.J. (1998). Plausibility and recovery from garden paths: An eye-tracking study. Journal of Experimental Psychology: Learning, Memory, and Cognition, 24, 940–961.

Pickering, M.J., Traxler, M.J. and Crocker, M.W. (in press). Ambiguity resolution in sentence processing. Journal of Memory and Language.

Pritchett, B. (1988). Garden path phenomena and the grammatical basis of language processing. Language, 64, 539–576.

Pritchett, B. (1992). Grammatical Competence and Parsing Performance. Chicago: University of Chicago Press.

Rayner, K., Carlson, M. and Frazier, L. (1983). The interaction of syntax and semantics during sentence processing: Eye movements in the analysis of semantically biased sentences. Journal of Verbal Learning and Verbal Behavior, 22, 358–374.

Rayner, K. and Duffy, S.A. (1986). Lexical complexity and fixation times in reading: Effects of word frequency, verb complexity, and lexical ambiguity. Memory and Cognition, 14, 191–201.

Rayner, K. and Frazier, L. (1989). Selection mechanisms in lexically ambiguous words. Journal of Experimental Psychology: Learning, Memory, and Cognition, 15, 779–790.

Rayner, K., Garrod, S. and Perfetti, C.A. (1992). Discourse influences during parsing are delayed. Cognition, 45, 109–139.

Rayner, K. and Morris, R.K. (1991). Comprehension processes in reading ambiguous sentences: Reflections from eye movements. In: G.B. Simpson (Ed.), Understanding Word and Sentence. Amsterdam: Elsevier, pp. 175–198.

Rayner, K., Pacht, J.M. and Duffy, S.A. (1994). Effects of prior encounter and global discourse bias on the processing of lexically ambiguous words: Evidence from eye fixations. Journal of Memory and Language, 33, 527–544.

Sereno, S.C., Pacht, J.M. and Rayner, K. (1992). The effect of meaning frequency on processing lexically ambiguous words. Psychological Science, 3, 296–300.

Spivey-Knowlton, M. and Sedivy, J. (1995). Resolving attachment ambiguities with multiple constraints. Cognition, 55, 227–267.

Spivey-Knowlton, M., Trueswell, J. and Tanenhaus, M. (1993). Context effects in syntactic ambiguity resolution: Discourse and semantic influences in parsing reduced relative clauses. Canadian Journal of Experimental Psychology, 37, 276–309.

Sturt, P. and Crocker, M.W. (1996). Monotonic syntactic processing: A cross-linguistic study of attachment and reanalysis. Language and Cognitive Processes, 11, 449–494.

Sturt, P., Pickering, M.J. and Crocker, M.W. (1999). Structural change and reanalysis difficulty in language comprehension. Journal of Memory and Language, 40, 136–150.

Tabor, W., Juliano, C. and Tanenhaus, M.K. (1997). Parsing in a dynamical system: An attractor-based account of the interaction of lexical and structural constraints in sentence processing. Language and Cognitive Processes, 12, 211–271.

Taraban, R. and McClelland, J.R. (1988). Constituent attachment and thematic role assignment in sentence processing: Influence of content-based expectations. Journal of Memory and Language, 27, 597–632.

Traxler, M.J. and Pickering, M.J. (1996). Case-marking in the parsing of complement sentences: Evidence from eye movements. Quarterly Journal of Experimental Psychology, 49A, 991–1004.

Traxler, M.J., Pickering, M.J. and Clifton, C. (1998). Adjunct attachment is not a form of lexical ambiguity resolution. Journal of Memory and Language, 39, 558–592.

Trueswell, J. (1996). The role of lexical frequency in syntactic ambiguity resolution. Journal of Memory and Language, 35, 566–585.

Trueswell, J., Tanenhaus, M.K. and Garnsey, S. (1994). Semantic influences on parsing: Use of thematic role information in syntactic disambiguation. Journal of Memory and Language, 33, 285–318.

Trueswell, J., Tanenhaus, M.K. and Kello, C. (1993). Verb-specific constraints in sentence processing: Separating effects of lexical preference from garden-paths. Journal of Experimental Psychology: Learning, Memory, and Cognition, 19, 528–553.

Tyler, L.K. and Marslen-Wilson, W.D. (1977). The on-line effects of semantic context on syntactic processing. Journal of Verbal Learning and Verbal Behavior, 16, 683–692.

Van Gompel, R.P.G., Pickering, M.J., Liversedge, S.P. and Traxler, M.J. (1999). [The source of processing difficulty in relative clause ambiguities]. Unpublished data.

Van Gompel, R.P.G., Pickering, M.J. and Traxler, M.J. (1999). Reanalysis in sentence processing: Evidence against current constraint-based and two-stage models. Manuscript submitted for publication.

COMMENTARY ON SECTION 4

Sentence Processing: Issues and Measures

Wayne S. Murray
University of Dundee

In the preceding chapters, the reader will find a rather biased sample of current work on sentence processing. But perhaps, at least partially because it shares many of my own prejudices, a sample that I would argue is none the worse for that bias and in fact benefits from it. A book, after all, is the place for developing themes and promoting approaches, whether or not these even-handedly address the range of views currently prevalent in the wider academic community.

This bias is reflected not only in the way that the chapters address the theme of this book — Reading as a Perceptual Process — but also in the issues that are tackled and the theoretical approaches that are adopted. Without question, the most influential approach to sentence parsing in recent years has centred around 'constraint satisfaction' accounts, and yet there is no proponent of that view represented here, only one chapter that tackles the issue head-on (from a negative viewpoint) and two chapters which mention it (again negatively) in passing. And yet the reader — or at least this reader — is left feeling that these chapters have had something important to say about the issue. Similarly, I will argue, these chapters appear to be converging on a consensus about what certain eye movement measures can, and cannot, tell us about the process of sentence parsing and the sorts of things that we should be looking for and thinking about in an eye movement record. Again, the emerging approach is not one that is entirely consonant with the 'standards' of the current literature.

Issues

A reader could be forgiven for believing that there is a 'cottage industry' in European psycholinguistics in the area of modifier attachment decisions. More specifically, in the attachment of a relative clause to a complex NP of the form

Reading as a Perceptual Process/A. Kennedy, R. Radach, D. Heller and J. Pynte (Editors)
© 2000 Elsevier Science Ltd. All rights reserved

'NP1 of NP2' — the now infamous " ... daughter of the Colonel who was on the balcony ... ". In fact to view it as a 'cottage' industry would be to seriously underestimate its magnitude, and that magnitude is adequately represented here: Four of the seven chapters focus precisely on this issue and one more exploits the ambiguity in passing.

Europe is, however, in a relatively unique position for work involving cross-linguistic comparisons, having a proliferation of different languages within a relatively restricted geographical region, and for this issue, in particular, cross-language comparisons have proved extremely informative. Ever since the original Cuetos and Mitchell (1988) study showed that preferences apparent in English were not reflected in Spanish, this has been a subject of hot (and sometimes heated) debate. It is an important issue for two reasons: it not only raises fundamental questions about the factors which drive parsing decisions, but it also strikes at the issue of whether it is possible to draw *any* general conclusions about parsing principles that are independent of the nature of a particular language. The 'English Disease' is still prevalent in psycholinguistics, with many researchers consciously or unconsciously assuming that what is true for English is likely to be generally true. Increasingly, however, this assumption is proving to be ill-founded or at least questionable. Even basically mono-lingual anglophones, such as myself, who become involved in a little cross- or other-linguistic research, are beginning to question whether English is even a 'normal' language, let alone a typical one. Arguably, English is so atypical in many ways, that there is a great risk in assuming either that the findings from English are likely to be replicated in other languages or even that what appears to be important to an anglophone will have a similar effect on the reader of another language.

Do the data from the studies reported here lead us to a general conclusion about the nature of the factor(s) influencing this type of modifier attachment? Arguably not. The strongest contender for that particular crown was probably Don Mitchell's 'tuning hypothesis'. That approach also had a particular intuitive appeal, with the suggestion that the parser might be driven by the simplest of all possible principles — go for the analysis most likely to be correct. However, Mitchell's own work showing parsing preferences which are at odds with the probabilities of a language (e.g., Mitchell and Brysbaert, 1998) does a good job of nailing down the lid on that coffin. It is worth mentioning that this is, of course, also a nail for the coffin lid of any statistically driven approach to parsing, including constraint–satisfaction approaches. Mitchell, Brysbaert, Grondelaers and Swanepoel here (Chapter 18) use the same hammer and nails on the 'Gricean account' of modifier attachment and appear to do a convincing job of shutting that lid, with the conclusion that it accounts for zero percent of the variance.

Should we conclude therefore, with Pynte and Colonna (Chapter 20), that given the diversity of findings in the literature, any approach in terms of general parsing principles is unlikely to be successful? Perhaps not. It certainly seems clear that the answer is unlikely to be simple, but a few consistencies appear to be emerging. The chapters by Konieczny and Hemforth, Pynte and Colonna, and Frenck-Mestre and Pynte all point to the importance of the salience of discourse entities and other 'higher level' effects in the resolution of this ambiguity. As Pynte and Colonna suggest, the successful implementation of some of these necessitates postulating some sort of delay or underspecification mechanism, and they provide a fascinating, if perhaps not entirely plausible, model of such a mechanism. However, to be fair, they do succeed in demonstrating that such a *principle* can produce some unexpected results that in fact match empirical findings.

There is, in fact, a long tradition of postulating some possibility for delay in the parsing process, or the more current manifestation — underspecification (e.g., Gorrell, 1995, 1998; Kennedy, Murray, Jennings and Reid, 1989; Sturt and Crocker, 1997; Weinberg, 1993). But while recent data on incremental interpretation (e.g., Murray and Rowan, 1998; Pickering and Traxler, 1998; Traxler and Pickering, 1996a,b) pose quite a challenge for such approaches, they do seem to steadfastly refuse to go away. Coming down firmly on both sides of the fence (see, for example, Kennedy et al., 1989 vs. Murray and Rowan, 1998), I'm inclined to suggest that perhaps both may be true. There are circumstances under which interpretation clearly proceeds very rapidly indeed, and yet in our lab and apparently in many others, there appears to be a certain lack of consistency in this. It is not uncommon to hear, "How come it showed up in first fixation duration last time, but this time we only get it in ... ?" This is an issue that I will return to below, but surely one of the great challenges facing all of us who wish to use eye movements as a sensitive index of on-going cognitive processes is to understand the exact nature of this 'elastic band' that apparently couples the eye to the language processor. What factors determine whether it will be tight or frustratingly saggy?

Konieczny and Hemforth raise another important issue related to the resolution of this, and presumably many other, ambiguities. Is it really the case that modifier attachment is unaffected by the nature of the modifier? Construal (Frazier and Clifton, 1996) suggests that it should be — at least for relative clauses and prepositional phrases expressing 'non-primary' relations. However, beginning with the findings of Britt, Perfetti, Garrod and Rayner (1992), it has become apparent that these two types of modifying expressions can behave quite differently. Indeed, recent work by Mandleberg (1999) in English has shown that even with very closely matched prepositional phrase and relative clause modifiers, attachment preference and the way in which this may be influenced by referential context varies greatly with modifier type. In the case of the German data reported here, however, there is an additional factor which may be playing a role. German relative clauses are mandatorily preceded by a comma, whereas prepositional phrases are not. As Konieczny and Hemforth speculate, the 'boundary' before the relative clause may serve to block certain types of regressions. Whether or not such a boundary effect is critically related to the presence of a comma is an empirical question certainly worthy of further research.

However, as Hill and Murray (Chapter 22) point out, there has in fact been scant attention paid to the role of punctuation in sentence parsing. Most researchers have either deleted sentence-internal punctuation with gay abandon, or have assumed that they necessarily understand the role it will play. The data reported in this chapter suggest that both approaches are seriously flawed. In some circumstances, punctuation appears to exert profound effects on the parser, while in others it is effectively 'transparent'. Perhaps even more worryingly, its local and global effects appear to be different. At an oculomotor level, the presence of a comma exerts a fairly consistent effect on eye movement parameters, and one not far divorced from effects of variation in spacing. However, this consistency across item types is not matched by the rather more specific effects of commas on processing difficulty and overall reading patterns. There goes that 'stretchy elastic band' again!

Hill and Murray's conclusion that commas are 'not just another constraint' placed on the parser is, however, consistent with the story coming out of the data in many of these chapters. The analysis dictated by frequency, availability or 'acceptability' appears not always to be the one pursued. Instead, it is frequently the case that one factor appears to exert an effect far more substantial than the strength of any constraint that it imposes. However, as Spivey and Tanenhaus (1998) demonstrated, constraint-based models have proved themselves remarkably adept at accounting for apparent all-or-none phenomena. But this is a facility that I suspect they will not demonstrate when it comes to accounting for the type of data reported by Van Gompel, Pickering and Traxler (Chapter 24).

Ambiguity has provided the staple diet of parsing research ever since its inception. Some of the earliest studies specifically set out to determine the 'costs' of ambiguity (e.g., Fodor, Garrett and Bever, 1968; Hakes, 1971), with the conclusion " ... that there is an increase in computational load associated with ambiguity, and that some sort of parallel processing is what accounts for that increase" (Fodor, Bever and Garrett, 1974, p. 367). However, the norm in more recent times has become comparisons of processing load in the alternate versions of locally ambiguous items at or after the point at which the ambiguity has been resolved. Van Gompel and colleagues have turned this logic on its head and shown that the processing of a continuing ambiguity can in fact be *easier* than when it is resolved (in either direction). Such findings clearly provide a major challenge for any model of the parsing process which suggests that more than one analysis is maintained with either a cost to multiple analyses or competition between them. It is interesting, though, that their proposed solution to this difficulty harks back to an age-old principle — the idea of a race with only one survivor (see also the chapter by Konieczny and Hemforth). The same principle was inherent in the development of the Garden

Path Model — the fuel that drove the parsing principles was the speed or facility with which the potential analyses could be computed. The difference is that Van Gompel and colleagues admit a much wider range of factors into the 'handicapping' process. In fact, they suggest no principled reason for excluding any. This brings us back to Pynte and Colonna's question of whether we can conclude that there are any *general principles* underlying parsing decisions or whether it is basically anarchic?

One principle that has maintained currency for a long time now is the suggestion that it is not so much syntactic principles or processes that drive parsing decisions but their interpretive consequences. Although it became perhaps a little lost in later versions of 'referential theory', Crain and Steedman's (1985) original proposal was that it was the interpretive consequences of an analysis which determined its choice, not anything to do with syntax. Syntactic preferences were seen as an epiphenomenon related to interpretive complexity. Clearly a number of the papers here concur with the suggestion that interpretive factors play a role, but the general conclusion seems to be that they do so when 'late' or 'arbitrary' decisions need to be made and there is a primacy in the role played by syntax. Nowhere is this clearer than in the chapter by Clifton, Bock and Rado. They examine one recent proposal derived from referential theory — the suggestion that focus operators such as 'only' facilitate the interpretation of ambiguous phrases as noun phrase modifiers (Ni, Crain and Shankweiler, 1996) — and find it seriously wanting. Like Paterson, Liversedge and Underwood (1999), they find evidence that the properties of 'only' facilitate recovery from a garden path, but not that it contributes to the choice of an initial analysis. However, before a syntax-first anti-anarchist rejoices that here at least is some restriction on the principles and sources of information that can guide parsing decisions, it should be borne in mind that Clifton et al. begin by doing a fairly convincing job of first demolishing the principles on which this referential claim is based. If 'only' does not in fact fulfil the referential role that Ni et al. suggest, then these data are silent on the general question of whether referential factors play a role in parsing decisions. It is, however, easy to agree with Clifton et al.'s final conclusion. As this and so many of the other chapters here demonstrate, it seems clear that analysis of the processes at the interface between syntax and semantics is likely to provide a focus for much of the most interesting and important future research.

Measures

It took a while to establish the ascendancy of Just and Carpenter's (1980) 'immediacy hypothesis', but these days one would be hard pressed to mount a case that there is anything other than a pretty close coupling between eye movement parameters and the on-going cognitive processing of what is being looked at. We have seen evidence of a number of 'high level' cognitive factors (such as, but not limited to, word frequency, syntactic disambiguation and pragmatic plausibility) influencing even the duration of the very first fixation falling on a word. This seems like pretty tight coupling indeed. And yet, as mentioned above, it is not always so. Sometimes such effects occur further downstream in the pattern of eye movements. Sometimes, in fact, very much further downstream. It seems unclear whether, or when, this reflects a rather looser coupling between eye movements and cognitive processes and when, or whether, it might reflect some sort of delay or underspecification in the cognitive process itself.

As Liversedge, Paterson and Pickering (1998) pointed out, readers faced with processing difficulty appear to have three choices: They can spend longer at the current point of regard and attempt to resolve the difficulty, making use of representations of previously read text held in memory. They can make use of the 'memory' afforded by the printed text and regress to a previously read region in order to check the appropriateness or accuracy of previously read information, or to use this in revising their current interpretation. (For a detailed discussion of this issue see Chapter 8.) Alternatively, they can 'put off' the problem and push on in the hope that an appropriate solution will be delivered by the next few words. This might even result in *faster* reading times in the region under consideration.

All of these possibilities assume tight coupling between the cognitive processes involved in reading and the location and duration of fixations. And from this perspective it is not too difficult to see how even very similar experiments might show quite different patterns of results with one, say, finding effects of a syntactic manipulation on the duration of the first fixation in a 'disambiguating region' and another finding rather 'later' effects on, say, first pass reading time in a subsequent region, the probability of regressions or even second pass reading. Readers may experience the *same difficulty* in the two experiments, but respond to it in different ways, presumably because of something to do with the nature of the task or the filler items or some other extraneous variable. If this is true, then two points need to be considered. First, we would be mistaken to assume that some sorts of eye movement measures *necessarily* index 'early' processes while others reflect only revision or repair. Certainly, the early measures must reflect early processes, but the converse is not necessarily true. Second, it suggests that some aspects of eye movement control are influenced by even 'higher level' cognitive factors, such as expectation. At the least, we have to postulate that readers can be encouraged to develop differences in reading style. While this is obviously trivially true, in that it is possible to modulate overall parameters, like average saccade size, in response to instruction or perceived text difficulty, it seems like an altogether more radical suggestion to propose that the reader would modulate the basic nature of their response to difficulty, switching on or off, for example, the 'press on' versus 'go back' procedure.

It might be suggested that this is an exaggeration and there really are processing differences between instances where the reader chooses one option rather than another. For example, it might be possible to find a first fixation duration effect of pragmatic plausibility if all of the experimental sentences are simple and the reader is 'primed' to expect a particular type of structure. However, with a bit of added syntactic complexity and maybe some more variation in the form of the 'background', the process runs to completion a little more slowly and first fixation duration then only reflects somewhat lower level effects. And, in fact, I have argued exactly that case (Murray, 1998). However, for every instance like this, there are a number of others where the coupling is not so obvious; where there is no discernible reason why the 'early' effects in one experiment don't show up in the same measure in another.

We may, in time, find that there is a systematic relationship between the nature of the 'difficulty', or the cognitive process which it stimulates, and the particular pattern of ocular response, but for now we seem a long way from the goal of being able to associate a particular pattern of eye movements with a certain type of cognitive process. To take, for example, the distinction suggested by Van Gompel et al. between processing 'load' (derived from competition in a constraint-based architecture) and reanalysis; it would be very appealing indeed if we could take the *pattern* of eye movements as evidence for one or other of these. For example, it could be the case that 'load' slows processing, but does not necessitate reinspection, whereas reanalysis might involve the 're-inputting' of material. But while it is tempting to say that such *principles* seem sensible, it is all too easy to see how such a distinction can rapidly become blurred. As suggested above, 're-inputting' can be from memory, and regressions occur in text where there is no obvious need for reanalysis. It is very easy to take an individual's eye movement record while reading a particular sentence and interpret their 'intentions' at various points in the sentence, but I wonder how often we get it right?

But are we really justified in *necessarily* assuming such a tight coupling between eye movements and the underlying cognitive process? There is some reason to believe that we may not be. If the 'immediacy hypothesis' is necessarily true, it is not clear why there is, for example, some apparent dissociation between 'local' eye movement patterns associated with a comma or double spacing (Chapter 22) and more global measures which show varying degrees of processing difficulty. Also, there seems to be an increasing amount of evidence for some distribution of processing across more than one word object at the same time. It is not just the sort of parafoveal on foveal effects reported, for example, by Kennedy (Chapter 8) that suggest that there is some form of parallel or distributed processing, but also the rather less controversial 'spill-over' effects of factors such as word frequency.

If the duration of a fixation on word N is modulated by the frequency of word $N - 1$, then this surely suggests that some processing of word $N - 1$ is occurring in parallel with the inspection of word N. It might be the case that although the eye moves to word N, its processing is not commenced until all processing of word $N - 1$ is completed, but this does not seem very parsimonious, especially in the context of the current evidence for first fixation and parafoveal effects of word N. It seems far more likely that there is some overlap in processing and in this case the location of the eye must be divorced from the cognitive processing of at least one word. In fact there might be overlapping processing of three words. The spillover effects suggest that the processing of word $N - 1$ continues, on at least some occasions, while word N is being inspected. The first fixation and gaze duration effects related to properties of word N suggest that it is being processed during these fixations. And if we admit the evidence for parafoveal on foveal effects, then it seems that at least some processing of word $N + 1$ is likely to have begun. In fact, there is some recent evidence from our lab (Boissiere, 1999) which suggests that, under at least some circumstances, parafoveal lexical processing may extend even two words to the right.

If all of these effects can be substantiated, it will be quite a challenge to success-fully model the nature of the processes involved. One could be pessimistic about this and conclude, with Sandy Pollatsek, that if one admits the possibility of the over-lapping processing of more than one word we will be reduced to concluding simply that 'stuff happens' (Pollatsek, 1999, pers. commun.). However, I'm more opti-mistic about the possibility of our successfully understanding how such a cascaded process might work, but there is certainly no denying that it will be a challenge.

However, for the moment, let's just assume that processing and eye location are (reasonably) tightly coupled. Let's also ignore Pynte and Colonna's suggestion that perhaps there can be some decoupling between eye position and processing consequences because of the nature of the parsing process itself. Under these circumstances, how do we best measure 'load' or 'difficulty'? The 'tradition' has been to look at the duration of initial fixations and a multi-fixation measure that is probably most appropriately labelled 'gaze'.

Inhoff and Radach (1998) point out the need for developing some 'trading standards' in the nature of the procedures and measures which we use. They cogently point out the potential dangers and confusions that can result from not doing so. Similarly, Liversedge, Paterson and Pickering (1998) point out the weaknesses or relying (solely) on particular sorts of multi-fixation measures of processing difficulty. However, Inhoff and Radach shy away from offering prescriptive suggestions and Liversedge et al. say that they specifically don't wish to claim that particular measures are better than others.

In contrast, I intend to be altogether more bold (or perhaps foolhardy). I could not agree more with these authors that some 'trading standards' are necessary — and probably overdue. I believe that there is sufficient evidence now to at least make a stab at what some of them should be. If I stick my neck out with a concrete proposal or two, I might be shot down, but if I am, it should at least stimulate a necessary and important discussion.

Gaze

The term 'gaze' has been defined as the summed duration of all fixations falling within a defined region, until the eye exits that region (in any direction). However, this term is normally only used in reading research when the region constitutes a single word. When the region is comprised of a number of words, this measure is frequently, and I will argue inappropriately, referred to as 'first pass reading time' (e.g., Rayner, Sereno, Morris, Schmauder and Clifton, 1989). Clifton et al. and Konieczny and Hemforth use that terminology here, while Frenck-Mestre and Pynte adopt the hybrid 'first pass gaze duration'.

Why do I argue that this is inappropriate? Well, for starters, why (confusingly) use two terms to refer to the same measure? The answer I will suggest lies in two questionable assumptions, both of which are related to processing. The first of these is that the term 'gaze' somehow relates to apperception. Thus, the amount of time spent looking at a word, or indeed any object, is assumed to be related to the time taken to identify it. One might achieve this with a single fixation, or with a somewhat larger or more difficult 'object' it may take a number of fixations probably directed to different parts of the object. The assumption, however, is that the object is likely to be inspected for just enough time to identify it, before the eye moves on. Total inspection time is assumed to be closely related to total identification time. (I will ignore the question raised by Inhoff and Radach of whether we should also be including saccade time in this measure, since, as they point out, it will probably make relatively little difference in the majority of instances.)

What makes this assumption questionable is, of course, the nature of that elastic coupling between the eye and the mind, with parafoveal and 'spillover' effects. Nonetheless, it does seem like a reasonable approximation, and if one includes instances with zero gaze (i.e., cases of word skipping) in the calculation of averages, then *average* gaze should be reasonably well related to average identification difficulty. I suspect the suggestion that we adopt a principle of including zeros in the calculation is likely to be controversial, but as far as I can see, it readily falls out of the above assumptions.

It might reasonably be suggested that this is crazy, since when a word is not fixated we don't know that it is in fact being identified. My response is that we don't *know* that when a word *is* inspected that it is being identified. We have good grounds for *assuming* that this is generally true, but know nothing of any specific instance. Similarly, we have good grounds for believing that most cases of word skipping involve the parafoveal identification of the word. Certainly, this is not identification in zero time, but the time required is included in the gaze on the previous word. Well, not quite — that gaze probably reflected less than the full time to identify that word (since there is likely to have been some parafoveal preview advantage there too). Thus, gaze duration in instances in which a word *is* inspected (assuming that some words are not) is likely to be an overestimate of identification time for the word. However, the *average* time, provided we include those zeros, is likely to be a pretty good estimate of the average identification time. Indeed, there is empirical evidence which suggests that the inclusion of zeros results in a measure more sensitive to processing load (Blanchard, 1985). The only systematic source of contamination will relate to the extent to which the mind may lag behind (or perhaps be ahead of) the eye.

In contrast, consider the consequences of ignoring zeros. Let's assume a concrete example of the two word string 'despite a'. Let's assume that in our sample of recordings 'despite' always attracts at least one fixation and has an average gaze duration of 265 ms. The word 'a', on the other hand only attracts fixations on 33% of occasions, but when it does, the average duration is 252 ms. Do we assume that 252 ms is a good estimate of identification time for 'a'? I suspect most would agree that the calculation including zeros (84 ms) is likely to be closer to the mark. The point is that if it's possible to identify a word without looking at it, calculation including only those cases where a fixation falls directly on the word is sure to provide a biased estimate and the extent of the bias will be directly related to the probability of skipping.

If you are still not convinced, perhaps one further calculation will do it. In the above example, assuming no regressions, average gaze on the string 'despite a' was 349 ms. How could this be made up of two 'sub-gazes' of 265 and 252 ms?

This brings us to the second assumption: If the gaze on a single word reflects time to identify it, then taking gaze on a string of words will reflect the time taken to process them. Seeing that this is an apperceptive process, we can consequently call it 'first pass reading time', on the assumption that first pass reflects the initial low level processing of that string — although in this case we are probably also assuming a bit of syntactic processing in addition to the word identifications. Again, with the caveats regarding a bit of elasticity in the system and the inclusion of zeros etc., this works fine, *provided we assume that this reflects the apperception of the 'object' as a whole*. However, this really isn't the case with a multi-word string — it normally isn't a single 'object'.

Liversedge et al. (1998) provide a number of interesting examples of what a reader might do in such circumstances, especially if this string poses some processing difficulty. However, the general principle is straightforward. Where the region consists of a number of 'objects', there is rather less certainty that the processing of all those objects will be completed before the eye leaves that region, than if only one object is involved. To take a concrete example, if the region were the string 'behind the fridge' and the eye landed on 'behind' and then immediately regressed to some previous words, would we assume that the duration of this fixation reflected the apperception of the entire string? I suspect not. We would probably be even less inclined to do so if, after regressing, the eye returned to inspect the word 'fridge' before moving on.

It is an open question as to what might constitute 'first pass reading time' in this instance. If we mean by that: the time to identify each of the words, then arguably it might be captured by something like the accumulated gaze on each of the three individual words. But of course that isn't normally what we mean. What we are usually trying to get at (at least in sentence parsing research) is some measure of immediate processing difficulty — lexical and syntactic and perhaps semantic. We assume that an 'early' measure, like gaze, will capture this better than later measures, such as total reading time (the sum of *all* fixations falling within a defined region). But while it's certainly true that gaze is an early measure, there is no guarantee that it will be a complete measure. Even ignoring the question of what prompted the regression in the example above, and whether this is in fact something that we wish to capture with our 'first pass' measure, it seems clear that the measure potentially fails to capture even the most basic identification process for part of the string. As Liversedge et al. aptly demonstrate, shorter gaze does not necessarily map onto decreased processing difficulty. In fact, it can easily mean the opposite. If all subjects in a 'difficult' condition immediately regressed after inspecting 'behind', in our example, and those in an 'easy' condition did not, then gaze would be shorter in the difficult condition.

The point is that 'gaze' seems to be an appropriate measure for the processing of an 'object' — normally in reading, but I suppose not necessarily, a single word. To the extent that the region being considered acts as more than one functional object, the measure becomes increasingly inappropriate. Changing the name does nothing to ameliorate this difficulty and, in fact, in this instance leads to a misapprehension. 'First pass reading time' effects have become something of a prerequisite for various sorts of parsing claims, but in fact it's not even clear what is meant by the term. Perhaps accumulated word gaze would come close, or perhaps accumulated *progressive* fixation duration, but both measures bring their own complications and I suspect they do not get at what the majority of sentence parsing researchers really mean by 'first pass reading time'. But one thing seems clear. It should not be confused with multi-word gaze. This seems to be a measure fraught with difficulty: it is not monotonically related to processing difficulty and cannot even be relied on to include the initial perceptual processing of the words in the string.

Proposal: Refer to any measure of accumulated fixation time before the eye exits a defined region (in any direction) as 'gaze'. The measure might (arguably) also include saccade time within this region. If a region is skipped, but it could conceivably have been inspected indirectly, then include zero as a valid measure.

Beware of the consequences of using this measure when the region includes more than one 'processing object' and certainly never refer to it as 'first pass reading time'.

Total pass reading time

It is interesting that the chapters here, even the one that comes from members of the group most instrumental in defining the 'reporting standard' prevalent in most of the current literature, seem to be converging on a new 'standard' measure of processing difficulty. The measure is not new, but using it as a reporting standard appears to be.

I believed that the measure first appeared in the literature as 'Total Pass (per word)' reading time in Kennedy, Murray, Jennings and Reid (1989), but I see from Van Gompel et al. (Chapter 24) that the same measure (unnamed) was in fact used by Duffy, Morris and Rayner (1988) in some of their regions. The measure was also independently developed by the lab in Freiburg, where it was termed 'Regression Path' reading time (e.g., Konieczny, 1996). In the chapters here it is referred to as 'Regression Path' by Konieczny and Hemforth, and Van Gompel, Pickering and Traxler; as 'Cumulative Region' reading time by Mitchell, Brysbaert, Grondelaers and Swanepoel; as 'Go Past' time by Clifton, Bock and Rado; and as a 'First Pass' reading time measure by Hill and Murray (we routinely calculate a number of 'First Pass' measures, but use this definition as the 'standard').

This measure cumulates the duration of all fixations, progressive and regressive, after the eye enters a region, until it exits it to the right. There seems to be an increasing amount of evidence which suggests that this definition has the potential to provide probably the most sensitive on-line measure of moment-to-moment processing load by incorporating both increased inspection time within a region and regressions resulting from processing difficulty. We routinely find this to be the most sensitive of the 'first pass' measures which we calculate and the results from a number of studies appear to converge on a similar conclusion (e.g., Brysbaert, 1994; Konieczny, 1996; Liversedge, Pickering and Traxler, 1996; Murray, Watt and Kennedy, 1994; Murray and Rowan, 1998). Also, of course, a similar conclusion emerges (with one small caveat) in the chapters here.

In addition to its apparent sensitivity to processing difficulty, the measure has one other outstanding characteristic — it does not 'lose' data. The total time taken to (initially) get to the end of a particular sentence region will simply be the sum of all of the 'Total Pass' reading times up to that point. As a 'first pass' measure, it is unique in this regard. Any gaze measure 'loses' the duration of regressions and reinspections of the region. They can, of course, be recovered with the addition of two more measures — 'first pass regression time' and 'initial region reinspection time' (which may or may not in fact include the first fixations falling on particular words) for each of the regions — but without all measures for all regions, part of the 'initial reading time' is lost. In fact, the measure was developed in our lab precisely to measure the totality of time spent processing a sentence up to some point in exactly the same way as might be reflected by 'cumulative' self-paced reading, where the reader has the option to regress before pressing on. There are obvious pitfalls in reporting measures which potentially leave a large proportion of the data unaccounted for. This is especially true if much of that data might be exactly what the study is concerned with (i.e., regressions resulting from a local processing difficulty).

Whether this is really a 'first pass' measure depends on what we mean by first pass. If we mean the first time that anything is inspected, then clearly it is not, since it incorporates a subset of reinspections. However, so does 'gaze'. The difference is that the reinspections here are not limited to those falling within a particular region. For that reason it's a bit peculiar to talk about this measure as being the first pass reading time *for that region*. Perhaps the best candidate for that would be accumulated progressive fixation time (i.e., the duration of each fixation, which falls further to the right than any previous one). This, however, has the drawback of assuming that saccades never overshoot and regressions never subserve initial identification. If, on the other hand, we mean the initial inspection time prompted by the material found in a region, then 'Total Pass' could be considered as a 'first pass' measure. The problem of course is that the term 'first pass' carries with it a great deal of theoretical 'baggage' at both the sentence processing and the oculomotor levels, and this is seldom, if ever, fully spelt out.

Pragmatically, however, this measure appears to provide what most researchers in sentence processing want from a 'first pass' measure. It sensitively reflects local processing difficulty in two out of the three possible response scenarios listed above ('stay longer' or 'regress'), and in the third ('press on'), it presumably reflects it a little later downstream. Its strength in accumulating different possible responses to difficulty is also its weakness in not distinguishing between them. But, as demonstrated by Konieczny and Hemforth and by Clifton et al. here, the addition of sub-measures focussing on various parts of this time can be very informative indeed, and such an approach may allow us to begin tackling the question, raised above, of whether differences in inspection pattern necessarily reflect different underlying processes. Also, the strength of routinely reporting a measure which includes the full data set should not be underestimated. The use of other 'first pass' measures frequently results in some part of the initial reading time falling between the cracks in the floorboards.

If, however, we are to standardise on the reporting of such a measure it would also be sensible to standardise on what to call it. My prejudice is obvious by the title to this section. I shy away from 'regression path' since the measure doesn't *necessarily* include regressions (i.e., if there are none launched from the region) and that sounds rather like the time taken *for* the regressions, not the total time taken to exit the region. 'Cumulative Region' reading time is alright in so far as it relates to the cumulative self-paced reading procedure mentioned above, but it doesn't imply anything about the process which ends the cumulation and it does sound rather like the sum of fixations falling *within* the region. I can see why Chuck Clifton likes the term 'Go Past', but to my ears (or eyes) it doesn't quite convey the sense that this is a 'first pass' measure. 'Total Pass', however, seems to me to convey the idea that this is a 'pass' measure and that it includes the totality of response required to pass. It also, incidentally, captures the fact that these measures 'total up'.

Proposal: Sentence processing research using eye movements should routinely report 'Total Pass Reading Time', whether or not it also reports other sub-measures. Like gaze, and for the same reasons, if a region is skipped, but it could conceivably have been inspected indirectly, then zero should be included as a valid measure. We should also settle on a single terminology for the measure. My vote is for 'Total Pass Reading Time', but for the sake of clarity I'll go along with any emerging consensus.

Conclusions

In addition to the specific topics tackled in each of the chapters in this section, the work reported here also raises a number of more general issues. Foremost amongst these is the question of whether we are right to continue looking for a (small) number of general parsing principles that drive the process in all instances and across a variety of languages. Increasingly, these and other studies are finding early effects of semantics and discourse related factors on the manner in which a sentence is processed. Are we right to consider these as just another set of 'constraints' to be added to syntactic 'preferences' or is it possible to derive a set of principles about what does and doesn't influence the initial analysis of a sentence and the manner in which the interface between syntax and semantics functions?

In order to answer this, and other questions about language processing, using eye movement technology, we need to have a good idea of the closeness of the coupling between eye movement parameters and the underlying cognitive process. While it is certainly clear that this coupling can be very tight, there is an increasing amount of evidence to suggest that it may, in some respects, or under some circumstances, also be rather loose. One important task for reading researchers is to better understand the nature of this coupling and whether different patterns of inspection are necessarily related to differences in the underlying cognitive process. A full understanding of the reading process and the way in which this is reflected in eye movement patterns and parameters will undoubtedly need to draw on findings from both the 'oculomotor' and the 'high level' ends of eye movement research.

However, we are now in a situation where eye movement recording appears to have become the 'technology of choice' for parsing research, and it is almost certainly a vain hope that the majority of researchers in this area will fully acquaint themselves with a good working knowledge of the more basic eye movement findings. For this reason, as well as many others, it is vitally important that we establish some generally recognised 'trading standards' concerning the types of measures that should be reported, the way that they should be calculated, and the sorts of conclusions which can be derived from them. Some consensus seems to be emerging in these chapters and in other recent research, and proposals are made here concerning the use and calculation of two types of measure. But, even if these proposals are accepted, they are no more than a beginning.

References

Blanchard, H.E. (1985). A comparison of some processing time measures based on eye movements. Acta Psychologica, 58, 1–15.

Boissiere, C. (1999). The Existence of Parafoveal Effects in Sentences. Unpublished Honours Dissertation, University of Dundee.

Britt, M.A., Perfetti, C.A., Garrod, S. and Rayner, K. (1992). Parsing in discourse: Context effects and their limits. Journal of Memory and Language, 31, 293–314.

Brysbaert, M. (1994). Sentence reading: Do we make use of non-audible cues? Paper presented at the Fourth Workshop on Language Comprehension, Giens, 13–14 May.

Crain, S. and Steedman, M. (1985). On not being led up the garden-path: The use of context by the psychological syntax processor. In: D.R. Dowty, L. Karttunen and A.M. Zwicky (Eds.), Natural Language Parsing: Psychological, Computational and Theoretical Perspectives. Cambridge: C.U.P., pp. 320–358.

Cuetos, F. and Mitchell, D.C. (1988). Cross-linguistic differences in parsing: Restrictions on the use of the Late Closure strategy in Spanish. Cognition, 30, 73–105.

Duffy, S.A., Morris, R.K. and Rayner, K. (1988). Lexical ambiguity and fixation times in reading. Journal of Memory and Language, 27, 429–446.

Fodor, J.A., Bever, T.G. and Garrett, M.F. (1974). The Psychology of Language. New York: McGraw-Hill.

Fodor, J.A., Garrett, M. and Bever, T.G. (1968). Some syntactic determinants of sentential complexity. II: Verb structure. Perception and Psychophysics, 3, 453–461.

Frazier, L. and Clifton, C., Jr. (1996). Construal. Cambridge, MA: MIT Press.

Gorrell, P. (1995). Syntax and Parsing. Cambridge: Cambridge University Press.

Gorrell, P. (1998). Syntactic analysis and reanalysis. In: F. Ferreira and J.D. Fodor (Eds.), Re-analysis in Sentence Processing. Dordrecht: Kluwer.

Hakes, D.T. (1971). Does verb structure affect sentence comprehension? Perception and Psychophysics, 10, 229–232.

Inhoff, A.W. and Radach, R. (1998). Definition and computation of oculomotor measures in the study of cognitive processes. In: G. Underwood (Ed.), Eye Guidance in Reading and Scene Perception. Oxford: Elsevier, pp. 29–54.

Just, M.A. and Carpenter, P.A. (1980). A theory of reading: From eye fixations to comprehension. Psychological Review, 87, 329–354.

Kennedy, A., Murray, W.S., Jennings, F. and Reid, C. (1989). Parsing complements: Comments on the generality of the principle of minimal attachment. Language and Cognitive Processes, 4, SI 51–76.

Konieczny, L. (1996). Human Sentence Processing: A Semantics Oriented Parsing Approach. Unpublished doctoral dissertation, University of Freiburg.

Liversedge, S.P., Paterson, K.B. and Pickering, M.J. (1998). Eye movements and measures of reading time. In: G. Underwood (Ed.), Eye Guidance in Reading and Scene Perception. Oxford: Elsevier, pp. 55–76.

Liversedge, S.P., Pickering, M.J. and Traxler, M.J. (1996). A comparative analysis of qualitatively different eye movement measures. Poster presented at CUNY Sentence Processing Conference, New York.

Mandleberg, H.J. (1999). The Effects of Referential Context and Pragmatic Plausibility on Syntactic Parsing. Unpublished Honours Dissertation, University of Dundee.

Mitchell, D.C. and Brysbaert, M. (1998). Challenges to recent theories of crosslinguistic variation in parsing: Evidence from Dutch. Syntax and Semantics, 31, 313–335.

Murray, W.S. (1998). Plausibility effects: A second look. Paper presented at First International Workshop on Written Language Processing, Sydney.

Murray, W.S. and Rowan, M. (1998). Early, mandatory pragmatic processing. Journal of Psycholinguistic Research (CUNY Special Issue), 27, 1–22.

Murray, W.S., Watt, S.M. and Kennedy, A. (1994). Influences of sensory form on syntactic processing options. Paper presented to Experimental Psychology Society, Exeter.

Ni, W., Crain, S. and Shankweiler, D. (1996). Sidestepping garden paths: Assessing the contributions of syntax, semantics and plausibility in resolving ambiguities. Language and Cognitive Processes, 11, 283–334.

Paterson, K.B., Liversedge, S.P. and Underwood, G. (1999). The influence of focus operators on syntactic processing of short relative clause sentences. Quarterly Journal of Experimental Psychology, 52A, 717–737.

Pickering, M.J. and Traxler, M.J. (1998). Plausibility and recovery from garden paths: An eye-tracking study. Journal of Experimental Psychology: Learning, Memory and Cognition, 24, 940–961.

Rayner, K., Sereno, S.C., Morris, R.K., Schmauder, A.R. and Clifton, C., Jr. (1989). Eye movements and on-line language comprehension processes. Language and Cognitive Processes, 4, SI 21–49.

Spivey, M.J. and Tanenhaus, M.K. (1998). Syntactic ambiguity resolution in discourse: Modeling the effects of referential context and lexical frequency. Journal of Experimental Psychology: Learning, Memory and Cognition, 24, 1521–1543.

Sturt, P. and Crocker, M.W. (1997). Thematic monotonicity. Journal of Psycholinguistic Research (CUNY Special Issue), 26, 297–322.

Traxler, M.J. and Pickering, M.J. (1996a). Plausibility and the processing of unbounded dependencies: An eye-tracking study. Journal of Memory and Language, 35, 454–475.

Traxler, M.J. and Pickering, M.J. (1996b). Case-marking in the parsing of complement sentences: Evidence from eye movements. Quarterly Journal of Experimental Psychology, 49A, 991–1004.

Weinberg, A. (1993). Parameters in the theory of sentence processing: Minimal commitment theory goes east. Journal of Psycholinguistic Research, 22, 339–364.

Section 5

Models and Simulations

Section Editor

Ralph Radach

CHAPTER 25

Saccade Planning in Reading with Central Scotomas: Comparison of Human and Ideal Performance

Timothy S. Klitz, Gordon E. Legge
University of Minnesota

and

Bosco S. Tjan
NEC Research Institute

Abstract

The presence of a central scotoma, often due to visual impairments such as age-related macular degeneration, disrupts the process of reading. We have examined reading with a central scotoma using two complementary approaches: ideal-observer analysis and visual-span simulation with human readers. We formulated Mr. Chips, an ideal-observer computer program that combines visual and lexical information optimally to read simple texts in the minimum number of saccades. To study human performance, we trained humans on a reading task with the same informational constraints as Mr. Chips. We measured saccade size and reading speed of human readers using a 'visual-span simulator'. We found that simulated central scotomas introduced to Mr. Chips, and to human readers, reduced the mean saccade size compared to reading with no central scotoma. Mr. Chips can increase his mean saccade size nearly 70% when he integrates information from both sides of the central scotoma, as opposed to reading with only one side of the central scotoma. Given unlimited time, the mean saccade size of human readers can also increase when integrating information on both sides of a central scotoma. However, when trying to maximize reading speed, human readers use information on only one side of the central scotoma (unless the scotoma is very small). In order for humans to maximize their reading speed, they compromise their saccade-planning performance relative to Mr. Chips.

Reading as a Perceptual Process/A. Kennedy, R. Radach, D. Heller and J. Pynte (Editors)
© 2000 Elsevier Science Ltd. All rights reserved

Introduction

Visual impairment usually has a major impact on reading. The primary focus in this chapter is low-vision readers with a central scotoma, that is, a blind spot in the center of the visual field. Central scotomas frequently result from age-related macular degeneration, a continually growing cause of vision loss. People with central scotomas usually have severe reading deficits, and often exhibit abnormal eye movements in reading (Bullimore and Bailey, 1995; Trauzettel-Klosinski, Teschner, Tornow and Zrenner, 1994). It is not yet known whether these abnormal eye movements are contributory to deficient reading (and thus should be corrected through rehabilitation), or are a consequence of reading with abnormal visual input (and thereby are optimal given the circumstances). Answers to these questions may have important implications in the area of low-vision rehabilitation.

A central scotoma splits the visual span, the number of letters that can be identified in a single fixation, into two visual 'islands' separated by the scotoma. If people confine their reading to only one side of the scotoma, they are using less than half of the available visual span. Can people with a central scotoma integrate the visual information present on both sides of a central scotoma?

We will address this issue using two complementary approaches: an ideal-observer analysis and a visual-span simulation with human readers. Mr. Chips is an ideal-observer computer program that combines visual and lexical information in an optimal way to read texts in the minimum number of saccades. At the present time, Mr. Chips deals specifically with the perceptual front–end constraints in reading and not with syntax or semantics. An ideal-observer approach allows us to establish a level of 'competence' (see Chomsky, 1965) for a reader that performs a saccade-planning task using finite visual and lexical information. We can establish the competence of an ideal reader with a central scotoma and compare it to the performance of a human reader with a simulated central scotoma. In order to systematically study human performance when reading with a central scotoma, we trained and tested normally-sighted readers on a reading task with the same informational constraints faced by Mr. Chips. This procedure involved the use of a 'visual-span simulator' (see below), which measures performance limits imposed by cognitive aspects of human readers, not captured by Mr. Chips.

With these two approaches, one a theoretical measure of competence (Mr. Chips) and the other an empirical measure of performance (human tested on the visual-span simulator), we will examine the impact of a simulated central scotoma on reading. Mr. Chips can clearly benefit from using visual information on both sides of a central scotoma because he is an ideal observer that can optimally use all the visual and lexical information present. The question we ask is: How *much* does Mr. Chips benefit from this integration across a central scotoma? With the visual-span simulator, we can ask whether human readers benefit in the same way by using information on both sides of a simulated central scotoma.

Mr. Chips: an ideal-observer model of reading

Mr. Chips is the name of a computer implementation of an ideal-observer model of reading. The name comes from the schoolmaster in the novel *Goodbye, Mr. Chips* (Hilton, 1934). Mr. Chips, the schoolmaster, was not a particularly brilliant man, but within the tiny world of his boarding school, he was very wise. Mr. Chips, the computer simulation, is fully competent, but only within the restricted domain of a simple reading task.

Ideal-observer models have been used in word recognition (e.g., Pelli, Farell and Moore, 1995), visual detection and discrimination (e.g., Geisler, 1989), and object recognition (e.g., Tjan, Braje, Legge and Kersten, 1995). An ideal observer is an algorithm that yields optimal performance on a task, given a specified set of information sources. An ideal-observer analysis is not intended as an exact model of how humans perform a task, but rather it establishes an upper bound (i.e., a level of competence) for human performance. We can then compare human performance to that of the ideal observer.

Mr. Chips makes optimal use of two sources of information: visual information and lexical information.[1] Visual information is obtained through a 'retina' (left side of Fig. 1). The retina is a linear array of character slots. Each slot can either be high resolution (individual letters can be identified) or low resolution (only a distinction between letters and spaces can be made).[2] In Fig. 1, the 'normal retina' has a visual span of 9 characters. The visual span is flanked by two peripheral regions of low-resolution character slots. Fig. 1 also illustrates a retina with three low-resolution slots in central vision, simulating a central scotoma. In the computer simulations in this chapter, all of the central scotomas are 'relative' scotomas, i.e., the scotoma is a region of blurred vision as opposed to a region of no vision (an

---

1 The model also makes use of oculomotor information, the accuracy of the landing sites of saccades performed by Mr. Chips. In planning saccades, Mr. Chips knows the mean (M) and the standard deviation (sd) of a Gaussian distribution of possible landing sites given an attempted saccade of size M. In all of the simulations discussed in the chapter, the standard deviation was set to zero, i.e., all saccades are 100% accurate. See Legge, Klitz and Tjan (1997) for a thorough analysis of the effects of oculomotor noise on the performance of Mr. Chips.

2 Note that the retina used in the Mr. Chips simulations is a simplified retina. O'Regan (1990, 1991) and others correctly point out that even in the foveal region, there is a decline in resolution as the eccentricity increases. However, for the purposes of this version of the Mr. Chips model, the effect on reading performance due to this simplification is likely quite small.

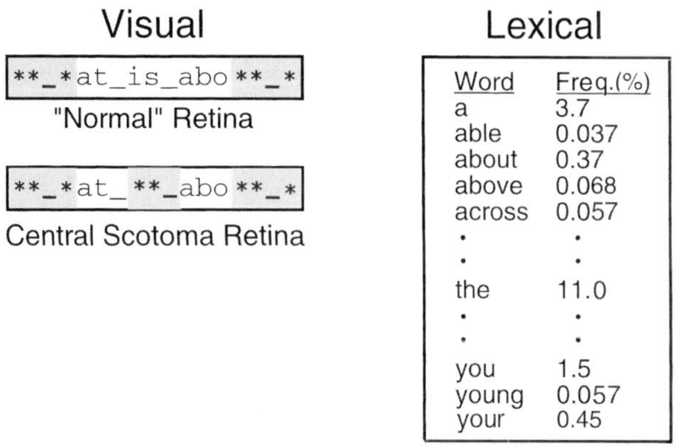

Visual   Lexical

```
**_*at_is_abo**_*
```
"Normal" Retina

```
**_*at_**_abo**_*
```
Central Scotoma Retina

Word	Freq.(%)
a	3.7
able	0.037
about	0.37
above	0.068
across	0.057
•	•
•	•
the	11.0
•	•
•	•
you	1.5
young	0.057
your	0.45

Fig. 1. Schematic of the information available to Mr. Chips, the ideal-observer model of reading. Mr. Chips relies on the integration of two sources of information: visual information ('normal retina' or central scotoma retina) and lexical information (words and their frequencies of occurrence).

absolute scotoma). Notice in Fig. 1 that with the normal retina, the word 'is' can be identified with certainty. However, in the central scotoma example, the word 'is' cannot be identified because both letters of the word are obscured by the central scotoma. As illustrated by the example in Fig. 1, the problem of reading with a central scotoma can be quite difficult. By changing the scotoma configuration of Mr. Chips's retina, we can change the visual information presented to him and examine the resultant change in saccade behavior.

The second source of information available to Mr. Chips is lexical information. Mr. Chips can use any lexicon that is assigned to him. The studies reported in this chapter used the 542 most frequent words in written English (Carroll, Davies and Richman, 1971) along with their frequencies of occurrence. More recently, we have been using much larger lexicons (for example, the 7500-word lexicon of *Grimm's Fairy Tales*) to more closely approximate the actual lexical abilities of human readers.

The goal of Mr. Chips is to recognize every word in a text in sequential order, with absolute certainty, in the minimum number of saccades. By minimizing the number of saccades, Mr. Chips maximizes the reading speed.[3]

In order to achieve the goal of minimizing the number of saccades, Mr. Chips makes saccades that minimize the uncertainty about the current word. In Fig. 1, the normal retina shows that the word 'abo**' is unknown because both 'above' and

---

3 Mr. Chips does not deal explicitly with fixation durations for each saccade. If we assume a standard fixation duration for each fixation, then the mean saccade size acts like a measure of reading speed.

'about' fit the visual information present. Mr. Chips will make a saccade of ten characters to place the last letter of the word in the first slot in the visual span. From his knowledge of the lexicon, Mr. Chips knows that the identity of the fifth letter will resolve the ambiguity.[4]

For the purposes of illustrating in more detail how Mr. Chips works, let us consider the example in Fig. 2A. Mr. Chips knows he has a visual span of size 1, that is, one high-resolution slot and four low-resolution slots. Here, Mr. Chips knows only that we have a four-letter word that begins with the letter 'c'. An examination of his 542-word lexicon indicates that there are five words that fit this pattern: 'call', 'came', 'city', 'cold', and 'come'. The conditional probabilities in Fig. 2 are the probabilities that c*** is each of the five possible words, based on word frequencies kept in the lexicon. Since the goal of Mr. Chips is to make a saccade to minimize the uncertainty of the current word, we need to quantify the concept of uncertainty. Guided by information theory, we define uncertainty as the entropy H:

$$H = -\sum_{i=1}^{k} p_i \log_2(p_i)$$

where p_i is the conditional probability of each possible word, and k is the number of possible words. In this case, the entropy is 2.10 bits of information (for reference, note that the entropy of two equally likely possible words is 1 bit, while the entropy of five equally likely candidate words is 2.31 bits).

In order to determine which saccade size, if executed, minimizes the entropy, Mr. Chips must consider all possible saccade sizes. In this example (see Fig. 2B), the range of saccades that keep the current word in the visual range are from -4 to $+3$. For each possible saccade size, Mr. Chips computes the expected entropy by considering all possible outcomes. Let us look at the example of a potential saccade of $+1$. A saccade of $+1$ will reveal the second letter of the word. As Fig. 2B shows, if the word is 'call', the letter 'a' will be revealed. But Mr. Chips will remain unsure whether the word is 'call' or 'came', with corresponding entropy of 0.76 bits. The same is true if the word is 'came'. If the word is 'city', then the letter 'i' is revealed. Since there is only one 4-letter word in the small lexicon beginning with 'ci', the uncertainty would be reduced to 0 bits. Similar calculations can be made for the outcomes of 'cold' and 'come' ($H = 0.79$). The overall expected entropy of a saccade of size $+1$ is the frequency-weighted average of all five possibilities. Here, the expected entropy is $H = 0.67$.

---

4 Of course, a saccade that reveals the fourth letter of the word also reduces the uncertainty to zero, but if two possible saccades reduce the uncertainty to the same amount, Mr. Chips will make the saccade that advances him furthest along in the text.

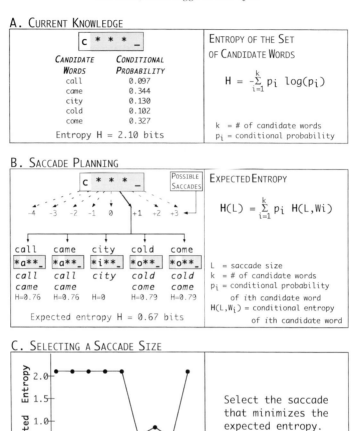

Fig. 2. Mr. Chips algorithm for making saccades through a text. Panel A shows the calculation of entropy for Mr. Chips's current situation. Panel B shows the calculation of the expected entropy after a series of possible saccades. Panel C graphically depicts the decision rule for Mr. Chips: select the saccade that minimizes the expected entropy.

We can do this same computation for all possible saccade lengths in the given range (see Fig. 2C). Then Mr. Chips chooses the saccade size that has the lowest expected entropy. In this case, he makes a saccade of size +3. This entropy analysis continues until the current word is identified, then Mr. Chips moves on to the next word.

Mr. Chips moves forward [5] through a string of text, using the visual and lexical information available to make saccades that minimize the entropy of the current

5 Although Mr. Chips's goal is to move forward through the text, Mr. Chips does occasionally

word. Using this algorithm, we can collect 'eye movement data' for a Mr. Chips simulation. We can compute the mean saccade size as the average of every saccade Mr. Chips makes while reading a string of text. In this chapter, we will present some of the key findings of Mr. Chips related to his performance in the presence of a simulated central scotoma. For a detailed review of simulation results from Mr. Chips, including word skipping, optimal viewing position, etc., see Legge, Klitz and Tjan (1997).

The performance of Mr. Chips

How does the performance of Mr. Chips vary with the introduction of a simulated central scotoma? How much benefit does Mr. Chips attain by integrating information on both sides of a central scotoma?

It has long been known that reading with a central scotoma can be quite difficult (Bullimore and Bailey, 1995; Faye, 1984; Legge, Rubin, Pelli and Schleske, 1985). However, to study eye movements in those with a central scotoma is non-trivial, especially if the person with a central scotoma does not have a stable location to fixate a word. In studies where eye movements were successfully recorded (Bullimore and Bailey, 1995; Trauzettel-Klosinski et al., 1994), mean saccade sizes dropped significantly for those with a central scotoma, as did reading speed. The number of regressions also increased in those with a central scotoma compared to those without a scotoma. In addition, the pattern of saccades in those with a central scotoma appears somewhat 'erratic'.

We can look at the performance of Mr. Chips with a retina containing a simulated central scotoma. We chose to test cases with a visual span of 9 and a scotoma centered in the clear visual area. We have estimated the visual span in reading to be about 9 characters for normal vision, based on human reading studies done by Legge, Ahn, Klitz and Luebker (1997), O'Regan (1990, 1991), and Rayner and Bertera (1979). The scotoma separated the visual span into two visual islands. For example, a scotoma of 1 character divides the visual span into two visual islands of four characters each, separated by the 1-character scotoma. Some people with a real central scotoma may choose to read above or below the scotoma, but for these simulations, we want to know how Mr. Chips performs when trying to integrate visual information on the left and the right sides of the simulated scotoma. Distribution of saccade sizes for scotomas of size 1, 3, and 7 characters are shown

---

move backwards in the text, a regression. Even though Mr. Chips is an ideal reader, regressions do occur. This is one of the emergent properties of Mr. Chips that matches well with the performance of normal human readers.

in Fig. 3, as well as the baseline case of no scotoma. Dark bars labeled '2 islands' are cases in which Mr. Chips uses visual information from both sides of the central scotoma to plan saccades.

The presence of a small 1-character scotoma has only a small effect on Mr. Chips, reducing the mean saccade size by about 12%, from 10.02 characters to 8.79 characters. However, as the scotoma size gets larger, the mean saccade size drops dramatically, a 66% drop from 10.02 to 3.40 characters at the largest scotoma size of 7 characters. Clearly, the presence of a large central scotoma can have a major effect on mean saccade size, even when Mr. Chips is allowed to use both sides of the central scotoma. In addition, the presence of a larger central scotoma increases the percentage of regressions to nearly 10% [6] and spreads the distribution of saccade sizes over a much wider range. The increased irregularity in Mr. Chips's saccades in the presence of a simulated central scotoma raises the *possibility* that corresponding irregular eye movements in patients with real central scotomas actually reflect adaptive eye movement strategies (because Mr. Chips's saccade strategies are always optimal, given the circumstances).

We can now ask if human readers with a simulated central scotoma gather and integrate information from both sides of a central scotoma when reading, or whether they read from only a single side of the central scotoma. The answer to this question is not clear from human eye movement studies. Guez, Le Gargasson, Rigaudiere and O'Regan (1993) and others have found that many patients with a central scotoma develop a preferred reading location to the left of their central scotoma. However, Fine and Rubin (1999) found in studies with normally-sighted subjects with simulated central scotomas that letter identification, word identification, and reading were all faster when subjects were presented information only to the right of the simulated central scotoma. In addition to questions about which side of the central scotoma is 'better' for reading, it is generally assumed that readers with a central scotoma cannot gather and use information from both sides of a central scotoma.

We can use Mr. Chips to compute the theoretical advantage to be gained in combining information from both sides of a scotoma, compared with one side only. The diagonal bars in Fig. 3 labeled '1 island' are simulations in which Mr. Chips is allowed to use only the visual information from one side of the central scotoma. [7] When reading with a 1-character central scotoma, Mr. Chips has a

---

6 When we include oculomotor noise in the simulations, the percentage of regressions can be much higher, up to 35% of the saccades.

7 For the presentation of data in Fig. 3, we have averaged the data from Mr. Chips when reading with only the information from the right side of the central scotoma and when reading with only the information from the left side of the central scotoma. Mean saccade sizes were nearly identical in the two cases for all sizes of a central scotoma.

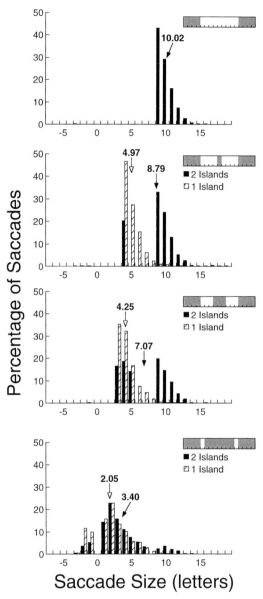

Fig. 3. Saccade size histograms for retinas with a visual span of 9 characters (top panel), and retinas with a central scotoma of 1, 3, or 7 characters (bottom three panels). Dark bars ('2 Islands') represent data from simulations when Mr. Chips integrates information from both sides of the central scotoma (when there is no central scotoma, the dark bars simply represent Mr. Chips's performance without a scotoma). Diagonal bars ('1 Island') represent simulations when Mr. Chips reads from only one side of a central scotoma. The arrows point to the mean saccade sizes for each of the two distributions (solid arrow for '2 Islands', open arrow for '1 Island'). Each distribution was based on a text of 2500 words.

mean saccade size about 77% larger with two sides (8.79 characters) as compared to one side of the central scotoma (4.98 characters). For a 3-character scotoma, the improvement of using both sides of the scotoma is 66% (7.07 versus 4.26 characters). For the 7-character scotoma, reading with both of the widely separated single-character islands (3.40 characters) is also 66% better than reading with only one of the single-character islands (2.05 characters).

These results make it clear that Mr. Chips benefits greatly from integrating visual information from both sides of a central scotoma, showing an average improvement of about 70% in mean saccade size compared with the use of one side only. The question remains whether human readers can do the same kind of integration.

Visual-span simulator and human readers

In order to make a quantitative comparison between Mr. Chips and human performance, we need to impose the same task constraints on human readers that are imposed on Mr. Chips. We have devised a reading task that achieves this goal. The apparatus, termed the 'visual-span simulator', is shown in Fig. 4. A human participant sits in front of a computer screen (Sony GDM-17E21). The display provides

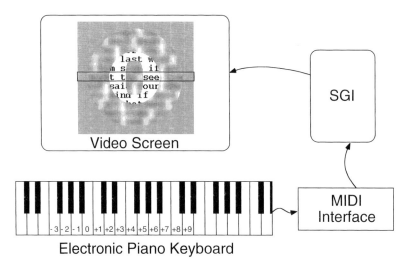

Fig. 4. Visual-span simulator apparatus. The experimental apparatus consists of a MIDI electronic keyboard, which sends output to a Silicon Graphics computer through a MIDI interface. The computer drives the visual presentation of a retinal configuration on the video screen. Participants in the experiment press keys on the MIDI keyboard to emulate eye movements on the video screen. The computer records saccade size (represented by the numbers on the keys of the keyboard in the figure), fixation durations, and reading speed.

the same information to a human participant that is available through Mr. Chips's 'retina'. Although the participant sees information displayed in a 2-D simulated visual span, in the current experiments, the participant is asked to attend only to the text along the horizontal diameter of the display. The region of the 'Video Screen' enclosed by the black rectangular box along the horizontal diameter, shown in Fig. 4, is the region participants use to read in this study. The box is for illustrative purposes only, and does *not* appear on the screen. In some trials, a simulated central scotoma is present, for example the 3-character scotoma shown in Fig. 4.

Human participants advanced the text through the retinal window on the screen by pressing keys on a MIDI electronic piano keyboard (Fatar SL-880). Each key on the keyboard represents a saccade of an integer size. Middle C is a saccade of 0, the next white key to the right is a saccade of +1, and so on. Keys to the left of Middle C represent backward saccades, or regressions. Generally, participants use their left hand to initiate backward saccades and their right hand to initiate forward saccades. Each time a key is pressed the Silicon Graphics O2 computer collects the MIDI keyboard signals, translates them into integer saccade sizes, and updates the screen. All of the saccade sizes are recorded by the computer, as well as durations for each fixation (i.e., the time between key presses).

The visual-span simulator has both advantages and disadvantages for studying reading. The obvious disadvantage is that human subjects are not making real eye movements to navigate through text. On the other hand, an important advantage of this setup is that we can rigorously control the visual presentation of information to the human reader, and investigate human performance using scotomas that would be difficult to simulate accurately with other methods. From a theoretical perspective, the visual-span simulator can be conceived as identical to Mr. Chips, except that human cognition is substituted for the entropy-minimization algorithm. In addition, the visual-span simulator allows a direct comparison between humans and Mr. Chips in terms of saccade size distributions, mean saccade sizes, and saccade landing sites. With the visual-span simulator, we get the added benefit of fixation duration and reading speed data, measures frequently used to study eye movements in reading. It is worth noting that although manual 'saccades' differ from eye movements as a method for transporting text through the visual field, low-vision reading frequently relies on manual methods (e.g., hand magnifiers) and other techniques besides eye movements for navigating through text (Harland, Legge and Luebker, 1998).

The data presented here are from one highly trained participant that had extensive practice using the experimental setup. Reading took place with both random words (the same lexicon as used by Mr. Chips) and real sentences (from *Aesop's Fables*). Since performance differences between the real and random texts turned out to be small, a thorough analysis of the real text versus random text question will not be addressed in this chapter.

We showed in the previous section that Mr. Chips could benefit by about 70% in mean saccade size by integrating information from both sides of a central scotoma. Can humans also benefit from integrating information to the left and right of a simulated central scotoma?

Our participant was asked to read with a retina that had a visual span of 9, and simulated central scotomas of 1, 3, and 5 characters. As a baseline for comparison, the participant also read with no central scotoma present. The participant was instructed to use three distinct strategies on the task. The first was the Chips emulation strategy, in which the participant tried to use the visual information from both sides of the central scotoma as well as knowledge about English words (lexical information) to plan saccades. In short, the participant was instructed to maximize saccade size and match Mr. Chips's behavior by using all available information.

While Mr. Chips (and the Chips emulation strategy) excel at maximizing mean saccade size, a more functional goal of human reading is to maximize reading speed. So, we compared the Chips emulation strategy to two other reading strategies that were computationally simpler, and *might* lead to higher reading speeds, despite being sub-optimal for maximizing saccade size.

The second strategy was a purely visual strategy. A purely visual strategy is one that guarantees that every letter in the text will appear in the clear regions of the retina and does not make any use of lexical inference. For the case of a visual span of 9 characters with no central scotoma, a strategy of moving 9 characters every saccade (9–9–9–9) will ensure that every letter will be seen. When there is a simulated central scotoma present, the same purely visual strategy cannot be successful. For example, if there is a 1-character central scotoma, the 9–9–9–9 strategy will result in every fifth letter being covered by the central scotoma. A modified strategy, alternating saccades of size 9 and size 4 (9–4–9–4) will guarantee that all of the letters will be uncovered on the two sides of the central scotoma. For a 3-character central scotoma, the purely visual strategy is 9–3–9–3. For the 5-character scotoma, the purely visual strategy is more difficult, with a saccade of size 9 interleaved with a series of smaller saccades (9–2–2–2–9).

A third reading strategy was a less efficient one-sided purely visual strategy, which restricted attention to only one side of the central scotoma. In the 1-character central scotoma example, a strategy of saccades of size 4 (4–4–4–4) places all the visual information in the clear region on one side of the central scotoma.

Table 1 shows the participant's reading performance using all three strategies, as well as the results for Mr. Chips, translated from Fig. 3. When there is no central scotoma, the human reader achieves only about a 4% gain in mean saccade size when using the Chips emulation strategy instead of a purely visual strategy (Mr. Chips's mean saccade size represents an 11% gain over a purely visual strategy). This small gain in mean saccade size is accompanied by a 26% decrease in reading

Table 1

Reading with the visual-span simulator compared to Mr. Chips

Scotoma size (characters)	Reading strategy	Reading speed (words/min)	Mean saccade size (characters)	Fixation duration (ms)
0	Chips emulation	112.5	9.39	1030
	Purely visual	152.2	9.00	630
	Mr. Chips	–	10.02	–
1	2 islands, Chips emulation	64.7	8.25	1460
	2 islands, purely visual	109.2	6.50	640
	1 island, purely visual	97.3	4.00	470
	Mr. Chips, 2 islands	–	8.79	–
	Mr. Chips, 1 island	–	4.97	–
3	2 islands, Chips emulation	38.3	5.95	1880
	2 islands, purely visual	46.3	6.00	1340
	1 island, purely visual	79.0	3.00	420
	Mr. Chips, 2 islands	–	7.07	–
	Mr. Chips, 1 island	–	4.25	–
5	2 islands, Chips emulation	23.7	3.91	1870
	2 islands, purely visual	22.2	3.75	1880
	1 island, purely visual	61.8	2.00	330
	Mr. Chips, 2 islands	–	3.40	–
	Mr. Chips, 1 island	–	2.05	–

Notes. (1) When the scotoma size is 0, there are no visual islands, so the purely visual strategy is neither '1 island' or '2 islands'. Reading takes place across the entire 9-character visual span. (2) Mr. Chips does not take time variables into consideration. As a result, no results are presented for fixation duration or reading speed for Mr. Chips.

speed. So, attempting to emulate Mr. Chips in planning saccades using all the visual and lexical information available, even in the absence of a scotoma, has a substantial reading speed cost.

What about reading with a simulated central scotoma? Can readers benefit from trying to integrate across a central scotoma? Comparing the data in Table 1 for reading with 1 visual island to reading with 2 visual islands, it is clear that mean saccade size increases substantially, an average increase of 92%, when integrating information from both visual islands. So, human readers *can* integrate visual information from both sides of a simulated central scotoma.

Is there a reading speed cost associated with the integration across a central scotoma? When the central scotoma is large (3 or 5 characters), reading speed is much slower (an average of 55% slower) when trying to integrate visual information on both sides of the scotoma. This is a cognitively challenging task that, despite gains in mean saccade size, leads to a substantial increase in fixation duration, and therefore a decrease in reading speed.

Table 1 shows, however, that the presence of a small 1-character central scotoma yields results different from those with a large scotoma. When the central scotoma is small (1 character), the mean saccade size still increased when integrating across both visual islands. However, reading *speeds* varied depending on the reading strategy used by the reader. If the participant used a purely visual strategy, reading speed was fast regardless of whether the participant read with one or two visual islands. Subjectively, when integrating across a 1-character scotoma, the text seemed to drift behind the scotoma, almost like reading text scrolling behind a small occluder. In this case, the reading speeds were actually quite fast compared to the purely visual cases when the scotoma is large. This is a special case in which integration took place quickly. However, if the participant tried to plan saccades deliberately (Chips emulation strategy), reading speed decreased substantially. So, despite the gains in mean saccade size, integration across the scotoma still has a large reading speed cost when actively planning saccades. Only in the unusual case when the words appear to flow behind a small occluder (a 1-character central scotoma) does the human reader benefit *both* in terms of reading speed and mean saccade size simultaneously.

It is clear that human readers can benefit (in mean saccade size) from integrating information on both sides of a simulated central scotoma IF readers are given sufficient time to process the information, or if the central scotoma is very small (a single-character scotoma). When the scotoma is larger, neither a Chips emulation strategy nor a purely visual strategy allows information to be rapidly integrated across the scotoma. Reading with only one side of the central scotoma greatly increases the reading speed achieved, but this comes at the cost of reducing the effective visual span, and therefore the mean saccade size, of the reader.

Conclusion

Our simulations show that an ideal reader with a simulated central scotoma improves reading performance (a 70% increase in mean saccade size) by integrating across a central scotoma. On the other hand, the task proves to be a very difficult one for human readers. Human performance when reading with a simulated central scotoma falls short of the competence level revealed by the ideal observer. Even with prolonged fixations, human saccades were only about 80% of the mean length of Mr. Chips's saccades when the human participant used the Chips emulation strategy. Although our participant could achieve larger saccades by gathering information from both sides of the simulated scotoma, he maximized reading speed by restricting reading to only one side of a central scotoma and ignoring the information on the other side. For humans to maximize reading speed, they compromise their saccade-planning performance relative to Mr. Chips. These results may help to explain some of the results from people with real central scotomas. Smaller mean saccade sizes may be accounted for by people reading from only one side of a central scotoma, effectively reducing the size of their visual span by more than half.

Acknowledgements

This work was supported by National Institutes of Health Grants EY02934 from the National Eye Institute and HD07151 from the National Institute of Child Health and Human Development. Bosco Tjan was at the Max-Planck Institute for Biological Cybernetics, Tuebingen, Germany when this work was completed. Preliminary results (Legge and Klitz, 1997) were also reported at the Minnesota Conference on Vision for Reach and Grasp, Minneapolis, Minnesota, October 1997.

References

Bullimore, M.A. and Bailey, I. (1995). Reading and eye movements in age-related maculopathy. Optometry and Vision Science, 72, 125–138.

Carroll, J.B., Davies, P. and Richman, B. (1971). The American Heritage Word Frequency Book. Boston, MA: Houghton Mifflin.

Chomsky, N. (1965). Aspects of the Theory of Syntax. Cambridge, MA: MIT Press.

Faye, E.E. (Ed.) (1984). Clinical Low Vision. Boston, MA: Little, Brown.

Fine, E.M. and Rubin, G.S. (1999). Reading with simulated scotomas: attending to the right is better than attending to the left. Vision Research, 39, 1039–1048.

Geisler, W.S. (1989). Sequential ideal-observer analysis of visual discriminations. Psychological Review, 96, 267–314.

Guez, J., Le Gargasson, J., Rigaudiere, R. and O'Regan, J.K. (1993). Is there systematic location for the pseudo-fovea in patients with central scotoma? Vision Research, 33, 1271–1279.

Harland, S., Legge, G.E. and Luebker, A. (1998). Psychophysics of reading. XVII. Low-vision performance with four types of electronically magnified text. Optometry and Vision Science, 75, 183–190.

Hilton, J. (1934). Goodbye, Mr. Chips. Boston, MA: Little, Brown.

Legge, G.E., Ahn, S.J., Klitz, T.S. and Luebker, A. (1997). Psychophysics of reading. XVI. The visual span in normal and low vision. Vision Research, 37, 1999–2010.

Legge, G.E., Klitz, T.S. and Tjan, B.S. (1997). Mr. Chips: an Ideal-Observer model of reading. Psychological Review, 104, 524–553.

Legge, G.E. and Klitz, T.S. (1997). Mr. Chips: an Ideal-Observer model for saccade planning in reading. Minnesota Conference on Vision for Reach and Grasp. Minneapolis, MN.

Legge, G.E., Rubin, G.S., Pelli, D.G. and Schleske, M.M. (1985). Psychophysics of reading. II. Low vision. Vision Research, 25, 253–266.

O'Regan, J.K. (1990). Eye movements and reading. In: E. Kowler (Ed.), Eye Movements and Their Role in Visual and Cognitive Processes. New York: Elsevier, pp. 395–453.

O'Regan, J.K. (1991). Understanding visual search and reading using the concept of stimulus 'grain'. IPO Annual Progress Report, 26, 96–108.

Pelli, D.G., Farell, B. and Moore, D.C. (1995). The role of letters in recognizing words. Manuscript submitted for publication.

Rayner, K. and Bertera, J.H. (1979). Reading without a fovea. Science, 206, 468–469.

Tjan, B.S., Braje, L.W., Legge, G.E. and Kersten, D. (1995). Human efficiency for recognizing 3-D objects in luminance noise. Vision Research, 35, 3053–3069.

Trauzettel-Klosinski, S., Teschner, C., Tornow, R.-P. and Zrenner, E. (1994). Reading strategies in normal subjects and in patients with macular scotoma assessed by two new methods of registration. Neuro-ophthalmology, 14, 15–30.

CHAPTER 26

Eye Fixation Durations in Reading: Models of Frequency Distributions

George W. McConkie
University of Illinois at Urbana-Champaign

and

Brian P. Dyre
University of Idaho

Abstract

Quantitative versions of three models of fixation-duration frequency distributions are presented: those proposed by Suppes (1989), McConkie, Kerr and Dyre (1994) and a modified version of that proposed by Harris, Hainline, Abramov, Lemerise and Camenzuli (1988). These, plus two additional versions of the Harris et al. model, were fit to a large set of eye-movement data from a group of adult readers. The McConkie et al. model fit the data best, though the fit appears to result primarily from the functions used rather than from the architecture proposed.

Reading as a Perceptual Process/A. Kennedy, R. Radach, D. Heller and J. Pynte (Editors)
© 2000 Elsevier Science Ltd. All rights reserved

Eye fixation durations in reading: models of frequency distributions

One of the most critical issues in understanding the relationship between eye behavior and cognitive processes during reading concerns the decision of when to move the eyes. The amount of time the eyes pause, referred to as the fixation duration or saccade latency, together with measures that accumulate durations of selected fixations, are the primary dependent variables for most eye-movement studies of language processing. However, at the present time the basis for the decision to move the eyes is unknown; hence, it is unclear what aspects of processing the fixation duration measures. A common assumption is that the eyes leave a word (or attention shifts from that word, initiating a saccade) only when the word has been identified. The study reported here examined the basis for this decision by comparing models of the frequency distributions of the durations of eye fixations, or saccade latencies.

In general, readers' fixation duration distributions appear to have three periods: a slow increase in frequency up to about 150 ms, a sharp rise to a peak around 200 ms, and a long tail that reaches near-zero frequency around 500 ms. Mathematical models have been proposed to account for the shape of the distribution of fixation durations (e.g., Harris, Hainline, Abramov, Lemerise and Camenzuli, 1988; McConkie, Kerr and Dyre, 1994; Suppes, 1989). These necessarily share some common features, including multiple-processing states and exponential decay functions. These models differ most, both formally and conceptually, in the manner in which they account for shorter fixation durations, and this has important implications for the cognitive processes underlying reading. The purpose of the work reported in this chapter was to competitively test these models to determine which holds the most promise for illuminating our understanding of the relationship between fixation durations and reading processes. A recently proposed model by Reichle, Pollatsek, Fisher and Rayner (1998) is not considered here because it is implemented as a procedural model, and no mathematical description of the fixation duration distribution is provided.

Models of fixation duration

Harris et al. (1988) reported that frequency distributions of fixation durations for both adults and children can be described by an exponential function with a randomly distributed onset time. This approach is mathematically equivalent to the convolution of two distributions, one based on an exponential function indicating a random waiting time until a saccade occurs, and the other based on a function indicating differing onset times for when this waiting period begins. We will refer to the onset time period as Stage 1 and the saccade waiting time as Stage 2.

Psychologically, this could represent a theory that assumes a variable time from the onset of a fixation until the start of the processing of information made available on that fixation, and that once processing begins the amount of processing time required before a saccade is executed can be represented as a random waiting time. Variability in the distribution of Stage-1 onset times is required to account for the rise in saccade frequencies early in the fixation. Although Harris et al. posited two sequential stages — an onset time period (Stage 1) and a waiting time period (Stage 2) — it is mathematically equivalent to reverse the order of the stages. Convolution implies a set of serial processes but the order of the processes is arbitrary. Hence, our reference to an onset distribution is a psychological interpretation, not a formal necessity.

Formally, a fixation has probability $D(t)\,dt$ of having a duration between times t and $t + dt$, where

$$D(t)\,dt = \left(\int_{-\infty}^{\infty} g(x)f(t-x)\,dx \right) dt \tag{1}$$

$$g(t)\,dt = \alpha e^{-\alpha t} \tag{2}$$

represents the distribution of random waiting times with α assumed to be a positive real number, and the form of the onset distribution, $f(t)$, is unknown, since Harris et al. did not postulate an exact form of this distribution of onset times. Therefore, it is necessary to complete the model by formalizing the onset time distribution of Harris et al. in order to determine how well the resulting model can account for readers' fixation durations. To model the onset distribution, the gamma distribution (Γ) was selected because it exhibits a finite onset time and an exponential tail and can be represented with only three parameters. This distribution is itself the convolution of two or more identical exponential distributions. Hence, the onset time of Stage 2 (or end of Stage 1) has probability $f(t)\,dt$ of occurring between times t and $t + dt$, where

$$f(t)\,dt = \begin{vmatrix} 0 & t < \tau \\[2ex] \dfrac{(t-\tau)^{\gamma-1} e^{\frac{-(t-\tau)}{\rho}}}{\rho^{\gamma}\Gamma(\gamma)} & t \geq \tau \end{vmatrix} \tag{3}$$

For Eq. 3, parameter ρ represents the decay rate of the exponential functions undergoing convolution. Parameter γ represents the number of exponential functions undergoing convolution (also known as the shape parameter) while parameter τ represents the onset time for the gamma distribution.

This model, which will be referred to as the *two-stage gamma model*, consists of the convolution of the two distributions described in Eqs. 2 and 3. It assumes that the system is in Stage 1 at the beginning of every fixation and remains in that stage for a varying period of time (distribution given by Eq. 3) until a move to Stage 2 occurs. No saccades occur while in Stage 1. Once in Stage 2, a saccade occurs after a varying period of time as determined by Eq. 2.

Suppes (1989) proposed a model of eye-movement control that described the fixation duration distribution as a mixture of an exponential distribution and a convolution of two exponential distributions (the convolution is equivalent to a gamma distribution with shape parameter equal to 2). This model proposes that saccade triggering occurs from either one of two *states* (as opposed to stages). State 1 is described by a single exponential and accounts for fixations of very short duration, while State 2 is described by the gamma function and accounts for fixations of longer duration. The system is in State 1 at the beginning of each fixation, and State 2 begins at some later time, but its onset does not override State 1; that is, both states continue to exist simultaneously, and a saccade can be issued from either. A mixture parameter determines the number of saccades that are triggered from either state. This model will be referred to as the *two-state mixture model*. Psychologically, it could represent a theory in which, beginning at some early time in the fixation (perhaps before new visual information from that fixation has arrived at higher brain centers), there is some likelihood that a saccade will be made as a result of previous processing or of oculomotor characteristics of the system. At some later time in the fixation, saccades are made based on processing of newly available information, greatly increasing their likelihood.

Formally, a fixation has probability $D(t)\,\mathrm{d}t$ of having a duration between times t and $t + \mathrm{d}t$, where

$$D(t)\,\mathrm{d}t = \frac{\omega}{\lambda_1}\mathrm{e}^{-\frac{t}{\lambda_1}} + \left[\frac{(1-\omega)t}{\lambda_2^2}\right]\mathrm{e}^{-\frac{t}{\lambda_2}} \qquad (4)$$

As can be seen in Eq. 4, the model consists of five parameters. Parameter ω represents the relative influence (weights) of the single vs. convoluted distributions, and thus can take any value between 0 and 1 inclusive. Parameters λ_1 and λ_2 represent the decay rates of the single exponential and gamma distributions, respectively. These parameters are allowed to take any positive value. A more general form of Suppes's model requires two additional parameters, τ_1 and τ_2, to represent the onset times for the exponential and gamma distributions, respectively. Because these parameters represent onset times they are restricted to being positive values only. This model is formally expressed as

$$D(t)\,\mathrm{d}t = \frac{\omega}{\lambda_1}\mathrm{e}^{-\frac{t-\tau_1}{\lambda_1}} + \left[\frac{(1-\omega)(t-\tau_2)}{\lambda_2^2}\right]\mathrm{e}^{-\frac{t-\tau_2}{\lambda_2}} \qquad (5)$$

McConkie et al. (1994) proposed an alternative, sequential two-state model based on an analysis of fixation durations represented as hazard (survival) functions. This model, which will be referred to as the *two-state transition model*, assumes that when a fixation begins, the system is in State 1. One can conceptualize State 1 of this model as a race between two processes, one that may trigger a saccade, and another that may trigger a transition to State 2. During State 1, the likelihood of making a saccade is very low, but slowly rises over time according to a linear hazard function. The likelihood of a transition to State 2 is also initially zero and rises according to a linear hazard function. However, it starts increasing later than the saccade process, and increases much more rapidly. If a transition is made to State 2, the likelihood of making a saccade is high and constant, suggesting a random, waiting time process (described by an exponential function) governing the time of the saccade. Psychologically, State 1 could represent the period prior to the processing of newly acquired visual information, with saccades resulting from the processing of previous information or from random activity in the oculomotor system. State 2 could represent the period after the system has begun to make use of this information in its processing.

This model requires five parameters. Formally, a saccade has probability $f_1(t) \, dt$ of being triggered from State 1 at a time between t and $t + dt$, where

$$
f_1(t) \, dt = \left| \begin{array}{ll} 0 & t < \tau_1 \\ 2\beta_1(t - \tau_1)e^{-\beta_1(t-\tau_1)^2} & \tau_1 \leq t < \tau_2 \end{array} \right. \tag{6}
$$

For Eq. 6, parameter β_1 represents the slope of the linear hazard function governing the State-1 saccade-triggering process and must be greater than zero to insure that the hazard function is rising. Parameter τ_1 represents the onset time of the linear hazard function.

Since the transition probability only applies to the population of fixations that has not yet been terminated by a State-1 saccade, the probability must be scaled by the proportion of the unterminated fixations. A transition to State 2 has probability $f_t(t) \, dt$ of occurring at a time between t and $t + dt$, where

$$
f_t(t) \, dt = \left| \begin{array}{ll} 0 & t < \tau_2 \\ 2\beta_2(t - \tau_2)e^{-\beta_1(t-\tau_2)^2} \left(1 - \int_0^t f_1(t) \, dt \right) & t \geq \tau_2 \end{array} \right. \tag{7}
$$

For Eq. 7, parameter β_2 represents the slope of the linear hazard function governing transitions to State 2 and must be greater than β_1 to insure that the hazard function rises more quickly than the saccade-triggering hazard. Parameter τ_2 represents the onset time of the transition linear hazard function. The term $1 - \int_0^t f_1(t) \, dt$ represents the proportion of fixations not yet terminated by a State-1 saccade. To insure that some saccades are triggered from State 1, it is assumed that $\tau_2 > \tau_1$, that is, the distribution with onset τ_1 starts at a shorter fixation duration than the distribution with onset τ_2.

If a transition is made to State 2, the likelihood of making a saccade is high and constant, suggesting a random, waiting time process governing the time of the saccade. The probability density function representing the distribution of durations for saccades triggered from State 2, $g(t)$, can thus be described by an exponential function (Eq. 2) with an onset time randomly distributed according to the State-1 transition distribution. This approach is mathematically equivalent to the convolution of the two distributions, $f_t(t)$ and $g(t)$. Hence, a fixation has probability $f_2(t)\,dt$ of being triggered from State 2 between times t and $t + dt$, where

$$f_2(t)\,dt = \left(\int_{-\infty}^{\infty} g(x) f_t(t - x)\,dx \right) dt \tag{8}$$

Putting together the saccade-triggering functions for State 1 and State 2, $f_1(t)$ and $f_2(t)$, respectively, a fixation has probability $D(t)\,dt$ of being triggered between times t and $t + dt$, where

$$D(t)\,dt = \begin{vmatrix} 0 & t < \tau_1 \\ f_1(t) & \tau_1 \leq t < \tau_2 \\ f_1(t)\left(1 - \int_{\tau_2}^{t} f_t(t)\,dt\right) + f_2(t) & t \geq \tau_2 \end{vmatrix} \tag{9}$$

The term $1 - \int_{\tau_2}^{t} f_t(t)\,dt$ represents the proportion of fixations that has not yet made the transition to State 2 and, hence, has a saccade likelihood based on the State-1 function.

If it is assumed that no saccades are initiated from State 1 ($f_t(t) = 0$ for all t), then this model would simply be another form of the general convolution model proposed by Harris et al. and described above: the fixation duration distribution results from the convolution of an onset distribution and an exponential distribution (Eq. 8), where the onset distribution is represented by a single linearly rising hazard function (Eq. 7). However, the addition of a non-zero probability for saccades to be triggered from State 1 allows the model to predict very short fixations. As fixation duration increases it becomes more likely that a transition will be made into State 2 before a saccade is ordered.

In the analyses reported below, the two-state transition model consistently fit the data better than the other two models. We wondered whether this advantage was due to the architecture of the model itself (i.e., saccades being initiated from either of two sequential states) or just due to the linear hazard functions used to describe the distributions of the model. To explore this question, two additional versions of the Harris et al. two-stage model were developed that employed linear hazard functions to describe the onset distribution. A *two-stage mixture model* represents the onset distribution as a mixture of two distributions, each defined by a unique linearly rising hazard function (see Eq. 10). For this model the distribution of onset times is simply a weighted average of the probabilities of each distribution. Hence, the onset has probability $f(t)\,\mathrm{d}t$ of occurring between times t and $t + \mathrm{d}t$, where,

$$f(t)\,\mathrm{d}t = \begin{vmatrix} 0 & t < \tau_1 \\ \omega\left[2\beta_1(t - \tau_1)e^{-\beta_1(t-\tau_1)^2}\right] & \tau_1 \le t < \tau_2 \\ \omega\left[2\beta_1(t - \tau_1)e^{-\beta_1(t-\tau_1)^2}\right] & t \ge \tau_2 \\ +(1 - \omega)\left[2\beta_2(t - \tau_2)e^{-\beta_2(t-\tau_2)^2}\right] \end{vmatrix} \tag{10}$$

For Eq. 10, parameter ω represents a weighting parameter governing the relative influence of the two distributions and can take any value between 0 and 1 inclusive. Parameters β_1 and β_2 represent the slopes of the linear hazard curves corresponding to each distribution. These parameters must be positive numbers to insure that the hazard curves rise over time. Parameters τ_1 and τ_2 represent the onset times for the two distributions. It is assumed that $\tau_1 < \tau_2$, that is, the distribution with onset τ_1 starts at shorter fixation duration than the distribution with onset τ_2.

Finally, a *two-stage race model* represents the onset distribution as a race between two distributions, each defined by a unique linearly rising hazard function (see Eq. 11). Formally, race models are represented as the sum of the hazard functions corresponding to each distribution in the race. Hence the onset has probability $f(t)\,\mathrm{d}t$ of occurring between times t and $t + \mathrm{d}t$, where

$$f(t)\,\mathrm{d}t = \begin{vmatrix} 0 & t < \tau_1 \\ 2\beta_1(t - \tau_1)e^{-\beta_1(t-\tau_1)^2} & \tau_1 \le t < \tau_2 \\ 2\left[\beta_1(t - \tau_1) + \beta_2(t - \tau_2)\right]e^{-\beta_1(t-\tau_1)^2-\beta_2(t-\tau_2)^2} & t \ge \tau_2 \end{vmatrix} \tag{11}$$

For Eq. 11, parameters β_1 and β_2 represent the slope of the linear hazard curves corresponding to each distribution, and τ_1 and τ_2 represent the onset times for the two distributions, as in the mixture model.

Both of these additional two-stage models assume that, at the beginning of each fixation, the system is in an initial Stage 1 from which no saccades can be issued, and that the transition to Stage 2 can occur on the basis of either of two underlying processes. These two processes each have a distribution of transition times that is specified by a linear hazard curve, with an onset time (the time at which the transition likelihood begins to rise above zero) and a slope. A psychological interpretation of the two-stage mixture or race models is somewhat different than that of the two-state transition model. Here we might suppose that the two processes constituting Stage 1 are two bases on which saccades can be ordered (for example, previous vs. new information, or perceptual vs. language processing factors). Stage 2 might then be associated with oculomotor activity, which requires a random waiting time before an ordered saccade is launched.

Thus, five models were tested in all, each having four to six parameters. These models represent theories that assume three different types of relationships between two underlying stages or states, representing the timing of stage/state periods, and the times and types of transitions from each of these. In two-stage models, the system passes from Stage 1 to Stage 2 before a saccade is made. In the two-state mixture model, the two states turn on at different times, existing concurrently, and a saccade can be issued from either state, though the momentary response likelihood is higher in State 2. In the two-state transition model, the system is initially in State 1, from which either a saccade can be triggered or a transition can be made to State 2. In State 2, the momentary response likelihood is higher. All the models assume the same exponential function for saccade production from the second stage or state.

Method

Fixation duration distributions predicted by the models were compared to eye fixation data obtained from eye-movement records collected during reading. In all, six data sets were used, four containing data from individual adult subjects (Kerr, 1992), one containing grouped adult data (McConkie, Kerr, Reddix and Zola, 1988), and one containing grouped data from five fifth-grade readers. [1] In all cases, subjects were reading continuous text, and asked questions about its content periodically. Data were collected using a Dual-Purkinje Image Eyetracker. For each of the data sets only data for the first fixation on a word following a forward saccade were included in the analyses. In addition, data corresponding to the first and last fixation on a line were eliminated from the analyses in order to avoid artifacts resulting from the return sweep of the eyes. Finally, fixations on which blinks or other irregularities occurred were excluded. After these exclusions between 33,049 and 46,159 fixations remained in each data set. Only data from the group of adult subjects are presented below; patterns from the other data sets were quite similar.

---

1 These data sets were collected by Michael Reddix (adult group data), Paul Kerr (individual adult readers) and David Zola (young readers). We acknowledge their contributions to the current study.

Predictions of each model were fit to the data using the method of maximum likelihood. In this method, a set of values is chosen for the parameters of a model. The frequency distribution based on these parameter values is then generated. The likelihood of each fixation, given the generated distribution, is calculated, and a loss value, indicating the summed log-likelihood of the entire set of data coming from this distribution, is computed. Optimal parameter values were obtained through an iterative process that allowed each of the model parameters to vary freely until an optimal solution (maximum likelihood) was reached. The optimization was performed using the IMSL Fortran 77 Math Library subroutine DBCPOL (Visual Numerics, 1999), which uses a direct search complex algorithm designed for fitting non-smooth multivariate functions. When optimizing models with many parameters (i.e., 4–6 in this case), it is possible for non-optimal solutions to be found based on local minima in the loss function. To avoid this problem, we performed ten fits of each model to each data set, with each fit starting from a different configuration of parameter values. The starting values were determined using the IMSL Fortran 77 Math subroutine DGGUES, which randomly spaces the values throughout the parameter space. The best fit of the ten attempts was considered to be the optimal configuration of parameters for a particular model. In all cases, the optimal configuration was obtained with several sets of starting values; often for all sets that allowed the model to converge on a solution.

Measures of goodness of fit, including Pearson's χ^2 test, maximum likelihood, and proportion of variance predicted, were used to evaluate the fit of every model. Without exception, the fit of every model was significantly rejected ($p < 0.05$) by the Pearson χ^2 test. This is not surprising, given the enormous size of the sample and degrees of freedom used to evaluate each model (around 40,000 fixations per data set and 49 degrees of freedom). As sample size and degrees of freedom become very large the Pearson χ^2 goodness of fit test becomes extremely sensitive to very minor deviations between the models' predictions and the data. It is not unusual for a well-fitting model to be rejected when it is fit to a large sample of data with many degrees of freedom. As a result it is impossible to make an absolute claim that a given model provides a good or poor fit to the data based on this test. Instead, the discussion will focus on the relative goodness of fit indices between competing models.

We optimized the models' parameters by minimizing negative log-likelihood (base 10). This measure can also be used as a metric of relative goodness of fit: low values correspond to relatively good fits while high values correspond to poor fits. To obtain a better sense of absolute goodness of fit, the proportion of variance in the observed frequency distributions predicted by each model was also calculated, using a sum of squared deviations. Of course, since the model was not optimized on the basis of this index its use here is simply as a way to communicate the general adequacy of the model.

Results

Fig. 1 shows the obtained frequency distribution for the group of adult readers, together with the distributions generated by each of the five models with optimal parameter values. These distributions were created using 10 ms fixation duration 'bins'. Distributions for the other data sets are quite similar: of the six data sets, four showed better fits than this, based on the total loss value divided by N, and one (5th-grade children) showed a slightly worse fit. Tables 1–5 present the optimal model parameter values for the adult readers, again showing a pattern quite similar to that from the other data sets. At the bottom of each table, the loss values and proportion of variance predicted by the models are also listed.

In absolute terms all the models fit each of the data sets quite well, accounting for a minimum of approximately 88% of the variability in fixation duration distributions. The results were very consistent across all six data sets: the two-state

Table 1

Best-fit parameters and likelihood for two-stage gamma model fit to the fixation duration distribution of a group of adult readers: 42754 fixations (50 bins)

Parameter	Best-fit value
τ	0.0000
γ	7.4000
ρ	0.0188
α	15.3000
$-\log_{10}(\text{likelihood})$	64190
R^2	0.8823

Table 2

Best-fit parameters and likelihood for two-state mixture model fit to the fixation duration distribution of a group of adult readers: 42754 fixations (50 bins)

Parameter	Best-fit value
τ_1	0.0383
λ_1	0.0872
τ_2	0.1200
λ_2	0.0486
ω	0.1350
$-\log_{10}(\text{likelihood})$	62343
R^2	0.9600

Table 3

Best-fit parameters and likelihood for two-state transition model fit to the fixation duration distribution of a group of adult readers: 42754 fixations (50 bins)

Parameter	Best-fit value
τ_1	0.0175
β_1	8.2200
τ_2	0.1080
β_2	210.0000
α	18.3000
$-\log_{10}(\text{likelihood})$	61582
R^2	0.9980

Table 4

Best-fit parameters and likelihood for two-stage mixture model fit to the fixation duration distribution of a group of adult readers: 42754 fixations (50 bins)

Parameter	Best-fit value
τ_1	0.0100
β_1	74.4000
τ_2	0.1100
β_2	228.0000
α	18.5000
ω	0.2610
$-\log_{10}(\text{likelihood})$	61585
R^2	0.9981

Table 5

Best-fit parameters and likelihood for two-stage race model fit to the fixation duration distribution of a group of adult readers: 42754 fixations (50 bins)

Parameter	Best-fit value
τ_1	0.0025
β_1	12.9000
τ_2	0.1140
β_2	203.0000
α	18.4000
$-\log_{10}(\text{likelihood})$	61591
R^2	0.9980

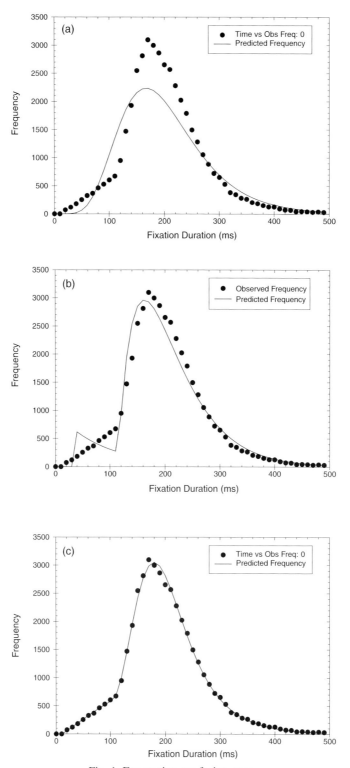

Fig. 1. For caption see facing page.

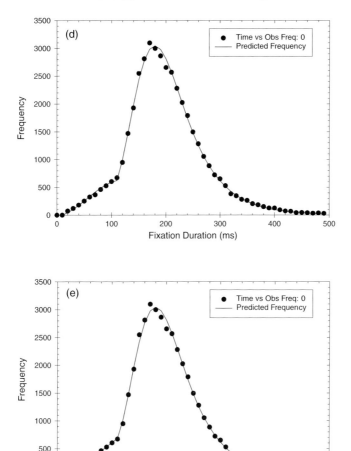

Fig. 1 (continued). Obtained frequency distribution of the durations of eye fixations for a group of adult readers, together with distributions produced by five models. (a) Two-stage gamma model, based on Harris et al. (1988). (b) Two-state mixture model (Suppes, 1989). (c) Two-state transition model (McConkie et al., 1994). (d) Two-stage mixture model, based on Harris et al. (1988). (e) Two-stage race model, based on Harris et al. (1988).

transition, two-stage race, and two-stage mixture models fit the data best and produced approximately the same likelihood values, followed by the two-stage gamma model and finally the two-state mixture model.

An examination of the predicted fixation duration distributions illustrates where the two-state mixture model and the two-stage gamma model failed. As Fig. 1b indicates, the two-state mixture model produces two discontinuities in the early part of the fixation duration distribution that are not exhibited by the data. These discontinuities result from the fact that the model produces fixation duration distributions from a mixture of an exponential distribution and a gamma function with shape parameter equal to two. Optimization of the model results in parameter values that fit the exponential distribution to very short fixations. However, the shape of the obtained distribution at very short fixations exhibits a linear increase rather than an exponential decay. Furthermore, the predicted distribution peaks too early and the peak is either too low or too high, depending on the data set. The two-stage gamma model (Fig. 1a) fits the early part of the fixation duration distribution more closely, but also tends to peak too low. The two-stage mixturetwo-stage mixture model, two-stage race, and two-state transition models all fit the data equally well (see Fig. 1c–e) and the predicted distributions do not show any systematic deviations from the observed data.

Discussion

The two-state transition model clearly provides a better fit to the data than either the two-stage gamma or the two-state mixture model. This is true for data from individuals as well as groups, and from children as well as adults. In fact, the fit to the data is quite impressive. Harris et al.'s (1988) proposal that the right tail of the fixation-duration frequency distribution can be well described with an exponential function is supported by this result. During the latter period of a fixation, the period of time until a saccade occurs can be considered as a random waiting time, described with a single parameter. That being confirmed, the second contribution of the current study is in considering how to model the left tail of the distribution in a psychologically appropriate manner. Here, all three models involved assume multiple states or stages and use convolution, in one way or another, to randomly delay the period at which the second stage or state comes into effect with its exponential distribution.

Neither of the models that attempt to fit the early period with exponential-based distributions, our elaboration of Harris et al.'s model using a gamma function, or Suppe's two-state mixture model, is very successful. Rather, success was achieved by assuming that two time-related processes take place early in the fixation: the likelihood of a saccade being initiated increases over time, something like the recovery from a refractory period, and the likelihood that a transition will be made to State 2 also increases over time. Both of these increases are implemented in a simple form at the level of hazard functions (Luce, 1986), consisting of linear increases over time. This is in contrast to the constant hazard level that underlies an exponential distribution, which is very successful in modeling the saccade likelihood in the later part of the fixation.

A critical difference between two-stage and two-state models is that the former postulates an initial period during which no saccades are issued, whereas the latter allows saccades to occur, albeit with low frequency, during the initial period. We had thought that this characteristic of two-stage models might make it difficult for them to fit the data in the early period of the fixation. The results of the model-fitting activity described above indicate that this expectation was incorrect. However, it is evident that for this model to be successful, the period of time that the system remains in Stage 1 before it is possible to make a transition to Stage 2 must be minimal; since some saccades occur after eye fixations of only 20 ms, transitions must be permitted within that period of time. This constraint is not present with a model such as the two-state transition model that allows saccades to be executed from the initial state.

A rise in saccade frequency early in the fixation can be achieved in either of two ways, which we will refer to as transition-based or growth-based. The first is the result of an increasing number of fixations over time in which a transition has been made to a stage or state in which saccades are either possible or more likely. Thus, an increase in saccade frequency is achieved without assuming any increase in the momentary likelihood of saccades occurring from fixations that are in a given state. All three models assume this type of increase. The second type is the result of an actual increase, or growth, over time in the momentary likelihood in a given state that a saccade will occur. The two-state transition model is the only one of the three models that assumes this type of growth process. The other models depend exclusively on transition-based increases.

The purpose of including two additional versions of the two-stage model was to determine whether the two-state transition model's ability to describe the fixation-duration frequency distributions was due to its architecture or its use of linear hazard distributions to model the early saccades. Two architectures often used in processing models were examined, a mixture and a race model, to describe the Stage-1 period, prior to the exponentially based Stage 2. These were selected as a means of providing variation in architecture, rather than on the basis of proposing reasonable alternative theories of the reading processes involved. As Tables 3–5 indicate, these two models were just as successful in fitting the data as was the two-state transition model. In fact, over the six data sets examined, each of these three models fit best at least once, and they were always very close in their obtained loss values. Thus, there is no empirical basis for selecting the two-state architecture over the two-stage architecture. Employing distributions based on two linearly increasing hazard functions, in any of the three architectures explored, leads to a very successful fit to the data. This supports the usefulness of these functions as a basis for fitting the fixation duration (or saccade latency) data from the early part of the fixation, and as a basis for convolution with the later exponential function. It also indicates that the type of growth-based increase in momentary saccade likelihood that is postulated in the two-state transition model is not required in order to fit this part of the distribution well. Transition-based increases are capable of modeling the data equally well.

One example of the potential usefulness of distributions based on linearly increasing hazard functions for fixation duration data is found in a recent article by Reichle et al. (1998) that describes E-Z Reader, a model of saccade control during reading. An examination of E-Z Reader's predictions for fixation duration distributions, which are based on gamma distributions, indicates prediction errors similar to those produced by the two-stage gamma model as shown in Fig. 1a. Both show a tendency to overpredict short and long fixations, thereby underpredicting fixations in the middle range. It is possible that the use of linear hazard functions could correct this defect in E-Z Reader and similar models.

While differing architectures did not systematically affect the overall fit of models based on the hazard function, it did affect the estimates for parameters that these models have in common. While the onset times for both hazard functions were quite similar across models, the slope values differed among them. Selection between architectures must be made, then, on the basis of the plausibility of the described architecture as a model of the underlying psychological processes and the plausibility of the parameter estimates as indicators of the behavior of these processes. In addition, with theory-based interpretations of the parameters, tests can be made of their behavior in response to the manipulations of selected text and task variables.

An interpretation of the parameters in the two-state transition model provides a basis for this type of testing. It is assumed that State 1 constitutes the period of time prior to the system's beginning to make use of new visual information made available on this fixation. The use of this information is delayed for two reasons: first, some time is required for transmitting the information from the retina to appropriate brain centers where it can influence higher processes, and second, even when information is available its influence may be blocked until needed (Blanchard, McConkie, Zola and Wolverton, 1984). If processing is still being based on information acquired during previous fixations, the actual use of (or attention to) the new information may be delayed. During this initial state, saccades result from processing of previously acquired information; saccade likelihoods are low because in most cases any necessary saccade has already been executed. The first hazard curve describes the frequency distribution of saccades issued from this state. The transition to State 2 occurs when the system begins to make use of newly acquired information. The second hazard distribution describes the frequency distribution of times at which this transition occurs (or a constant delay following that time). Thus, it describes the variation in transition times. Once in State 2, the likelihood of making a saccade in any interval of time, for surviving fixations, remains a constant, giving a random waiting time until a saccade occurs. This could be interpreted either as a truly random process, or as the result of a largely deterministic process operating in each of a large set of fixations, yielding a set of times distributed as a random waiting time.

Within this framework, the parameter estimates take on psychological meaning. For example, β_1, the slope parameter for State 1 should not be affected by information from the current fixation, but only that from prior fixations. The onset parameter for State 2, τ_2, indicates the time at which transitions to State 2 first occur, or the time at which new information made available on a fixation first begins to have its effect on eye-movement decisions. This is estimated at 108 ms. Whether lexical or syntactic characteristics of the text perceived on the current fixation affect the parameters for the transition function, the second hazard curve, depends on whether or not the transition depends on characteristics of the currently perceived text, or only on completion of processing of prior information. We expect that the primary effect of currently perceived text characteristics will be on the α parameter, which controls the decay rate of the exponential describing the latter part of the fixation period.

Further work is required in order to test such specific hypotheses about the psychological meanings of the parameters of the models. For the present time, however, it seems clear that the fixation-duration frequency distribution is fit very well by a variety of models in which activities in the early period are represented by distributions derived from two linearly increasing hazard curves, representing growth processes (but not necessarily growth in the momentary saccade likelihood from a given state or stage), and the latter period is represented by an exponential distribution, representing a stable state.

Acknowledgements

This research was conducted at the Beckman Institute for Advanced Science and Technology and supported by PHS Grant HD28181 to George McConkie. This chapter was written while he was on sabbatical leave at Beijing Normal University in Beijing, China, partially supported by a Senior Scholar Grant from the Chiang Ching-kuo Foundation.

References

Blanchard, H.E., McConkie, G.W., Zola, D. and Wolverton, G.S. (1984). Time course of visual information utilization during fixations in reading. Journal of Experimental Psychology: Human Perception and Performance, 10, 75–89.

Harris, C.M., Hainline, L., Abramov, I., Lemerise, E. and Camenzuli, C. (1988). The distribution of fixation durations in infants and naive adults. Vision Research, 28, 419–432.

Kerr, P.W. (1992). Eye Movement Control During Reading: The Selection of Where to Send the Eyes. Unpublished doctoral dissertation. Doctoral Dissertation, University of Illinois at Urbana-Champaign. Dissertation Abstracts International, #9305577.

Luce, R.D. (1986). Response Times: Their Role in Inferring Elementary Mental Organization. New York: Oxford University Press.

McConkie, G.W., Kerr, P.W. and Dyre, B.P. (1994). What are 'normal' eye movements during reading: toward a mathematical description. In: J. Ygge and Lennerstrand (Eds.), Eye Movements in Reading. Oxford: Elsevier, pp. 331–343.

McConkie, G.W., Kerr, P.W., Reddix, M.D. and Zola, D. (1988). Eye movement control during reading, I. The location of initial eye fixations on words. Vision Research, 28 (10), 1107–1118.

Reichle, E.D., Pollatsek, A., Fisher, D.L. and Rayner, K. (1998). Toward a model of eye movement control in reading. Psychological Review, 105 (10), 125–157.

Suppes, P. (1989). Eye-movement models for arithmetic and reading performance. In: E. Kowler (Ed.), Eye Movements and their Role in Visual and Cognitive Processes. Amsterdam: Elsevier, pp. 455–477.

Visual Numerics (1999). Chapter 8: Optimization. In: IMSL Math/Library Users Guide Volume 2 [On-line]. Available: http://www.vni.com/products/imsl/MATHVol_2.pdf

CHAPTER 27

Eye Movement Control in Reading: Updating the E-Z Reader Model to Account for Initial Fixation Locations and Refixations

Keith Rayner
University of Massachusetts

Erik D. Reichle
Carnegie Mellon University

and

Alexander Pollatsek
University of Massachusetts

Abstract

In this chapter, we describe recent work in which we (Reichle, Rayner and Pollatsek, 1999) updated the E-Z Reader model (Reichle, Pollatsek, Fisher and Rayner, 1998) to account for initial landing positions in words and refixations during reading. Prior simulations by Reilly and O'Regan (1998) suggested that fixation locations are primarily determined by word length information, and that the identification of words plays only a minimal role in deciding where to move the eyes. This claim appears to be problematic for the E-Z Reader model in that within the model lexical access is the engine that drives the eyes forward during reading. However, we show that a newer version of E-Z Reader which still assumes that lexical access is the engine driving eye movements, accurately predicts the locations of fixations and within-word refixations.

Reading as a Perceptual Process/A. Kennedy, R. Radach, D. Heller and J. Pynte (Editors)
© 2000 Elsevier Science Ltd. All rights reserved

Introduction

Many researchers interested in eye movements in reading have focused primarily on how low-level oculomotor factors influence *where* readers fixate next (O'Regan, 1990, 1992), while others (Just and Carpenter, 1980, 1987) have been primarily interested in how higher-level linguistic factors determine *when* readers move their eyes. Although there is some evidence to suggest that the decisions of where to move next and when to move are made somewhat independently (Rayner, 1998; Rayner and McConkie, 1976; Rayner and Pollatsek, 1981), we believe that it is important to understand both aspects of eye movement control during reading. There is now ample evidence that both oculomotor and linguistic variables play a role in influencing eye movements during reading. Thus, the real challenge is to develop a theoretical framework that is comprehensive enough to account for both aspects of eye movement control during reading. To this end, we developed a computational model of eye movement control in reading which we called the *E-Z Reader* model (Reichle et al., 1998). Although a number of studies have been conducted in our laboratory to examine which variables influence the decision of where to move the eyes next (Morris, Rayner and Pollatsek, 1990; Pollatsek and Rayner, 1982; Rayner, Fischer and Pollatsek, 1998; Rayner and McConkie, 1976; Rayner and Pollatsek, 1981; Rayner, Sereno and Raney, 1996), the E-Z Reader model primarily dealt with the issue of when to move the eyes. When dealing with where to move the eyes, the original model only dealt with decisions about which words to fixate or skip.

We (Reichle, Rayner and Pollatsek, 1999) have recently updated the E-Z Reader model to account more specifically for where readers fixate in reading. In this chapter, we will first review the general findings regarding where readers fixate in words. Then, we will describe our recent modeling work in which we updated the E-Z Reader model to account for initial landing position effects and refixations in reading.

Where do readers fixate?

Although there are differences among various theories concerning when to move the eyes (see Rayner, 1998, and Rayner et al., 1996, for discussion), there seems to be some agreement that low-level visual information obtained from parafoveal vision is an important factor in determining where to fixate next (Rayner, 1998). Specifically, it is widely assumed that word boundaries, defined by the spaces surrounding the fixated word ($word_n$) and the next word ($word_{n+1}$), are important cues utilized in determining where to fixate next. For example, when the spaces between words are removed or filled in with extraneous characters, readers move their eyes a shorter distance than when such information is available (McConkie and Rayner, 1975; Morris et al., 1990; Pollatsek and Rayner, 1990; Rayner, 1986; Rayner and Bertera, 1979; Rayner and Pollatsek, 1981; Rayner, Reichle and Pollatsek, 1998). Given that reading is slowed by the lack of effective space information and that saccade lengths are shorter when space information is not available, it seems appropriate to conclude that spaces are functional for eye guidance.

Recently, however, Epelboim, Booth and Steinman (1994) challenged the argument that spaces between words are functional for eye guidance and suggested that the primary reason that unspaced text interferes with reading is that the removal of spaces interferes with word identification. Their argument is based on the assumption that if readers normally relied on space information to guide eye movements during reading that they should be virtually helpless when spaces are removed and the pattern of eye movements should be altered dramatically. They claimed, based on experiments in which readers read unspaced text, that the pattern of saccades was only minimally altered and that reading unspaced text was surprisingly easy even though reading speed was cut in half for most readers in their experiment (see Rayner and Pollatsek, 1996, for evidence that reading is slowed considerably by the absence of space information). While we agree with part of their claim (that word identification is interfered with when spaces are removed), data from recent experiments from our lab (Rayner et al., 1998) make it clear that both eye guidance and word identification processes are disrupted when space information is not available. In these experiments, we compared reading when spaces were available and when they were not. More specifically, we examined fixation time on high- and low-frequency words when space information was available and when it was not. The absence of space information dramatically increased the processing time of low-frequency words in comparison to high-frequency words supporting the idea that word identification is disturbed by the absence of space information (as readers are unsure where words begin and end). However, the pattern of where readers' eyes land on a target word (i.e., the histogram of landing positions) clearly indicated that the lack of space information disrupts eye guidance as the initial fixation position shifted dramatically to the beginning of words (when spaces were not available, readers adopted a much more conservative strategy of only moving their eyes short distances). Thus, the results of the experiments by Rayner et al. (1996) provide clear confirmation of the fact that space information is functional for eye guidance in reading.

A number of other studies have also demonstrated that initial landing position effects are evident in the eye movement record. Typically, the locations of initial fixations on a word are approximately normally distributed (with the tails of the distributions being truncated at the word boundaries) with the means of the distributions falling slightly to the left of center when reading orthographies printed from left to right. This effect was originally called the *preferred viewing location* by Rayner (1979). It is interesting to note that the preferred viewing location effect holds for languages printed from right to left. Deutsch and Rayner (1999) recently reported that for Israeli readers reading Hebrew text, the preferred viewing location is slightly to the right of center of words of various lengths. Indeed, the distributions of landing positions for various word lengths for readers of Hebrew look very similar to those of English readers (except that they are mirror images of each other).

An important qualification to the preferred viewing location effect was first reported by McConkie, Kerr, Reddix and Zola (1988) and subsequently confirmed by Rayner et al. (1996). Namely, as the distance between the prior fixation location (the *launch site*) and the current fixation location (the *landing site*) increases, the mean of the distribution shifts towards the beginning of the word, and the distribution becomes more variable. Although the length of the target word affects neither the mean nor the variance of the distributions, the leftward deviation that results from increasing the distance between the launch site and target site is decreased the longer the duration of the fixation on the launch site. These regularities, and the fact that word identification is faster when the center of the word is fixated, led O'Regan (1981, 1992) and O'Regan and Lévy-Schoen (1987) to suggest that readers aim their initial saccade towards the center of the targeted word (to what he originally termed the *convenient viewing position,* but more recently called the *optimal viewing position*; O'Regan, 1992), so as to facilitate word identification as much as possible. However, because of oculomotor error, readers' saccades often miss the target at the center of the word. This error stems from two sources: (1) a systematic range error that causes the eyes to undershoot distant targets and overshoot near targets, and (2) random error that is due to oculomotor variability. As with other forms of motor error, the variability associated with the latter source of error increases with the length of the movement trajectory (i.e., saccade) and decreases with preparation (i.e., fixation duration on the launch site word).

McConkie et al.'s (1988) analysis provides a framework for understanding how low-level, oculomotor variables affect where the eyes initially fixate on a word during reading. Therefore, we (Reichle et al., 1999) recently added assumptions based on McConkie et al.'s work to the E-Z Reader model to determine whether the model can account for the locations of initial fixations and within-word re-fixations. With respect to this issue, Reilly and O'Regan (1998) recently used a predecessor of the E-Z Reader model, the model of Morrison (1984), which was subsequently modified and expanded by Pollatsek and Rayner (1990) and Rayner and Pollatsek (1989), to argue against certain types of models of eye movement control. Specifically, Reilly and O'Regan (1998) reported that a computer simulation of the original Morrison model (which they called the *attention shift strategy*) had difficulty generating many of the characteristics of the fixation location distributions that are normally observed in reading (McConkie et al., 1988; McConkie, Zola, Grimes, Kerr, Bryant and Wolff, 1991; Rayner, 1979; Rayner et al., 1996). Given Reilly and O'Regan's findings, we were interested in the extent to which the E-Z Reader model could account for landing position effects. In this chapter, we describe our recent updates to the original E-Z Reader model (see Reichle et al., 1999, for further detail). We begin by describing the additional assumptions that were incorporated into the model and then describe the simulation results.

Updating the model: additional assumptions

The model described by Reichle et al. (1999) is an updated version of the E-Z Reader model (Reichle et al., 1998). Because the core model remains unchanged, many of the details of the model will not be specified in this chapter (the interested reader should consult Reichle et al., 1998, 1999). In the E-Z Reader model, eye movements are influenced by five processes: (1) a familiarity check on a word, f; (2) the subsequent completion of lexical access on a word, lc; (3) an early stage of saccadic programming; (4) a late stage of saccadic programming; and (5) saccades. The first two processes are assumed to be jointly determined by each word's frequency of occurrence (taken from Francis and Kuçera, 1982) and the predictability of the word in a given context (as determined empirically). We conceptualized these processes as being the product of a single cognitive module that is responsible for word recognition. In the model, the familiarity check indicates that lexical access is imminent and serves as a cue to the motor system to begin programming a saccade to the next word. The completion of lexical access (i.e., the process of uniquely identifying a word) is the signal to shift covert spatial attention to the next word. This distinction between f and lc is consistent with several two-stage models of lexical access (Paap, Newsome, McDonald and Schvaneveldt, 1982; Van Orden, 1987) and allows the model to decouple the signal to program a saccade from the signal to shift attention. If attention and eye movement programming are not decoupled, it is difficult to explain 'spillover' effects in reading or how the difficulty of the fixated word affects the intake of parafoveal information (see Pollatsek and Rayner, 1990, and Reichle et al., 1998, for further discussion).

The two stages of saccadic programming, as well as the actual saccades, are the products of an oculomotor module that plans and executes eye movements. The distinction between early and late stages of saccade programming follows from the notion of Morrison (1984) (based on Becker and Jürgens, 1979) that the program to make an eye movement can be canceled by a subsequent program if a second program is initiated soon enough after the first.[1] Thus, during the course of programming a saccade, there is a 'point of no return': before this point, the program is labile, and can be canceled by subsequent saccadic programs; after the point of no return, the program is nonlabile and the saccade will be executed. This feature of the E-Z Reader model is essential because it provides the basis for word skipping. Word skipping occurs when $word_n$ is fixated, but the first stage of lexical access, f, has completed on $word_{n+1}$. Because f signals the oculomotor system to begin planning a saccade to $word_{n+2}$, the labile program to move the eyes to $word_{n+1}$ is canceled, and $word_{n+1}$ is skipped.

As noted above, the E-Z Reader model was originally designed to account for eye movements at the level of whether or not individual words were fixated or skipped. In our more recent work (Reichle et al., 1999), the model was refined so that it could make predictions about the locations of fixations at the level of individual letter positions. To do this, our data base of the Schilling, Rayner and Chumbley (1998) sentence corpus was expanded to include the length of each word (measured in characters). This information was then used to calculate each word's center, which was assumed to be the functional target of any saccade targeted to that word. Thus, both inter-word and intra-word saccades targeted to $word_n$ were assumed to be directed towards the center of $word_n$.

Although the assumed saccade target is the center of a word, simulated saccades (like real saccades) are prone to two types of error: (1) systematic range error, which causes saccades to undershoot distant targets and overshoot near targets, and (2) random variability associated with oculomotor movements. To determine the predicted location of each fixation in the simulation, the absolute distance (in terms of number of character spaces, where letters, punctuation, and blank spaces are all assumed to occupy a single character) between the current fixation and the saccade target was calculated. This value is the planned saccade length, or PSL. The systematic range error, or SRE, is given by Eq. 1:

$$SRE = (\Psi_b - PSL) \cdot \Psi_m \tag{1}$$

where Ψ_b is a free parameter that represents the *optimal saccade length*, or the saccade length for which the saccade neither undershoots nor overshoots the intended target. Because McConkie et al. (1988) found that the optimal saccade length tended to be around seven characters, Ψ_b was fixed at a value of 7. Similarly, Ψ_m is a free parameter that modulates the effect of the systematic range error.

---

1 Becker and Jürgens (1979) found that saccades occasionally moved the eyes to positions in between the initial fixation target location (which was canceled) and the location of a second fixation target (that was presented subsequently). We did not attempt to simulate these intermediate, or 'blend', saccades because they occur infrequently and because doing so would increase the complexity of the model and our modeling effort.

Because McConkie et al. (1988) estimated this value to be slightly less than half a character, we fixed the value of Ψ_m at 0.4 characters. Thus, for every character that a planned saccade extends beyond 7, the length of the saccade that is executed will fall short by almost half a character.

The second source of saccade variability, the random error associated with oculomotor movements, E, is a random deviate sampled from a Gaussian distribution, with $\mu = 0$, and σ given by Eq. 2:

$$\sigma = \beta_b + (\beta_m \cdot \text{PSL}) \tag{2}$$

where β_b and β_m are free parameters that adjust the oculomotor variability as a linear function of the planned saccade length. The actual saccade length is then given by Eq. 3:

$$\text{Saccade length} = \text{PSL} + \text{SRE} + E \tag{3}$$

As noted above, in the updated version of the model, our assumptions regarding fixation locations were taken directly from McConkie et al. (1988). However, the model (as described up to this point) is identical to E-Z Reader 5 (Reichle et al., 1998). Thus, our decision to add McConkie et al.'s assumptions about the source of saccadic errors should be conceptualized as an attempt to specify our model more precisely rather than as an attempt to develop another version of the model. For the sake of exposition, however, we will refer to the updated version of the model as E-Z Reader 6.

Finally, one additional modification was necessary to update our model: in E-Z Reader 5, the rate of lexical processing was modulated as a function of *eccentricity*, or the distance between the word being processed and the word being fixated (see equation 6 in Reichle et al., 1998). Because the original model only made predictions about whether words were skipped or not, it made sense to measure eccentricity in terms of the number of words intervening between the fixation point and the word being processed. However, because E-Z Reader 6 (Reichle et al., 1999) predicts the character that is being fixated, it makes more sense to define eccentricity in terms of the number of characters intervening between the point of fixation and the word being processed. More specifically, eccentricity, x, was redefined as the number of character spaces between the current fixation location and the center of the word being processed. The lexical processing rate is then adjusted using Eq. 4:

$$\text{duration}(x) = \text{duration}_0 \cdot \varepsilon^x \tag{4}$$

where duration_0 represents the time (in ms) required to complete each of the lexical processing components (i.e., the familiarity check, f, and the completion of lexical access, lc; see Reichle et al., 1998) when the center of the word is fixated, and ε

is a free parameter (actually, two free parameters, because different values are used for f and lc) that modulates duration. The eccentricity parameters were originally adopted to enhance the model's psychological plausibility; consequently, it was important to select values that would modulate the lexical processing rate no less than in our previous simulations. Because the mean word length in the Schilling et al. (1998) sentence corpus was 5.82 characters, values of ε were selected so that the processing rate at an eccentricity (as previously defined) of n words was on average greater than the processing rate at an eccentricity of 5.82 n characters.

Simulation results

Modeling the initial landing position in words during reading

To evaluate how well the model can reproduce the McConkie et al. (1988) results, we (Reichle et al., 1999) ran E-Z Reader 6 on our standard sentence corpus (i.e., the Schilling et al. sentences that were used in all of our previous simulations) using 1000 statistical subjects. [2] In the simulation, the initial landing positions were recorded for all 4-, 5-, 6-, and 7-letter words (excluding the first and last words of each sentence) for cases where the initial fixations followed saccades from launch sites 1-, 3-, 5-, and 7-character spaces to the left of the word boundaries. Histograms were then constructed to evaluate the predicted landing site distributions as a function of word length and launch site. These distributions excluded simulation trials in which a word was skipped due to oculomotor error under our assumption that, with real readers, these inadvertent skips would often lead to regressions. (In fitting the E-Z Reader model to the Schilling et al. data, all trials on which readers actually made inter-word regressions were eliminated.) Statistical trials on which a word was undershot due to oculomotor error were included, however, and were expected to inflate the predicted number of refixations. Because our corpus of sentences was relatively small, the empirical distributions were somewhat noisy, so that comparing them to the predicted distributions would be of little value. Instead, our emphasis was on showing that the distributions were consistent with those typically observed when extremely large data bases are analyzed (McConkie et al., 1988).

The landing site distributions for 5- and 6-letter words (see Reichle et al., 1999, for all four word lengths), as a function of four different launch sites, are shown

---

2 Although our sentence corpus was not rich enough to examine the fixation location distributions within the corpus, the properties of the distributions that we wanted to simulate have been reported in several places (e.g., McConkie et al., 1988, 1991; Rayner et al., 1996) and appear to be quite robust.

in Fig. 1. Consistent with prior reports (McConkie et al., 1988; Rayner et al., 1996; Reilly and O'Regan, 1998), the figure shows the percentage of initial landing positions with respect to how far away their launch sites were. Both the locations of the fixations and launch sites are indicated with respect to their distance (in number of character spaces) from the left word boundaries, with the blank space to the left of the words being designated as zero. The values of the two new parameters were estimated from McConkie et al. (1988): $\Psi_b = 7$, and $\Psi_m = 0.4$. The remaining parameters were selected to give reasonably good fits. [3]

The landing site distributions are quite similar to those reported by McConkie et al. (see their figs. 1 and 2). That is, the distributions are roughly normal in shape, with tails truncated at the word boundaries and means located near the center of the words. As the launch sites move further away from the left word boundary, the centers of the distributions shift leftward, and their variability increases. This second result is evident if one compares the relative heights of the distributions; as saccade length increases, so does the variability of the landing sites, thereby reducing the modes of the distributions. However, we also found that the variability of the distributions did not change markedly as a function of word length (see Reichle et al., 1999). This is also congruent with previous reports (McConkie et al., 1988; Rayner et al., 1996).

E-Z Reader 6 thus appears to do a fairly good job of predicting the locations of initial fixations on a word. However, it failed to explain several well-known properties of initial fixation locations. For example, it did not account for the finding of McConkie et al. (1988) that the magnitude of the systematic range error varied as a function of how long the launch site word is fixated. That is, as the fixation duration on the launch site increases, the extent to which the eyes overshoot or undershoot the subsequent word tends to decrease. The updated model cannot handle this result because the magnitude of the systematic range error is determined by a single, fixed parameter, Ψ_m. To handle the effect, we (Reichle et al., 1999) modified our assumption about the systematic range error so that the value of Ψ_m varied as a function of the fixation duration on the launch site word. We did this via

---

3 The slope (β_m) and intercept (β_b) parameters for the random error component of the saccades (see Eq. 2) were set equal to 0.11 and 0.85, respectively. The remaining parameters (as described in Reichle et al., 1998) and their values are: the slope ($f_b = 150$ ms) and intercept ($f_m = 12$ ms) parameters of the function relating the familiarity check duration, $t(f)$, to the logarithm of word frequency; the parameter ($\Delta = 0.85$) that determines how much additional time (i.e., a multiple of $t(f)$) is needed for the completion of lexical access, $t(lc)$; the parameter ($\theta = 0.5$) that attenuates the effect of predictability on $t(f)$; and the parameters that determine how long it takes to complete the labile ($t(m) = 135$ ms) and nonlabile ($t(M) = 50$ ms) stages of inter-word saccadic programming. The intra-word saccadic programming parameters, $t(r)$ and $t(R)$, were set equal to $t(m)$ and $t(M)$, respectively.

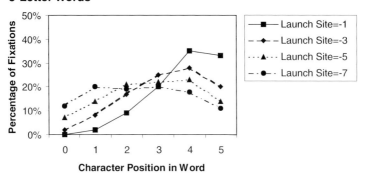

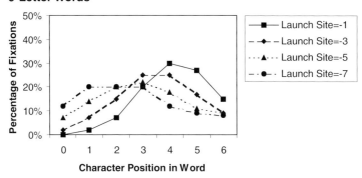

Fig. 1. Predicted landing site distributions on 5- and 6-letter words as a function of launch site. The locations of fixations and launch sites are indicated by numbers representing ordinal position, from left to right, with the blank space to the left of the word being zero. Adapted from Reichle et al. (1999) with permission from Elsevier Science.

Eq. 5:

$$\Psi_m = [\Omega_b - \ln(FD)]/\Omega_m \qquad (5)$$

In Eq. 5, the parameter that modulates the systematic range error, Ψ_m, is a linear function of the natural logarithm of the fixation duration (FD; in ms) on the launch site word. Ω_b and Ω_m are free parameters that determine how much the fixation duration affects the systematic range error. Eq. 5 is consistent with McConkie et al.'s (1988) account of the relationship between the launch site fixation duration and the systematic range error: as the fixation duration on the launch site increases, the eye guidance system presumably has more time to accurately locate the functional target of the upcoming saccade. This explanation was based on the fact that launch site fixation duration affected the magnitude of the systematic range error, but not the error due to oculomotor movement (Coëffé and O'Regan, 1987).

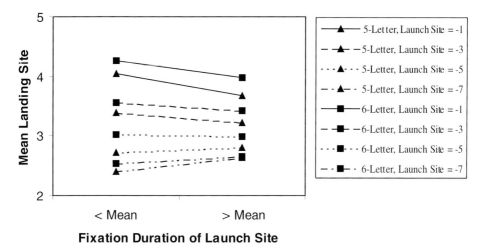

Fig. 2. Predicted landing site distribution means for 5- and 6-letter words as a function of the launch site location and fixation duration. The locations of the landing site means and launch sites are indicated by numbers representing ordinal position, from left to right, with the blank space to the left of the word being zero. The launch sites are sorted by fixation duration (above and below the mean value). Adapted from Reichle et al. (1999) with permission from Elsevier Science.

In the updated model, the values of the two new parameters were hand-chosen to provide reasonable fits ($\Omega_b = 7.3$; $\Omega_m = 4.5$). We then ran another simulation using 1000 statistical subjects and our standard sentence corpus. The predicted fixation locations for 4-, 5-, 6-, and 7-letter words were then sorted according to: (1) the location of the launch site; and (2) the fixation duration on the launch site. The latter was done first calculating the mean predicted fixation duration on launch site words (241 ms), and then dividing the predicted fixation locations into two groups: those following short launch fixations (i.e., fixation durations less than 241 ms), and those following long launch fixations (i.e., fixation durations longer than 241 ms). The means of the fixation location distributions were then calculated within each group, and compared to determine whether or not the magnitude of the systematic range error was affected by the launch site fixation duration. The means of the landing site distribution for 5- and 6-letter words (conditional upon whether the launch site fixation duration was above or below 241 ms) are presented in Fig. 2 (see Reichle et al., 1999, for all word lengths).

Fig. 2 shows that the landing site distribution means tend to converge towards the center of words as the fixation duration on the launch site word increases. This is clearly evident in the range of mean values; that is, the means of the 'below average' groups were more spread out (i.e., show a larger range of values) than the means in the 'above average' groups. This indicates that, as we had intended, the systematic range error can be made to be sensitive to the fixation duration on the launch site word.

Modeling refixations in reading

Up to this point, we have not addressed refixations (i.e., making another fixation on a word before moving to another word). Because the process of refixation is one of the least understood components of eye movement control (Rayner, 1998), it has often been sidestepped by various theories. For example, Reilly and O'Regan (1998) used a probability function to generate predictions about how often and where the eyes refixate so that the locations of these refixations could be used as launch sites in their study of landing site distributions. Typically, the probability of making a refixation is greatest following fixations on the beginning of the word, decreases towards the center of the word, and rises slightly near the end of the word, thus yielding an asymmetrical V-shaped function (see Rayner et al., 1996, fig. 3). Although Reilly and O'Regan (1998) correctly predict this type of function (see their fig. 3), their simulation does not provide a functional account of why the eyes behave in this manner. They maintain that "lexical processing is not assumed to affect the likelihood of refixating" and that "it is simply the eye's landing position which, when it deviates from the 'optimal' position, makes a refixation more likely" (Reilly and O'Regan, 1998, p. 307). However, Rayner et al. (1996) demonstrated that even when landing position was equated that readers refixated more often on low-frequency words than on high-frequency words (see Hyönä and Pollatsek, 1998, and Rayner, 1998, for other evidence that lexical processing influences refixation probability on a word).

In the E-Z Reader model, the same process underlies both inter- and intra-word saccades: a 'horse race' between the competing eye movement programs — one targeted on the next word by the completion of the familiarity check, f, and the other targeted on the same word and triggered by an 'automatic' signal whenever a fixation begins. In the case of refixations, f is slower than the completion of the labile stage of an automatically programmed saccade, whereas in the case of an inter-word saccade, f beats the end of this labile stage and it is canceled and the inter-word saccade program 'wins'. Thus, the original E-Z Reader model could explain when and why intra-word saccades (i.e., refixations) occur, but it could not specify how they are modulated by the location of the initial fixation. However, the updated model gives a reasonably good account of how the initial fixation location can modulate the probability of a refixation without making any additional assumptions. Remember that in E-Z Reader 6, the rate of lexical processing (f and lc) is modulated as a function of the distance between where the eyes are currently fixated and the center of the word that is being processed (see Eq. 4). As a result, the familiarity check completes most rapidly when the center of the word is fixated, and takes longer as the fixation deviates to either side of the word. Because refixations occur when the labile program to make an intra-word saccade completes before the familiarity check (i.e., f), our assumption about eccentricity means that refixations should be more likely to occur when the initial fixation is near the beginning or end of a word. This, in turn, should give rise to a symmetric V-shaped refixation function.

In sum, the E-Z Reader model explains the probability of a refixation as being primarily due to one cause: the speed of lexical identification (more technically, to the speed of the familiarity check process). The speed of this process is influenced both by linguistic variables, such as the frequency of a word in the language and by its predictability, and by physical factors, such as where one is fixating on a word. However, there is another factor that will influence refixations: undershoots. That is, according to the model, some of the time when an initial fixation is near the end of word$_n$, it is because word$_{n+1}$ was the target, but there was an undershoot. In those cases, the succeeding fixation will be on word$_{n+1}$ or word$_{n+2}$. As a result, the probability of refixation should in general be somewhat greater when the initial fixation is near the beginning of a word than when the initial fixation is near the end of a word (all else being equal).

To provide more quantitative tests of these predictions, we ran E-Z Reader 6 on our sentence corpus (using 1000 statistical subjects) and calculated the probability that a saccade from a particular location would be a refixation as a function of the landing position of the initial fixation on a word. Once again, we ran the simulation for 4-, 5-, 6-, and 7-letter words (see Fig. 3).

As Fig. 3 indicates, the updated model was largely successful in producing the V-shaped refixation functions. Although refixations are more likely to occur after the eyes have fixated the beginning of the word, the probability of making

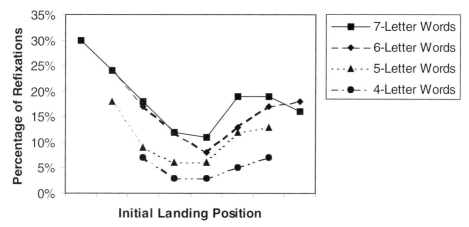

Fig. 3. Predicted percentages of refixations on 4-, 5-, 6-, and 7-letter words following initial fixations at different locations. The locations of the initial fixations are indicated by the marks along the *x*-axis, with the middle of the words located at mid-axis. Adapted from Reichle et al. (1999) with permission from Elsevier Science.

a refixation first decreases to a low-point near the center of the word, and then increases towards the end of the word. Moreover, the low-frequency, long words tended to be refixated more often than the high-frequency, short words, again consistent with Rayner et al. (1996). However, the overall conditional probability of making a refixation was only approximately correct. For example, Rayner et al. (1996) found that nearly 38% of the first fixations that landed in the space immediately to the left of 7-letter words were followed by refixations, as compared to the predicted value of 20%. Finally, although the probability of making a refixation drops slightly following initial fixations that land on the final letter of 7-letter words, Rayner et al. observed a similar pattern in that the probability functions tended to become less regular near the ends of long words (those longer than 6 characters in length). This suggests that some of the initial fixations that land near the end of long words are intended for subsequent words, and hence unlikely to result in refixations.

While E-Z Reader 6 gives a fairly good general account of refixations, it is likely to be incomplete because it only treats words as complete units. However, there is some evidence that the morphemic composition of words can affect both the probability of a refixation and the location of a refixation (see Chapter 4). Thus, morphemes, as well as words, could be cognitive units whose processing triggers eye movements. For the case of morphemes, however, the issue of where the eye movement would be directed is unclear. That is, it would be ideal to have the saccade targeted to something like the middle of the next morpheme. However, it seems unlikely that the eye movement system can actually locate this spot in the text quickly enough given that there are no spaces delineating morphemes. One simple strategy might be to direct the saccade towards the end of the word in hopes that it would be a reasonable location for processing the second morphemic unit. It is beyond the scope of the present chapter to include the processing of morphemes into the model (not to mention the fact that it would be a major change to the model).

How well does the updated model predict what the original model was designed to predict?

In the process of updating the model to account for initial fixation locations and refixations, we (Reichle et al., 1999) added assumptions to the original model that changed the process by which eccentricity affects word identification and we also posited that the 'wrong' word can sometimes be fixated. Because E-Z Reader was designed to explain individual fixation durations and gaze durations on words as well as the probability of skipping and refixating words, it is quite possible that either change could harm the fit of the model. In particular, the deliberate introduction of the possibility that the 'wrong' word is fixated should affect the skipping and refixation probabilities. It could also presumably affect fixation durations because there are now fixations actually made on one word when the processing of a different word is determining the duration of the fixation. The issue, then, is whether these changes weaken the fit of the model. Table 1 shows the performance of the updated model (E-Z Reader 6) in predicting the mean gaze durations, first fixation durations, single fixation durations, probability of skipping, making a single fixation, and making two fixations, for five frequency classes of words. These values are presented along side of the observed values, and the values that were reported in our earlier simulation (E-Z Reader 5; see Reichle et al., 1998).

The data in Table 1 indicate that the model's performance was only slightly degraded by the addition of McConkie et al.'s (1988) assumptions regarding oculomotor error. Of course, we could have improved the updated model's overall performance by finding optimal values for the parameters that were added to account for the initial landing site distributions and refixations instead of simply setting the parameters equal to values that were estimated from other sources. [4] We did not do so for the sake of simplicity, and because we wanted to show that the general outcome of the simulations does not depend upon specific parameter values.

Discussion

There have recently been a number of attempts to provide computational and more quantitative models of eye movement control in reading (see Chapters 25 and 26). Undoubtedly, this trend will lead to greater understanding of the process of skilled reading. Our primary goal in the present chapter was to demonstrate that the assumptions of McConkie et al. (1988) are not inconsistent with the basic E-Z Reader framework, and that, by combining the two approaches, one can gain a further understanding of eye movement control in reading (see Reichle et al., 1999). Within the context of the E-Z Reader model, we have tried to explain several basic aspects of eye-movement control related to the locations of initial fixations and within-word refixations: namely, the distributions of these fixations, how these distributions are affected by low-level oculomotor variables, and the etiology of refixations. Prior to this point, the E-Z Reader model did a fairly good job of accounting for when the eyes move (both within and between words) and where the eyes fixate at the level of individual words (Reichle et al., 1998; see also Rayner et al., 1998). By adding a few assumptions about the relationship between the oculomotor system and saccadic accuracy, the updated model also explains where

---

4 The results of simulations not reported in this chapter support this claim.

Table 1

Comparison of the overall performance of E-Z Reader 5 with E-Z Reader 6 (adapted from Reichle et al. (1999) with permission from Elsevier Science)

Frequency class	Mean frequency	Gaze duration			First-fixation duration			Single-fixation duration		
		Obs	EZ5	EZ6	Obs	EZ5	EZ6	Obs	EZ5	EZ6
1	3	293	291	286	248	251	253	265	274	272
2	45	272	271	268	234	253	252	249	263	263
3	347	256	257	247	228	246	240	243	252	245
4	4889	234	226	216	223	223	215	235	224	217
5	40700	214	211	206	208	210	206	216	210	210

Frequency class	Mean frequency	Probability of skipping			Prob. of making single fixation			Prob. of making two fixations		
		Obs	EZ5	EZ6	Obs	EZ5	EZ6	Obs	EZ5	EZ6
1	3	0.10	0.09	0.06	0.68	0.73	0.78	0.20	0.17	0.17
2	45	0.13	0.16	0.11	0.70	0.76	0.80	0.16	0.07	0.09
3	347	0.22	0.27	0.21	0.68	0.68	0.74	0.10	0.04	0.04
4	4889	0.55	0.49	0.44	0.44	0.50	0.53	0.02	0.01	0.03
5	40700	0.67	0.68	0.64	0.32	0.32	0.34	0.01	0.00	0.02

Obs = observed performance (see Reichle et al., 1998, table 5), as calculated from our corpus of the Schilling et al. (1998) sentences. EZ5 = predicted performance of E-Z Reader 5 (see Reichle et al., 1998, table 5) using the following parameter values: $f_b = 195$ ms; $f_m = 17$ ms; $\Delta = 0.70$; $t(m) = 150$ ms; $t(M) = 50$ ms; $\varepsilon_1 = 1.25$; $\varepsilon_2 = 1.75$; and $\theta = 0.5$. The within-word motor programming parameters, $t(r)$ and $r(R)$, were assumed to have the same values as $t(m)$ and $t(M)$, respectively. Root-mean-square deviation = 0.198. EZ6 = predicted performance of E-Z Reader 6 (i.e., the updated model with the added McConkie et al. 1988 assumptions) using the following parameter values: $f_b = 150$ ms; $f_m = 12$ ms; $\Delta = 0.85$; $\theta = 0.5$; $t(m) = 135$ ms; $t(M) = 50$ ms; $\varepsilon_1 = 1.09$; and $\varepsilon_2 = 1.13$. The new parameters and their values were: $\Psi_b = 7$; $\beta_b = 0.85$; $\beta_m = 0.11$; $\Omega_b = 7.3$; and $\Omega_m = 4.5$. Root-mean-square deviation = 0.218.

the eyes fixate within words. Finally, and most importantly, the model provides a unified theory about why these various aspects of eye-movement control operate as they do. The model thus provides a tool for understanding how both oculomotor and linguistic variables affect eye movement control during reading.

While the model does a good job of accounting for a great deal of data, we realize that it is incomplete, and that there is still considerable room for improvement. For instance, the model can be criticized for its large number of free parameters (in this chapter, a total of 10), and for its overall complexity. There are several ways to address these criticisms. First, although we did attempt to maintain our minimalist approach in our modeling work, we did not make a serious effort in E-Z Reader 6 either to minimize the number of parameters or to find optimal fits. Hence, there is undoubtedly some redundancy in the model. As mentioned, we did not take steps to remedy these shortcomings because our goal was to simply provide an existence proof that, with the appropriate assumptions, the regularities that are due to low-level oculomotor factors are not problematic for the model.

With respect to the second criticism (that the model is too complex), it is worth emphasizing that the task of reading is itself very complex. As the classic quote of Huey (1908) indicates, "to [understand] what we do when we read would almost be the acme of a psychologist's achievements, for it would be to describe very many of the most intricate workings of the human mind." As it currently stands, we view the current model as a functional description of part of the processes that go on in the mind during reading, and how these processes give rise to the many regularities in eye movement behavior. If one considers the process of reading from the perspective of cognitive-neuroscience, it is immediately clear that the task involves the coordinated activity of at least three large-scale cortical networks; namely, the cortical regions involved in: (a) language processing; (b) visual–spatial attention; and (c) working memory (Mesulam, 1990, 1998). Because the current model places emphasis on only the first two of these areas, the argument could be made that the model is overly simplistic. In the end, however, any definition of 'complex' is relative; what matters is how well the model serves as a framework both for (1) organizing and understanding existing data and (2) guiding further research (Hintzman, 1991). By this standard, then, the E-Z Reader Model is clearly a success.

Acknowledgements

This work was supported by Grant HD26765 from the National Institutes of Health. The first author was also supported by a Senior Scientist Award (MH01255) from the National Institute of Mental Health. We thank Ronan Reilly and Timothy Klitz for their comments on an earlier version of the chapter.

References

Becker, W. and Jürgens, R. (1979). An analysis of the saccadic system by means of double-step stimuli. Vision Research, 19, 967–983.

Coëffé, C. and O'Regan, J.K. (1987). Reducing the influence of nontarget stimuli on saccade accuracy: predictability and latency effects. Vision Research, 27, 227–240.

Deutsch, A. and Rayner, K. (1999). Initial fixation location effects in reading Hebrew words. Language and Cognitive Processes, 14 393–421.

Epelboim, J., Booth, J.R. and Steinman, R.M. (1994). Reading unspaced text: implications for reading eye movement. Vision Research, 34, 1735–1766.

Francis, W.N. and Kuçera, H. (1982). Frequency Analysis of English Usage: Lexicon and Grammar. Boston: Houghton Mifflin.

Hintzman, D.L. (1991). Why are formal models useful in psychology? In: W.E. Hockley and S. Lewandowsky (Eds.), Relating Theory and Data: Essays in Honor of Bennet B. Murdock. Hillsdale, NJ: Erlbaum, pp. 175–194.

Huey, E.B. (1908). The Psychology and Pedagogy of Reading. New York, NY: Macmillan.

Hyönä, J. and Pollatsek, A. (1998). Reading Finnish compound words: eye fixations are affected by component morphemes. Journal of Experimental Psychology: Human Perception and Performance, 24, 1612–1627.

Just, M.A. and Carpenter, P.A. (1980). A theory of reading: from eye fixations to comprehension. Psychological Review, 87, 329–354.

Just, M.A. and Carpenter, P.A. (1987). The Psychology of Reading and Language Comprehension. Boston, MA: Allyn and Bacon.

McConkie, G.W., Kerr, P.W., Reddix, M.D. and Zola, D. (1988). Eye movement control during reading, I. The location of the initial eye fixations on words. Vision Research, 28, 1107–1118.

McConkie, G.W. and Rayner, K. (1975). The span of the effective stimulus during a fixation in reading. Perception and Psychophysics, 17, 578–586.

McConkie, G.W., Zola, D., Grimes, J., Kerr, P.W., Bryant, N.R. and Wolff, P.M. (1991). Children's eye movements during reading. In: J.F. Stein (Ed.), Vision and Visual Dyslexia. London: Macmillan Press, pp. 251–262.

Mesulam, M.M. (1990). Large-scale neurocognitive networks and distributed processing for attention, language, and memory. Annals of Neurology, 28, 597–613.

Mesulam, M.M. (1998). From sensation to cognition. Brain, 121, 1013–1052.

Morris, R.K., Rayner, K. and Pollatsek, A. (1990). Eye movement guidance in reading: the role of parafoveal letter and space information. Journal of Experimental Psychology: Human Perception and Performance, 16, 268–281.

Morrison, R.E. (1984). Manipulation of stimulus onset delay in reading: evidence for parallel programming of saccades. Journal of Experimental Psychology: Human Perception and Performance, 10, 667–682.

O'Regan, J.K. (1981). The 'convenient viewing position' hypothesis. In: D.F. Fisher, R.A. Monty and J.W. Senders (Eds.), Eye Movements: Cognition and Visual Perception. Hillsdale, NJ: Erlbaum, pp. 289–298.

O'Regan, J.K. (1990). Eye movements and reading. In: E. Kowler (Ed.), Eye Movements and their Role in Visual and Cognitive Processes. Amsterdam: Elsevier, pp. 395–453.

O'Regan, J.K. (1992). Optimal viewing position in words and the strategy-tactics theory of eye movements in reading. In: K. Rayner (Ed.), Eye Movements and Visual Cognition: Scene Perception and Reading. New York, NY: Springer, pp. 333–354.

O'Regan, J.K. and Lévy-Schoen, A. (1987). Eye-movement strategy and tactics in word recognition and reading. In: M. Coltheart (Ed.), Attention and Performance, XII. Hillsdale, NJ: Erlbaum, pp. 363–384.

Paap, K.R., Newsome, S.L., McDonald, J.E. and Schvaneveldt, R.W. (1982). An activation–verification model for letter and word recognition: the word superiority effect. Psychological Review, 89, 573–594.

Pollatsek, A. and Rayner, K. (1982). Eye movement control in reading: the role of word boundaries. Journal of Experimental Psychology: Human Perception and Performance, 8, 817–833.

Pollatsek, A. and Rayner, K. (1990). Eye movements and lexical access in reading. In: D.A. Balota, G.B. Flores d'Arcais and K. Rayner (Eds.), Comprehension Processes in Reading. Hillsdale, NJ: Erlbaum, pp. 143–163.

Rayner, K. (1979). Eye guidance in reading: fixation location in words. Perception, 8, 21–30.

Rayner, K. (1986). Eye movements and the perceptual span in beginning and skilled readers. Journal of Experimental Child Psychology, 41, 211–236.

Rayner, K. (1998). Eye movements in reading and information processing: 20 years of research. Psychological Bulletin, 124, 372–422.

Rayner, K. and Bertera, J.H. (1979). Reading without a fovea. Science, 206, 468–469.

Rayner, K., Fischer, M.H. and Pollatsek, A. (1998). Unspaced text interferes with both word identification and eye movement control. Vision Research, 38, 1129–1144.

Rayner, K. and McConkie, G.W. (1976). What guides a reader's eye movements? Vision Research, 16, 829–837.

Rayner, K. and Pollatsek, A. (1981). Eye movement control in reading: evidence for direct control. Quarterly Journal of Experimental Psychology, 33A, 351–373.

Rayner, K. and Pollatsek, A. (1989). The Psychology of Reading. Hillsdale, NJ: Erlbaum.

Rayner, K. and Pollatsek, A. (1996). Reading unspaced text is not easy: comments on the implications of Epelboim et al.'s study for models of eye movement control in reading. Vision Research, 36, 461–470.

Rayner, K., Reichle, E.D. and Pollatsek, A. (1998). Eye movement control in reading: an overview and model. In: G. Underwood (Ed.), Eye Guidance in Reading and Scene Perception. Oxford: Elsevier, pp. 243–268.

Rayner, K., Sereno, S.C. and Raney, G.E. (1996). Eye movement control in reading: a comparison of two types of models. Journal of Experimental Psychology: Human Perception and Performance, 22, 1188–1200.

Reichle, E.D., Pollatsek, A., Fisher, D.L. and Rayner, K. (1998). Toward a model of eye movement control in reading. Psychological Review, 105, 125–157.

Reichle, E.D., Rayner, K. and Pollatsek, A. (1999). Eye movement control in reading: accounting for initial fixation locations and refixations within the E-Z Reader model. Vision Research, 39, 4403–4411.

Reilly, R.G. and O'Regan, J.K. (1998). Eye movement control during reading: a simulation of some word-targeting strategies. Vision Research, 38, 303–317.

Schilling, H.E.H., Rayner, K. and Chumbley, J.I. (1998). Comparing naming, lexical decision, and eye fixation times: Word frequency effects and individual differences. Memory and Cognition, 26, 1270–1281.

Van Orden, G. (1987). A rows is a rose: spelling, sound, and reading. Memory and Cognition, 15, 181–198.

COMMENTARY ON SECTION 5

Five Questions about Cognitive Models and Some Answers from Three Models of Reading

Arthur M. Jacobs
Catholic University Eichstaett

Introduction

"Modeling is a way of life" Don Norman once said during a talk in Paris (approximately april 1983). As a student of experimental psychology working in the field of eye movements and reading at that time, I was impressed because the field I worked in seemed comparatively bare of people sharing Norman's approach to life and science: back in 1983 there was hardly any formal model of the sensori-motor and cognitive processes involved in eye movement control during reading to be found.

The three chapters in this section are impressive examples showing that this field of research is finally moving 'in Norman's direction' after having spent a considerable time developing and quarreling about methodological issues. The modeling work referred to in these chapters also is representative of the richness, creativity and heterogeneity of the cognitive modeling approach per se: it almost covers the whole range from pre-quantitative, verbal–graphical ('boxological') models to (quantitative) mathematical and algorithmic/simulation models (for a recent classification approach to cognitive models, see Jacobs and Grainger, 1994 or Grainger and Jacobs, 1998). Klitz et al. (Chapter 25) present a simulation model of impaired reading. Rayner et al. (Chapter 27) who started with a pre-quantitative model (Morrison, 1984), now present the updated version of a hybrid quantitative model (mixture between mathematical and simulation model), the E-Z reader model of eye movement control in reading. McConkie and Dyre (Chapter 26) present a mathematical model of fixation duration distributions during reading.

Reading as a Perceptual Process/A. Kennedy, R. Radach, D. Heller and J. Pynte (Editors)
© 2000 Elsevier Science Ltd. All rights reserved

Three types of cognitive models: Alternatives or complements?

One can distinguish three types or formats of cognitive models: prequantitative models that mainly come in the form of boxes-and-arrows ('boxological') models, mathematical models that try to capture the modeled aspect of reality in a set of equations, and algorithmic (computational, simulation) models that try to simulate cognitive reality by help of a computer program (Jacobs and Grainger, 1994). While both latter model types allow quantitative predictions, mathematical models use closed-form expressions that can be solved analytically, a feature lacked by simulation models of complex, non-linear, dynamic cognitive processes. While these different formats present a number of advantages and disadvantages discussed in Jacobs and Grainger (1994), mathematical models can be seen as the most explicit type of models, followed by simulation and prequantitative models (cf., Estes, 1975).

However, one of the strengths of mathematical models, abstractness, can also be regarded as a weakness: they abstract from as much detail as possible and thus fail to yield transparent possible answers with regard to the question of 'how a cognitive process could function' (Grainger and Jacobs, 1998; Jacobs, Rey, Ziegler and Grainger, 1998). If providing possible answers with regard to the 'How-question' is the central level of analysis of Cognitive Psychology, then simulation models should be the central modeling tool in our field (Marr, 1982; see also debate Broadbent, 1985 vs. Rumelhart and McClelland, 1985). Recent developments in the fields of word recognition, attention, or memory and a look through the issues of Psychological Review or Behavioral and Brain Sciences of the last 20 years support this notion. Nevertheless, also prequantitative, boxological and mathematical models have their role to play in cognitive psychology: the first can be helpful descriptive tools for summarizing heterogeneous results from a wide variety of experimental paradigms into a single 'functional organization', while the latter "*remain our principal vehicle for the flights of imagination that smooth our experiences and extract from varying contexts the relationships that would hold among events under idealized noise-free conditions*" (Estes, 1975; cf. Jacobs, 1994, 2000; Jacobs and Grainger, 1994). Thus, all three types of cognitive models can be helpful in the inquiry of cognitive processes and can complement each other. I think that the three models in this chapter support this claim.

Five questions about cognitive models

For any model in cognitive psychology, a number of questions must be asked and answered in order to evaluate its usefulness. The five questions I propose are the condensed result of more than 10 years of actively asking questions to cognitive modelers who submitted their work to the journals for which I served as a reviewer. I hope they are inter-subjectively criticizable and therefore useful.

(1) What is (counts as) the model?
(2) What is the model a model for?
(3) Are the model parameters psychologically interpretable?
(4) Can the model be evaluated in comparison to other models?
(5) Can the model be identified and falsified?

Let us filter the three present models through these questions to illustrate the points and obtain some answers.

Form and extent of a model: what is the model?

The first question obviously must be what the model is, i.e., what form and extent the model takes. The question is less trivial than it may seem. After having determined a model's format — which is relatively easy in the present three cases — a trickier business is to determine whether the model is of 'the model is the theory' vs. 'the model is not the theory' kind. That is, one must decide how much of the authors' 'theory' of the investigated cognitive process is actually formalized by or implemented in the model (Jacobs and Grainger, 1994; McCloskey, 1991).

McConkie and Dyre propose a model in the tradition of mathematical models, popularized during the big years of learning theory (e.g., Estes, 1950) and not unusual in the fields of eye movement and reading research (Jacobs, 1993; McConkie, Kerr, Reddix, Zola and Jacobs, 1989; Nazir and Jacobs, 1991; Nazir, O'Regan and Jacobs, 1991; Nazir, Jacobs and O'Regan, 1998): models that consist of one or more equations attempting to describe how the dependent variables of interest (here: probability of fixations and their durations) change with the experimental conditions, with time, or with space. Mathematically, the model successfully describes the fixation duration frequency distribution as a sum of two distributions: one derived from two linearly increasing hazard curves, representing growth processes, and one exponential distribution representing a stable state.

However, although I have classified McConkie and Dyre's model as a mathematical model [1], would all readers agree that the model is entirely defined by equations (6) to (11), or, are some of the statements in the text, e.g., "it is assumed that State 1 constitutes the period of time prior to the system's beginning to make use of new visual information made available on this fixation" (p. 698) also a relevant part of

---

1 Note that according to Myung and Pitt (1998), this model would qualify as a statistical model, i.e., 'a parametric family of probability distributions of experimental data'. Myung and Pitt thus distinguish statistical from algebraic mathematical models and from network (computational or simulation) models.

the model? Perhaps, some even consider statements like "we expect that the primary effect of currently perceived text characteristics, such as the cultural frequency of words lying within the perceptual span region will be on the alpha-parameter, which controls the decay rate of the exponential describing the latter part of the fixation period" as being part of the model.

Thus, either the model contains more than can be or is described in equations (6) to (11) and then it may no longer count as a pure mathematical model, or, the model can be considered as one of the 'the model is not the theory' kind (Jacobs and Grainger, 1994). In both cases, problems with regard to answering questions four and five will arise, because it is unclear which part(s) of the model can be compared and falsified and which cannot. Much like the famous 'non-implemented' parts of simulation models (e.g., McCloskey, 1991), the 'non-equated' parts of mathematical models (or the theories they are part of) must be considered and taken into account in a complete evaluation of the model (see questions 4 and 5).

Klitz et al.'s 'Mr. Chips' is a simulation model, a computer algorithm trying to capture the crucial functional aspects of the modeled aspect of reality, that is, saccade planning in reading with and without central scotomas. Any model should simplify the modeled aspect of reality as much as possible: Mr. Chips achieves this by focussing on the perceptual front–end constraints in reading, combining simple visual and lexical information, but leaving aside any semantic, syntactic or contextual information that might intervene in guiding a good reader's eyes.

As for McConkie and Dyre's mathematical model, one must ask which non-implemented parts may belong to the model or the theory, respectively. The question becomes crucial in combination with questions 2–5, because when potentially getting into trouble having to answer questions like what Mr. Chips is a model for, whether it is psychologically plausible, whether it is comparable to alternative models, and finally, whether it is falsifiable, its authors might recur to the often-applied simulation modeler's stratagem and answer something like: "Well, this is not part of the implemented model" [2].

Rayner et al.'s model can be considered a hybrid between a mathematical and a simulation model. On the one hand, the original E-Z reader models 1 to 5 (Reichle, Pollatsek, Fisher and Rayner, 1998) are described by a set of six equations with eight parameters (five of which are free), if I am not mistaken. On the other hand, the equations are combined in a computer program that is used to run 'monte-carlo simulations' with 100 or 1000 'modeled participants' in order to generate the theoretical data. There are other examples of hybrid models in the literature on

---

2 I have no intention to suspect Klitz et al. of using this stratagem. I only use their simulation model as an example for a stratagem that might be applied (and in my experience as reviewer actually has been applied often). They may forgive me for having been used as a possible example case.

reading. The 'Activation–Verification Model' (AVM; Paap and Johansen, 1994) is one. As long as models of cognition use only non-interactive, feedforward processing, summarizing their behavior in a set of equations is possible and useful (Grainger and Jacobs, 1994, 1998). When using interactive feedback processes operating on hundreds or thousands of units, as in localist connectionist models of the interactive activation family (Grainger and Jacobs, 1996; McClelland and Rumelhart, 1981; Ziegler, Rey and Jacobs, 1998), it becomes virtually impossible to summarize the model's behavior in a set of equations, and even if it was possible, the mathematical model would not be tractable and hardly useful.

The 'price' Rayner et al. have paid for their mathematically tractable hybrid model is similar to Paap and Johansen: apart from oversimplifications and incompletenesses (Reichle et al., 1998, p. 149) that restrict the plausibility but increase the falsifiability of many cognitive models, Rayner et al. renounce on any feedback processes that would make the model mathematically untractable (see question 3).

What is the model a model for?

The second question is what the model is supposed to be a model for. Is it supposed to be a model of a possible (hypothetical, unobservable) cognitive architecture, process, or system, a model of a real (observed) function relating a dependent to an independent variable, or both?

Clearly, McConkie and Dyre's model is foremost a model of an observable distribution of a dependent variable across time. But, if I read the paper correctly, it is also more: a model of the hypothetical process(es) triggering a saccade. McConkie and Dyre's model belongs to the popular family of two-state, two-process, or two-stage models in cognitive psychology (Townsend and Ashby, 1983; Dunn and Kirsner, 1988). It postulates the operation of two distinct processes for triggering a saccade. Early in a fixation, 'early' saccades may be triggered from State 1, without the benefit of new information from the current fixation, either because it has not yet arrived at critical brain centers, or because, even though available, it has not yet been attended. 'Normal' saccades, however, are triggered only after a transition is made to State 2. Presumably, this transition occurs due to the influence of information from the current fixation. Hence, the two-state transition model includes a mechanism for explaining saccades that occur before visual information from the current fixation has an influence. In summary, the model is a model of a function plus a model of the hypothetical processes triggering a saccade. As the authors state, the model fits the data well, but this appears to result primarily from the (three) functions used in the model rather than from the architecture, that is, the process-structure, proposed. This duality makes the evaluation of the model complicated, as we will see in points 4 and 5 below. A problem arising from this is that whereas the model may well be specified with respect to its mathematical-functional part, it is certainly under-specified with respect to its architectural-process assumptions.

Mr. Chips, on the other hand, is a process model: it specifies how elementary visual and lexical information processing within the visual span guides eye movements in reading. However, as stated by the authors, Mr. Chips "is not intended as an exact model of how humans perform a task, but rather it establishes an upper bound (a level of competence) for human performance". Thus, Mr. Chips is a model for 'an ideal observer', i.e., an algorithm that yields optimal performance on a task [3], given a specified set of information sources. While ideal-observer models are useful tools for quantifying human performance relative to an optimality criterion, their usefulness for understanding human cognition is limited by the psychological plausibility of the assumptions specifying 'optimal performance' (see question 3 below).

E-Z reader is also a process model, but both more abstract and general than Mr. Chips: basically, it specifies how lexical access, the 'magical moment' of reading (Grainger and Jacobs, 1996; Jacobs and Carr, 1995), guides the eyes through words in a text. However, whereas the model seems well-specified with respect to assumptions about eye movement control, the central process of lexical access is under-specified in comparison with current computational models of word recognition (Coltheart and Rastle, 1994; Grainger and Jacobs, 1996; Paap and Johansen, 1994). One question therefore is whether E-Z reader also counts as a model of lexical access and therefore can be evaluated with respect to predictions concerning possible effects of factors known to affect this process.

Psychological interpretability of model parameters, plausibility of model

McConkie and Dyre raise the critical issue of the psychological interpretability and plausibility of their model and its parameters in the last part of their article. The issue is far from being trivial (Jacobs, 1993); to see this, it suffices to try to answer the question "What determines the psychological interpretability of a parameter in a mathematical or computational/algorithmic model [4]?" Klitz et al.'s minimalistic, ideal-observer model does not seem to adjust any free parameters to obtained data, while Rayner et al.'s 6th variant of E-Z reader offers a wealth of ten free parameters. Since these latter two groups of authors do not bring up the

---

3 Optimality is defined here as: recognize every word in a text in sequential order, with absolute certainty, in the minimum number of saccades.

4 For reasons of simplicity and page numbers I shall focus on the question of interpretability of free parameters. However, especially with respect to computational models, the question of the interpretability of fixed parameters is just as critical.

problem, in discussing it I shall focus on McConkie and Dyre's model. I agree with McConkie and Dyre that answering this question of parameter interpretability is difficult if the model is not backed by a clear theory specifying which independent or model-inherent variables affect which parameter under which conditions and for what reasons.

At least three questions can be asked to determine the psychological interpretability of a parameter. The first two are: Does the parameter systematically change with an independent variable and is this factor itself psychologically meaningful within the context of the model or other models? For example, McConkie and Dyre speculate that word frequency could affect the parameter which controls the decay rate of the exponential describing the latter part of the fixation period (alpha), but they emphasize that further work is necessary in order to solve the problem of the psychological meaning of the parameters of their model. One problem generated by this example is that word frequency is a factor whose psychological meaning is unclear. This is because its locus of effect is hotly debated by current computational models of word recognition; as concerns perceptual identification and lexical decision tasks, models of the interactive activation family localize the effect in perceptual encoding (McClelland and Rumelhart, 1981; Grainger and Jacobs, 1994, 1996; Jacobs and Grainger, 1992), whereas verification models view it as a result of a decision bias (Paap and Johansen, 1994). Similarly, as concerns the naming task, dual-route models (Coltheart and Rastle, 1994) — by virtue of its interactive activation component — localize the effect in the encoding level, whereas the pre-quantitative model of Balota and Chumbley (1985) localizes it in a later production stage.

With respect to McConkie and Dyre's model, the problem then is that first they would have to demonstrate that their alpha-parameter changes systematically with word frequency. Secondly, they would have to specify to which of the above theoretical camps they belong and, say they chose the 'perceptual encoding' camp, what their alpha-parameter has to do with perceptual encoding. But even if these two problems were successfully solved, a third question can be asked with regard to the interpretability of a parameter: does the parameter exclusively change with one factor? Suppose the alpha-parameter in McConkie and Dyre's model would have been demonstrated to change systematically with word frequency, but also with three other factors (say, bigram frequency, orthographic neighborhood density, and word consistency). Then, the question of its psychological interpretability would be far from being answered. Thus, with regard to mathematical models, the interpretability of a parameter depends on whether psychologically meaningful factors exist that change it systematically and — ideally — exclusively. Furthermore, the theory for which the model provides an implementation, must specify why and how a given parameter changes with a given factor.

In this context one can also ask the question whether the cognitive model as a whole is psychologically plausible. Both Mr. Chips and E-Z reader contain assumptions that seem implausible in the light of current empirical and computational evidence from reading research. For example, both Mr. Chips and E-Z reader neglect facts about the optimal viewing position in reading words (Chapter 1; O'Regan and Jacobs, 1992; Nazir et al., 1991, 1998), about the effects of orthographic similarity on lexical access (Andrews, 1997; Grainger and Jacobs, 1996), or about the role of top-down feedback in word recognition (Coltheart and Rastle, 1994; Grainger and Jacobs, 1994, 1996; Jacobs and Grainger, 1992; McClelland and Rumelhart, 1981; Zicgler et al., 1998). Of course, both models represent first steps towards more plausible models of reading and such restrictions concerning their plausibility stem from their attempts to remain as simple as possible and their focussing on the process of eye movement control. One challenge for future models of reading therefore is to integrate models as Mr. Chips or E-Z reader with computational models of word recognition, such as the DRC (Coltheart and Rastle, 1994), the revised AVM (Paap, Johansen, Chun and Vonnahme, 2000), or the MROM (Grainger and Jacobs, 1996) and MROM-p (Jacobs et al., 1998), that neglect eye movement control but are more specific and presumably more plausible with respect to orthographic, phonological, and lexical processes.

Model comparability and evaluation: 10 criteria but how to apply them?

Whereas both Rayner et al. and Klitz et al. focus on testing their own model against their own data sets, McConkie and Dyre provide an example of what I consider to be the best — but unfortunately not easily applicable and rarely applied — strategy of model evaluation: the so-called strong inference approach (Jacobs and Grainger, 1994, 1999; Jacobs et al., 1998). In this approach, alternative models are compared with respect to the same data sets (ideally coming from independent sources) and evaluated with regard to the same criteria. However, this presupposes that the models are comparable in a meaningful and transparent way and that standard, widely accepted criteria for model evaluation exist.

Both premises have their own problems as well as problems resulting from their interaction. As concerns model comparability, trying to compare the three models of saccade control in reading in this chapter with respect to a set of formal criteria of model evaluation is useless: the models are just too heterogeneous with respect to even the most fundamental criteria, that is, potential and actual descriptive adequacy, horizontal and vertical generality, simplicity and falsifiability, and explanatory adequacy (for more details on these criteria, see Jacobs and Grainger, 1994; Jacobs et al., 1998; Myung and Pitt, 1998).

Rayner et al. refer to two other criteria models should fulfill (Hintzman, 1991): organize and make understandable existing data and guide research. However, much as the eight criteria mentioned above, I am unable to apply these two additional criteria in a reasonably comparative manner to the three models of this chapter: because the models are not comparable. Ideally, two models are comparable if they differ by one and only one aspect (parameter or structural component of the model), the change of which leads to qualitatively or quantitatively different falsifiable predictions. A crucial experiment can then be designed to definitely test between the two models. If the models differ by more than one parameter or architectural assumption, as is even the case with the five models compared by McConkie and Dyre, if I'm not mistaken, then determining which model is the best and why it is the best becomes complicated, as demonstrated in McConkie and Dyre's article [5].

Model identifiability and falsifiability

The questions of model identifiability and falsifiability can nicely be illustrated using the E-Z reader model which, although it has ten free parameters, still can be considered as overly simplistic, as the authors argue. The E-Z reader model would be identifiable, if their authors could show that the model's parameters are uniquely determined in light of observed outcomes and thus are meaningfully interpretable (Bamber and van Santen, 1985; Myung and Pitt, 1998). The question of model falsifiability is intimately related to the problems of model simplicity and identifiability. Let me ask a simple question to illustrate the point: is a good model one that includes a maximum of possible outcomes? Or is it one that excludes a maximum of possible outcomes? Everything else being equal between two models, the answer is as simple as the question: the better of the two is the one that places the greatest restrictions on how the empirical data can turn out to be, if the model is correct. A good empirical law is one that prohibits a maximum of outcomes. The same is true for a good cognitive model.

Put differently, the question of model falsifiability asks whether there exist potential outcomes that are contradictory to the model. This brings us back to my question 1 above, because one cannot answer the question of model falsifiability without having a clear notion of what exactly counts as 'the model'. In addition, only falsifying an identifiable (or identified) model makes sense.

To facilitate model testing and the tricky problem of falsifiability, a pragmatic heuristic is to ask cognitive modelers to indicate a 'strongest falsificator' for the

---

5 Nevertheless, with respect to mathematical models such as McConkie and Dyre's, meaningful model comparisons are possible if one respects a standard procedure and a number of necessary criteria. Recently, Myung and Pitt (1998) proposed five selection methods for deciding between several mathematical models on the basis of two criteria, the number of free parameters and the functional form of the model.

model: an effect that the model excludes under all initial conditions (Jacobs and Grainger, 1999) [6].

If I am not mistaken, none of the models in this section is discussed with respect to these related problems, and the questions of whether any of the three models is identifiable and falsifiable must await future research.

Outlook

In summary, one big challenge for cognitive modelers remains the development of a set of standard procedures and criteria that allow rational comparisons and evaluations of models. The five questions posed in this chapter to three models of reading perhaps illustrate the complexity of the problem, but also show ways how to solve it.

One promising way to more rational model comparisons and evaluations is followed by Rayner et al. who use a modeling principle called nested modeling (Grainger and Jacobs, 1996, 1998; Jacobs, 1994; Jacobs and Grainger, 1994; Myung and Pitt, 1998): they test increasingly complex and general variants of the E-Z reader model arriving at the 6th variant in the present chapter. More formally, this principle requires that a new model either includes the old one as a special case by providing formal demonstrations of the inclusion, or dismisses with it, after falsification of the core assumptions of the old model. The leading idea is that, although a single model cannot be more or less true (i.e., it can only be true or false, the latter being the rule), a new model M' can very well represent a better approximation to reality than the old model M. This would be the case if it can be shown that the empirical content of model M' is greater than that of model M (Grainger and Jacobs, 1998). This seems to be the case for E-Z reader 6 in comparison to its precursors.

In conclusion, when constructing or testing their models, cognitive modelers can facilitate the task of model evaluation by following a few useful principles or stratagems, such as nested modeling (Rayner et al.), strong inference (McConkie and Dyre), or ideal-observer analysis (see Klitz et al.). In addition, they could facilitate theory progress by trying to specify what exactly counts as 'the model', what the model exactly is 'a model for', why and how the model's parameters necessarily depend on specific independent variables, whether there exists a unique set of parameters that fits a crucial pattern of data, and whether there is a logically possible pattern of data that the model excludes (i.e., by which it is falsified). While some may

---

6 Examples for such strongest falsificators can be found in the models of Grainger and Jacobs (1996) or Levelt, Roelofs and Meyer (2000).

feel that trying to answer the five questions posed in this chapter could be damaging to a creative cognitive modeling process, others may feel the contrary. At least, this is my experience from the last 10 years of reviewing and doing 'cognitive models'.

References

Andrews, S. (1997). The effect of orthographic similarity on lexical retrieval: Resolving neighborhood conflicts. Psychonomic Bulletin and Review, 4, 439–461.

Balota, D.A. and Chumbley, J.I. (1985). The locus of word frequency effects in the pronunciation task: Lexical access and/or production? Journal of Memory and Language, 24, 89–106.

Bamber, D. and van Santen, J.P.H. (1985). How many parameters can a model have and still be testable? Journal of Mathematical Psychology, 29, 443–473.

Broadbent, D.E. (1985). A question of levels: Comment on McClelland and Rumelhart. Journal of Experimental Psychology: General, 114, 189–192.

Coltheart, M. and Rastle, K. (1994). Serial processing in reading aloud: Evidence for dual-route models of reading. Journal of Experimental Psychology: Human Perception and Performance, 20, 1197–1211.

Dunn, J.C. and Kirsner, K. (1988). Discovering functionally independent mental processes: The principle of reversed association. Psychological Review, 95, 91–101.

Estes, W.K. (1950). Toward a statistical theory of learning. Psychological Review, 57, 94–107.

Estes, W.K. (1975). Some targets for mathematical psychology. Journal of Mathematical Psychology, 12, 263–282.

Grainger, J. and Jacobs, A.M. (1994). A dual-read out model of word context effects in letter perception: Further investigations of the word superiority effect. Journal of Experimental Psychology: Human Perception and Performance, 20, 1158–1176.

Grainger, J. and Jacobs, A.M. (1996). Orthographic processing in visual word recognition: A multiple read-out model. Psychological Review, 103, 518–565.

Grainger, J. and Jacobs, A.M. (1998). On localist connectionism and psychological science. In: J. Grainger and A.M. Jacobs (Eds.), Localist Connectionist Approaches to Human Cognition. Mahwah, NJ: Erlbaum, pp. 1–38.

Hintzman, D.L. (1991). Why are formal models useful in psychology? In: W.E. Hockley and S. Lewandowsky (Eds.), Relating Theory and Data: Essays in Honor of Bennet B. Murdock. Hillsdale, NJ: Erlbaum, pp. 175–194.

Jacobs, A.M. (1993). Modeling the effects of visual factors on saccade latency. In: G. d'Ydewalle and J. van Rensbergen (Eds.), Perception and Cognition: Advances in Eye Movement Research. Amsterdam: North-Holland, pp. 349–361.

Jacobs, A.M. (1994). On computational theories and multilevel, multitask models of cognition: The case of word recognition. Behavioral and Brain Sciences, 17, 670–672.

Jacobs, A.M. (2000). Simulative Methoden. In: T. Herrmann, W. Deutsch and G. Rickheit (Eds.), Handbuch der Psycholinguistik. De Gruyter (in press).

Jacobs, A.M. and Carr, T.H. (1995). Mind mappers and cognitive modelers: Toward cross-fertilization. Behavioral and Brain Sciences, 18, 362–363.

Jacobs, A.M. and Grainger, J. (1992). Testing a semi-stochastic variant of the interactive activation model in different word recognition experiments. Journal of Experimental Psychology: Human Perception and Performance, 18, 1174–1188.

Jacobs, A.M. and Grainger, J. (1994). Models of visual word recognition: Sampling the state of the art. Journal of Experimental Psychology: Human Perception and Performance, 20 (6), 1311–1334.

Jacobs, A.M. and Grainger, J. (1999). Modeling a theory without a model-theory, or, computational modeling 'after Feyerabend'. Behavioral and Brain Sciences, 22, 46–47.

Jacobs, A.M., Rey, A., Ziegler, J.C. and Grainger, J. (1998). MROM-P: An interactive activation, multiple read-out model of orthographic and phonological processes in visual word recognition. In: J. Grainger and A.M. Jacobs (Eds.), Localist Connectionist Approaches to Human Cognition. Mahwah, NJ: Erlbaum, pp. 147–188.

Levelt, W.J.M., Roelofs, A. and Meyer, A.S. (2000). A theory of lexical access in speech production. Behavioral and Brain Sciences (in press).

Marr, D. (1982). Vision. San Francisco: Freeman.

McClelland, J.L. and Rumelhart, D.E. (1981). An interactive activation model of context effects in letter perception: Part I. An account of basic findings. Psychological Review, 88, 375–407.

McCloskey, M. (1991). Networks and theories: The place of connectionism in cognitive science. Psychological Science, 2, 387–395.

McConkie, G.W., Kerr, P.W., Reddix, M.D., Zola, D. and Jacobs, A.M. (1989). Eye movement control during reading: II. Frequency of refixating a word. Perception and Psychophysics, 46, 245–253.

Morrison, R.E. (1984). Manipulation of stimulus onset delay in reading: Evidence for parallel programming of saccades. Journal of Experimental Psychology: Human Perception and Performance, 10, 667–682.

Myung, I.J. and Pitt, M.A. (1998). Issues in selecting mathematical models of cognition. In: J. Grainger and A.M. Jacobs (Eds.), Localist Connectionist Approaches to Human Cognition. Mahwah, NJ: Erlbaum, pp. 327–355.

Nazir, T.A. and Jacobs, A.M. (1991). Effects of target discriminability and retinal eccentricity on saccade latencies: An analysis in terms of variable criterion theory. Psychological Research/Psychologische Forschung, 53, 281–289.

Nazir, T.A., Jacobs, A.M. and O'Regan, J.K. (1998). Letter legibility and visual word recognition. Memory and Cognition, 26, 810–821.

Nazir, T.A., O'Regan, J.K. and Jacobs, A.M. (1991). On words and their letters. Bulletin of the Psychonomic Society, 29, 171–174.

O'Regan, J.K. and Jacobs, A.M. (1992). The optimal viewing position effect in word recognition: A challenge to current theory. Journal of Experimental Psychology: Human Perception and Performance, 18, 185–197.

Paap, K. and Johansen, L. (1994). The case of the vanishing frequency effect: A retest of the verification model. Journal of Experimental Psychology: Human Perception and Performance, 20, 1129–1157.

Paap, K.R., Johansen, L.S., Chun, E. and Vonnahme, P. (2000). Neighborhood frequency does affect performance on the Reicher task: Encoding or decision? Journal of Experimental Psychology: Human Perception and Performance (in press).

Reichle, E.D., Pollatsek, A., Fisher, D.L. and Rayner, K. (1998). Toward a model of eye movement control in reading. Psychological Review, 105, 125–157.

Rumelhart, D.E. and McClelland, J.L. (1985). Levels indeed! A response to Broadbent. Journal of Experimental Psychology: General, 114, 193–197.

Townsend, J.T. and Ashby, F.G. (1983). Stochastic Modeling of Elementary Psychological Processes. New York: Cambridge University Press.

Ziegler, J.C., Rey, A. and Jacobs, A.M. (1998). Simulating individual word identification thresholds and errors in the fragmentation task. Memory and Cognition, 26, 490–501.

Author Index

Subject Index